ANTARCTIC PRESS

POSEFILE

ULTIMATE EDITION

REFERENCE MANUAL FOR ILLUSTRATORS

VOL.1

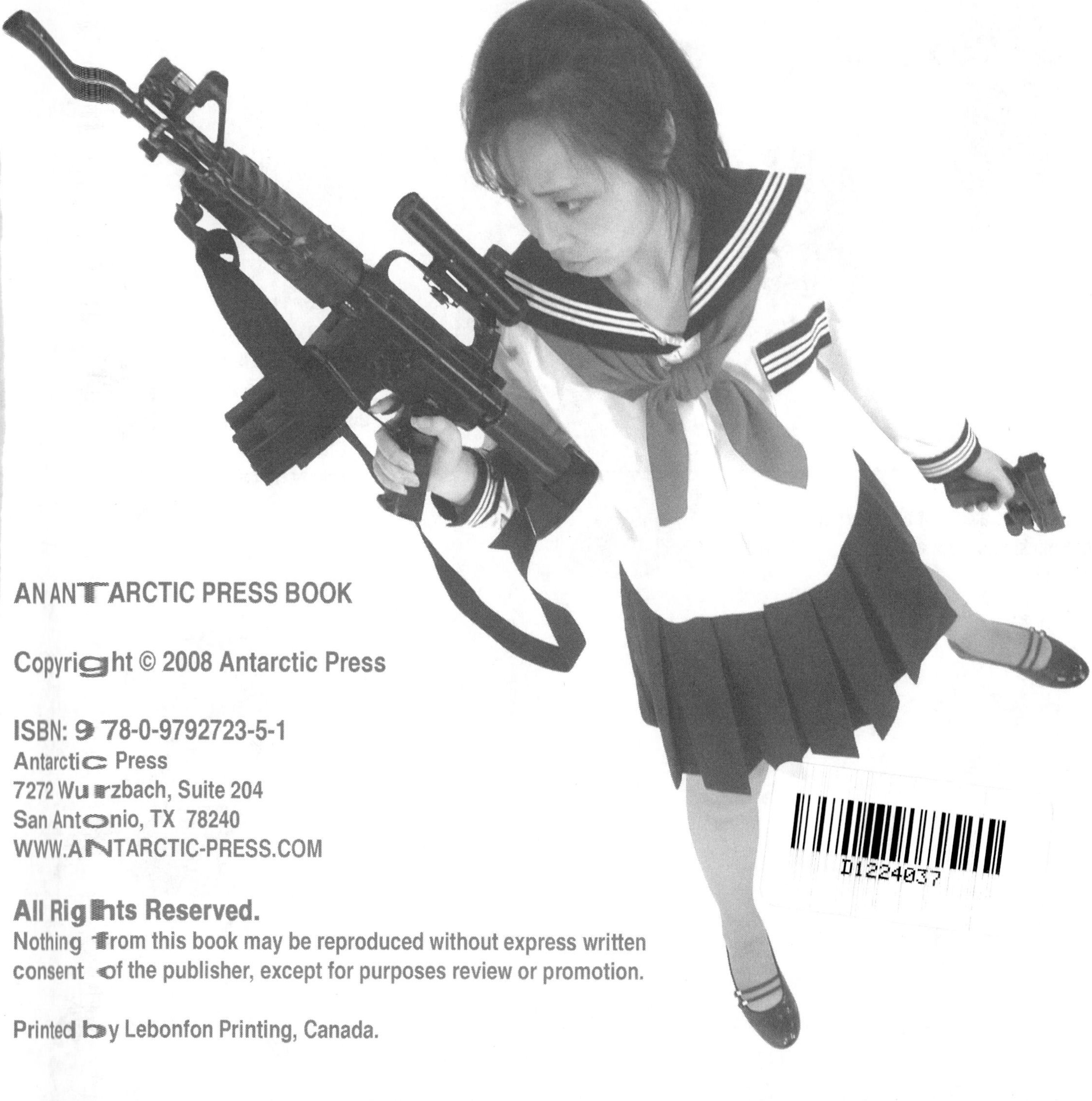

AN ANTARCTIC PRESS BOOK

ISBN: 978-0-9792723-5-1
Antarctic Press
7272 Wurzbach, Suite 204
San Antonio, TX 78240
WWW.ANTARCTIC-PRESS.COM

Printed by Lebonfon Printing, Canada.

HOW TO USE THIS POSEFILE:

Welcome to Antarctic Press's POSEFILE: ULTIMATE EDITION, the photo reference book for illustrators! For each pose, there are 24 images, taken from 3 different levels and from 360 degrees around so that no matter what your needs are, you're sure to find it here!

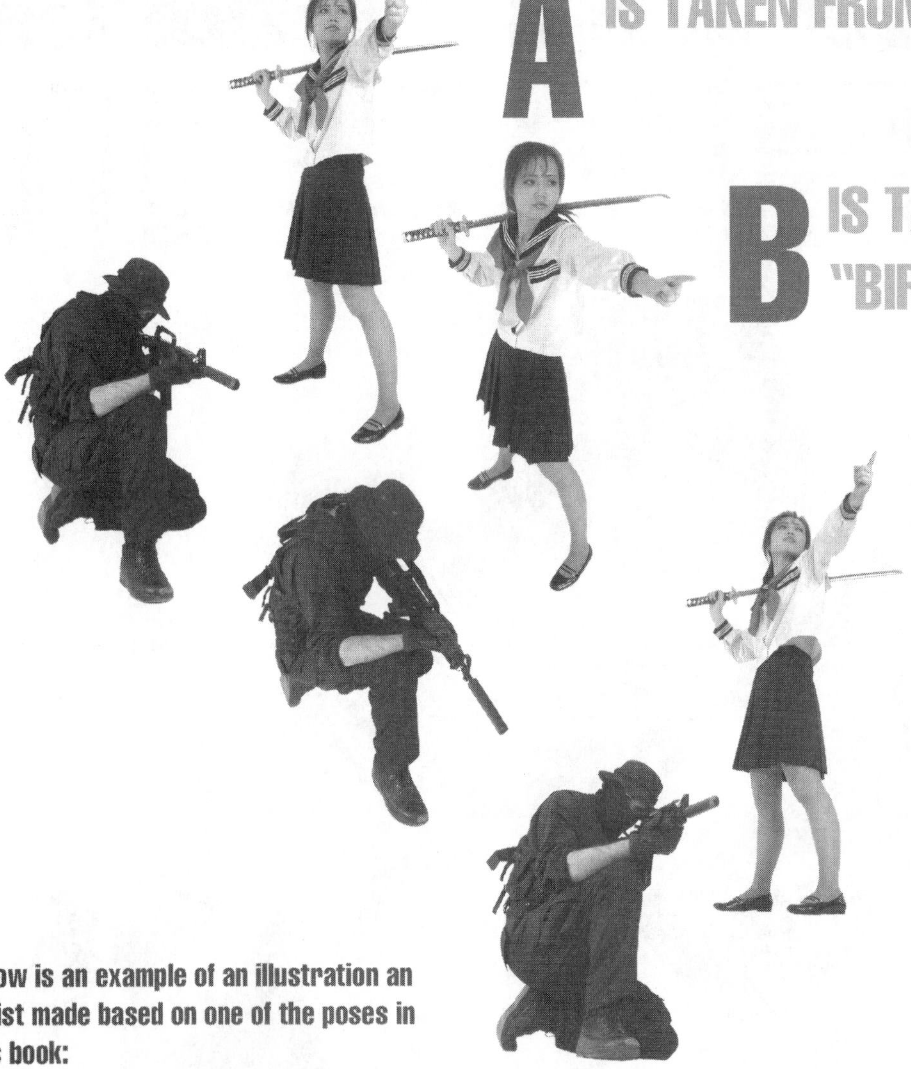

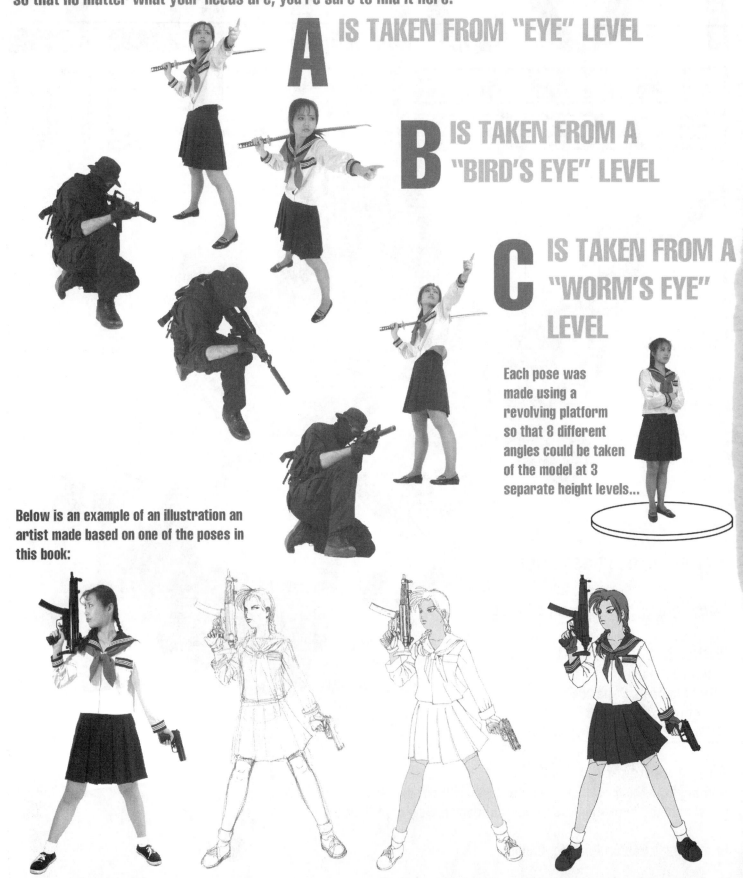

A IS TAKEN FROM "EYE" LEVEL

B IS TAKEN FROM A "BIRD'S EYE" LEVEL

C IS TAKEN FROM A "WORM'S EYE" LEVEL

Each pose was made using a revolving platform so that 8 different angles could be taken of the model at 3 separate height levels...

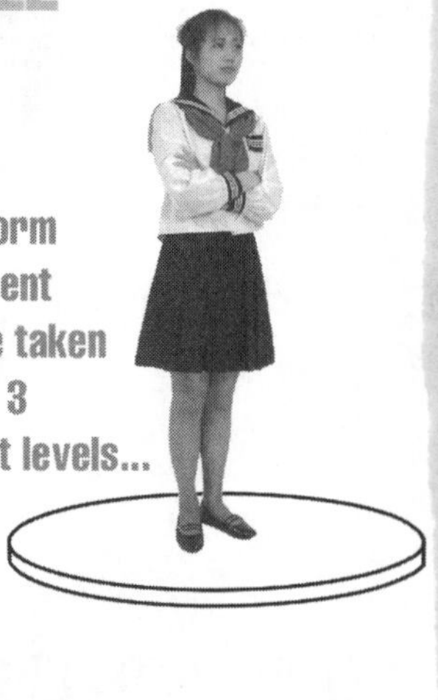

Below is an example of an illustration an artist made based on one of the poses in this book:

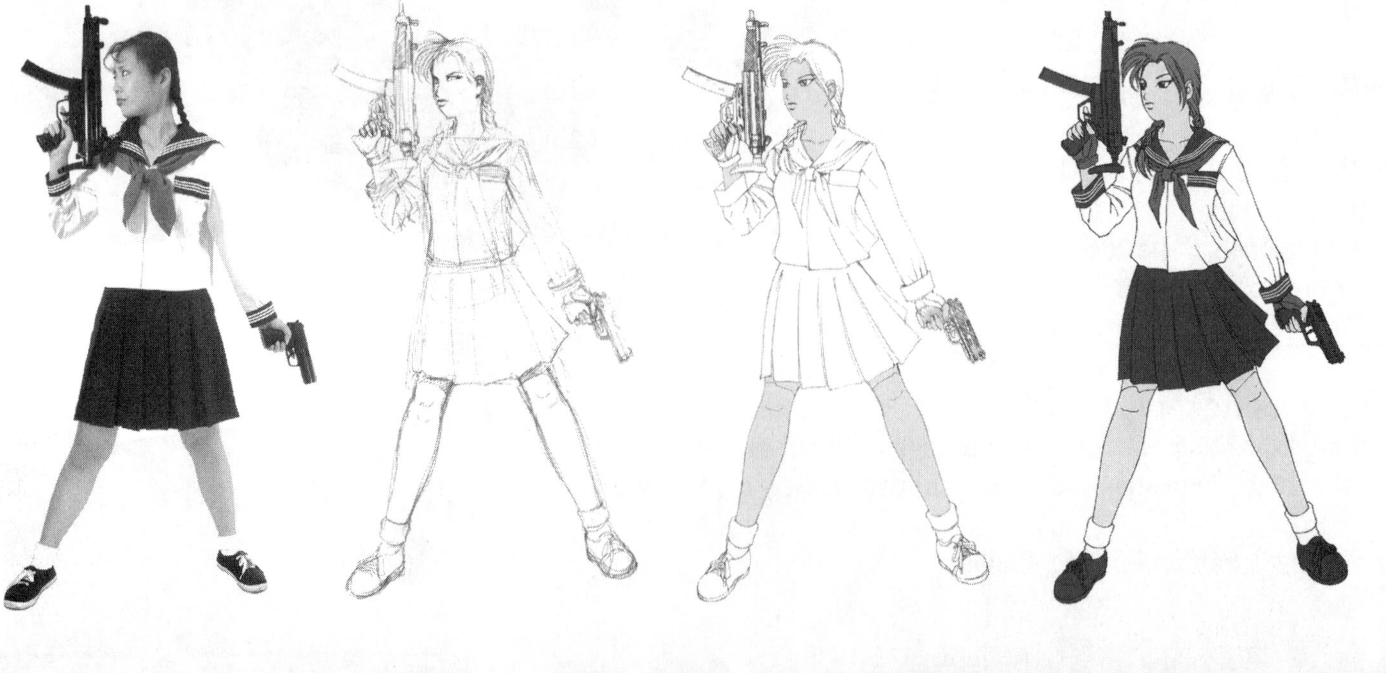

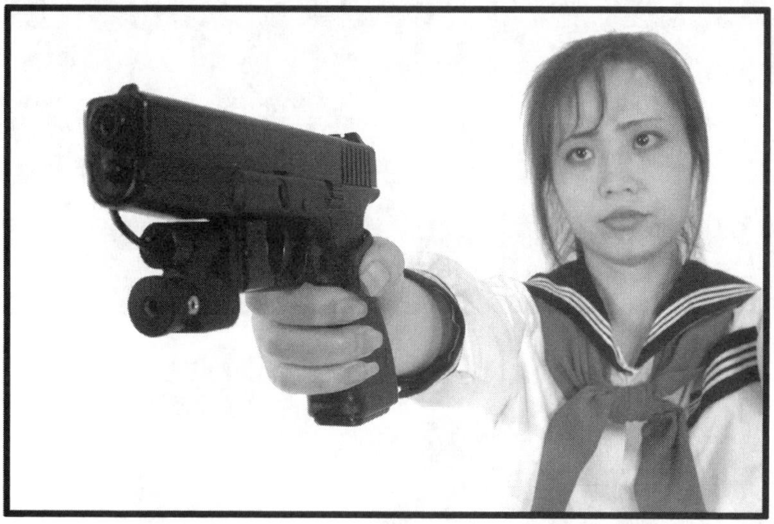

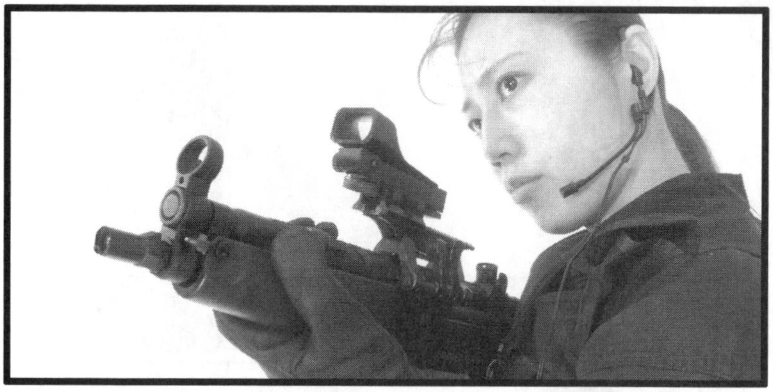

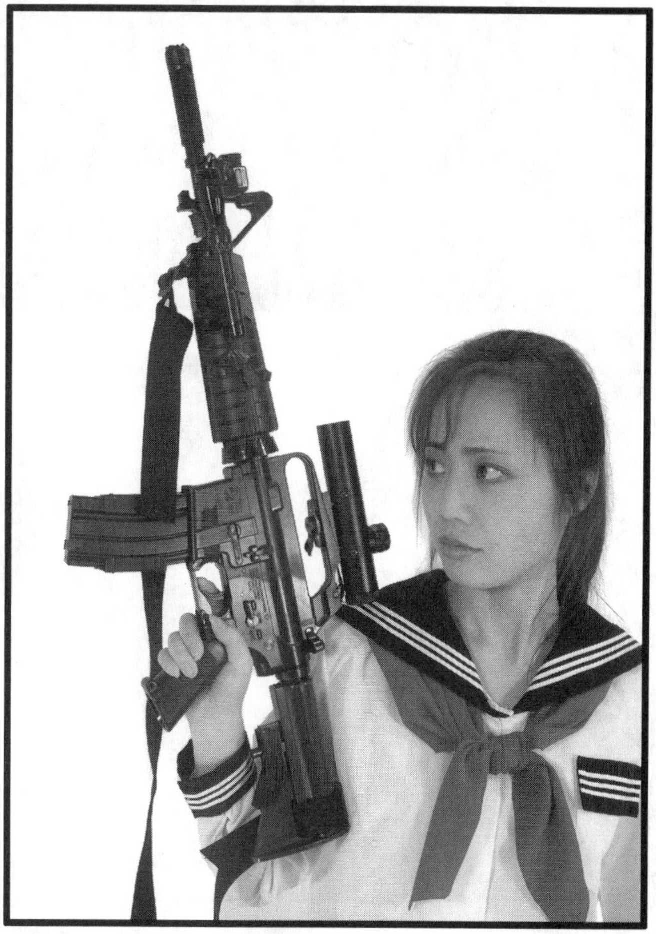

POSEFILE

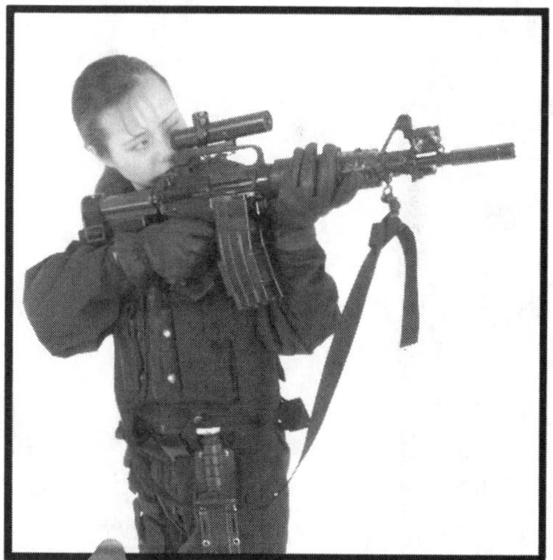

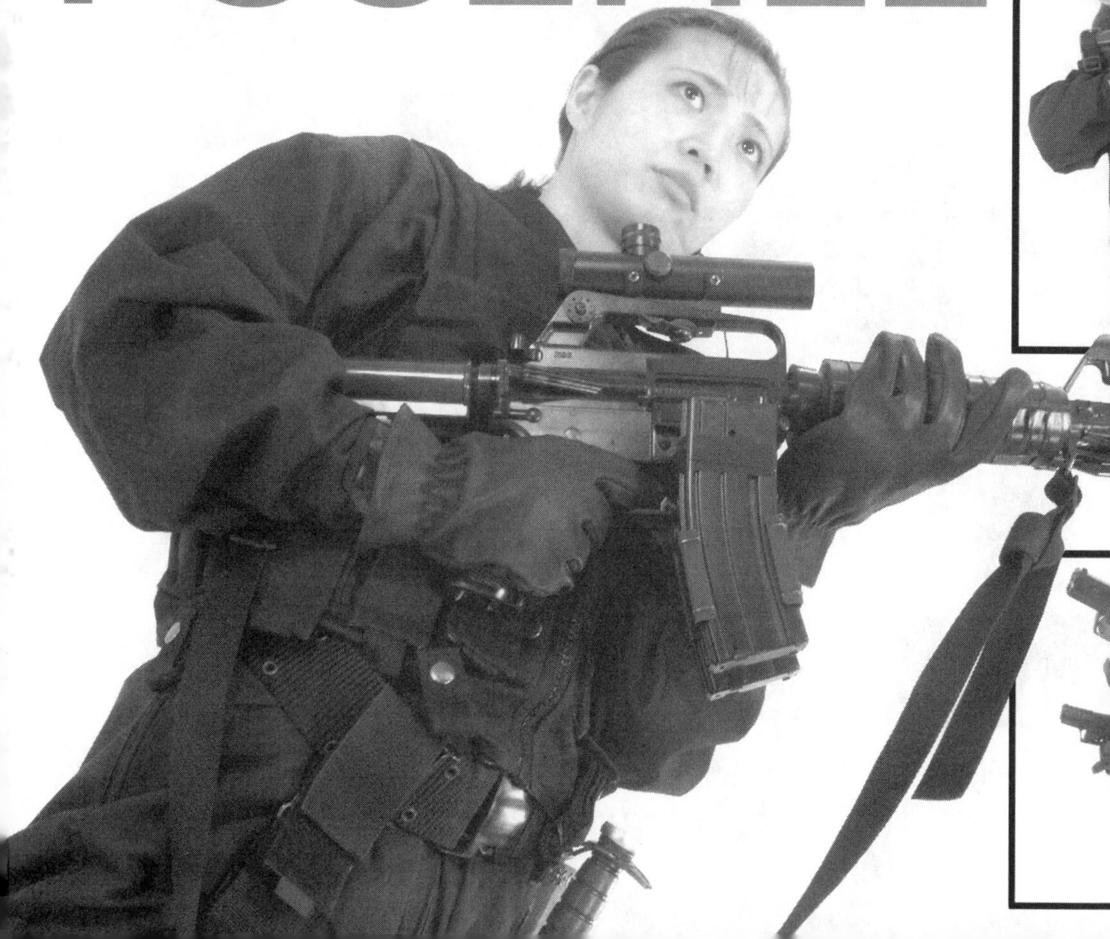

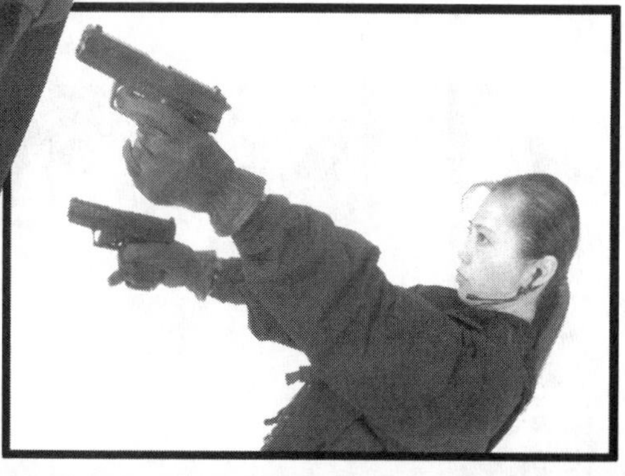

POSEFILE / ULTIMATE EDITION: COMBAT POSES

CONTENTS:

SCHOOL UNIFORM

Part 1: FEMALE MODEL: ACTION/CASUAL/FIGHTING STANCE/MISC:

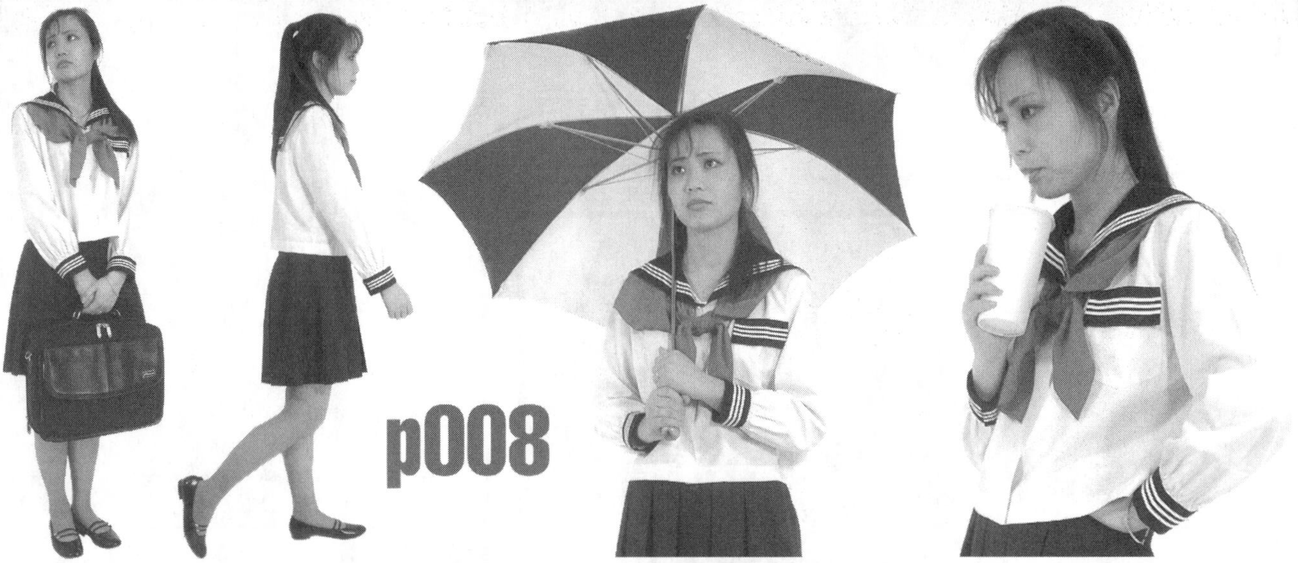

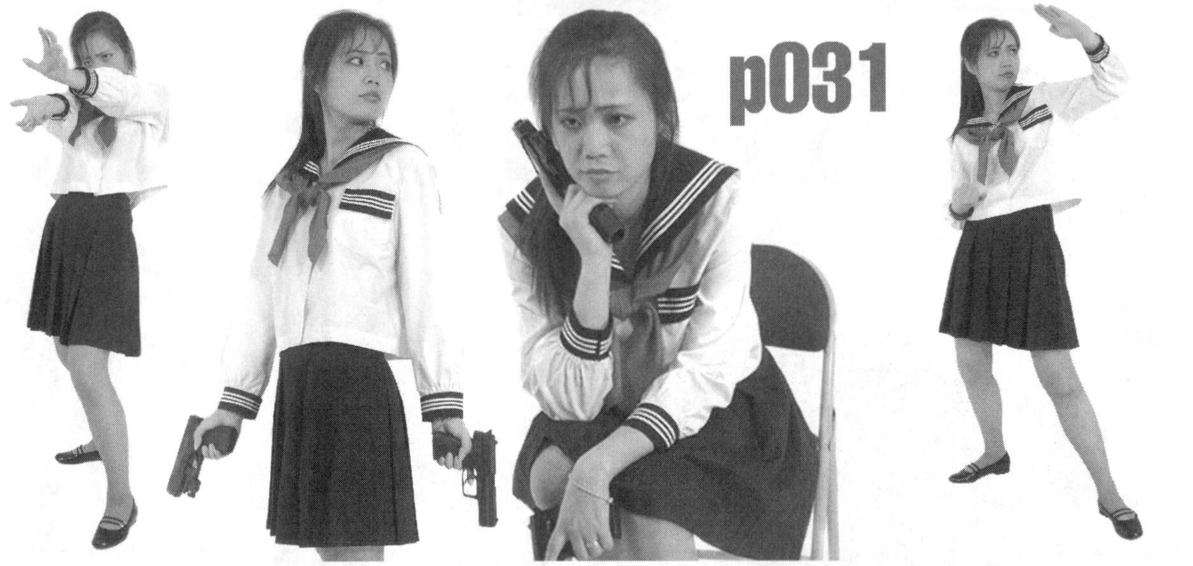

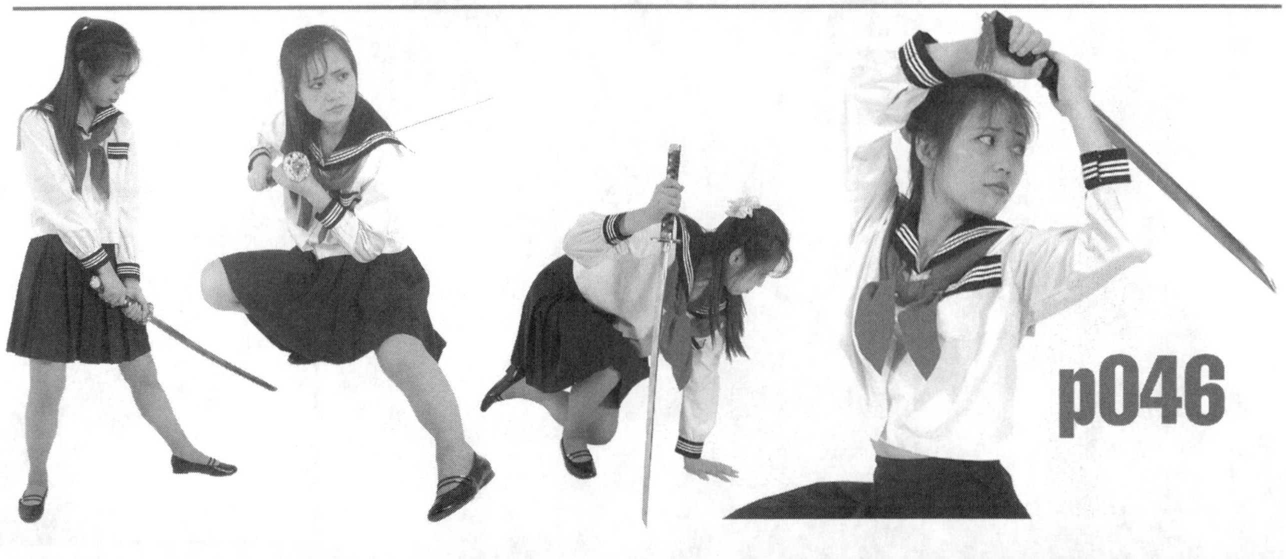

TACTICAL GEAR

SWAT / SPECIAL FORCES / TACTICAL UNITS / COVERT OPERATIONS

COLT M16 A2: M16 A1: XM177 E2: M653: M203 grenade launcher: H&K MP5 A2/A3 H&K USP / MICRO UZI / FRANACHI SPAS 12 shotgun / WALTHER P99 / FN P90 / BROWNING HI-POWER / GLOCK 17 / N6 TACTICAL KNIFE / WEAPONS POSES v.1

TACTICAL GEAR

p076

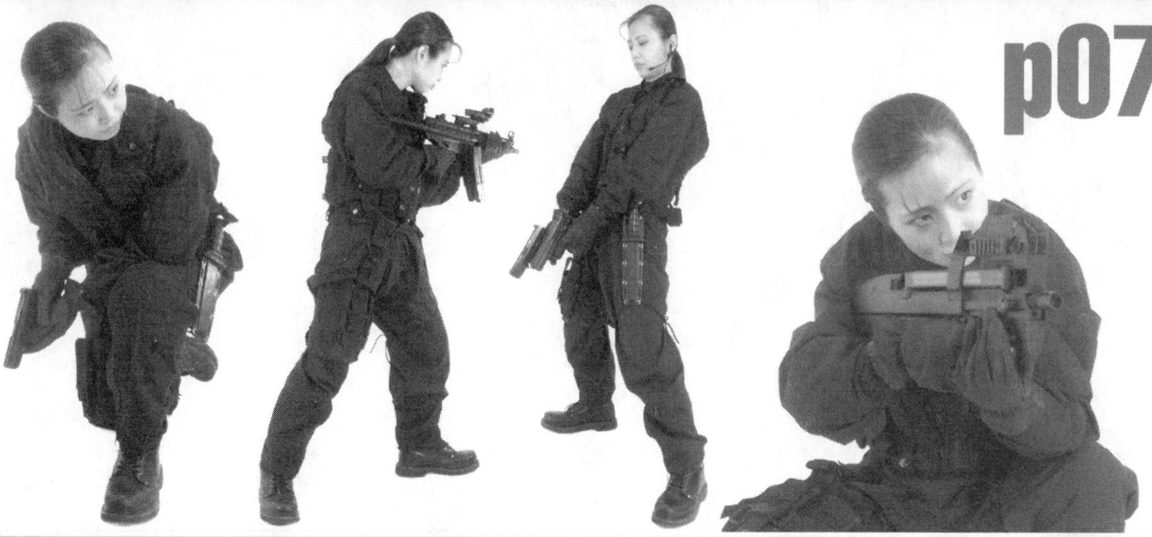

p126

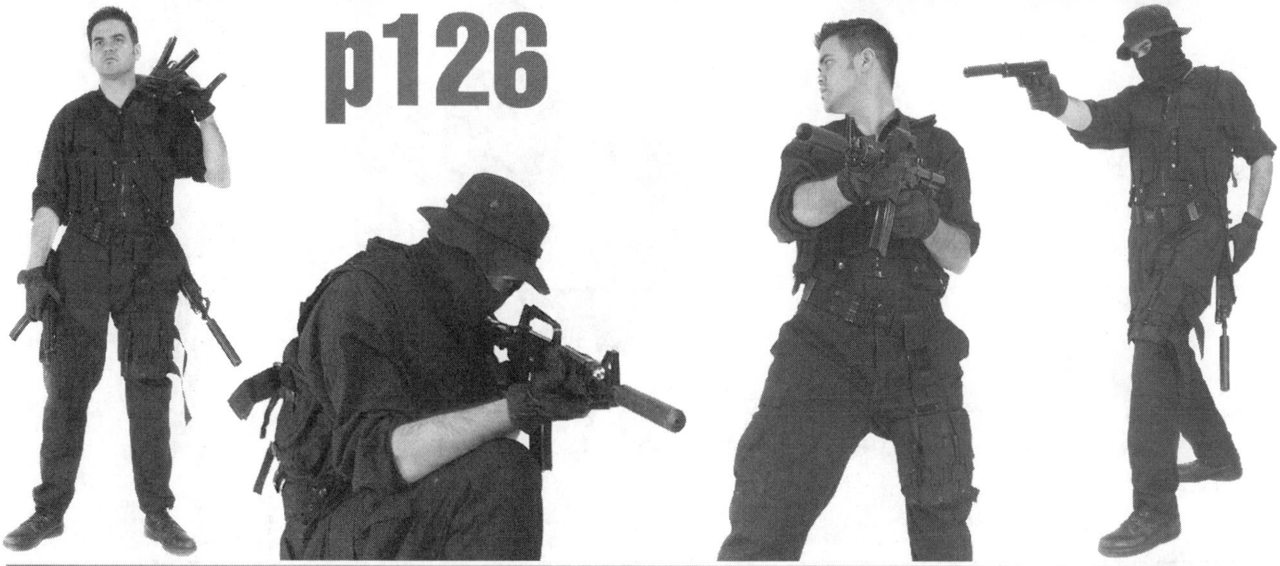

p164

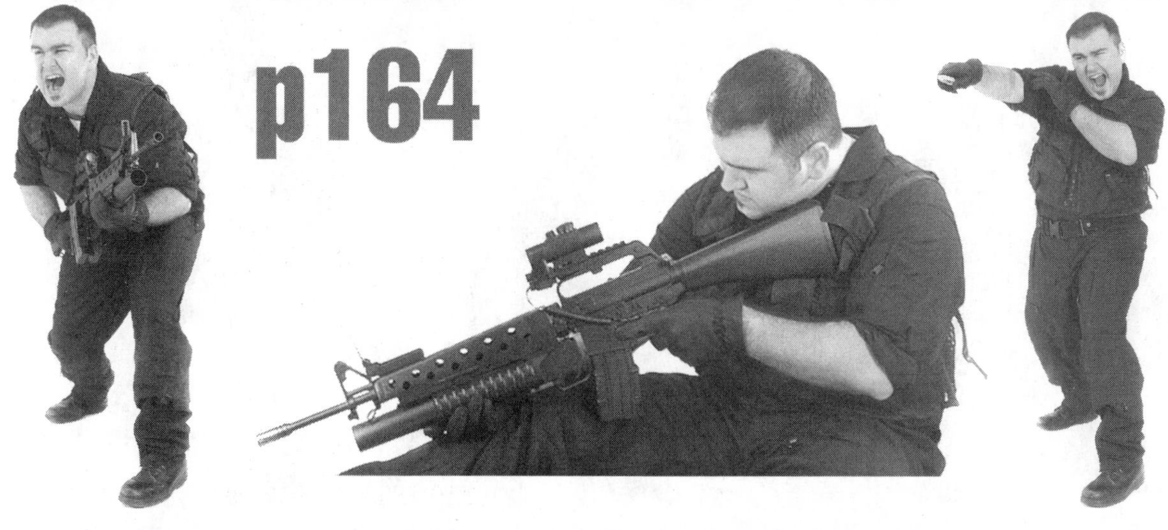

POSEFILE / ULTIMATE EDITION: ACTION POSES

TABLE OF CONTENTS

SUPERHERO STYLIN'

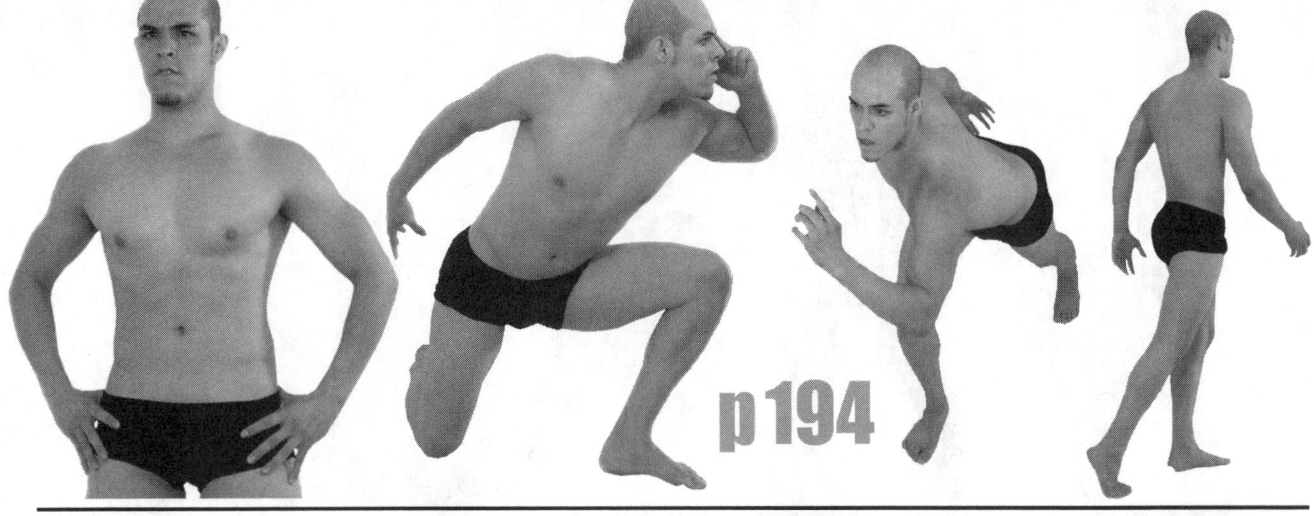

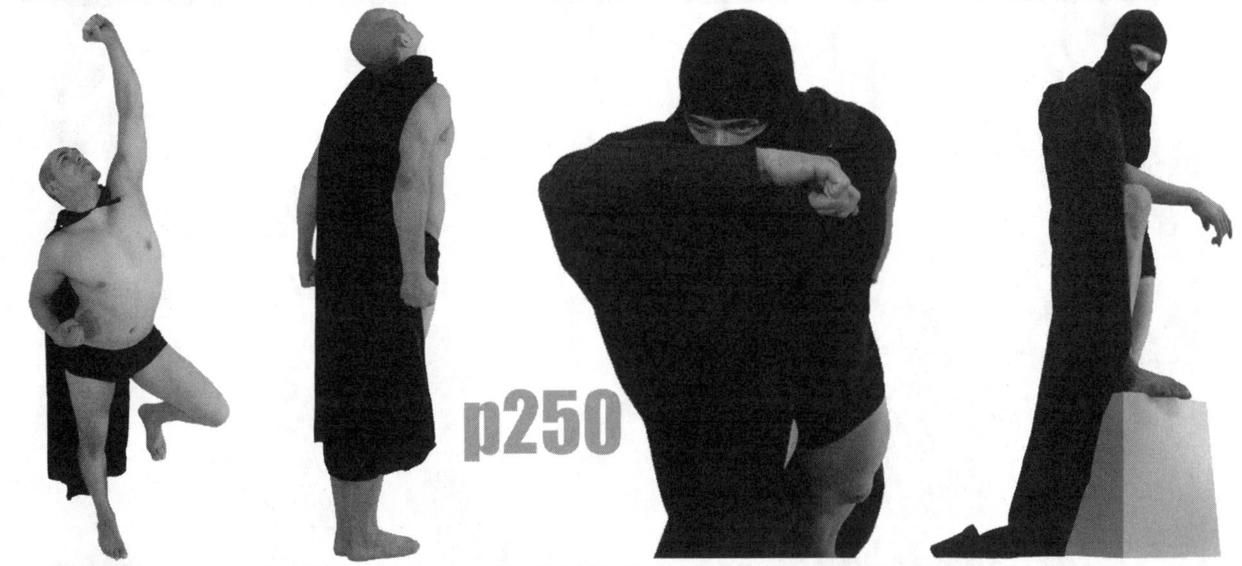

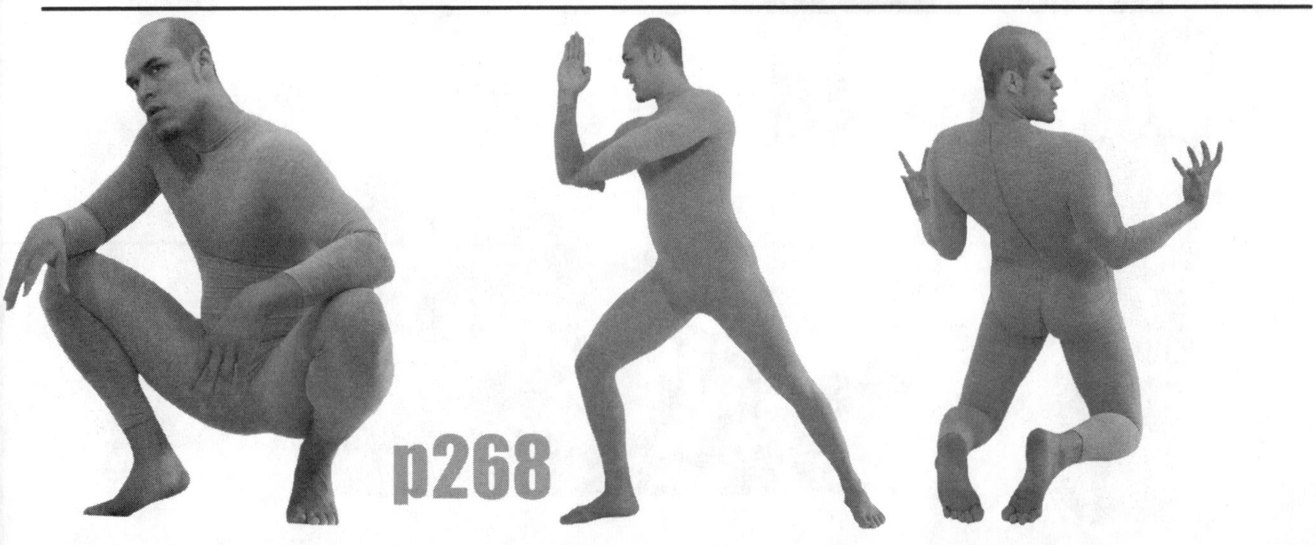

TABLE OF CONTENTS

WEAPONS AND GEAR

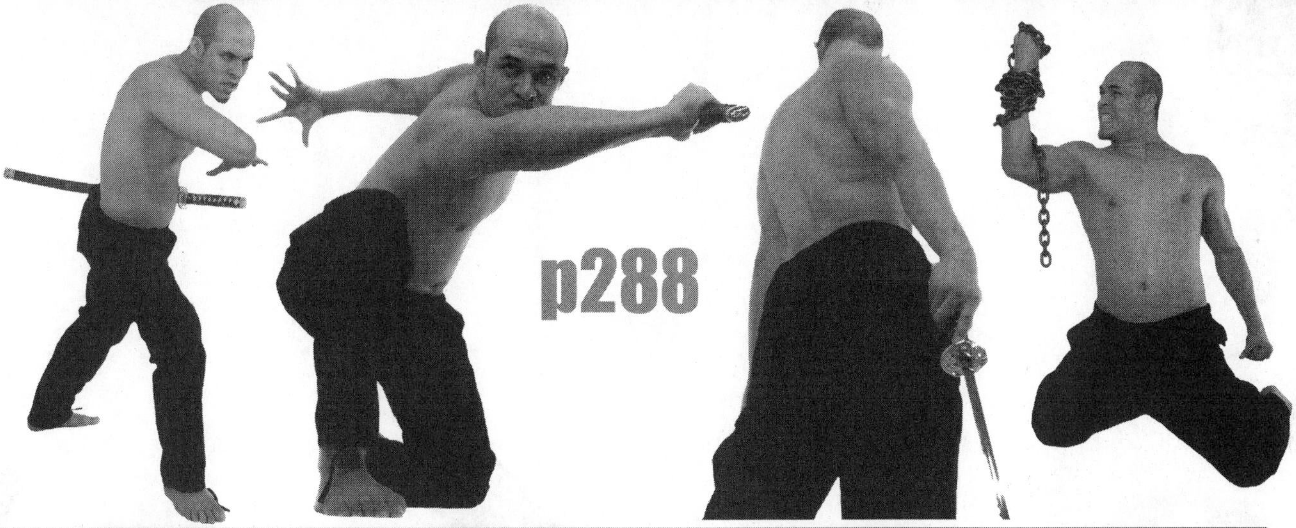

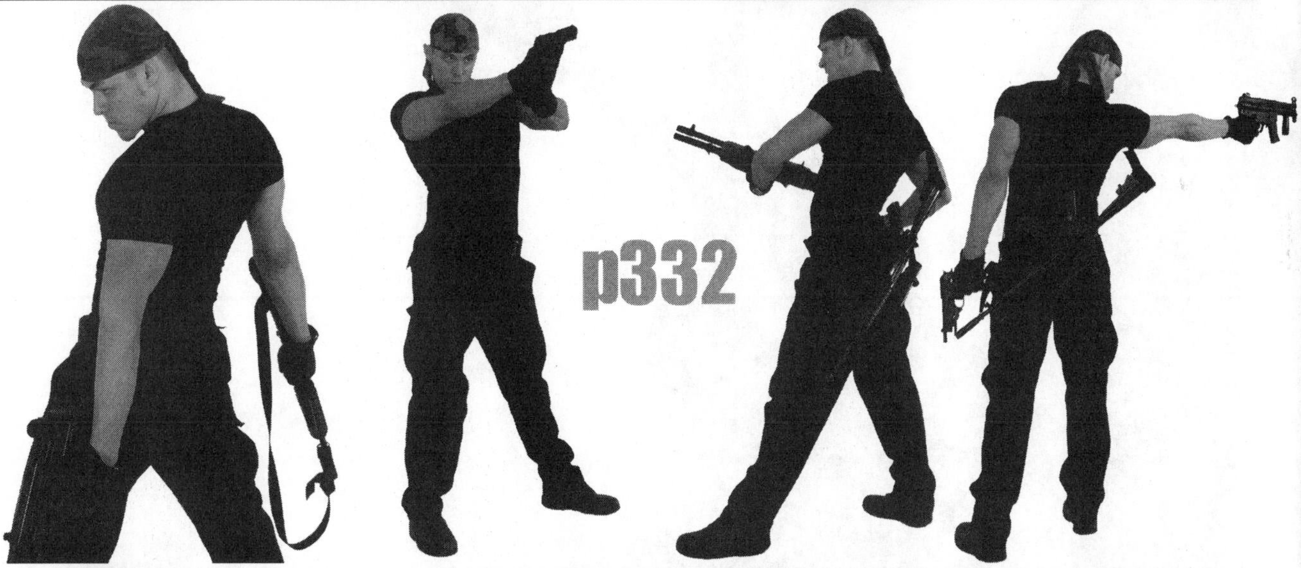

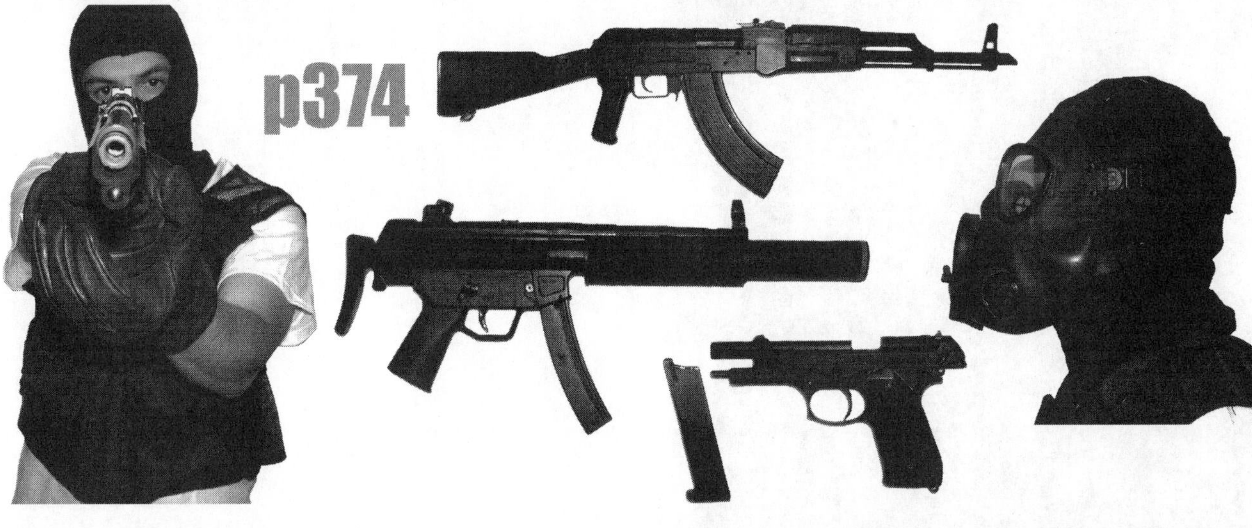

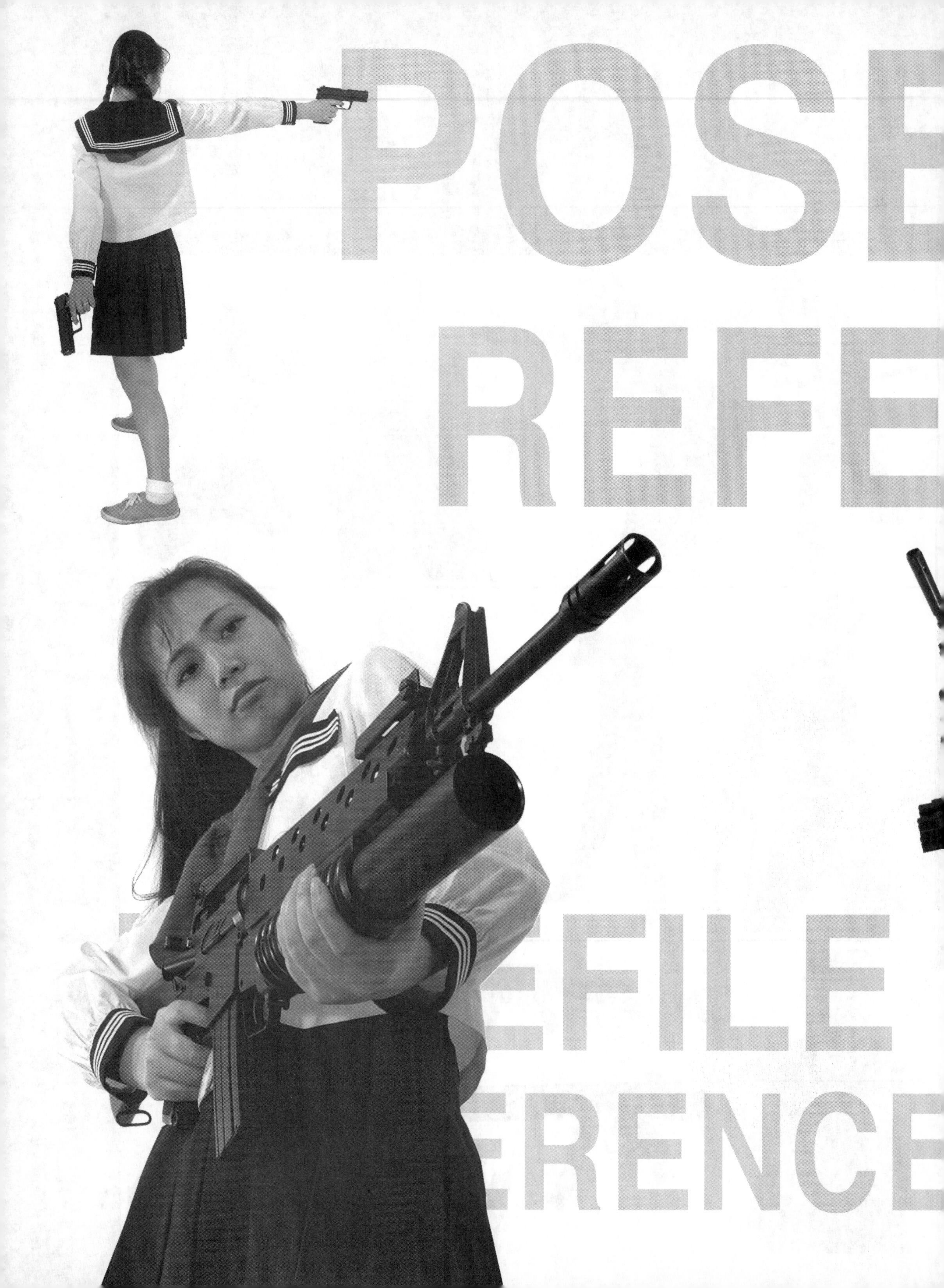
POSE
REFE
EFILE
ERENCE

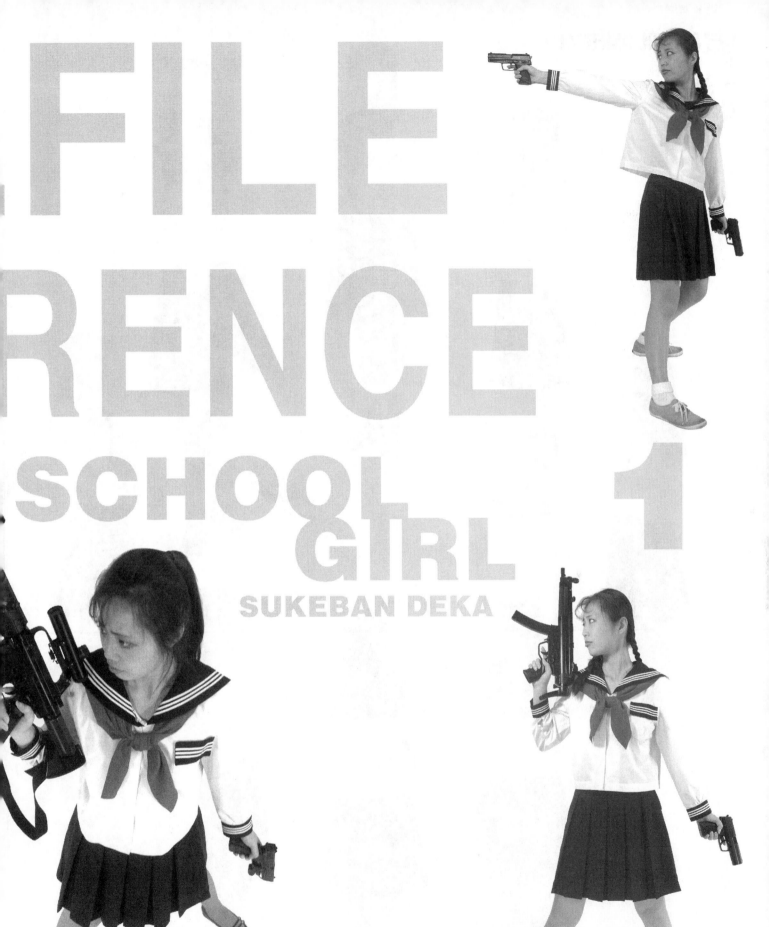

FILE
RENCE

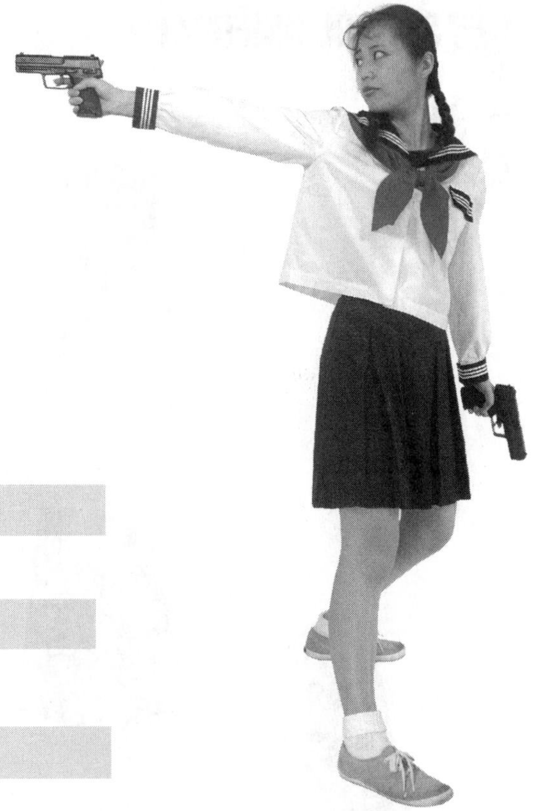

SCHOOL GIRL 1

SUKEBAN DEKA

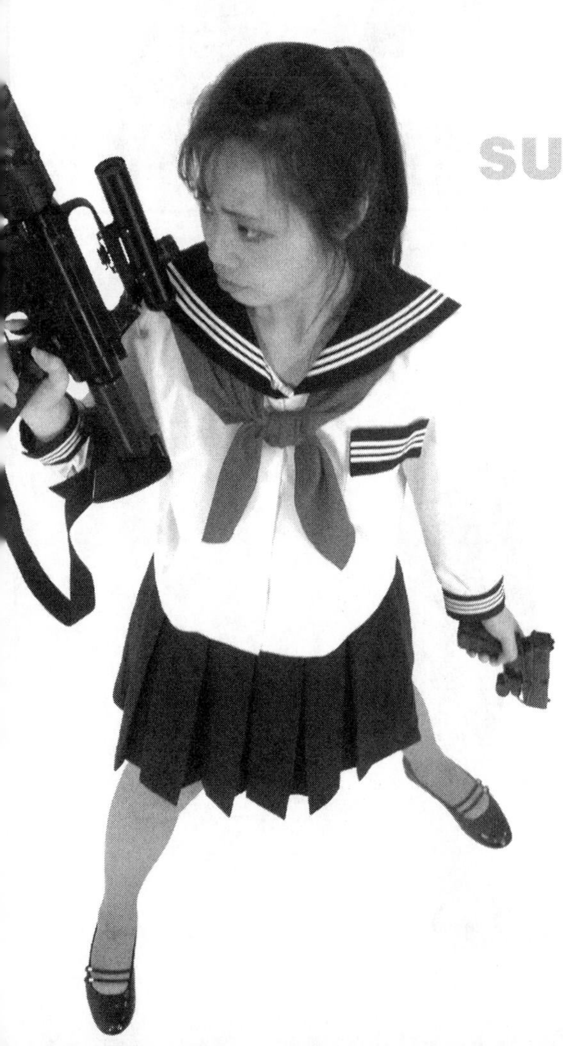

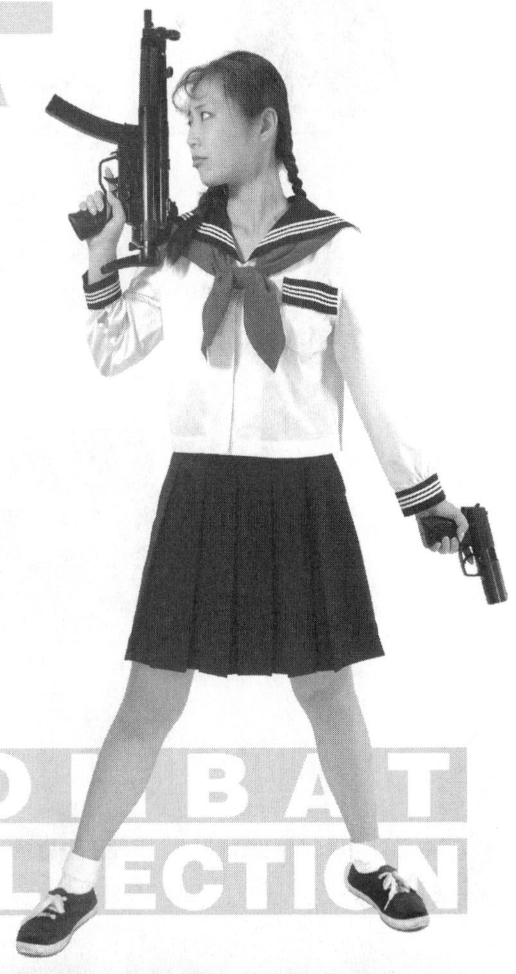

COMBAT COLLECTION

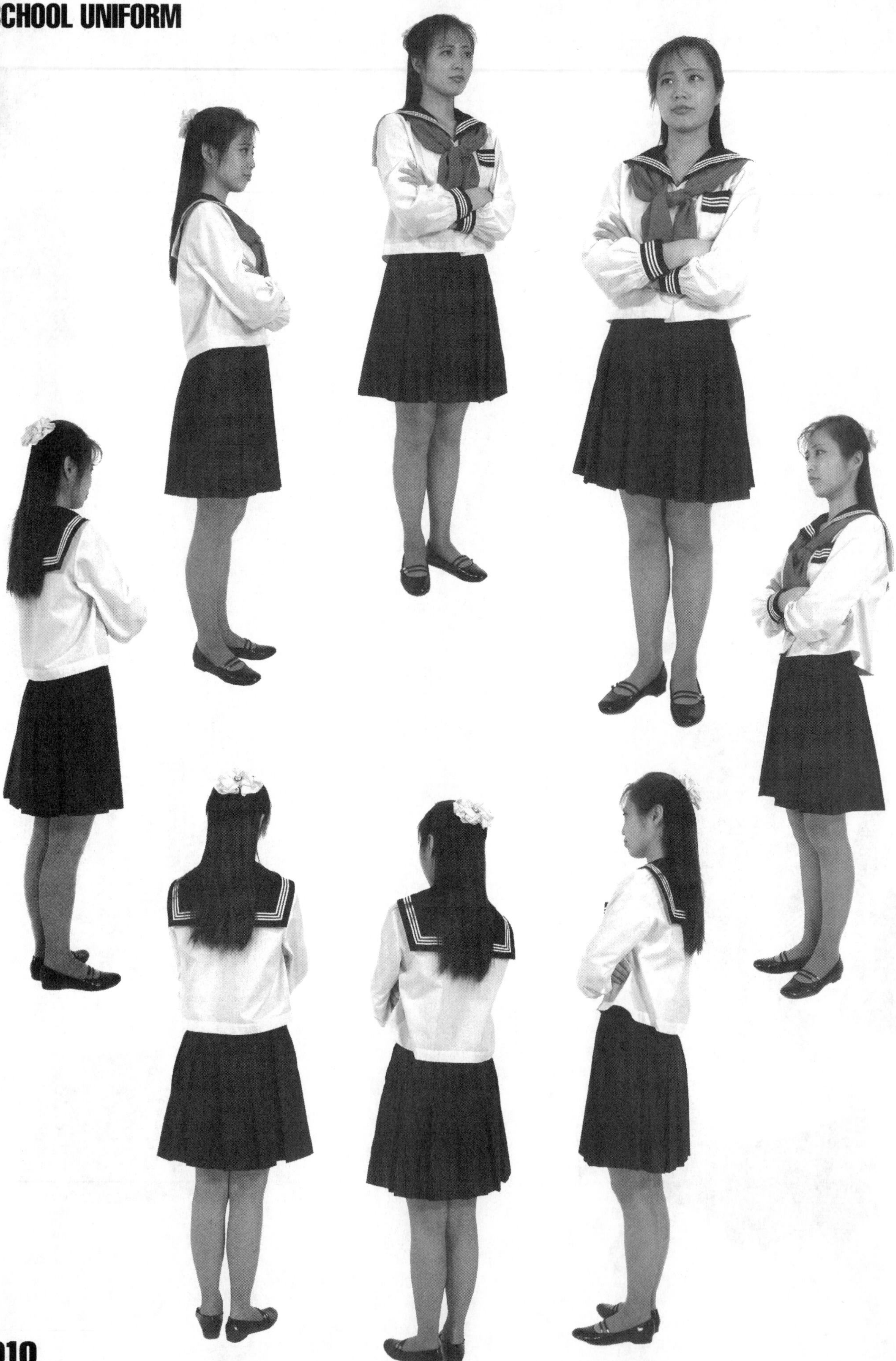

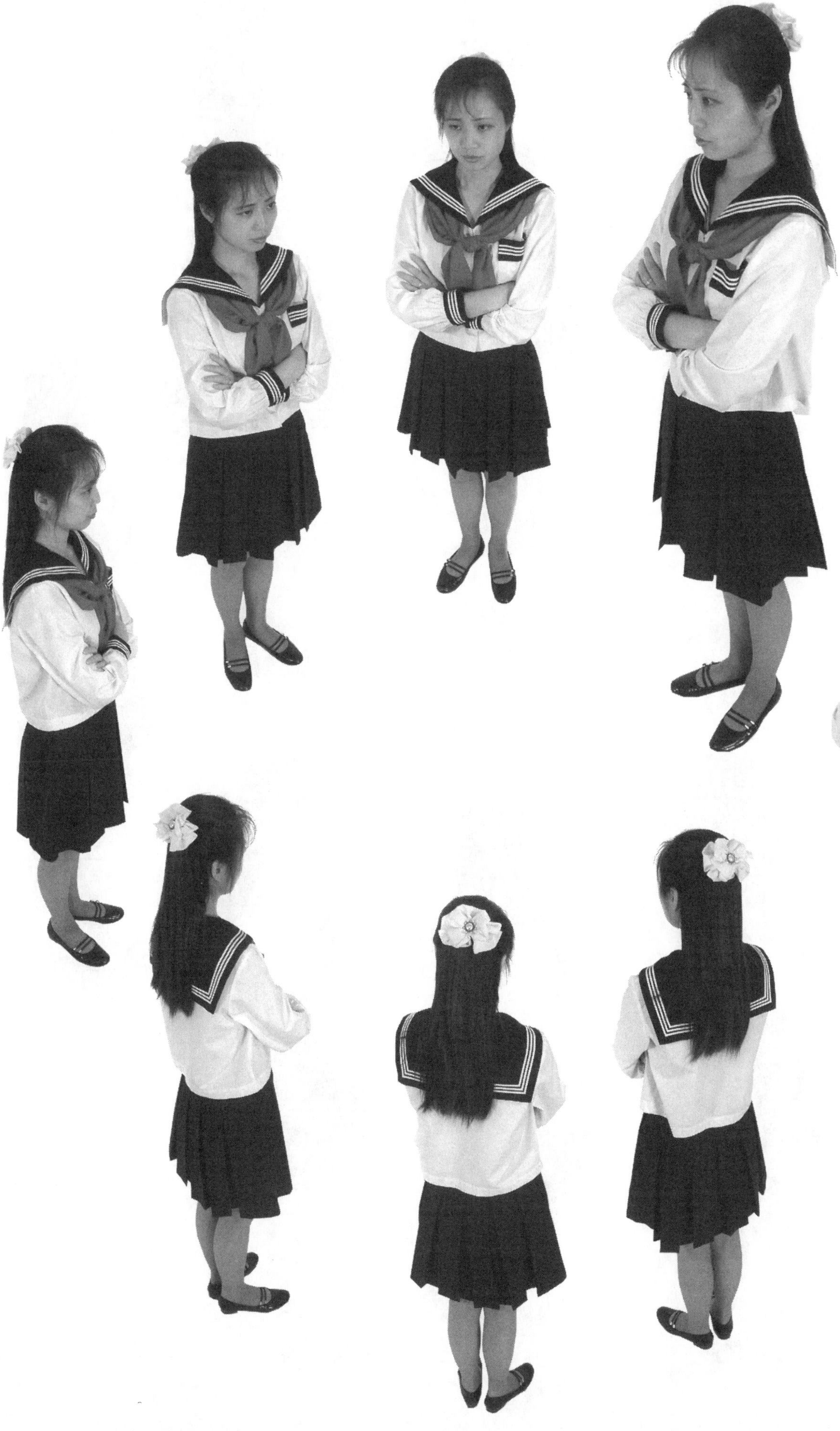

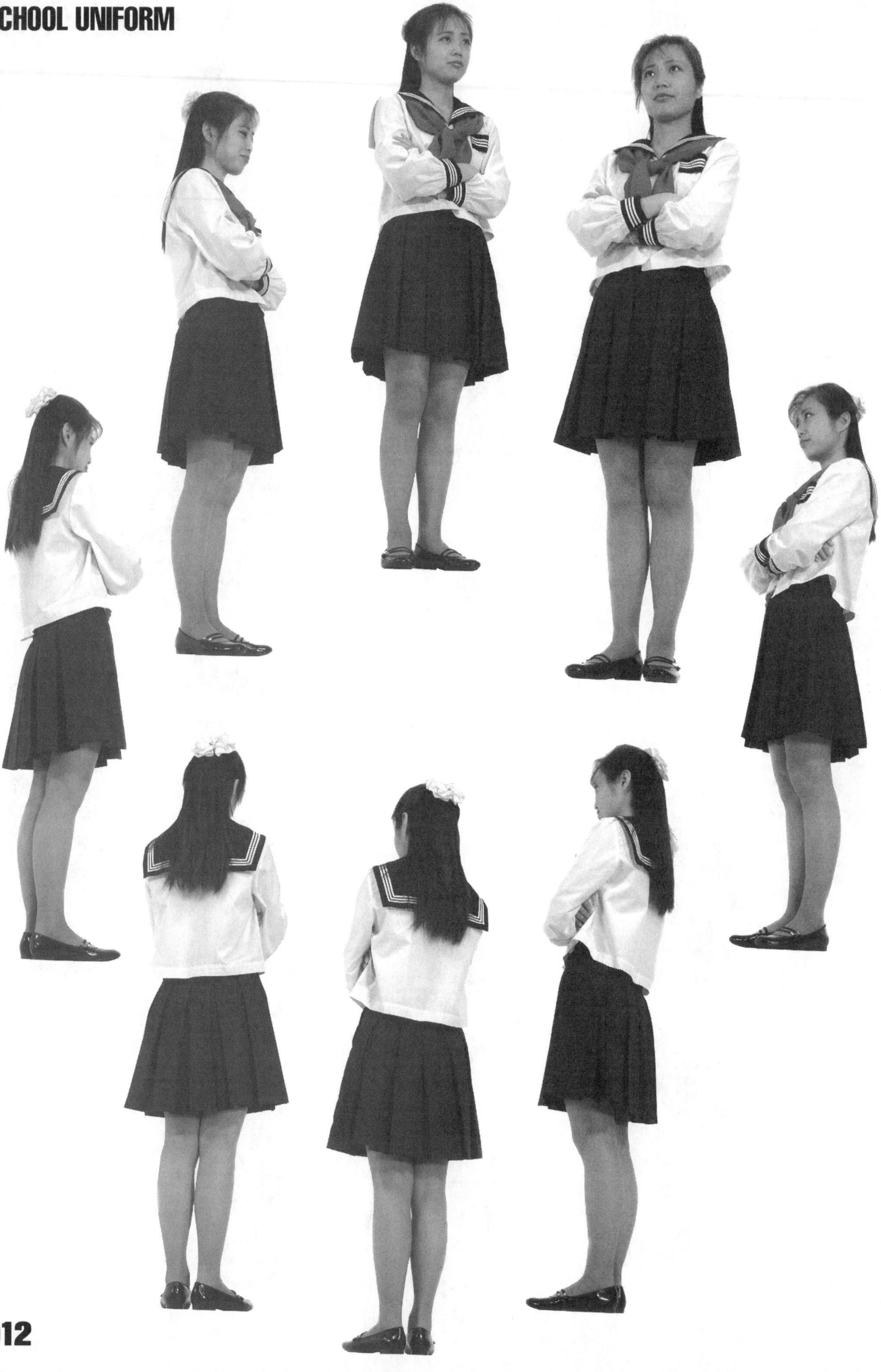

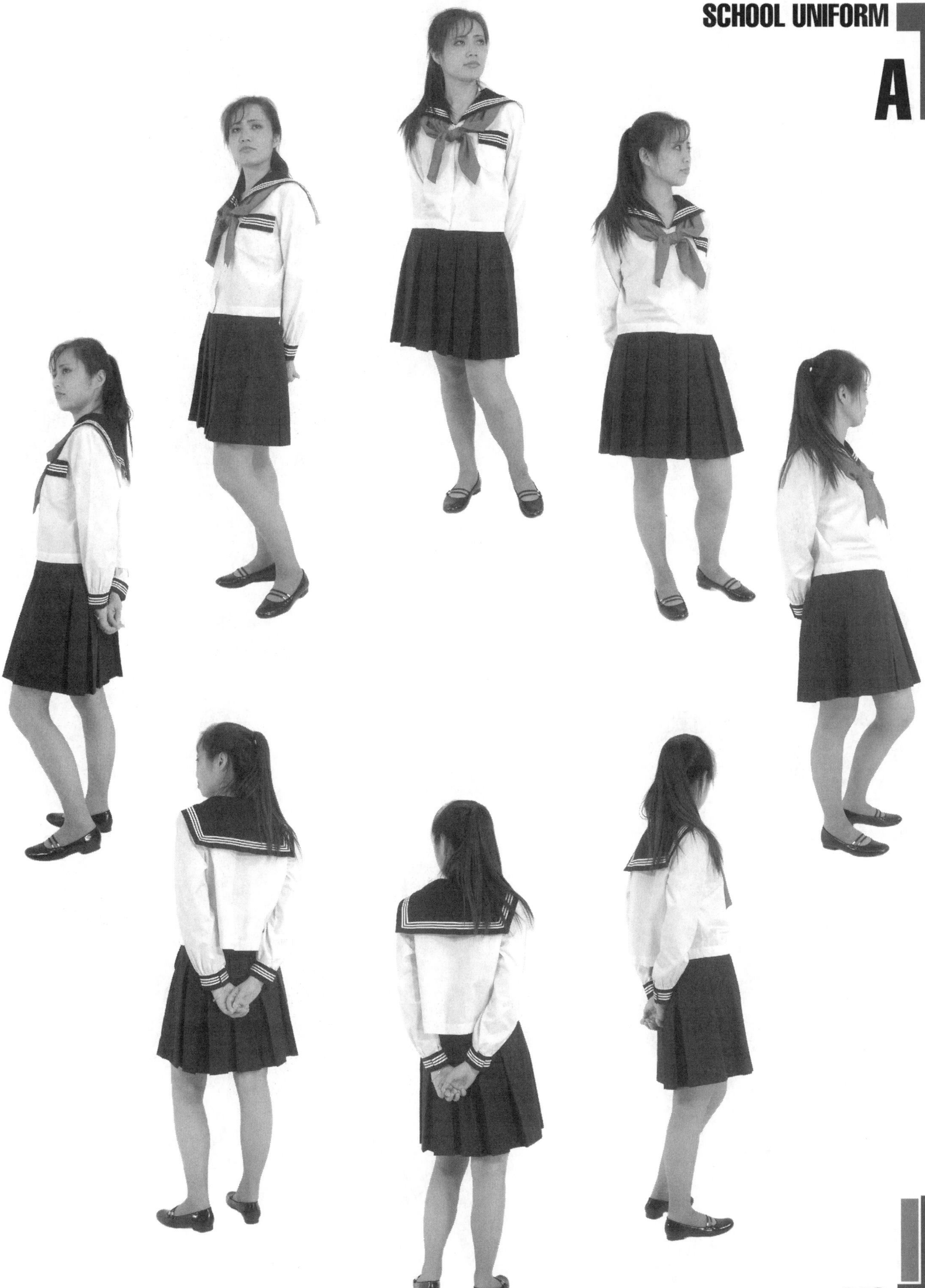

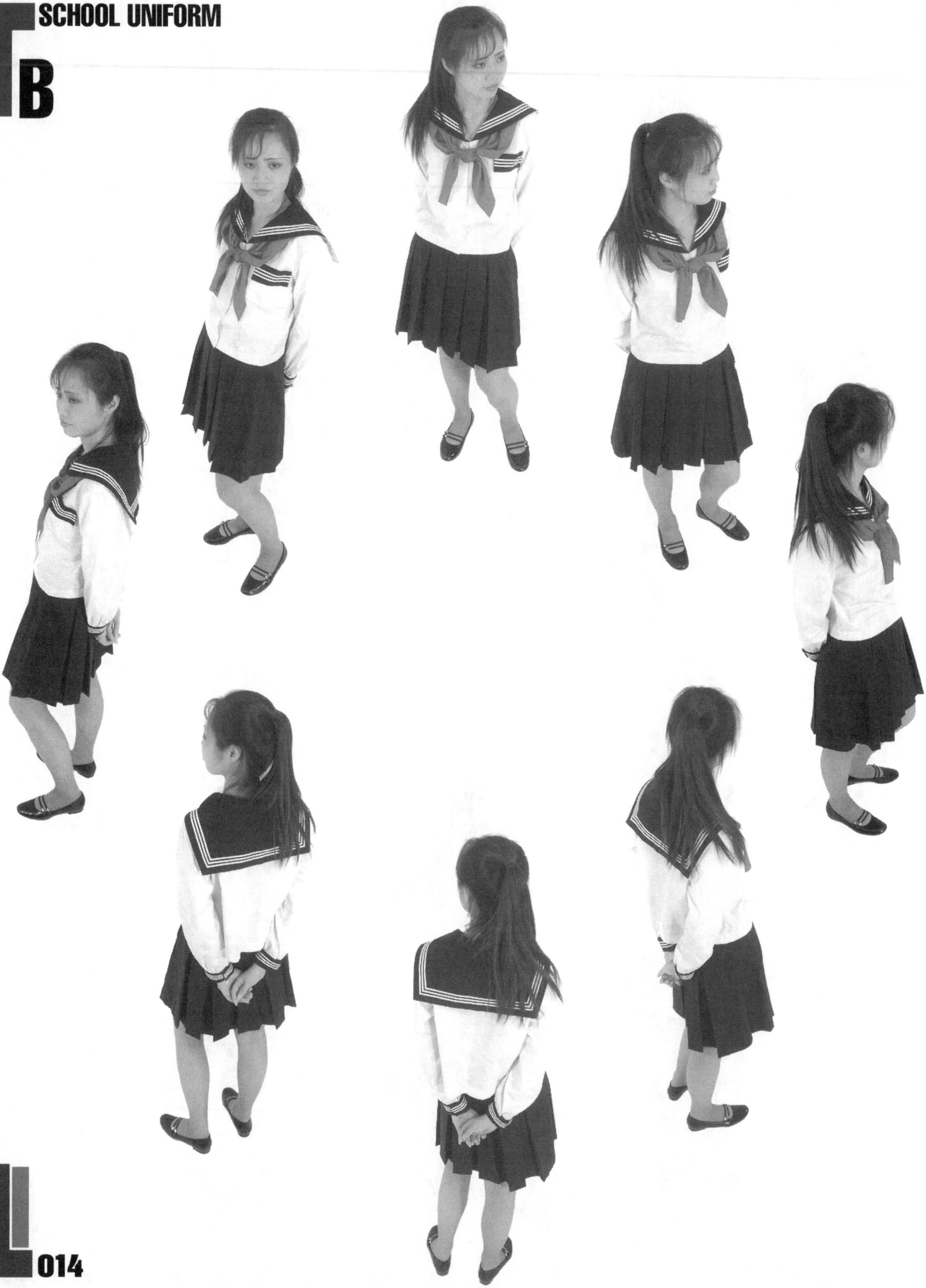

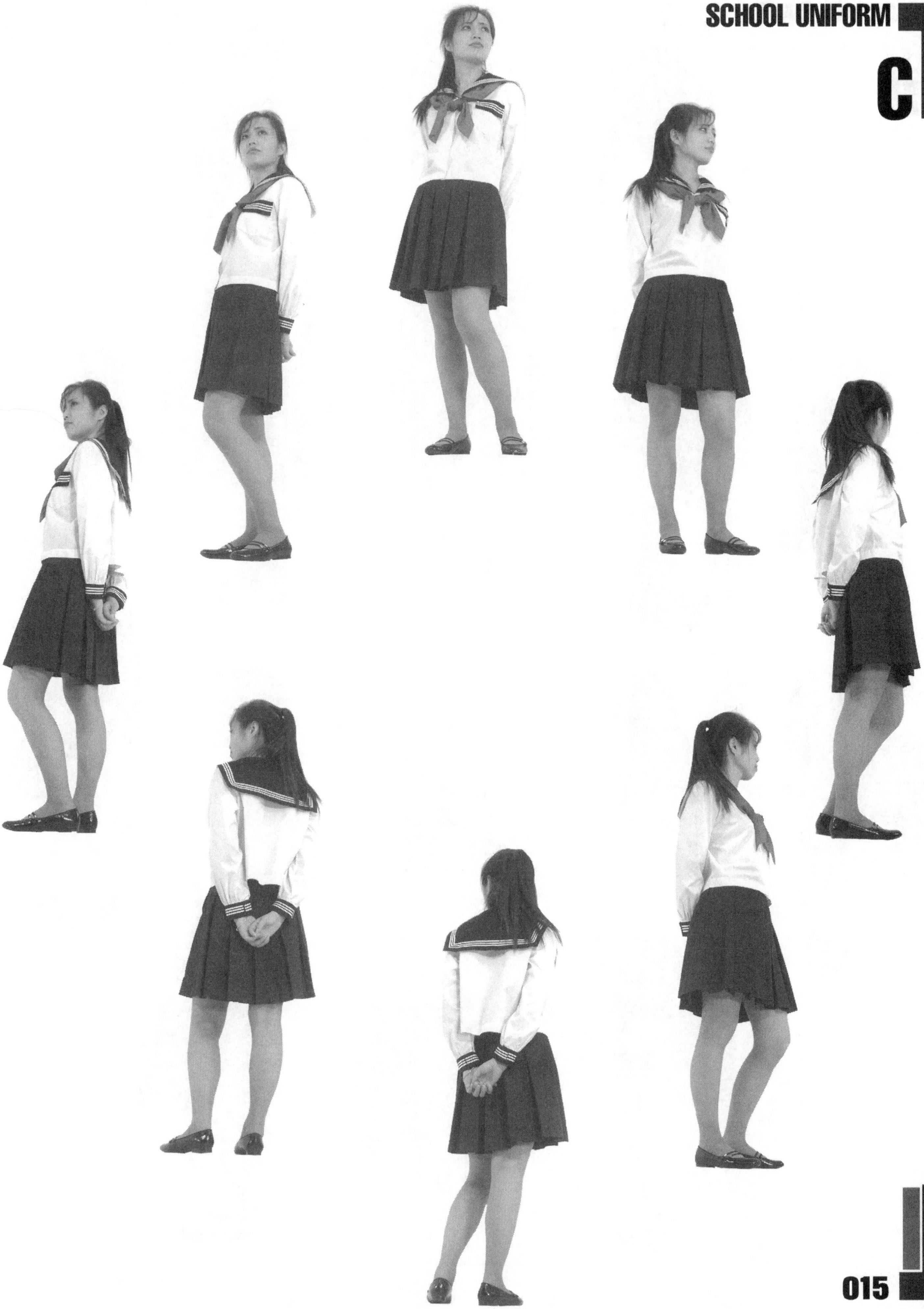

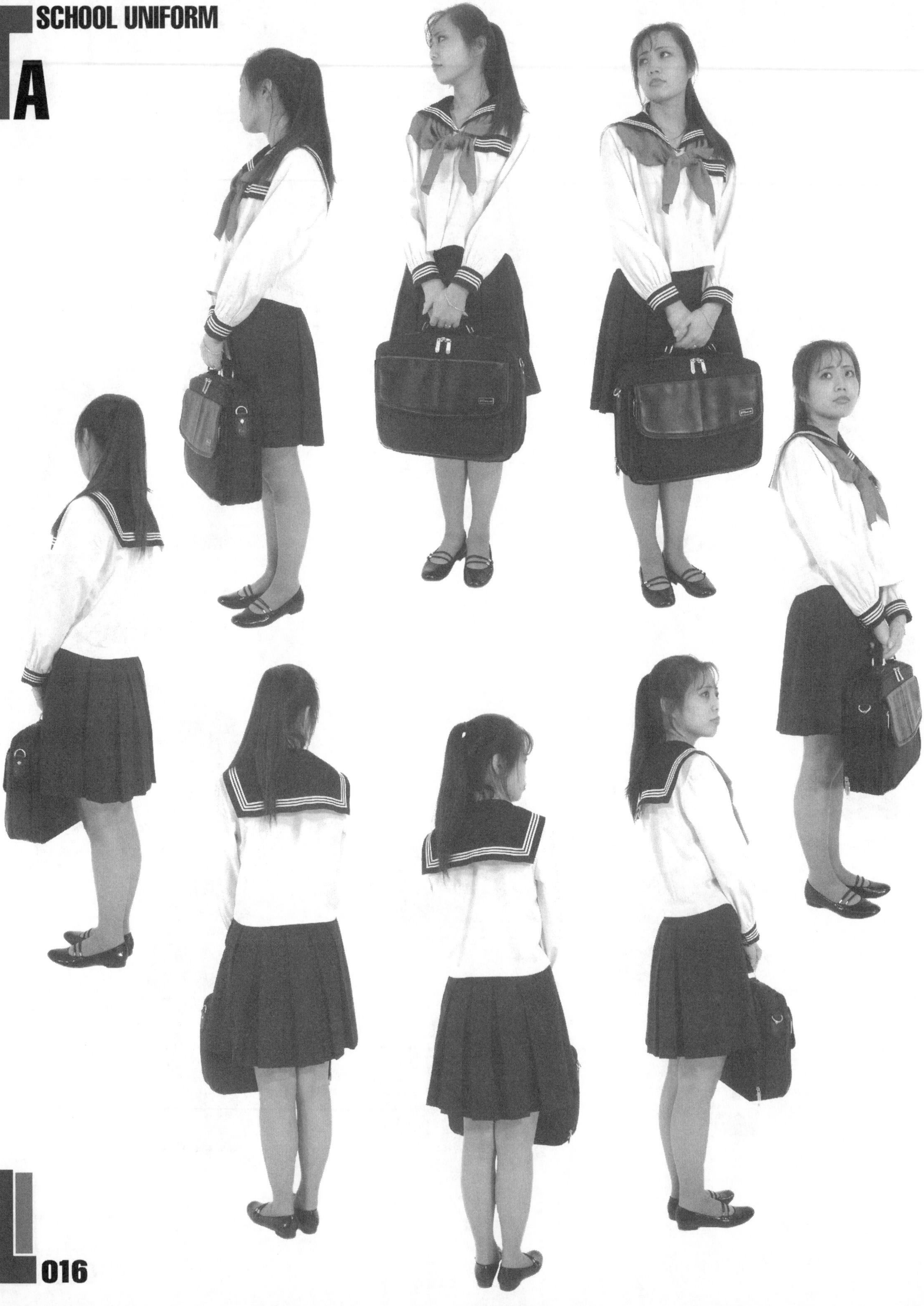

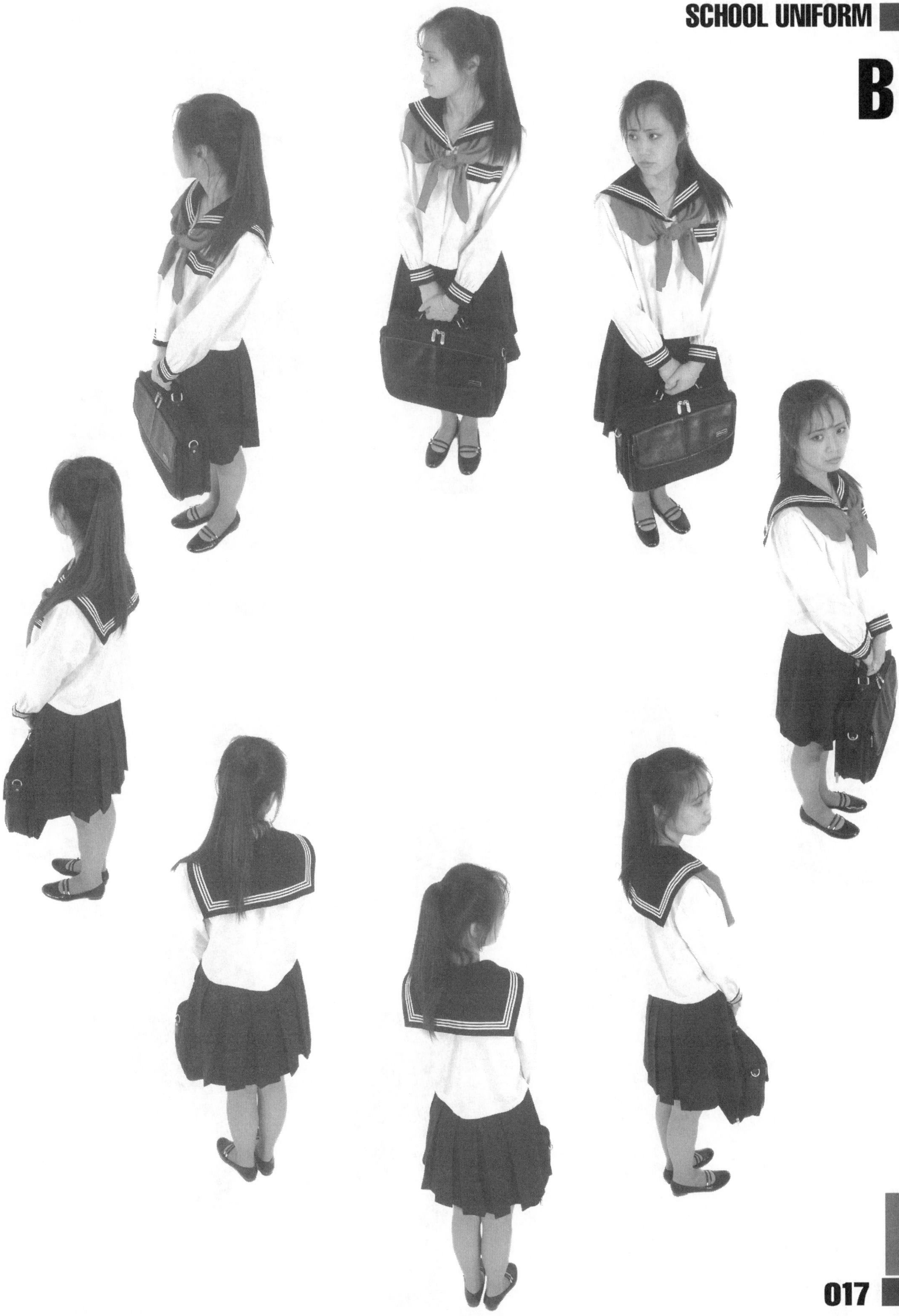

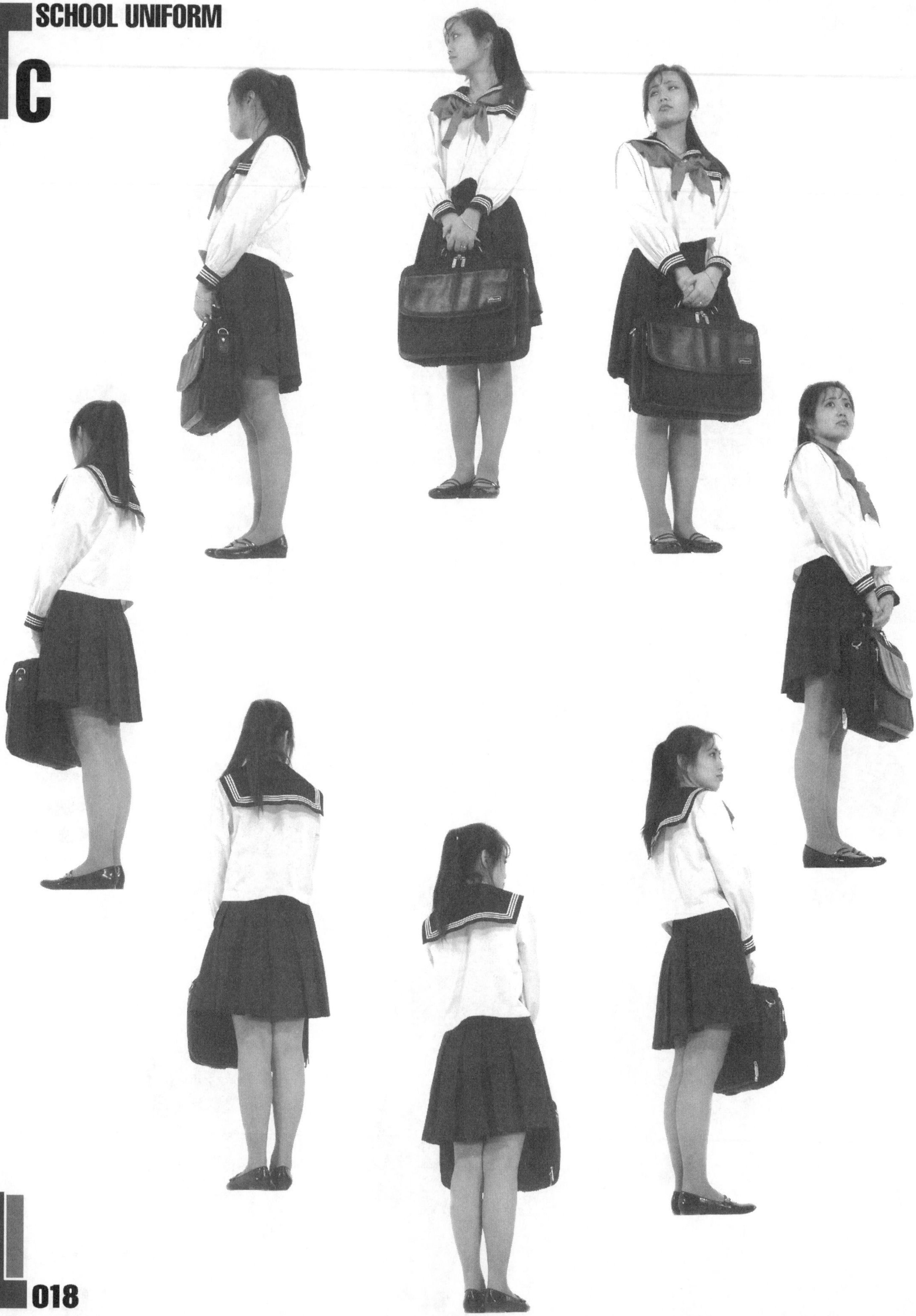

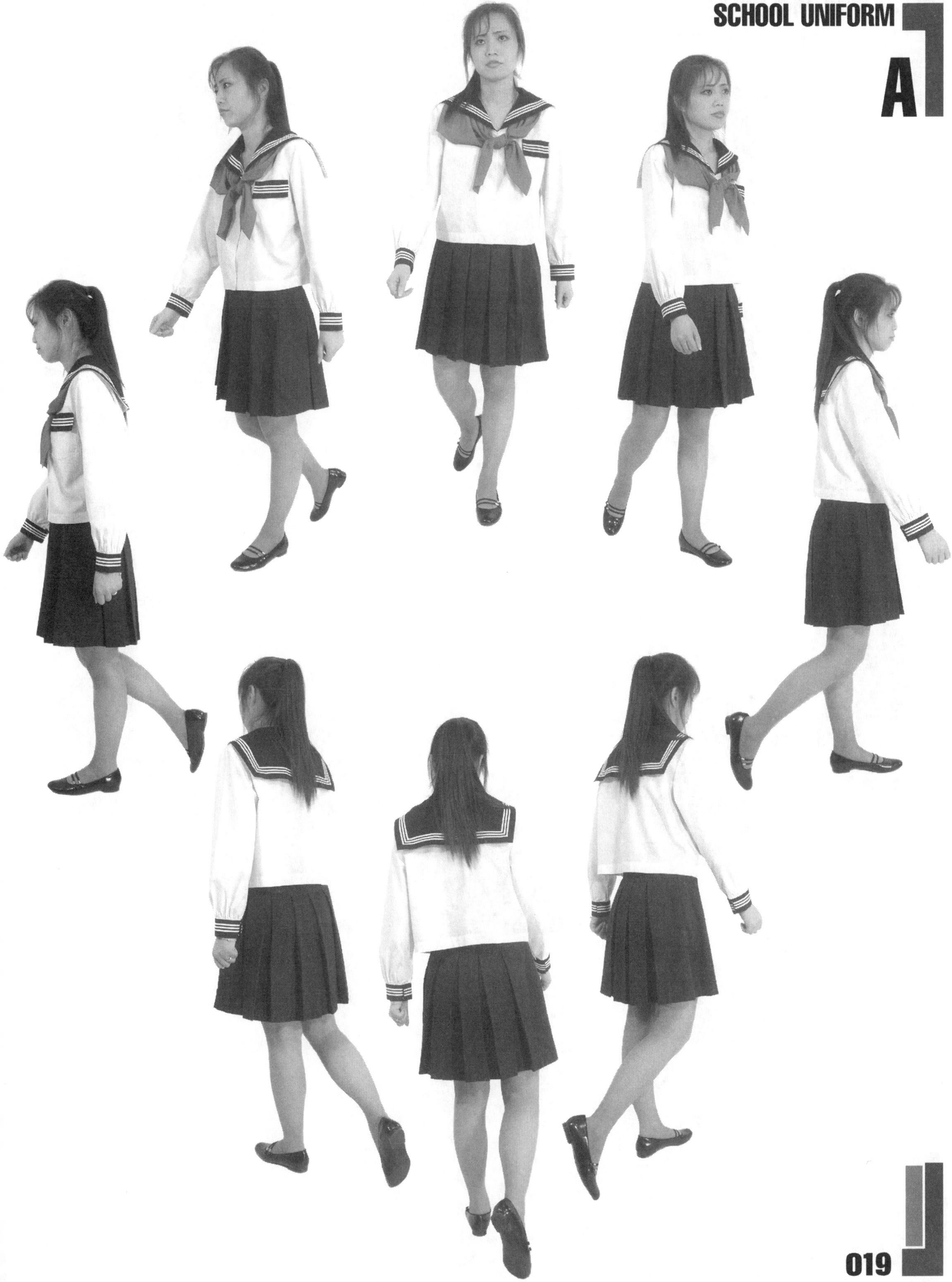

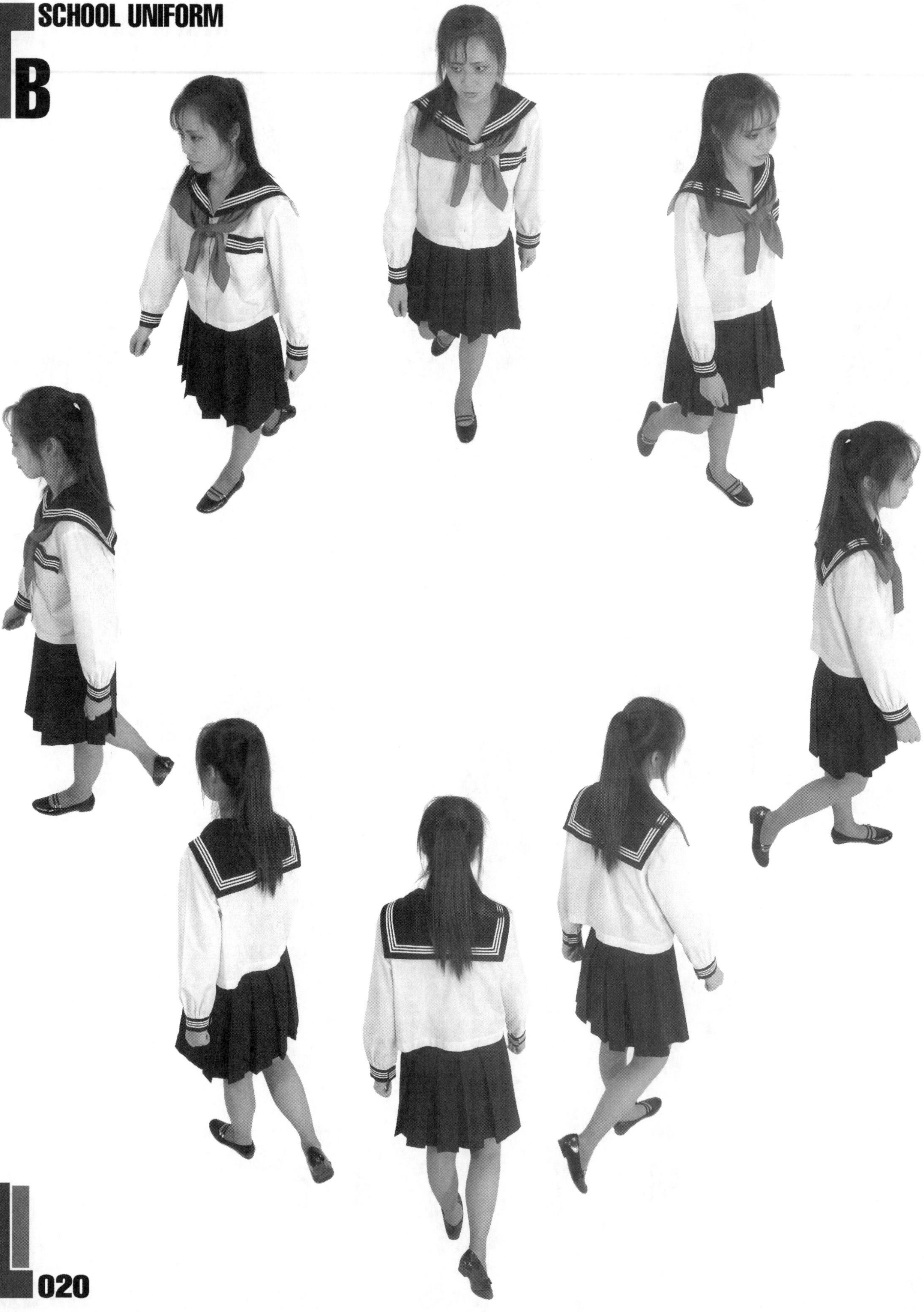

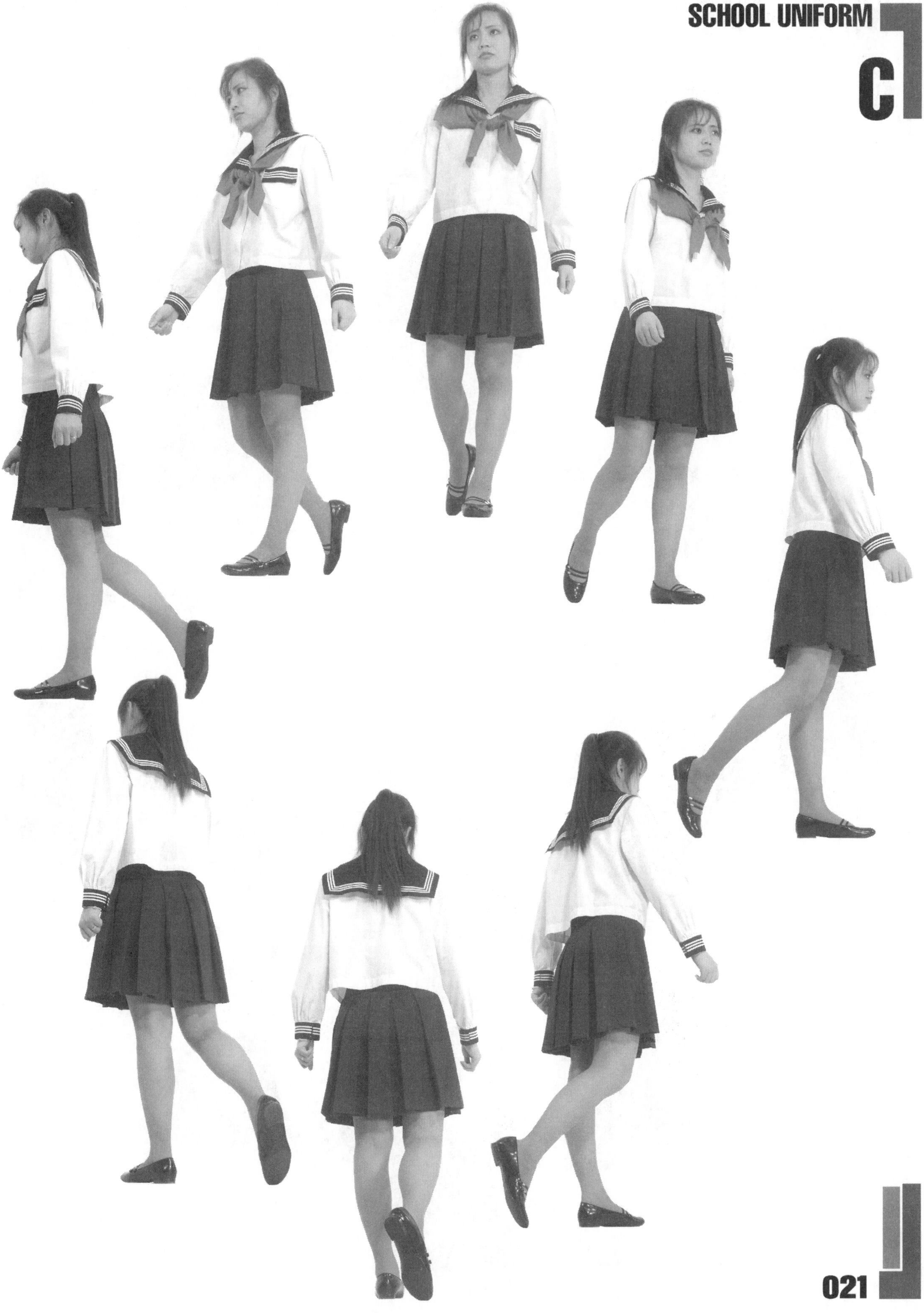

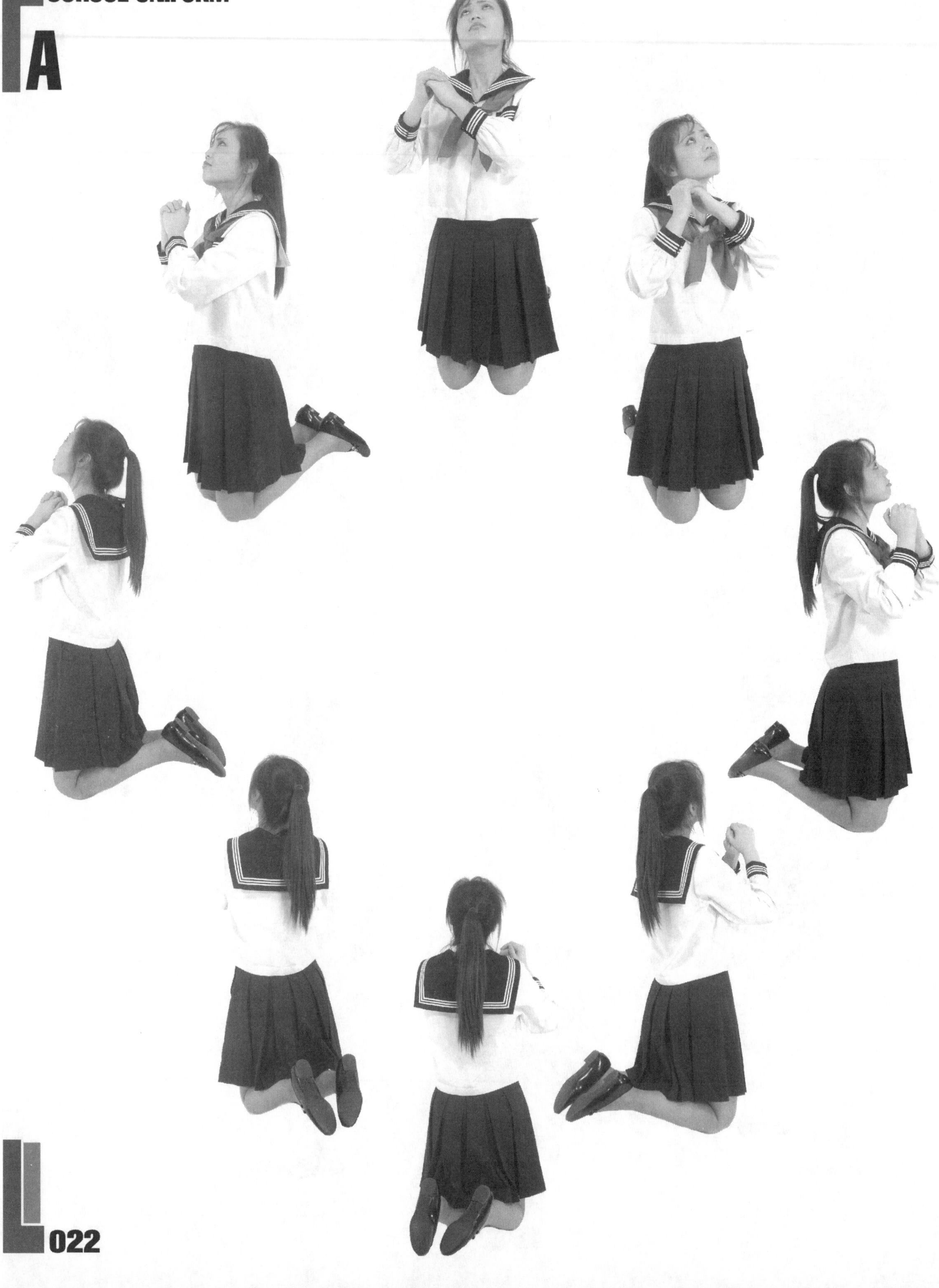

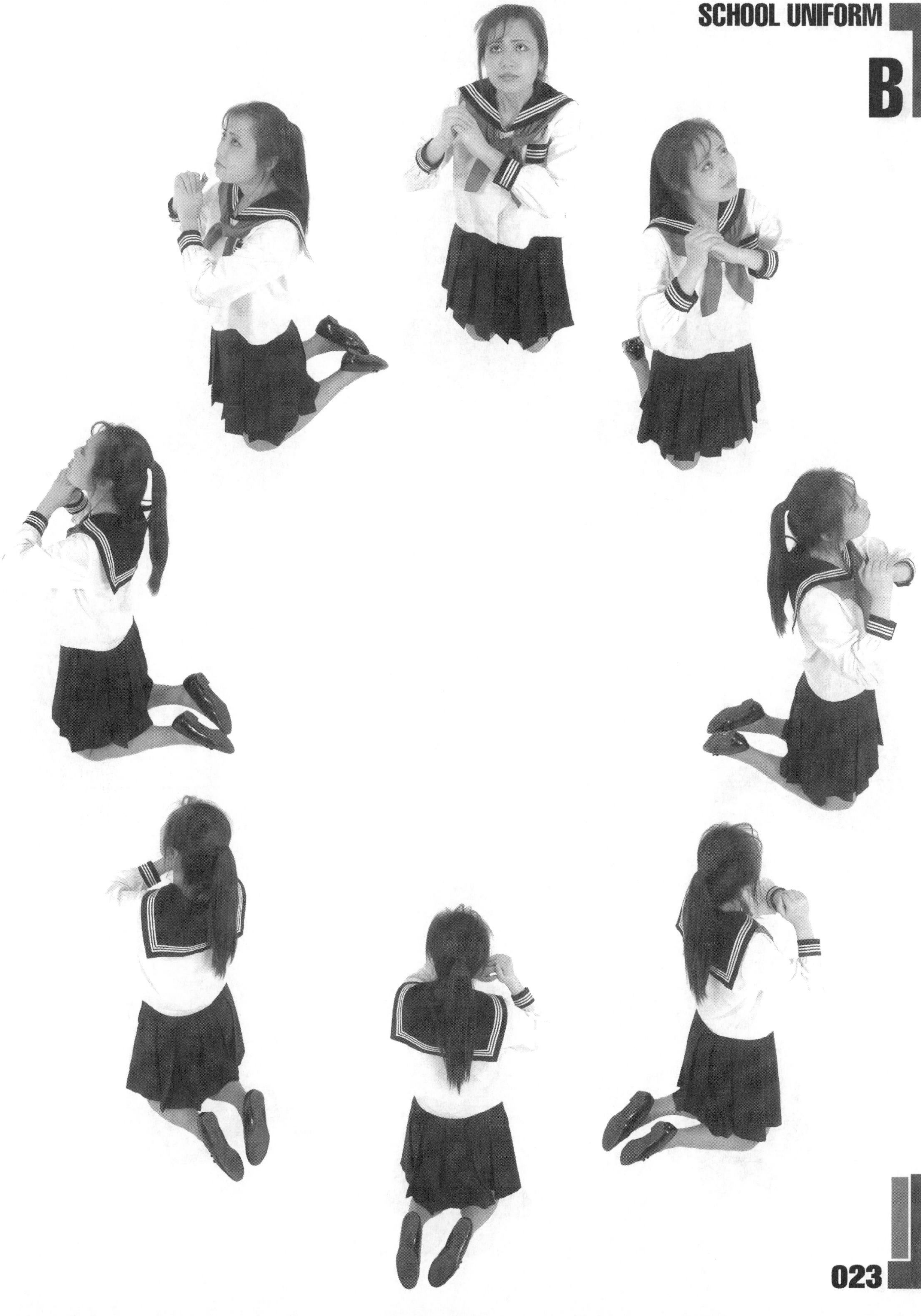

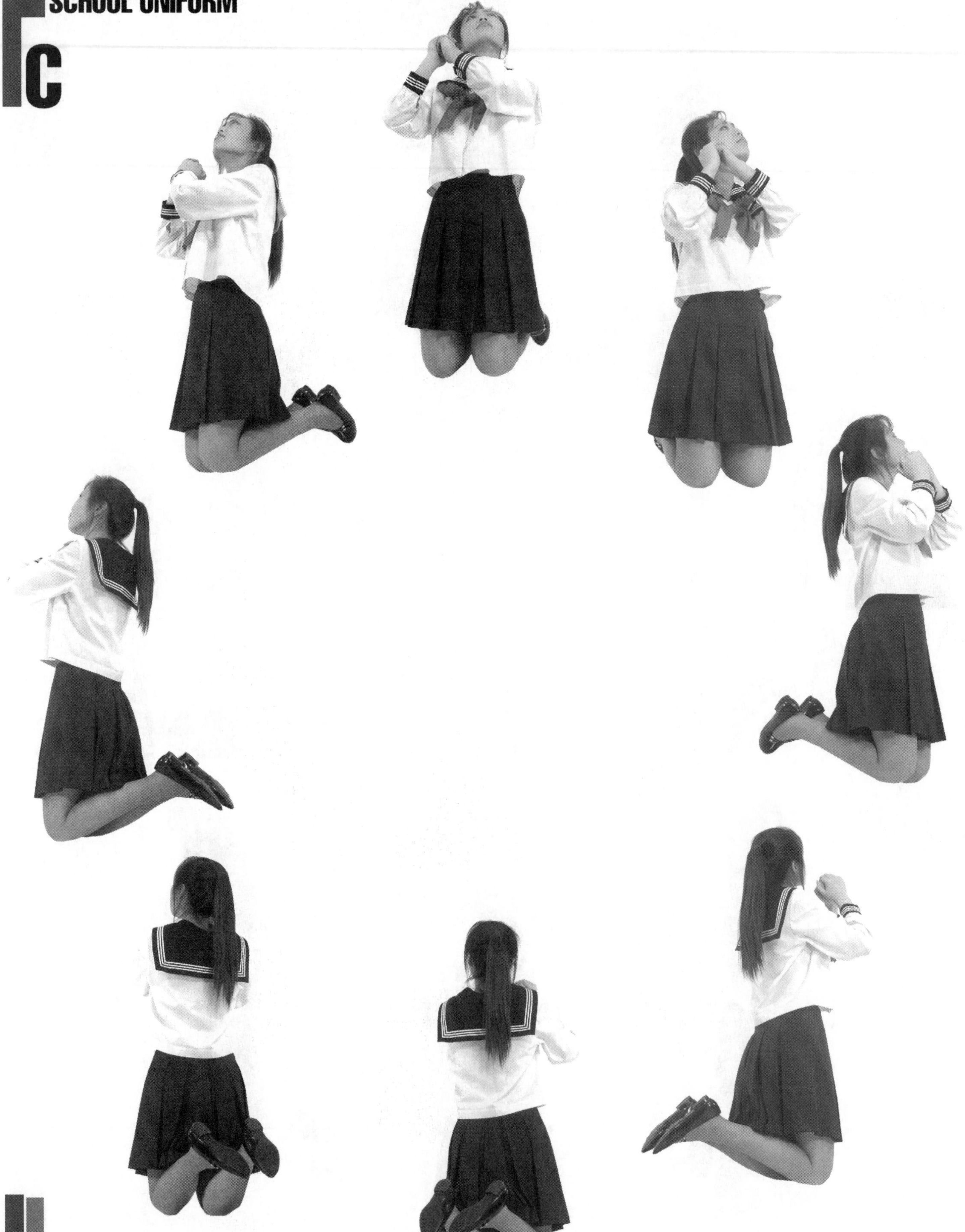

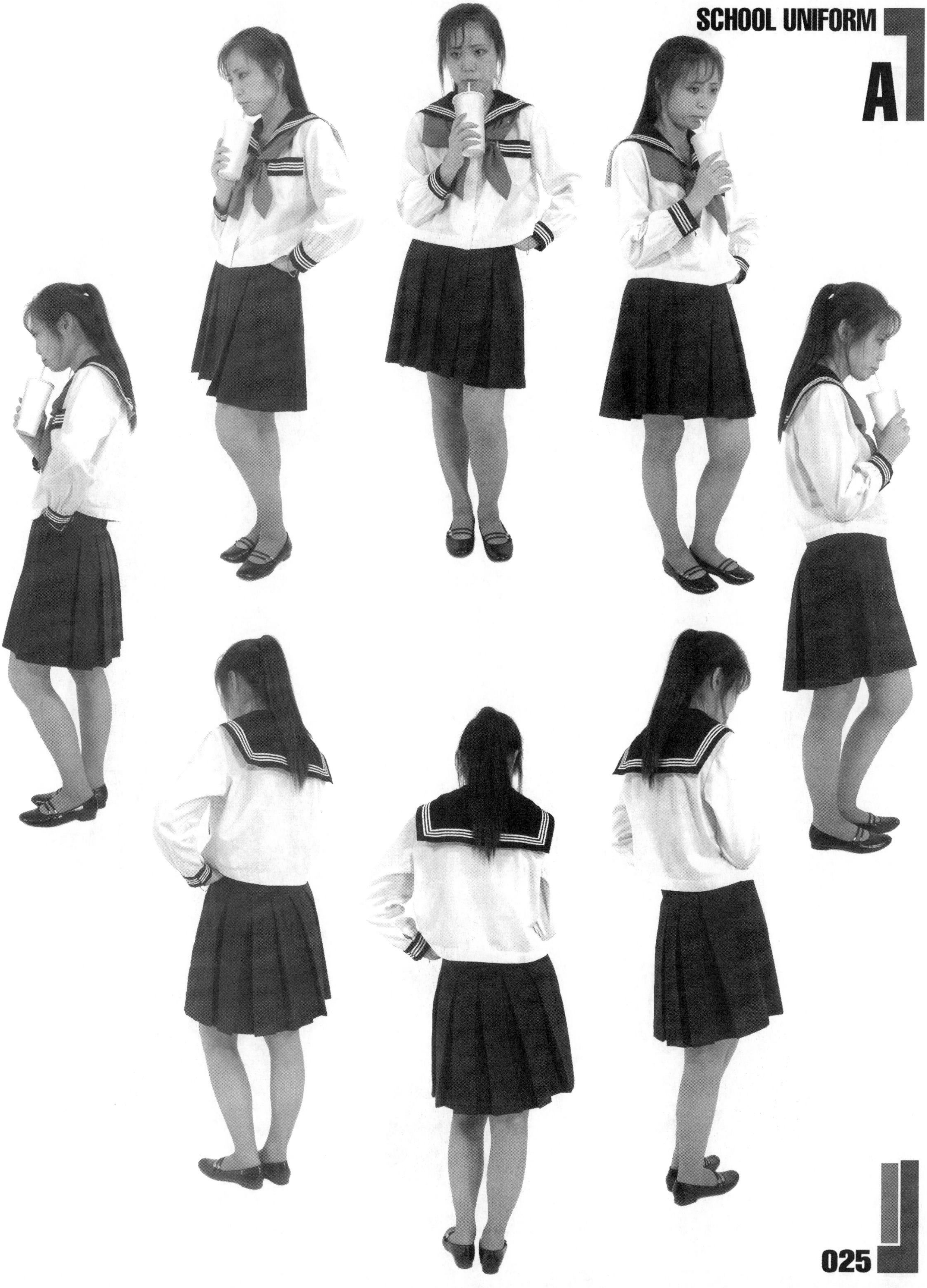

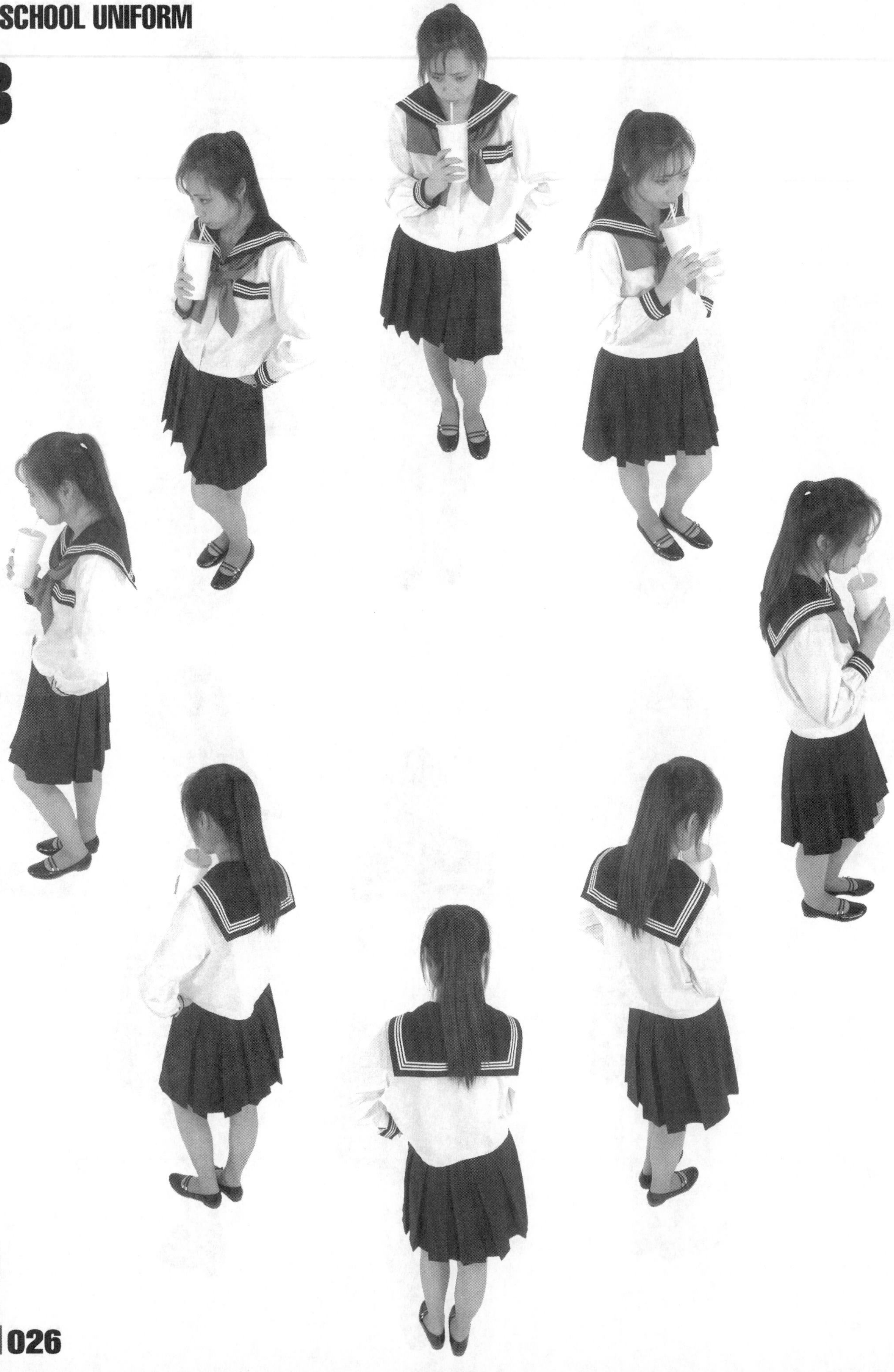

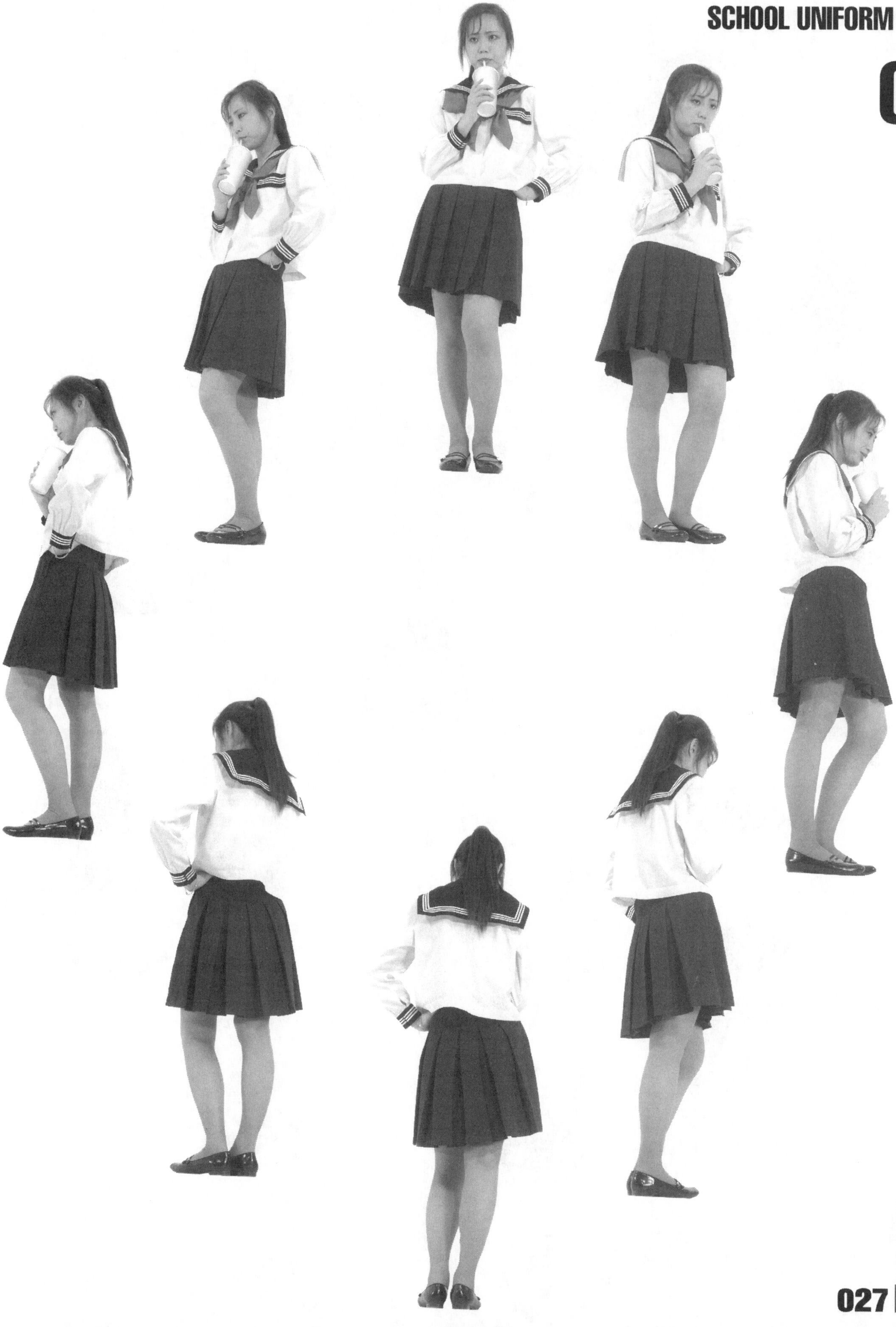

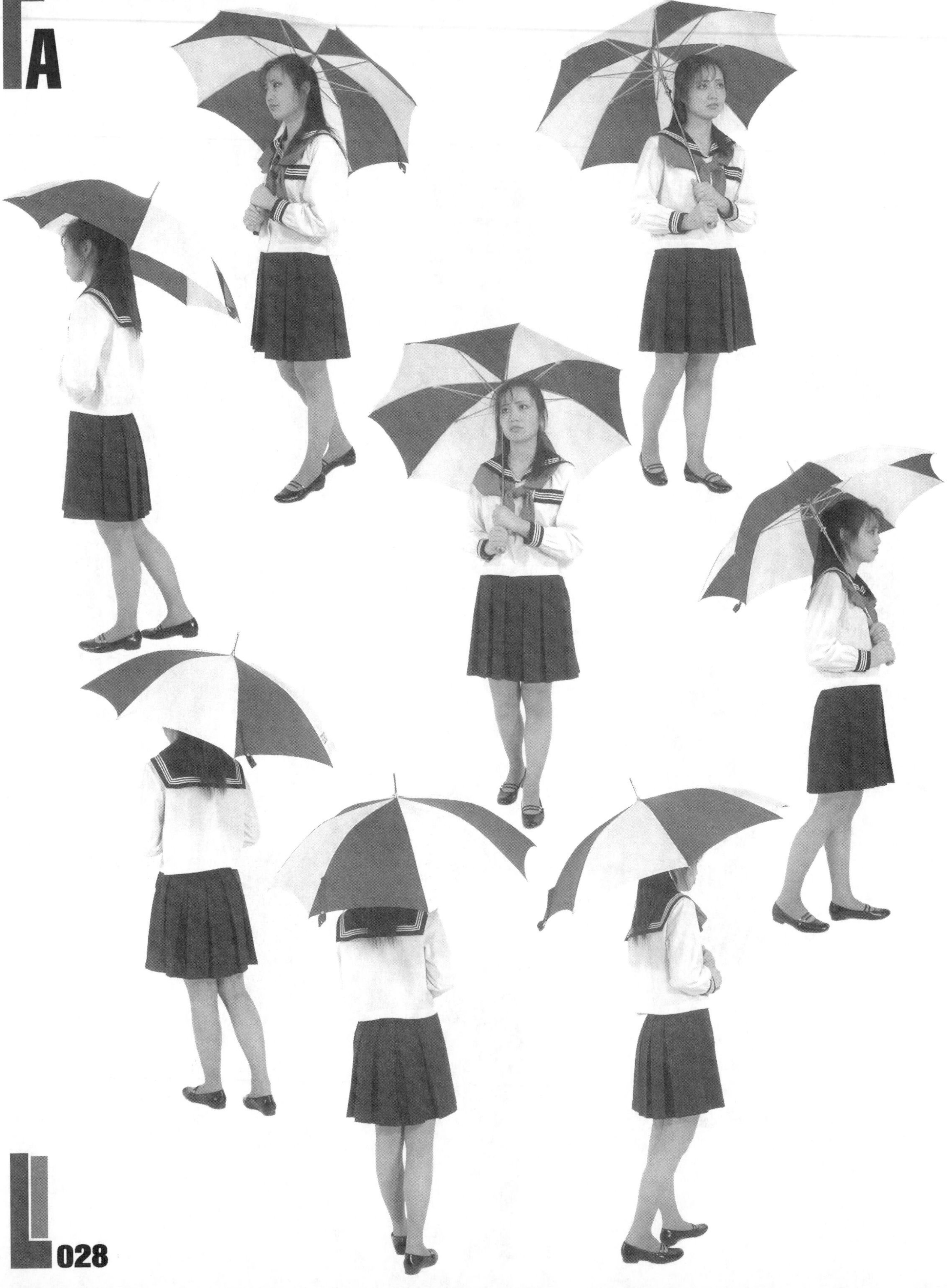

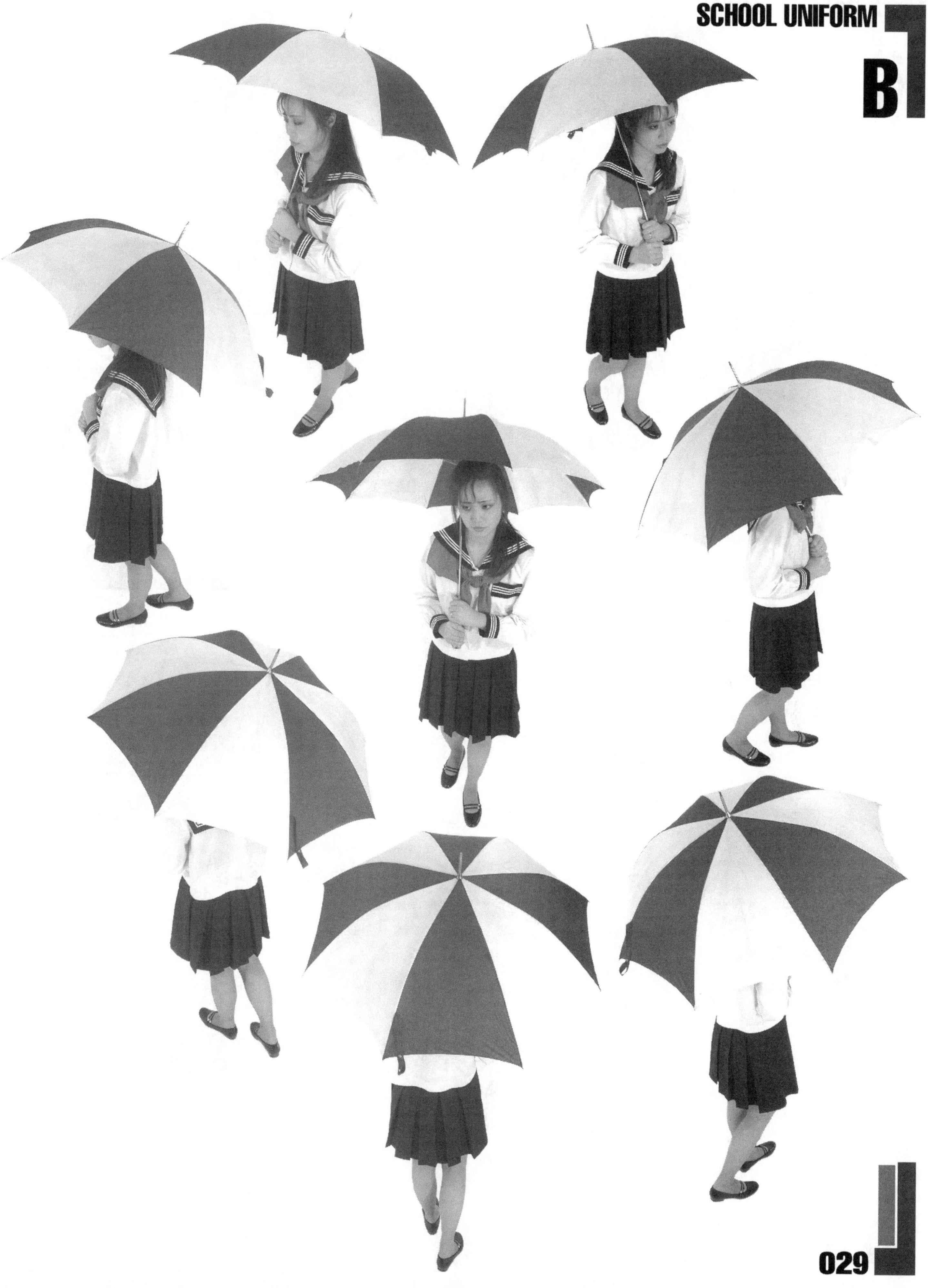

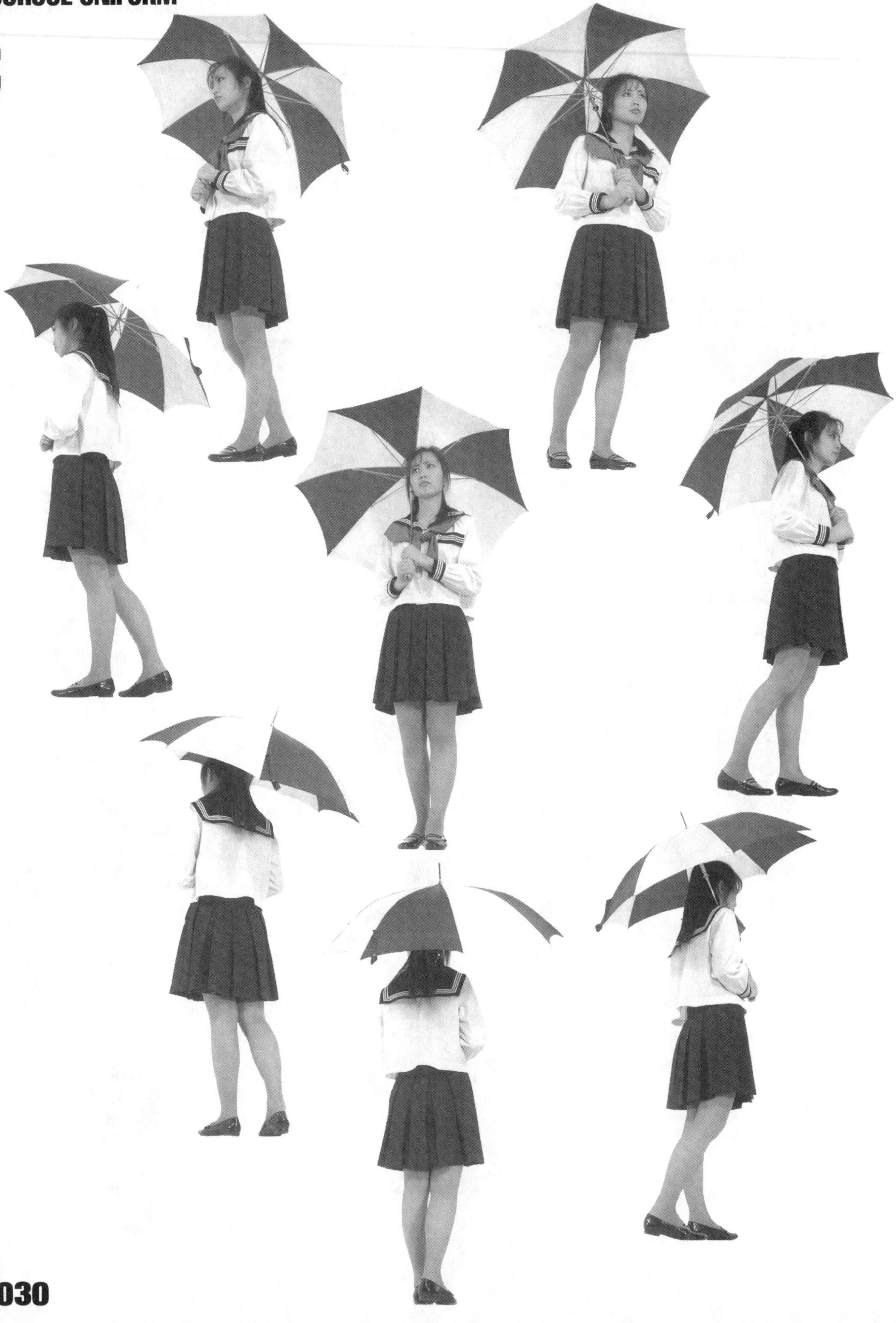

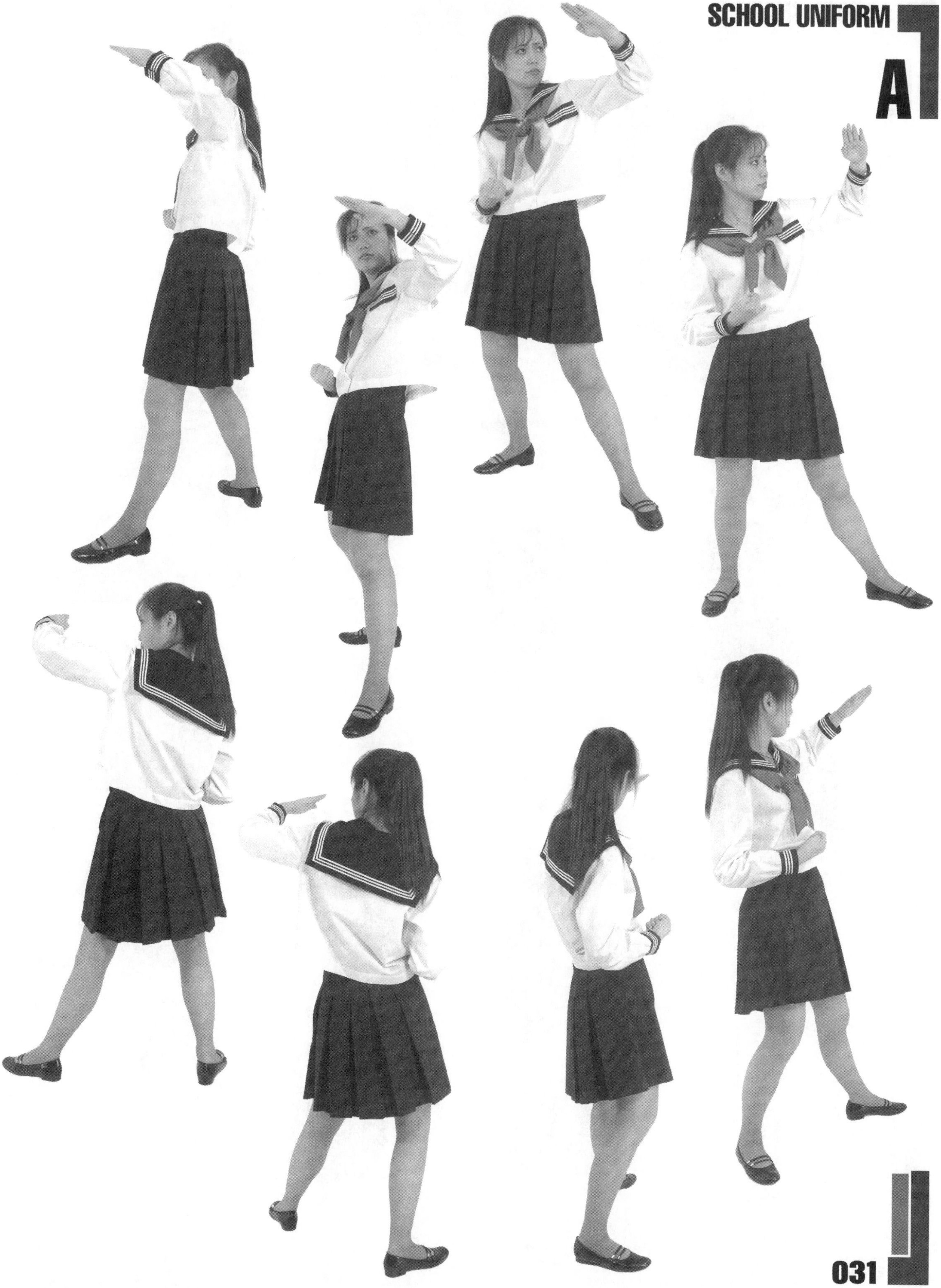

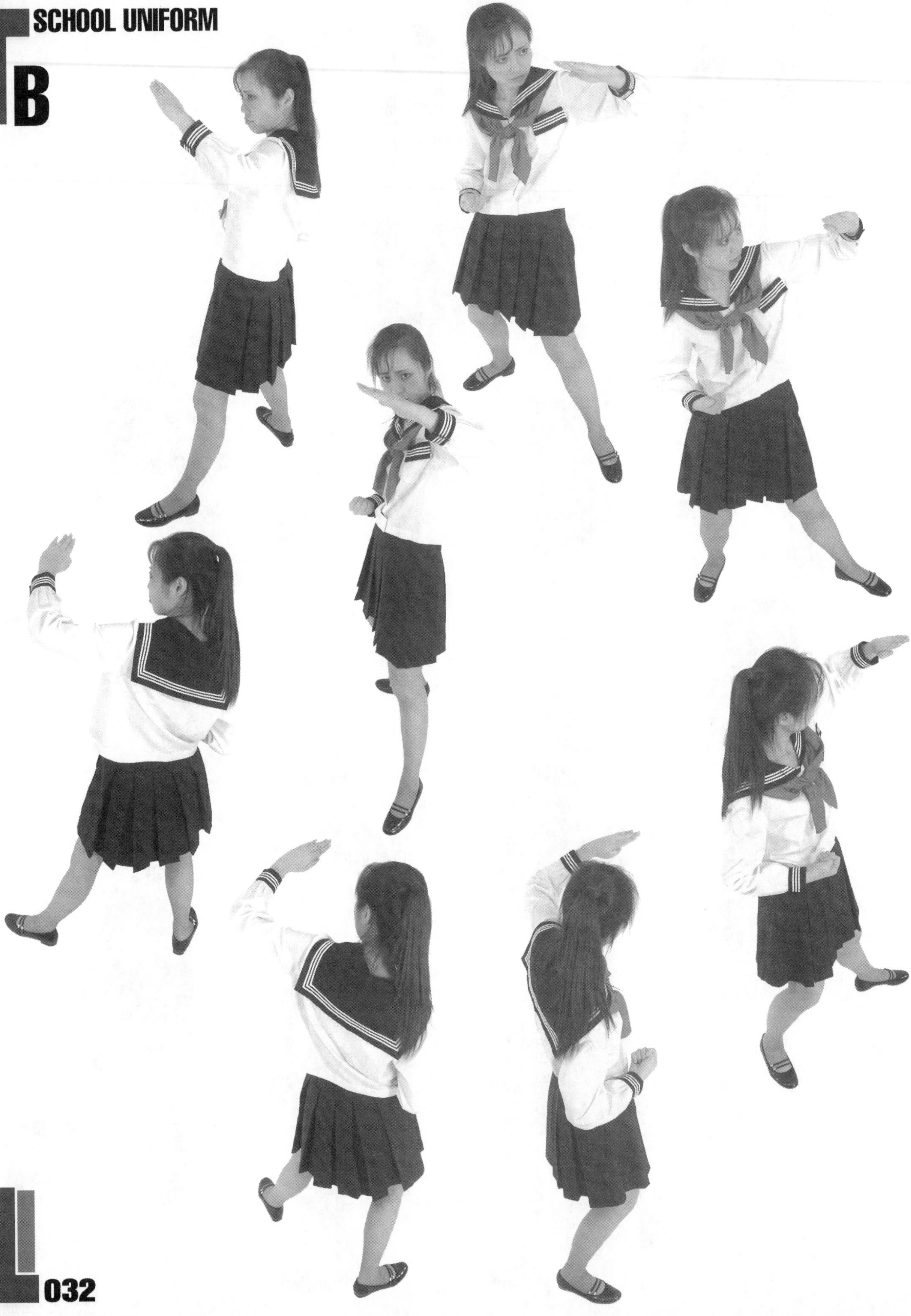

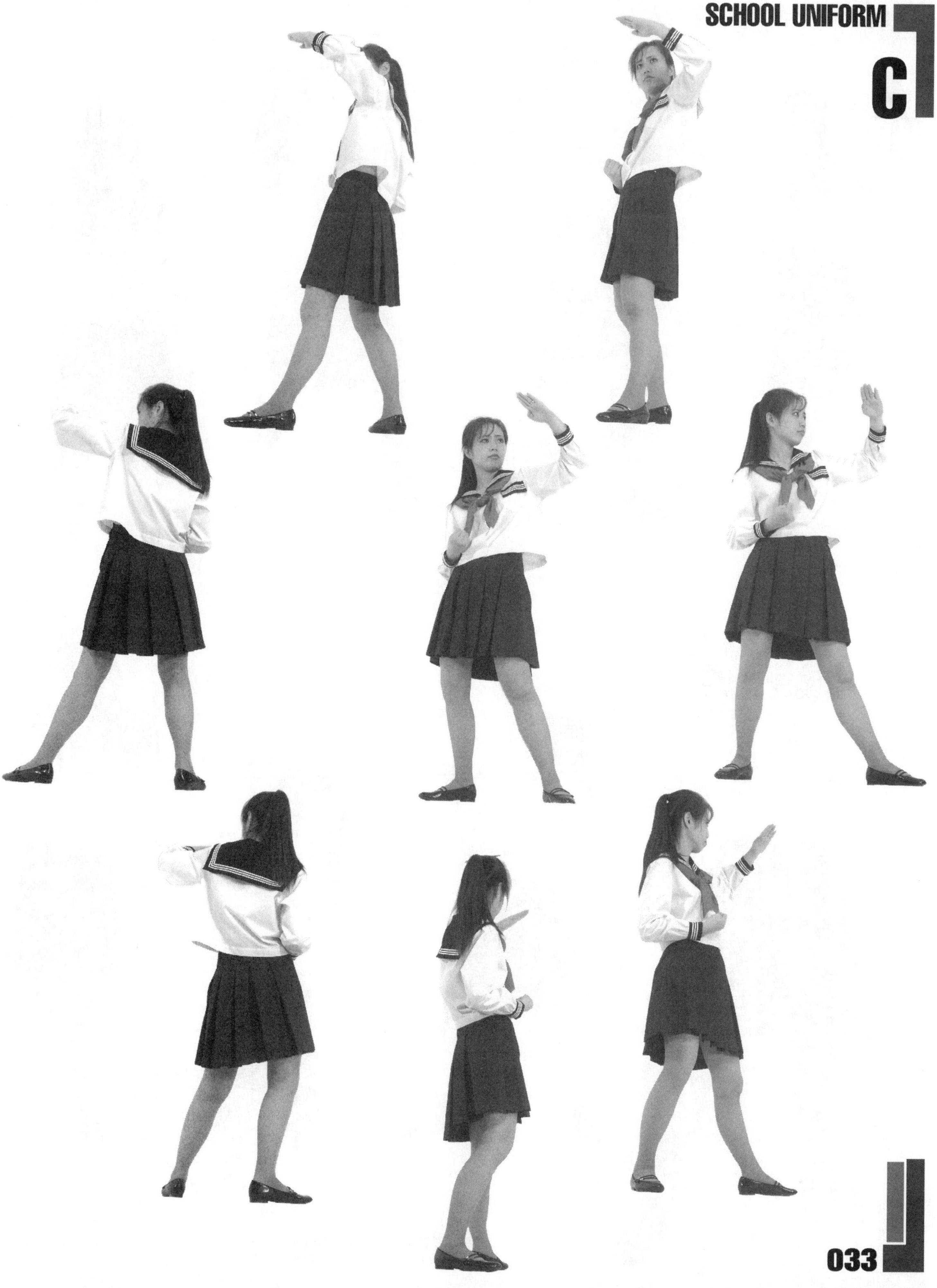

A

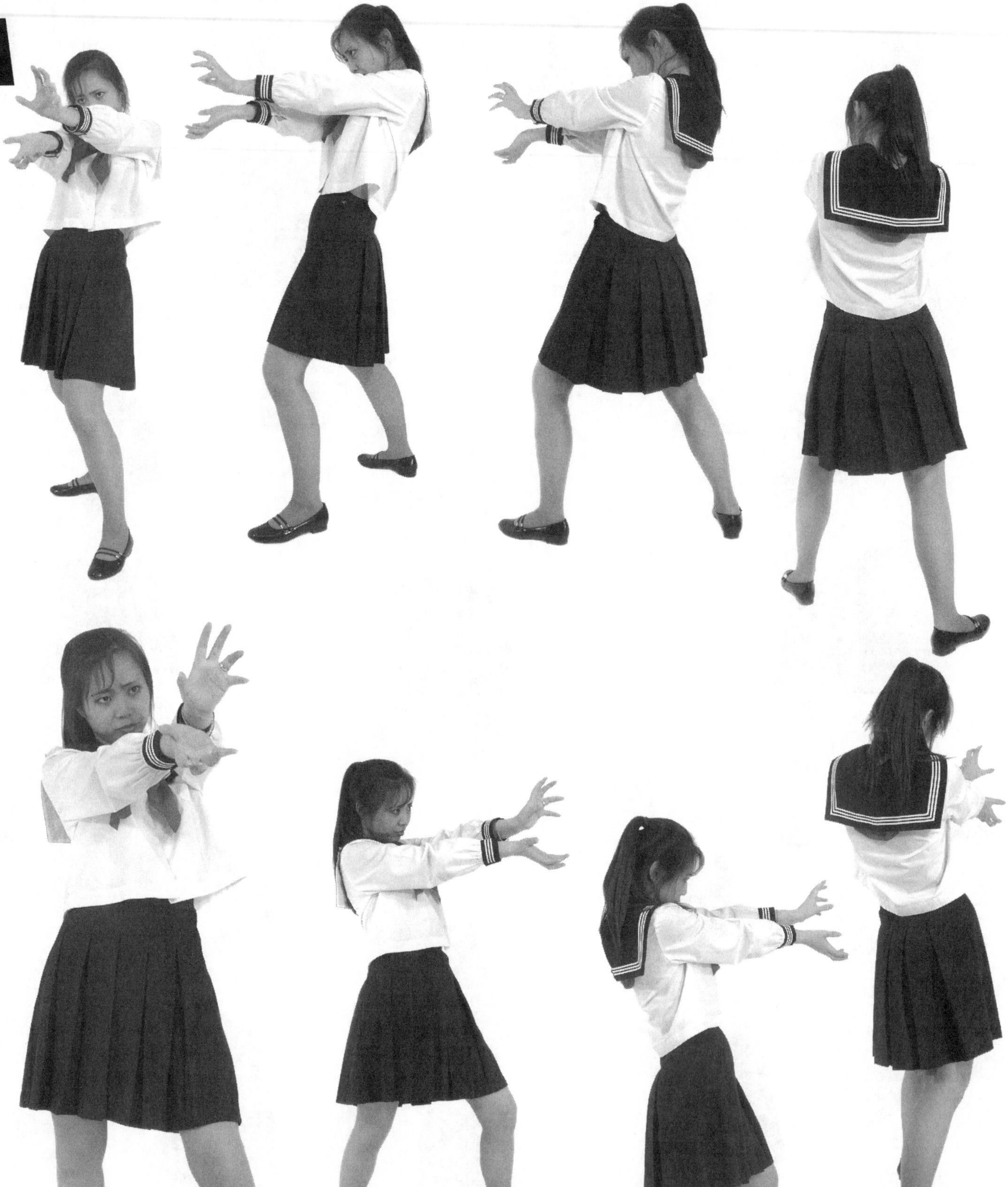

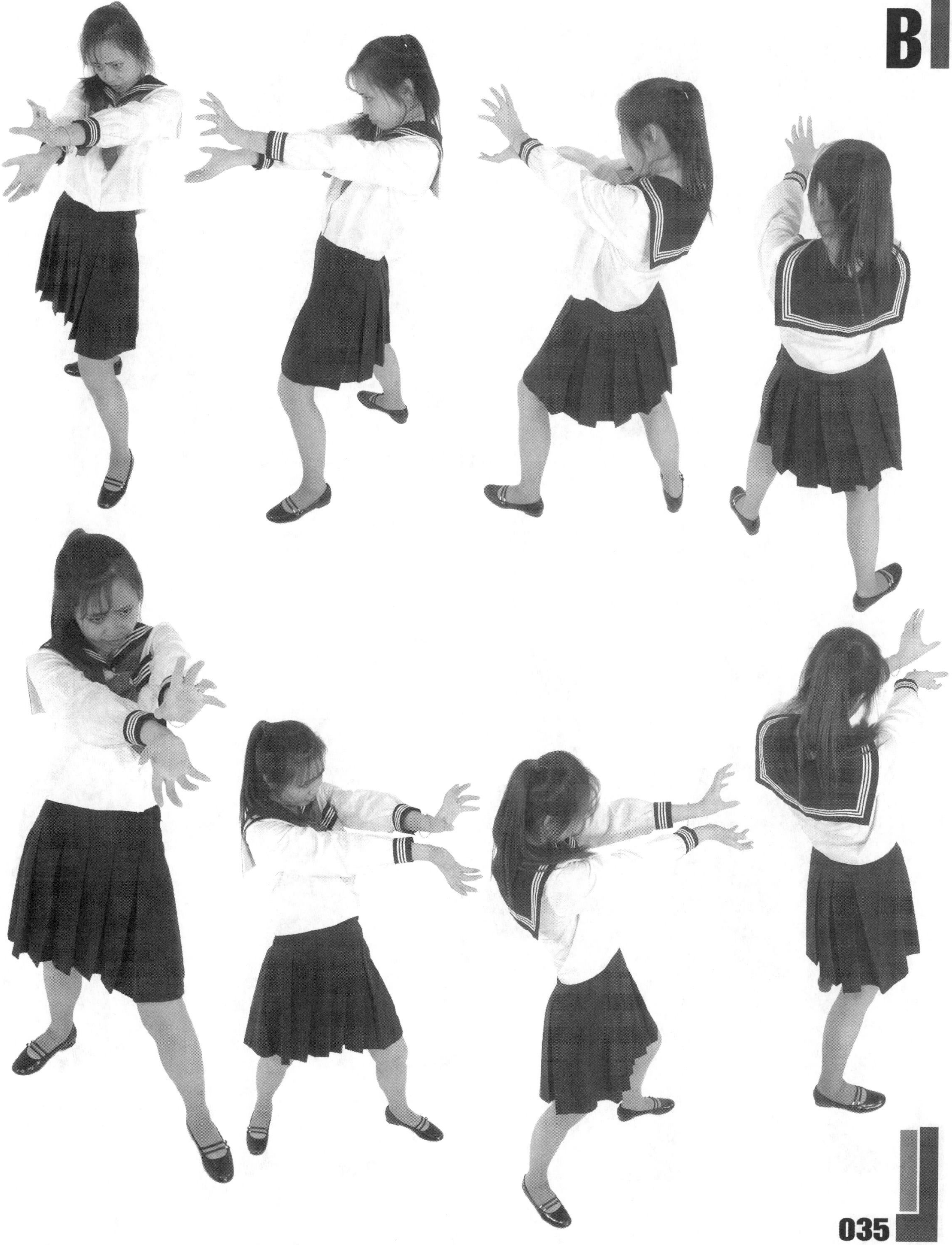

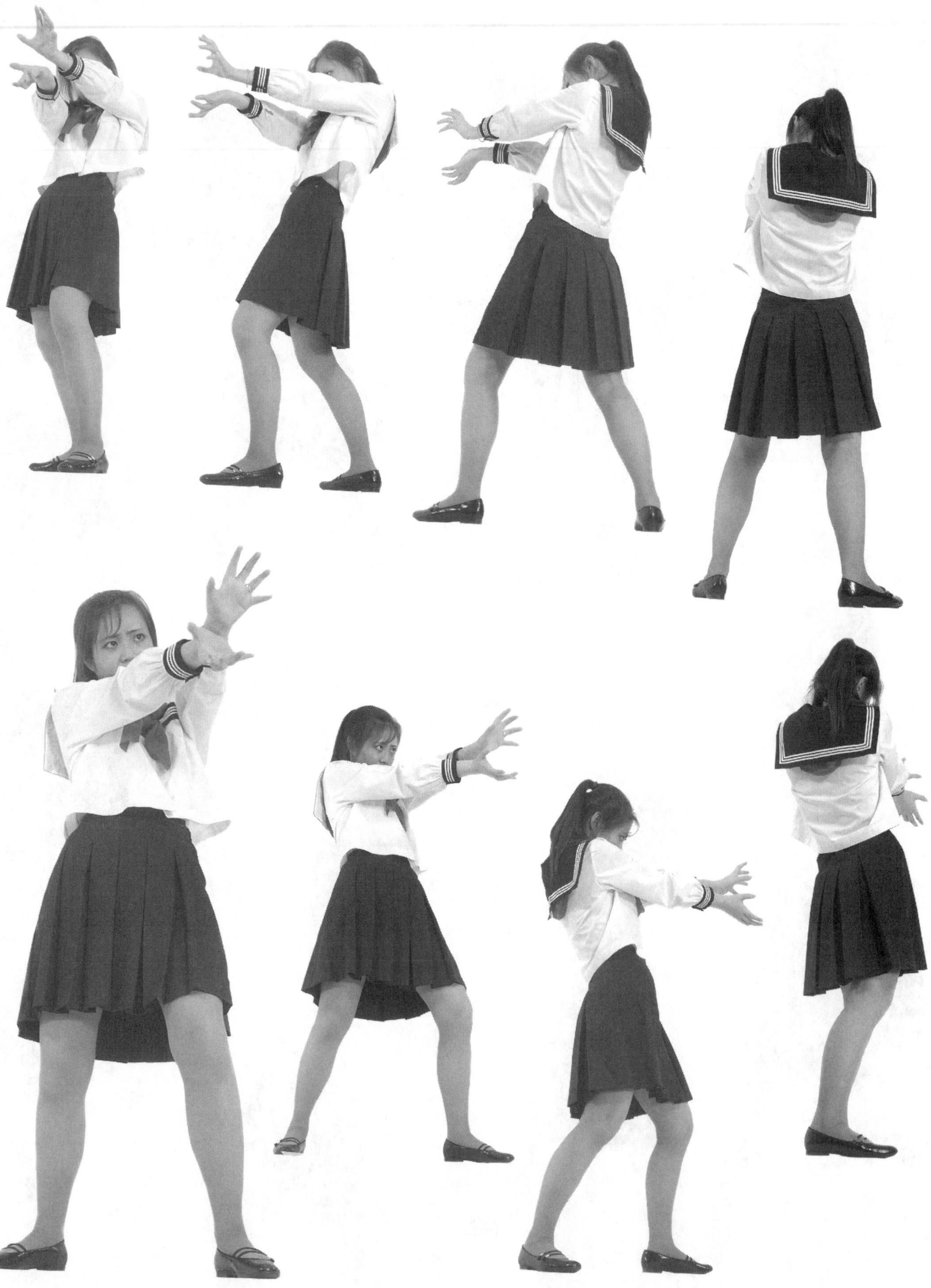

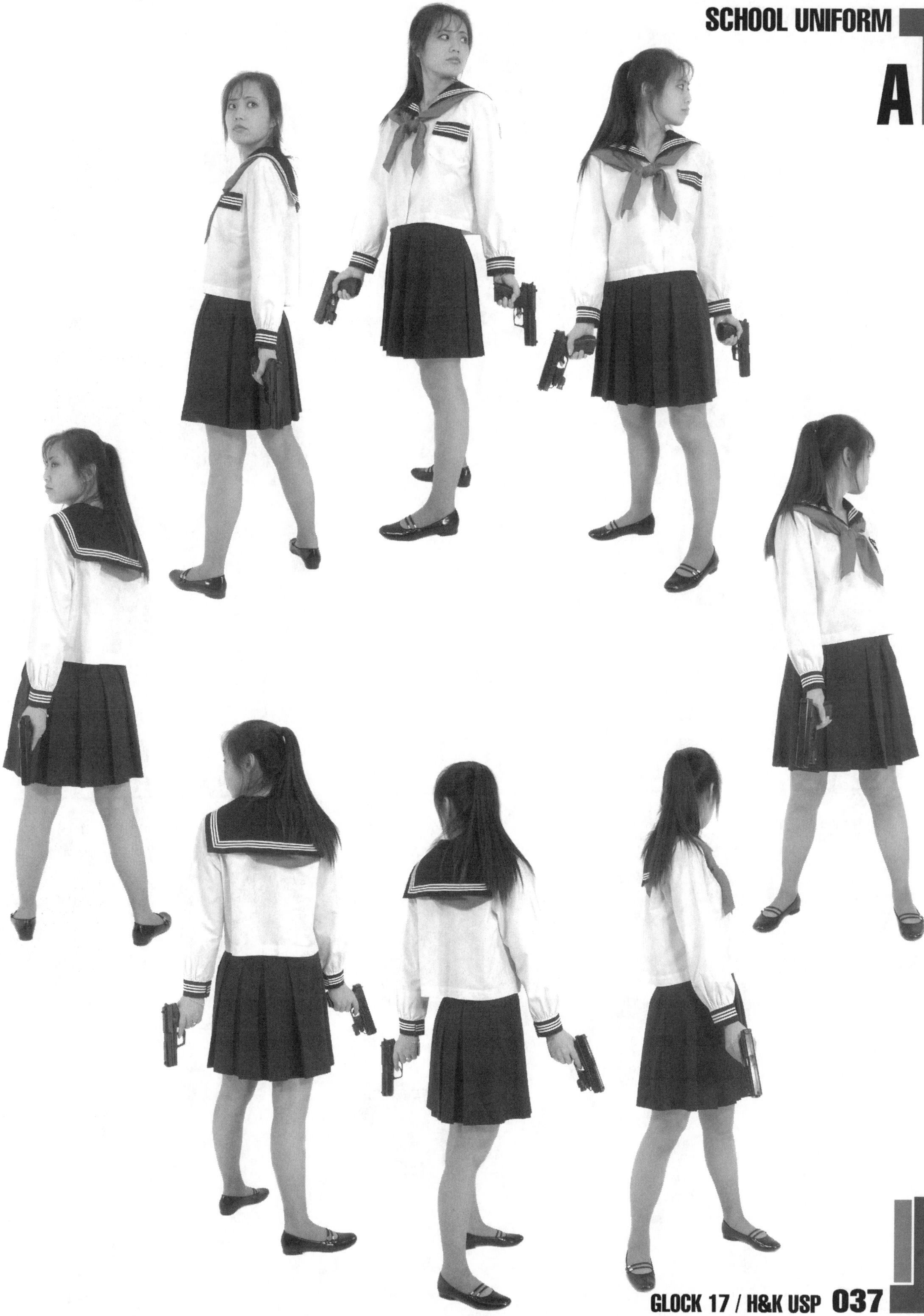

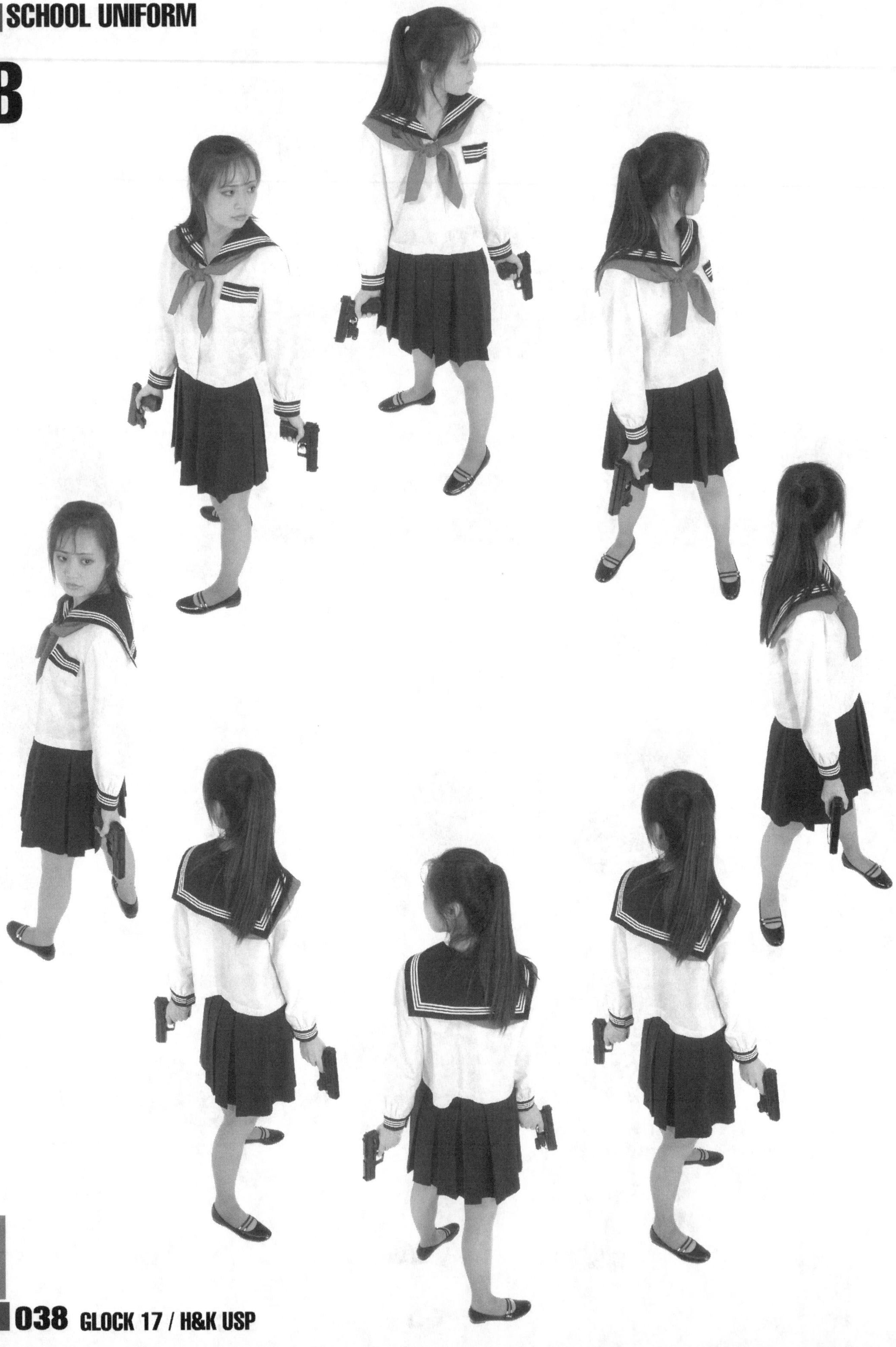

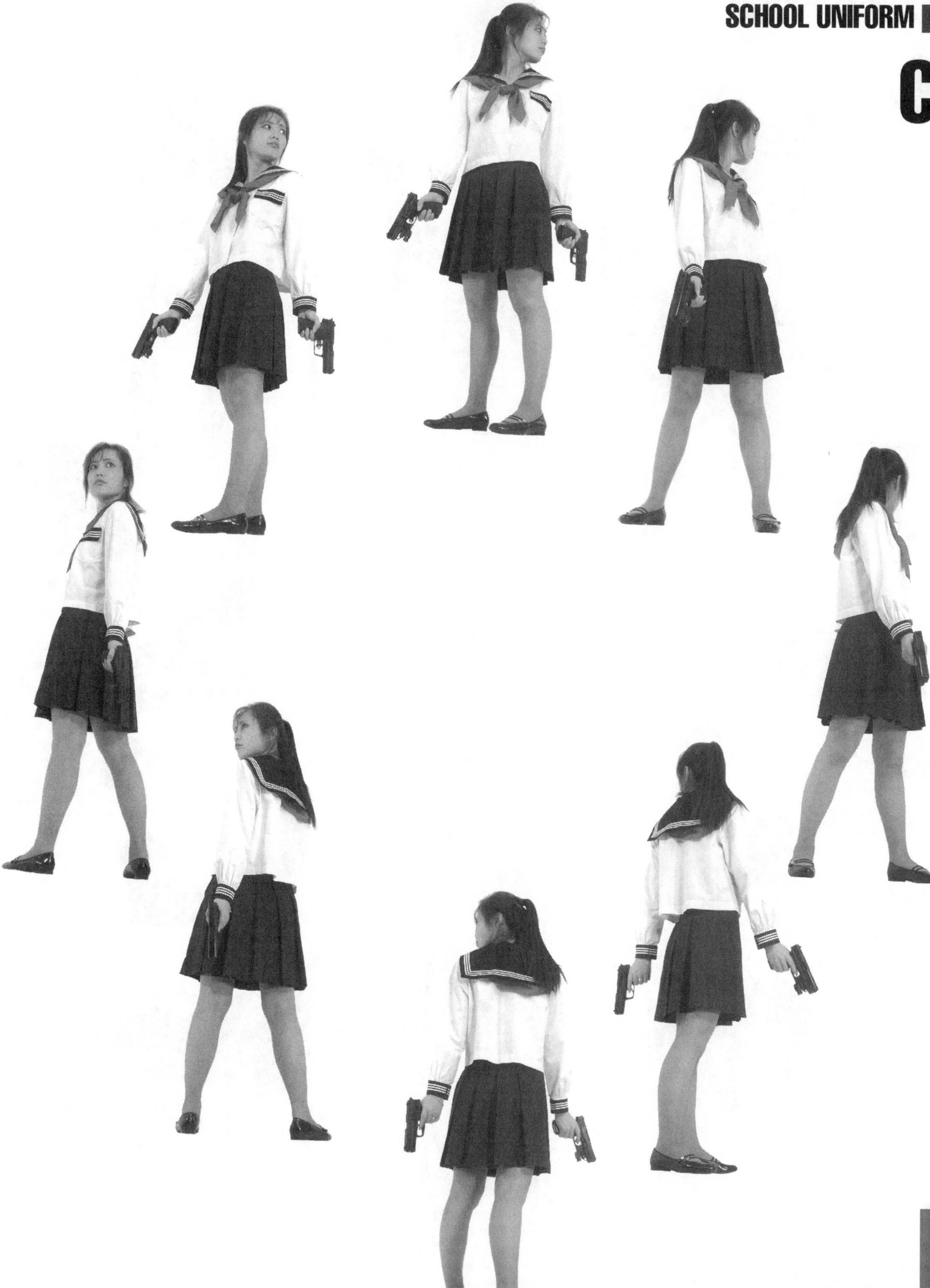

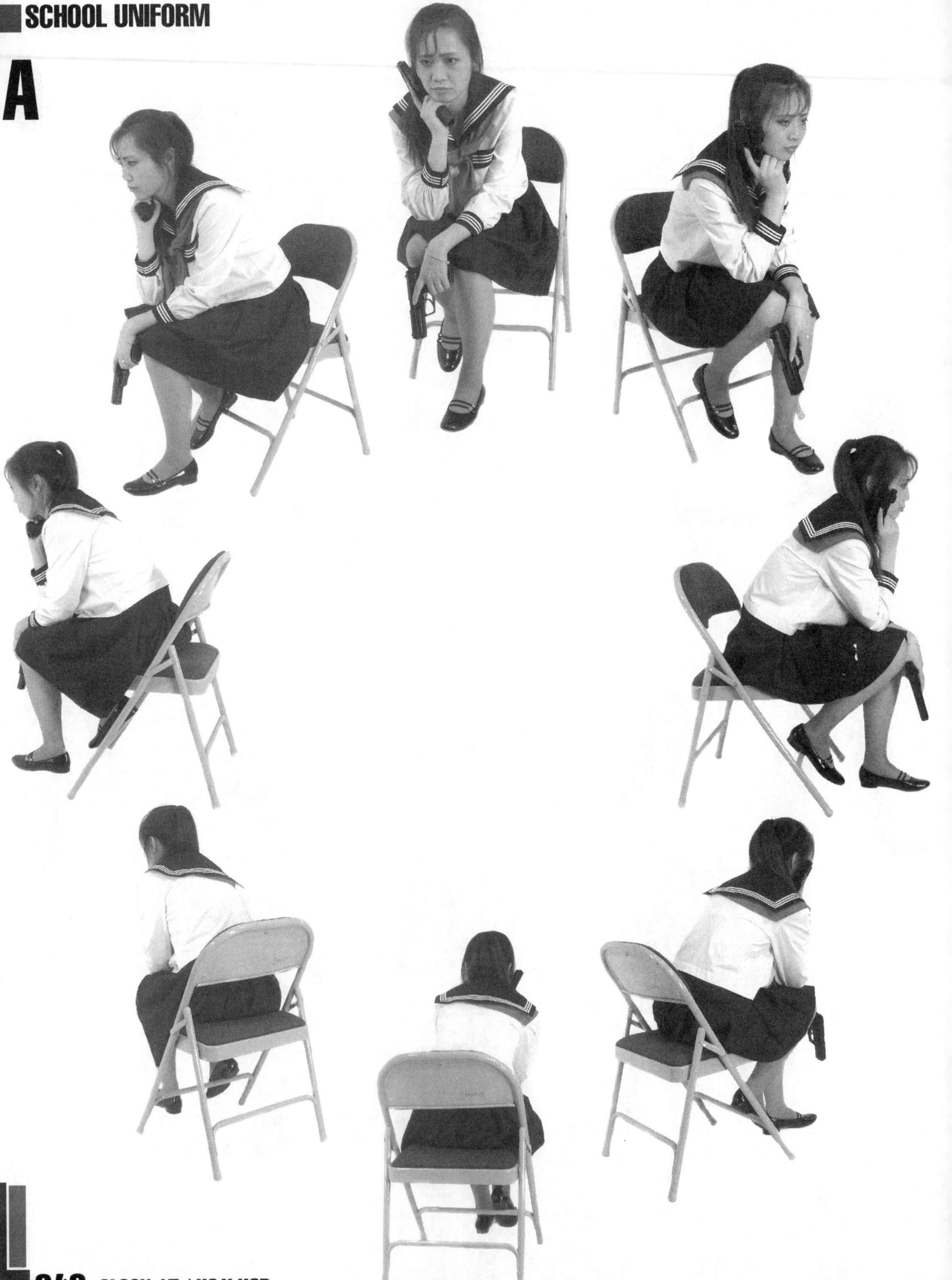

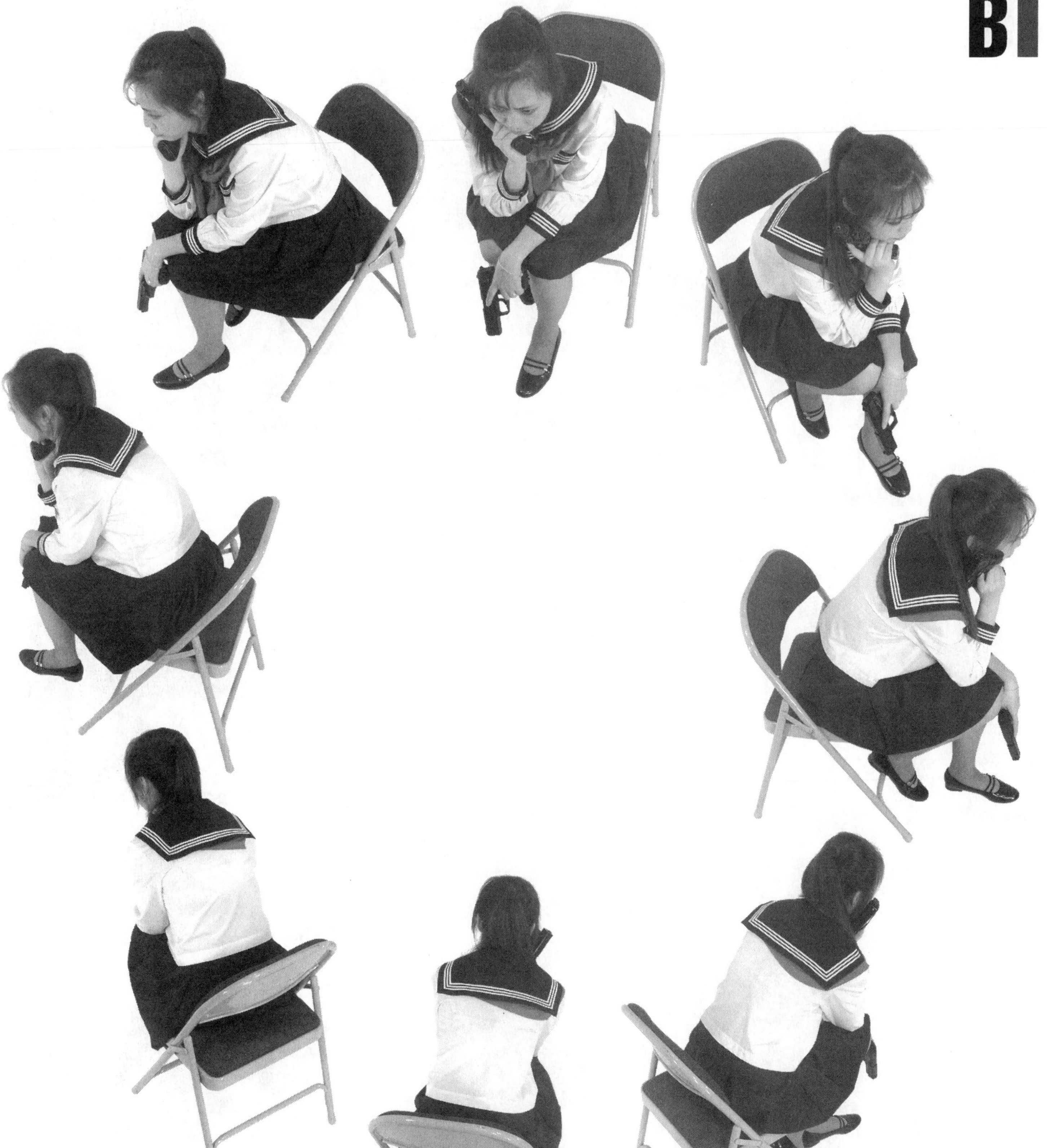

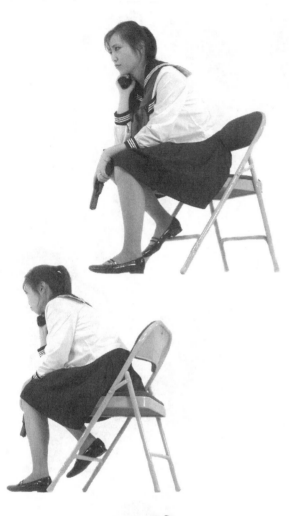

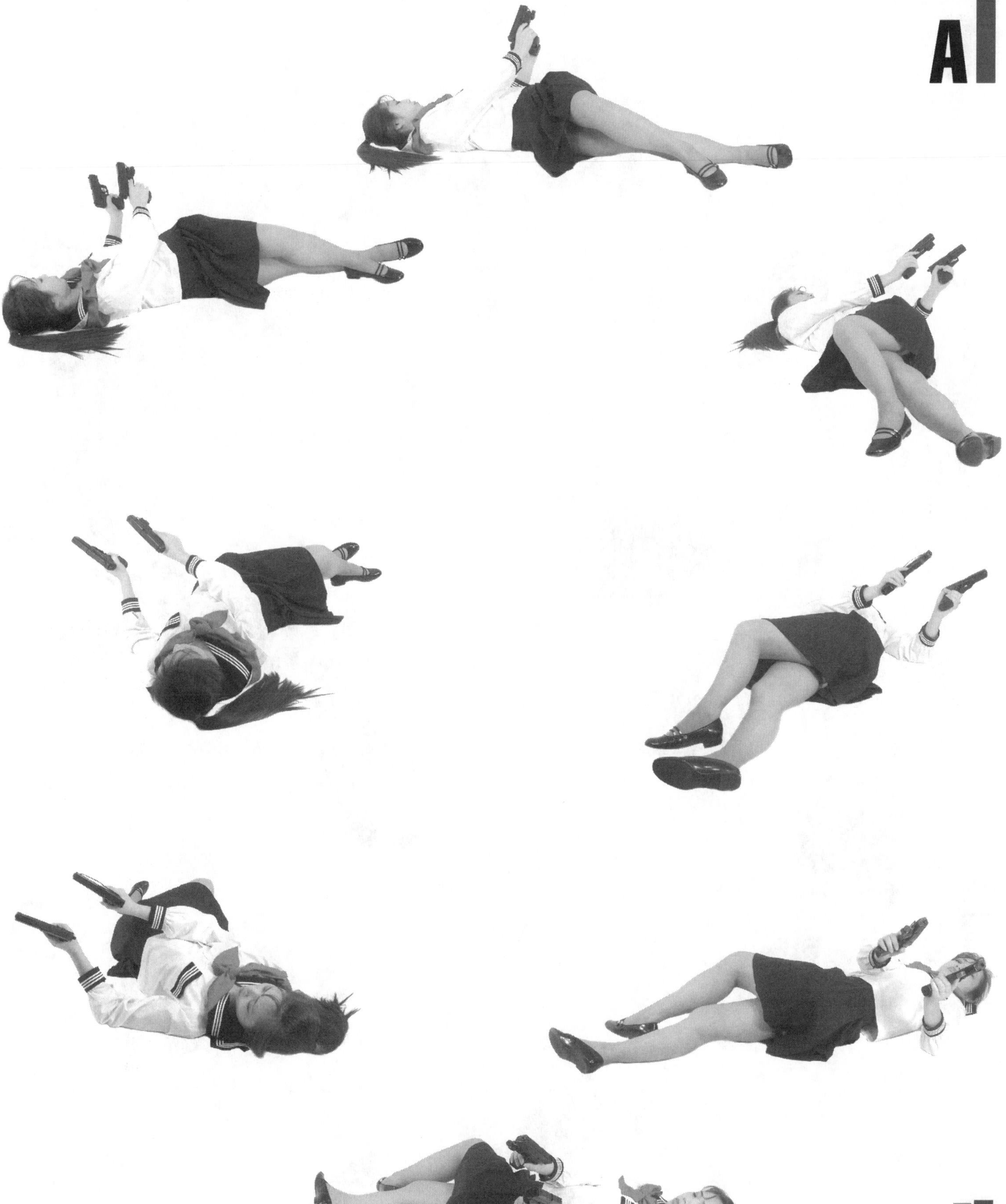

SCHOOL UNIFORM

B

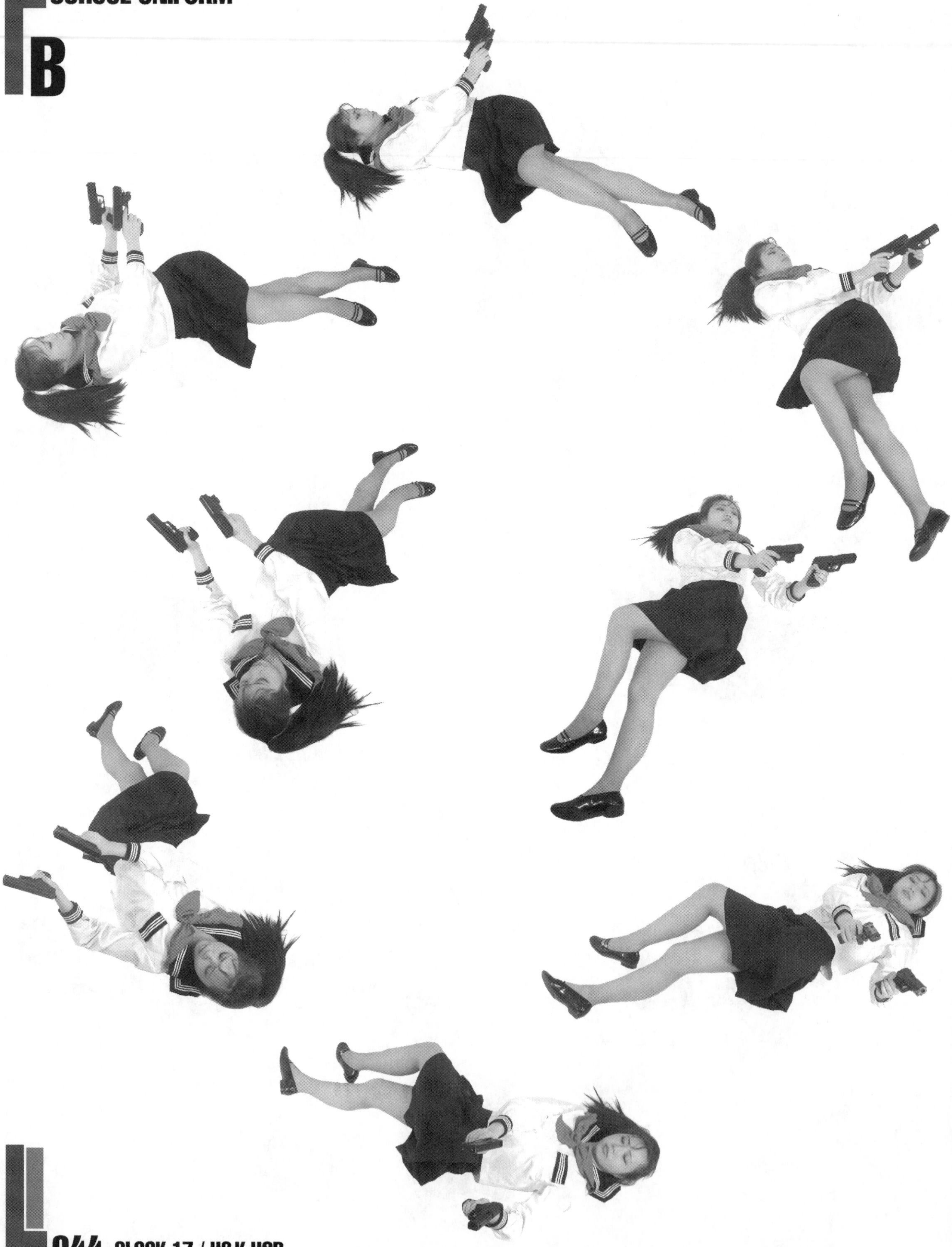

044 GLOCK 17 / H&K USP

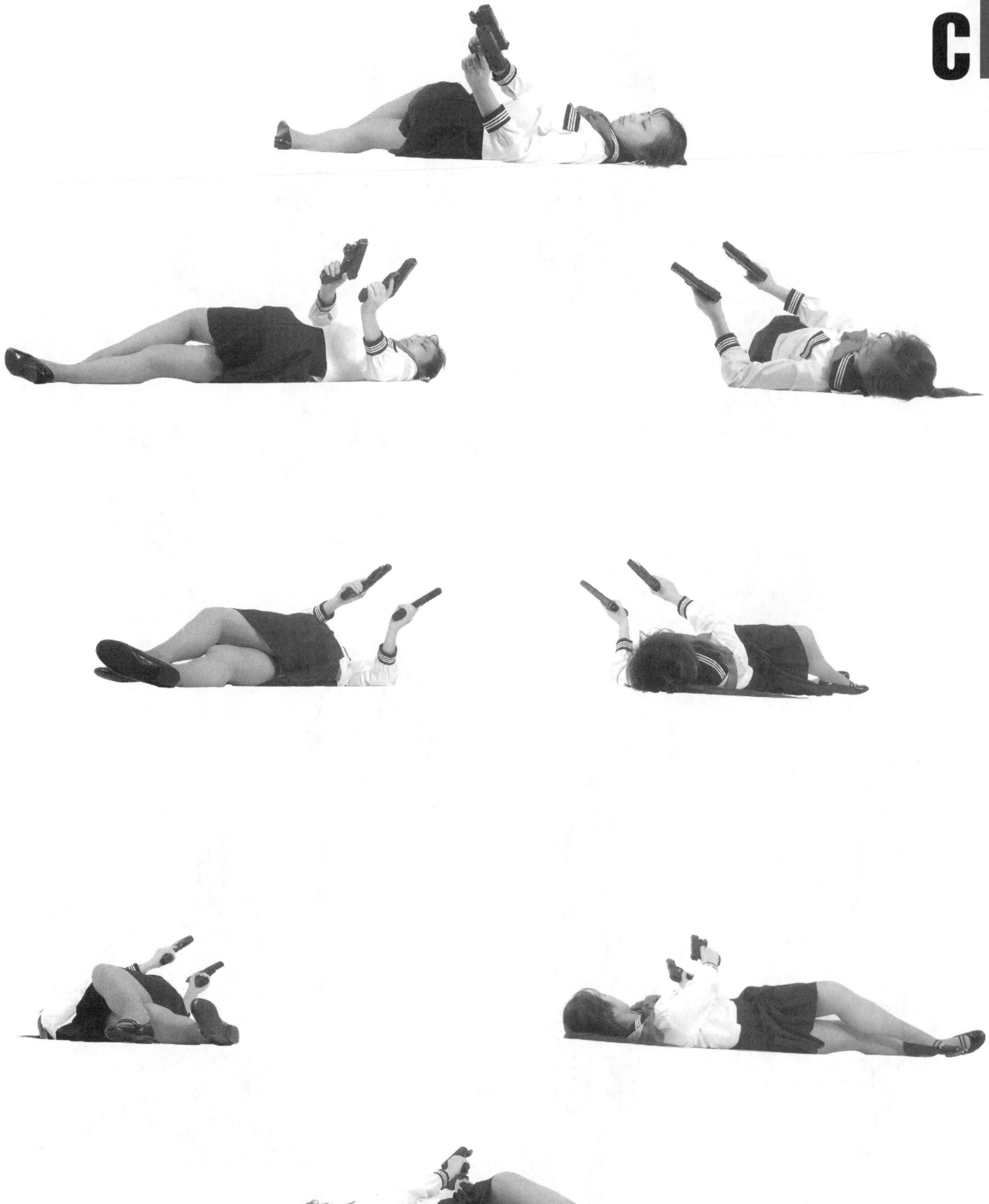

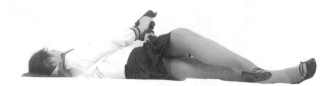

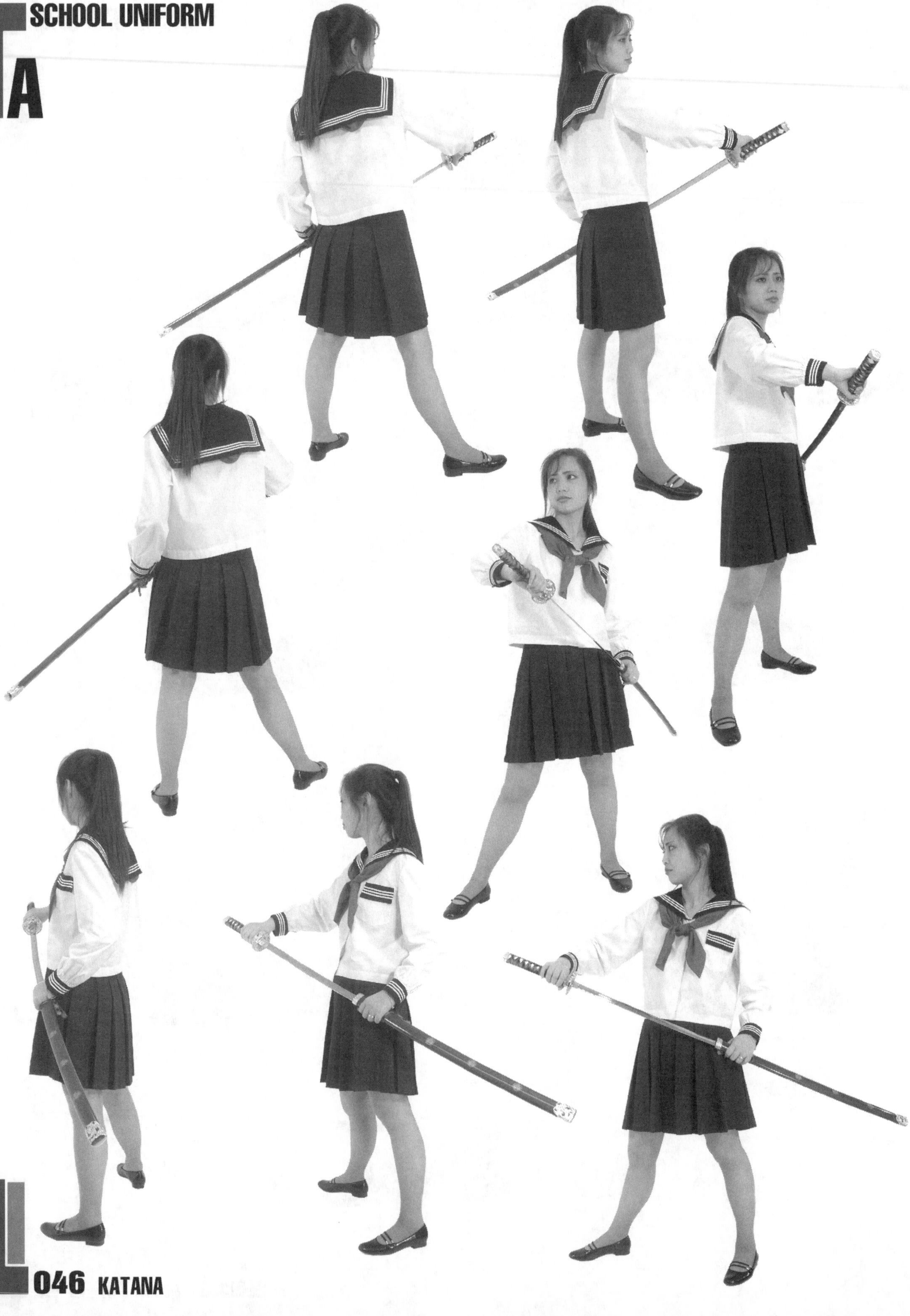

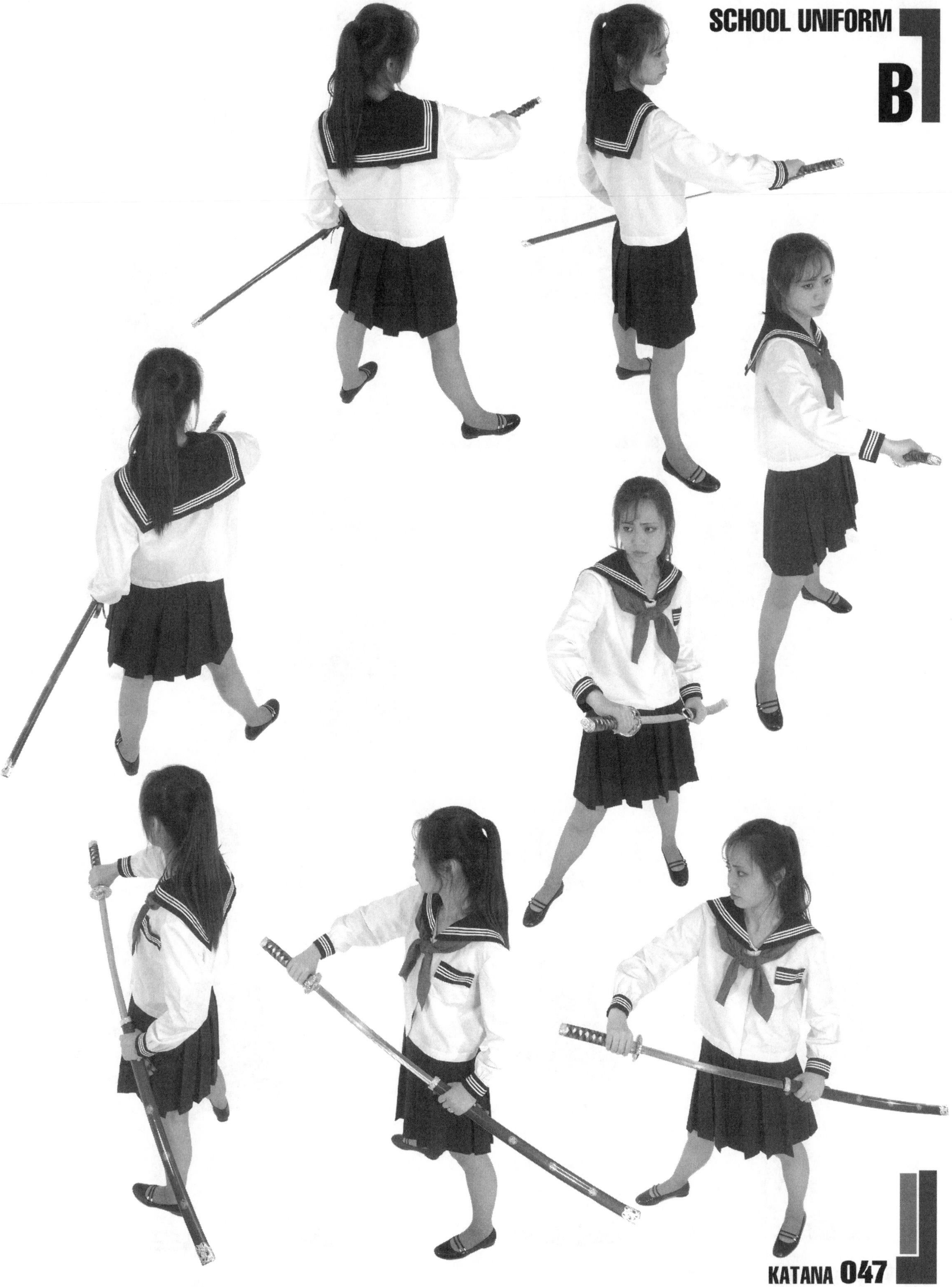

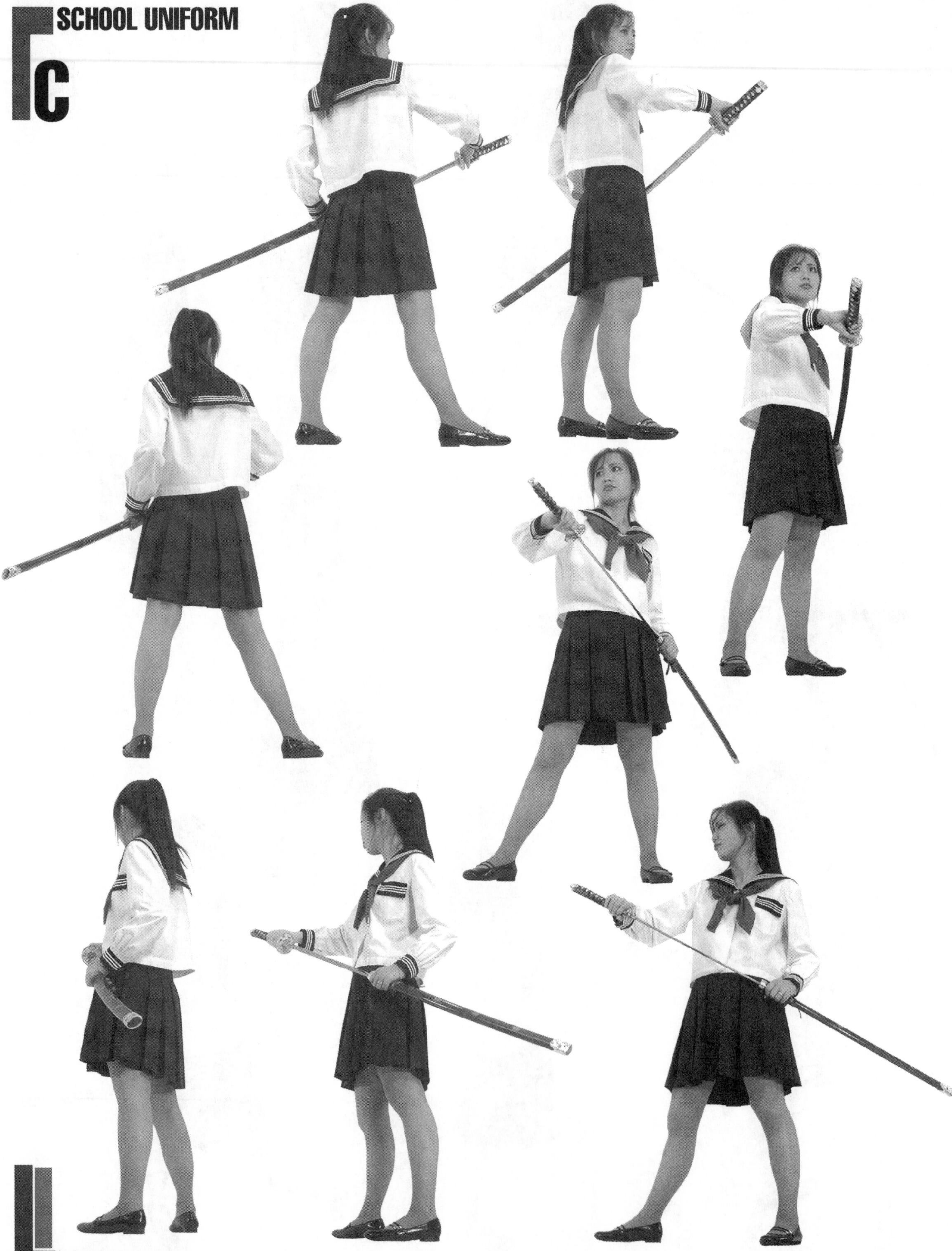

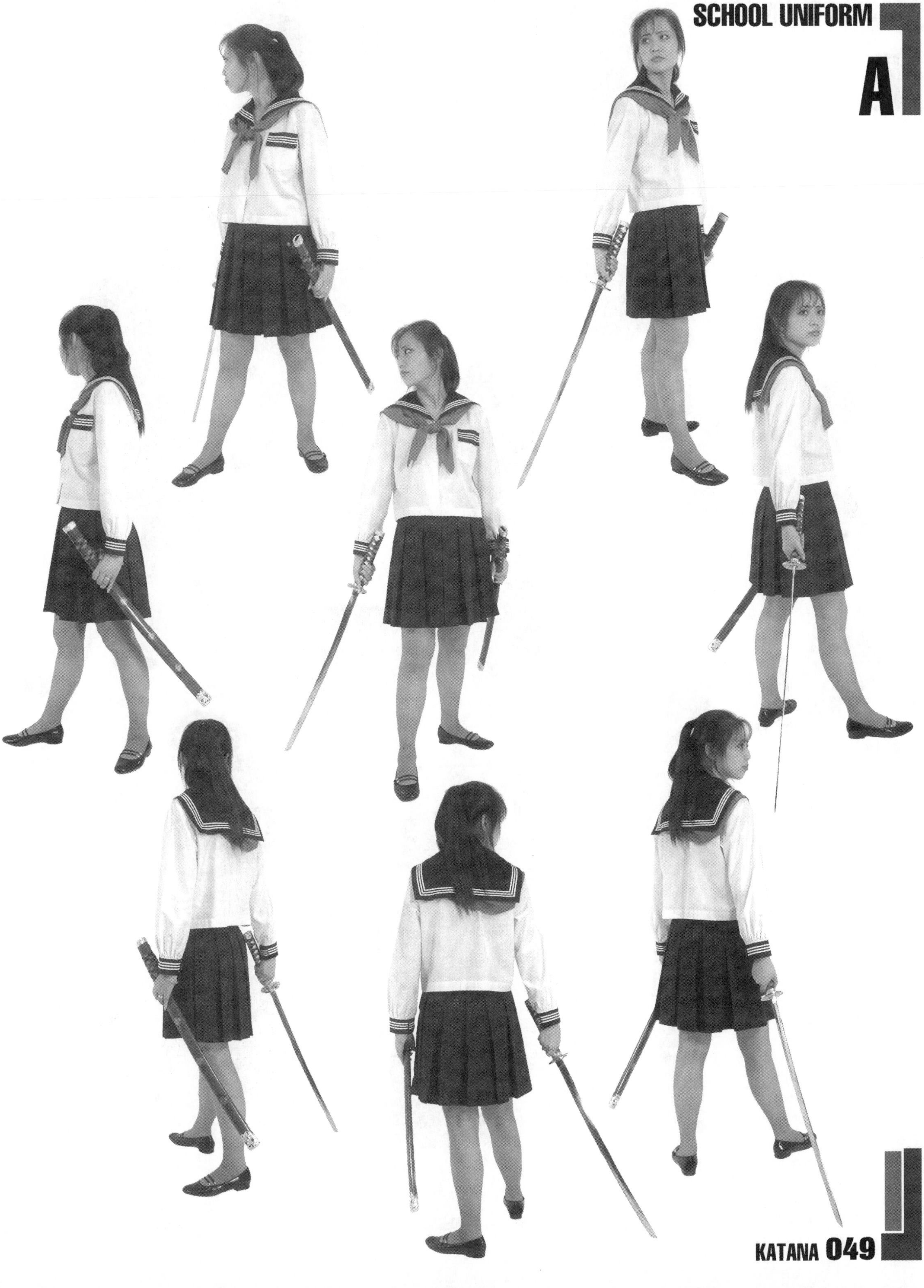

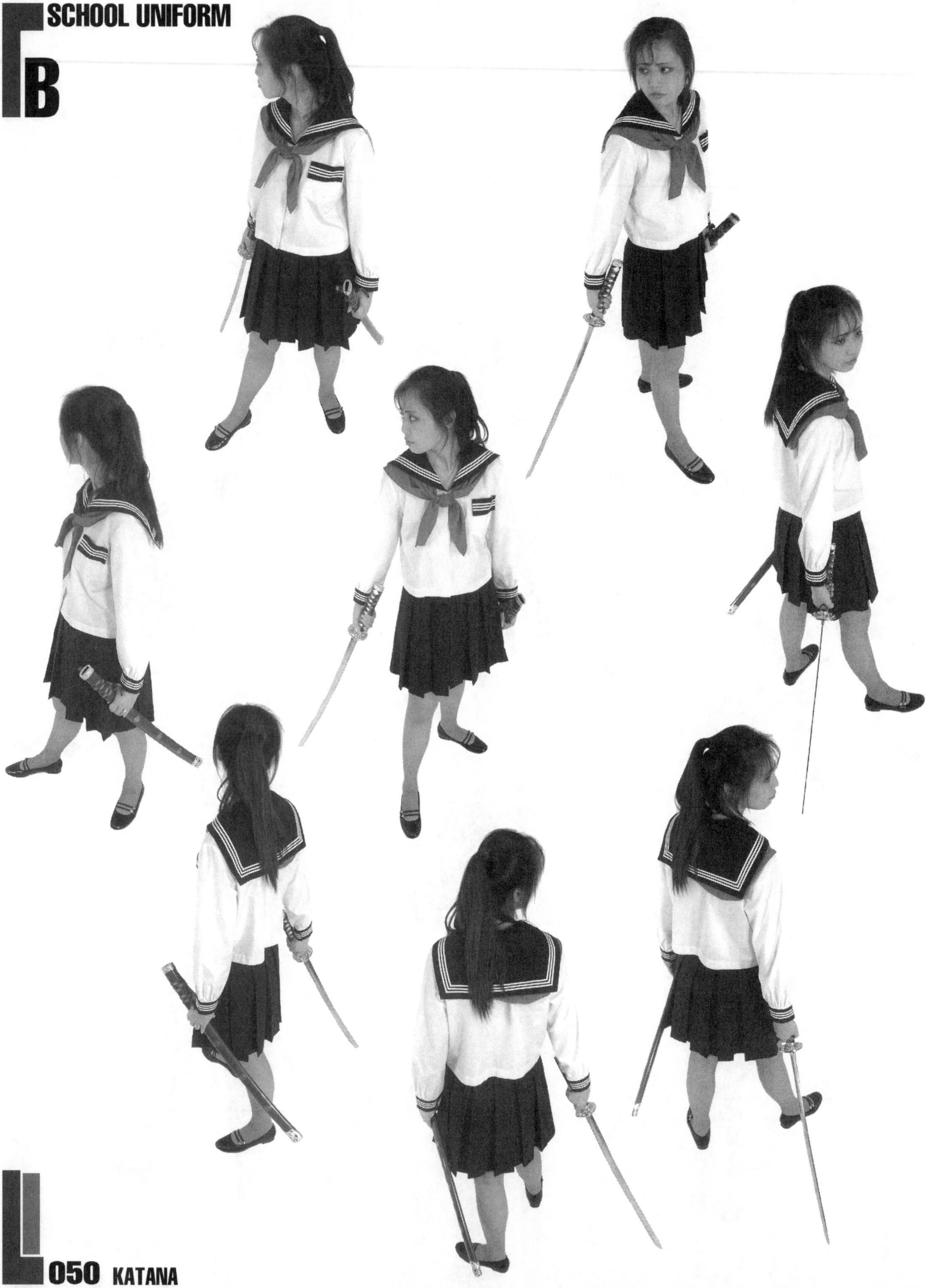

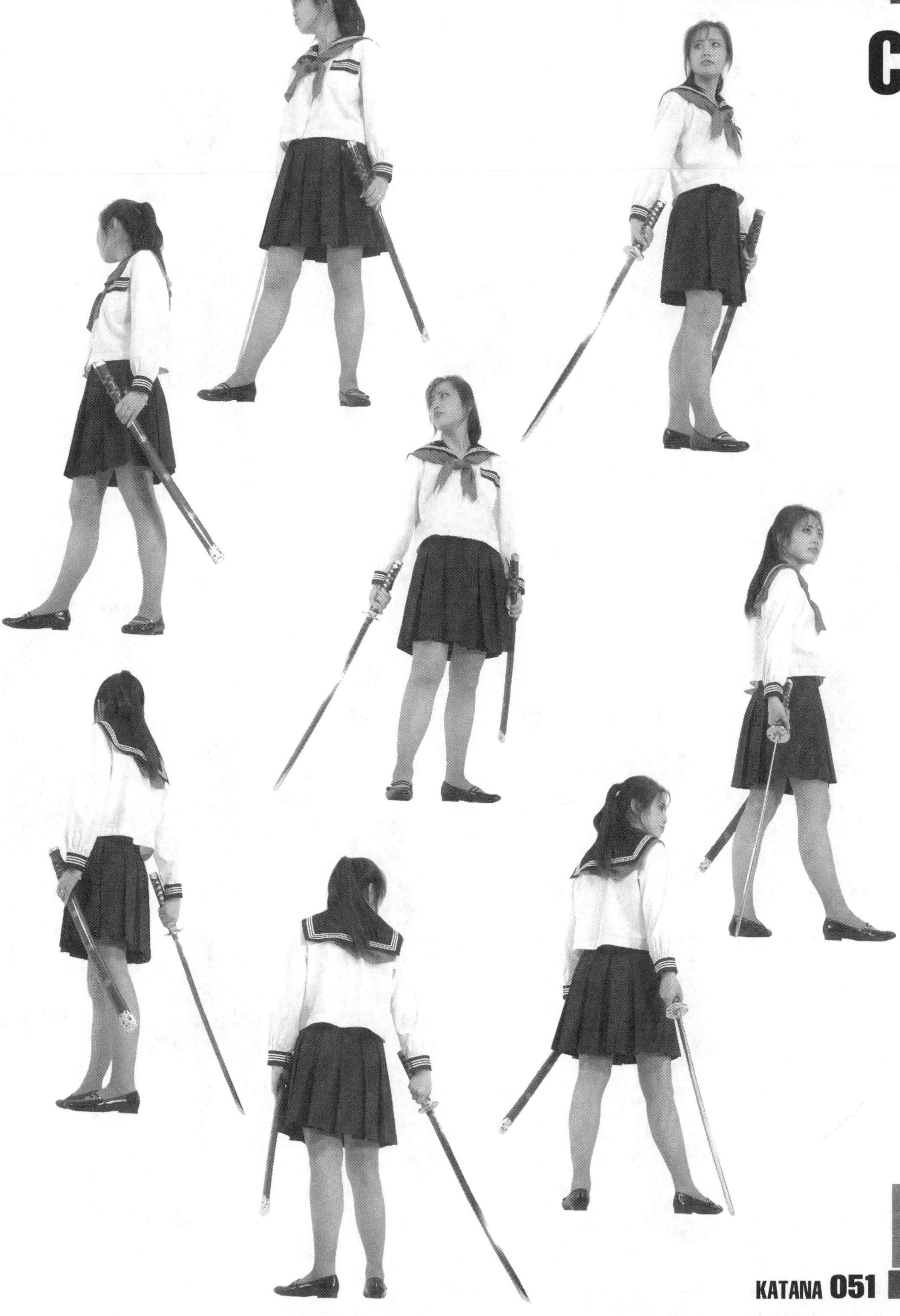

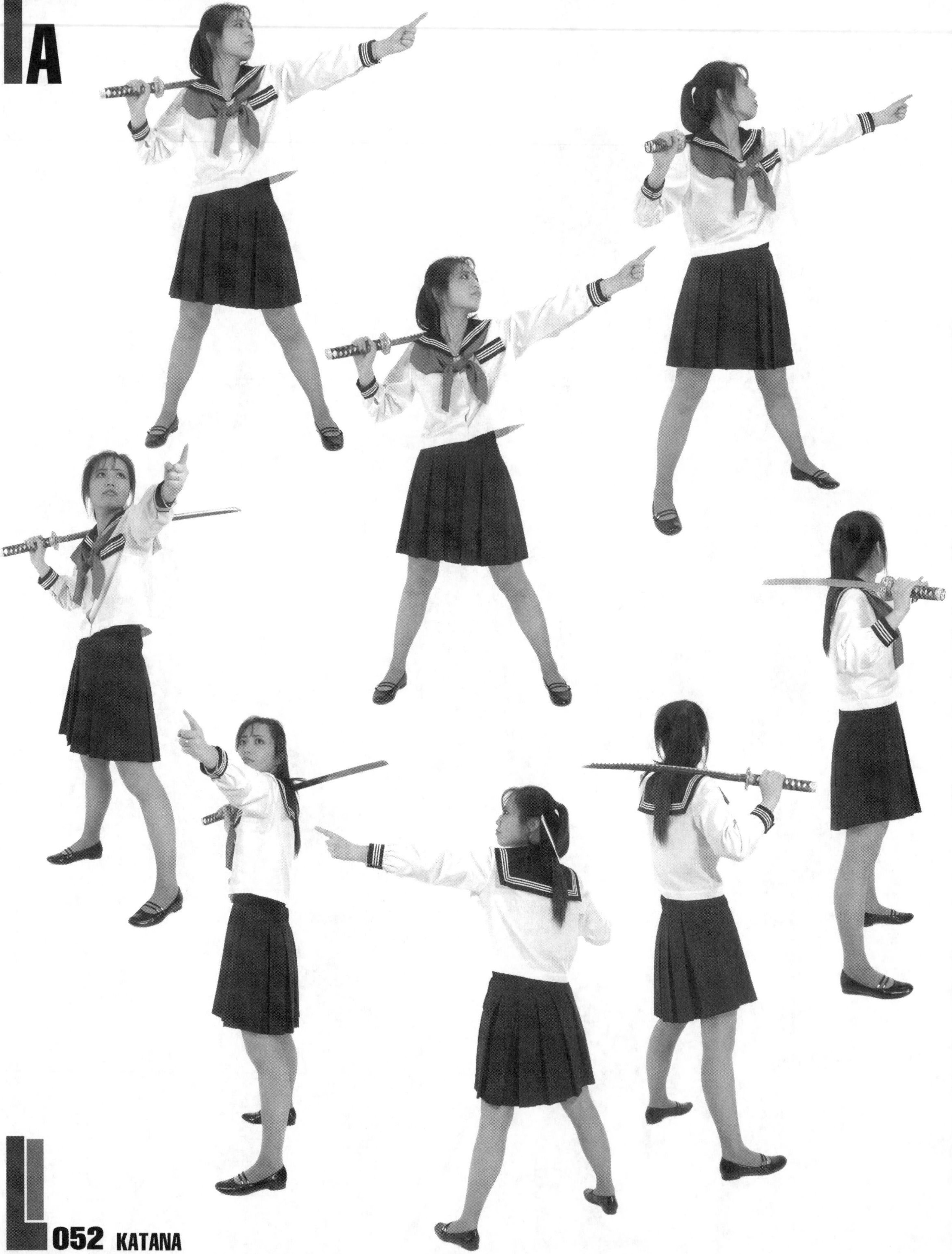

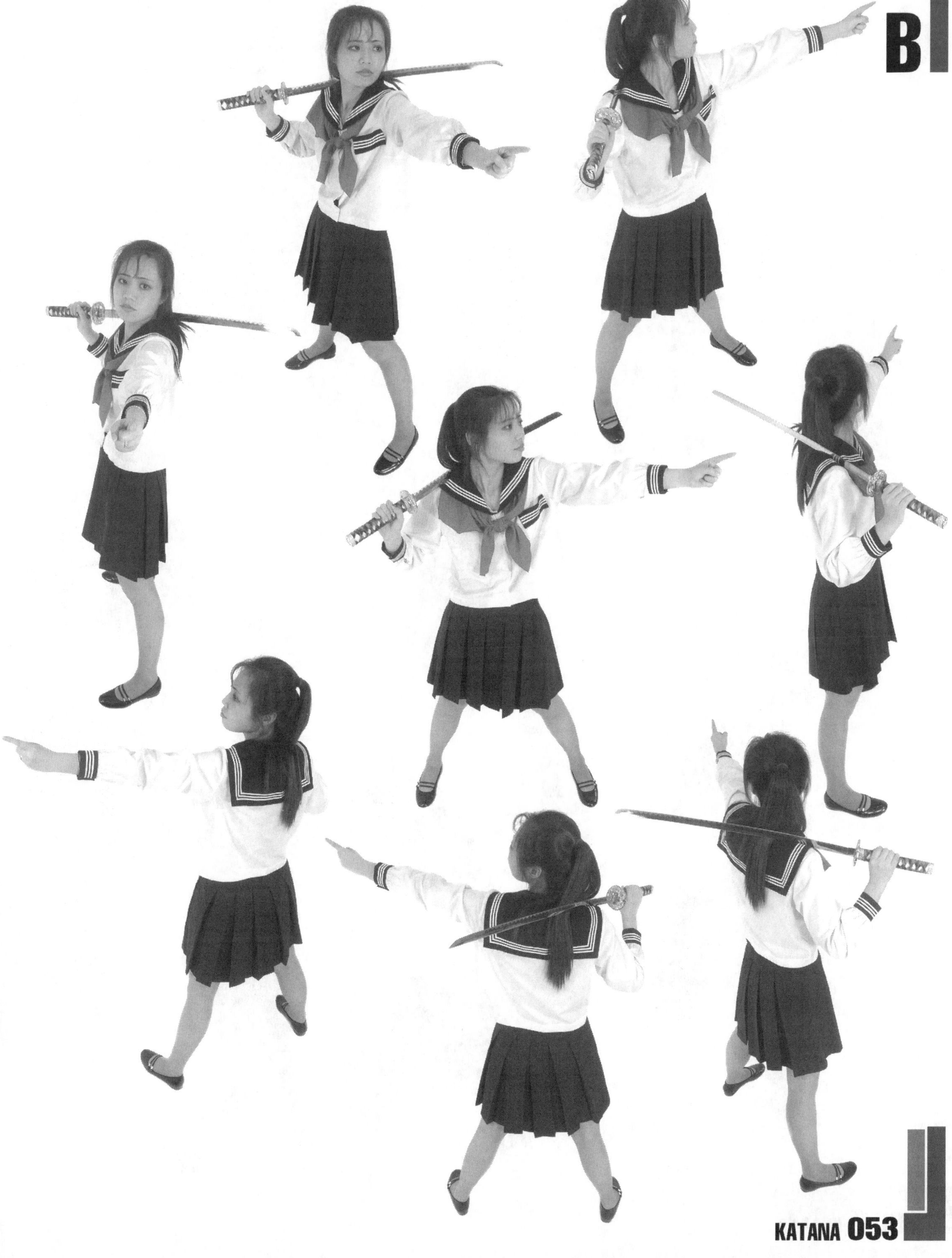

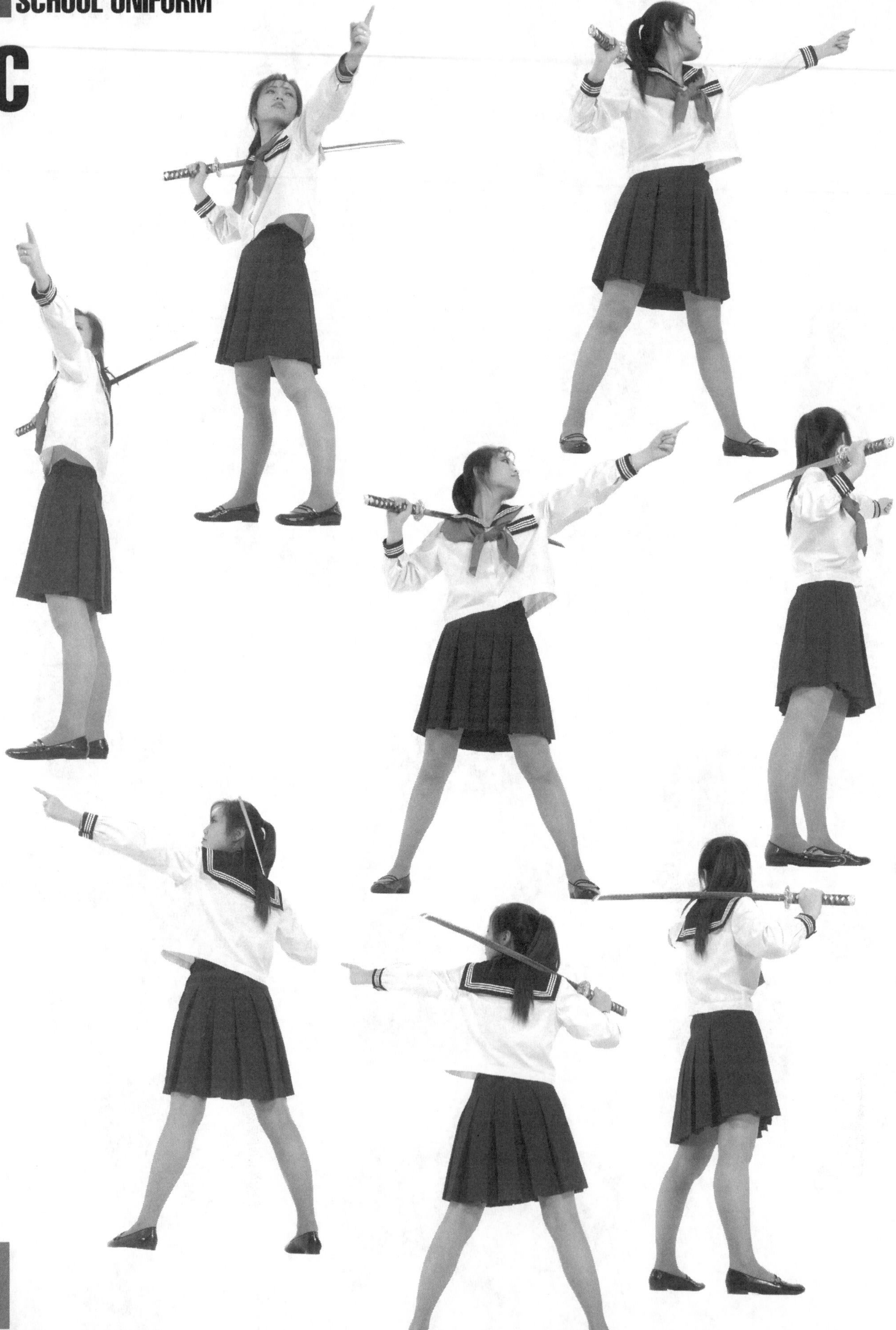

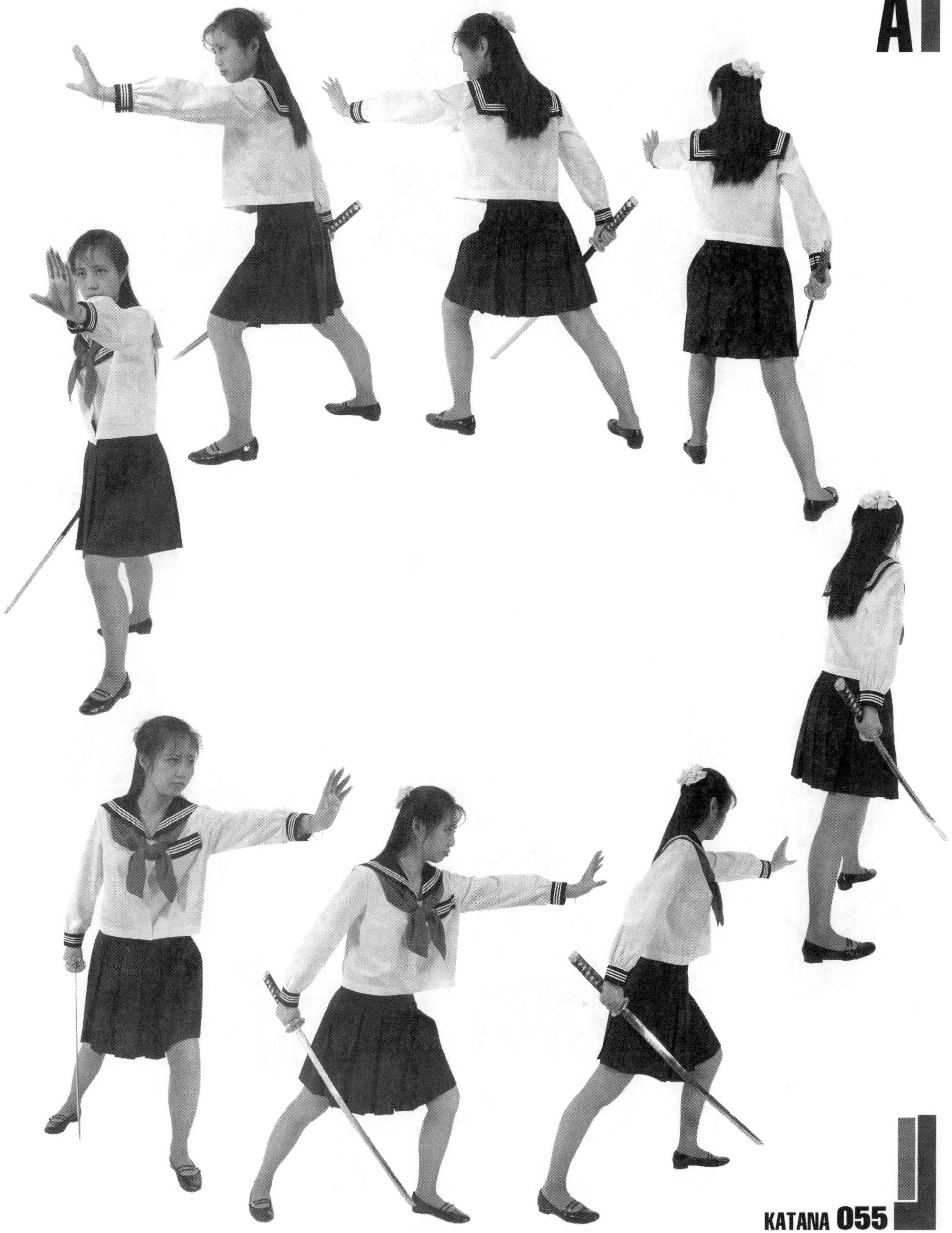

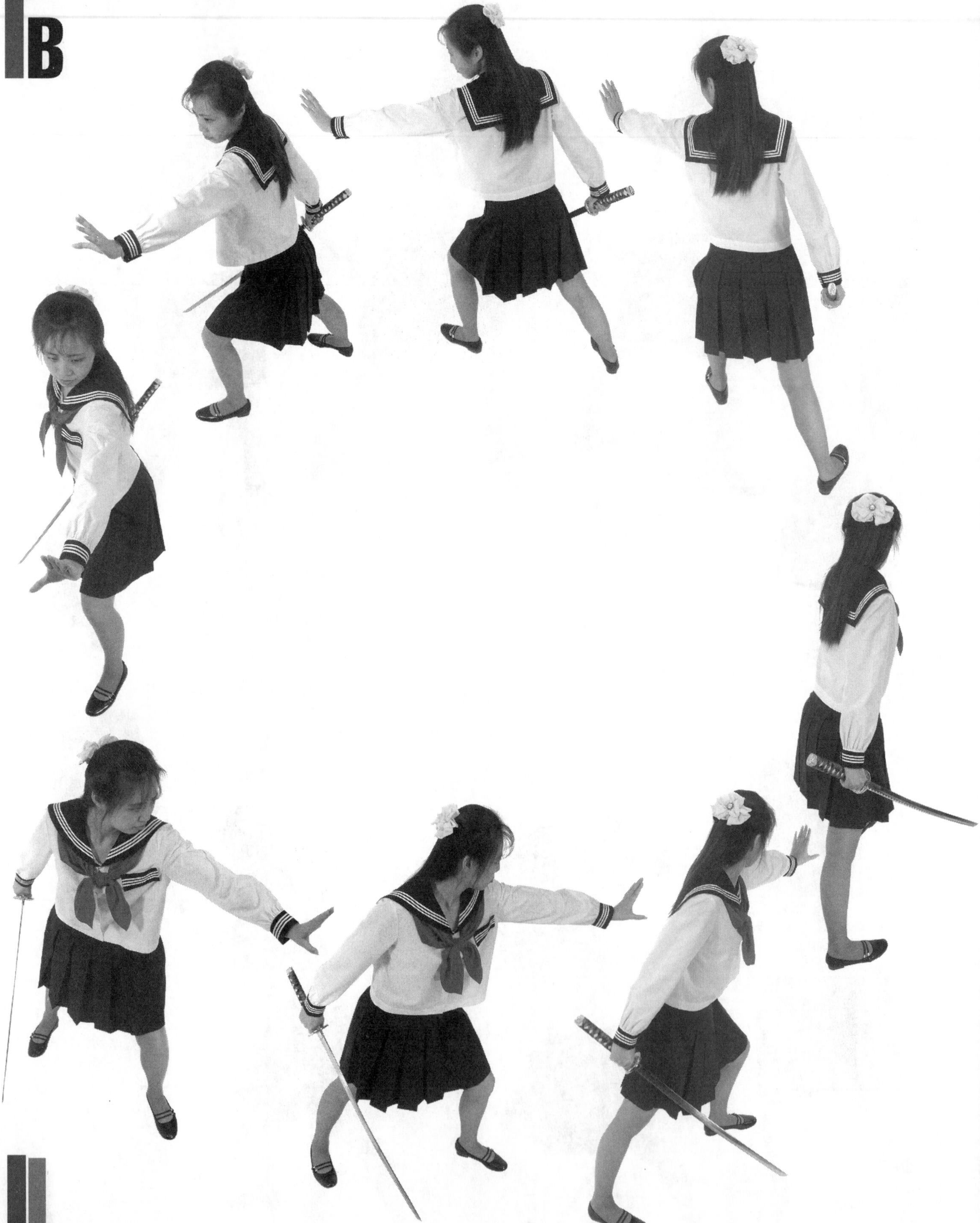

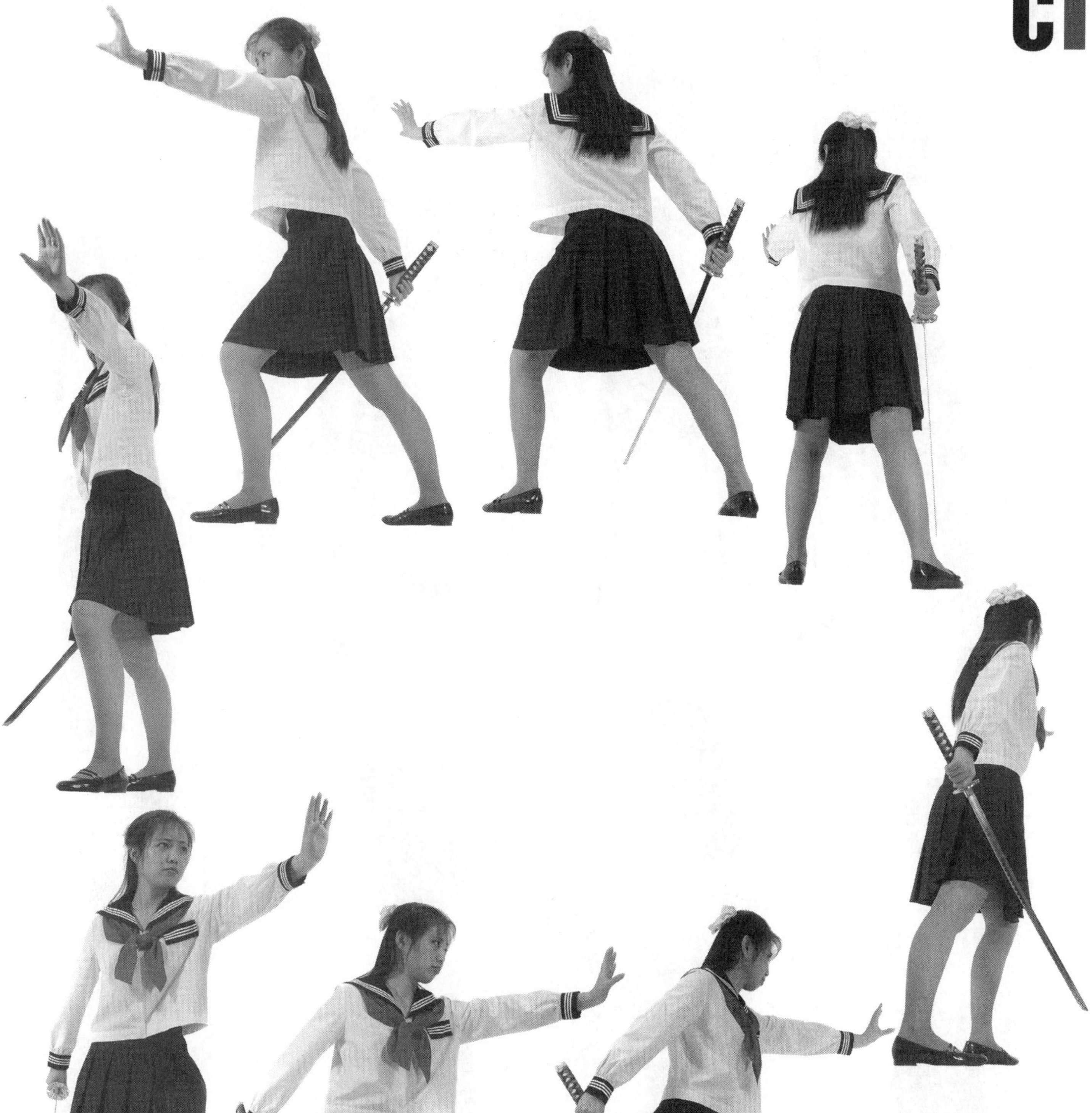

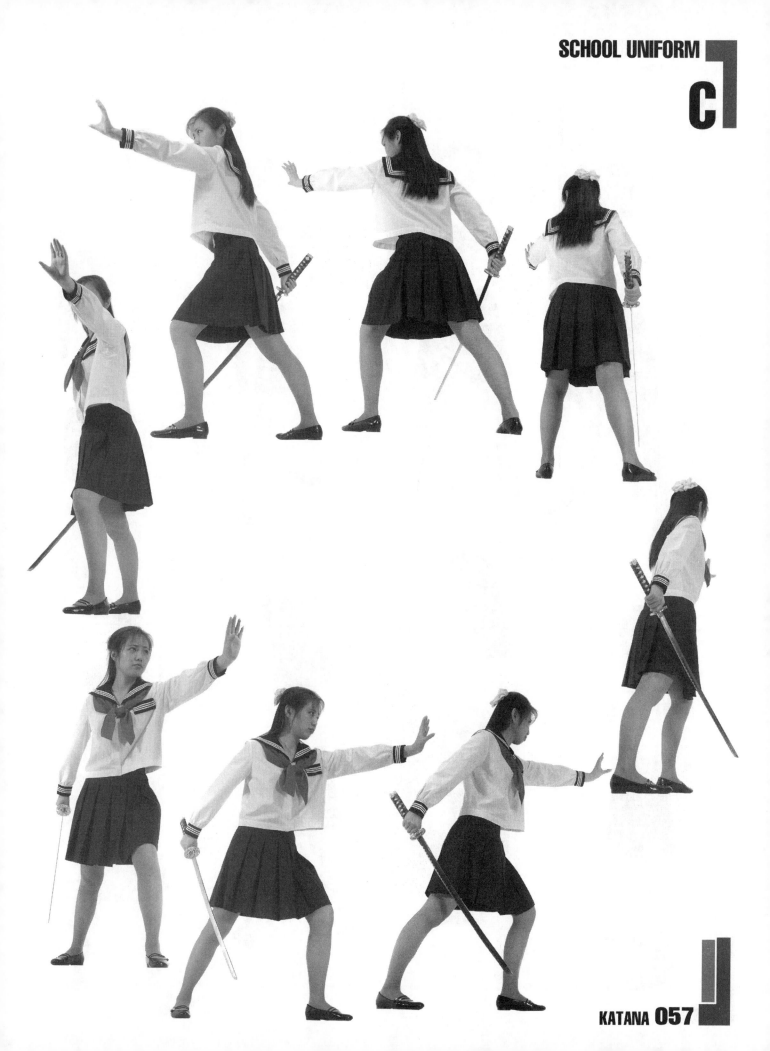

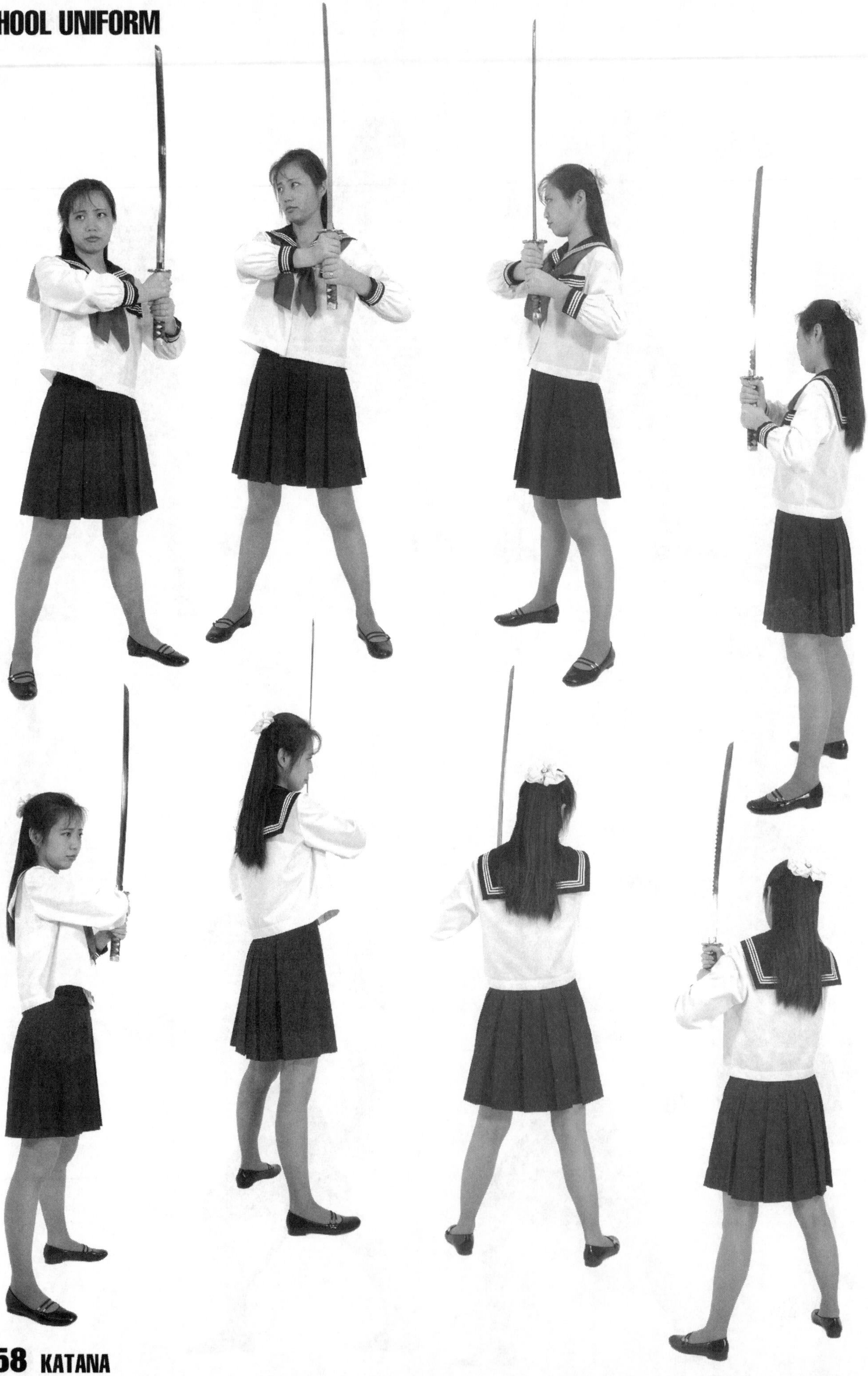

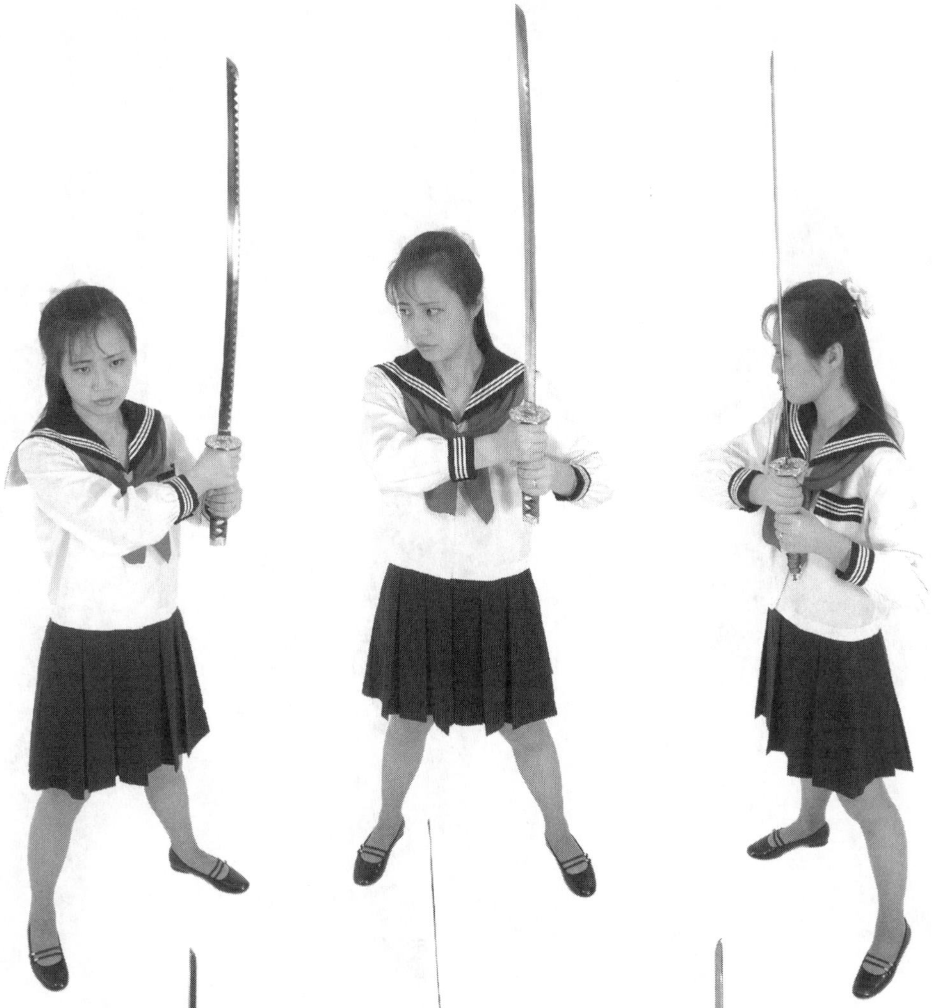

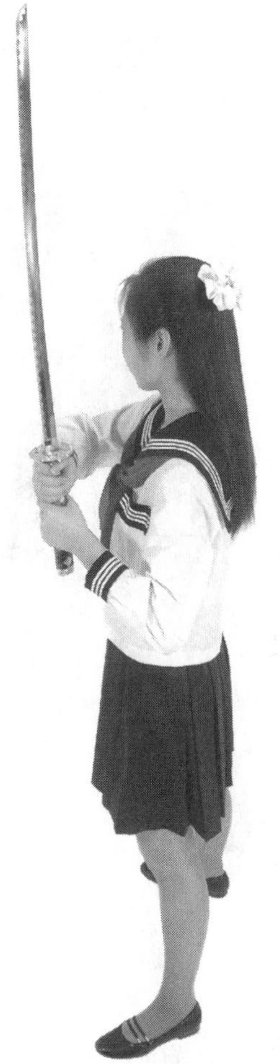

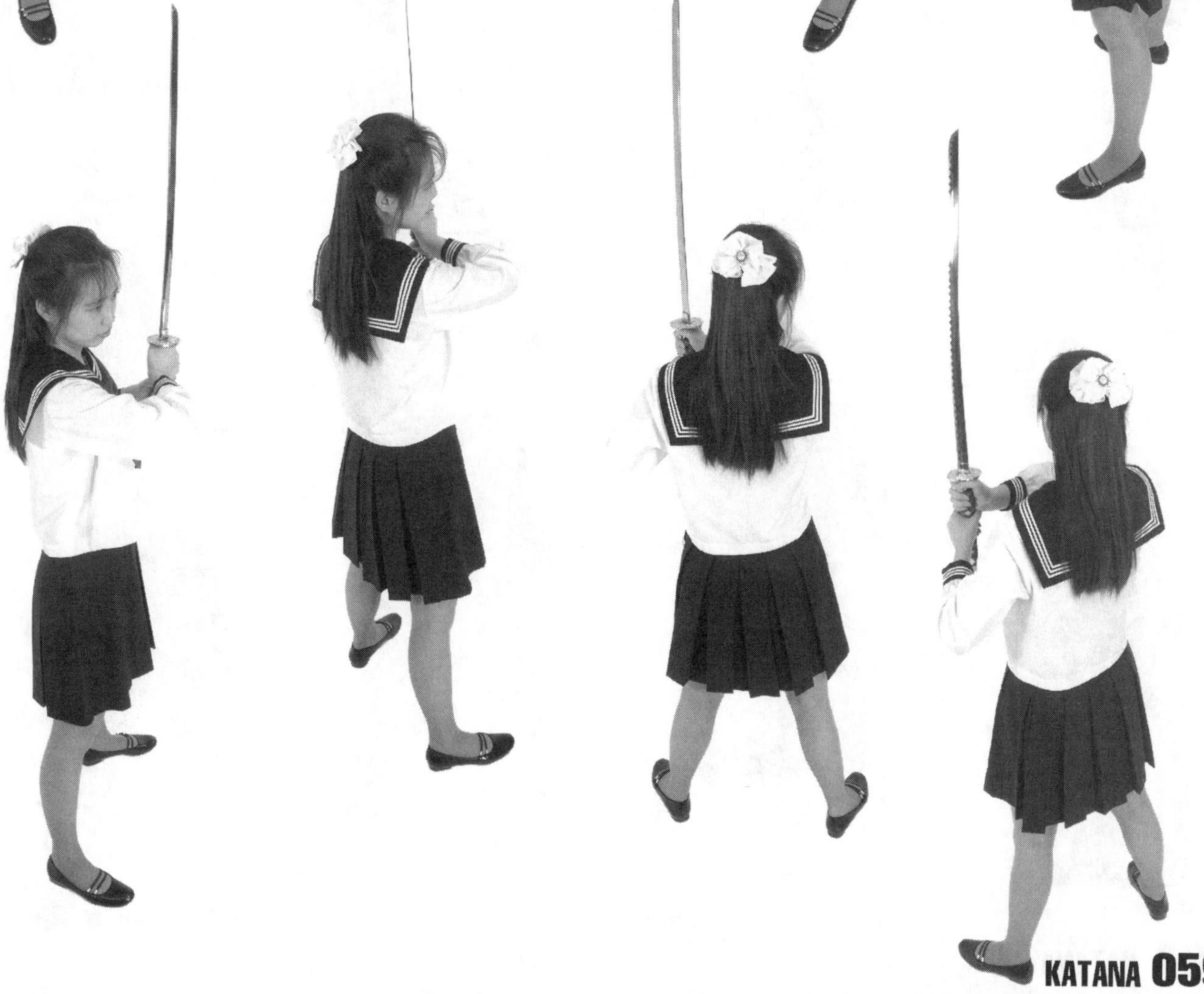

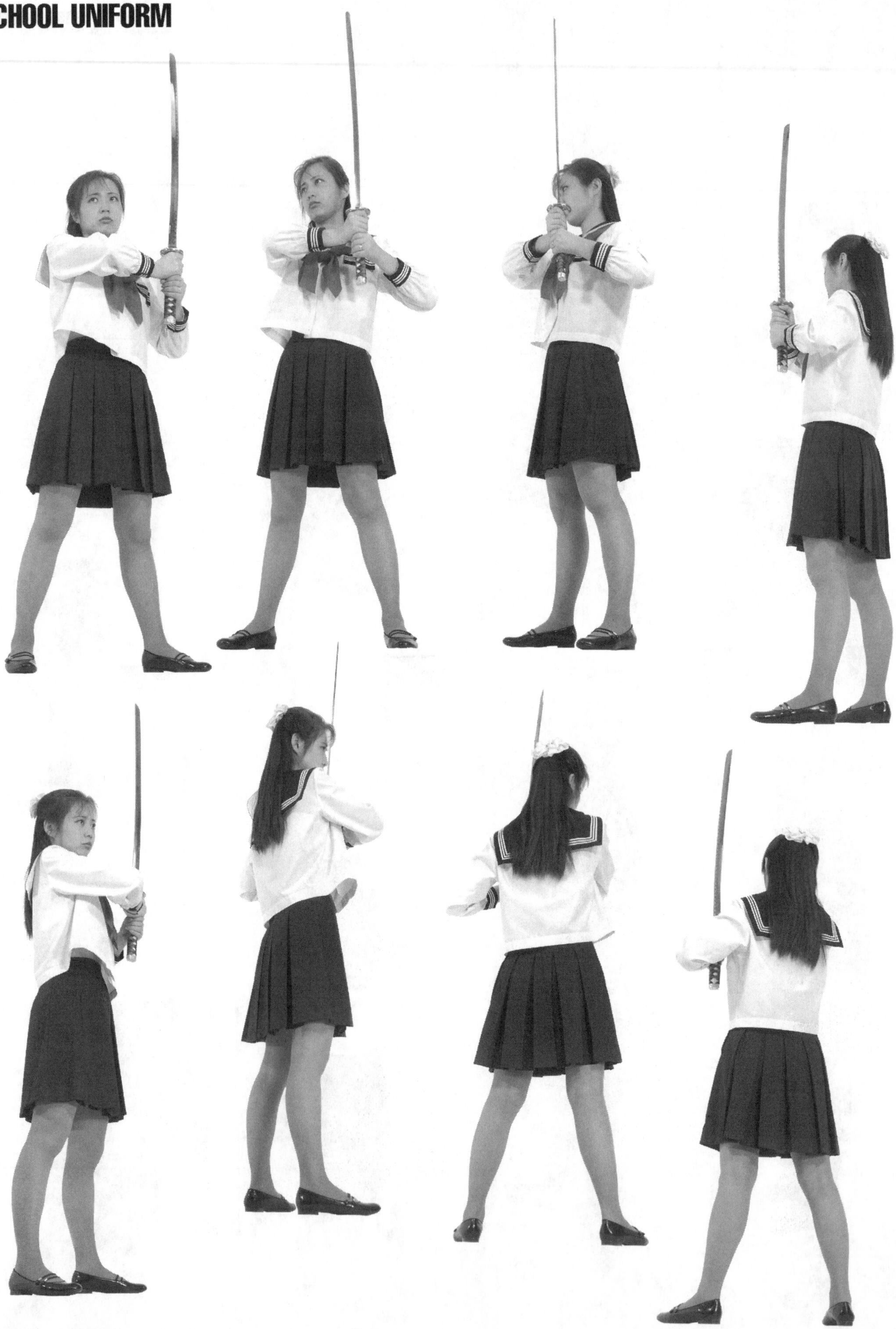

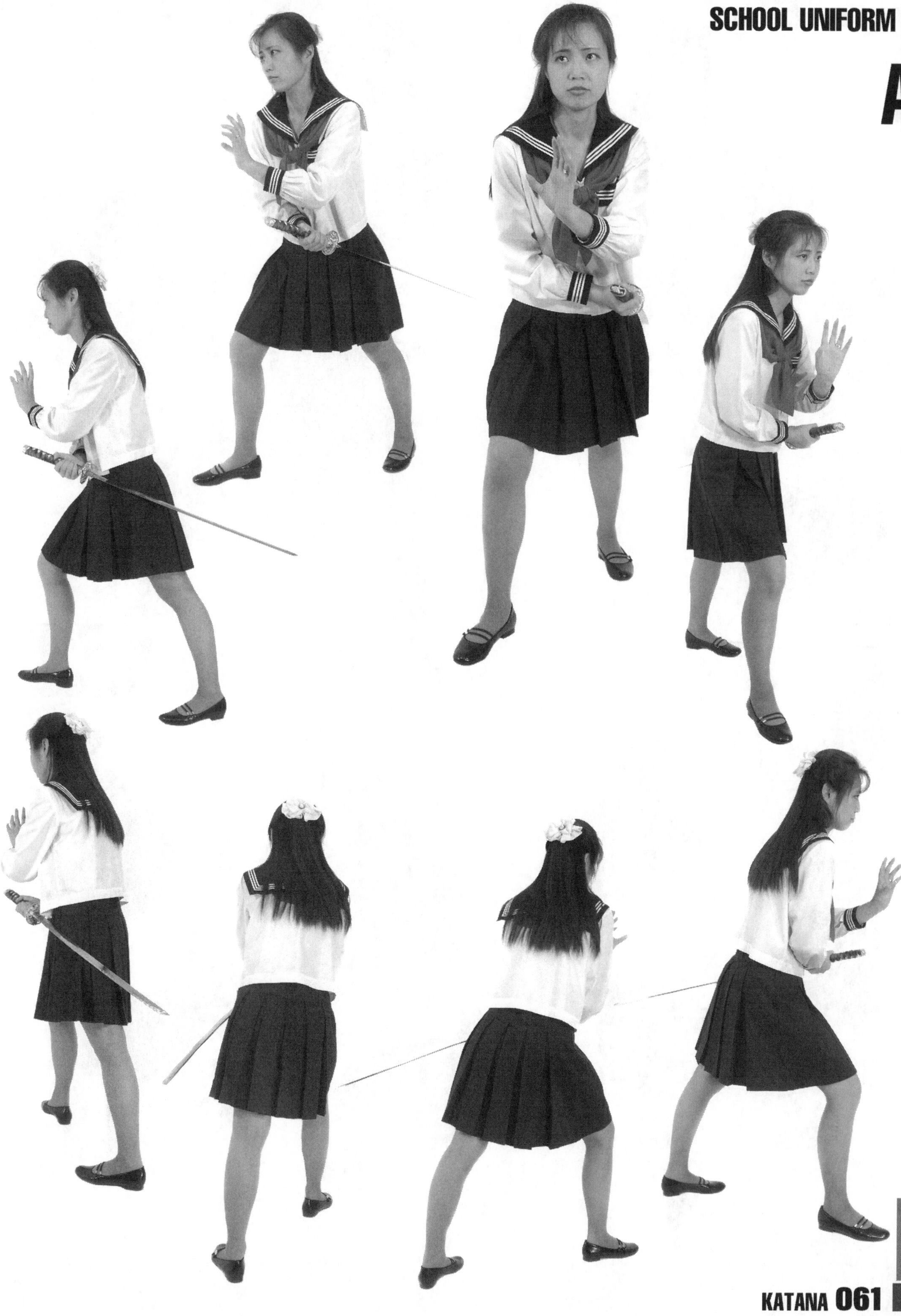

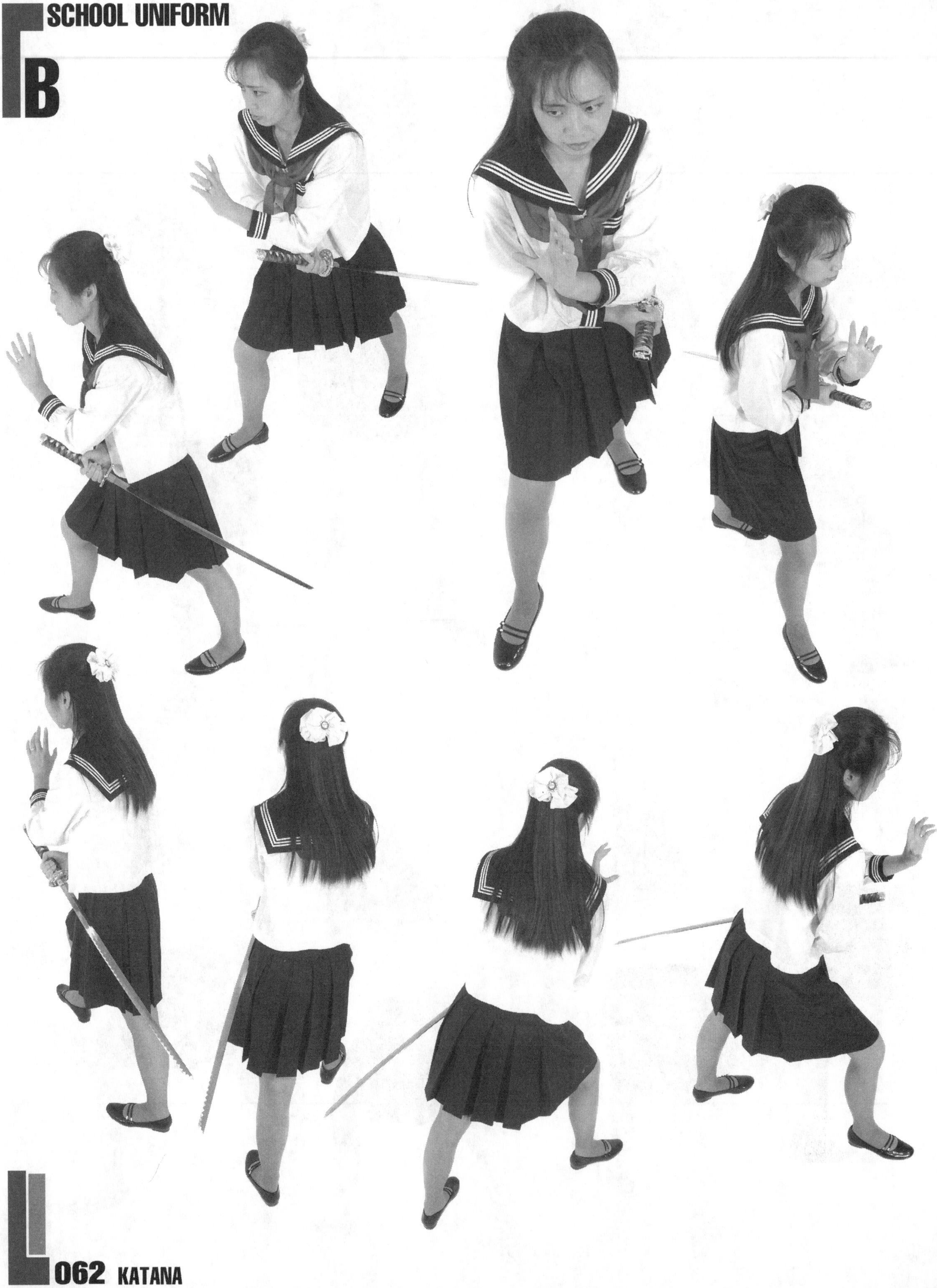

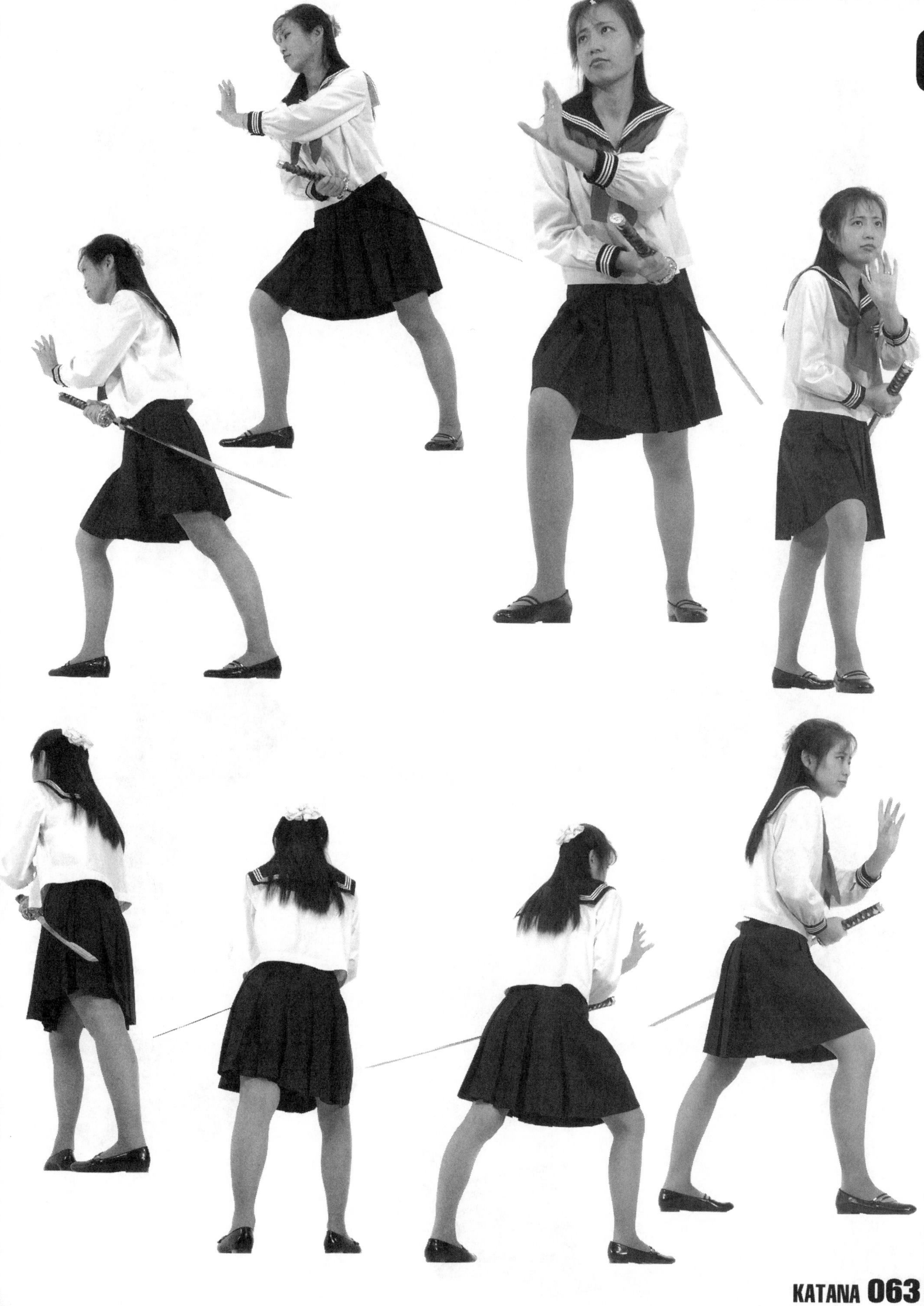

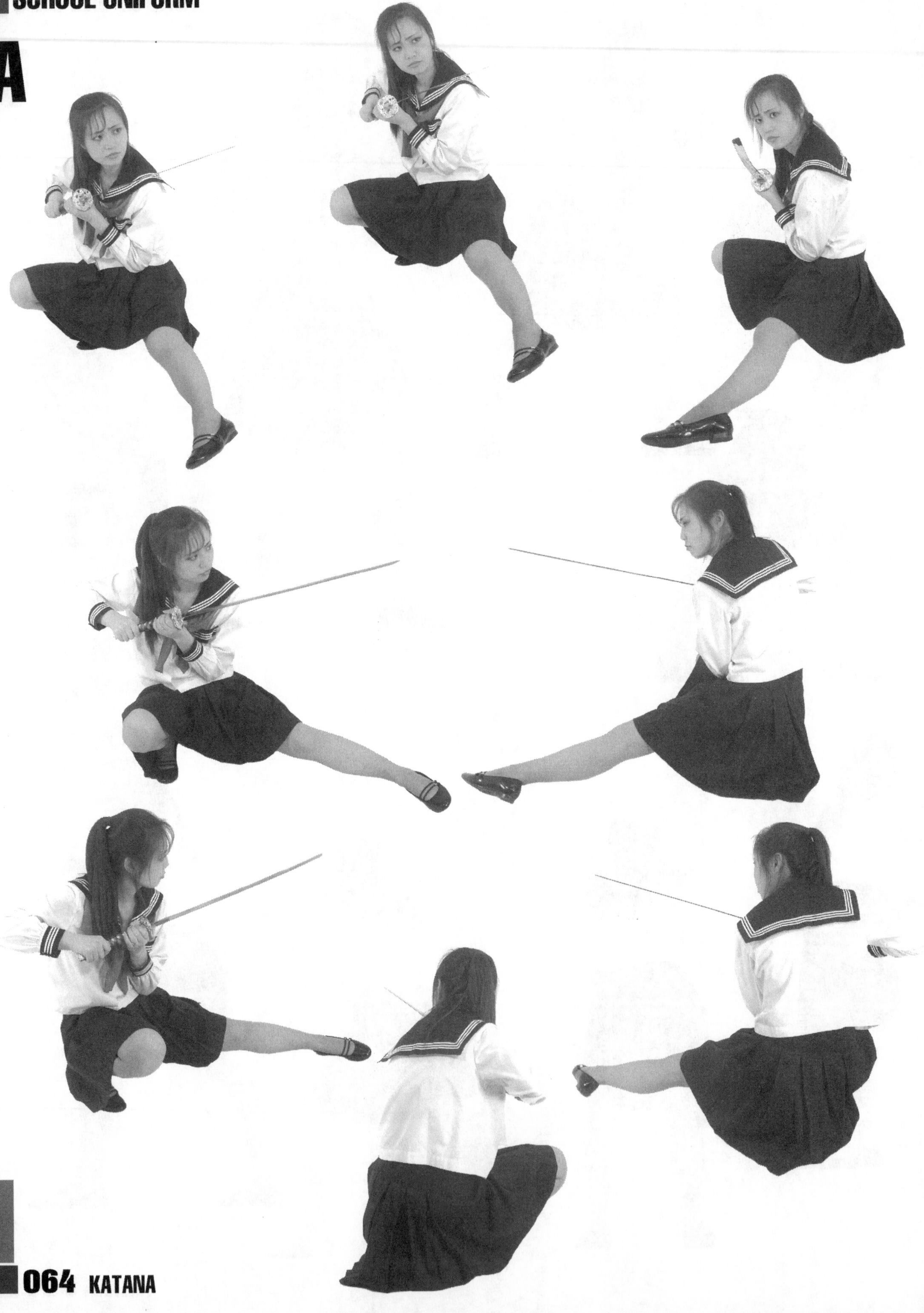

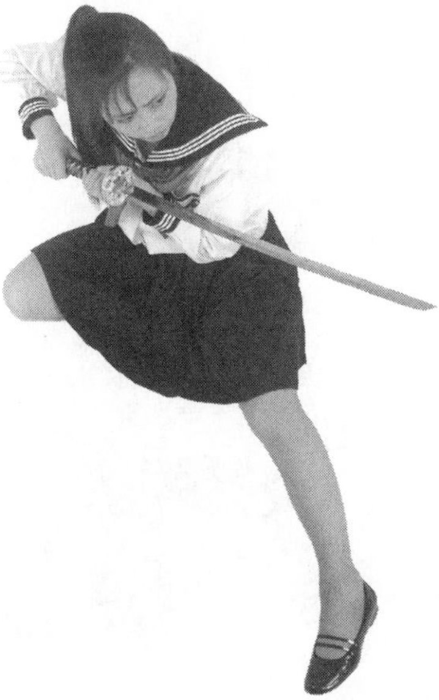

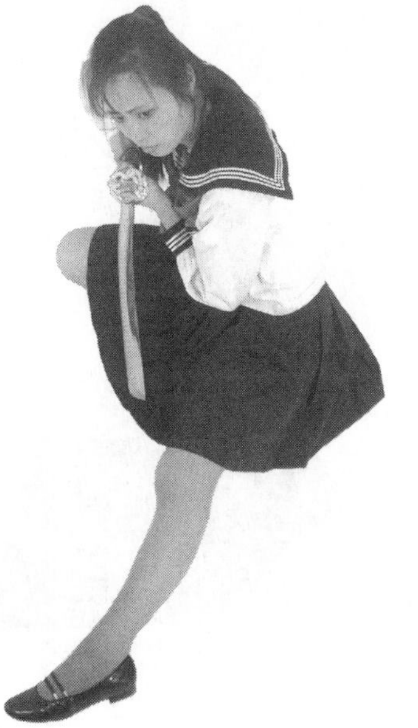

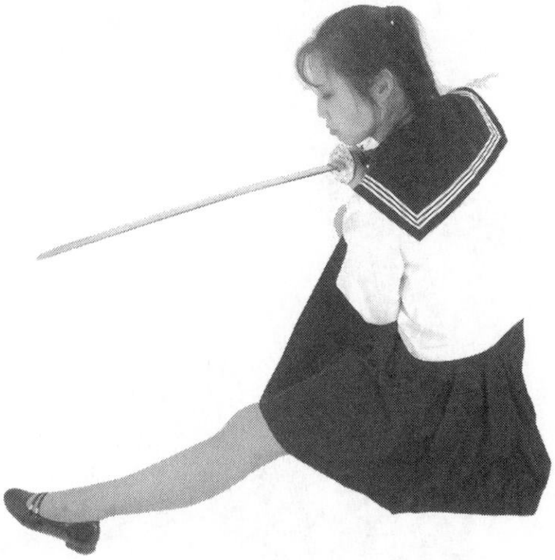

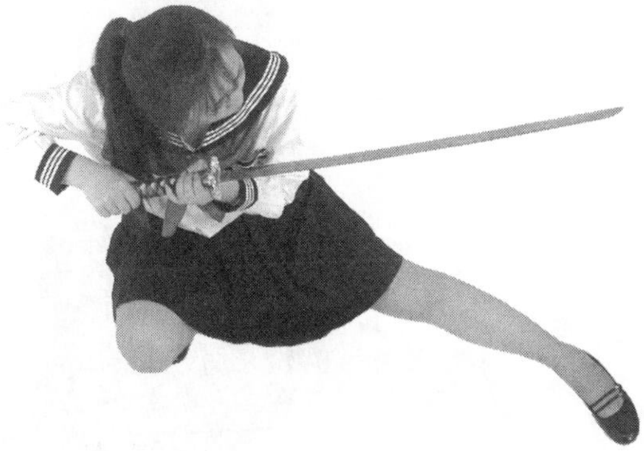

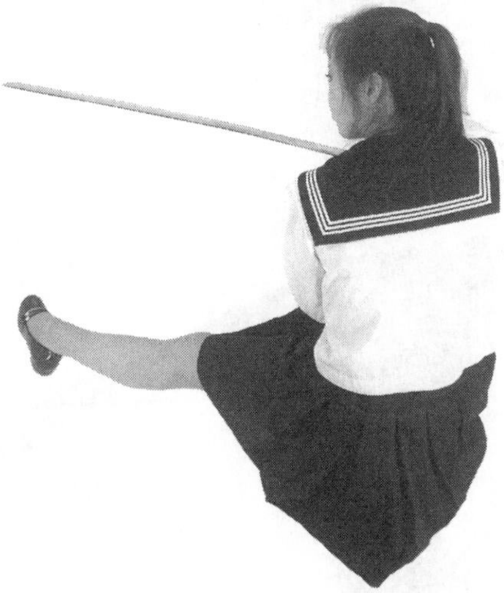

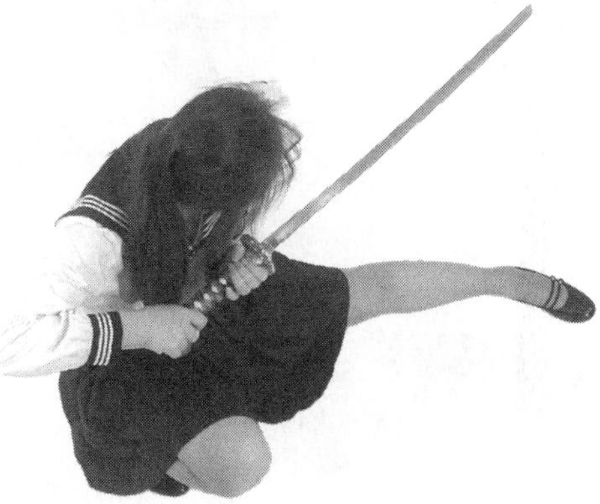

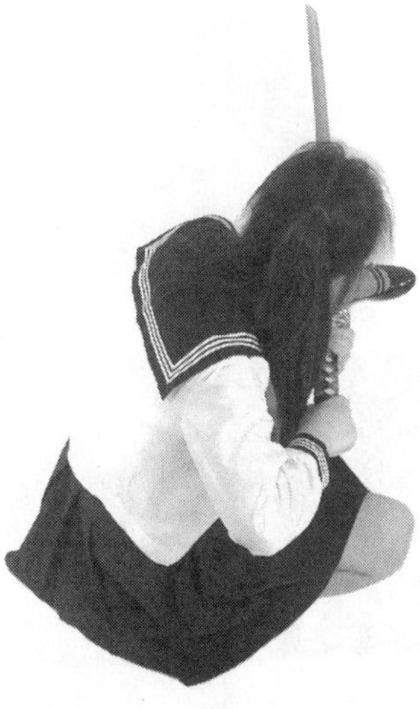

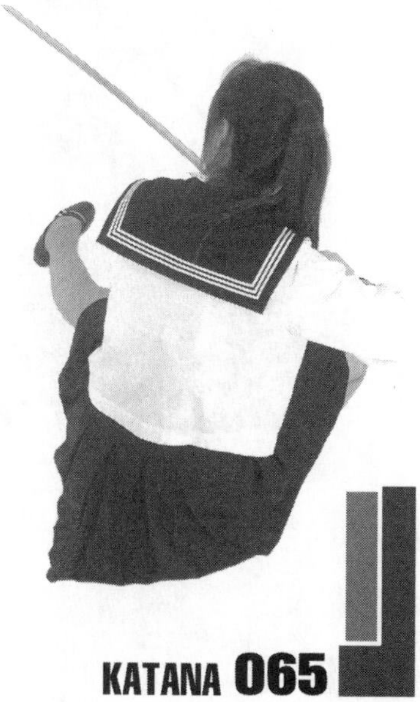

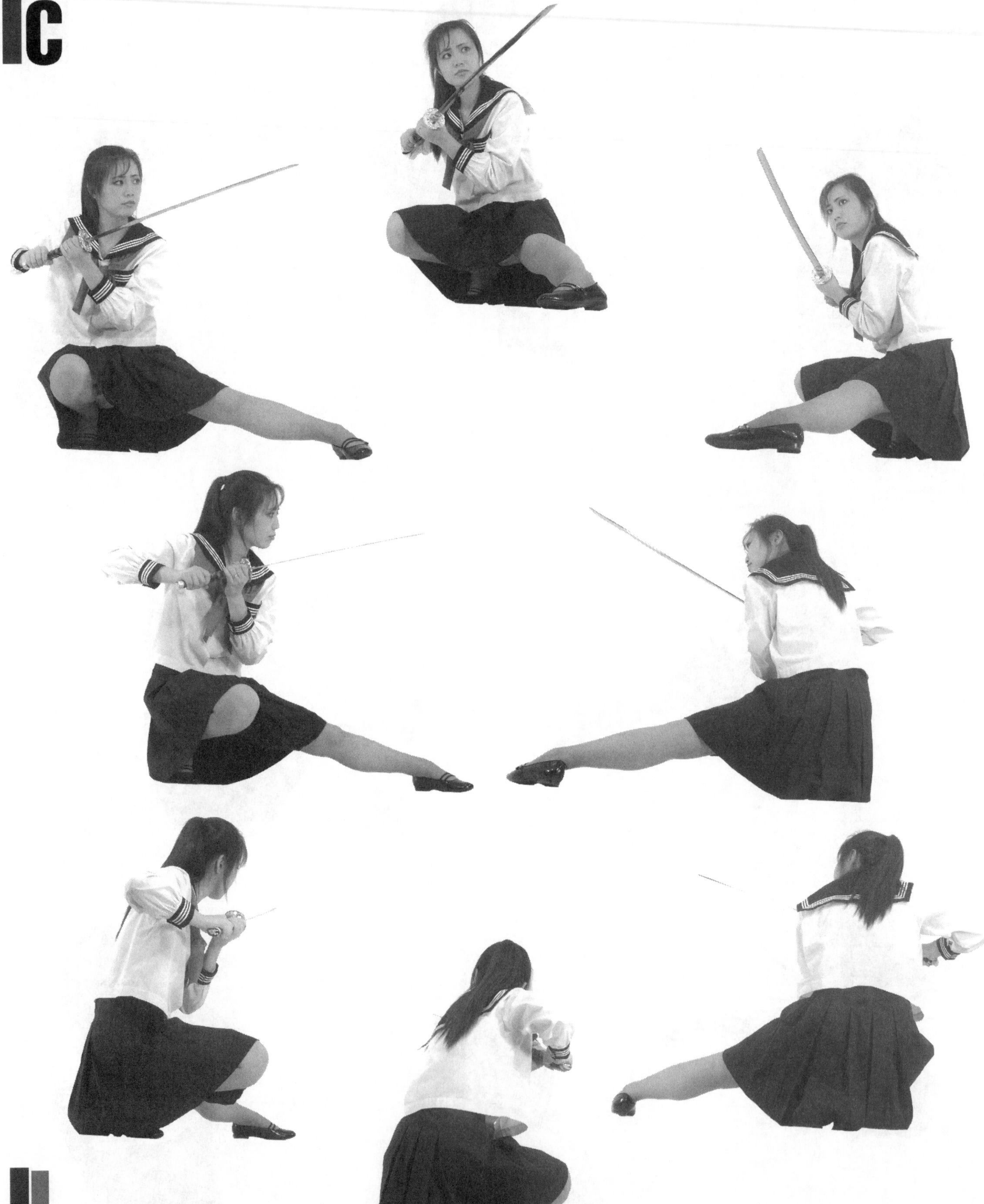

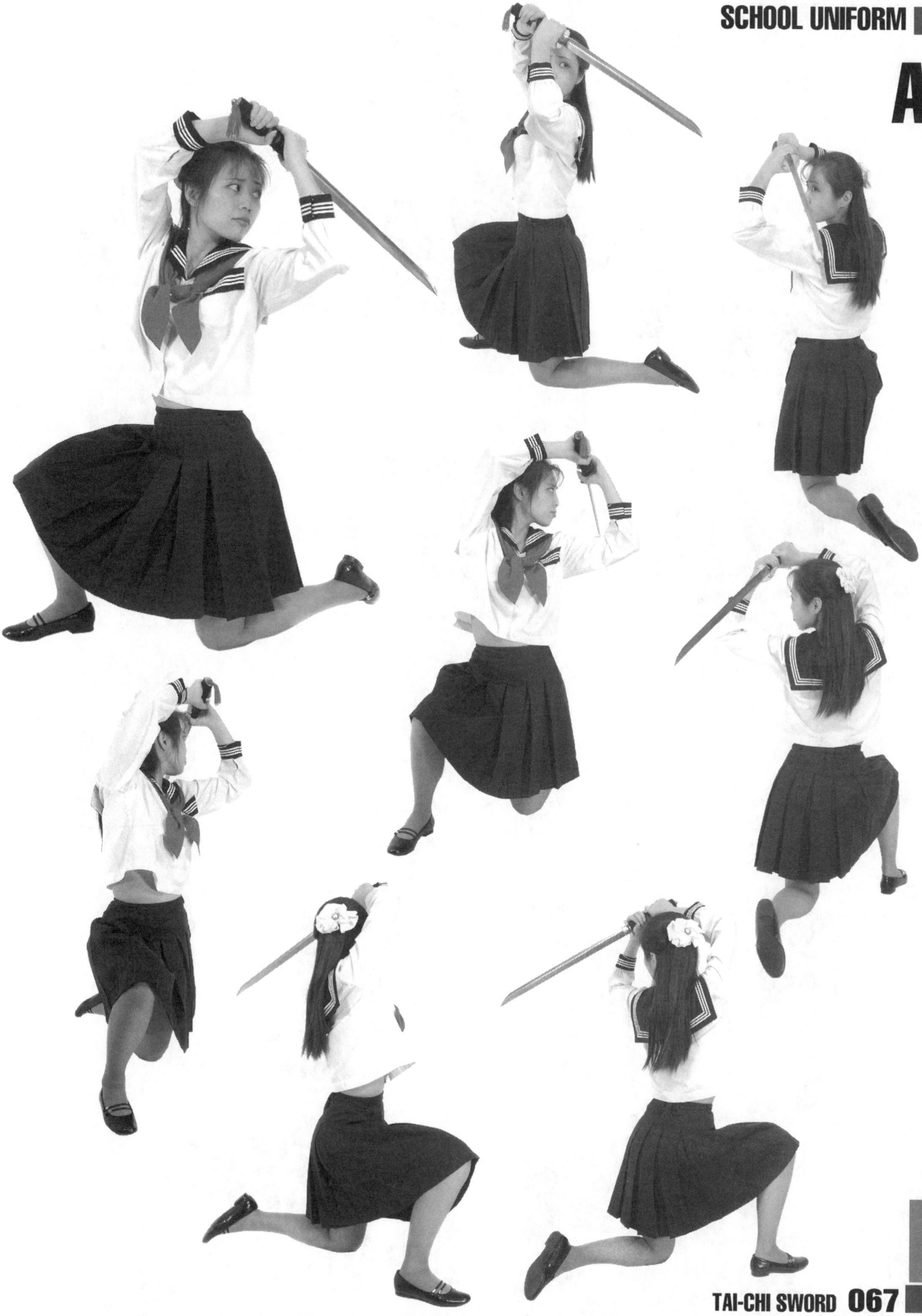

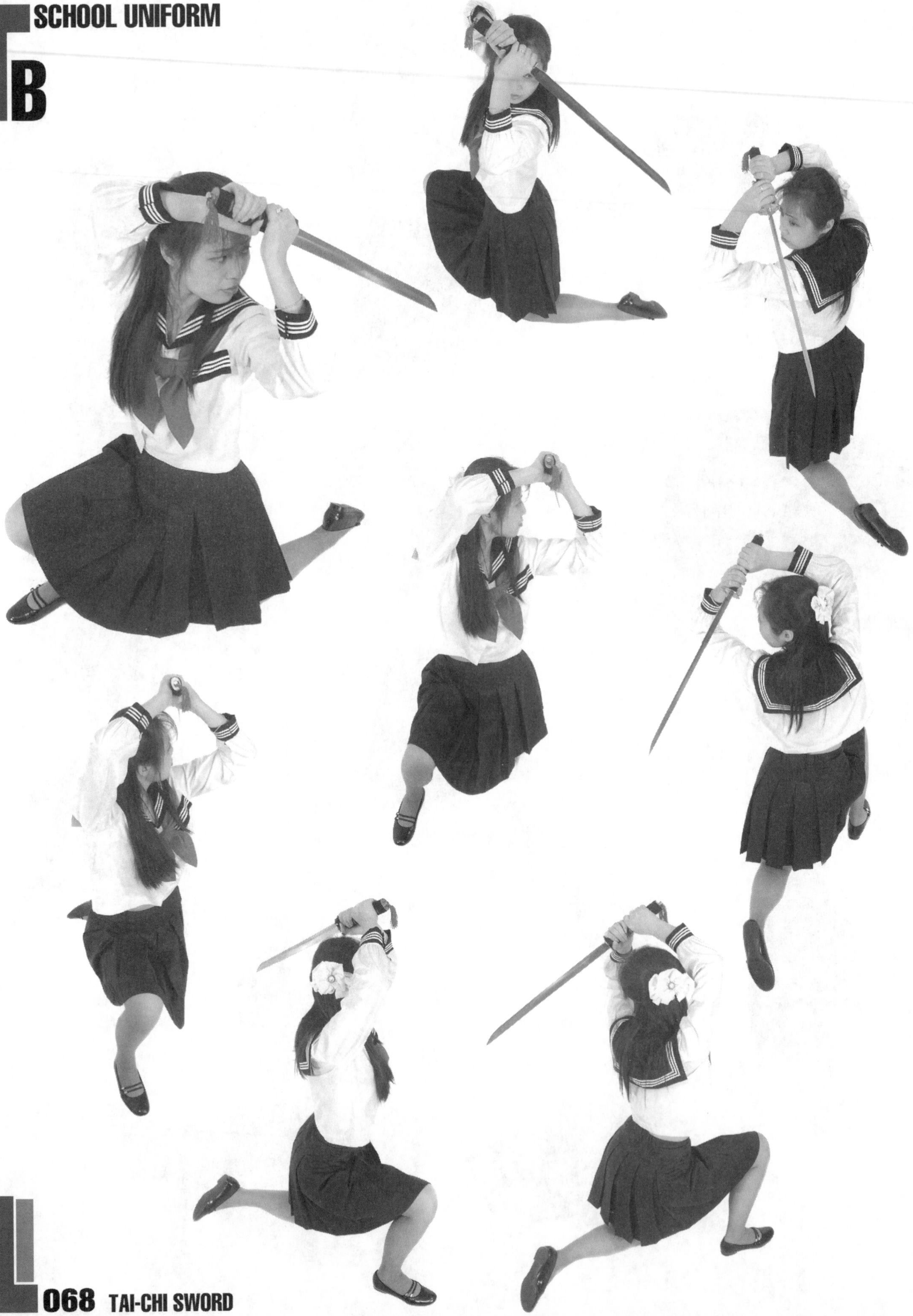

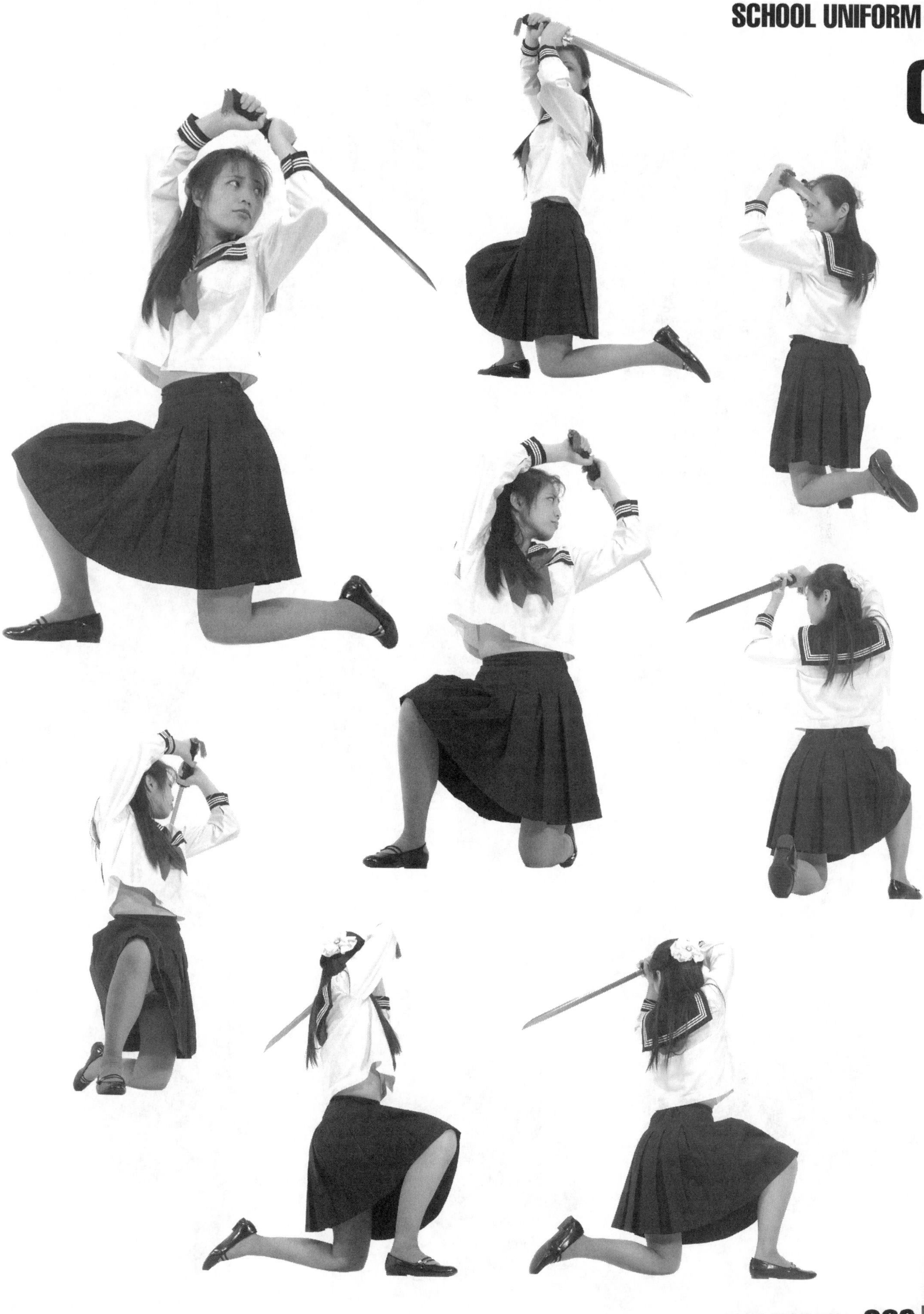

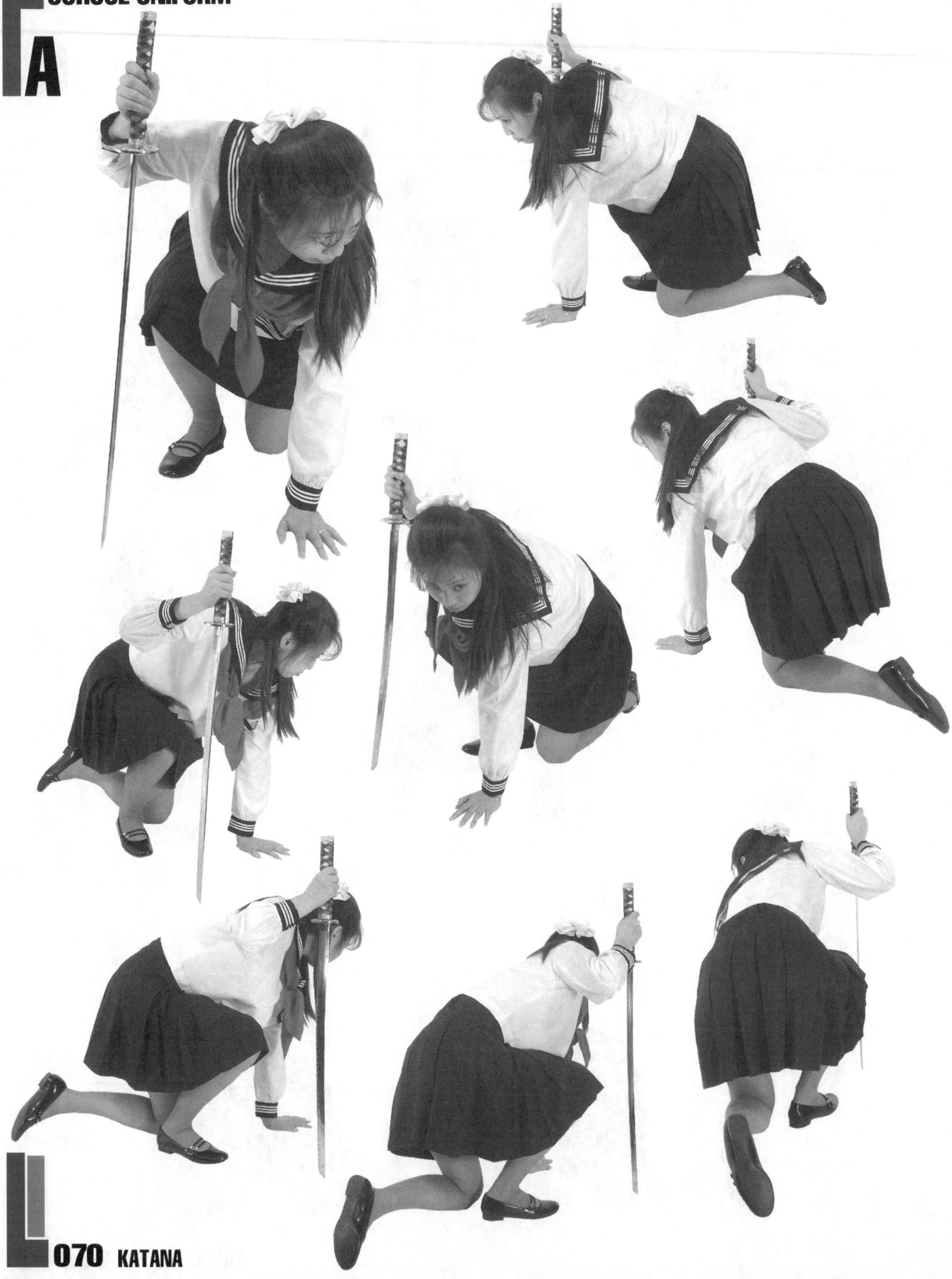

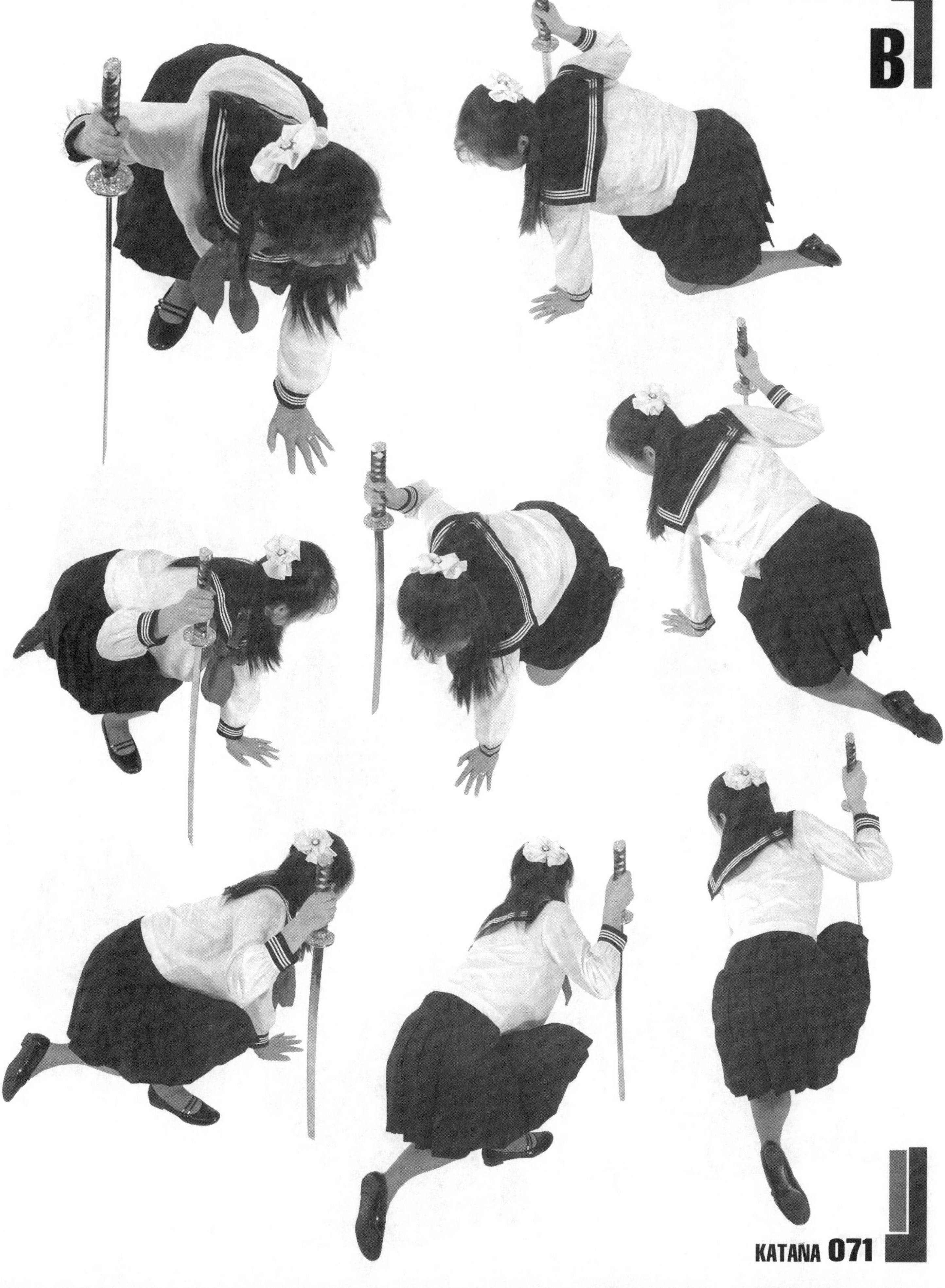

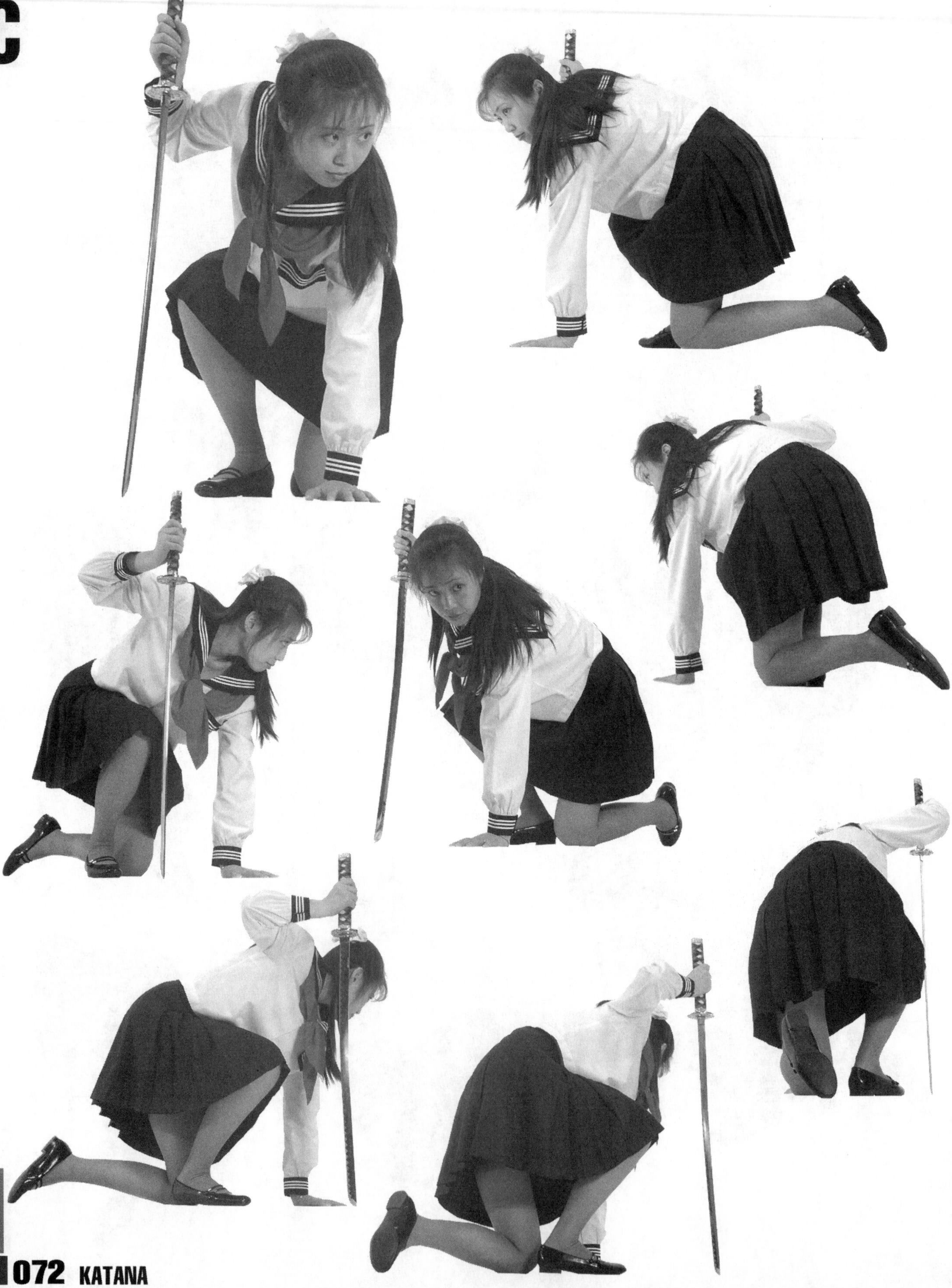

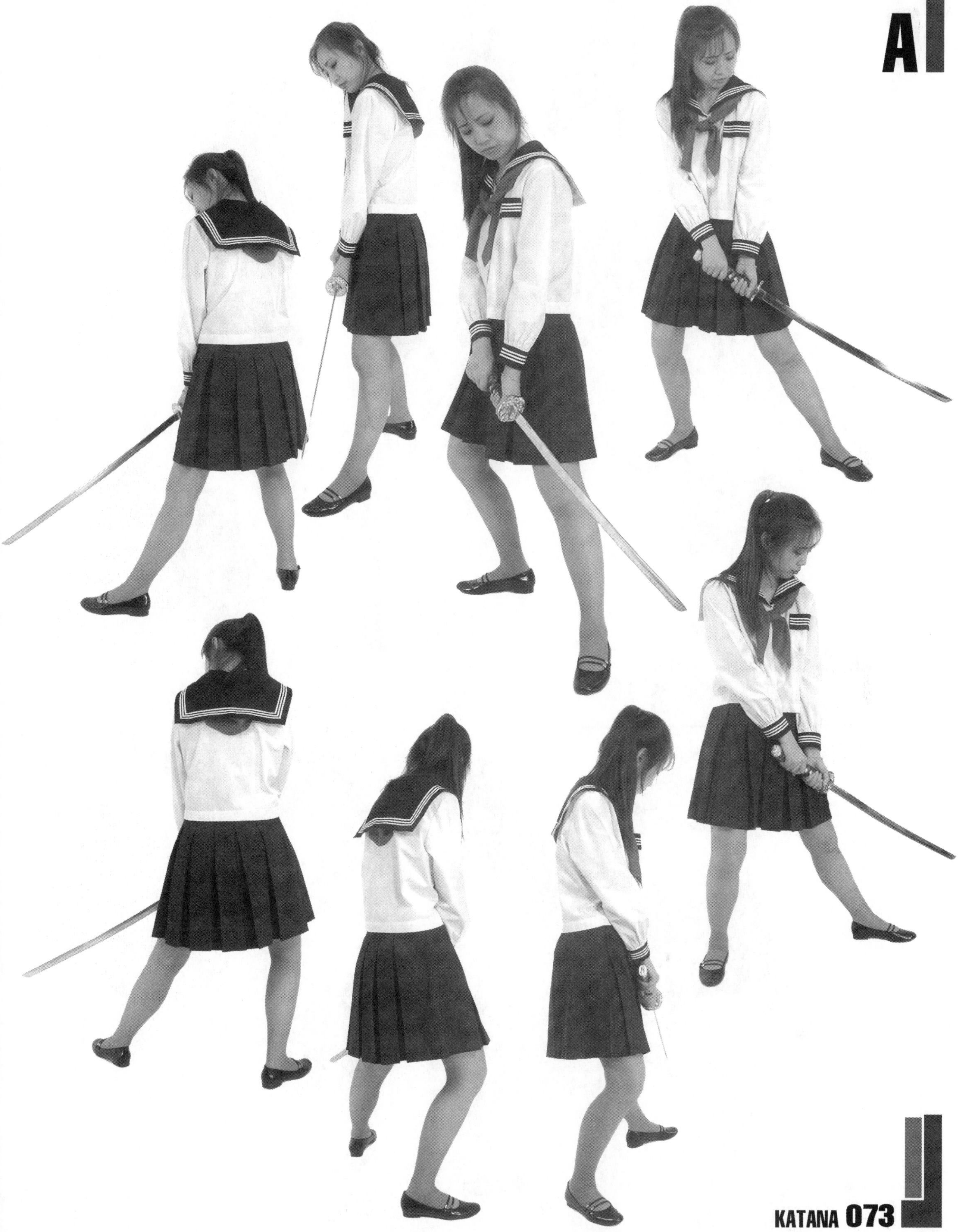

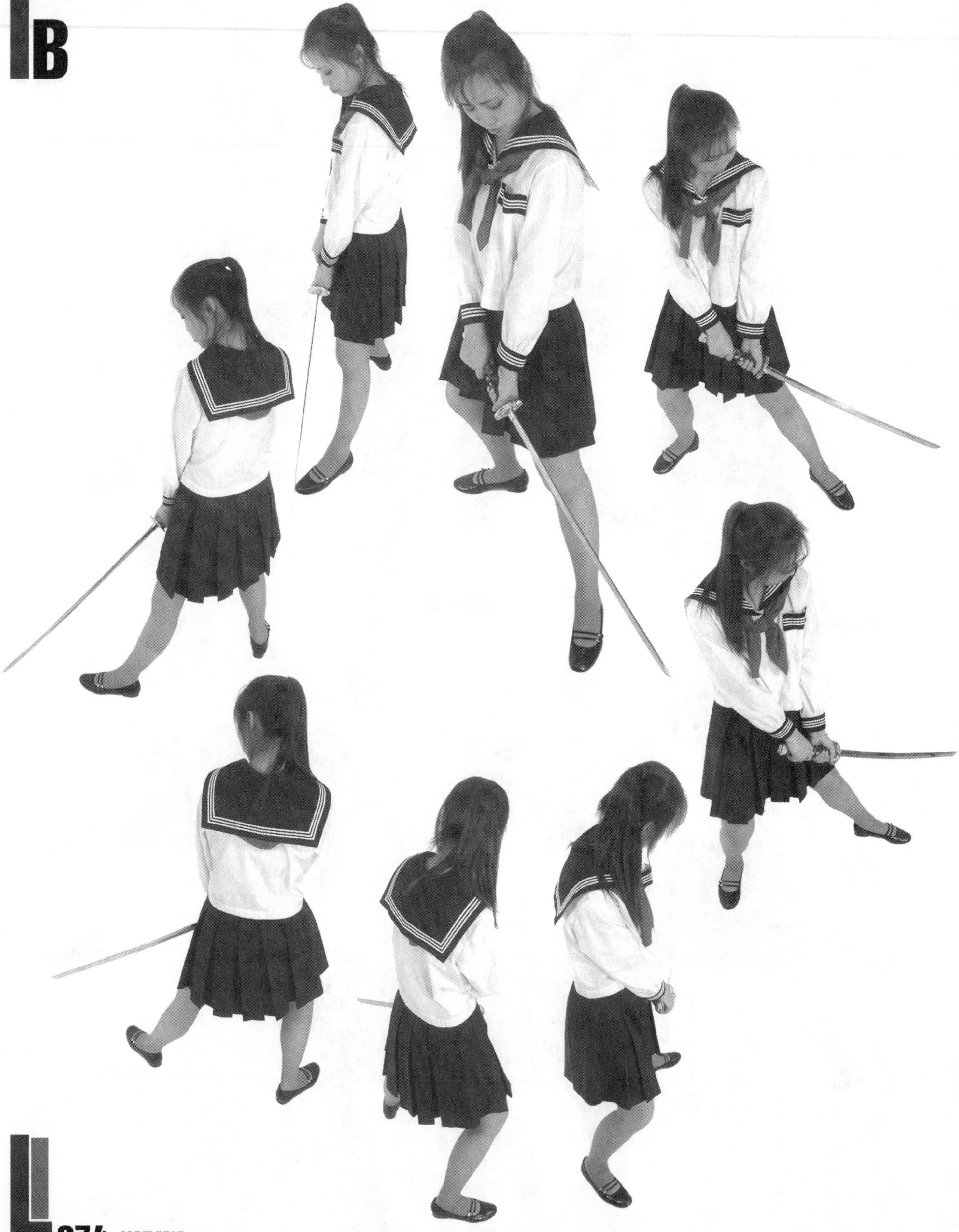

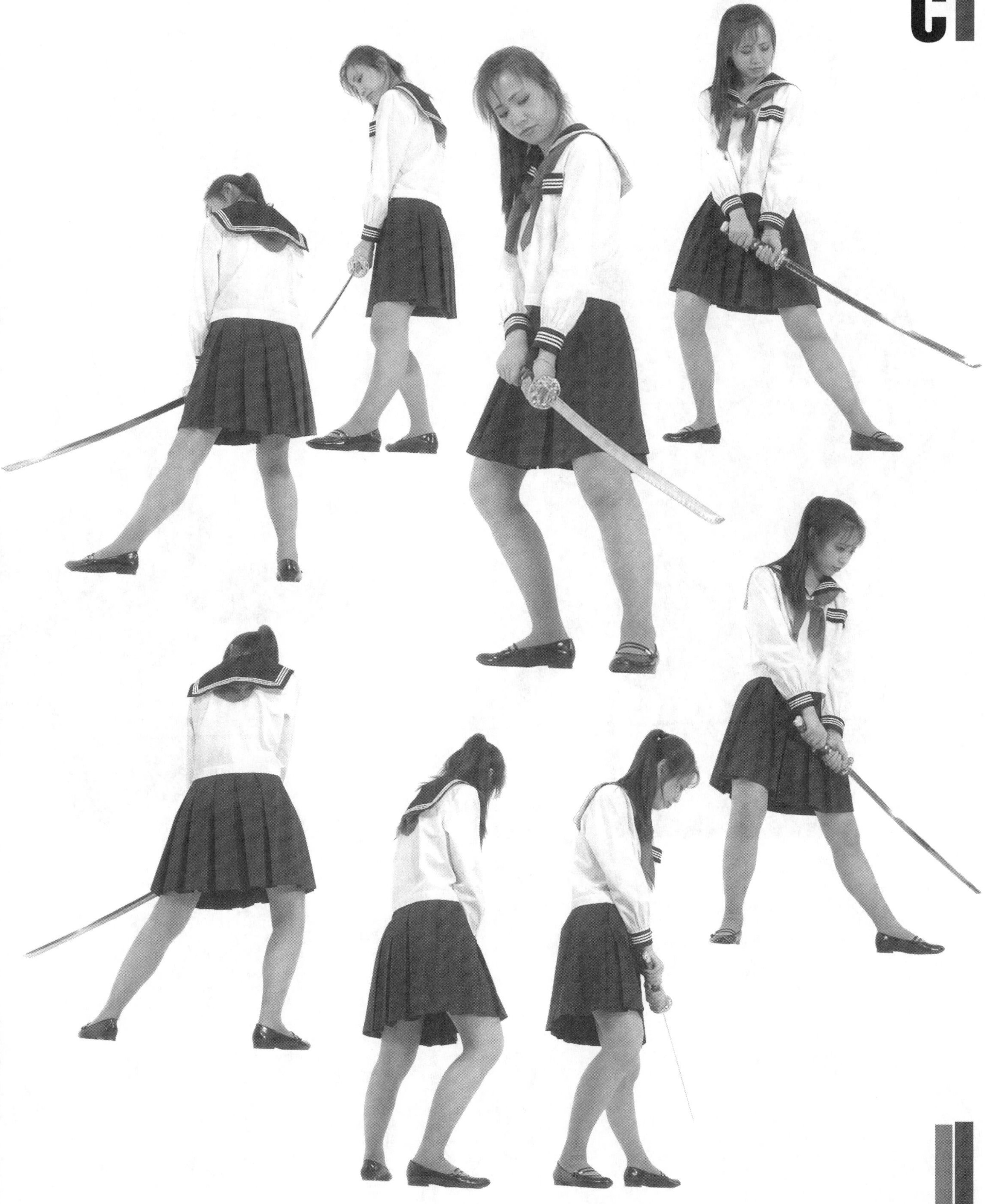

POSE

REFE

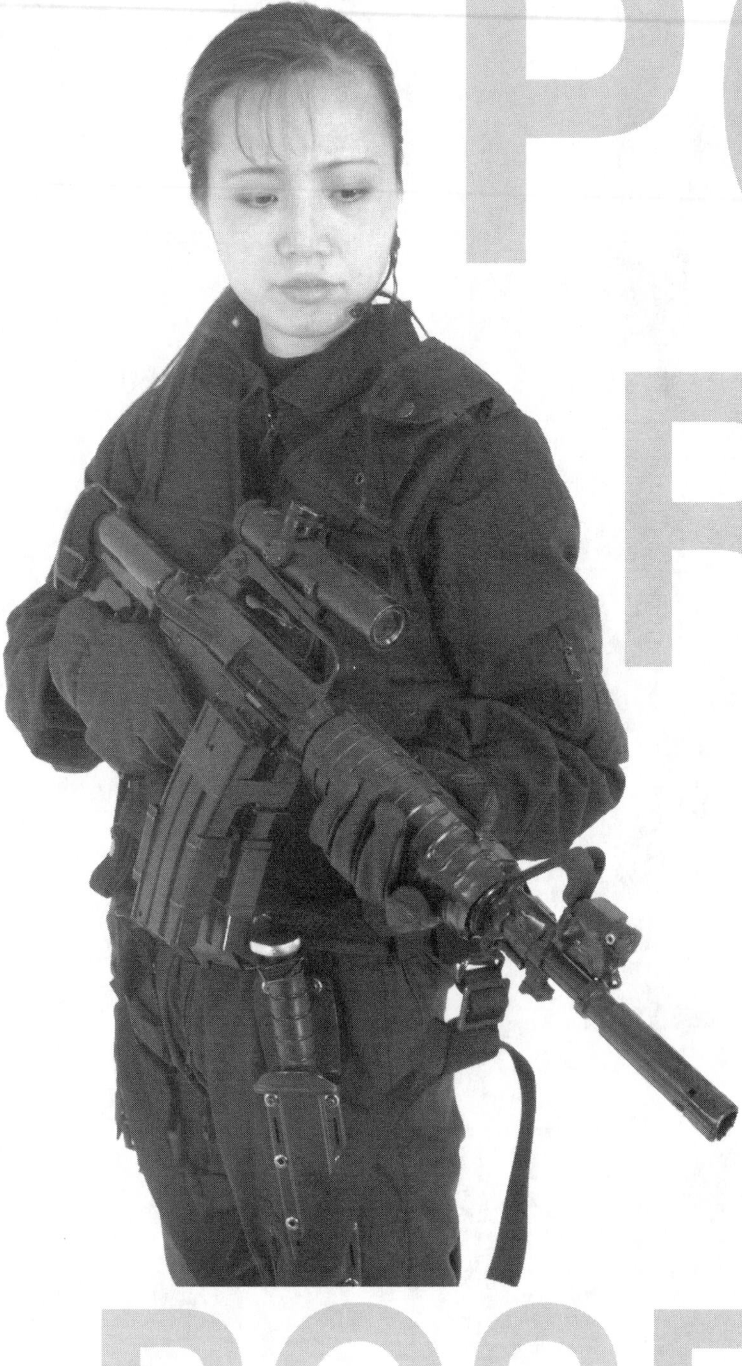

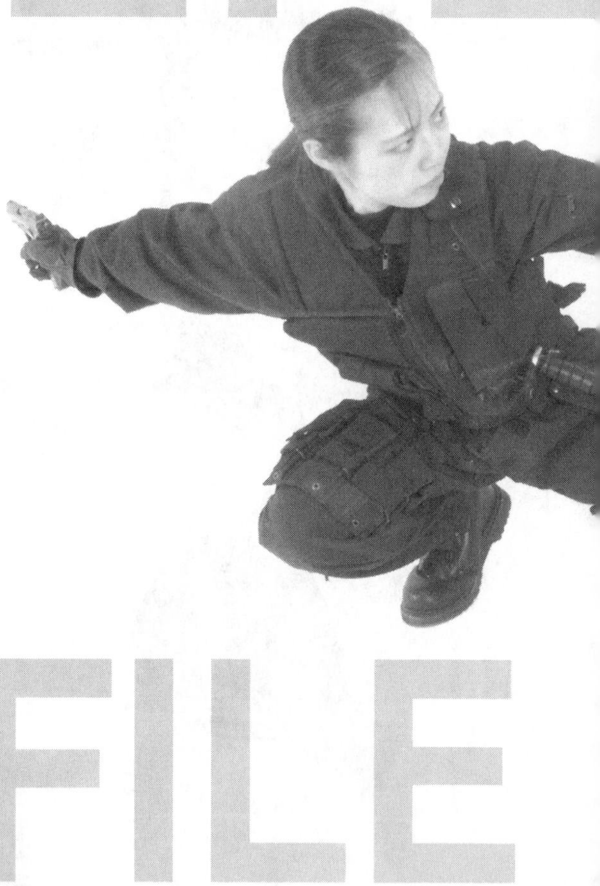

POSEFILE

REFERENC

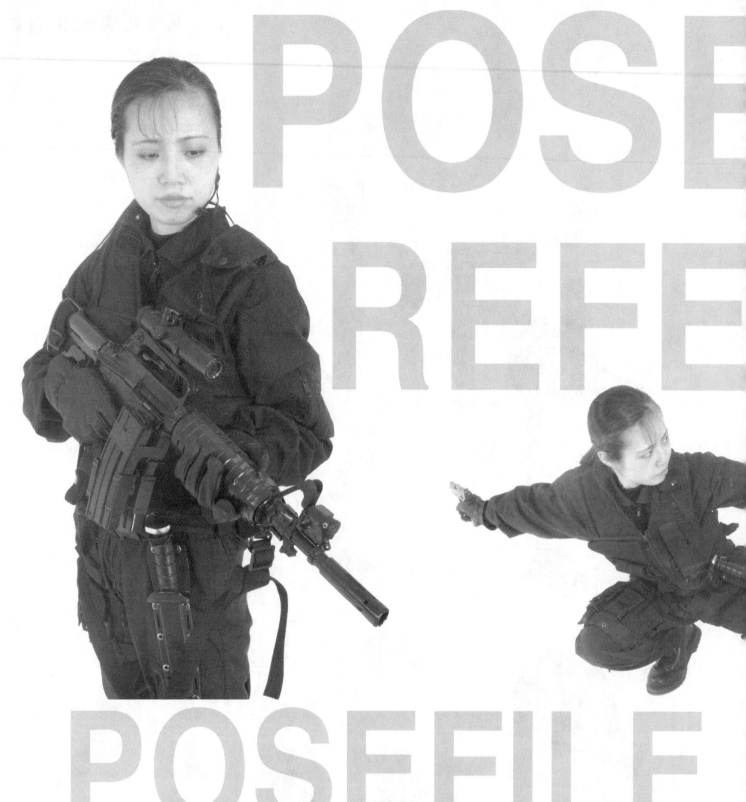

FILE

RENC

1

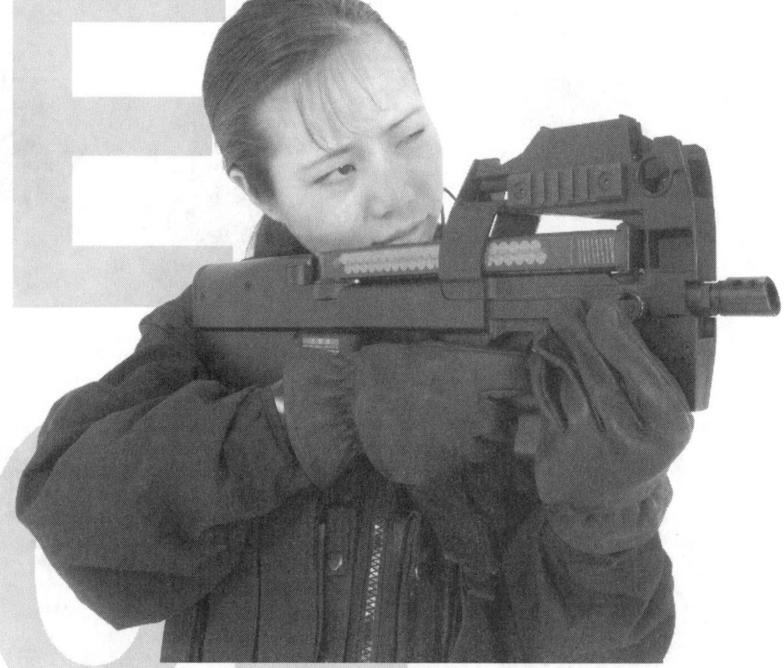

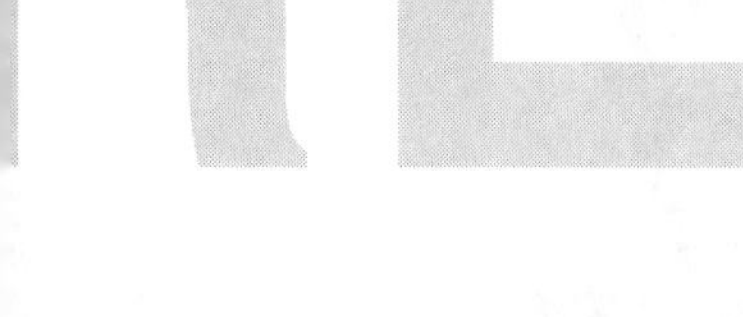

TACTICAL GEAR
COMBAT POSE
(FEMALE)

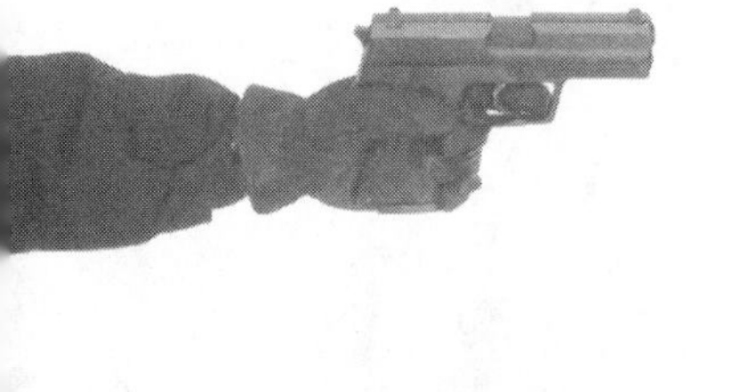

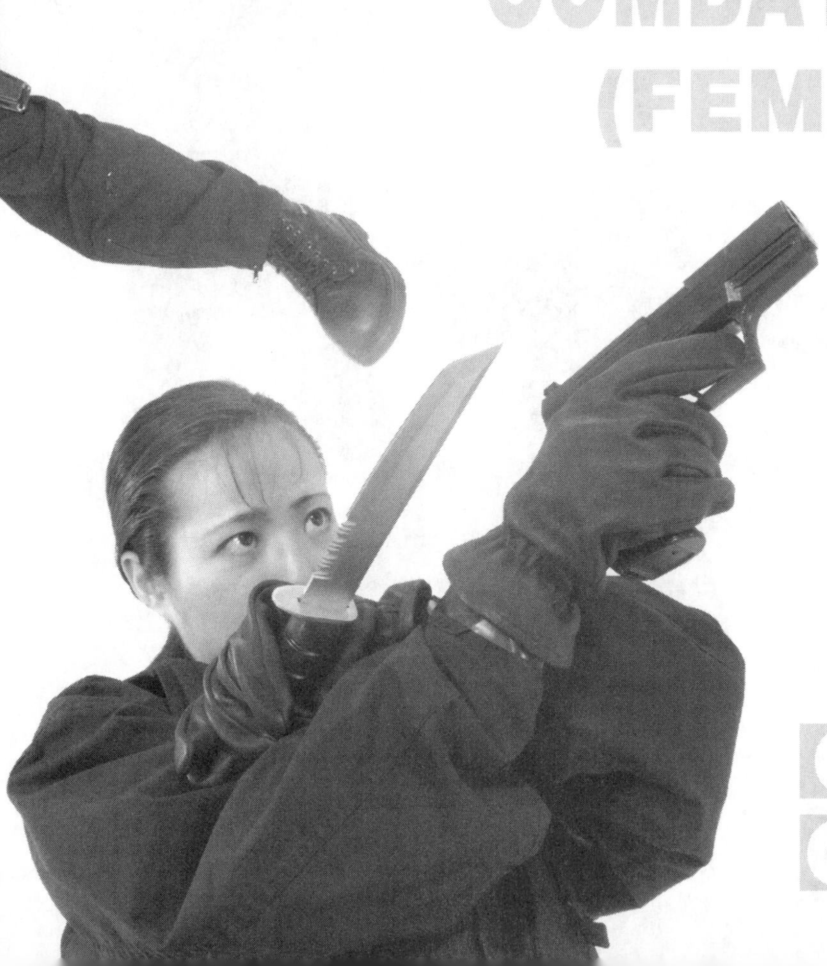

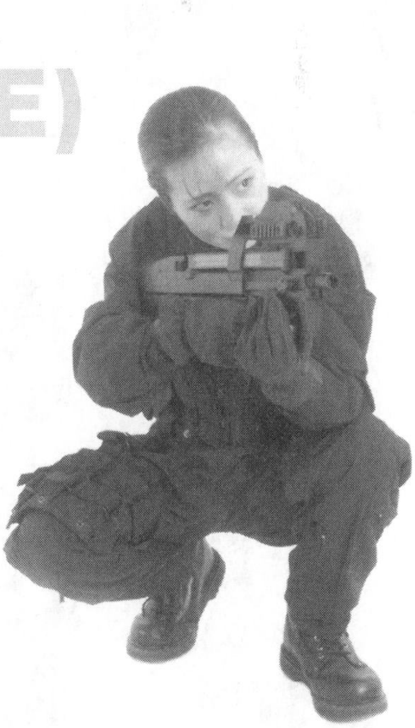

COMBAT COLLECTION

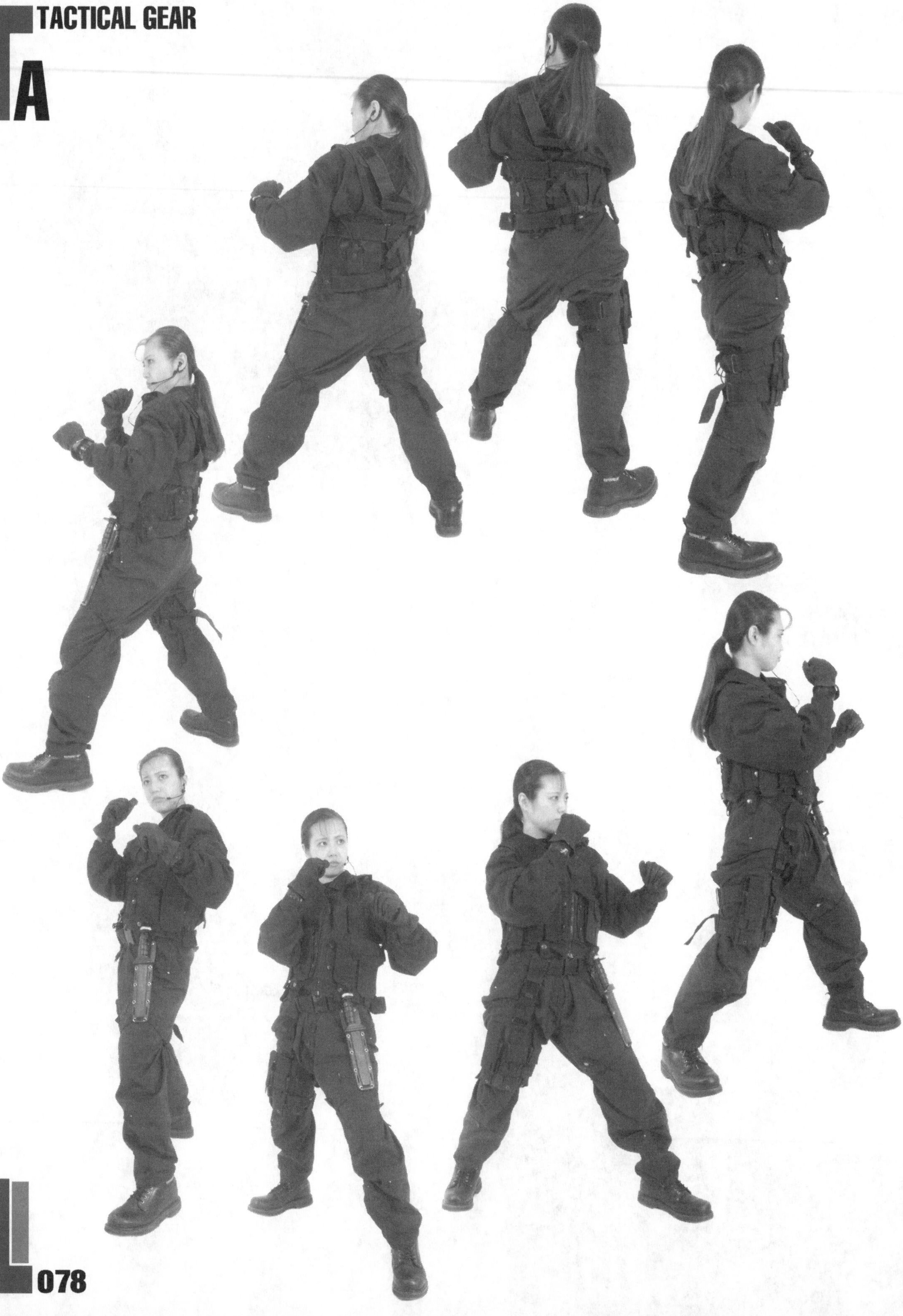

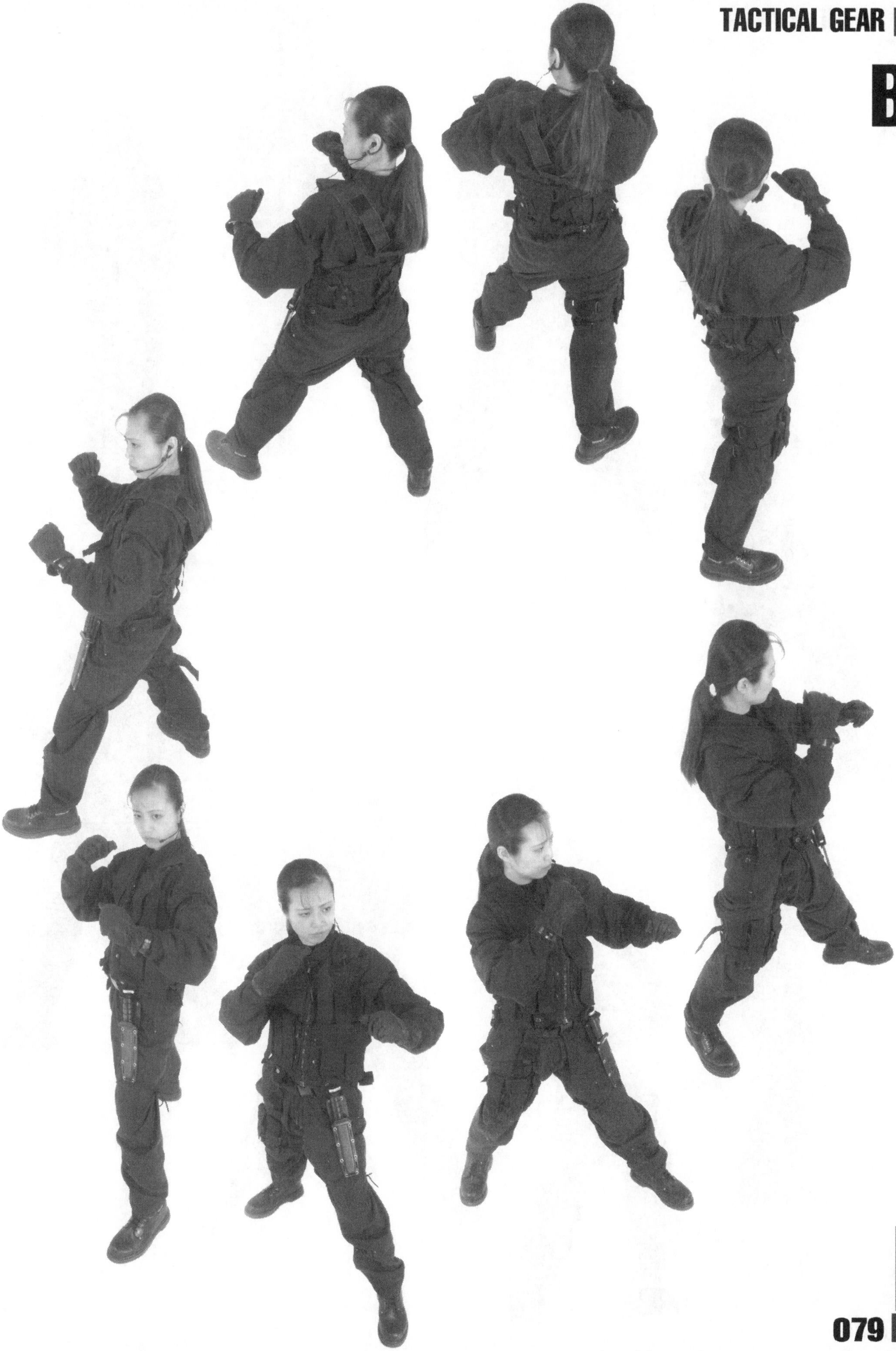

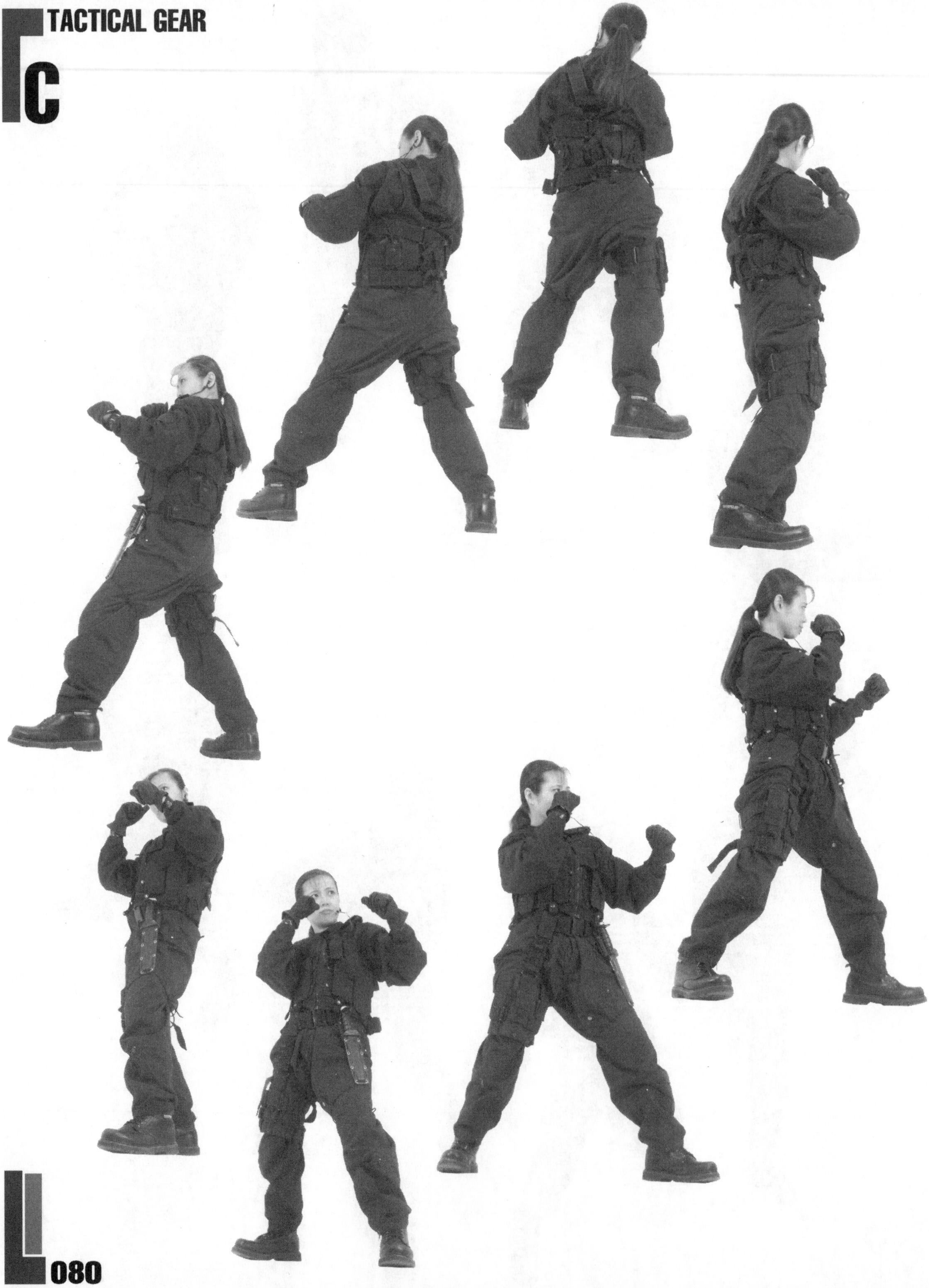

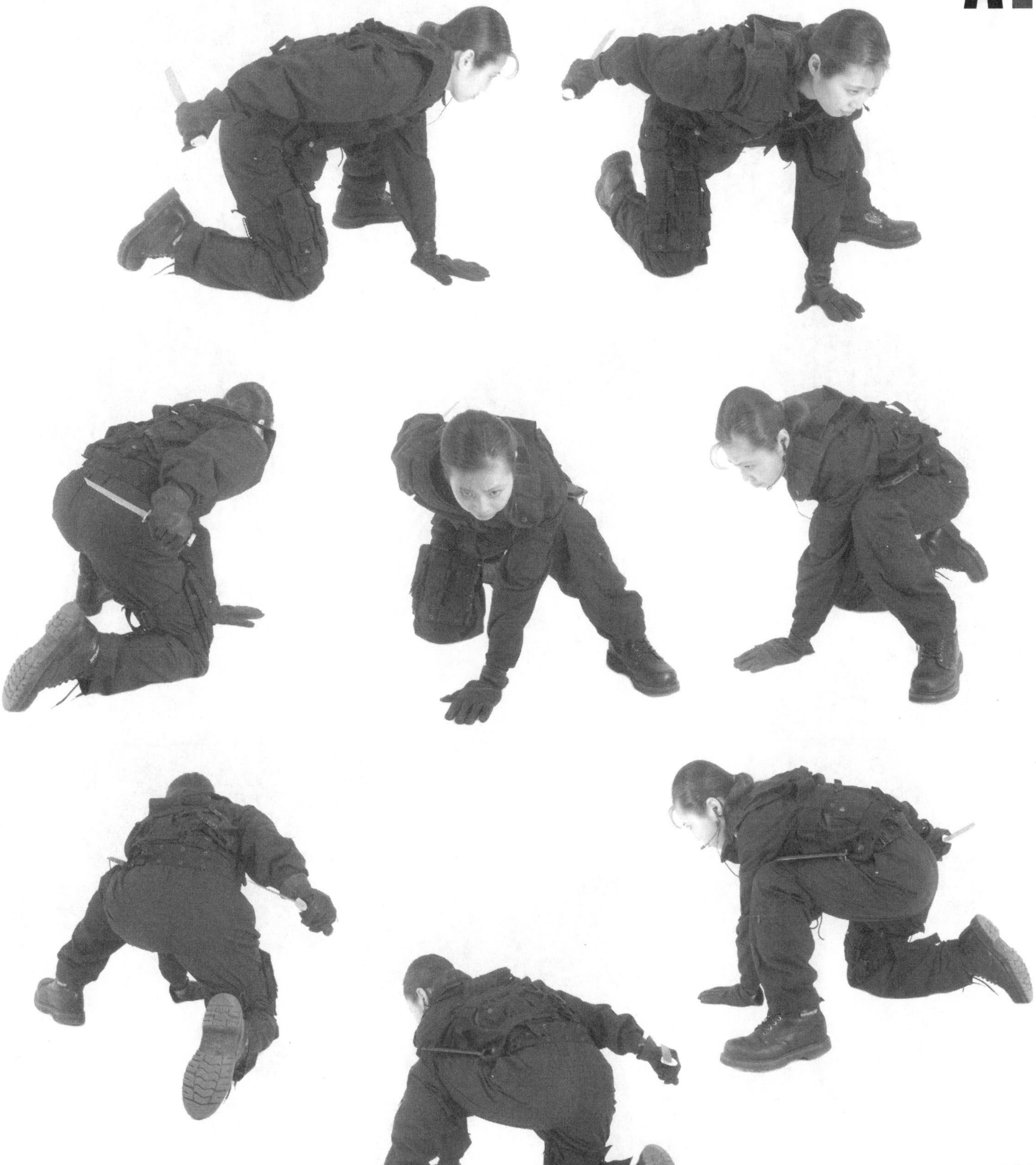

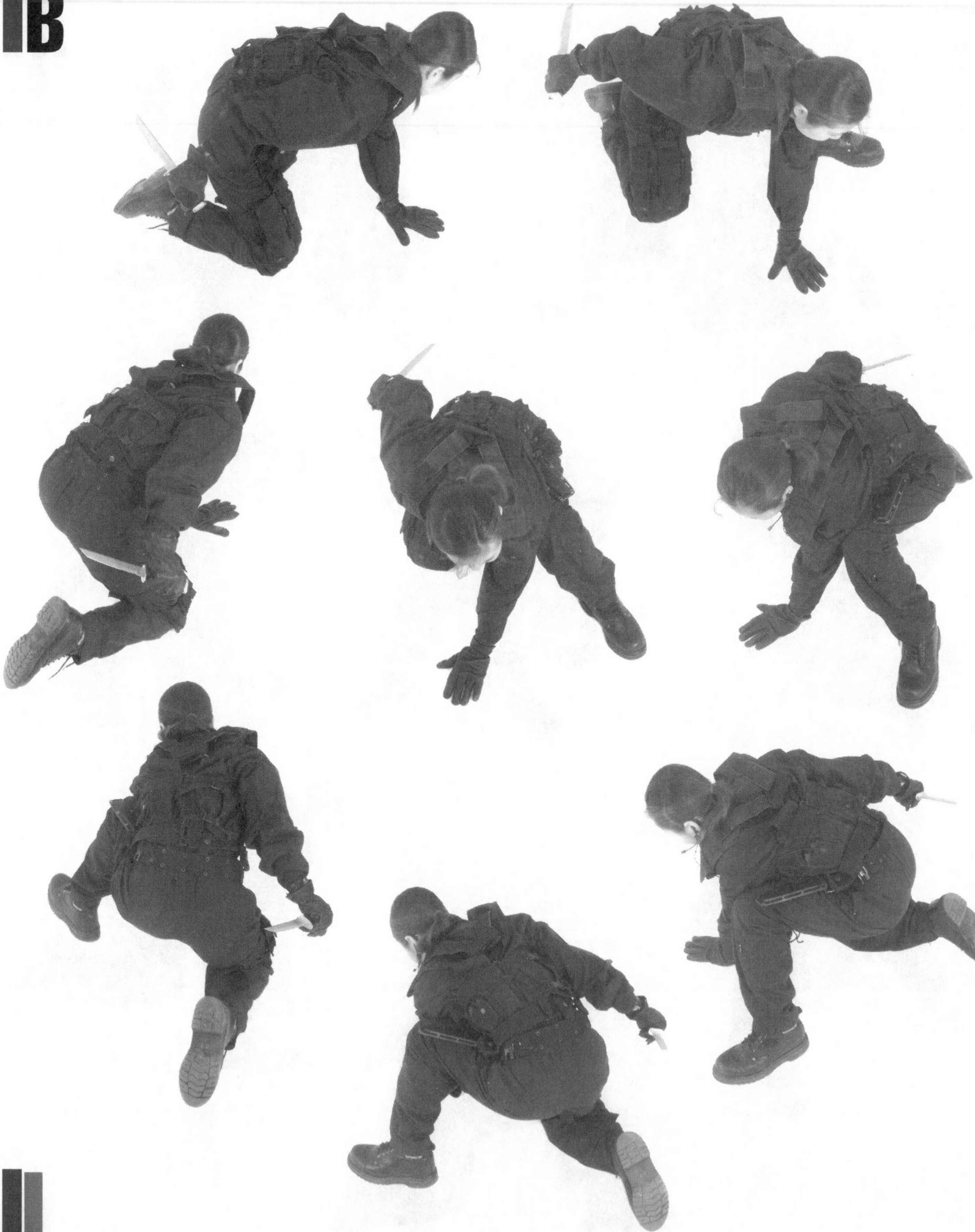

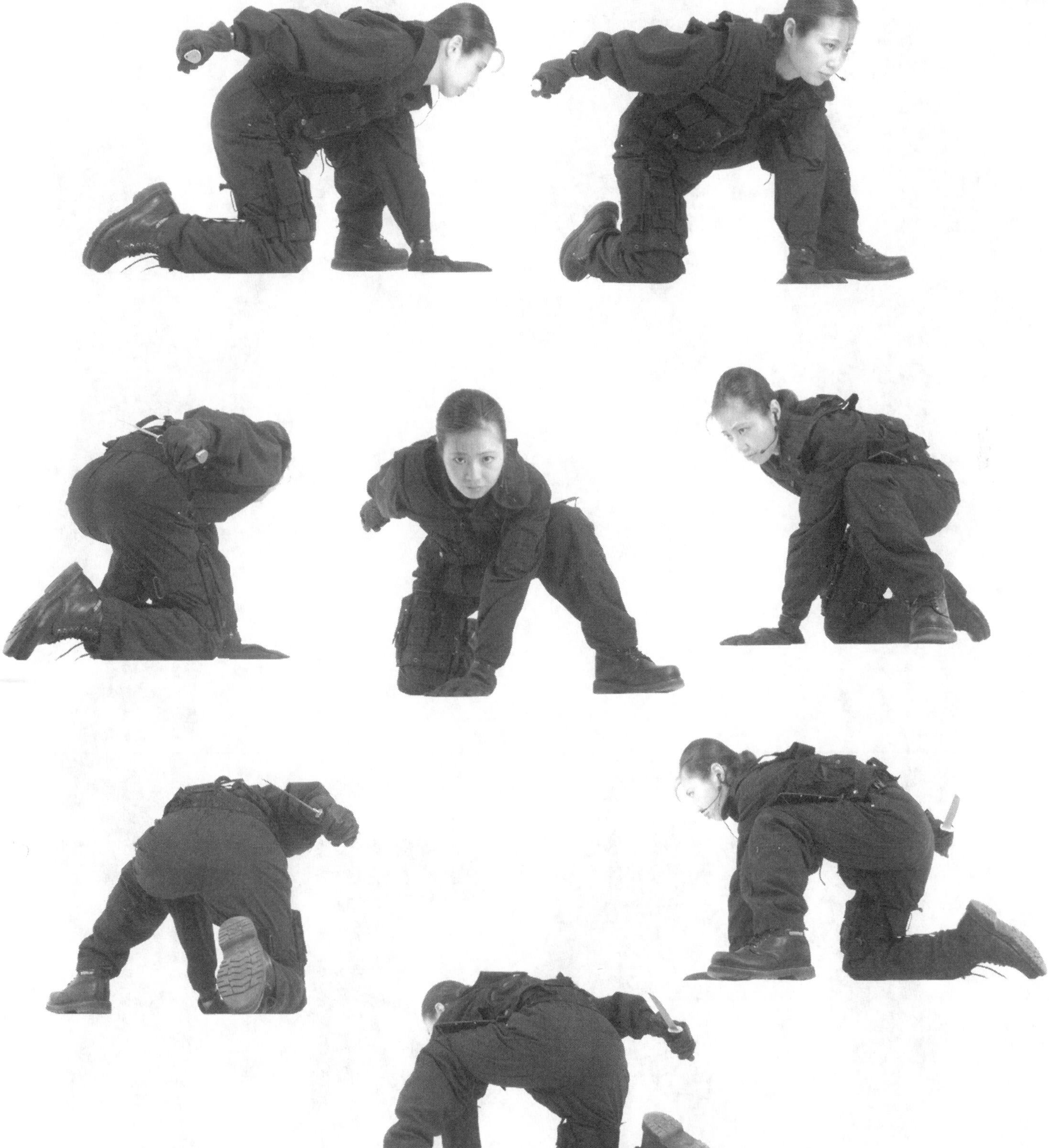

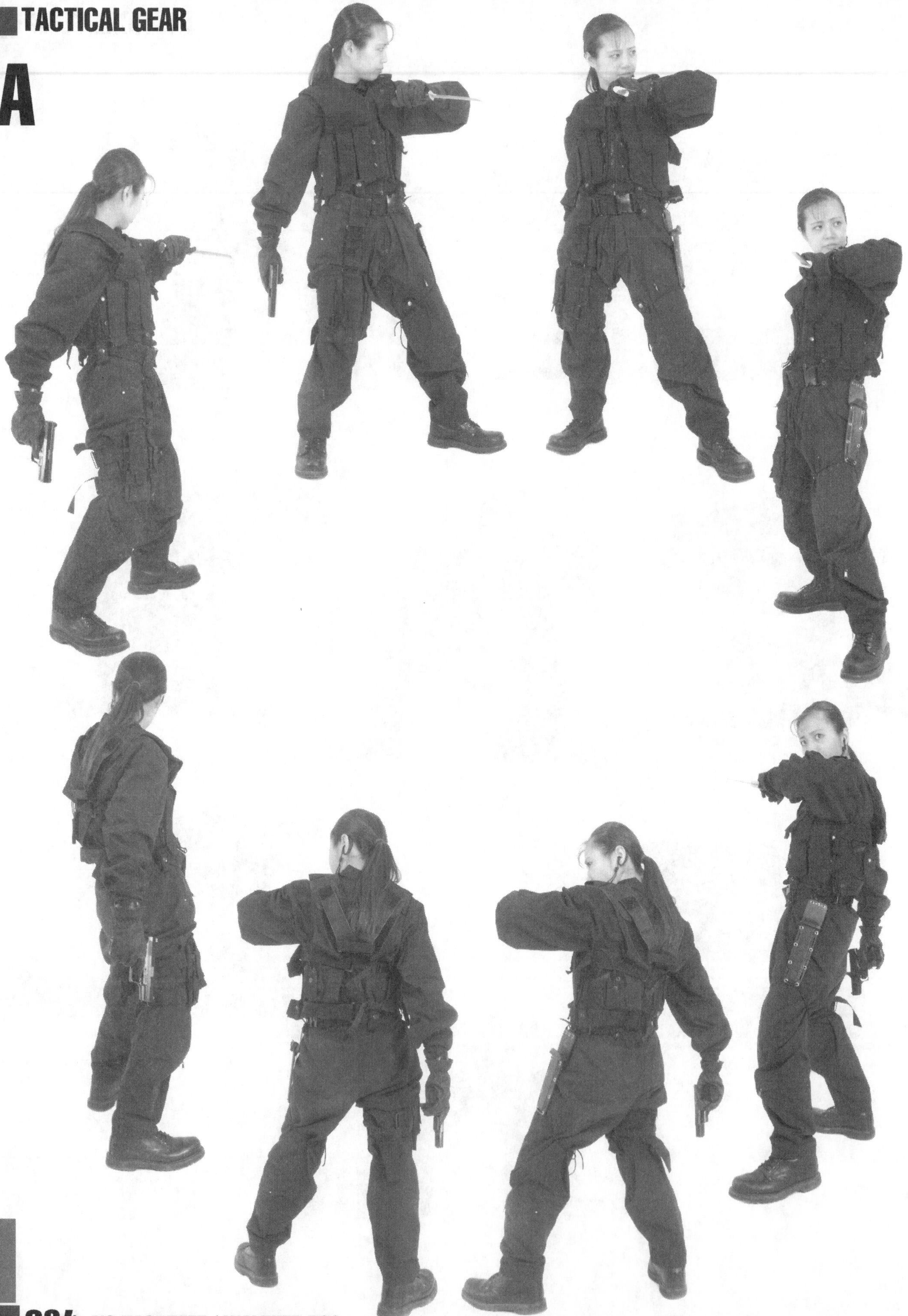

 N6 TAC KNIFE / WALTHER P99

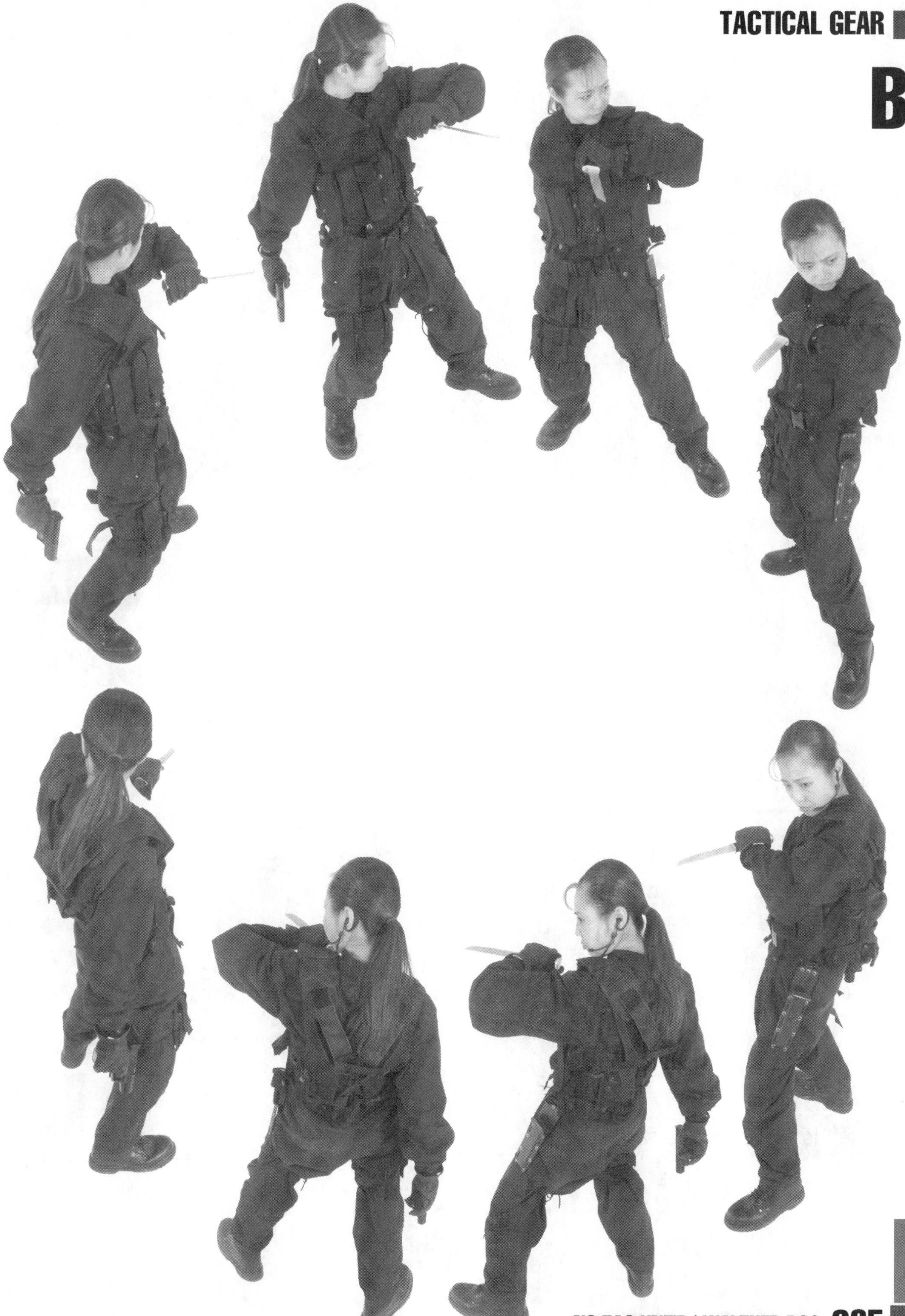

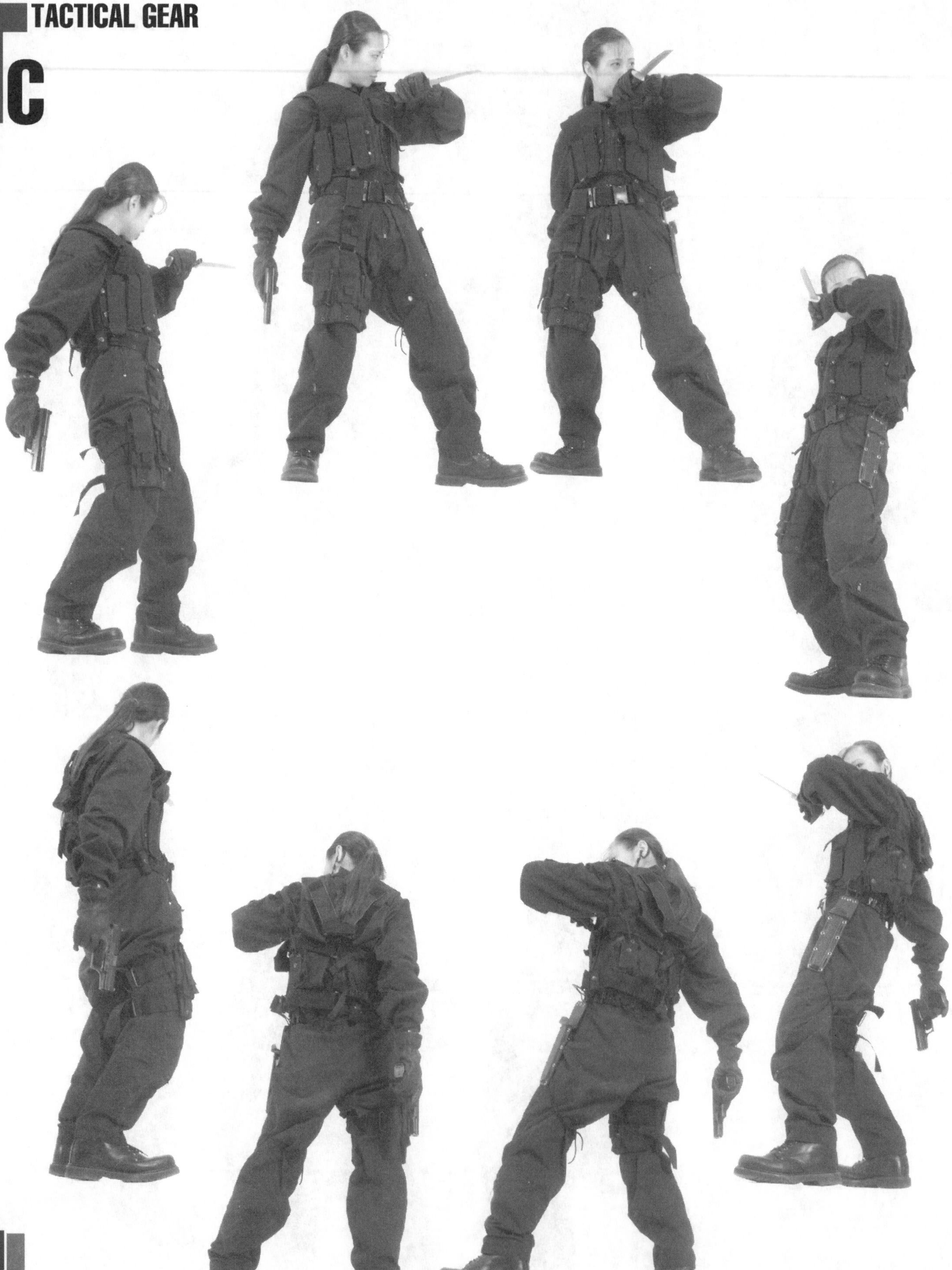

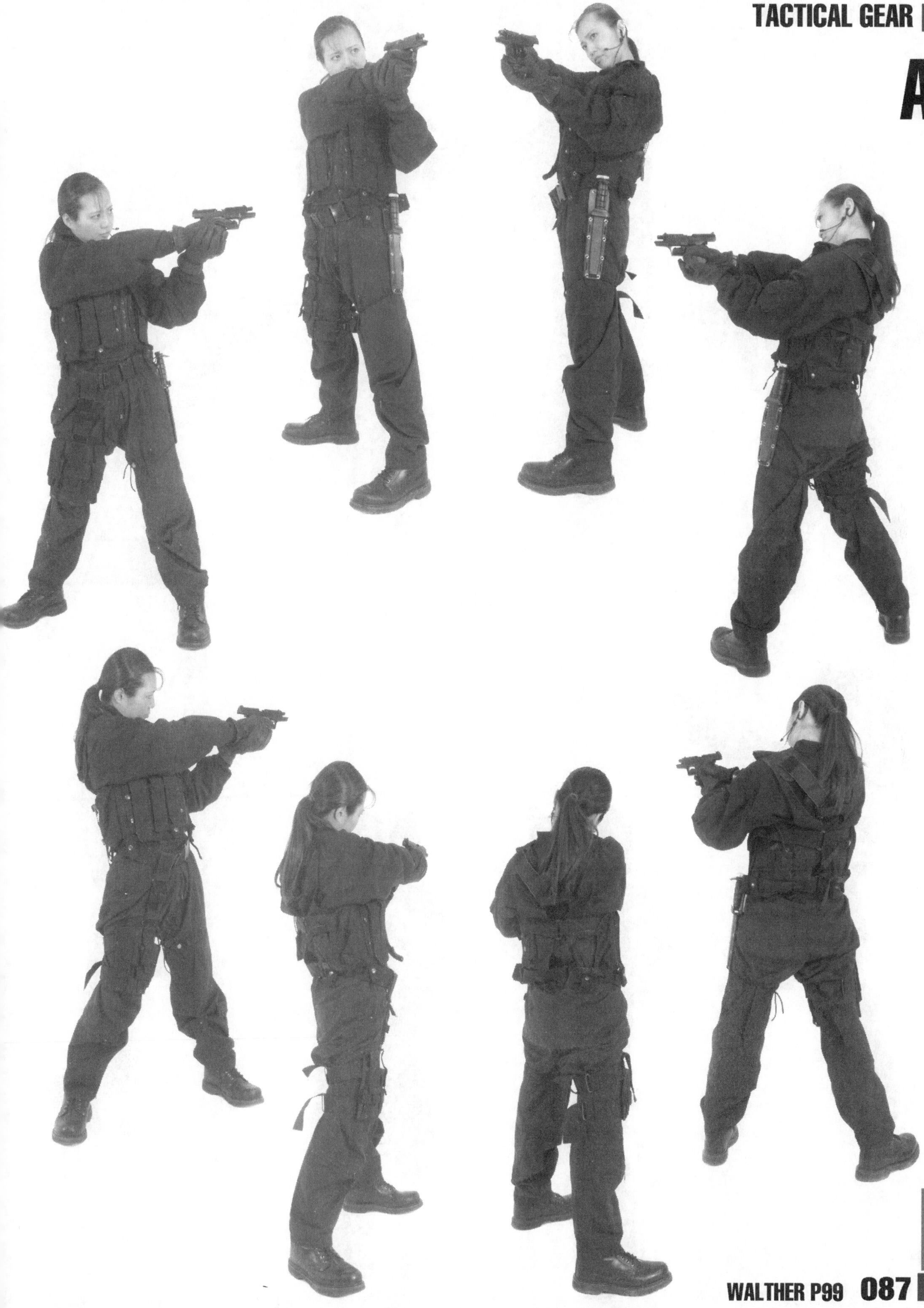

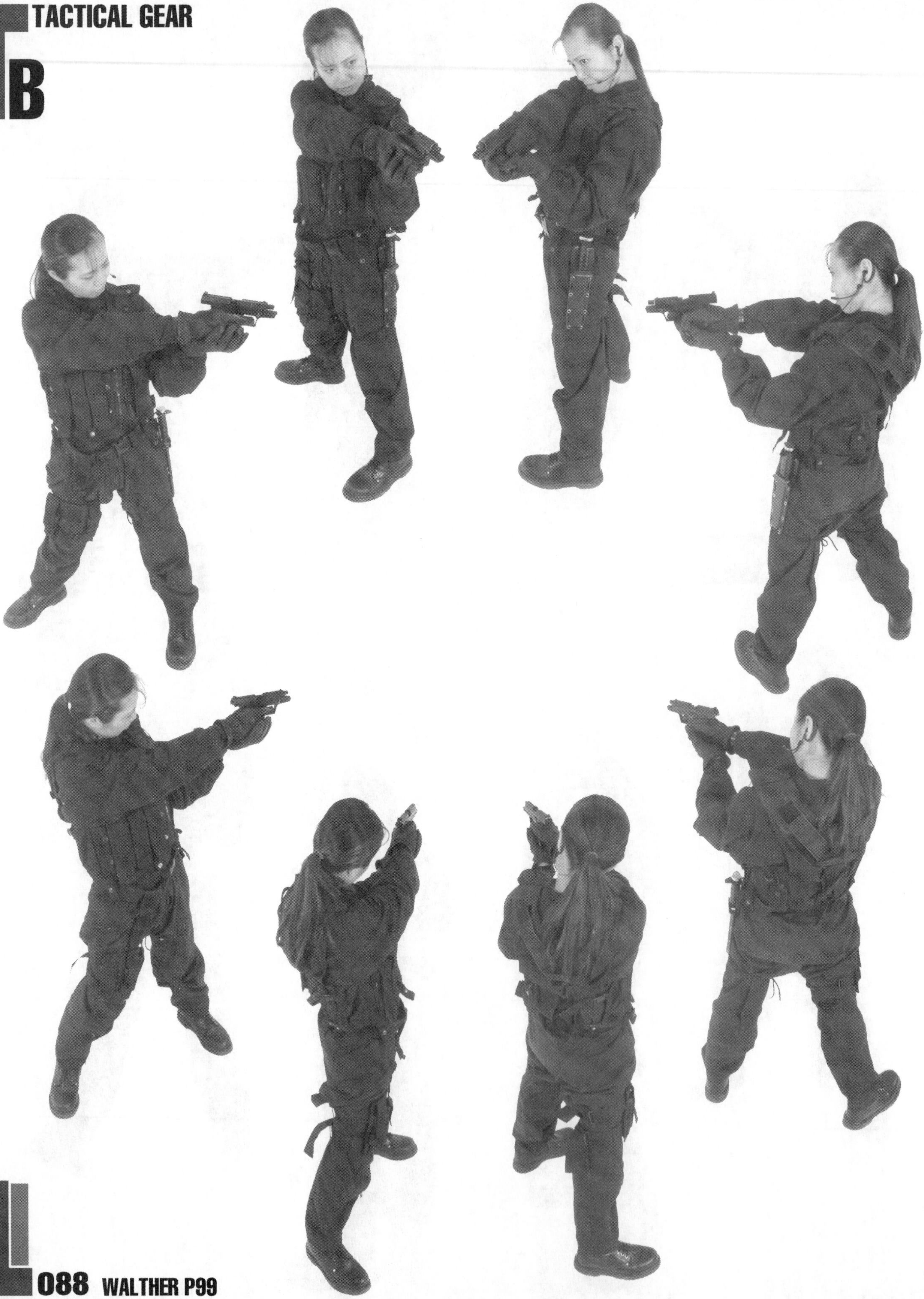

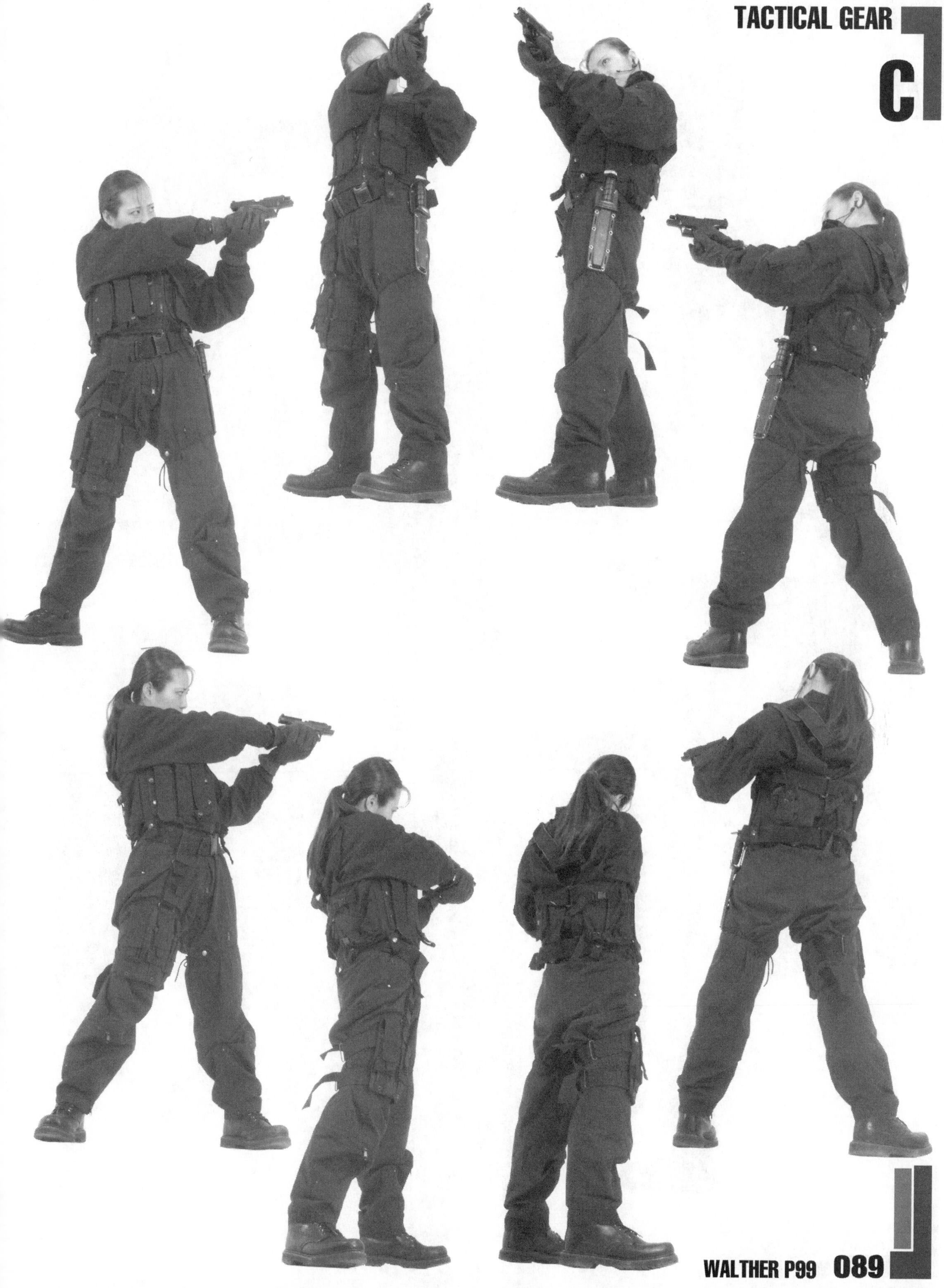

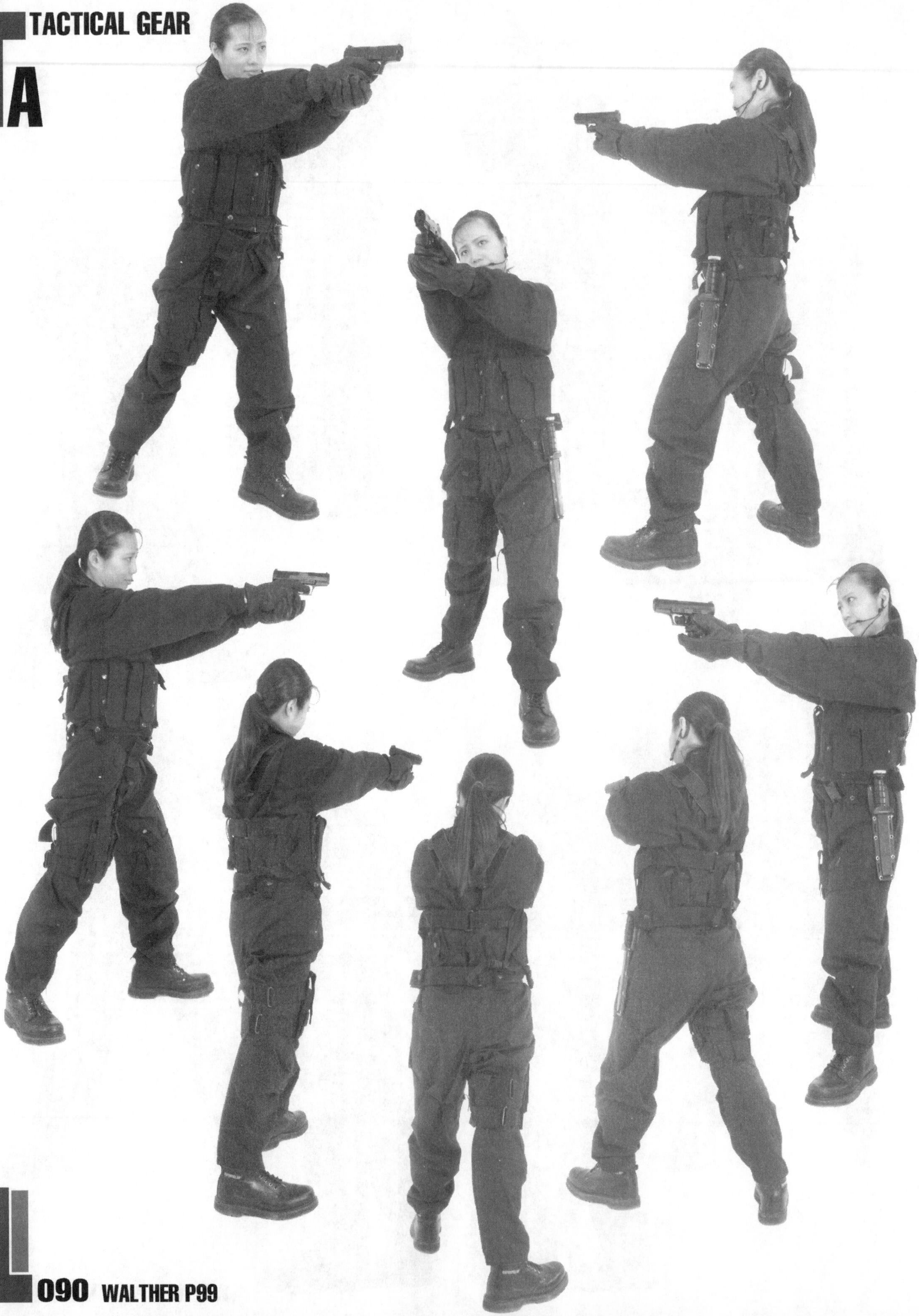

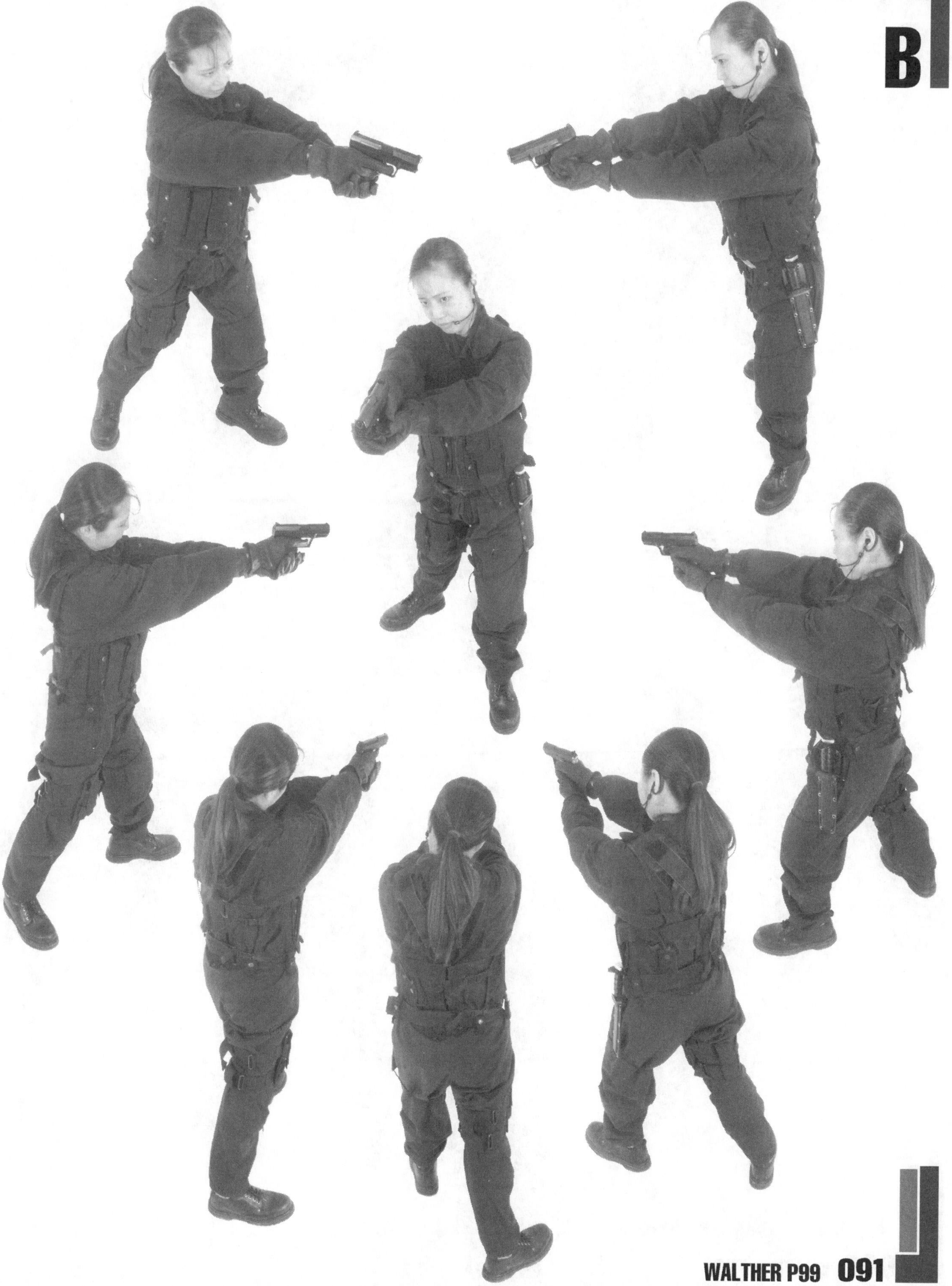

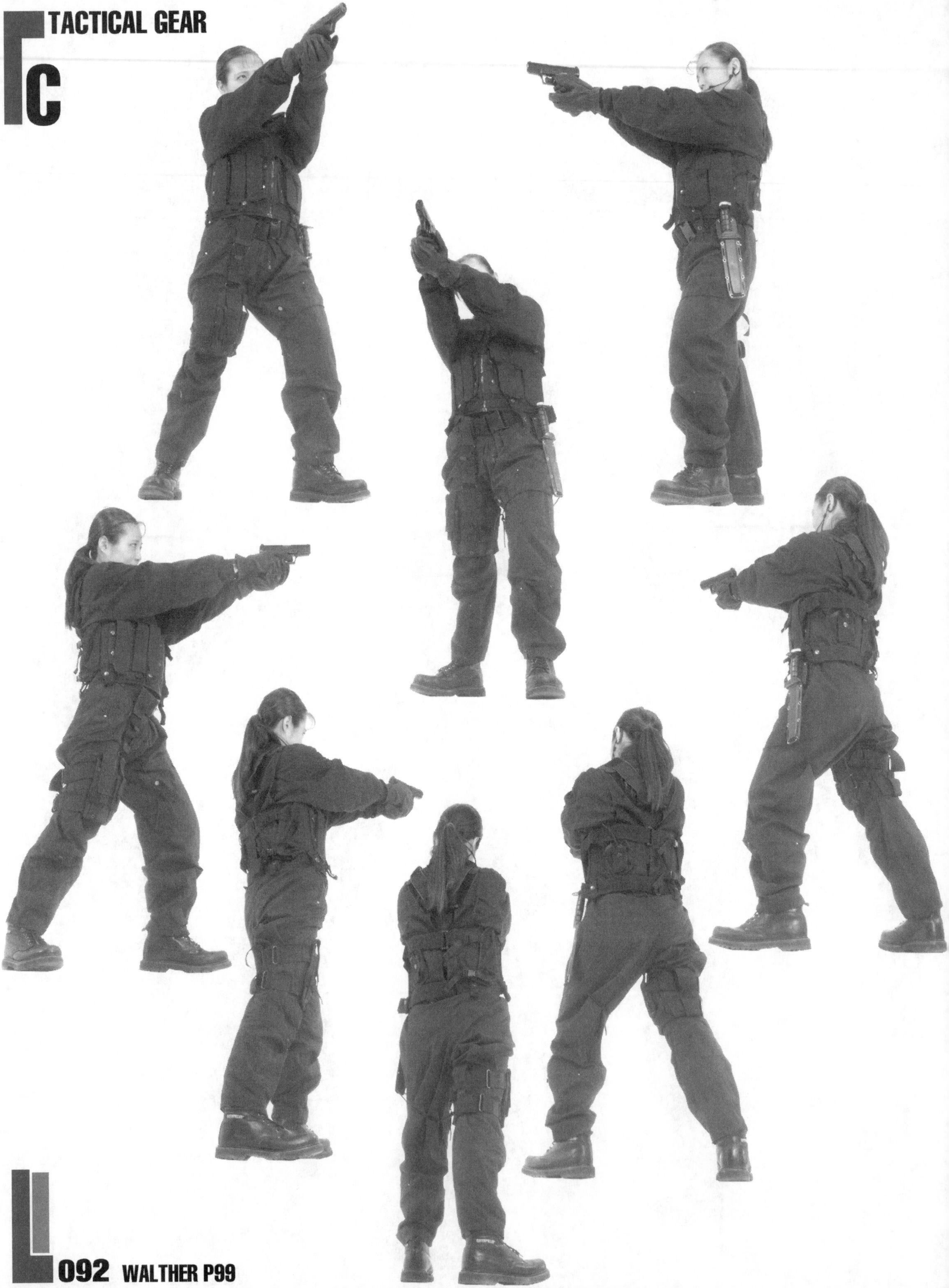

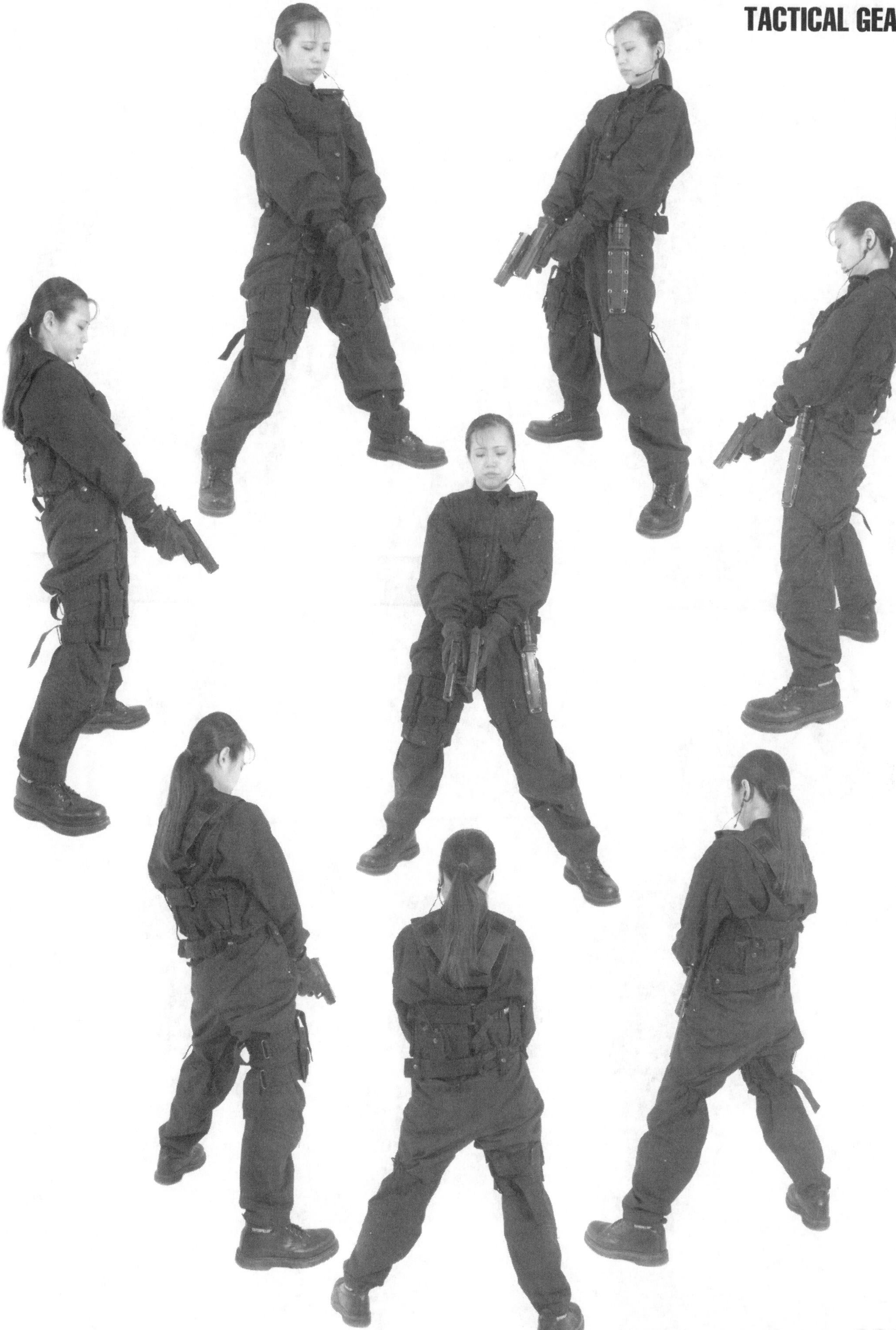

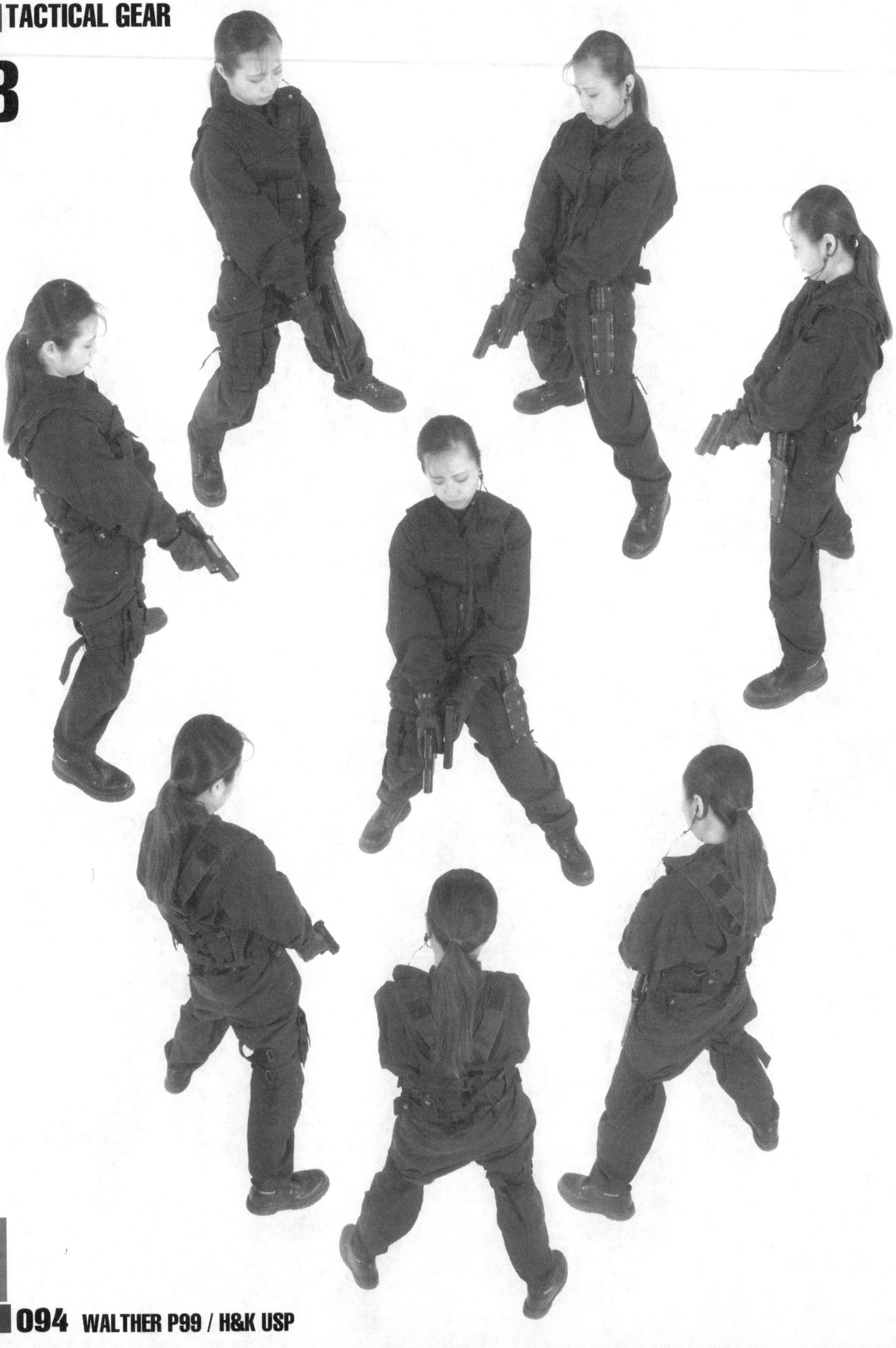

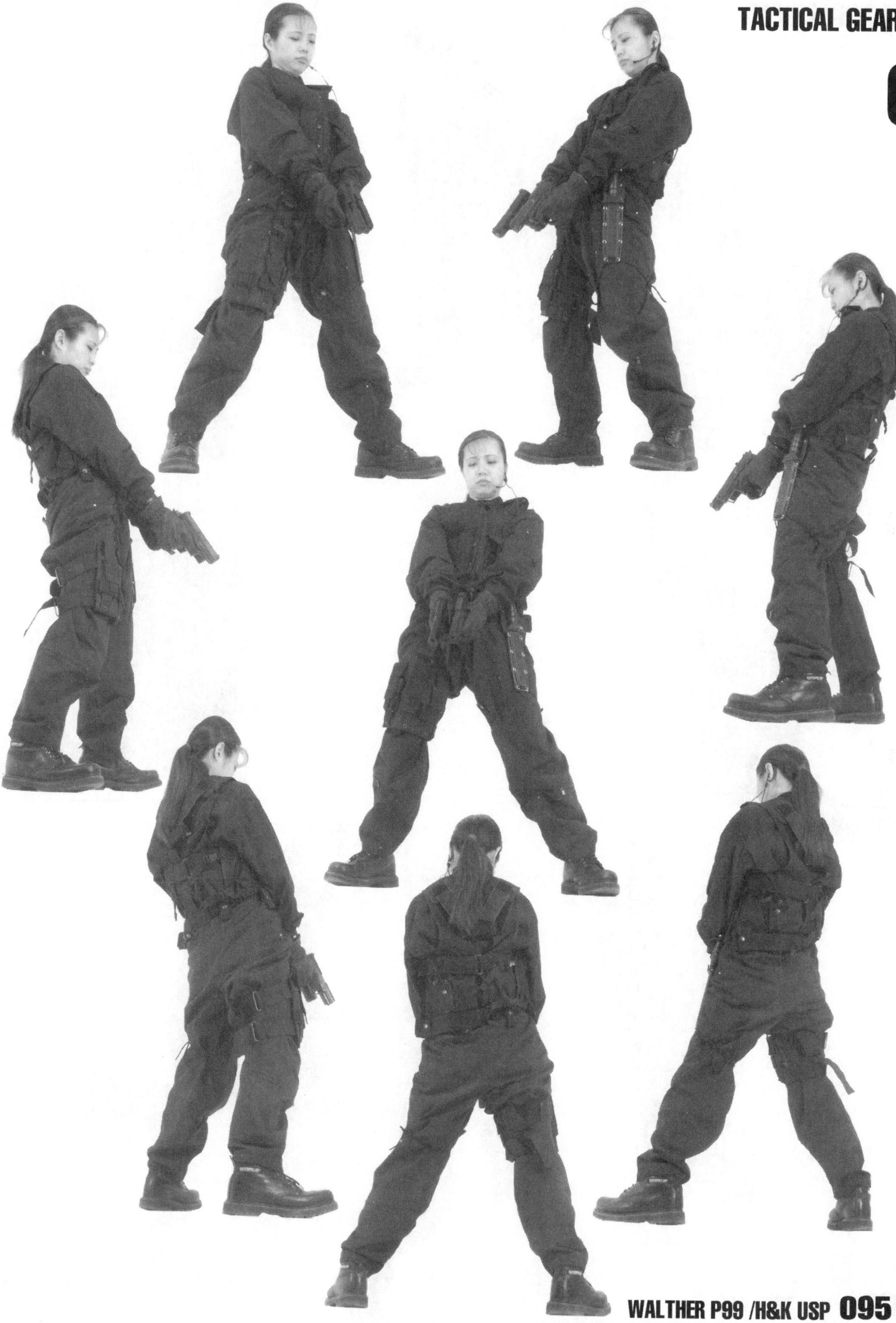

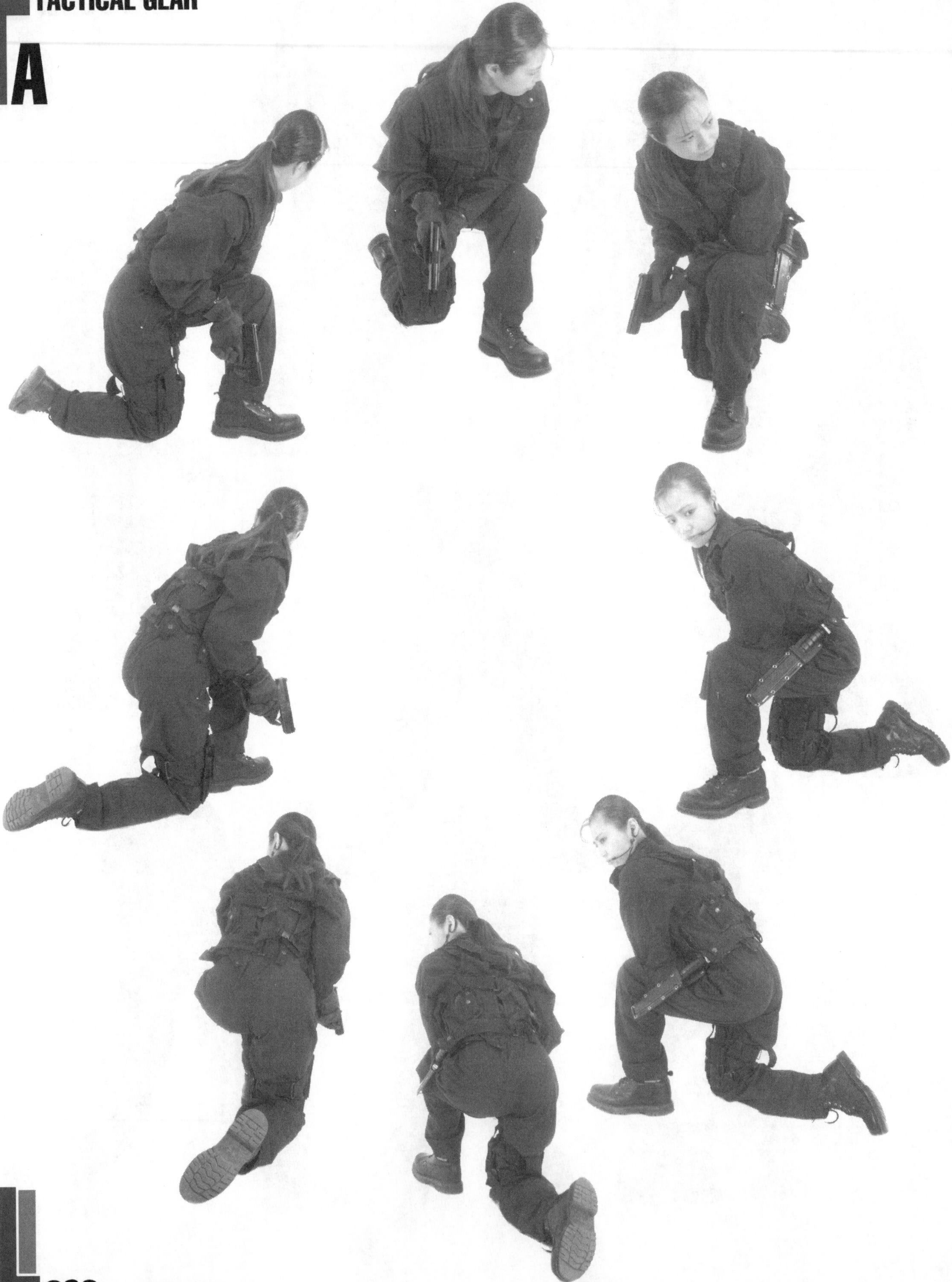

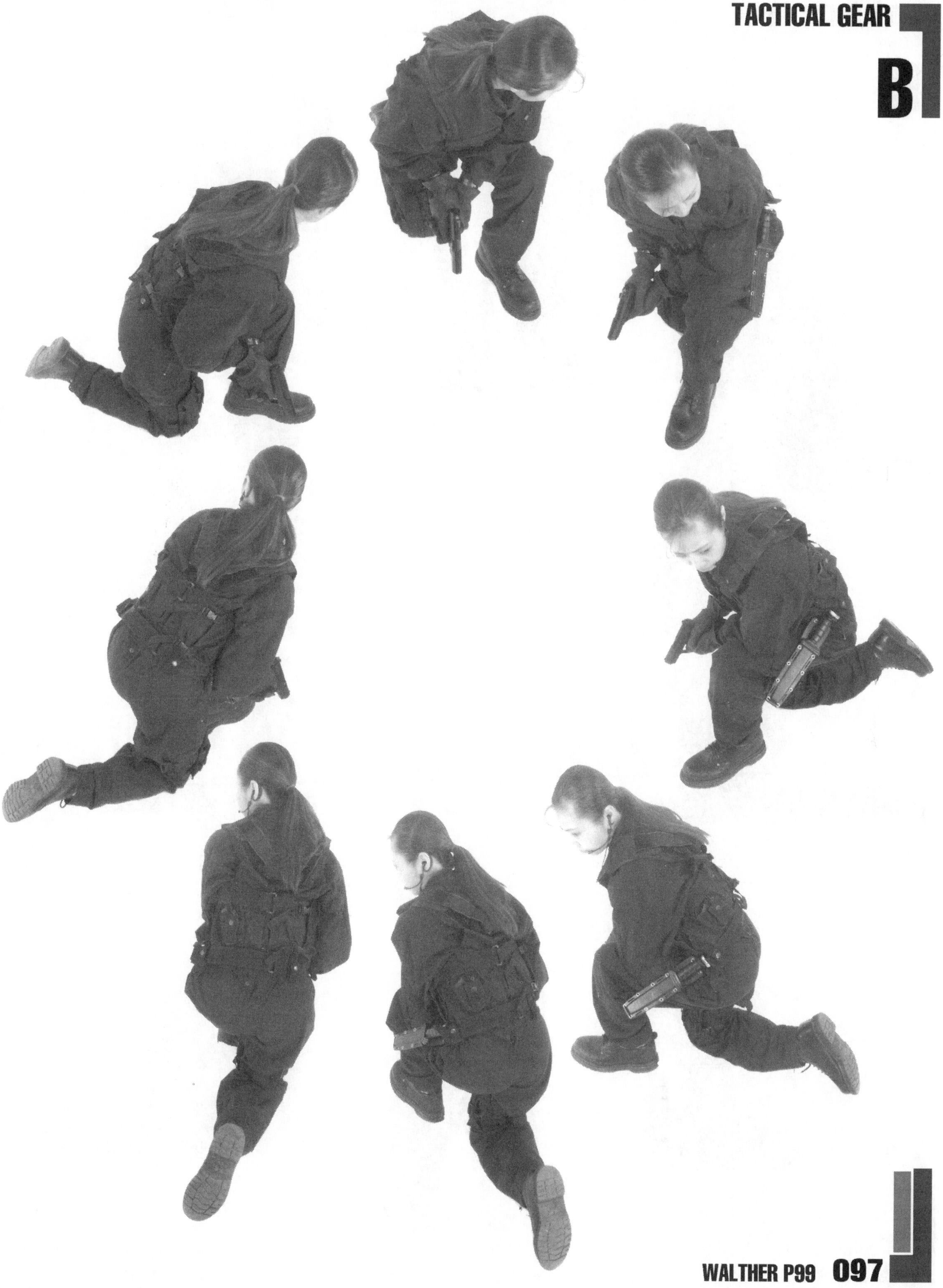

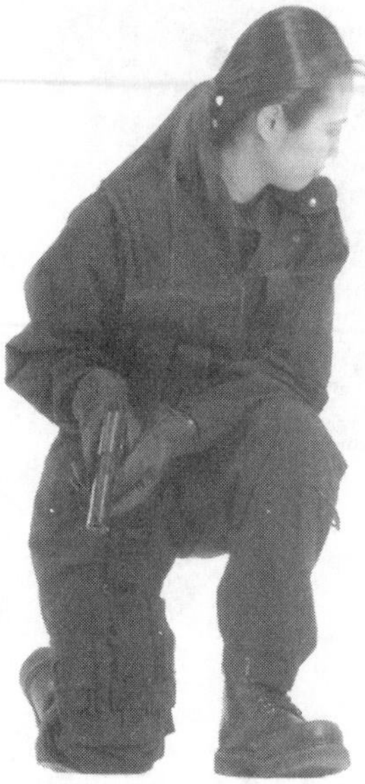

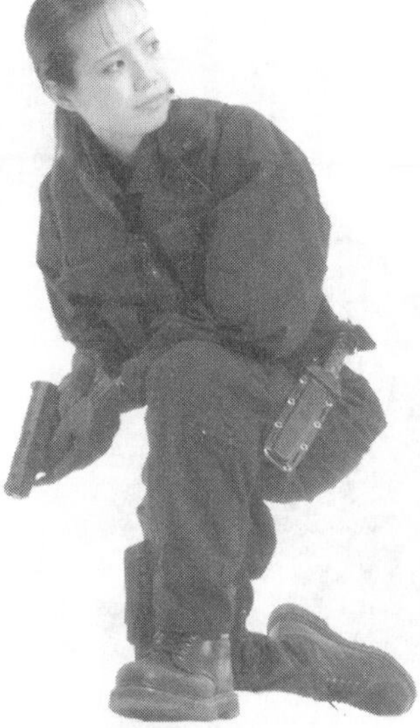

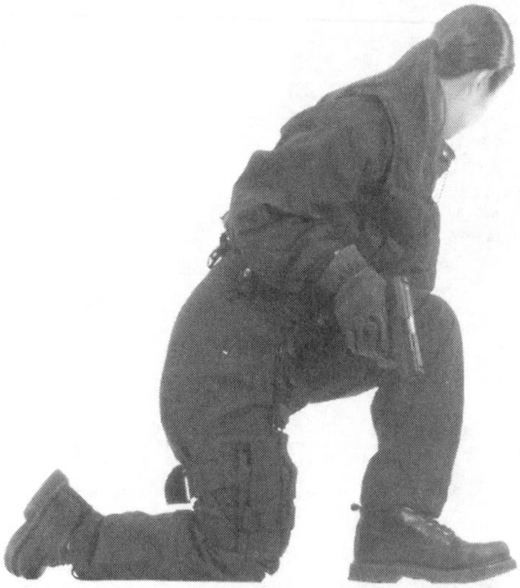

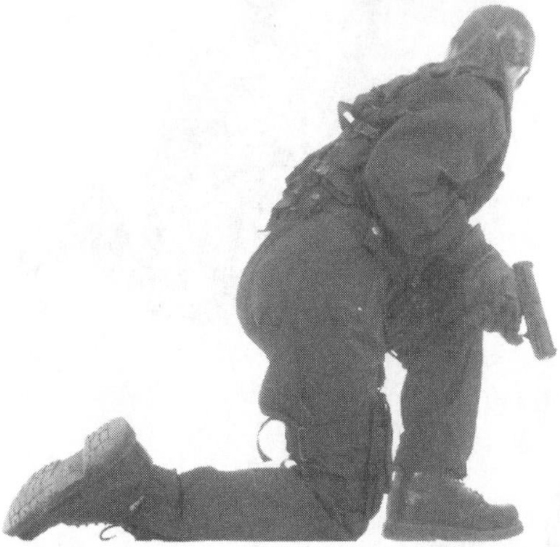

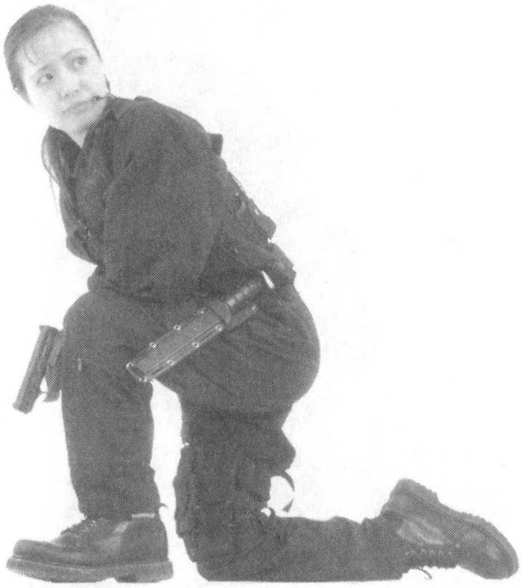

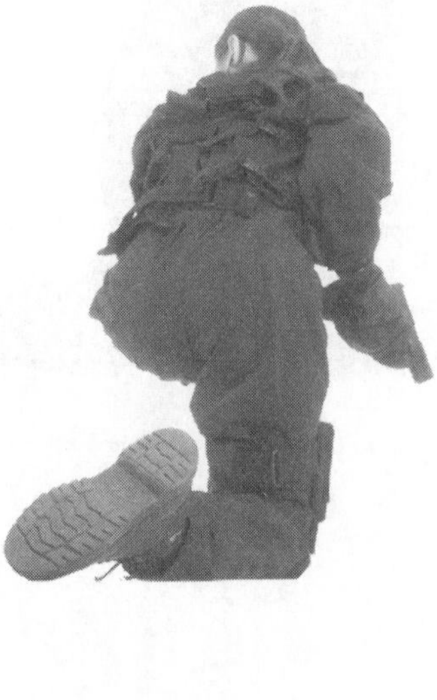

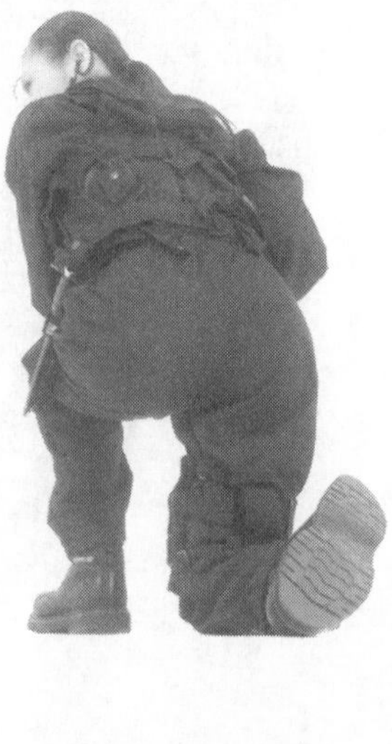

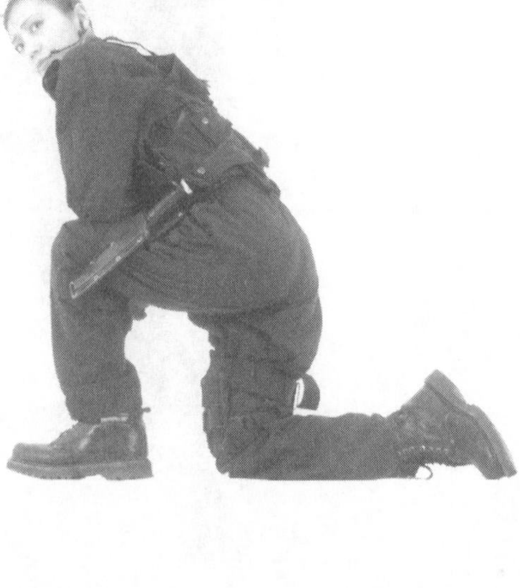

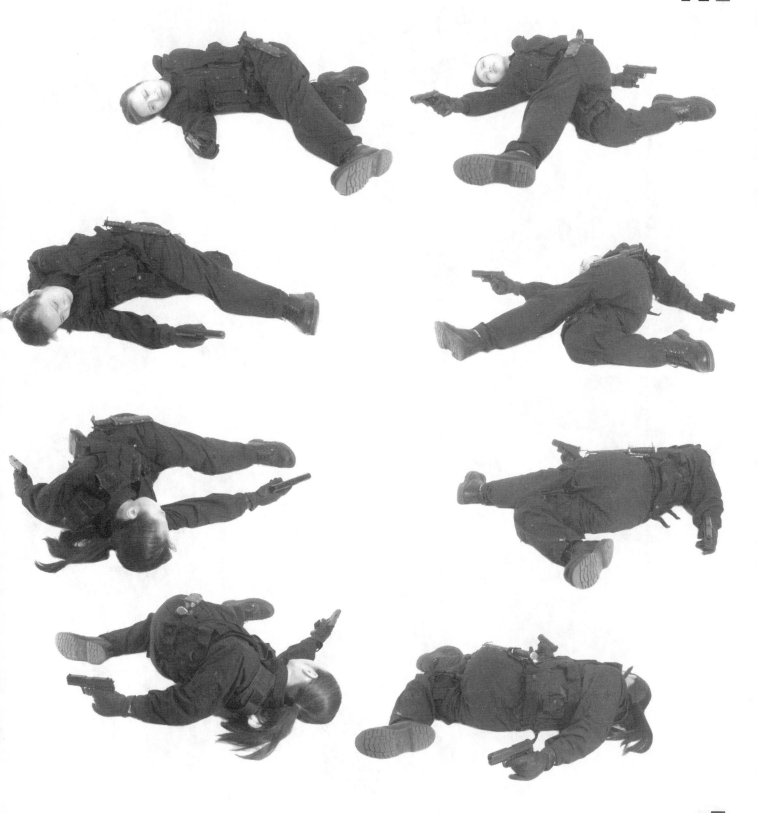

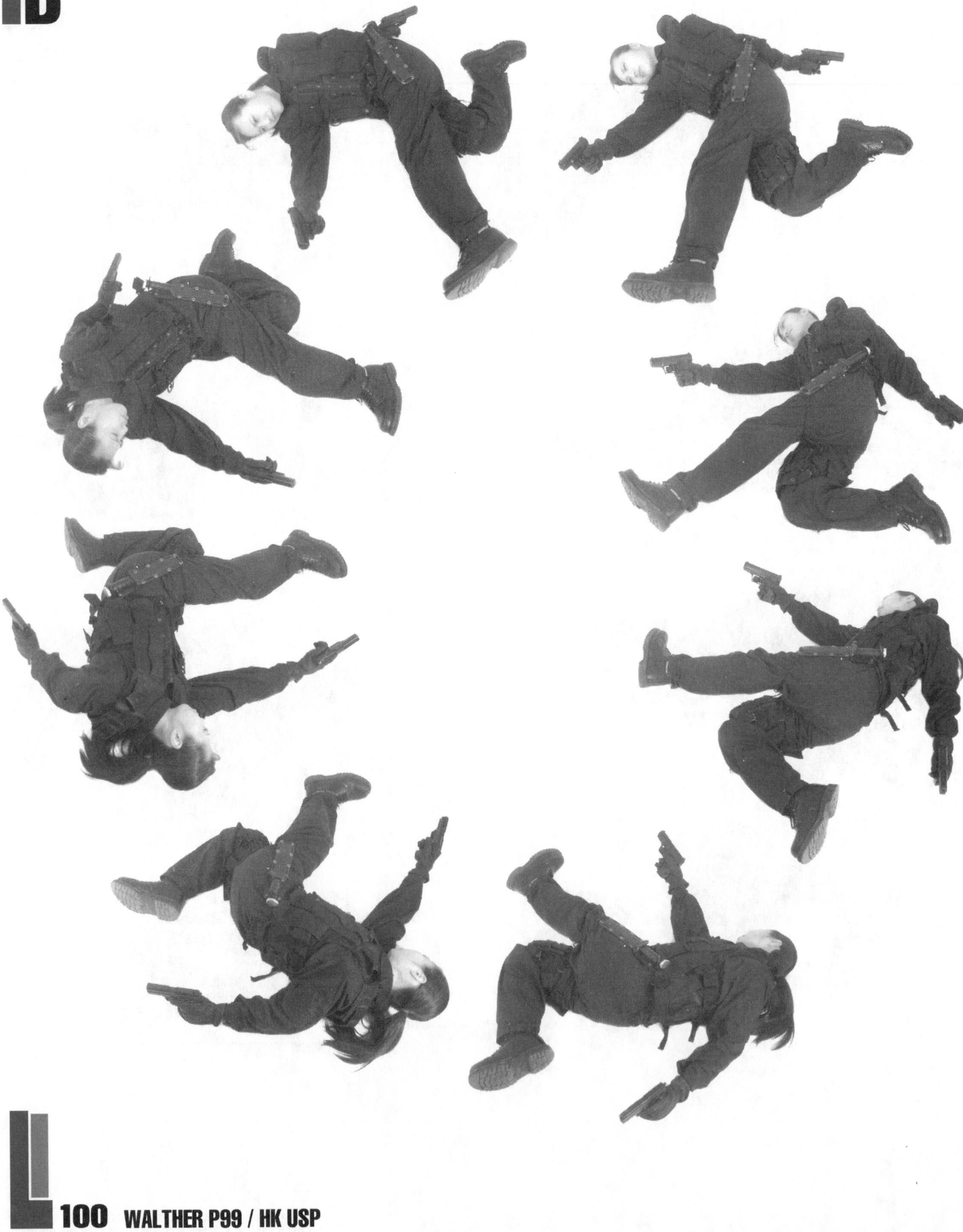

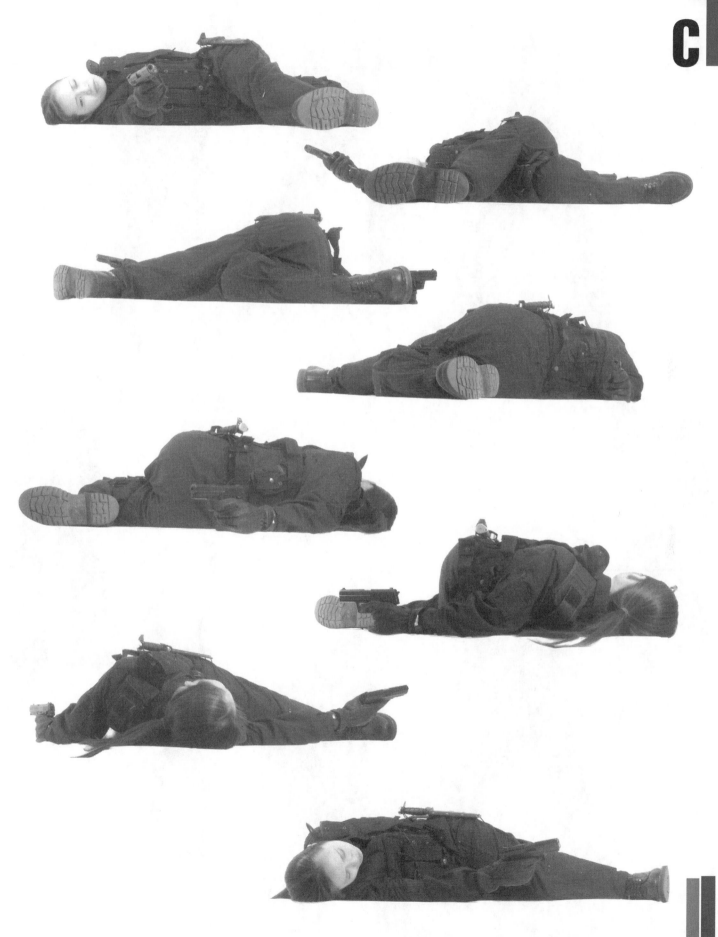

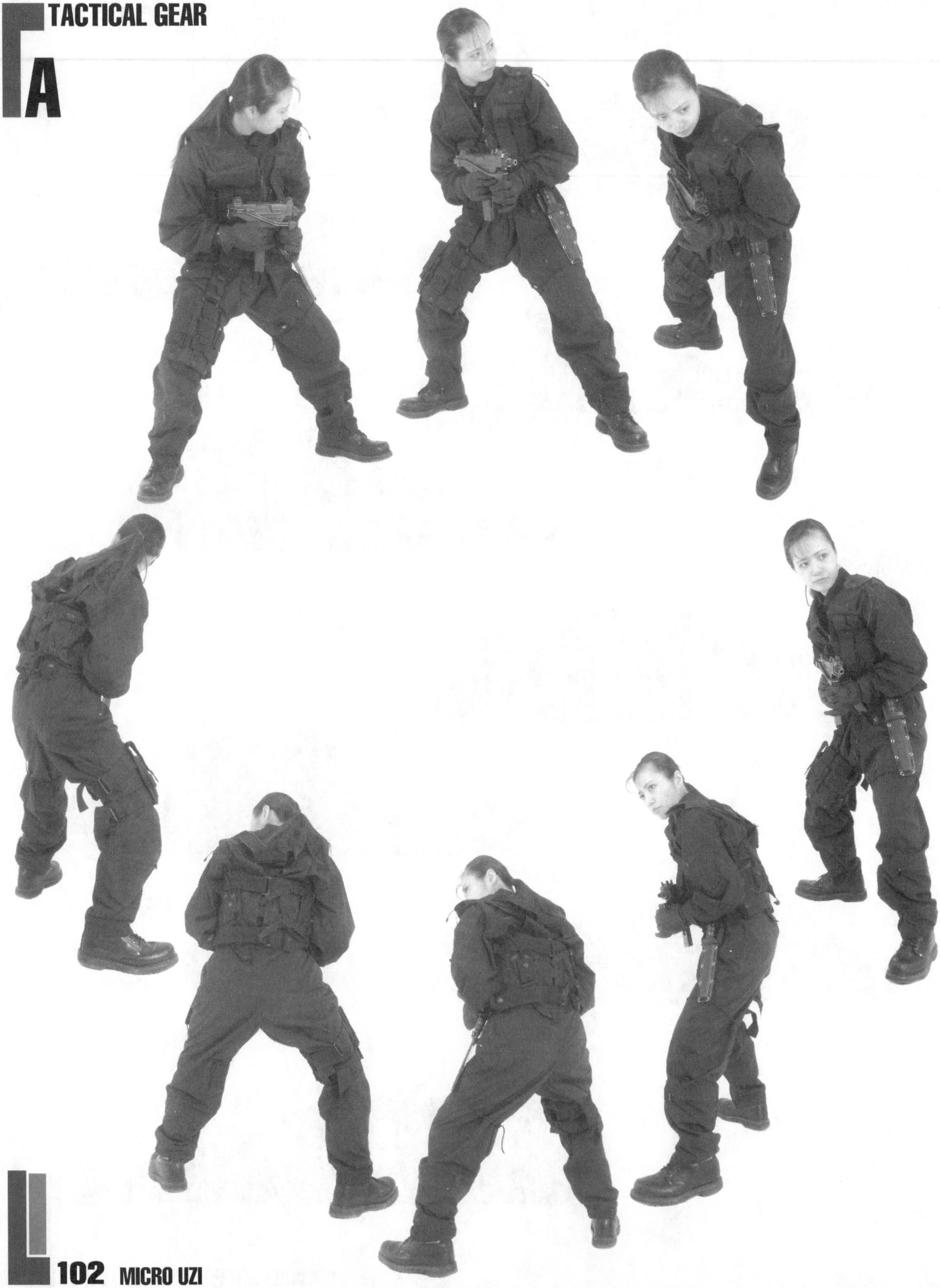

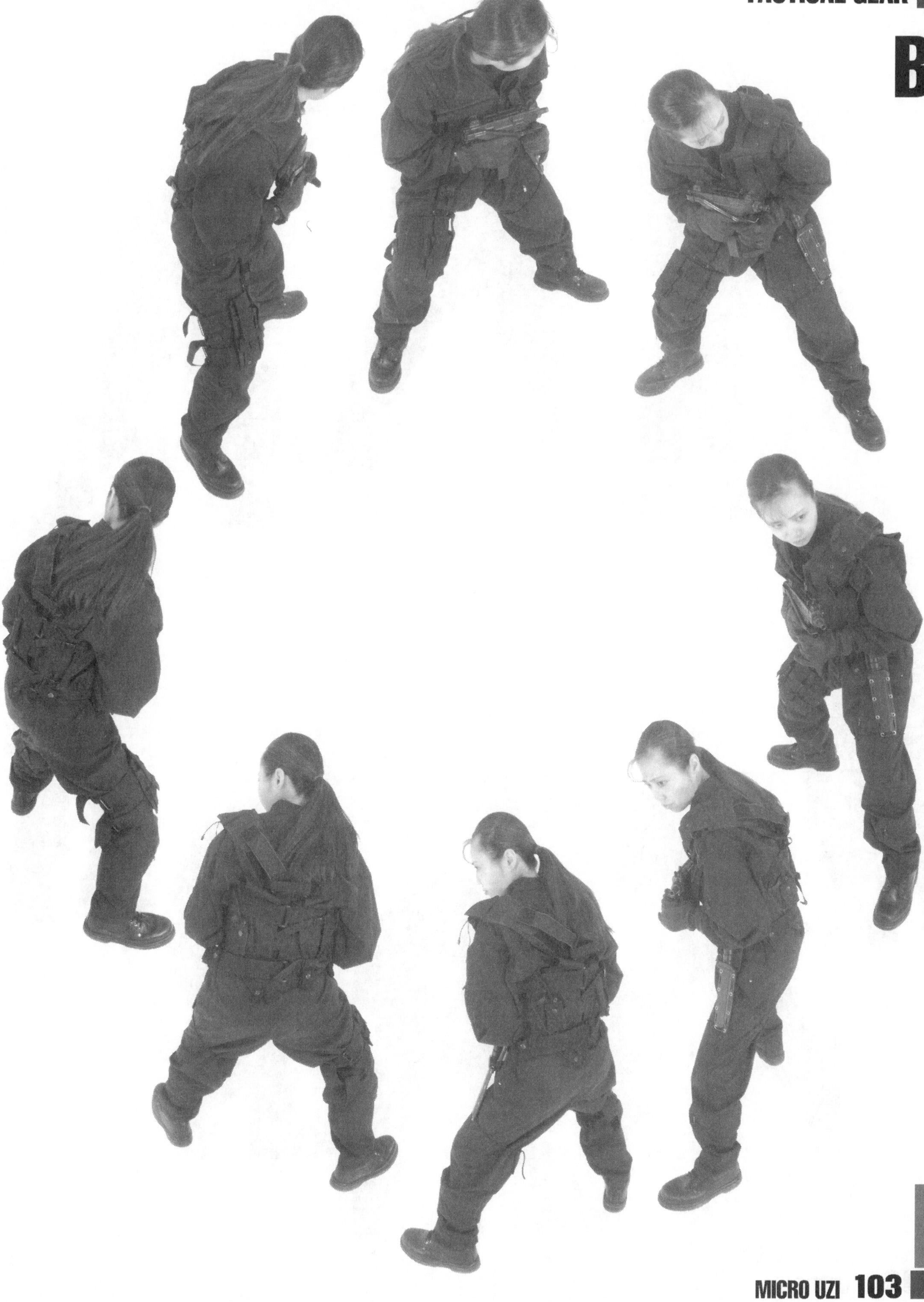

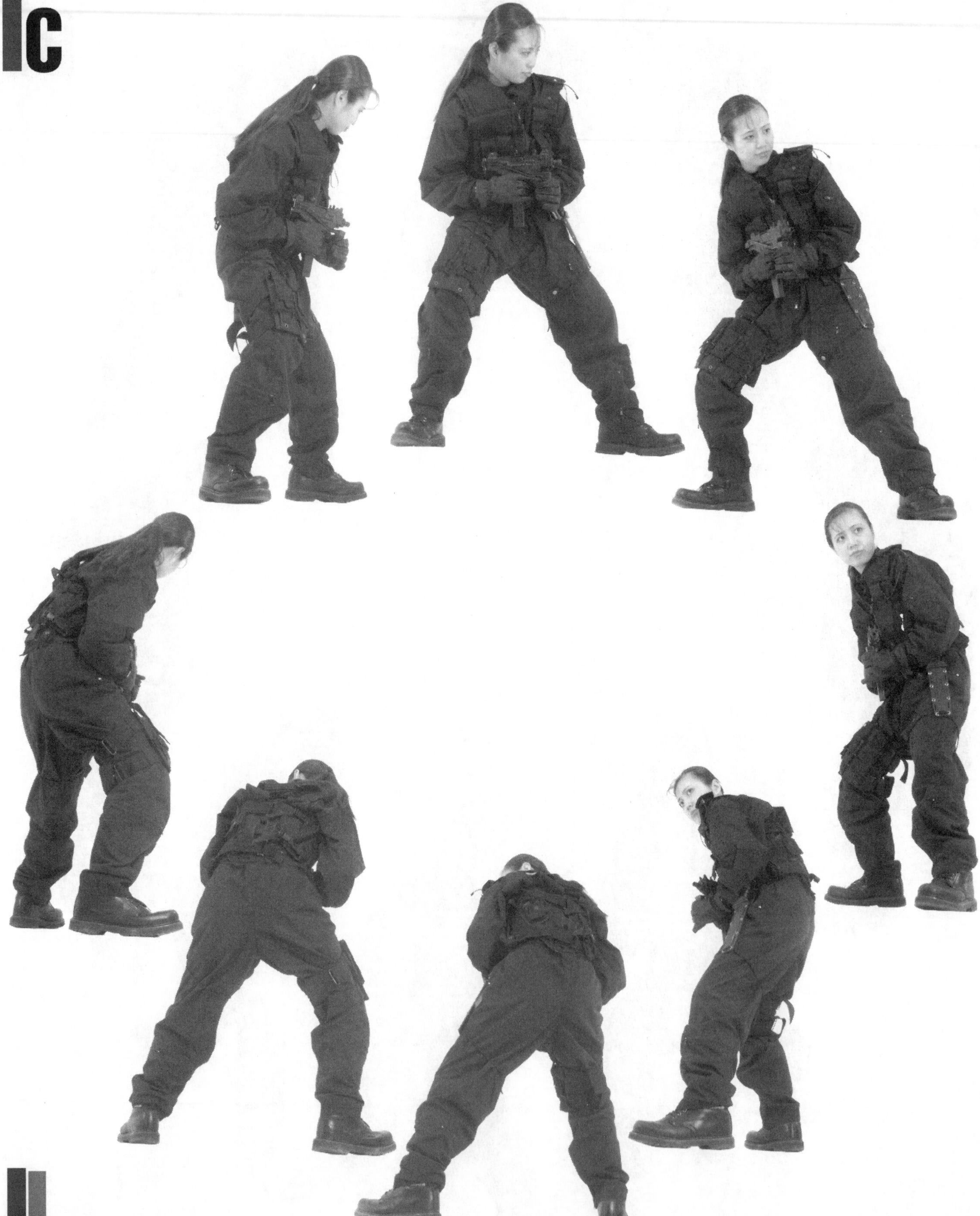

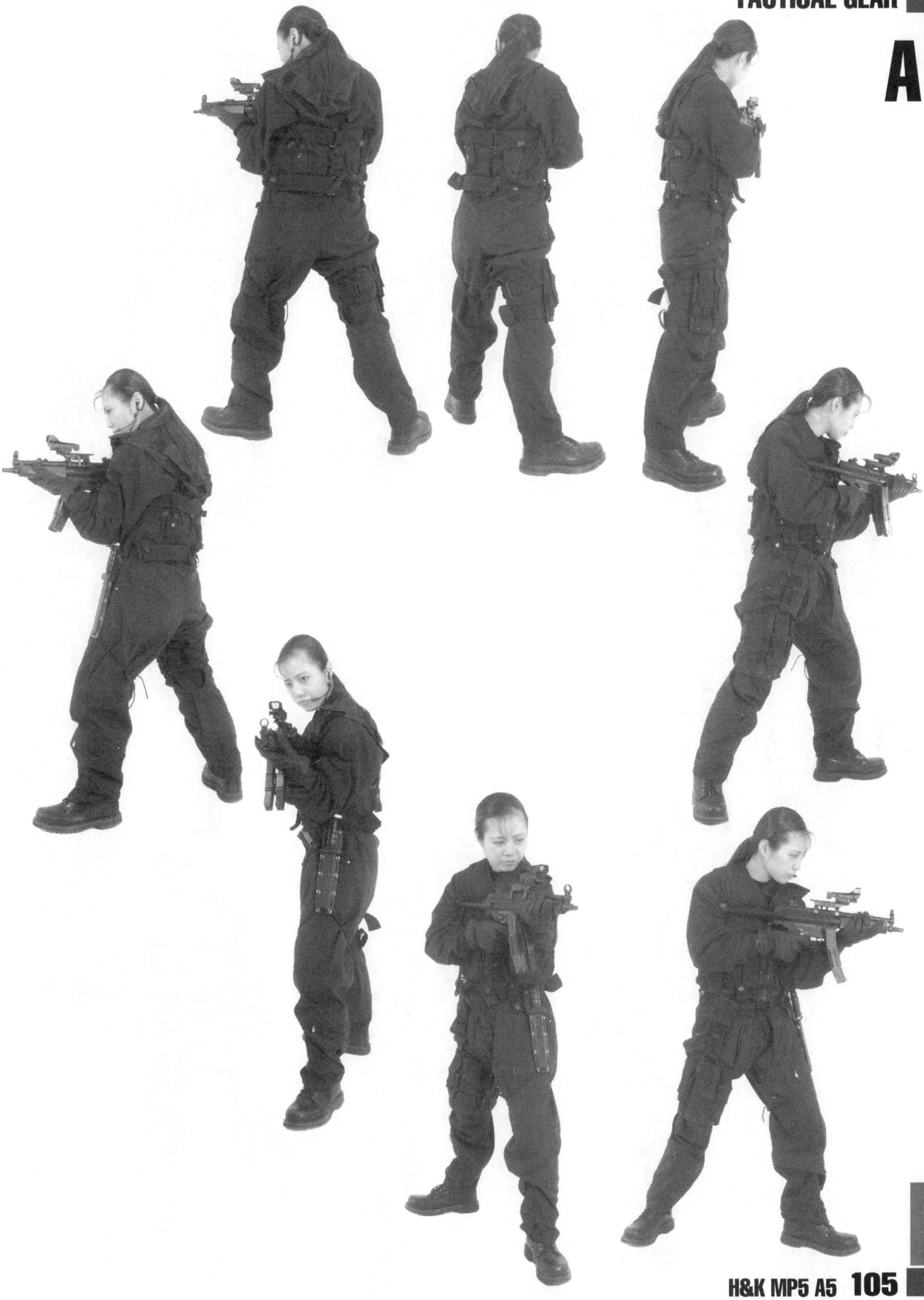

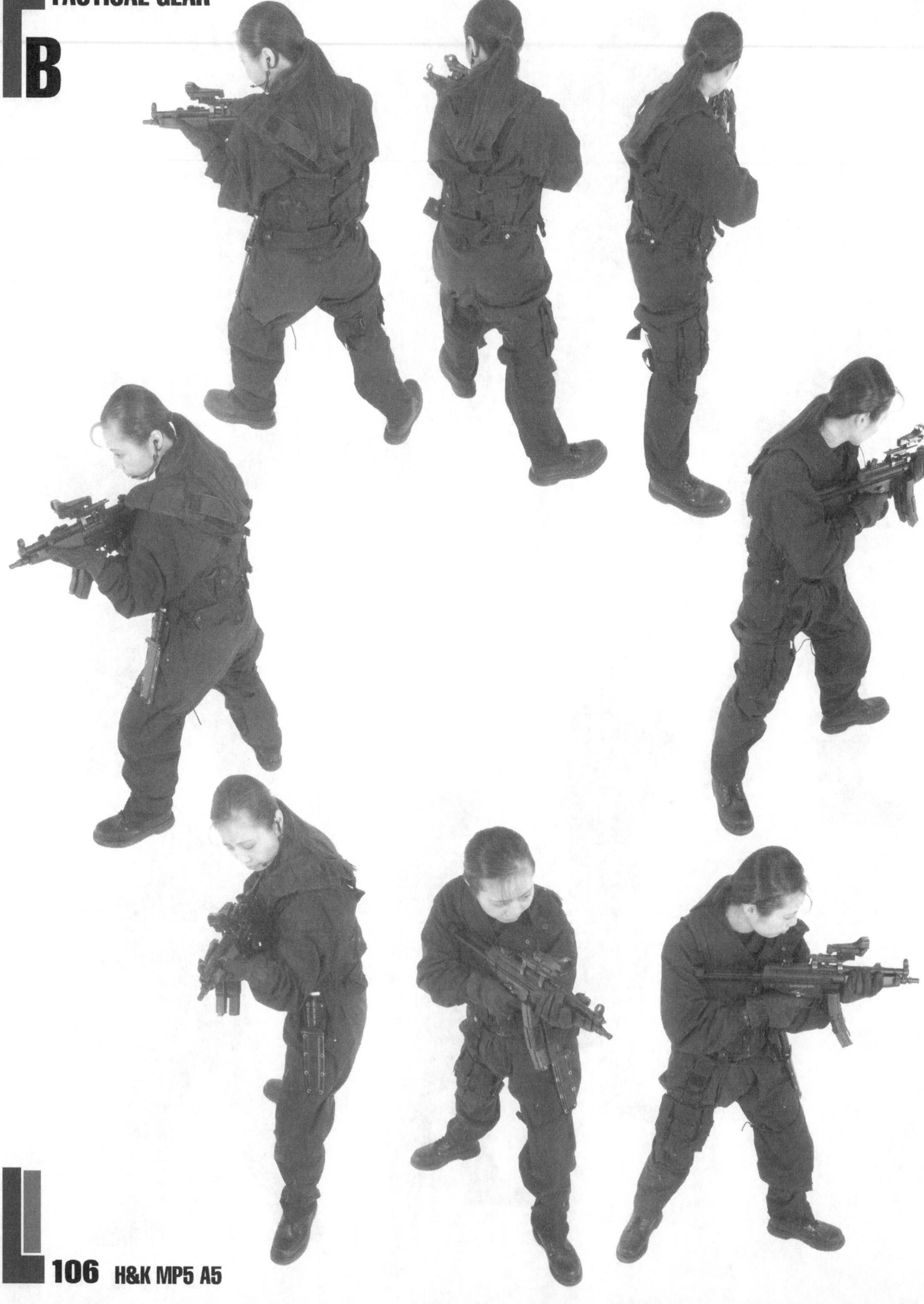

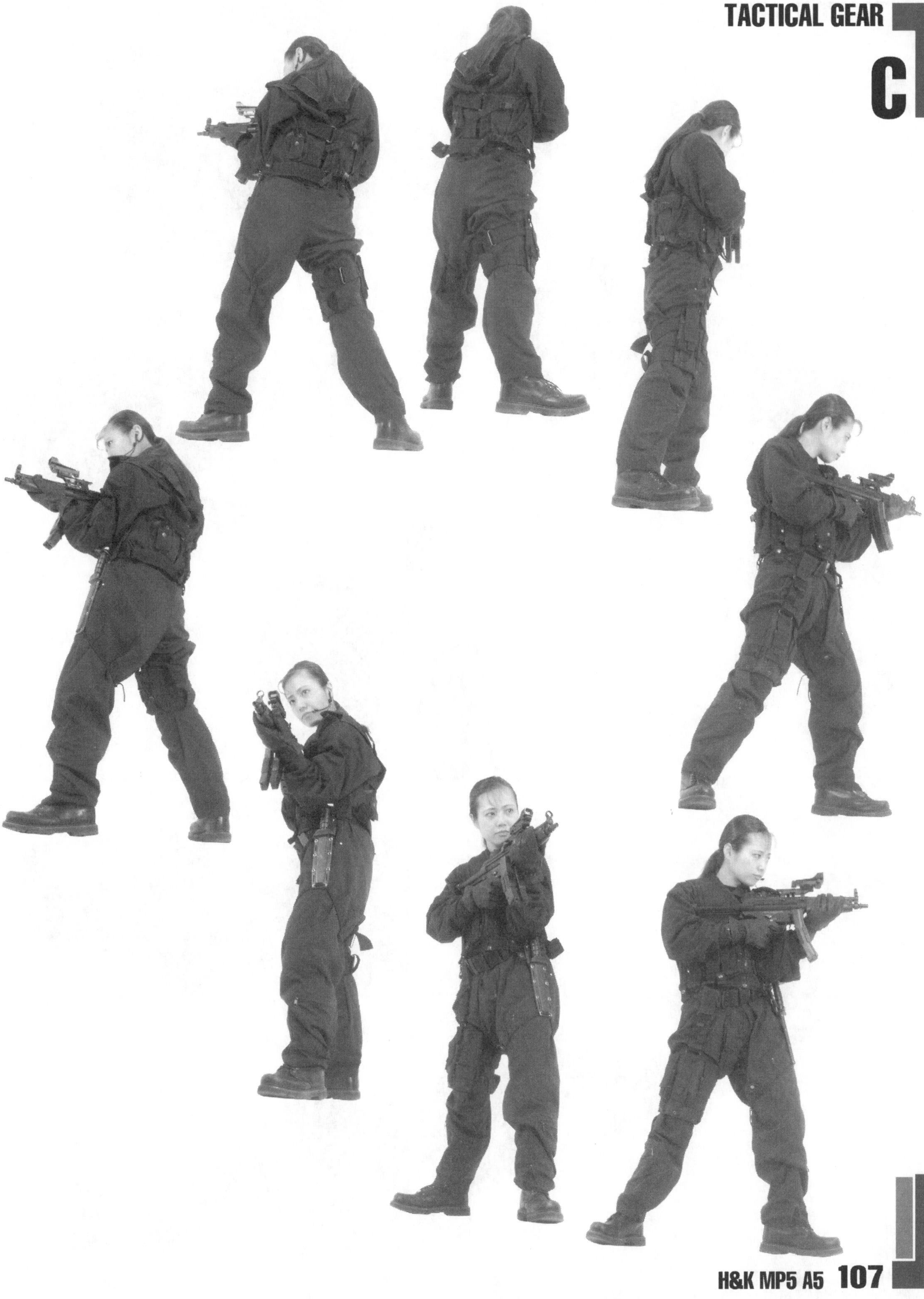

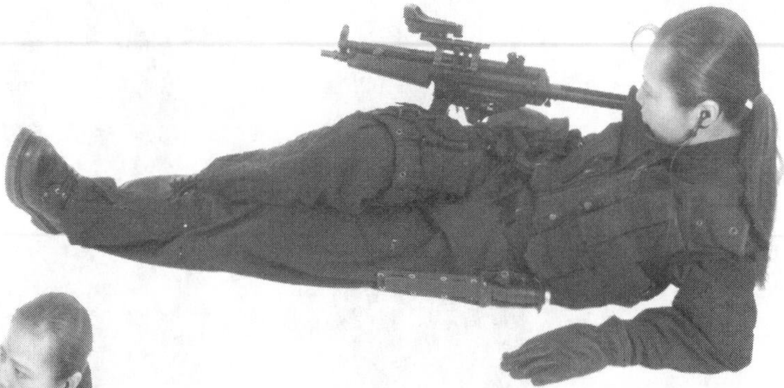

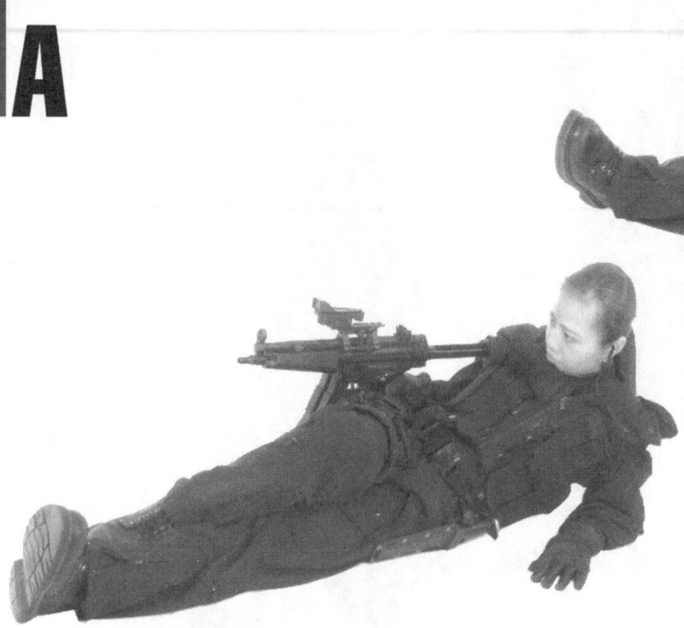

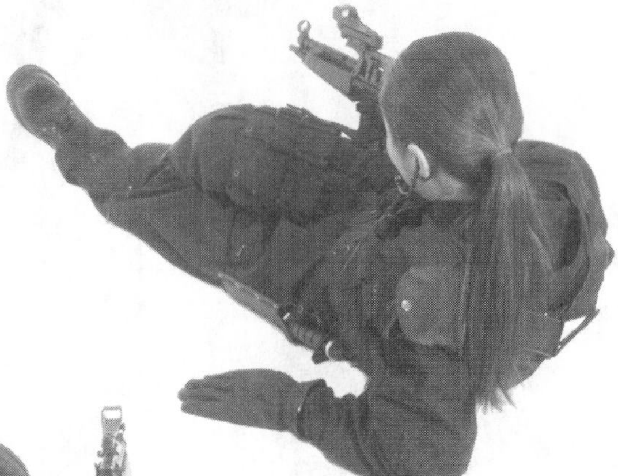

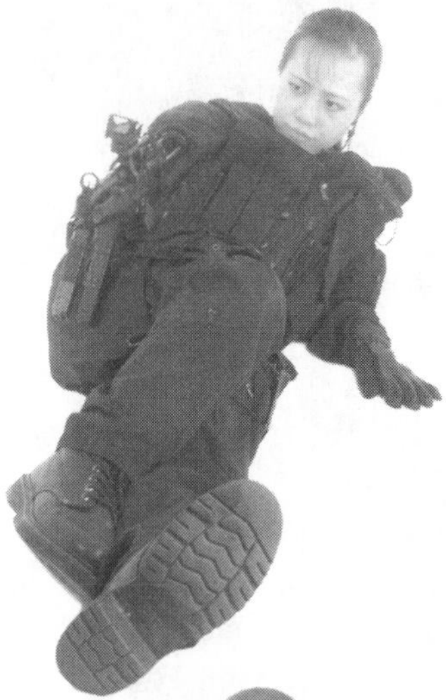

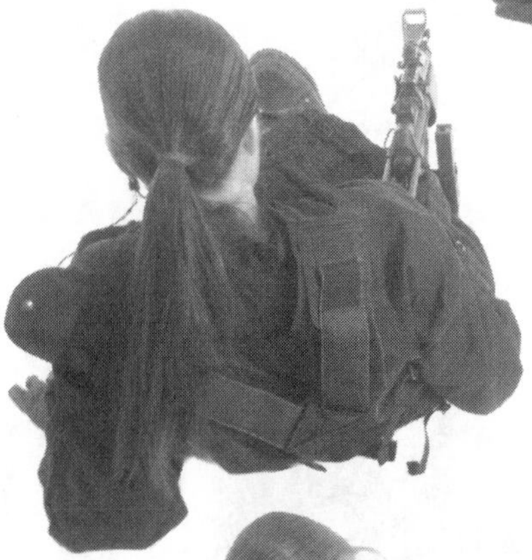

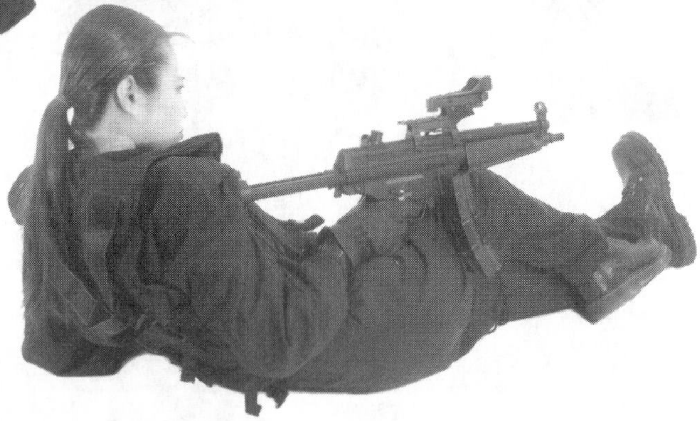

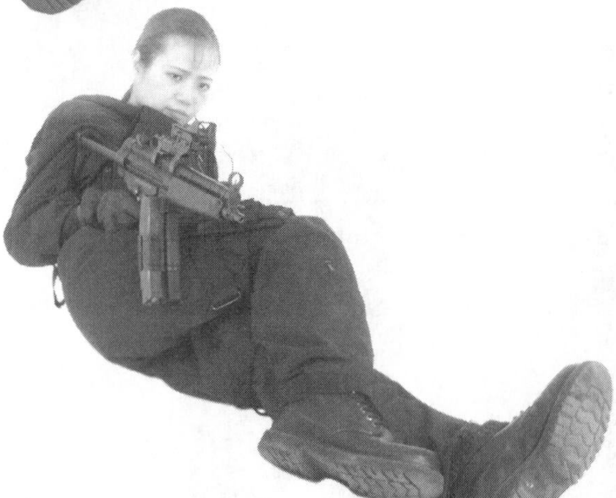

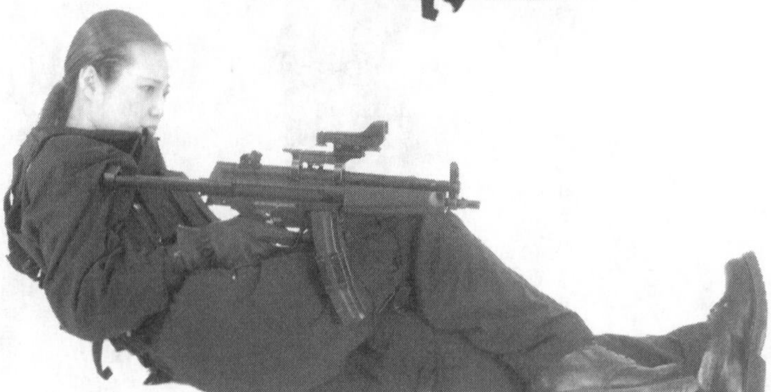

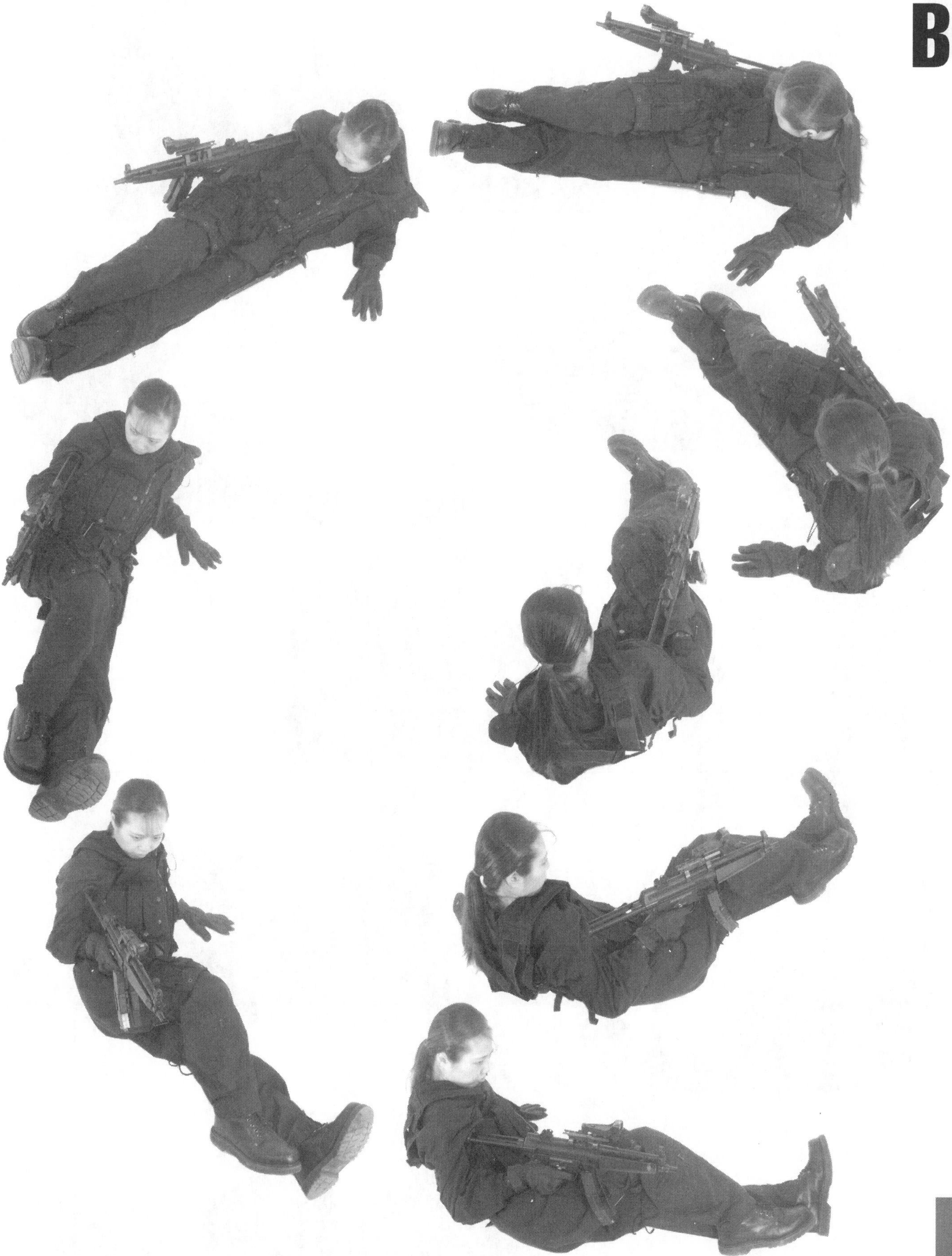

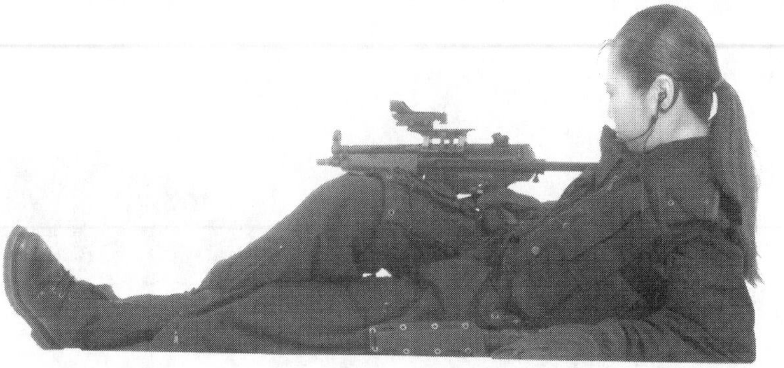
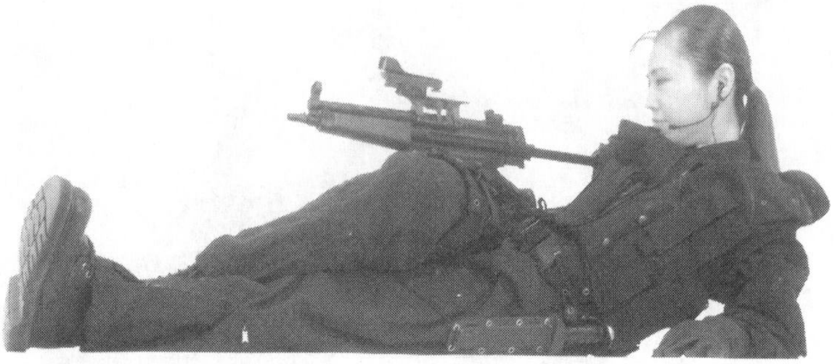
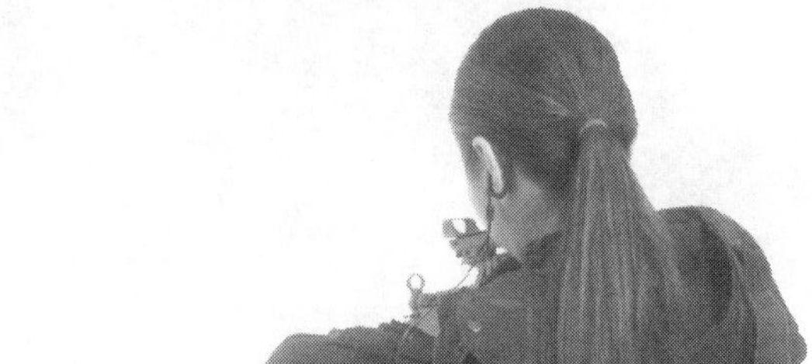
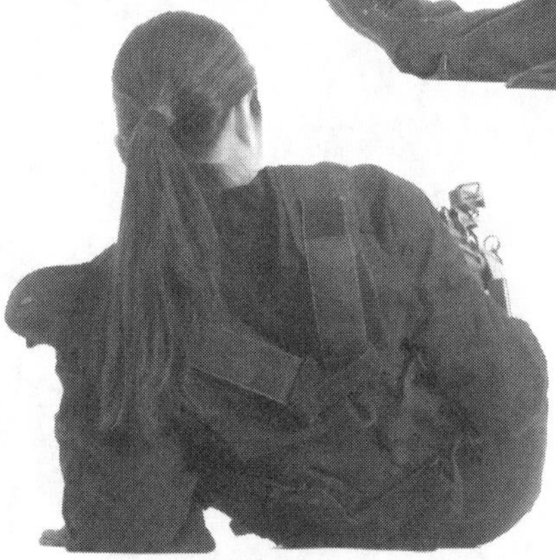
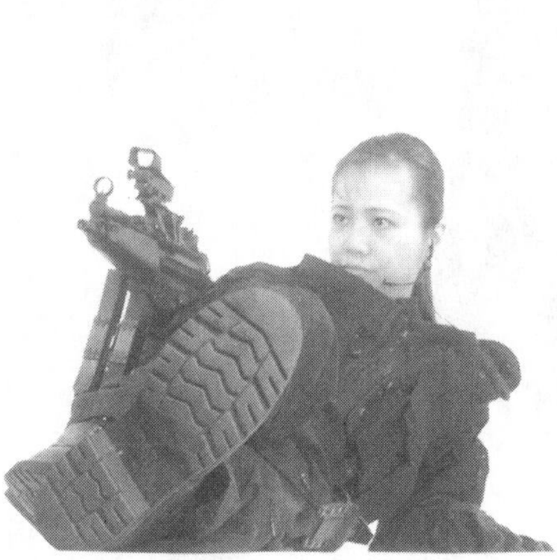
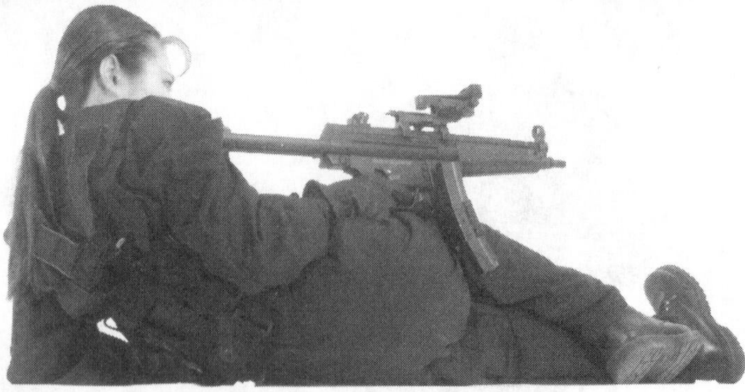
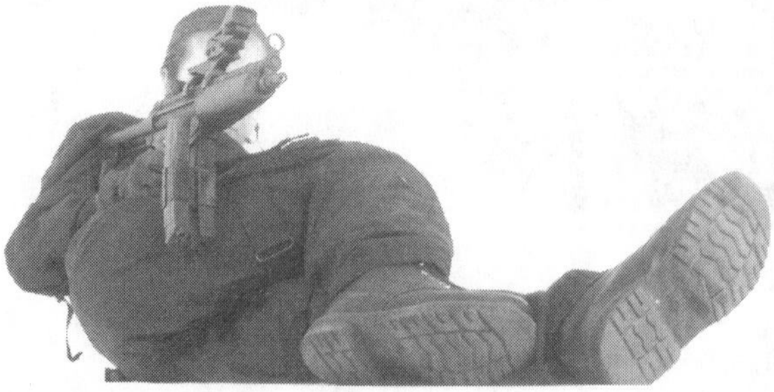
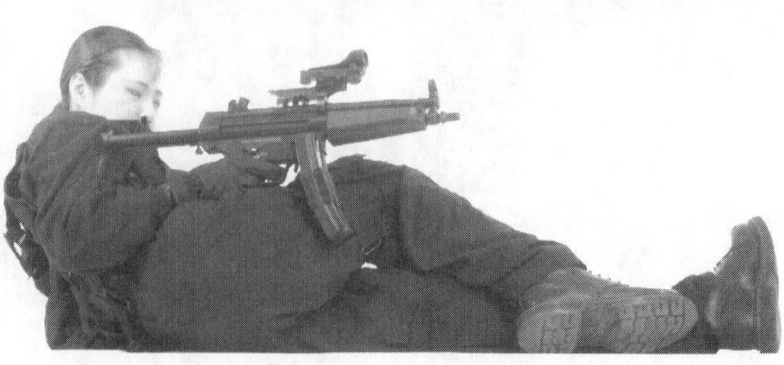

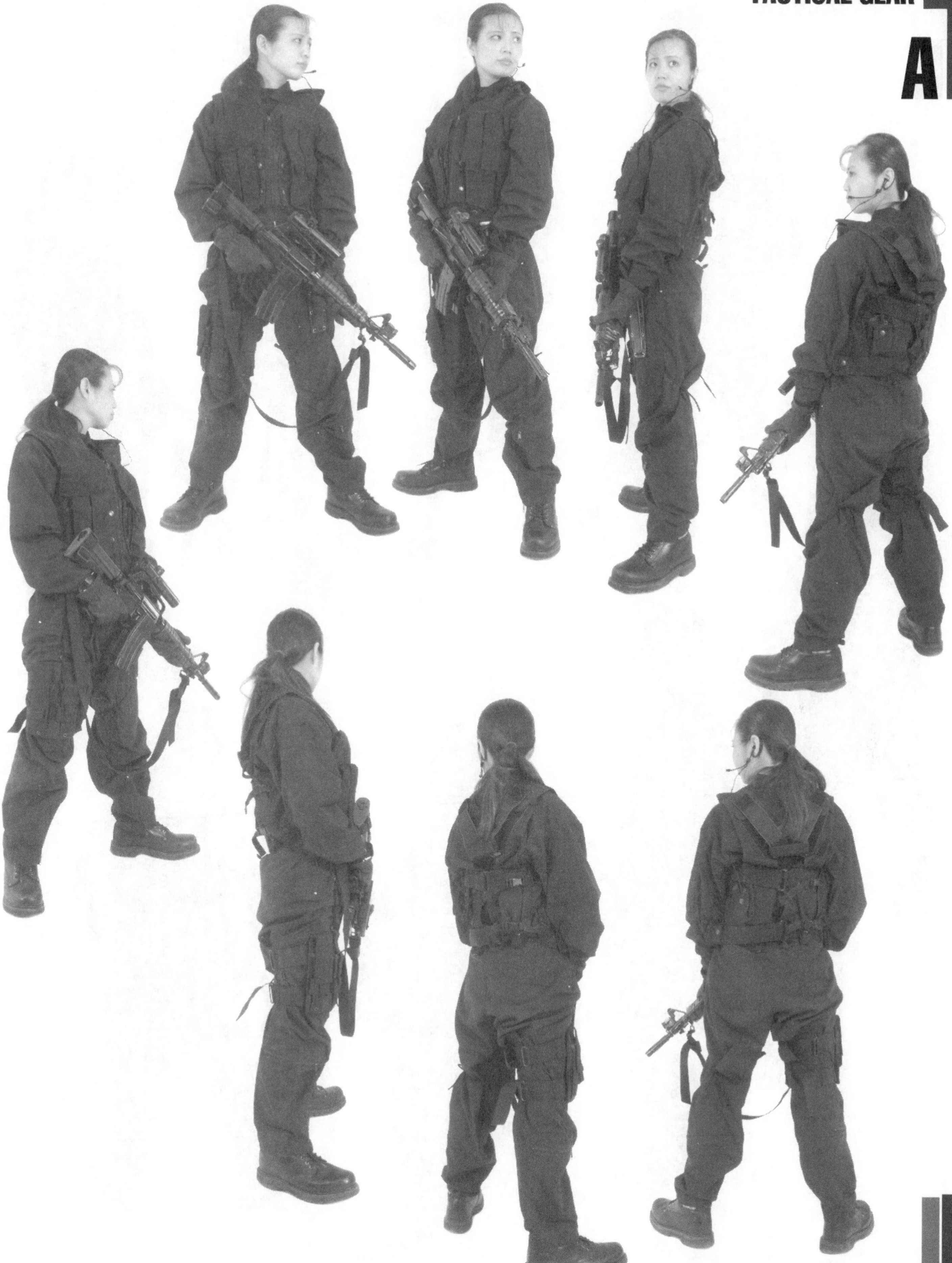

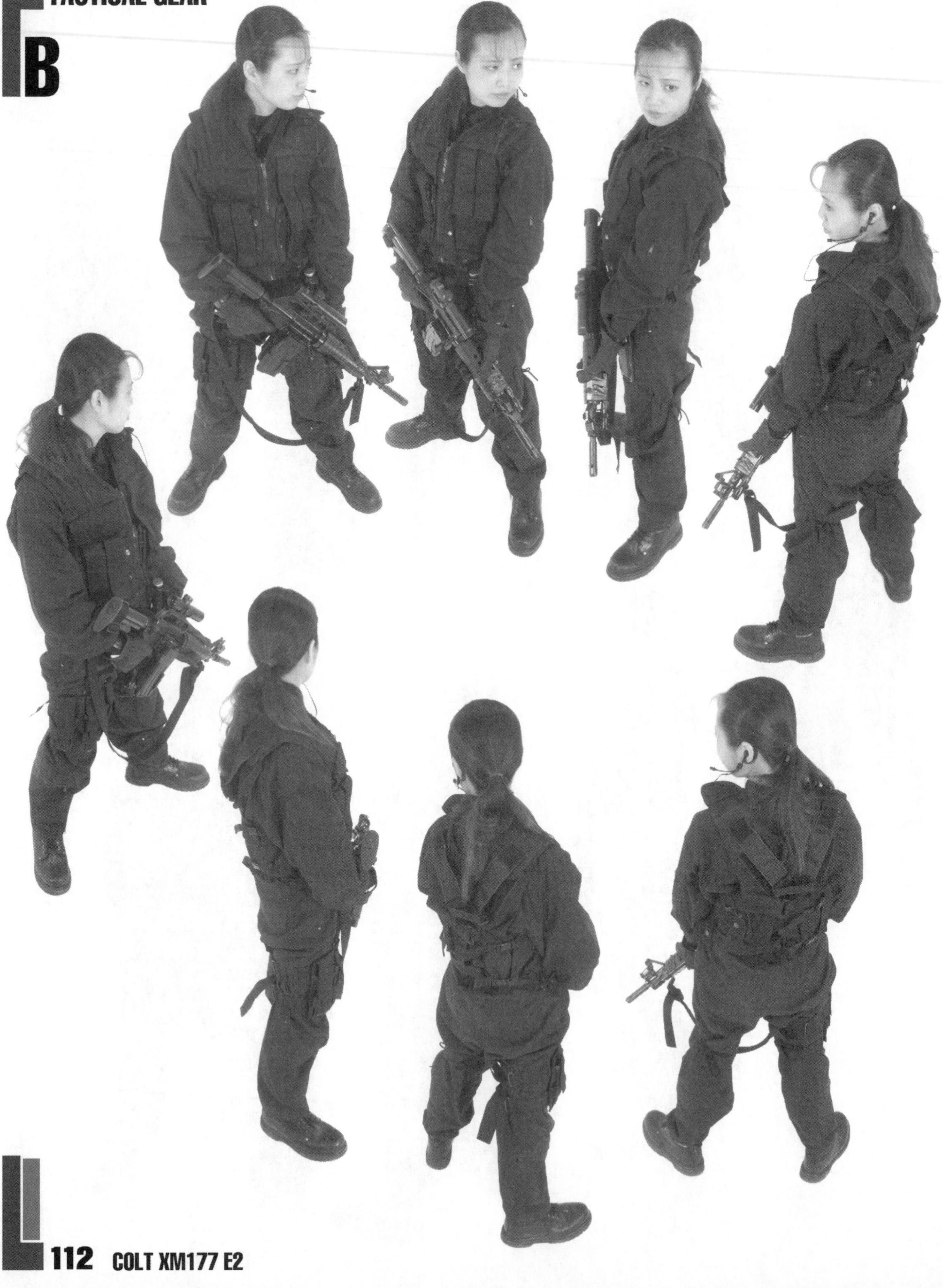

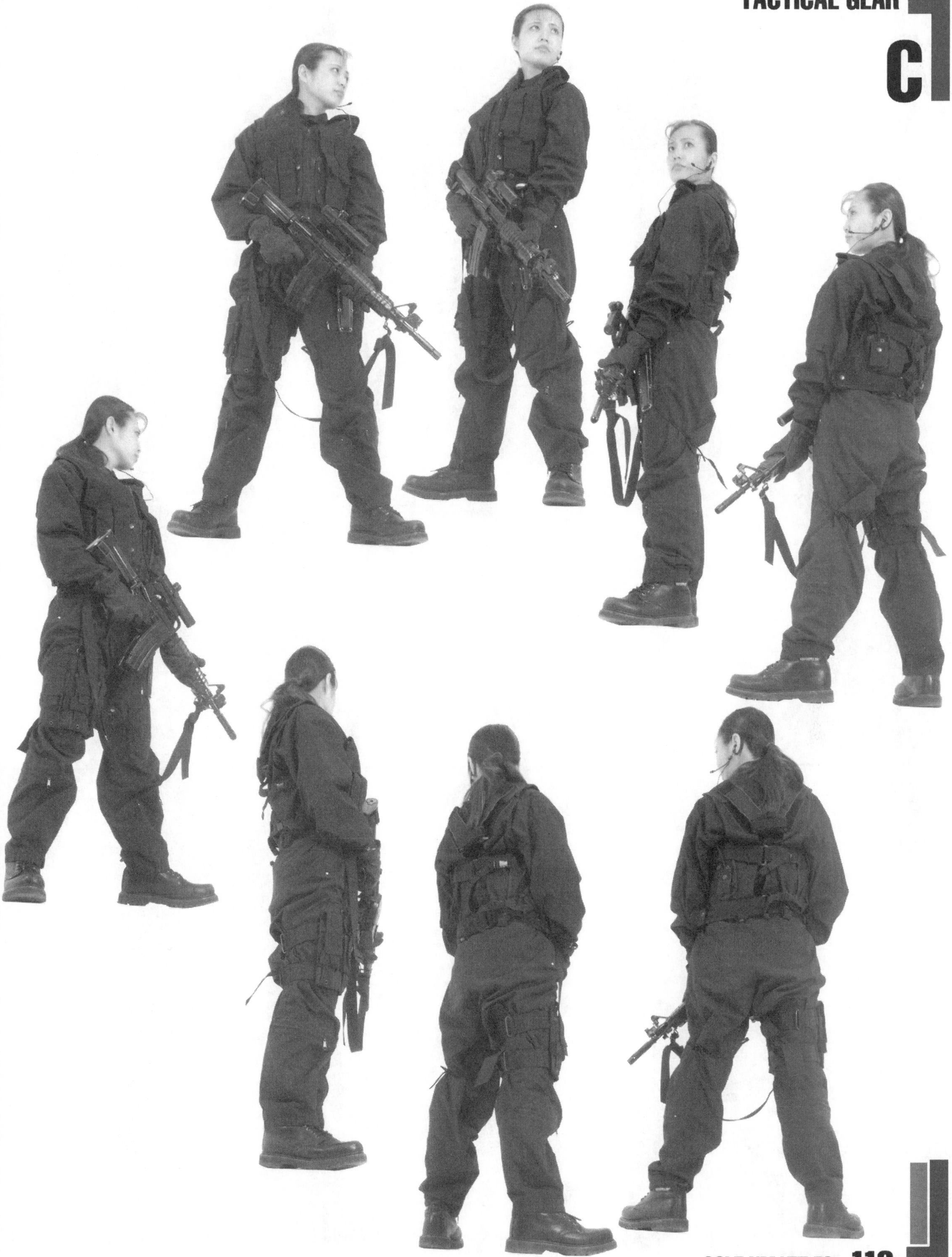

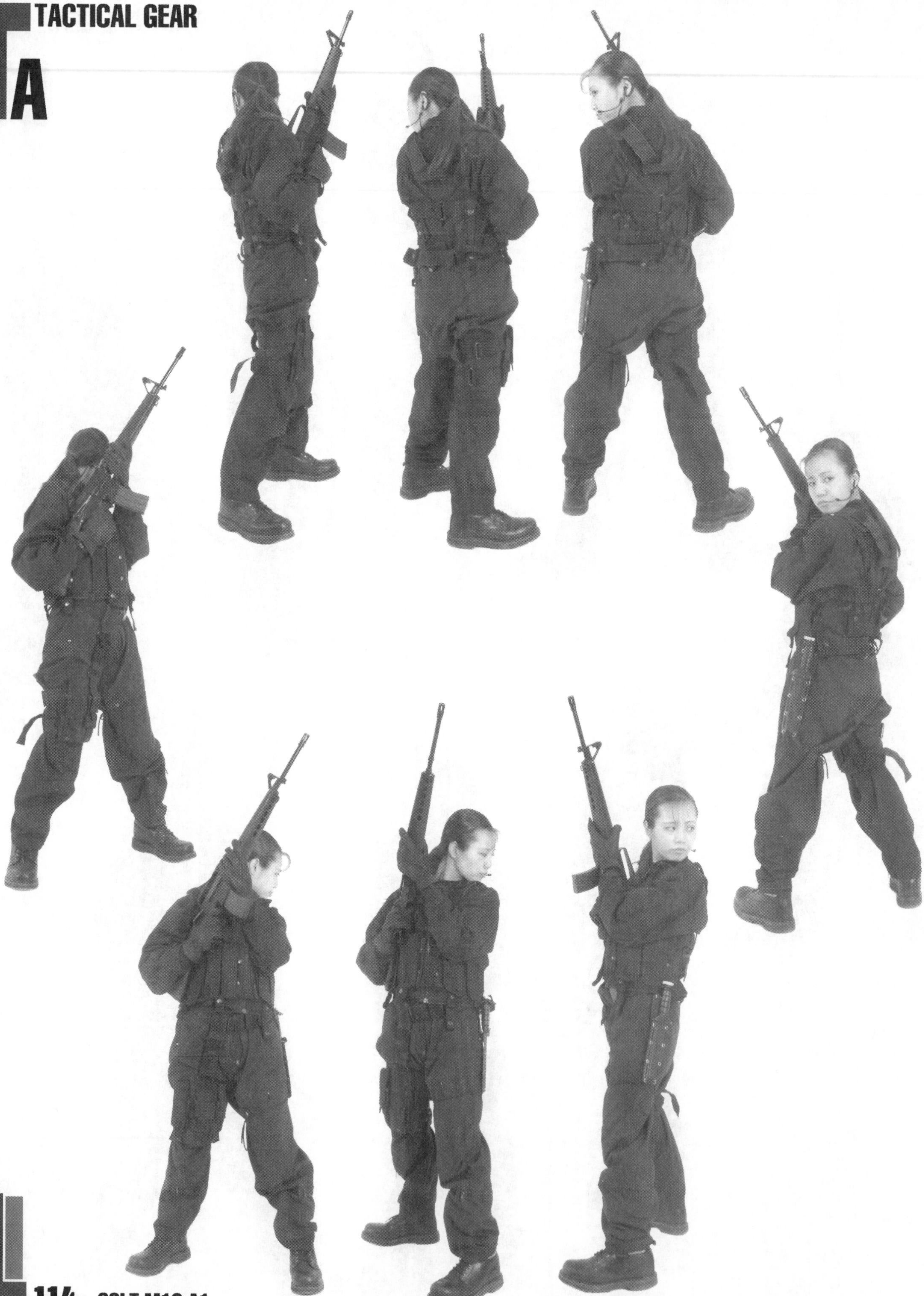

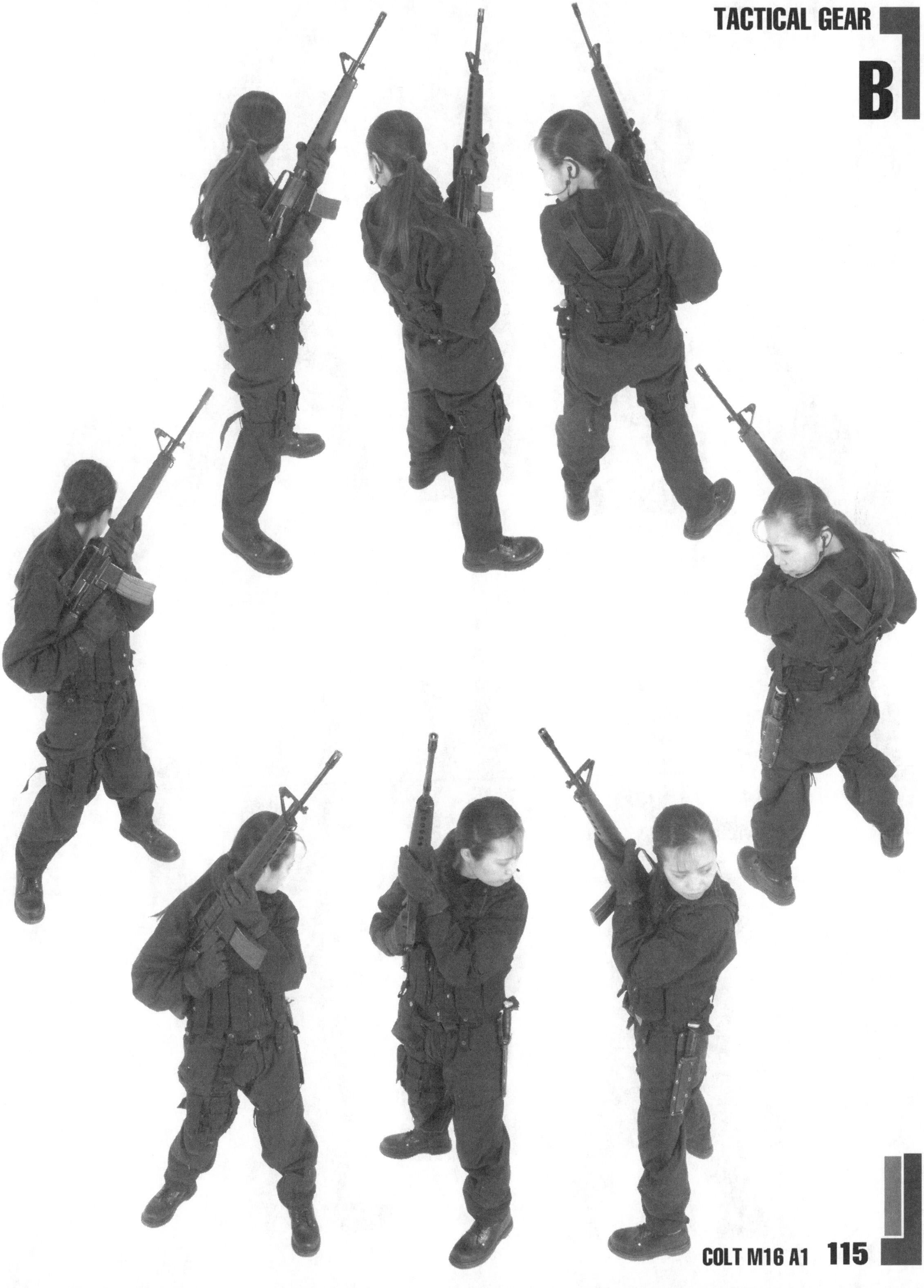

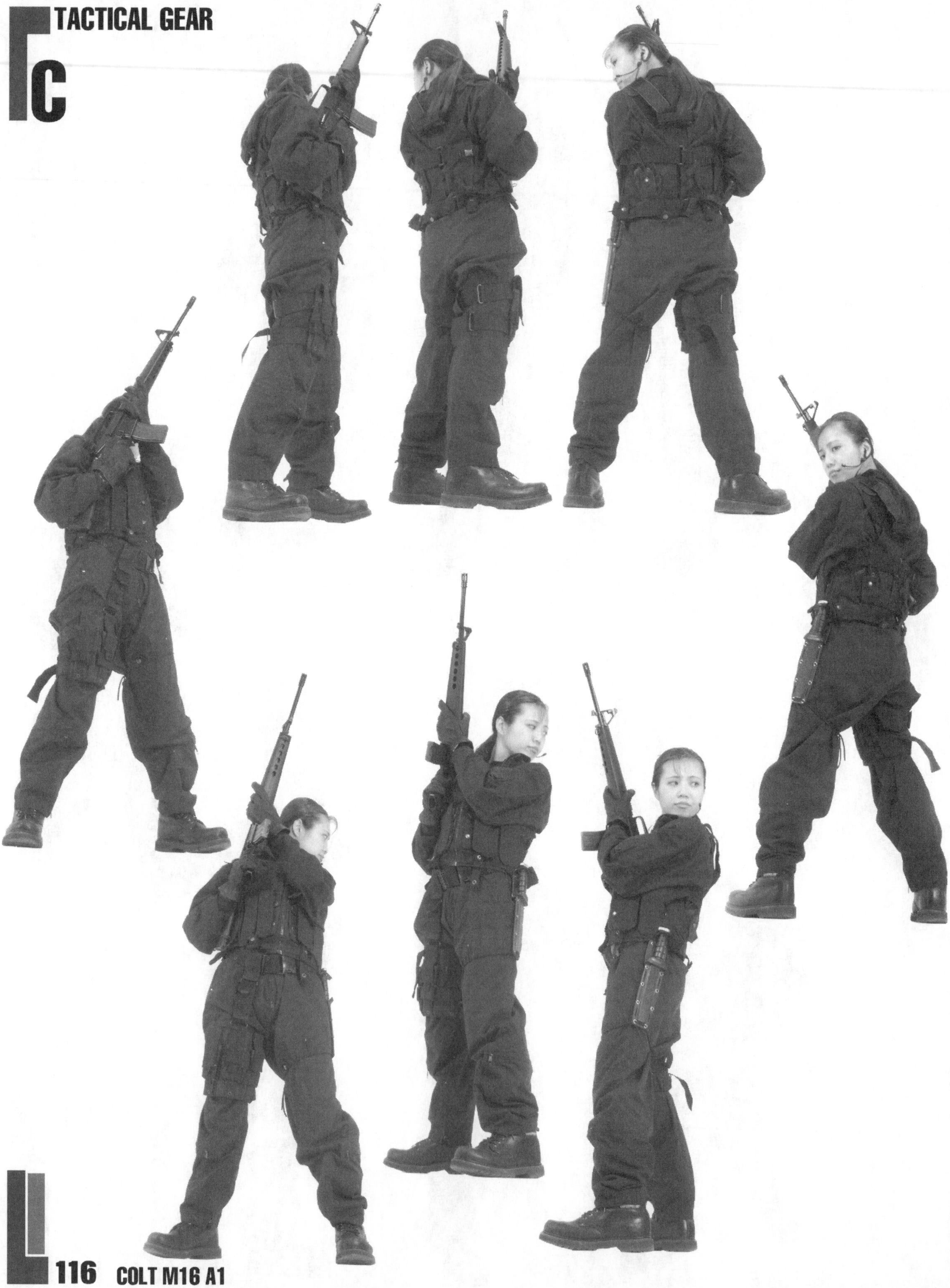

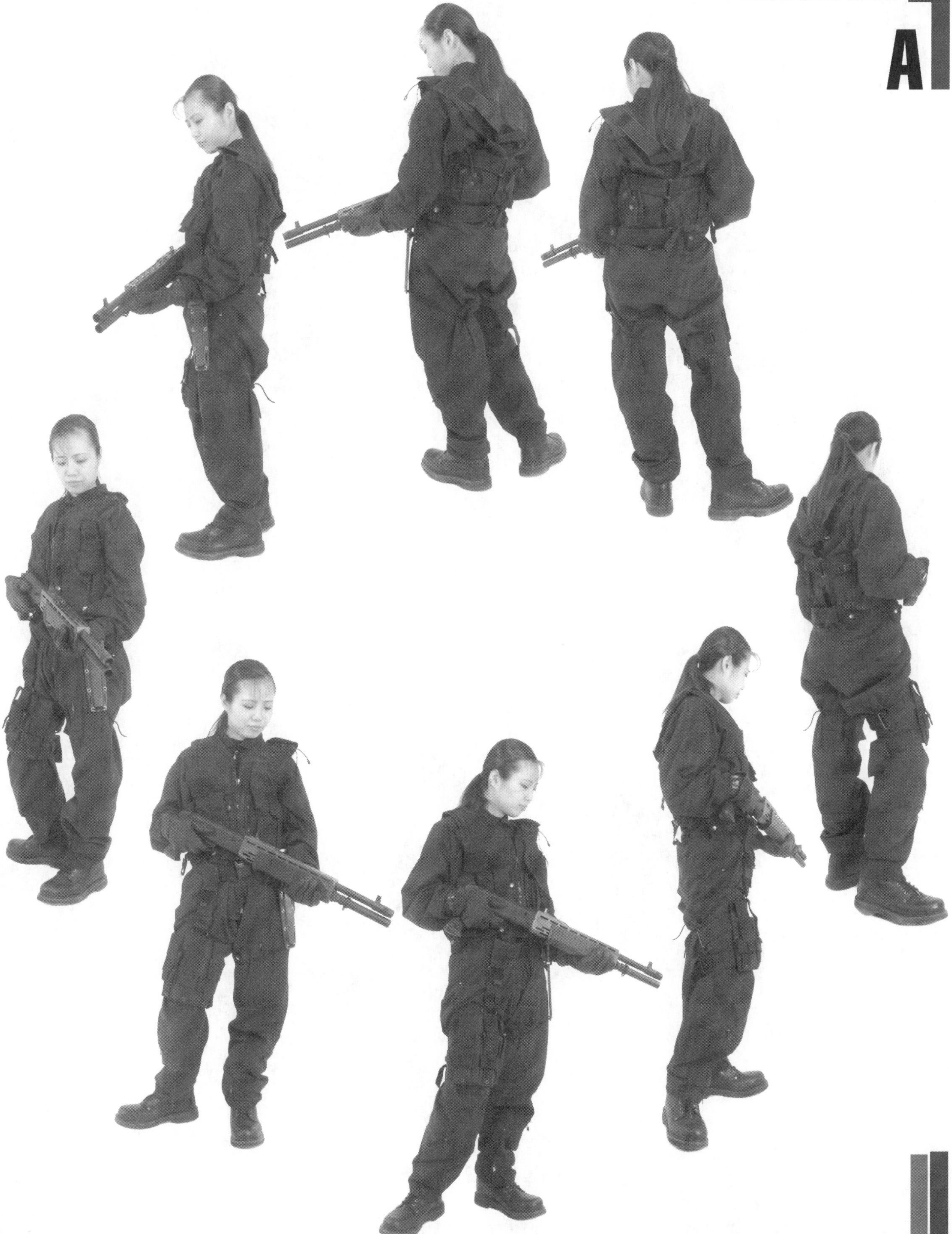

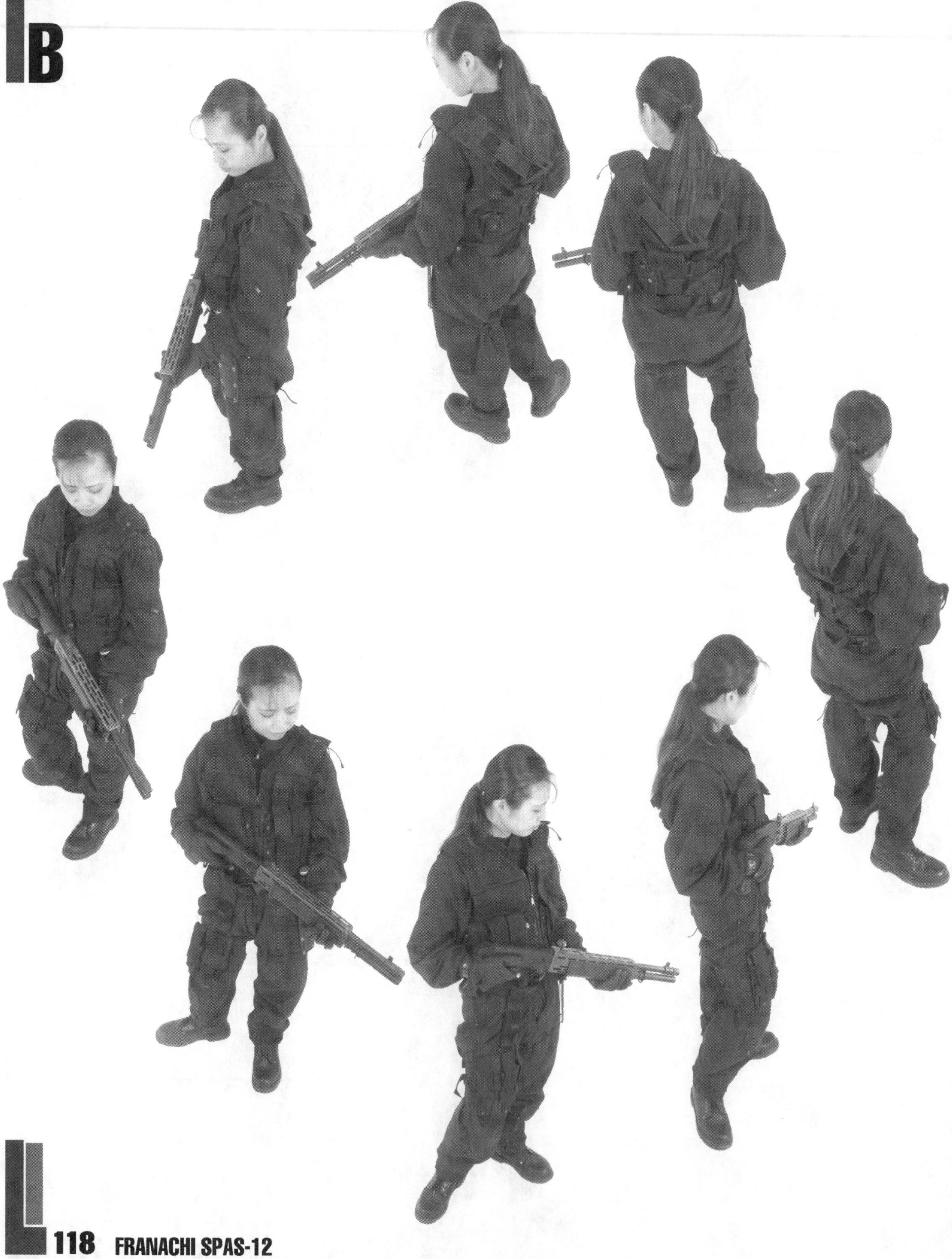

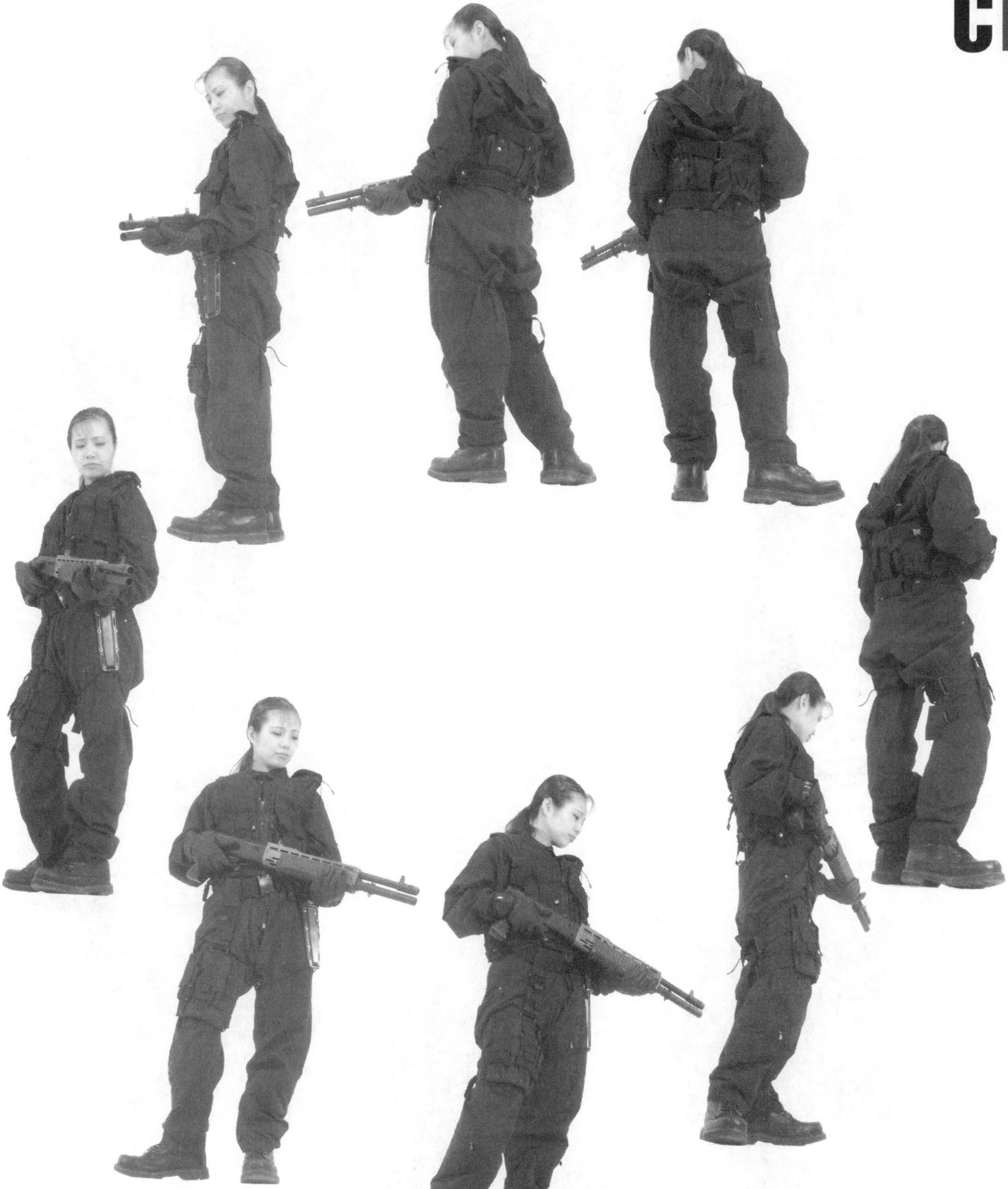

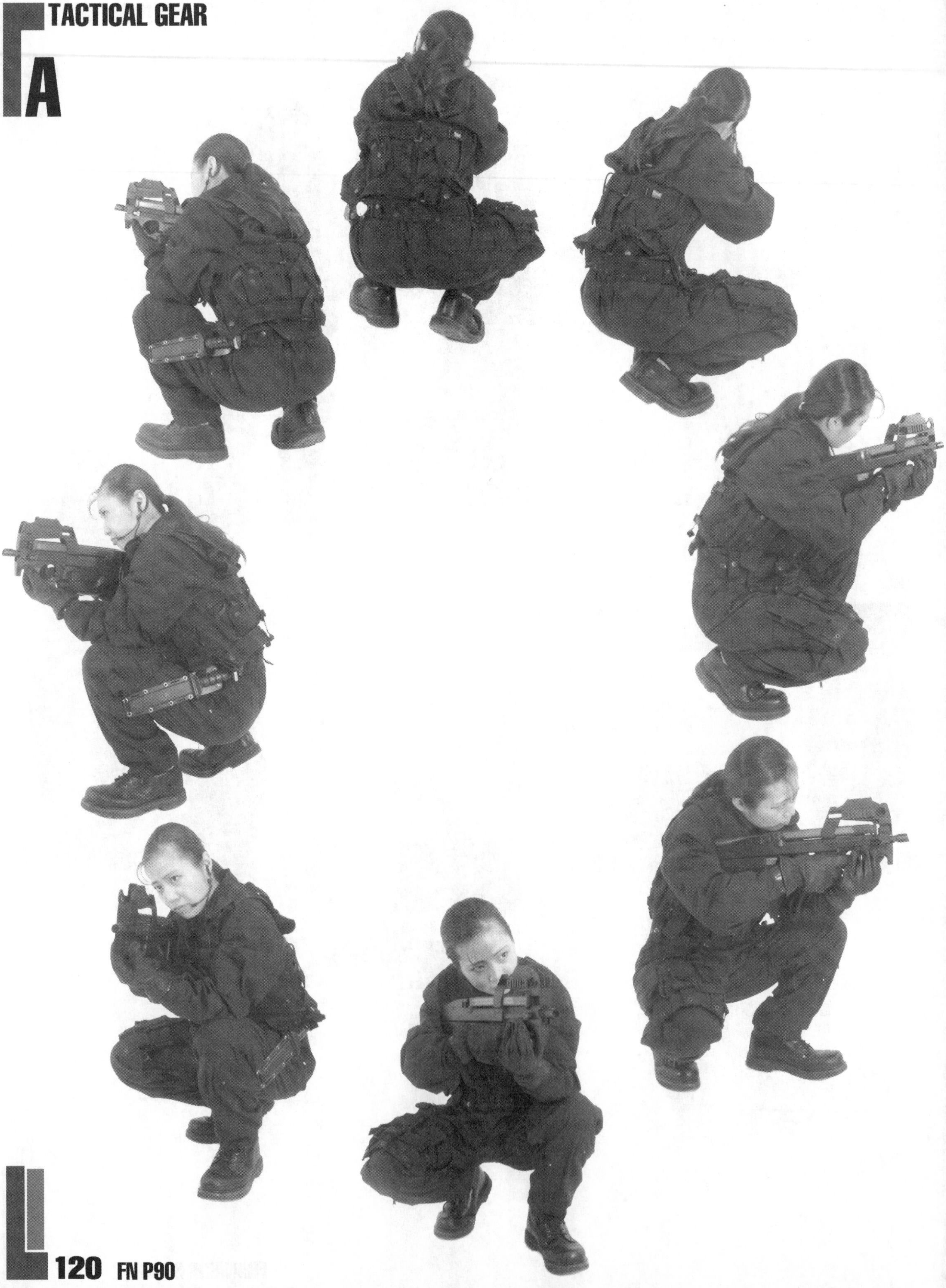

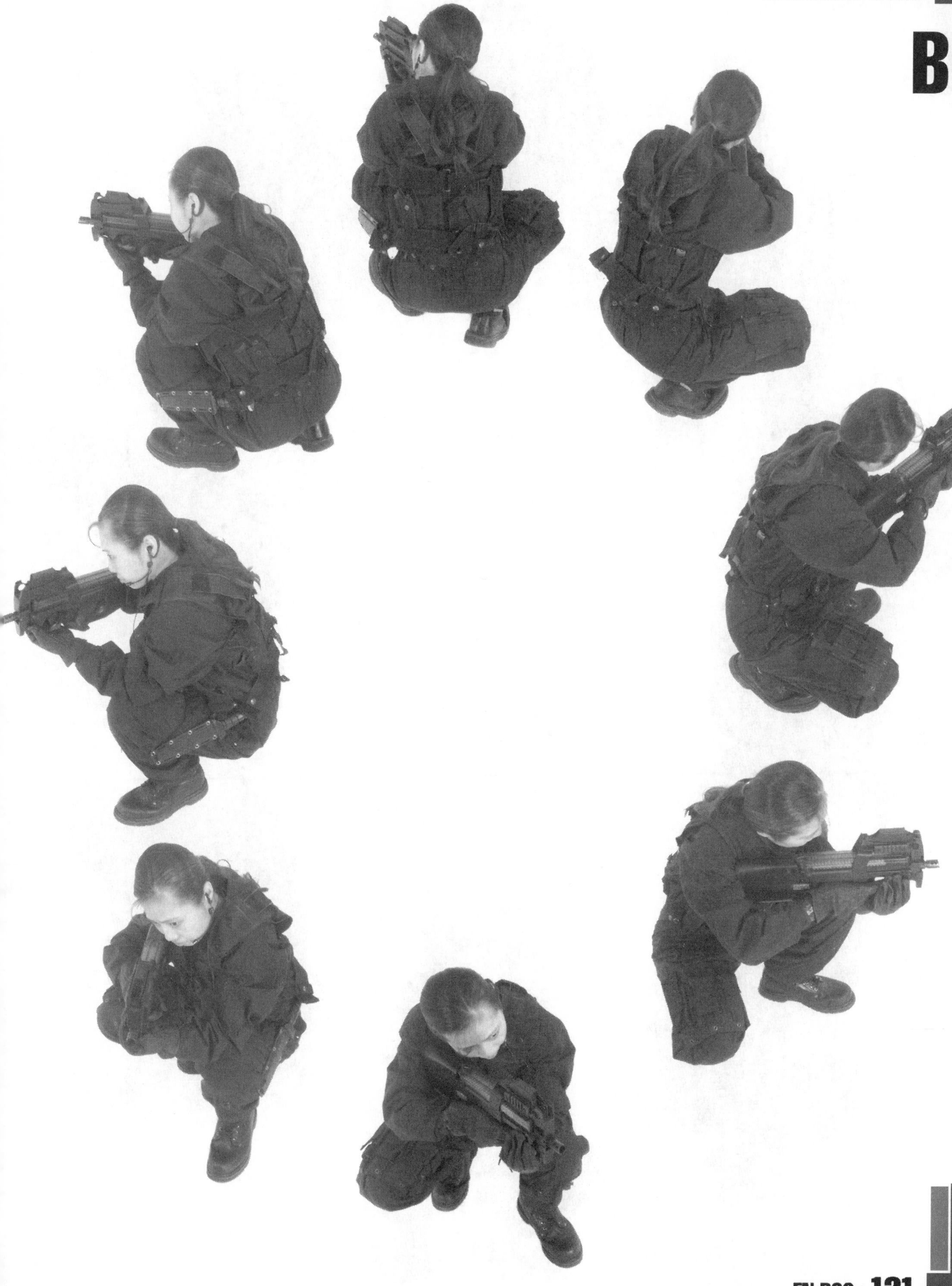

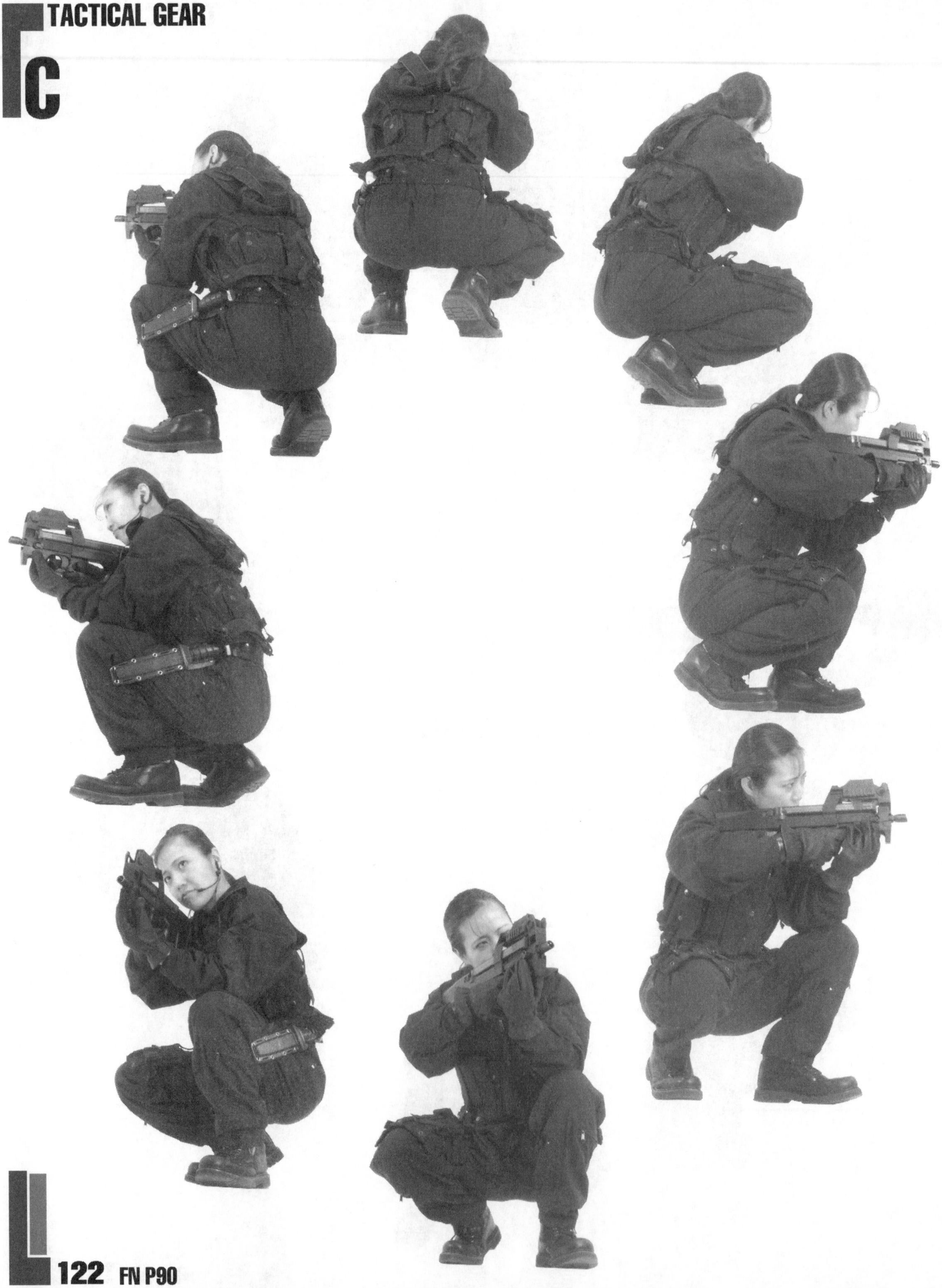

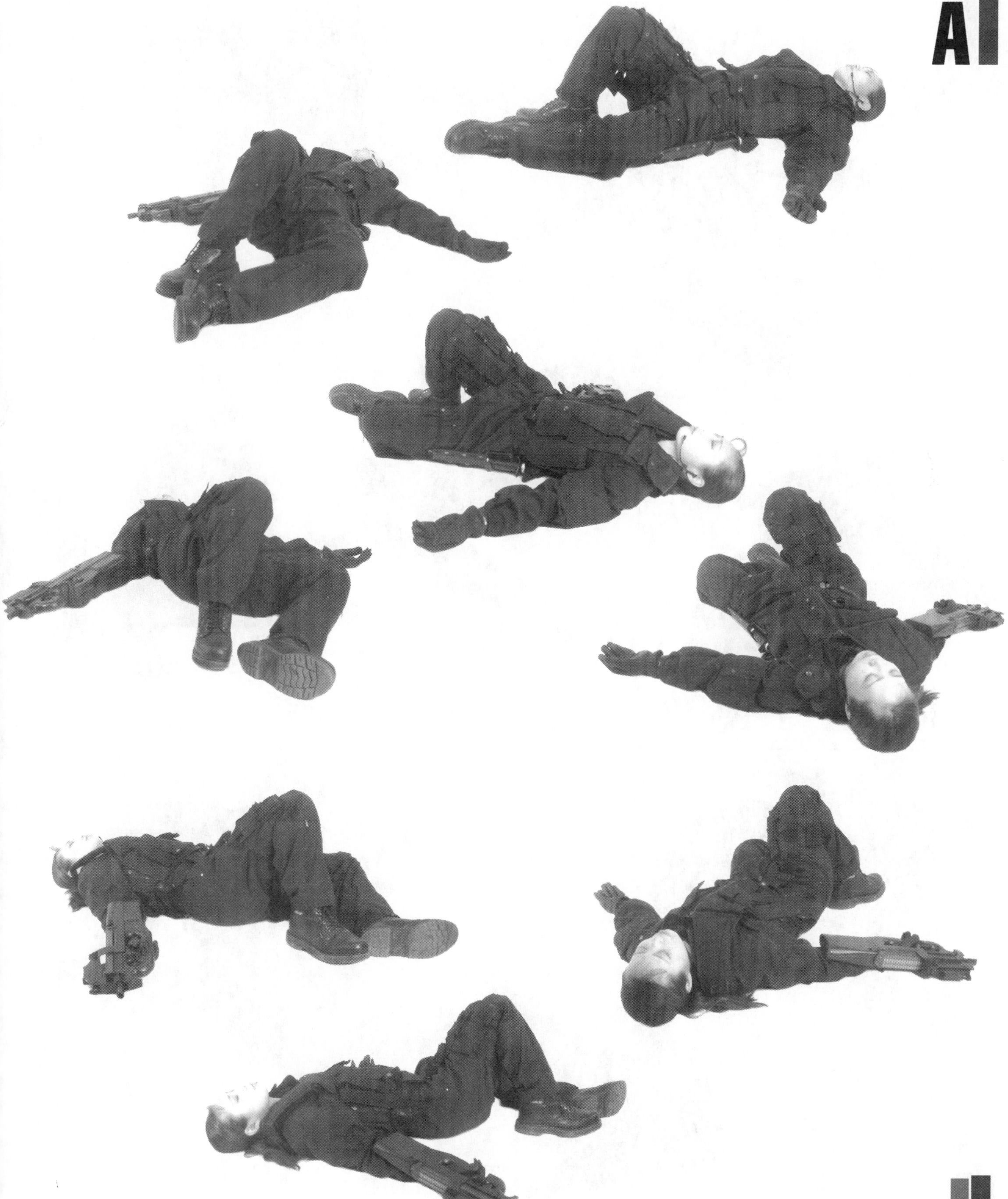

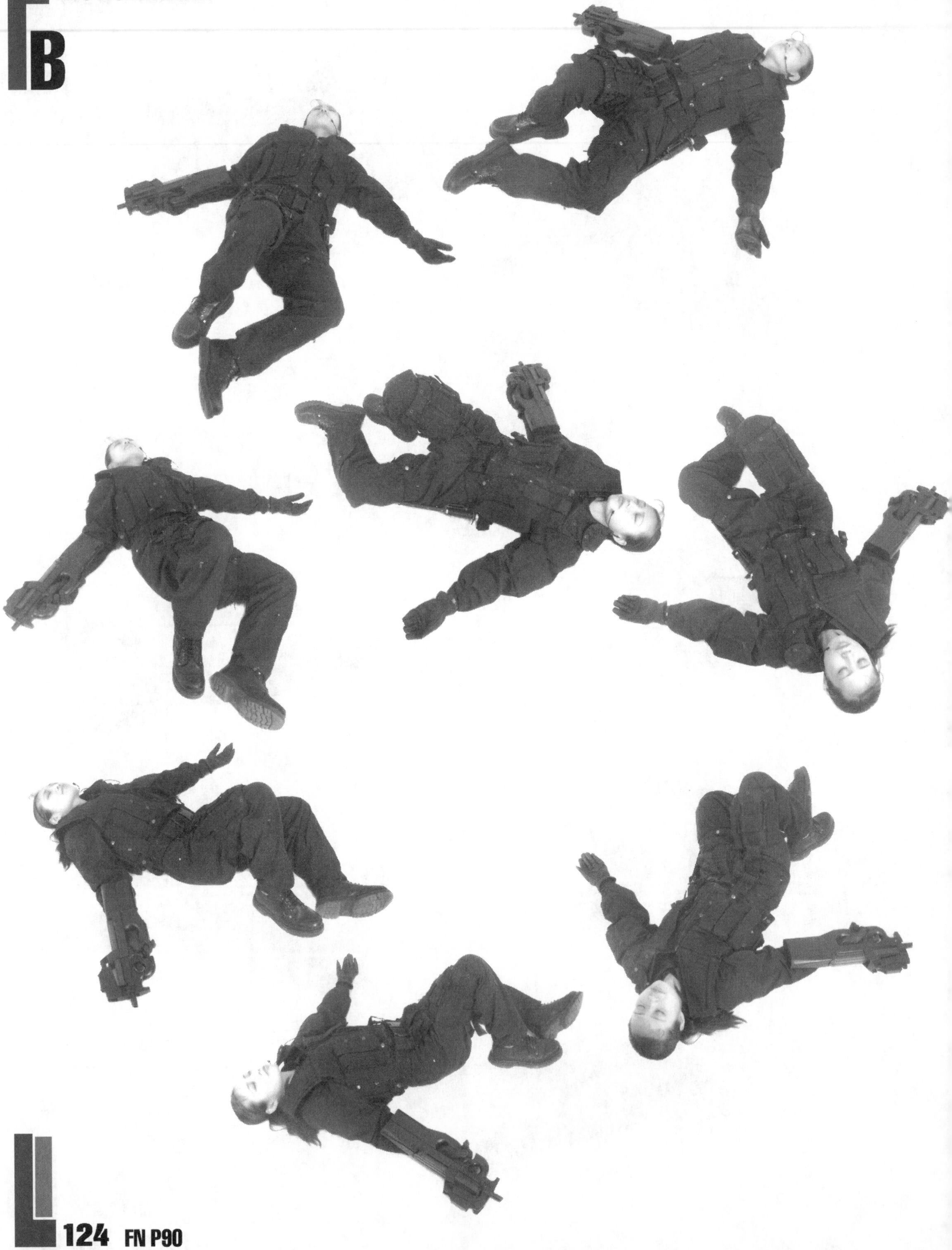

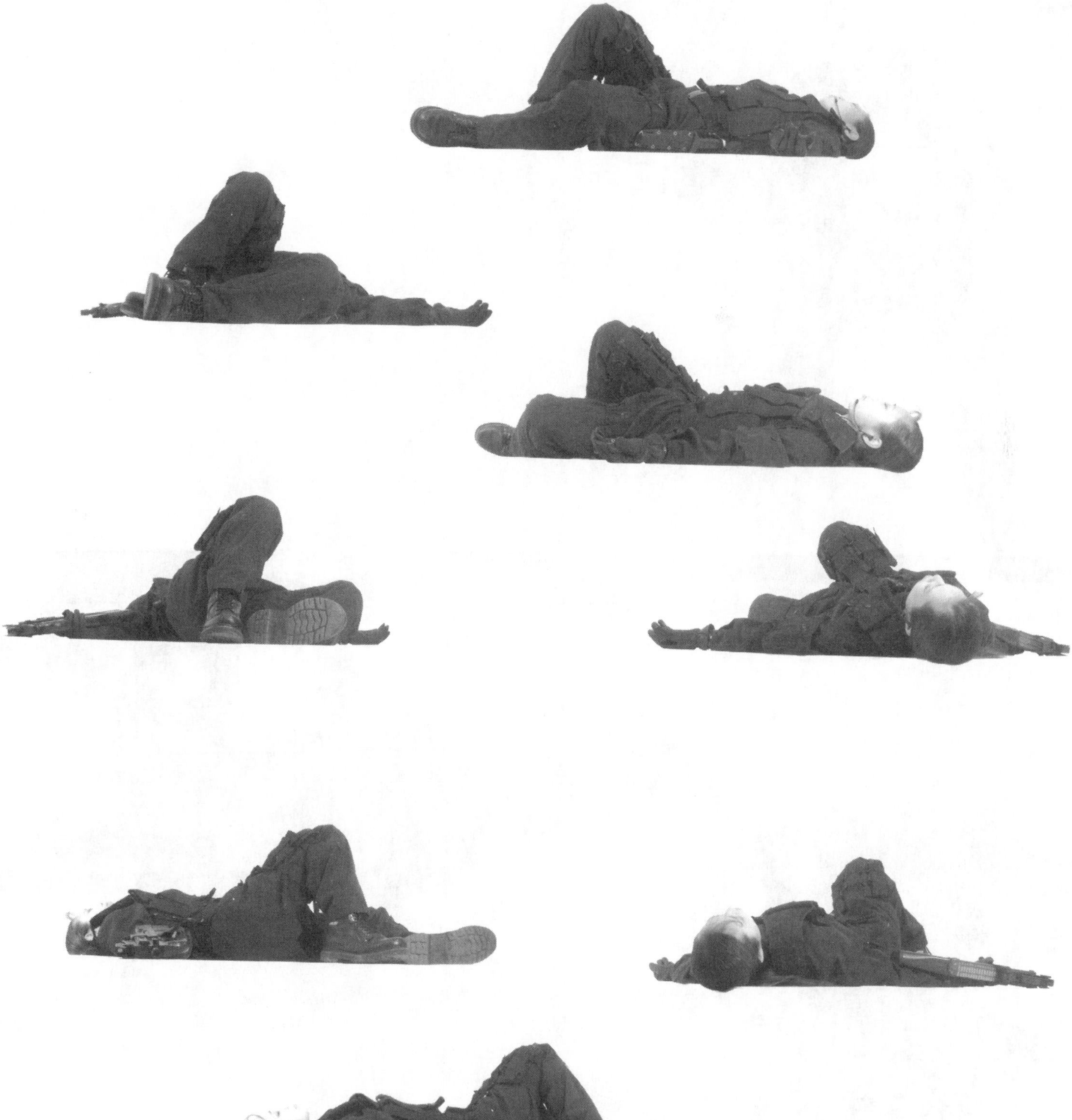

POSE
REFE

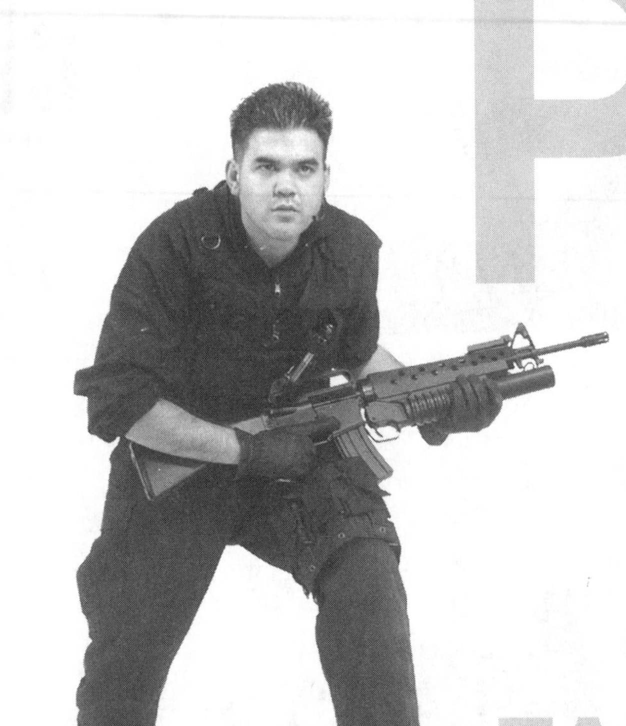

TACTICAL GEAR COMBAT POSE (MALE)

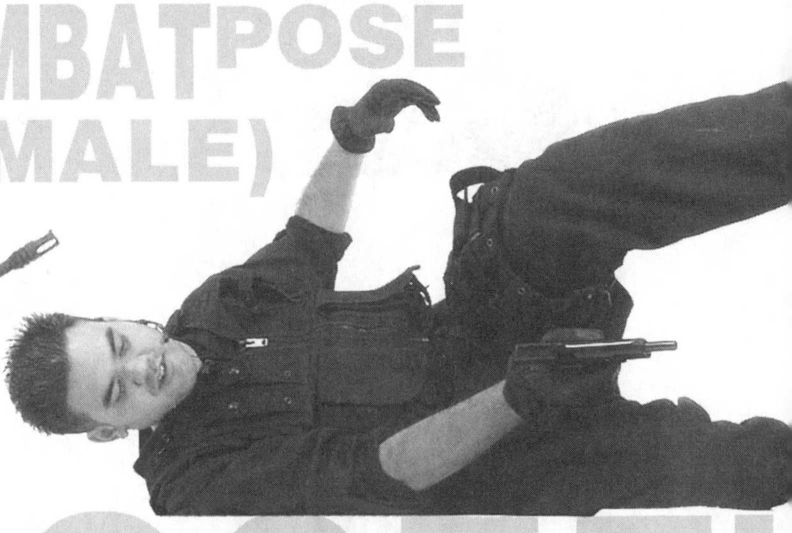

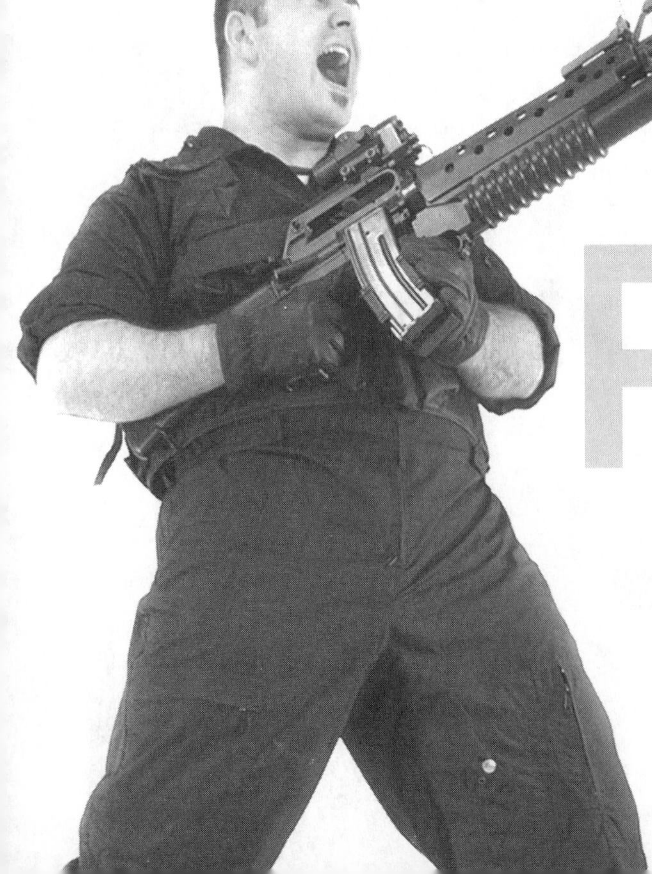

POSEFI
REFERE

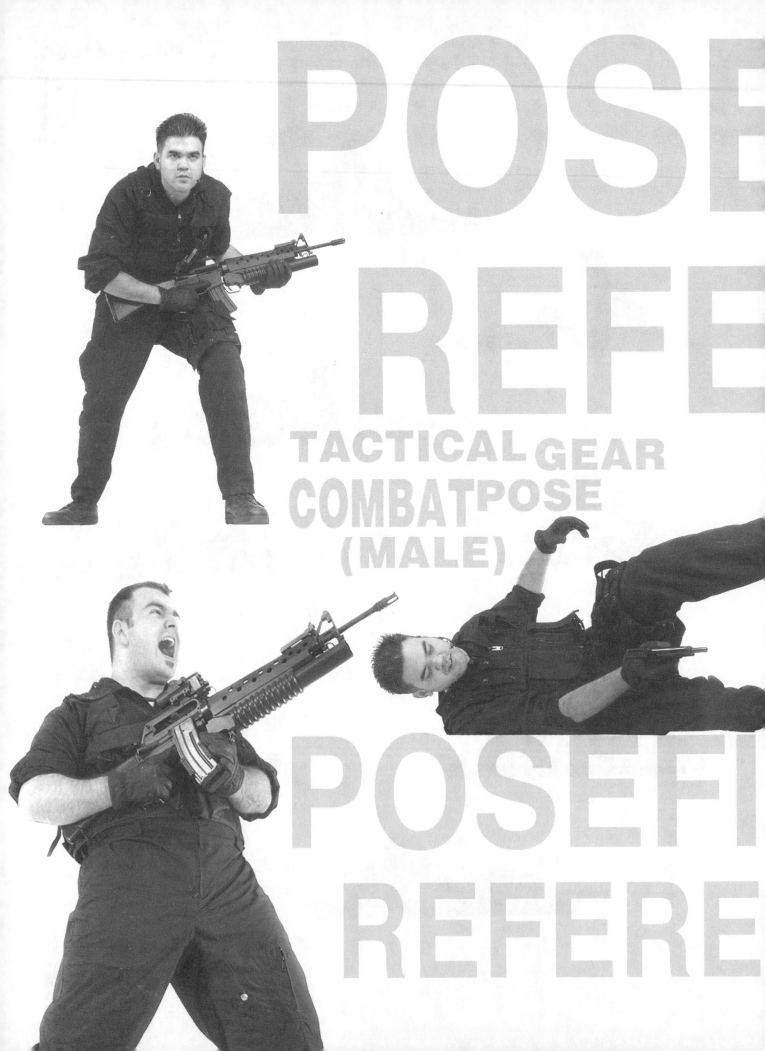

FILE

RENCE

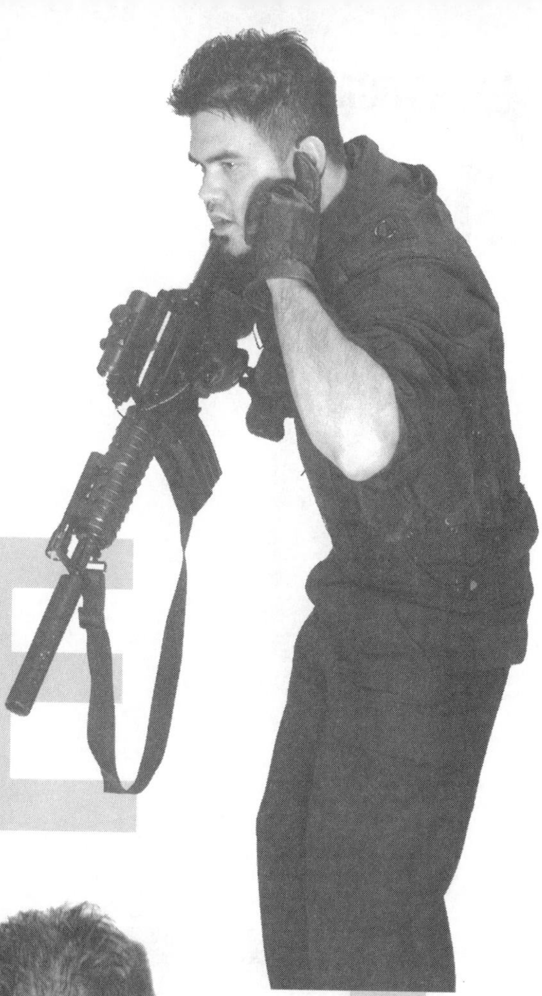

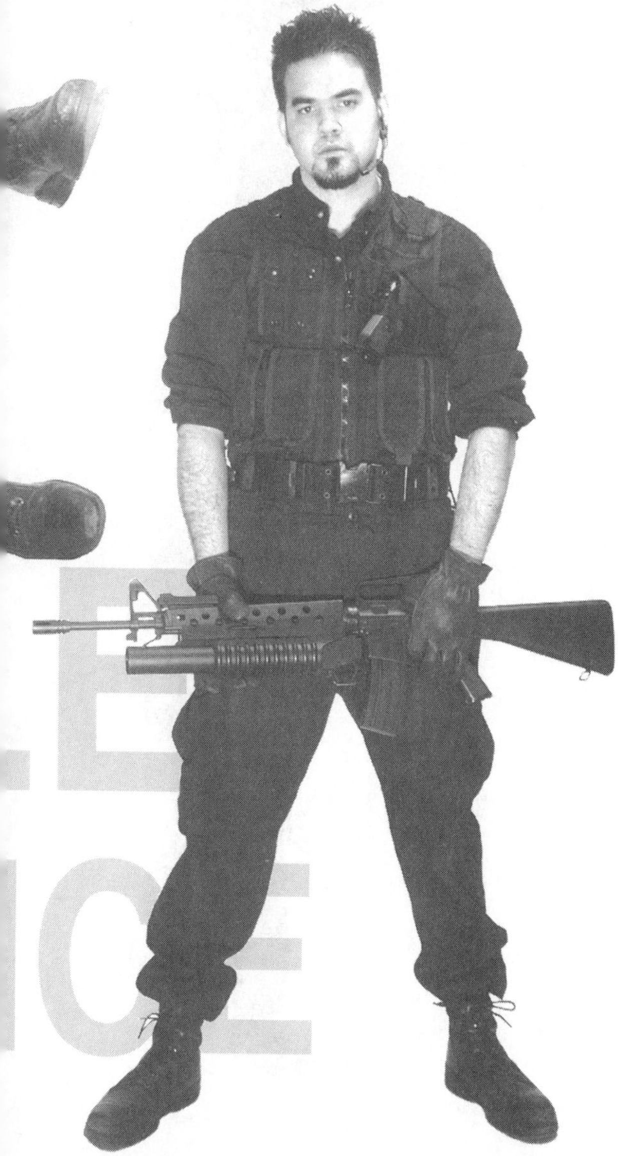

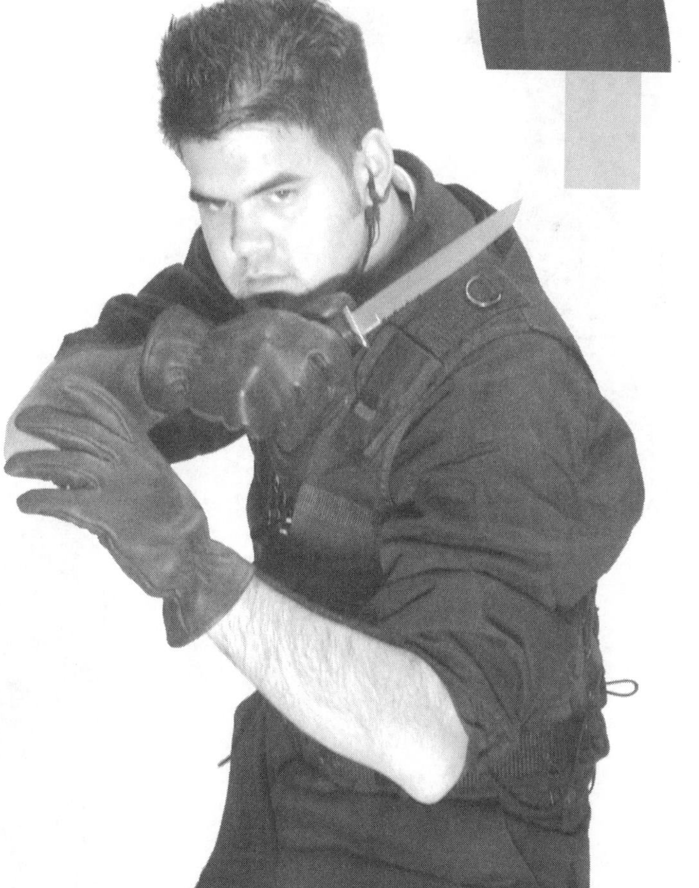

COMBAT
COLLECTION

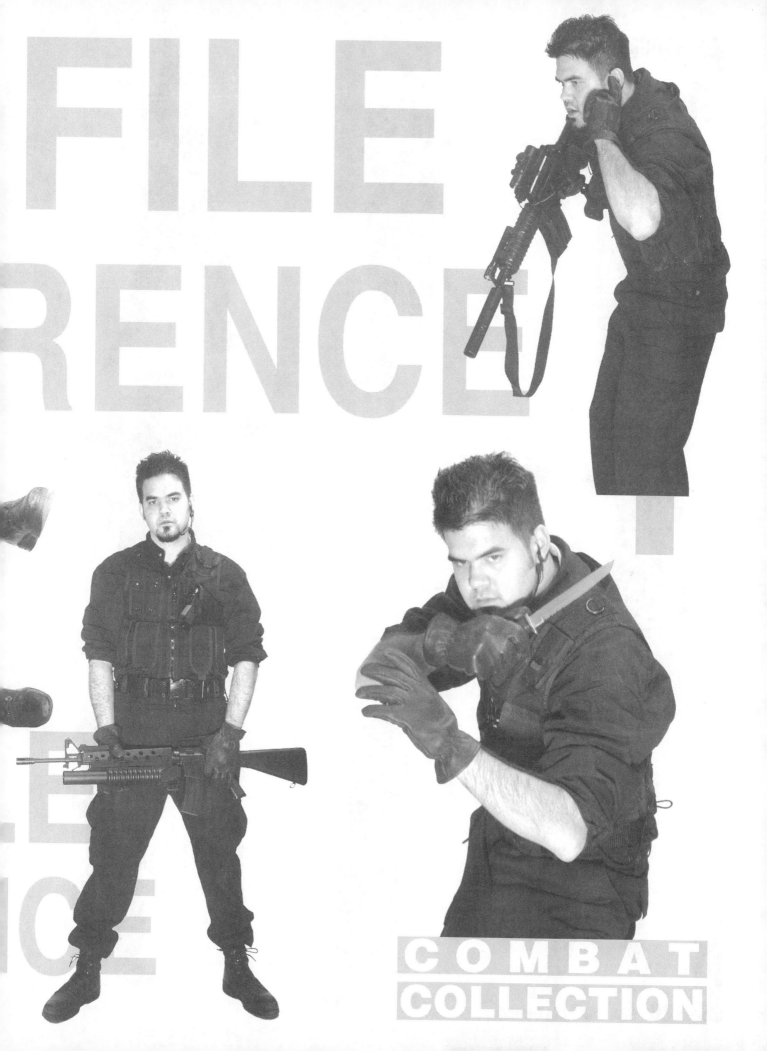

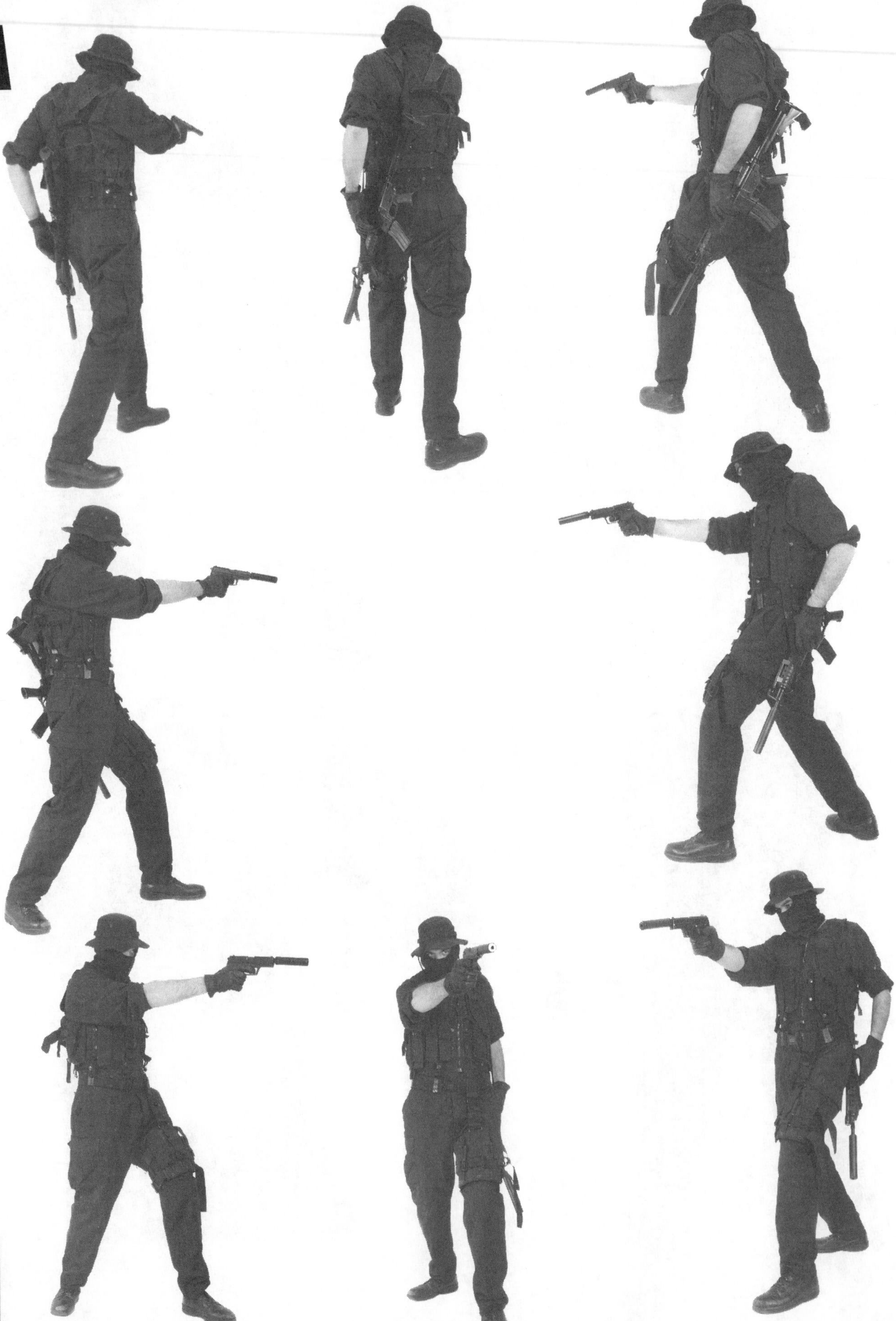

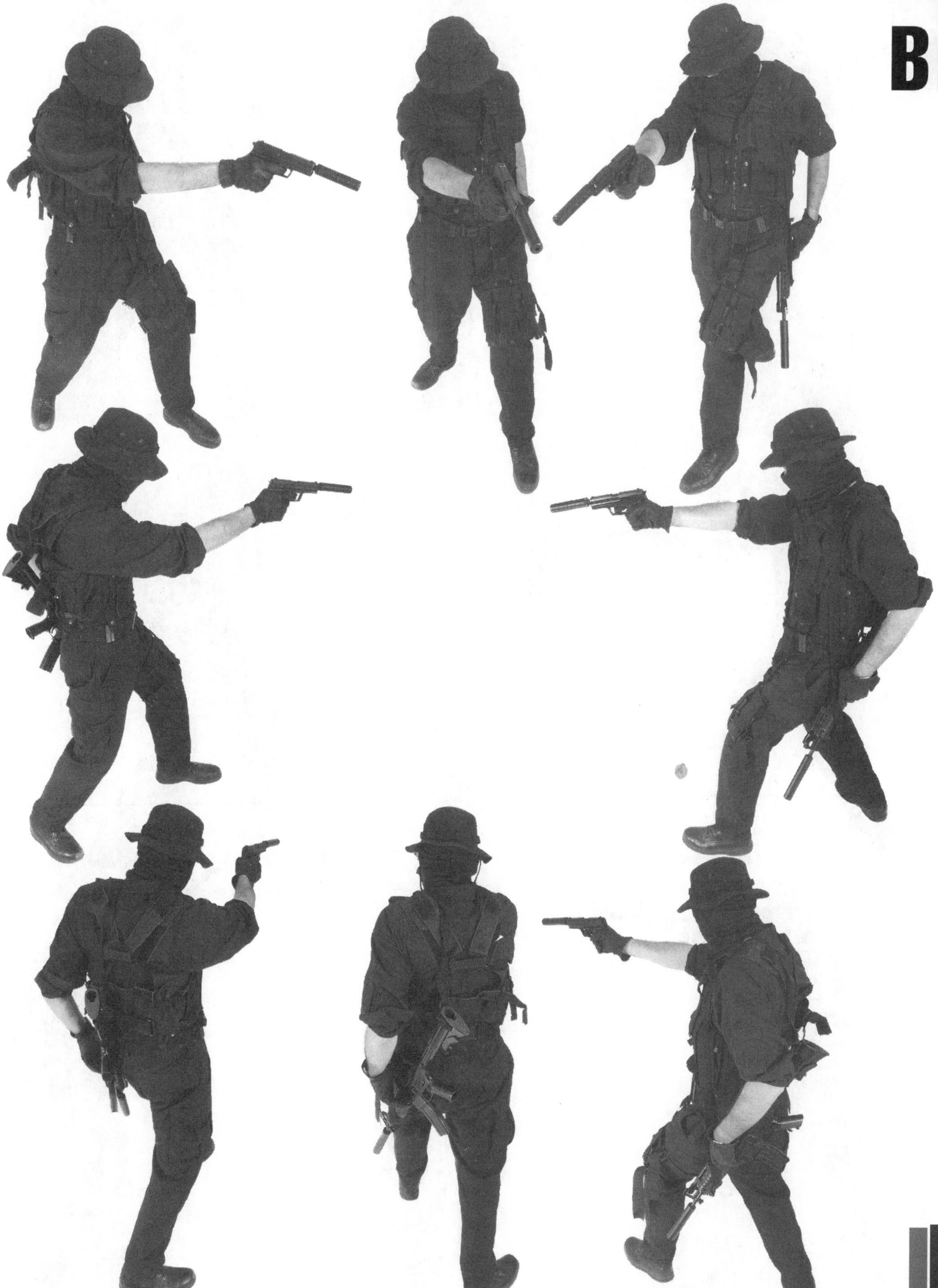

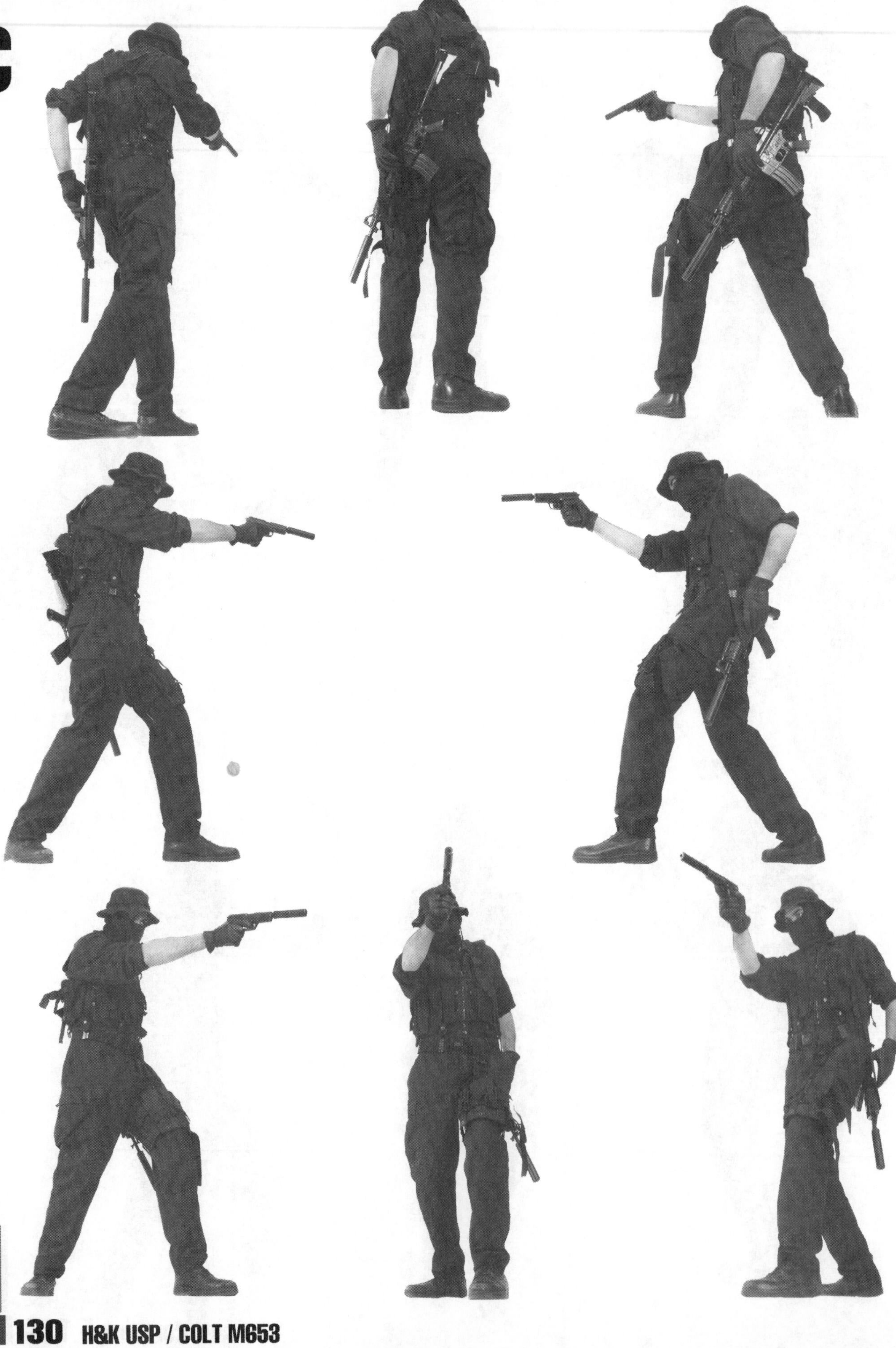

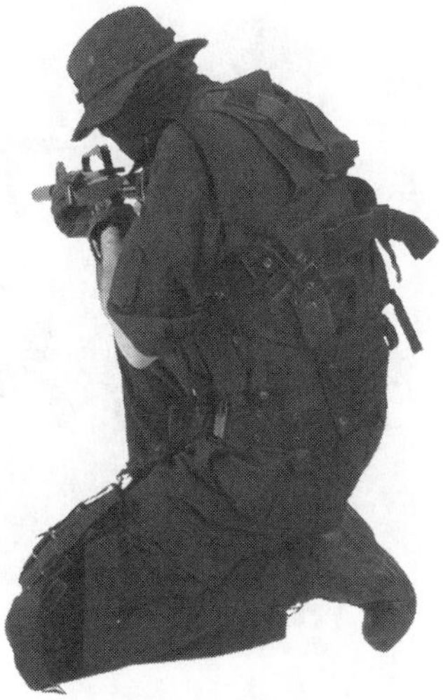

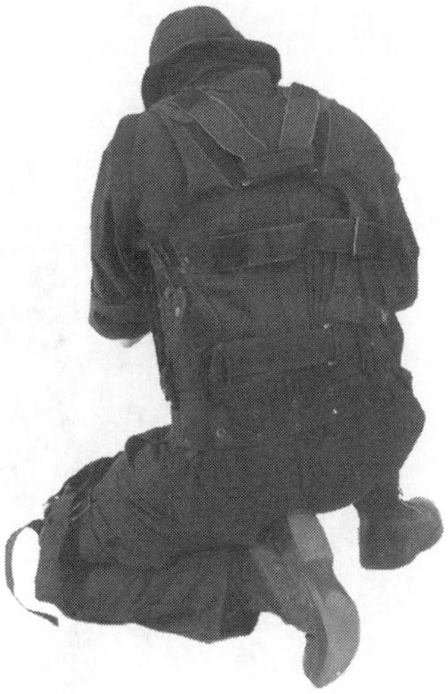

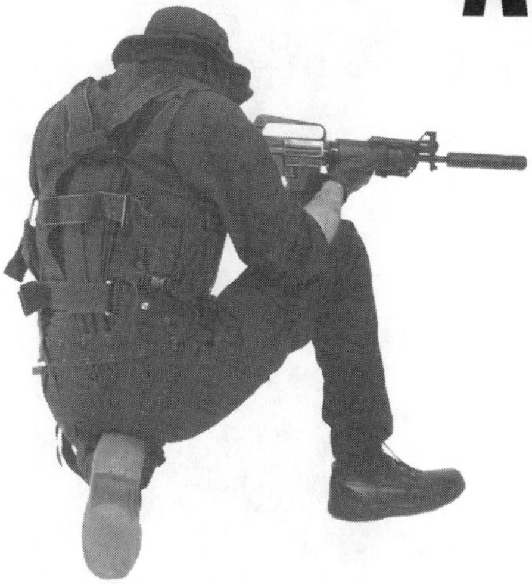

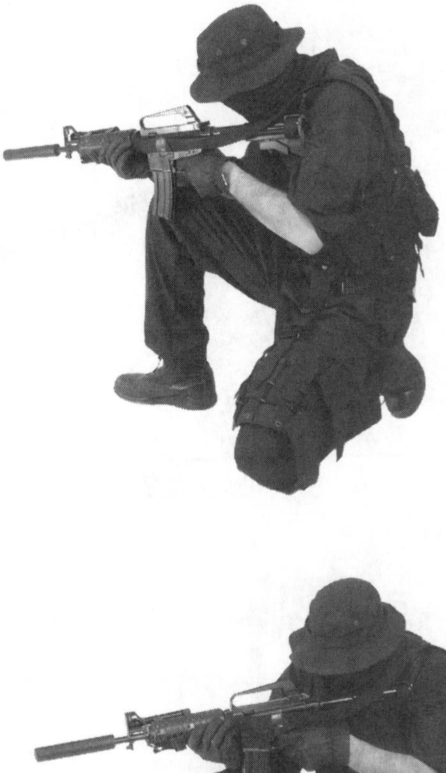

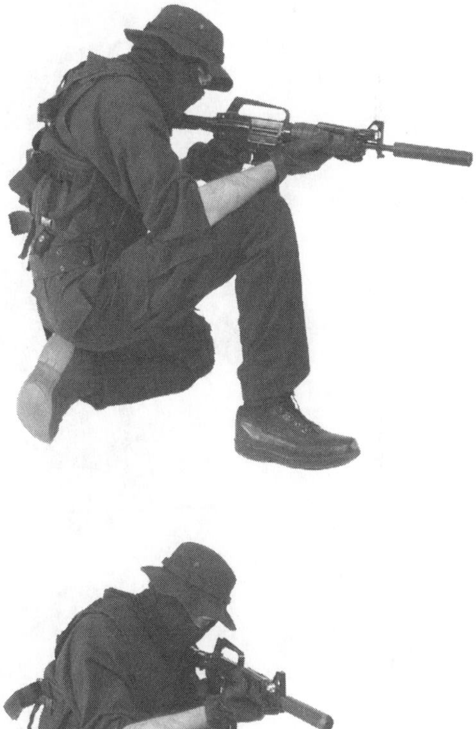

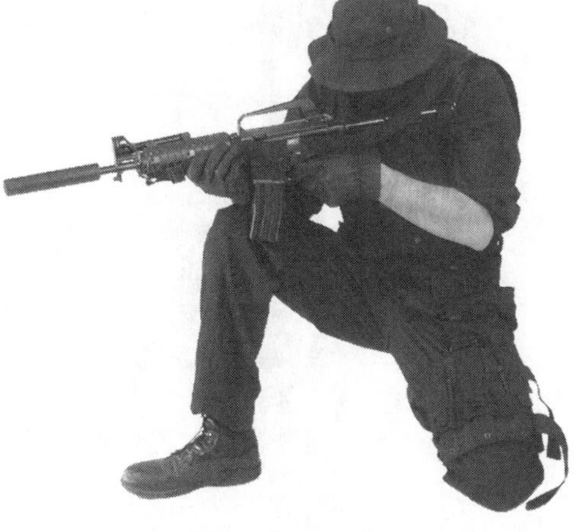

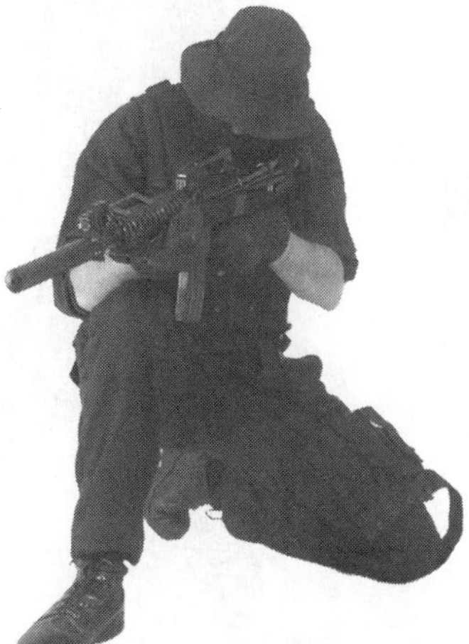

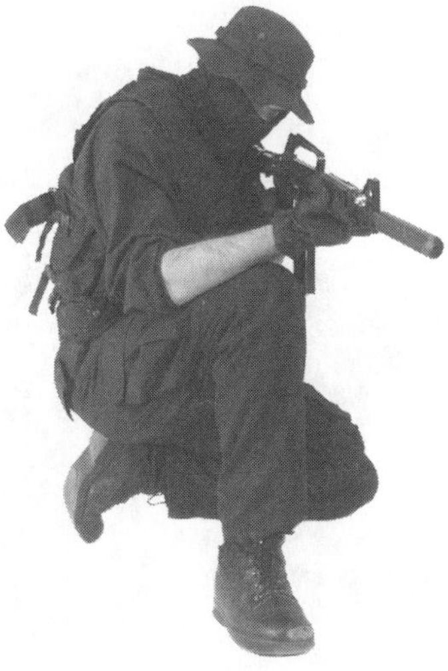

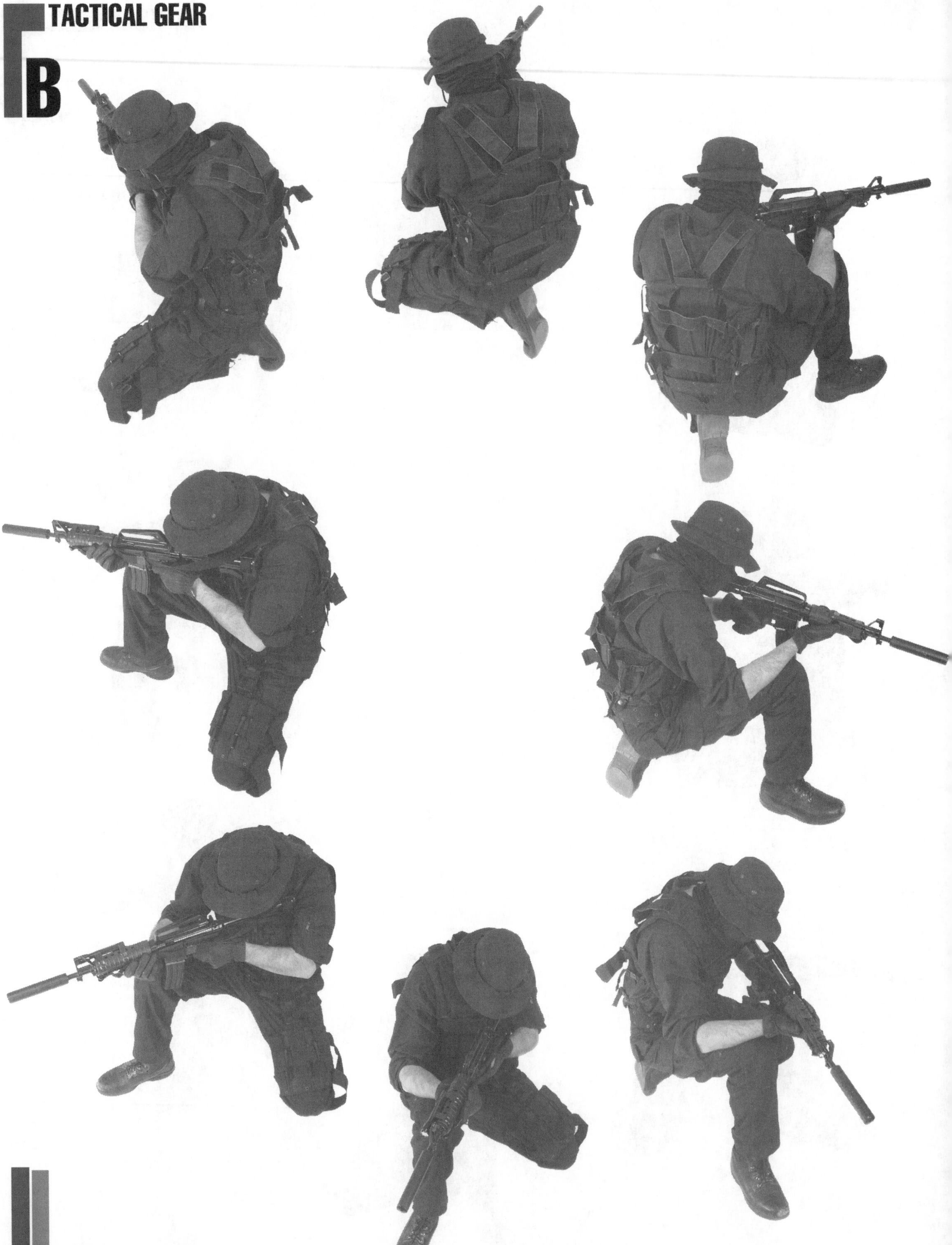

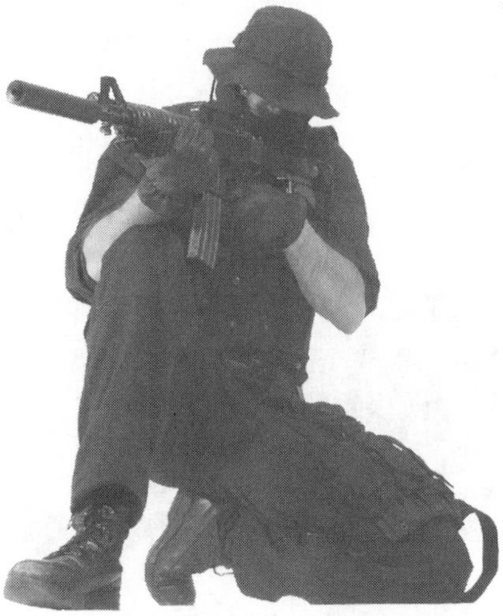

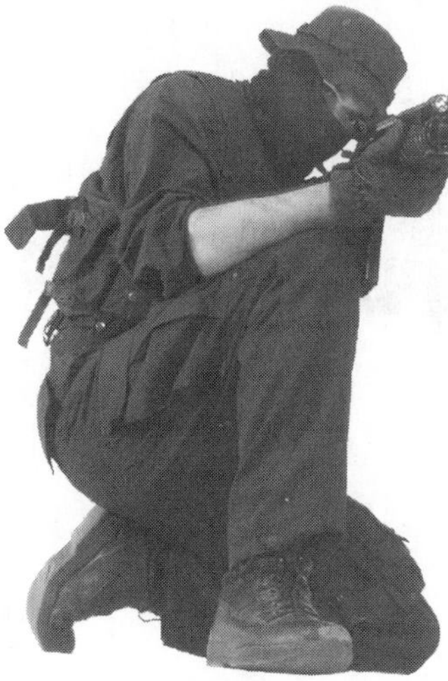

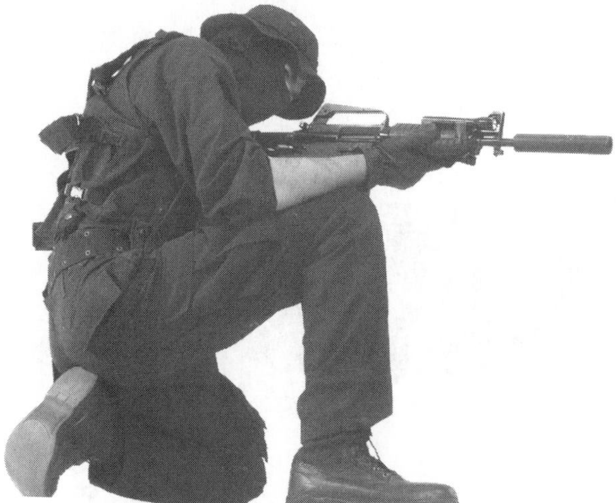

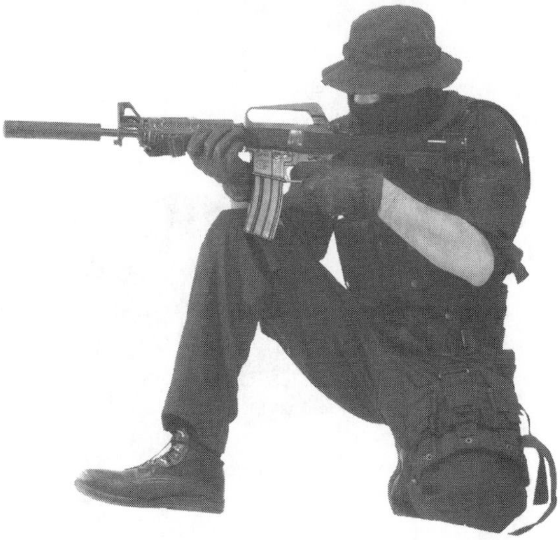

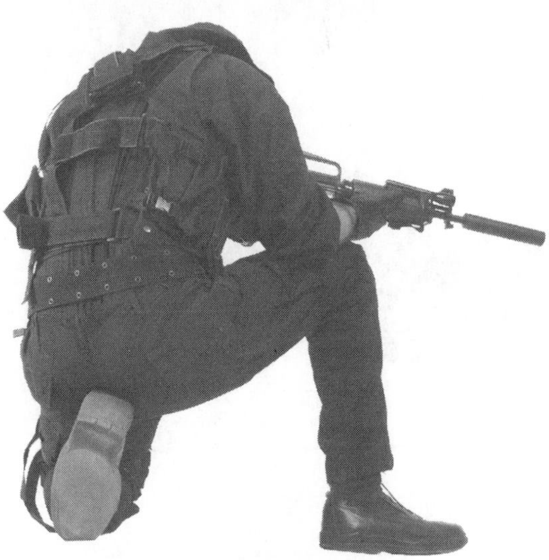

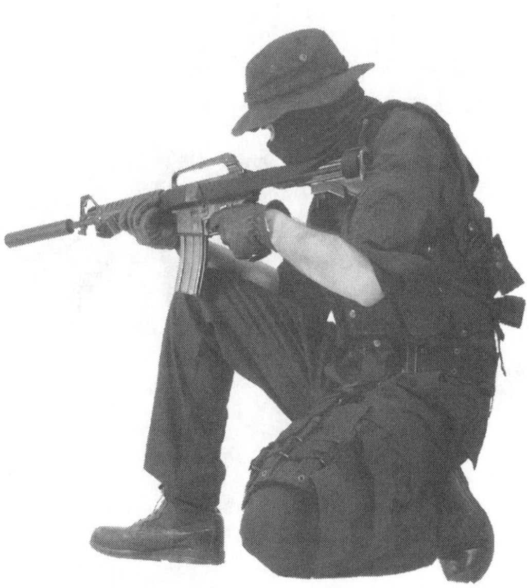

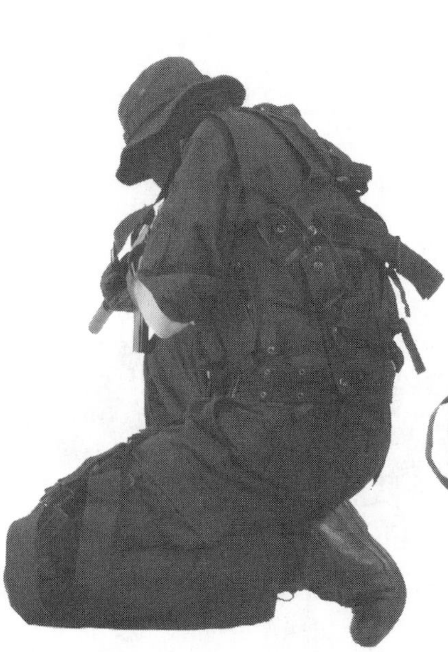

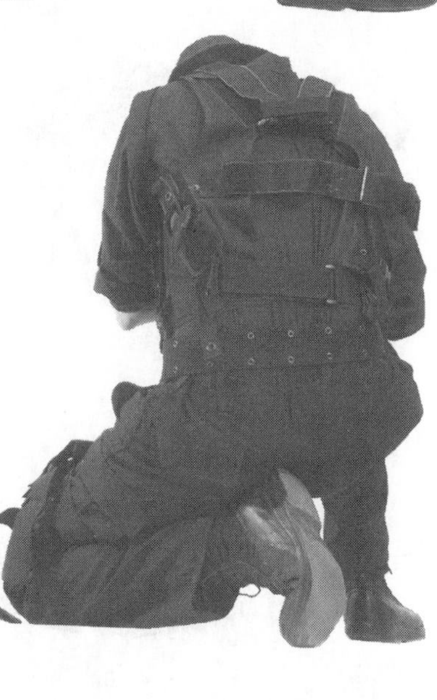

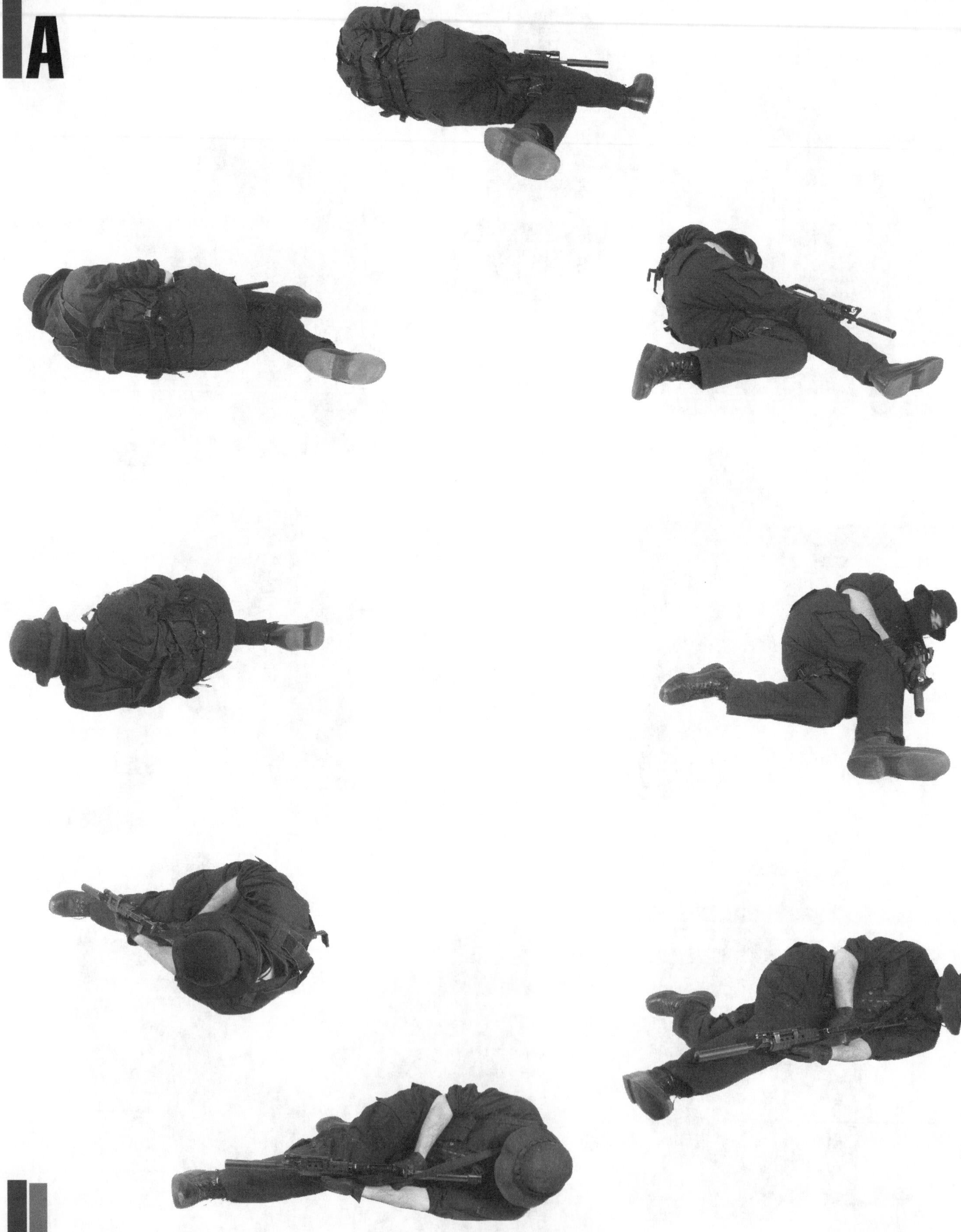

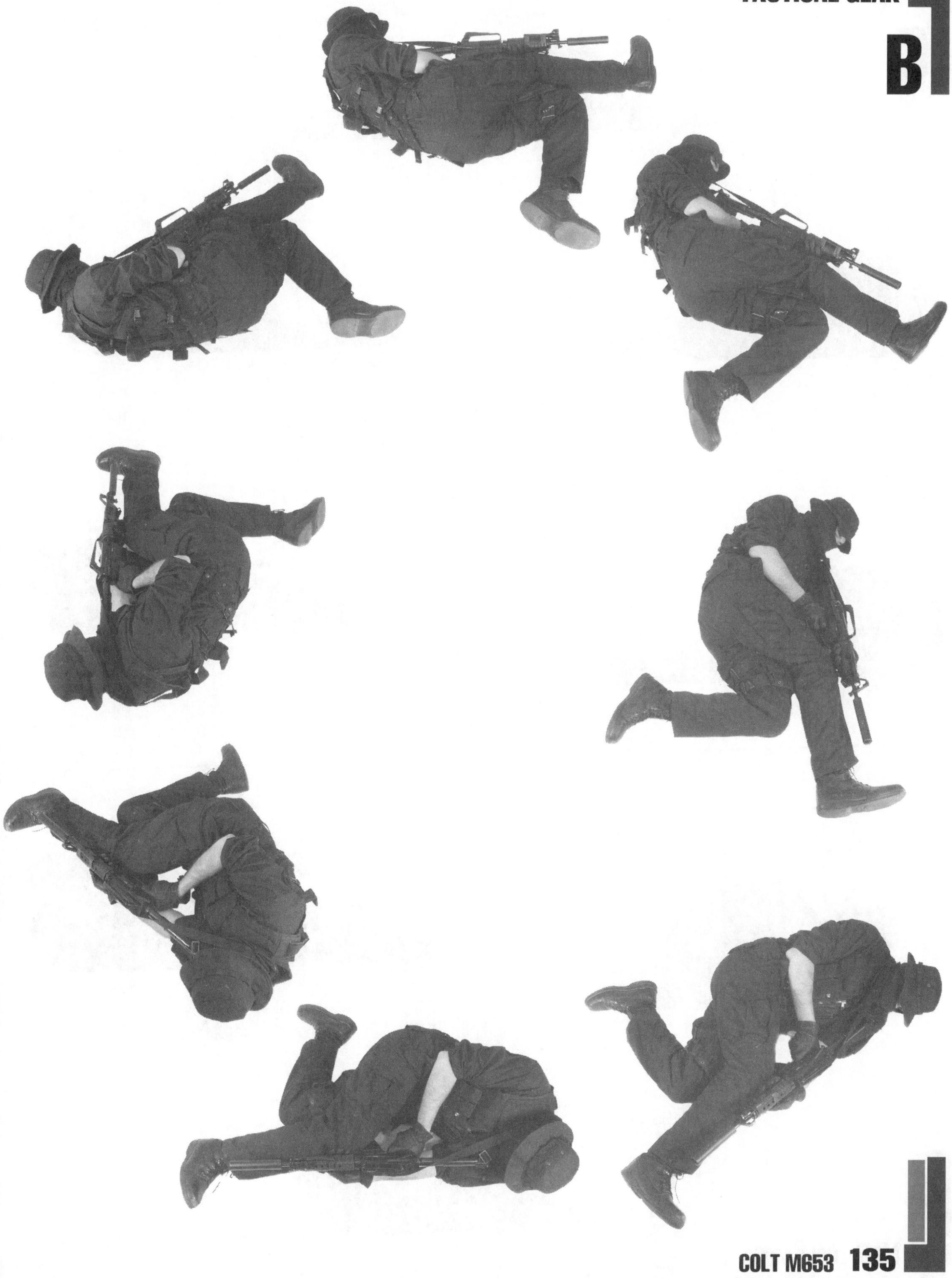

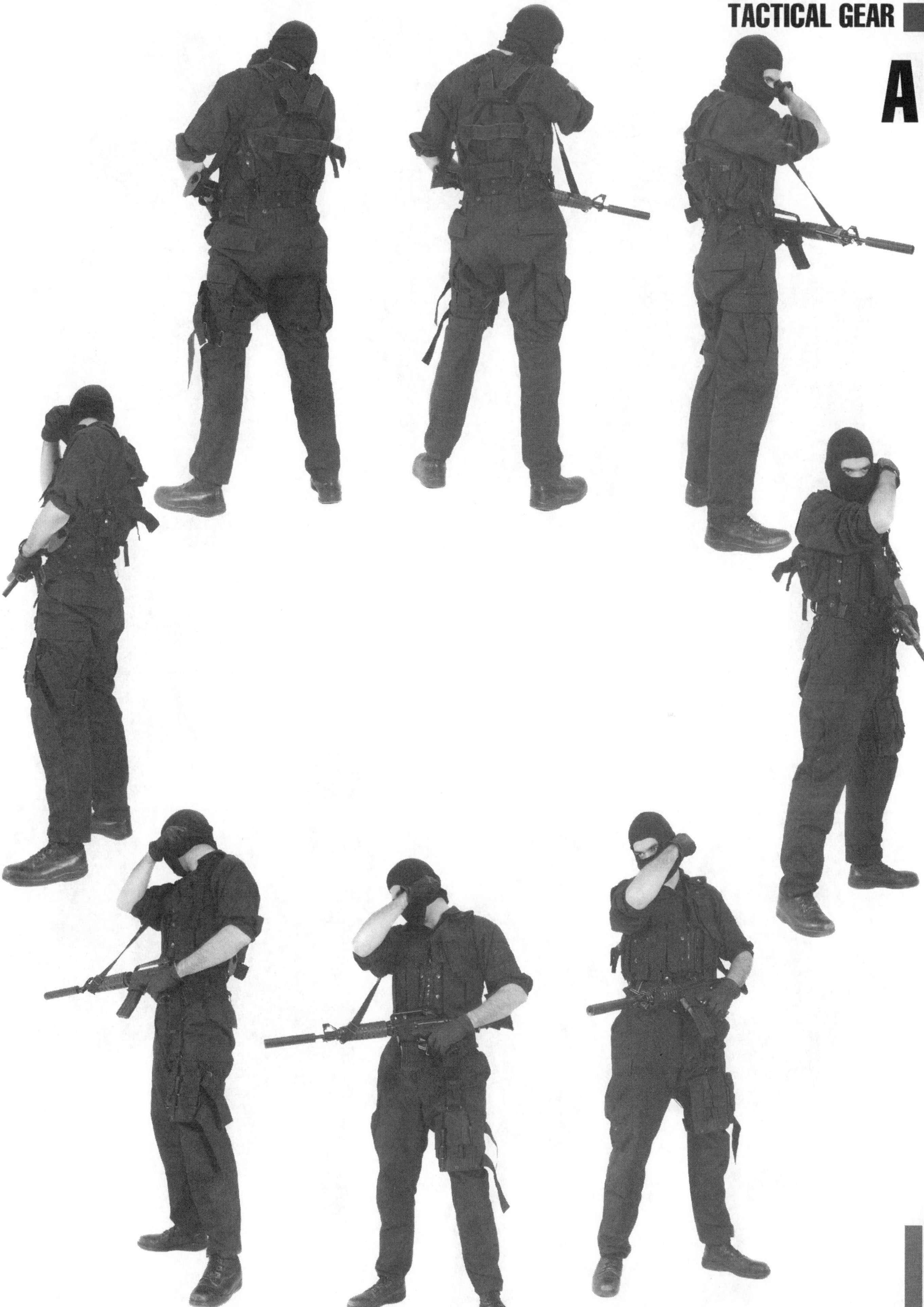

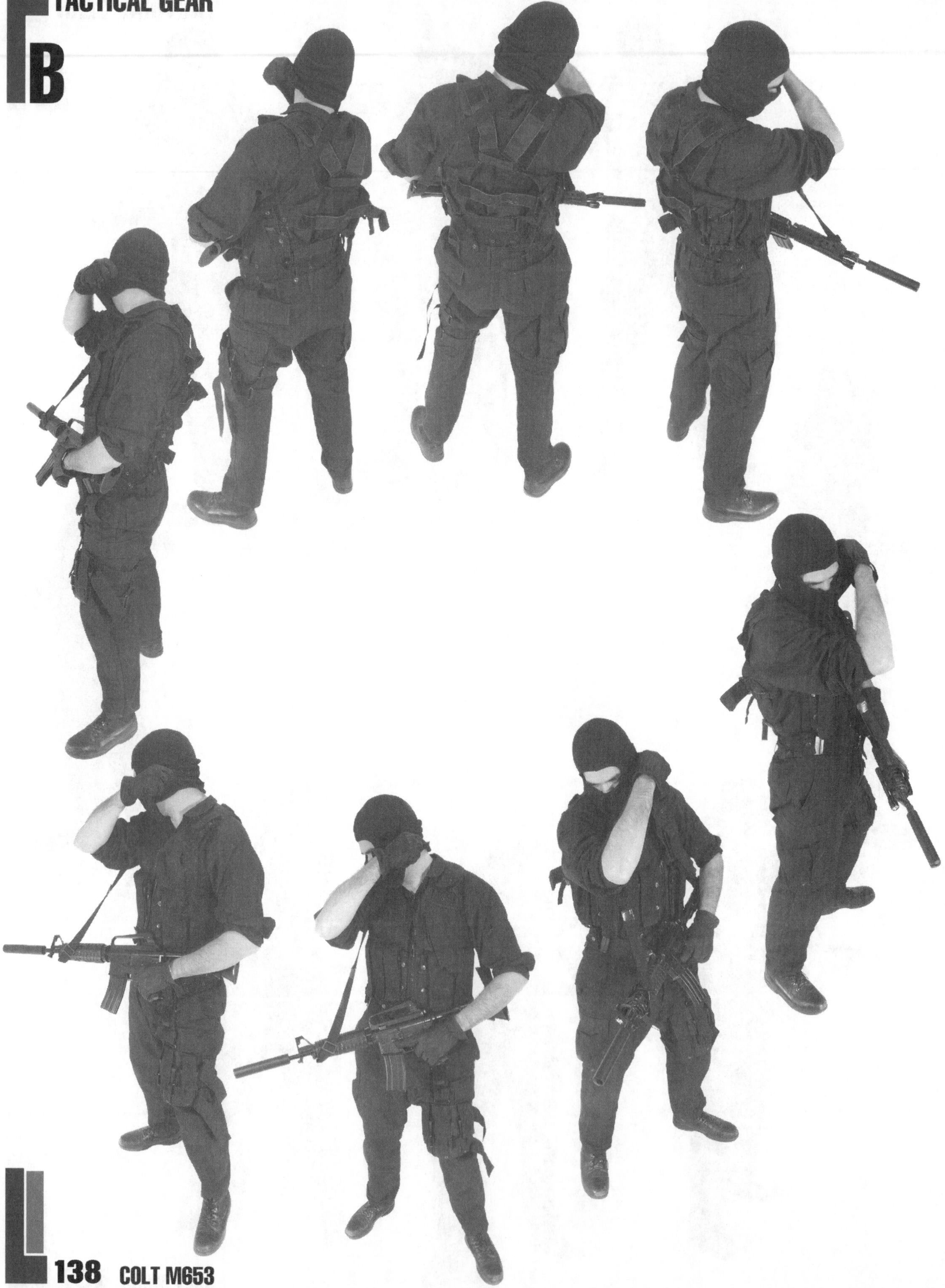

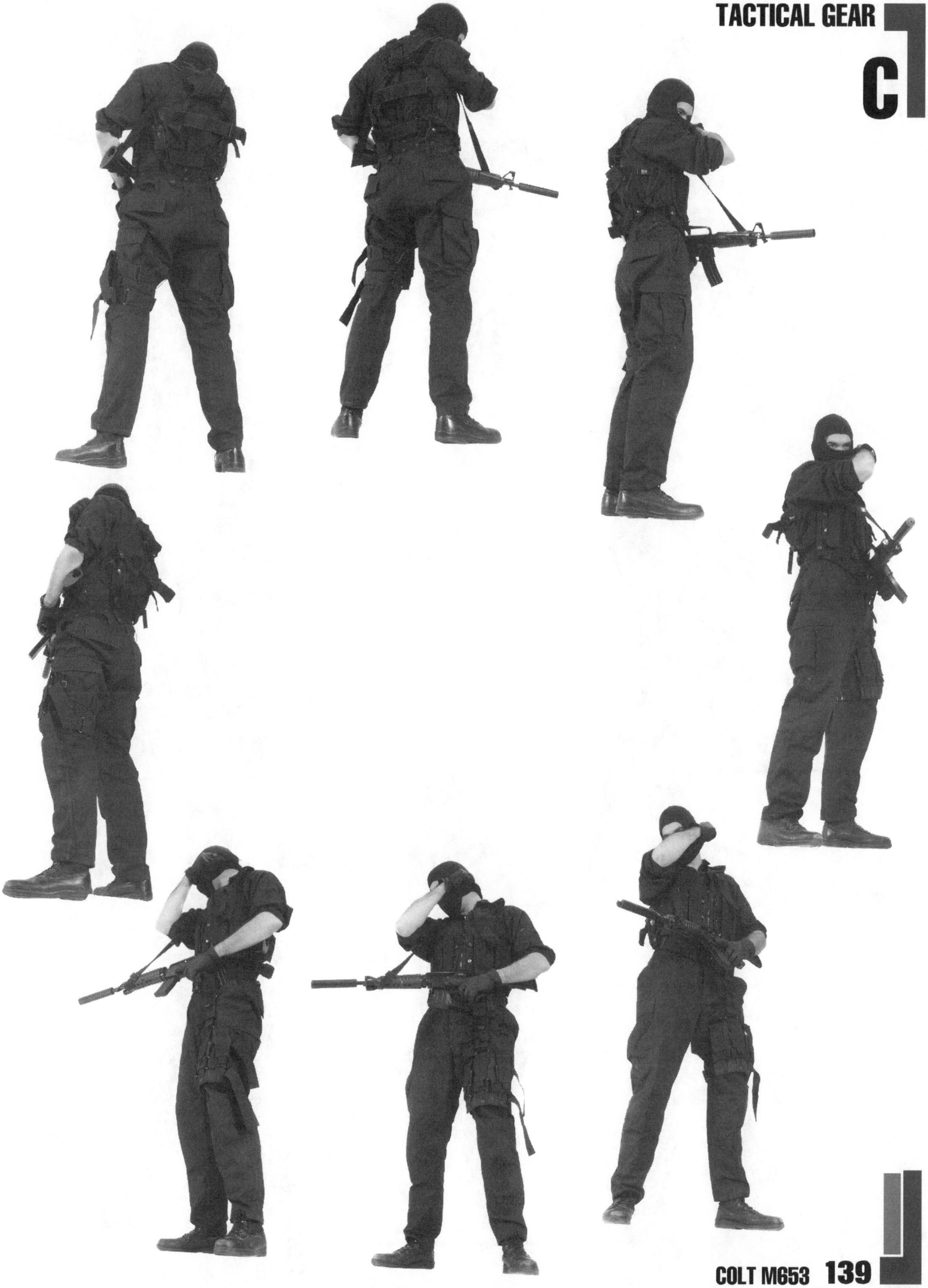

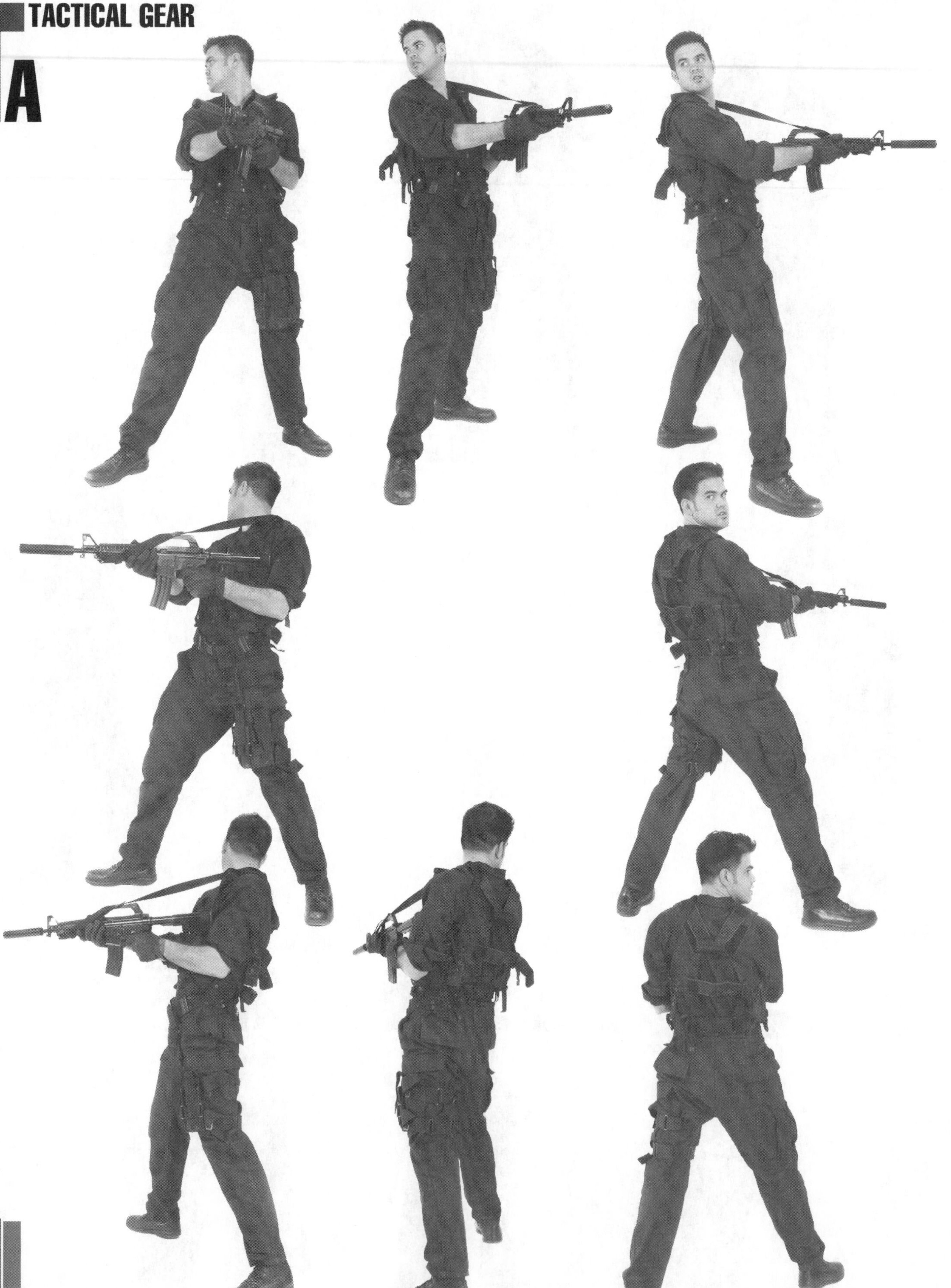

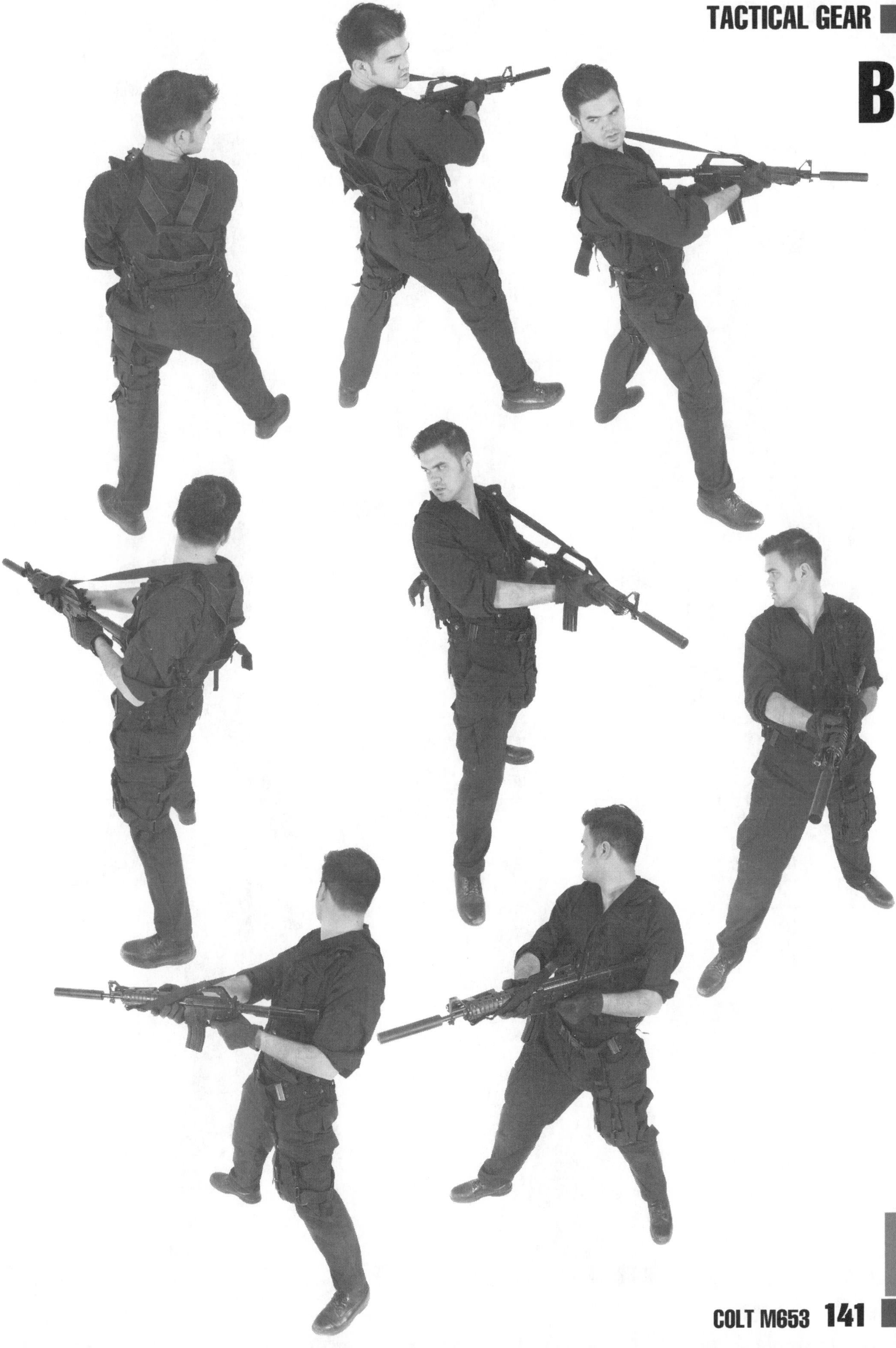

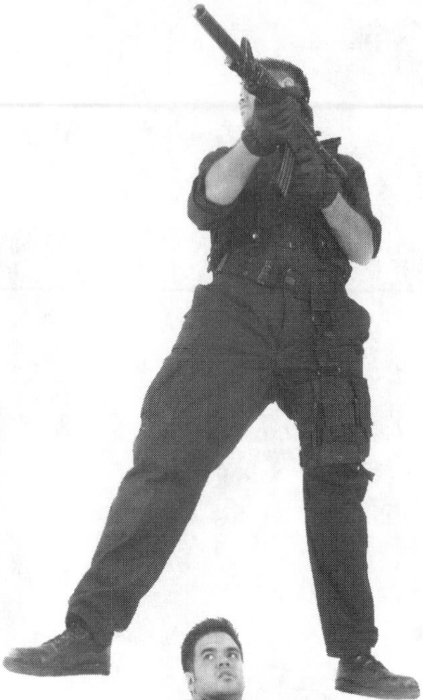

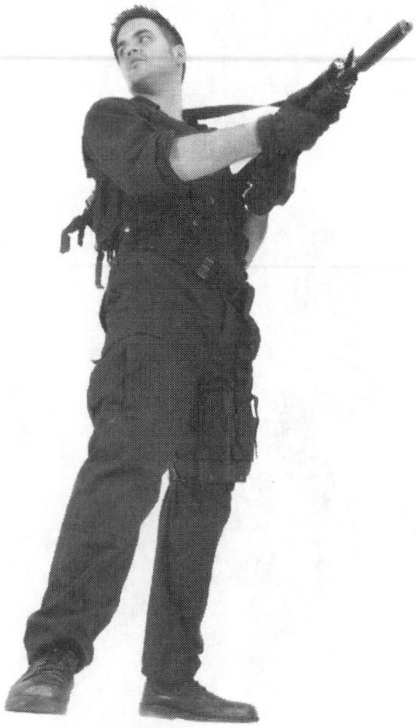

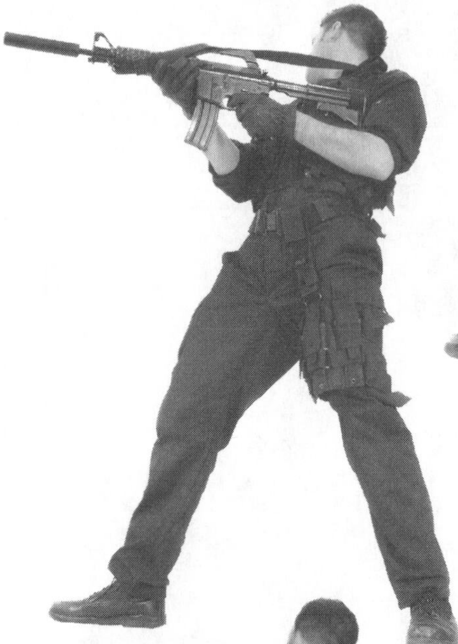

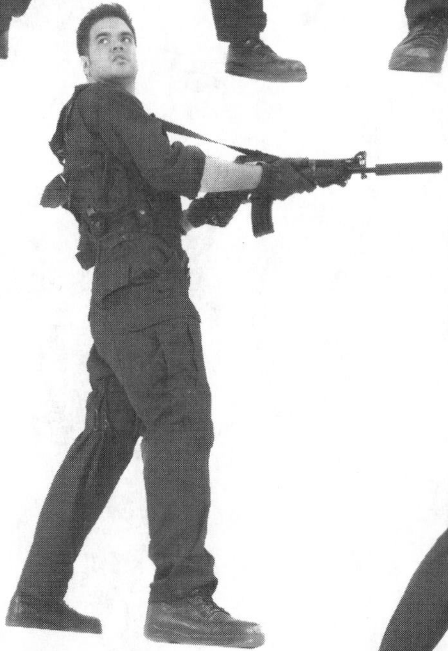

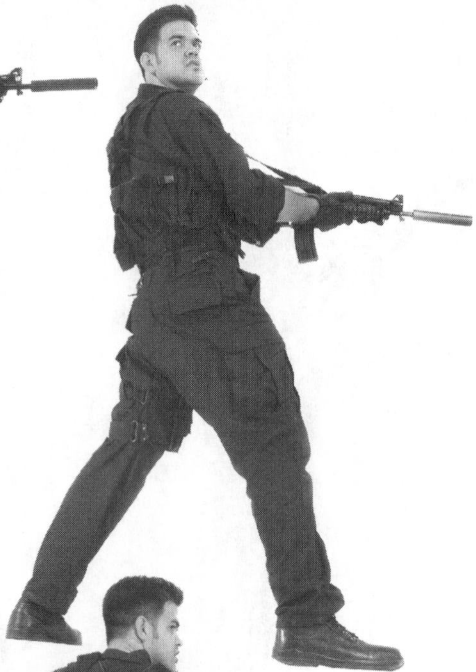

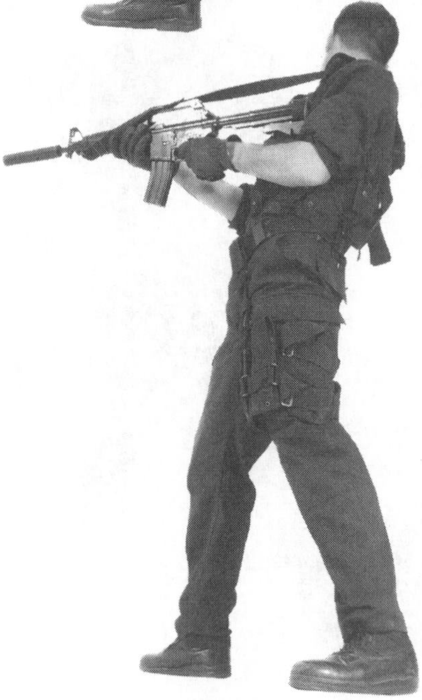

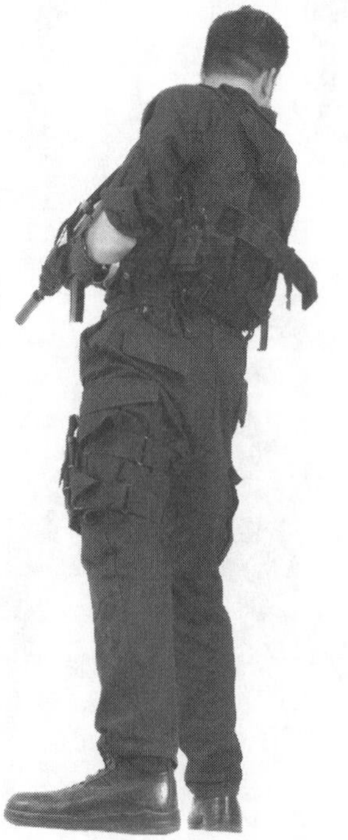

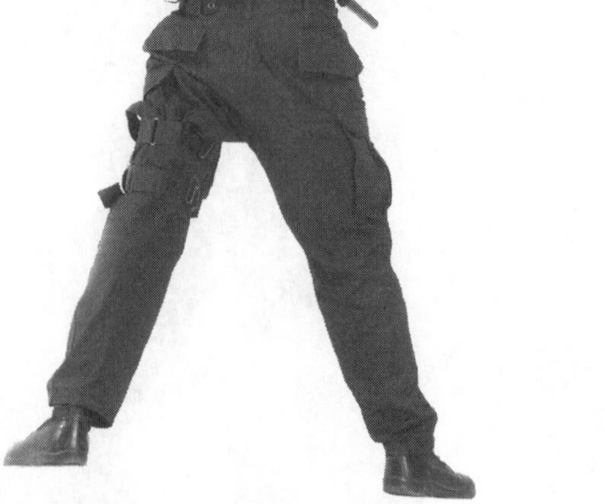

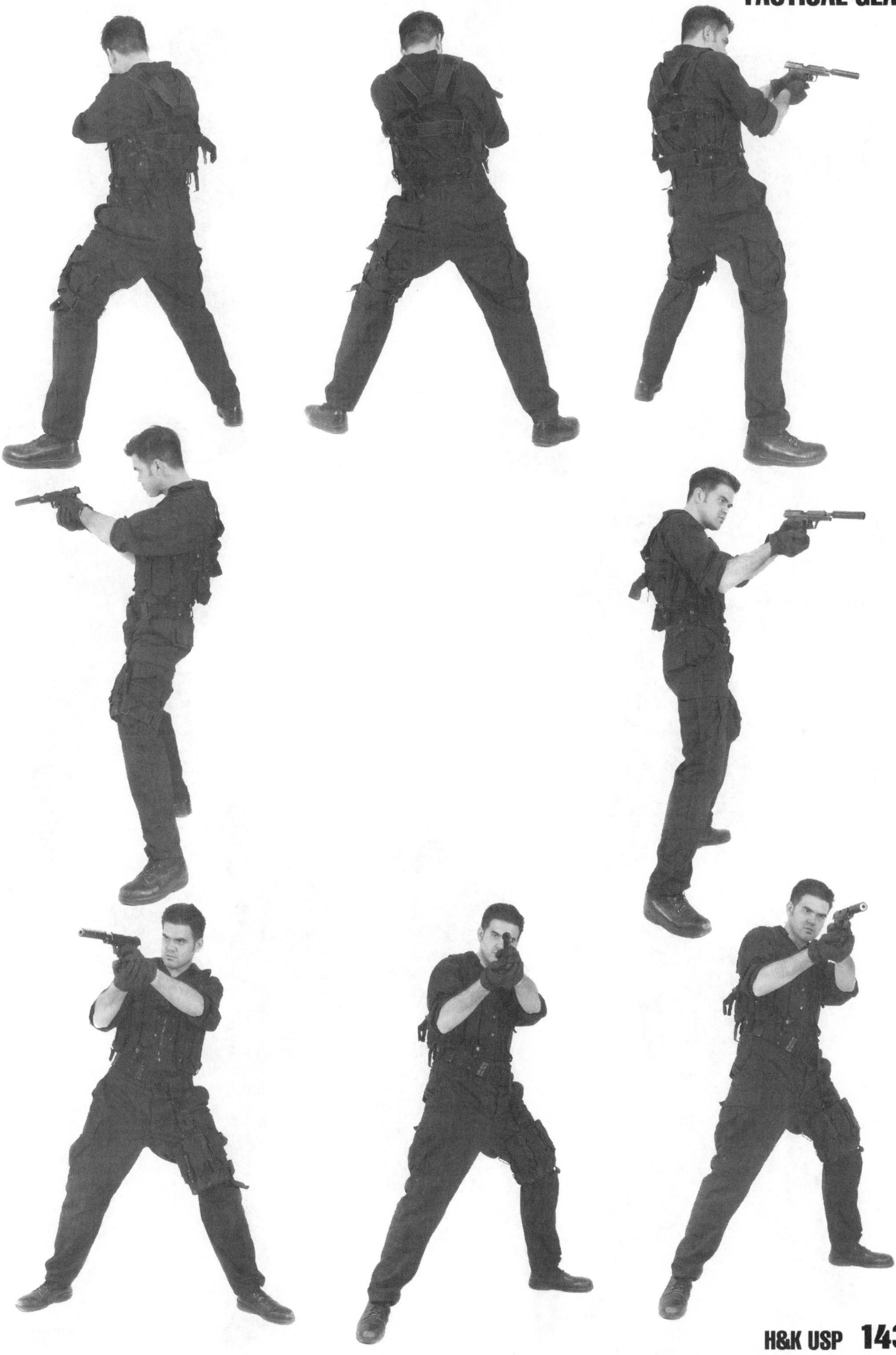

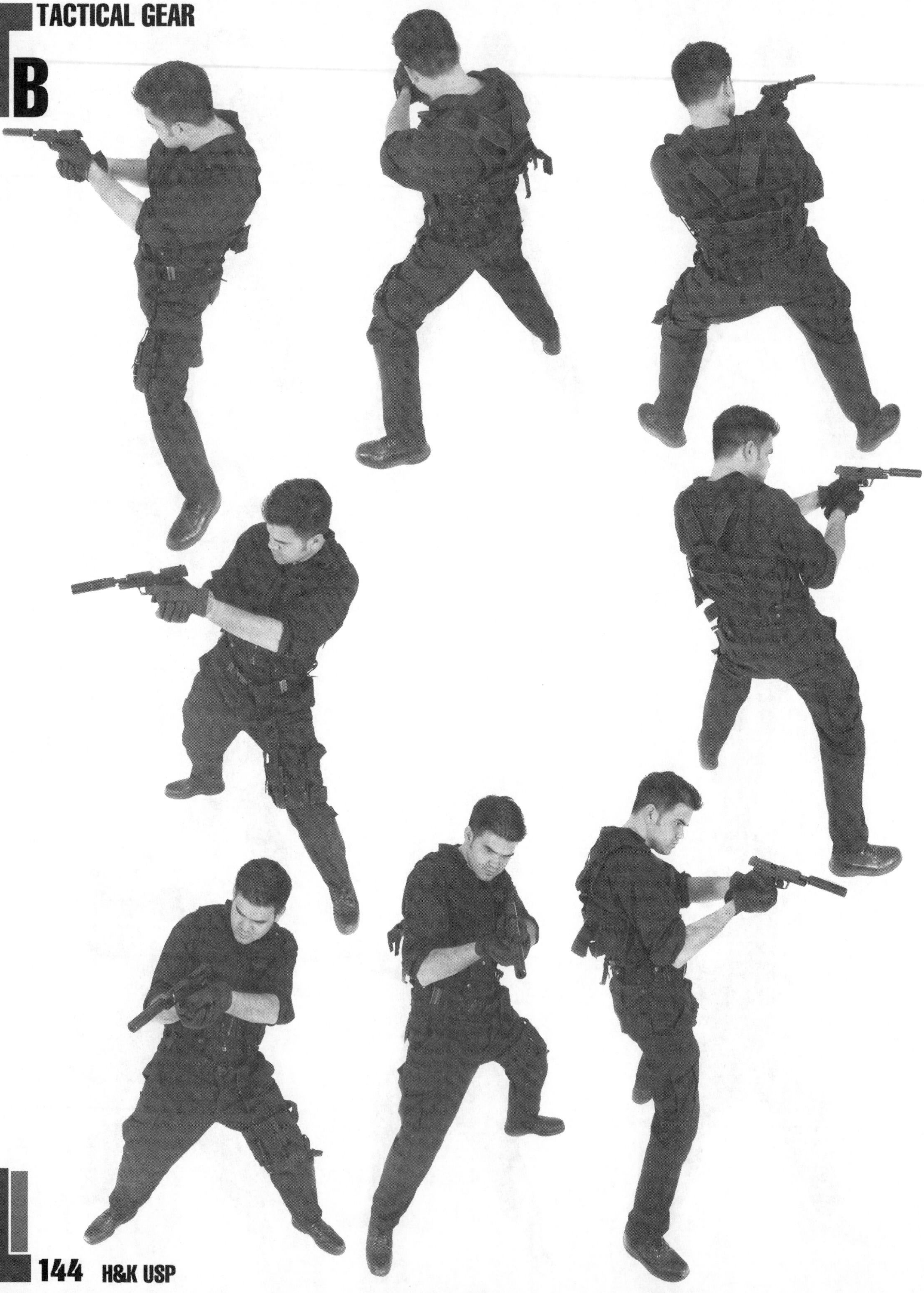

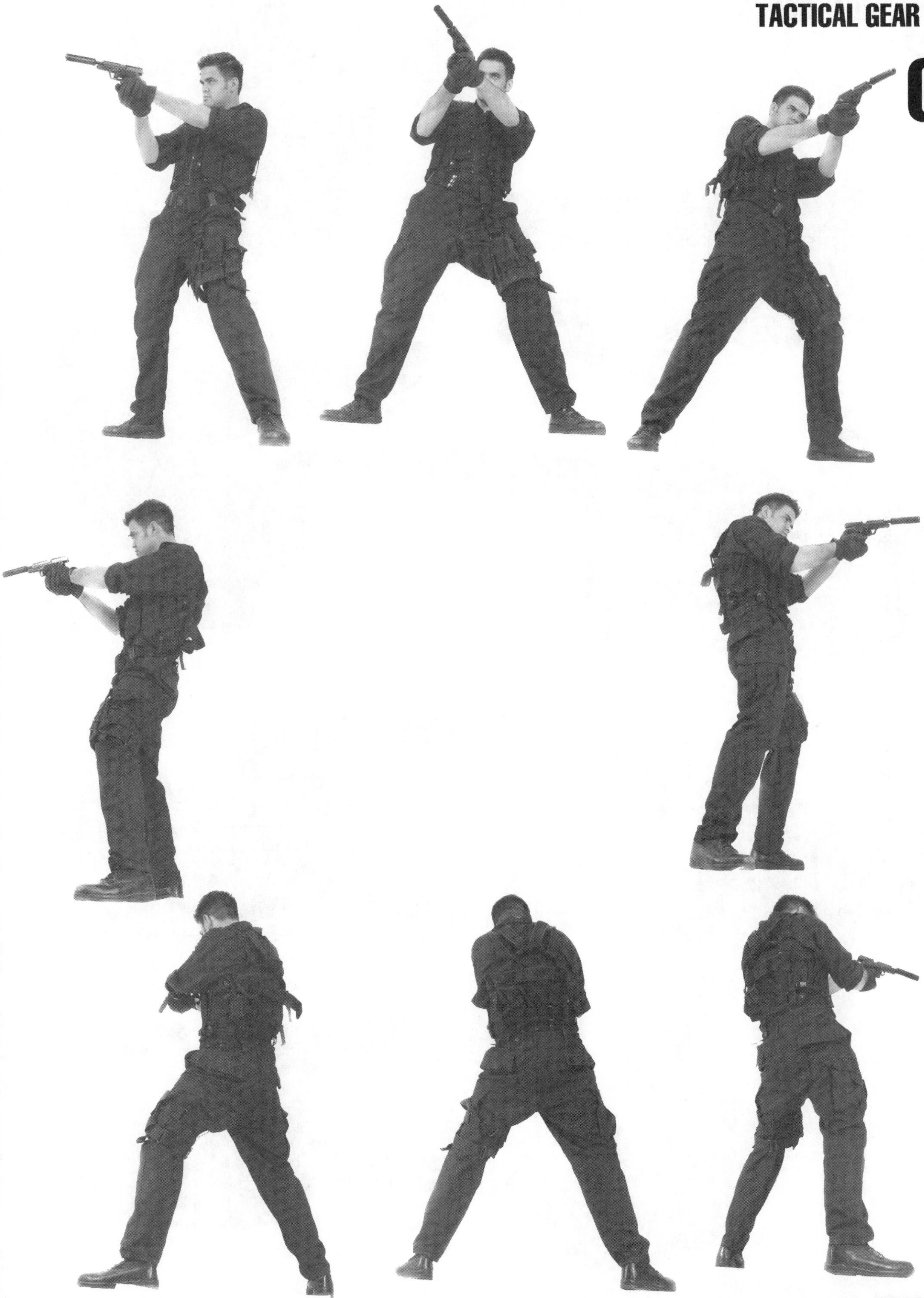

A

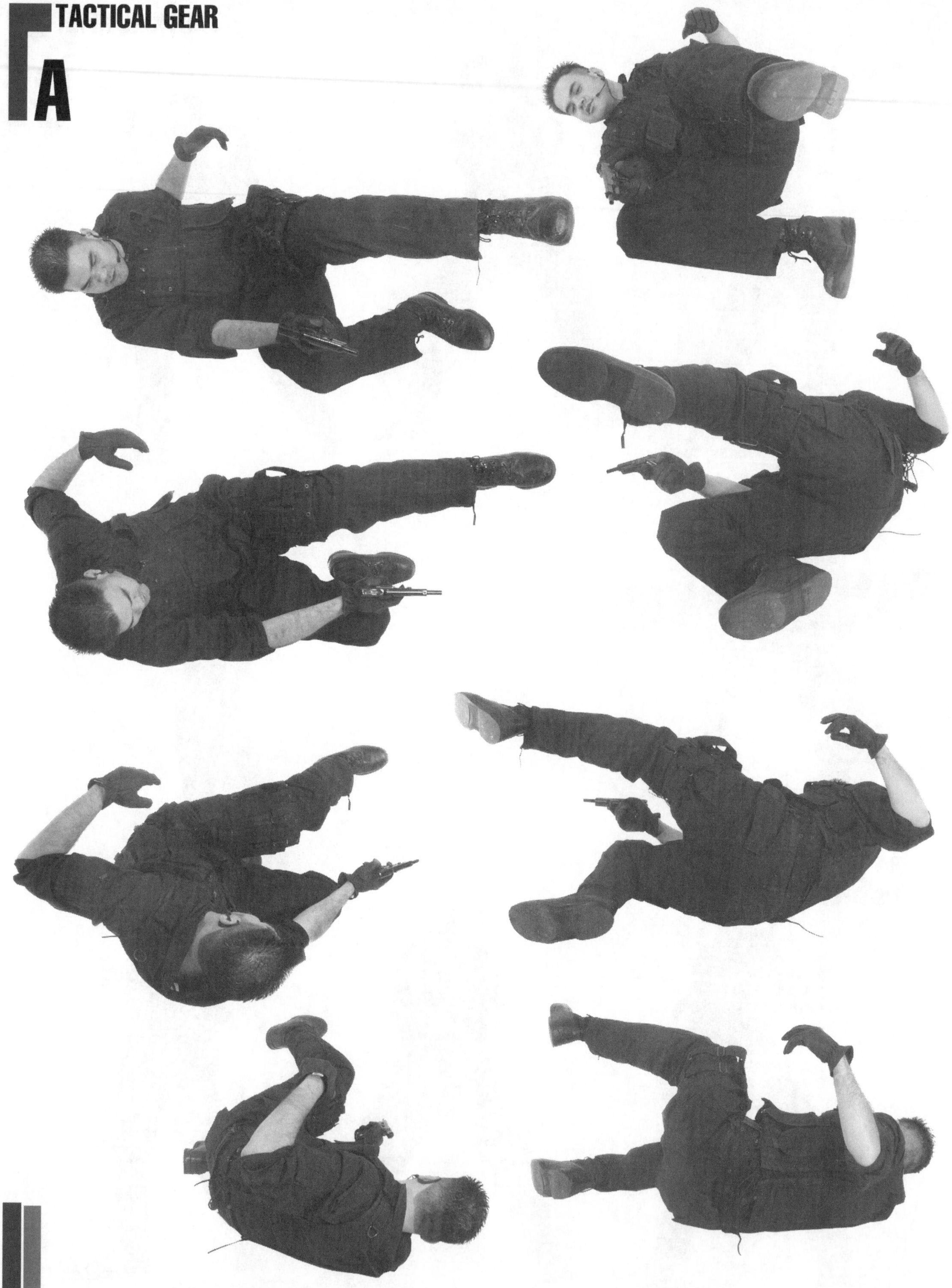

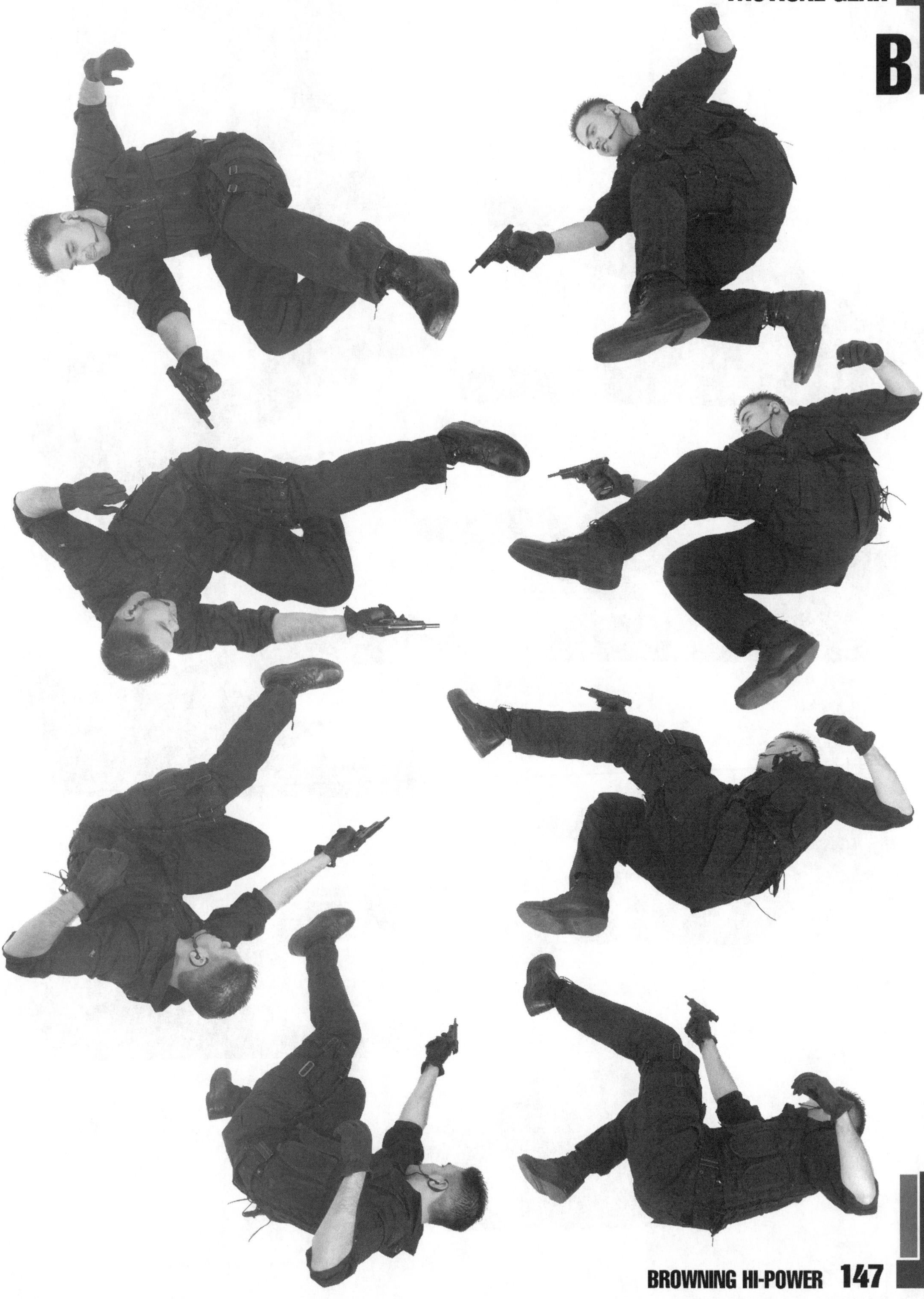

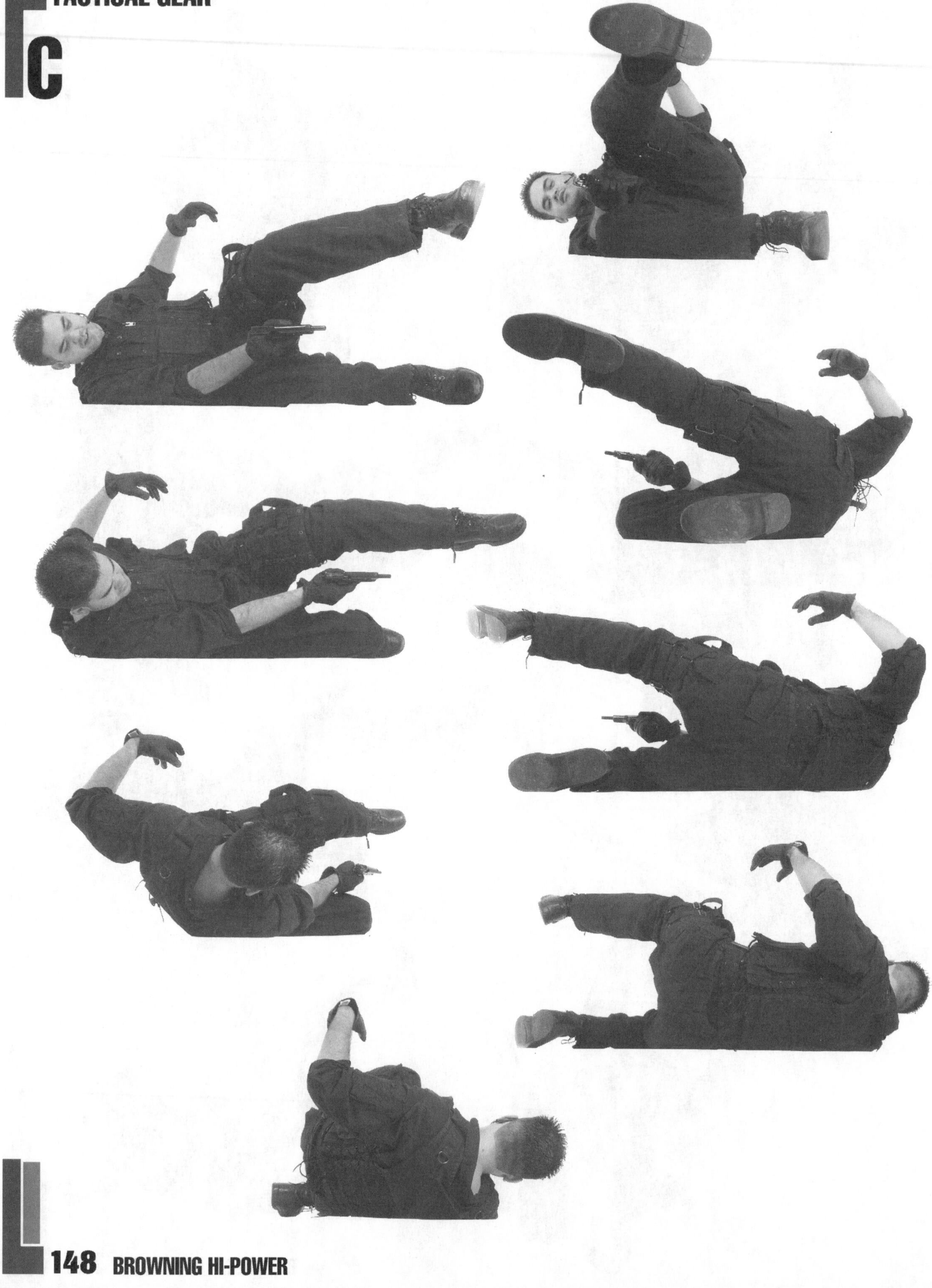

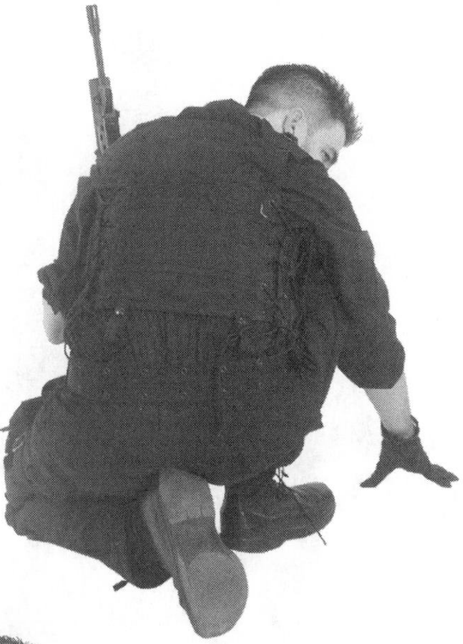
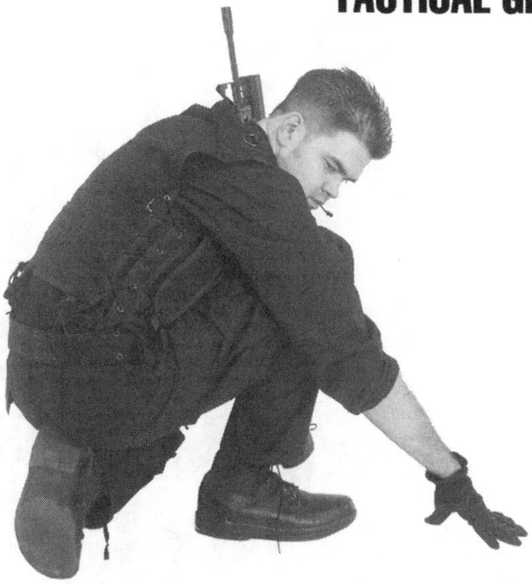
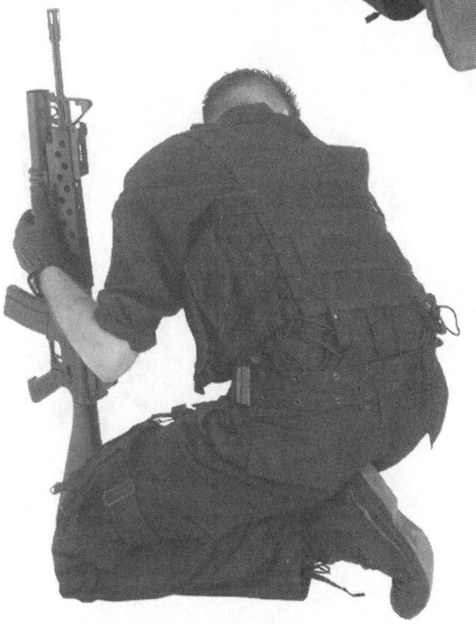
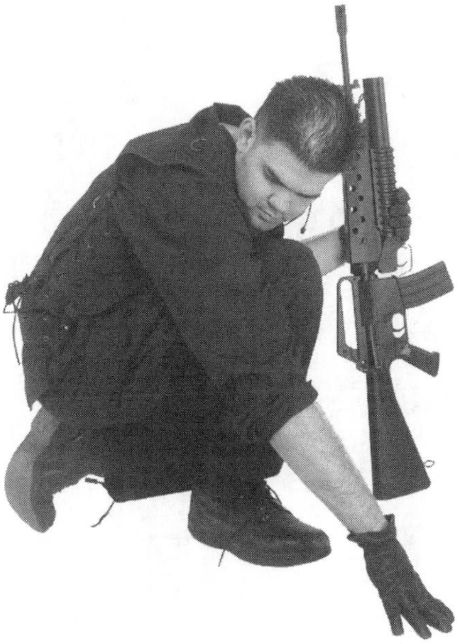
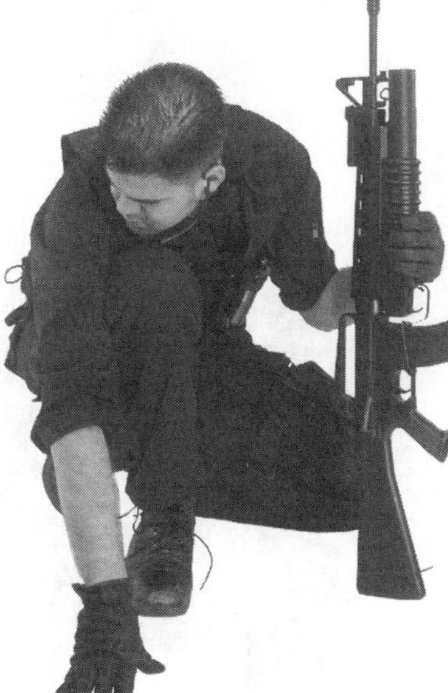
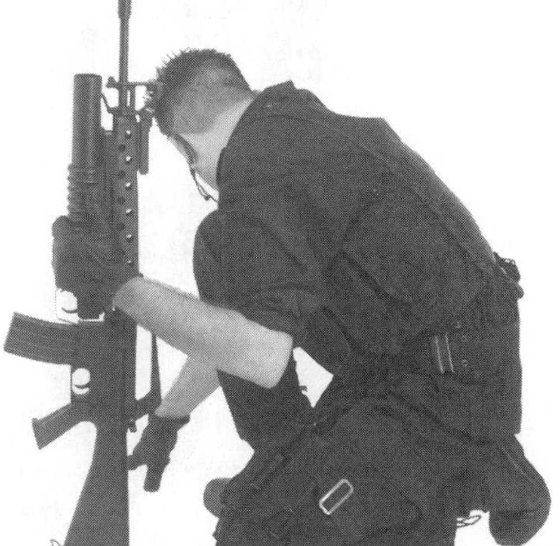
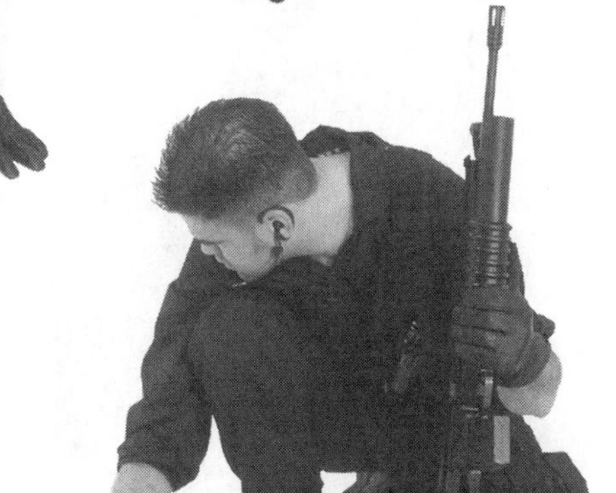
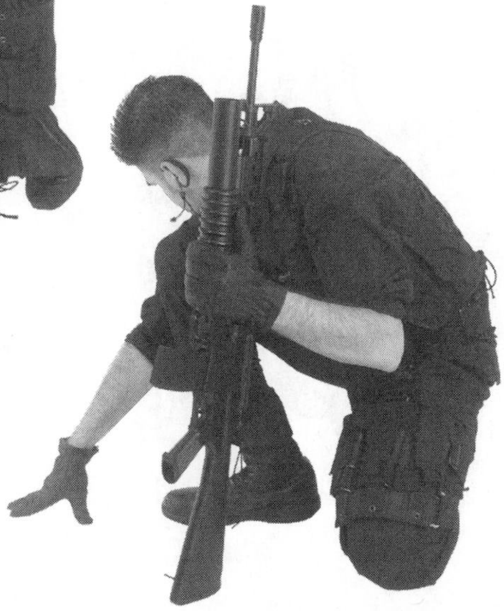

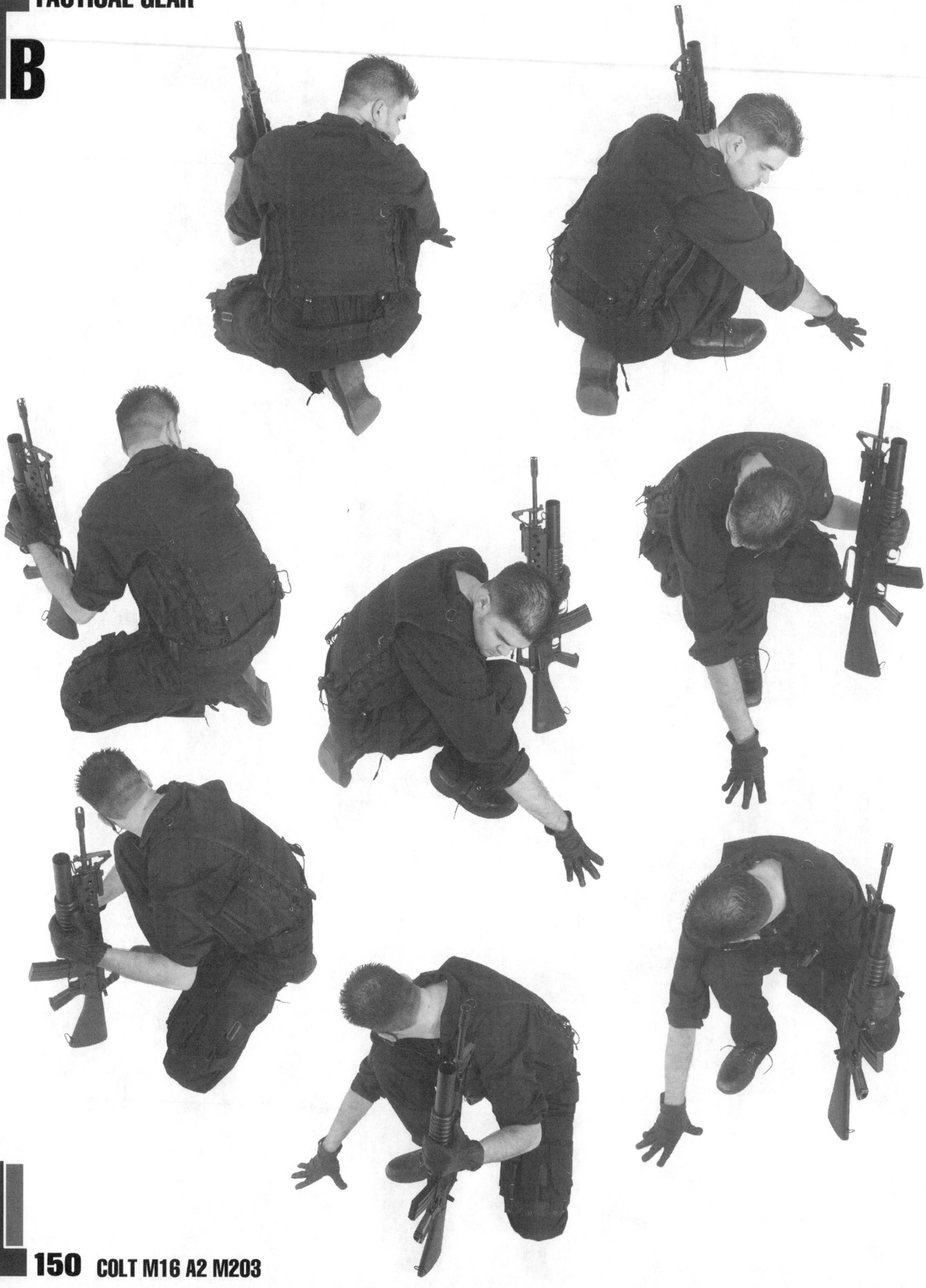

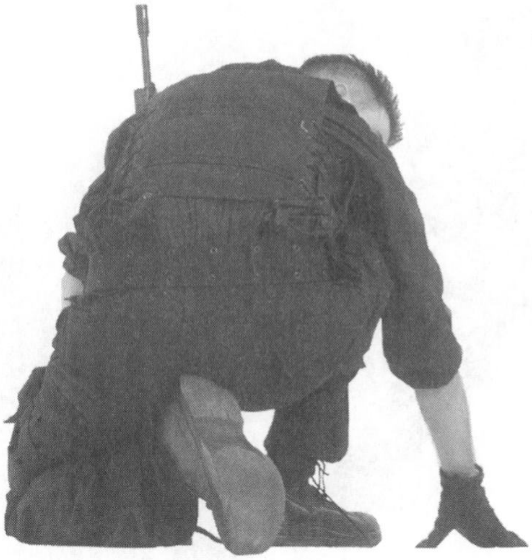

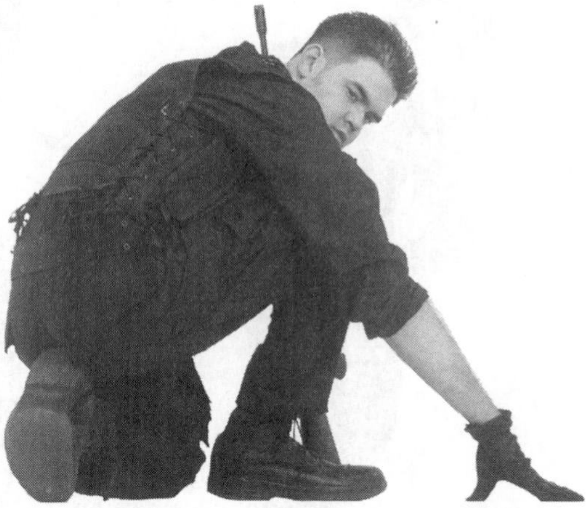

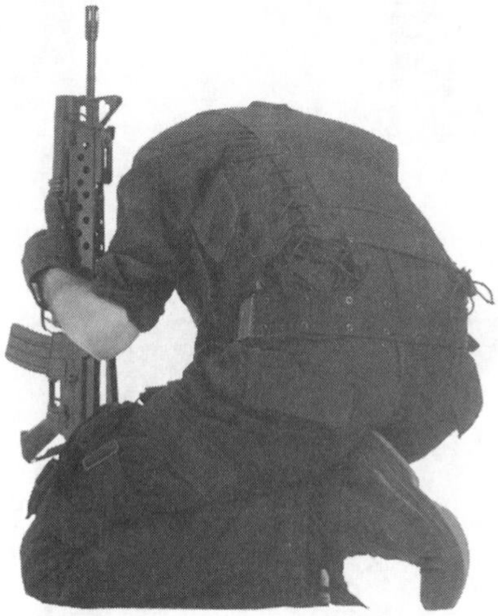

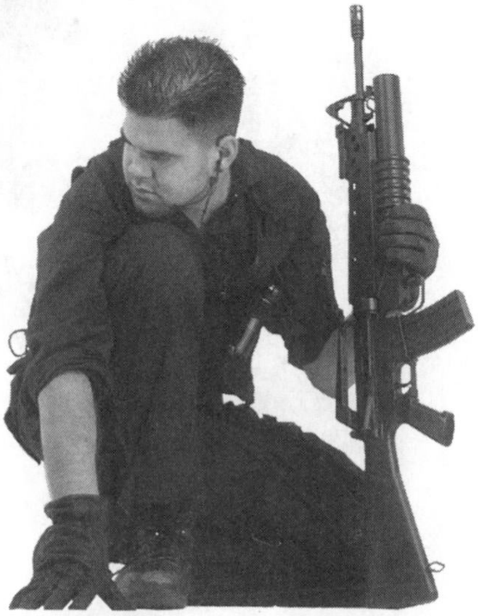

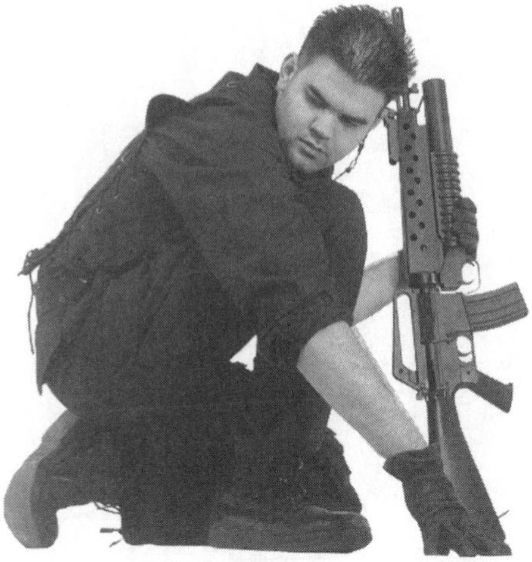

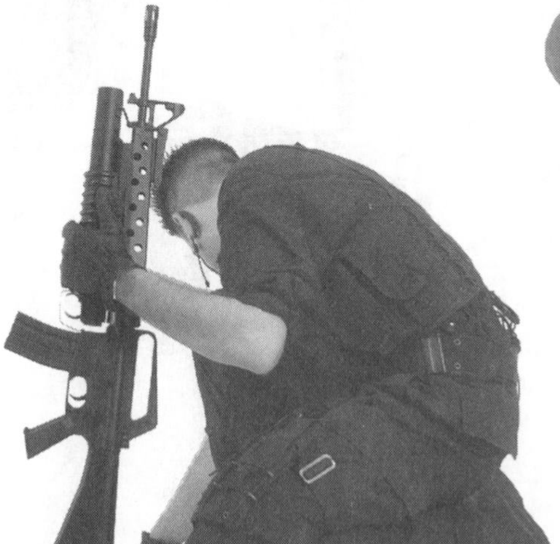

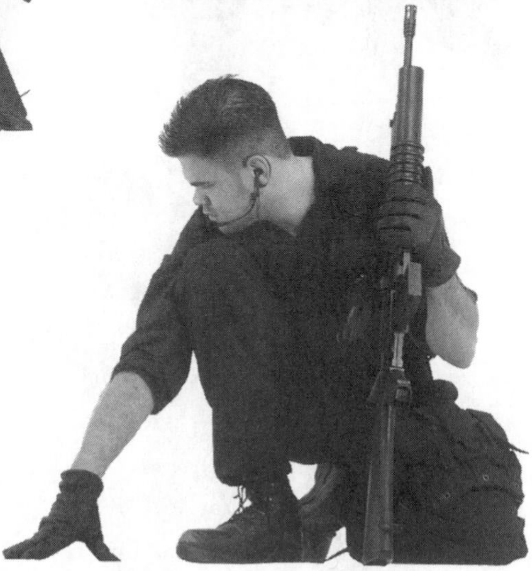

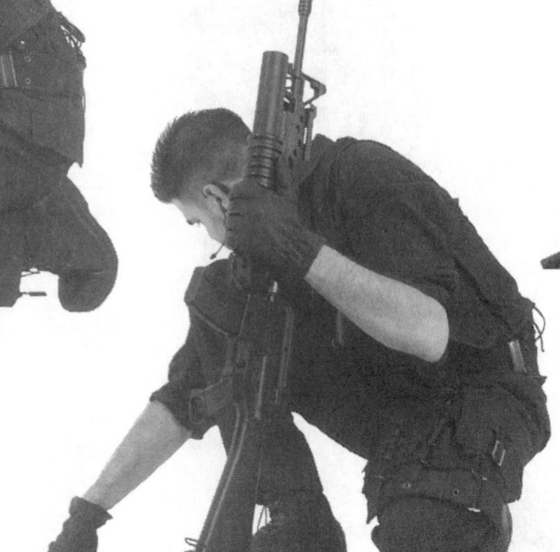

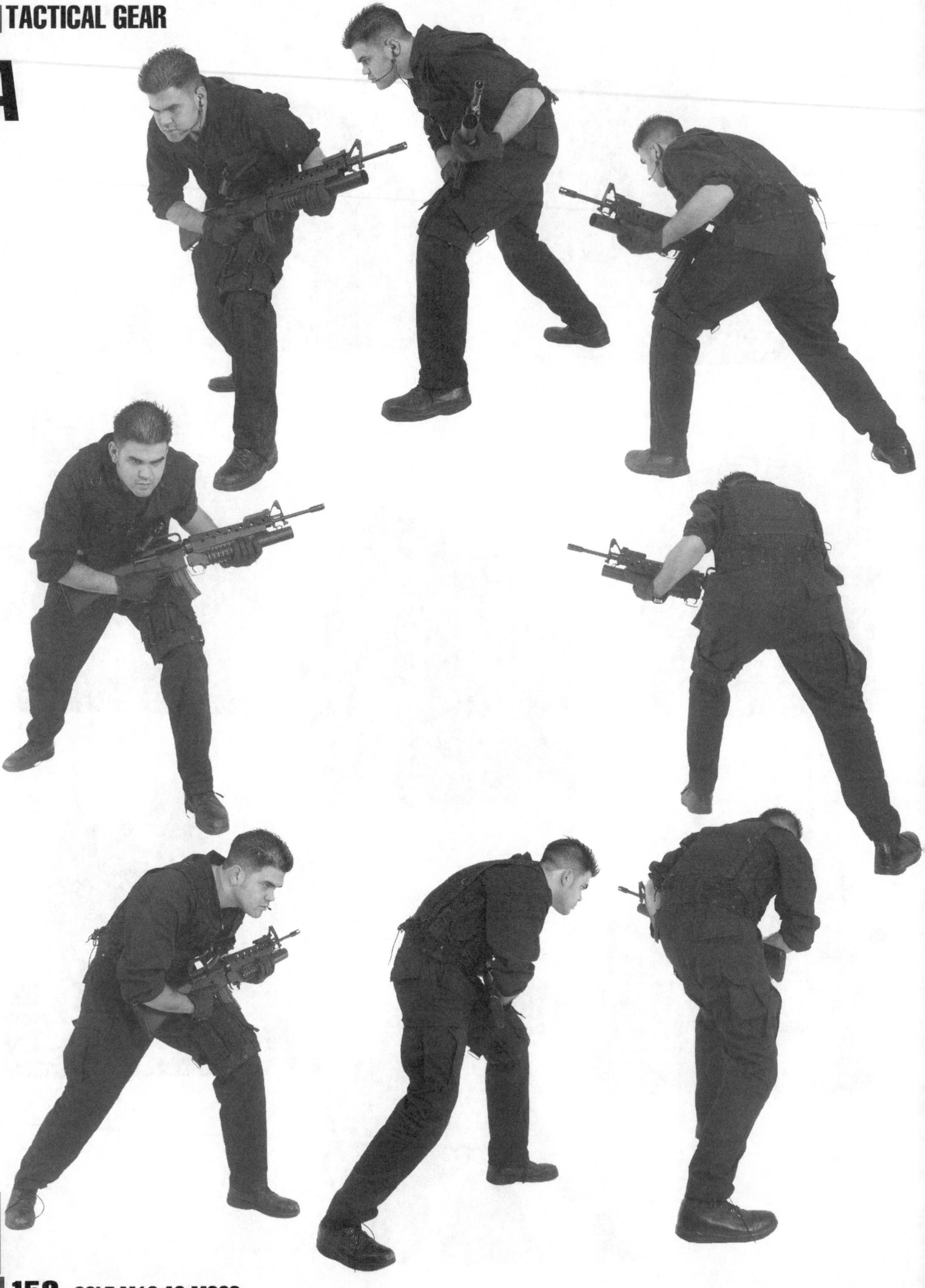

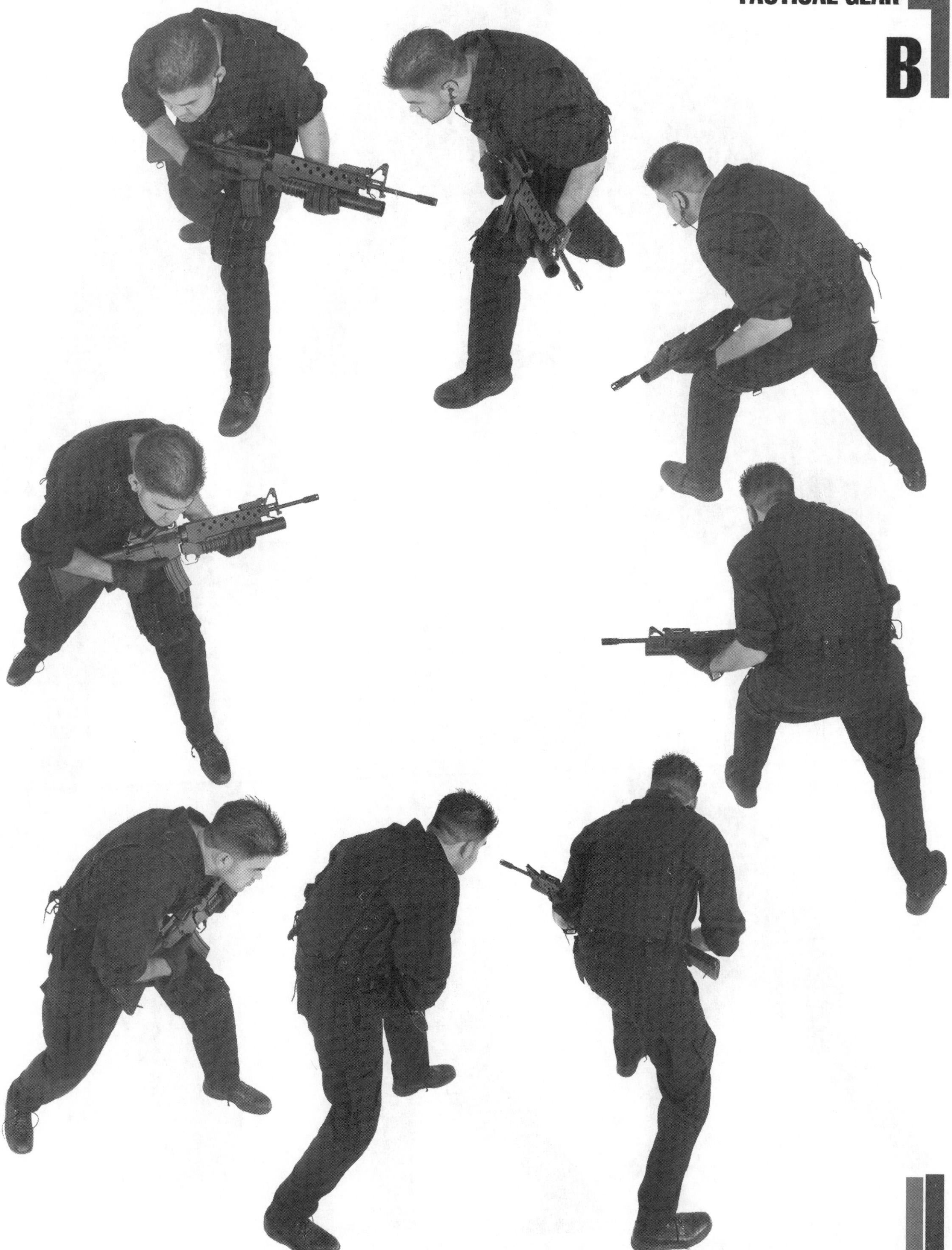

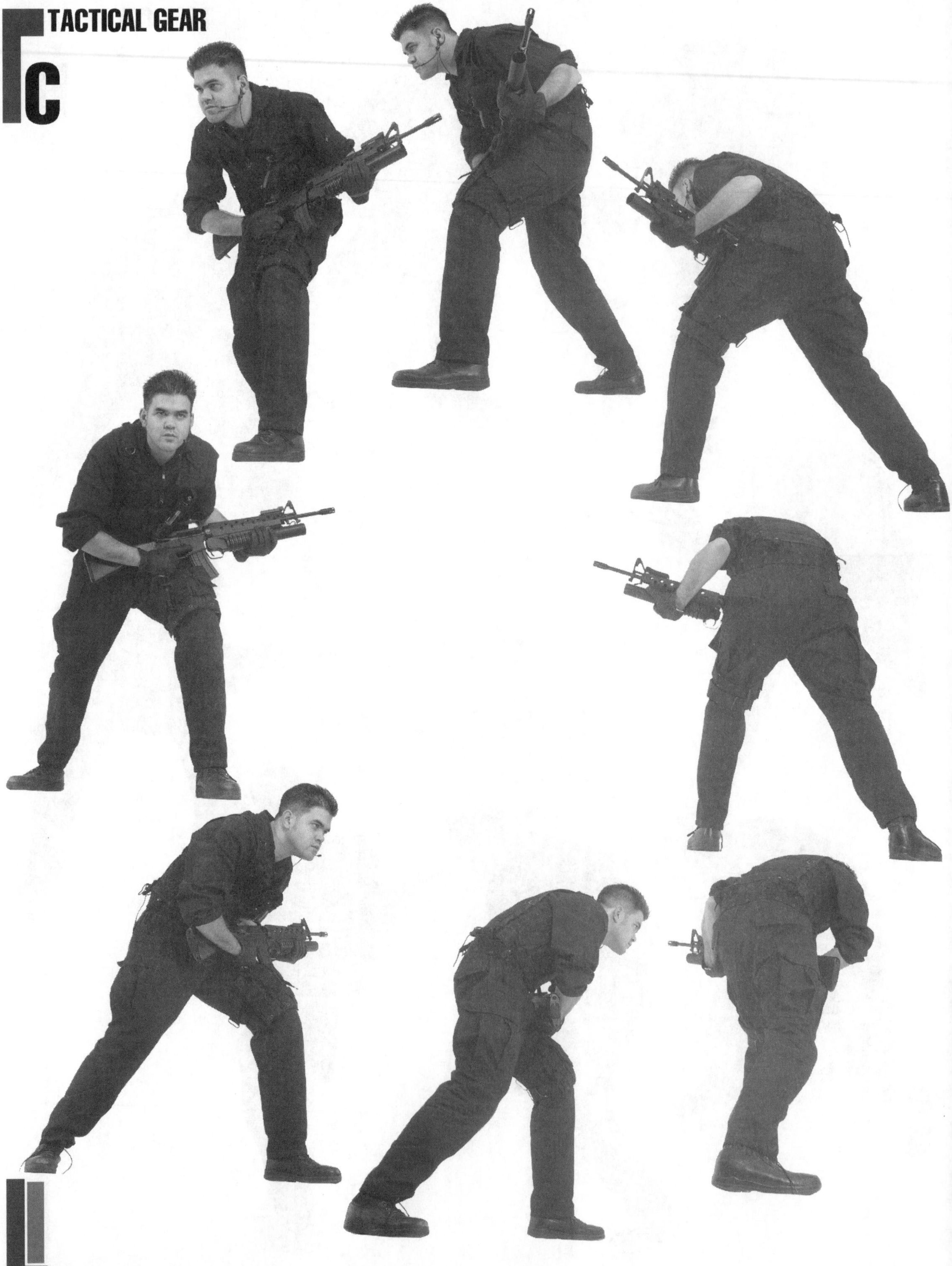

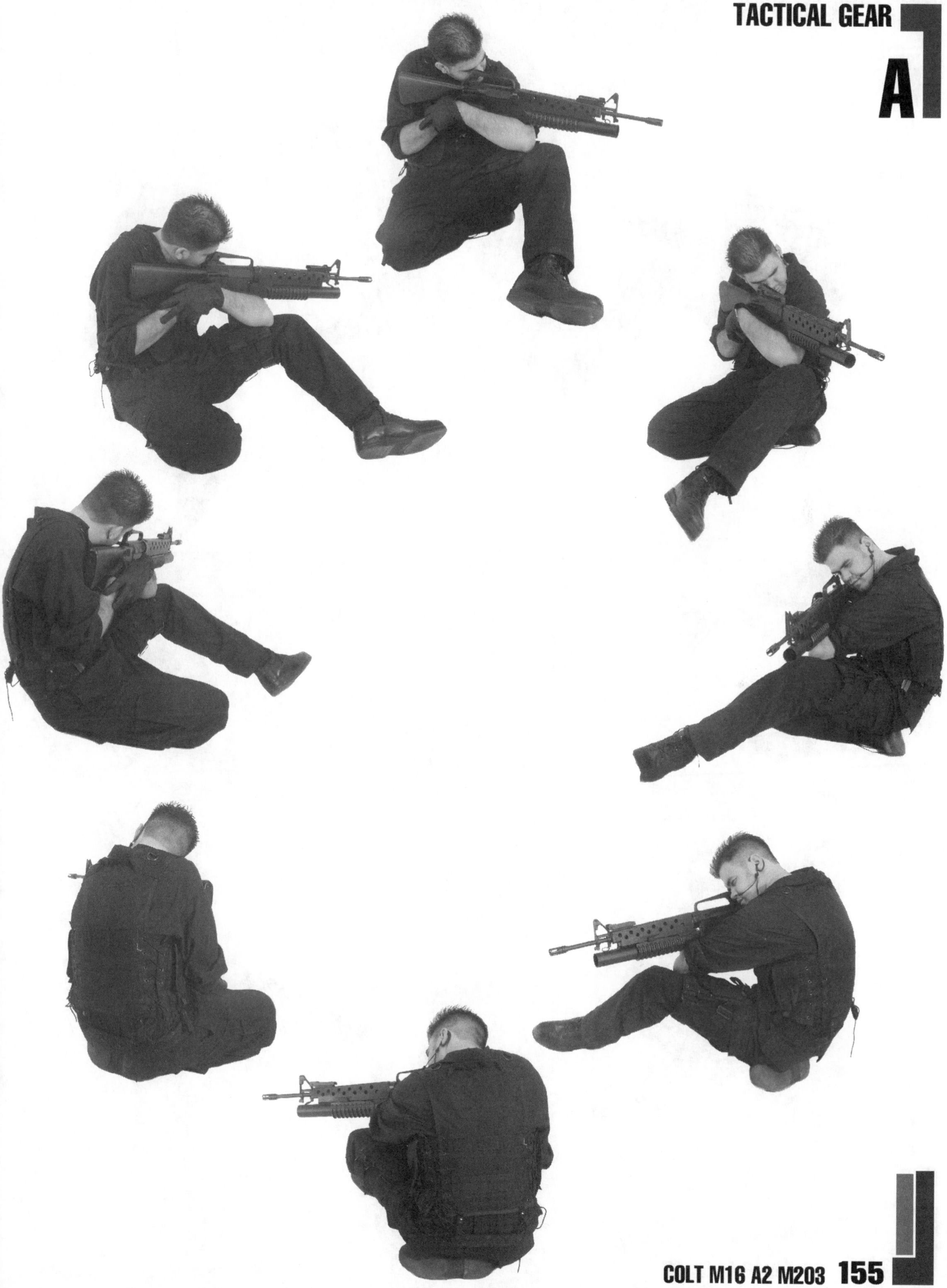

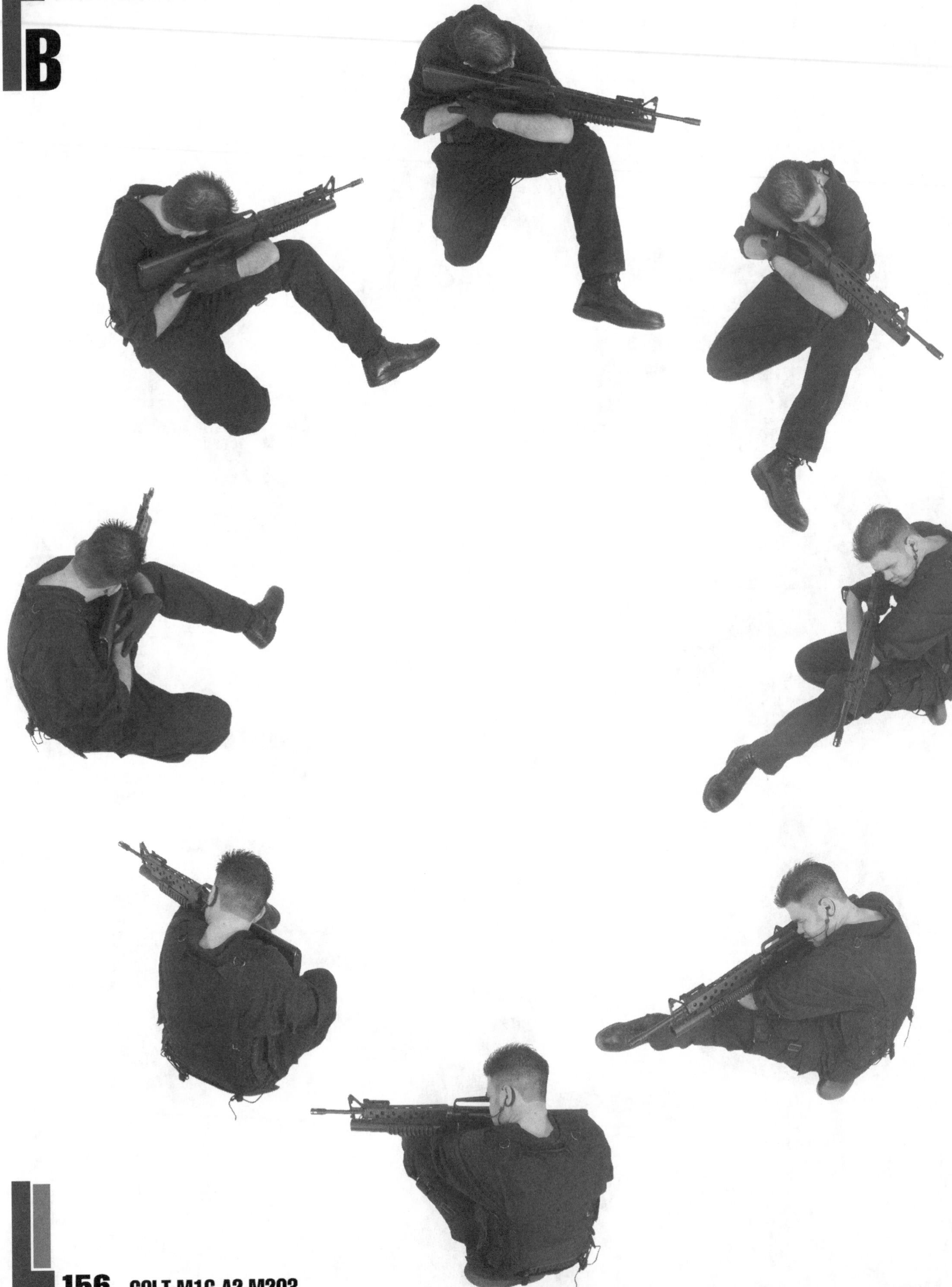

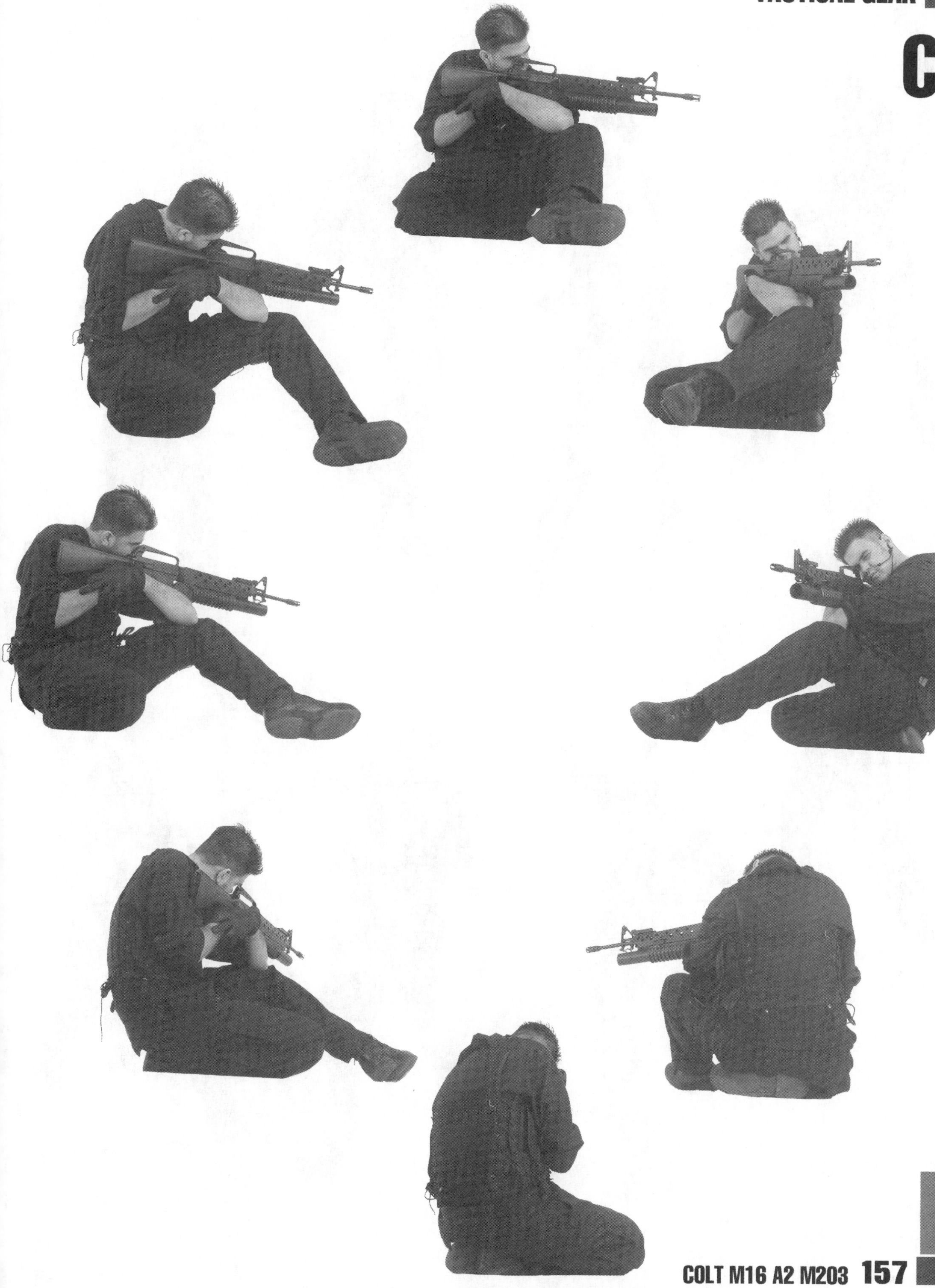

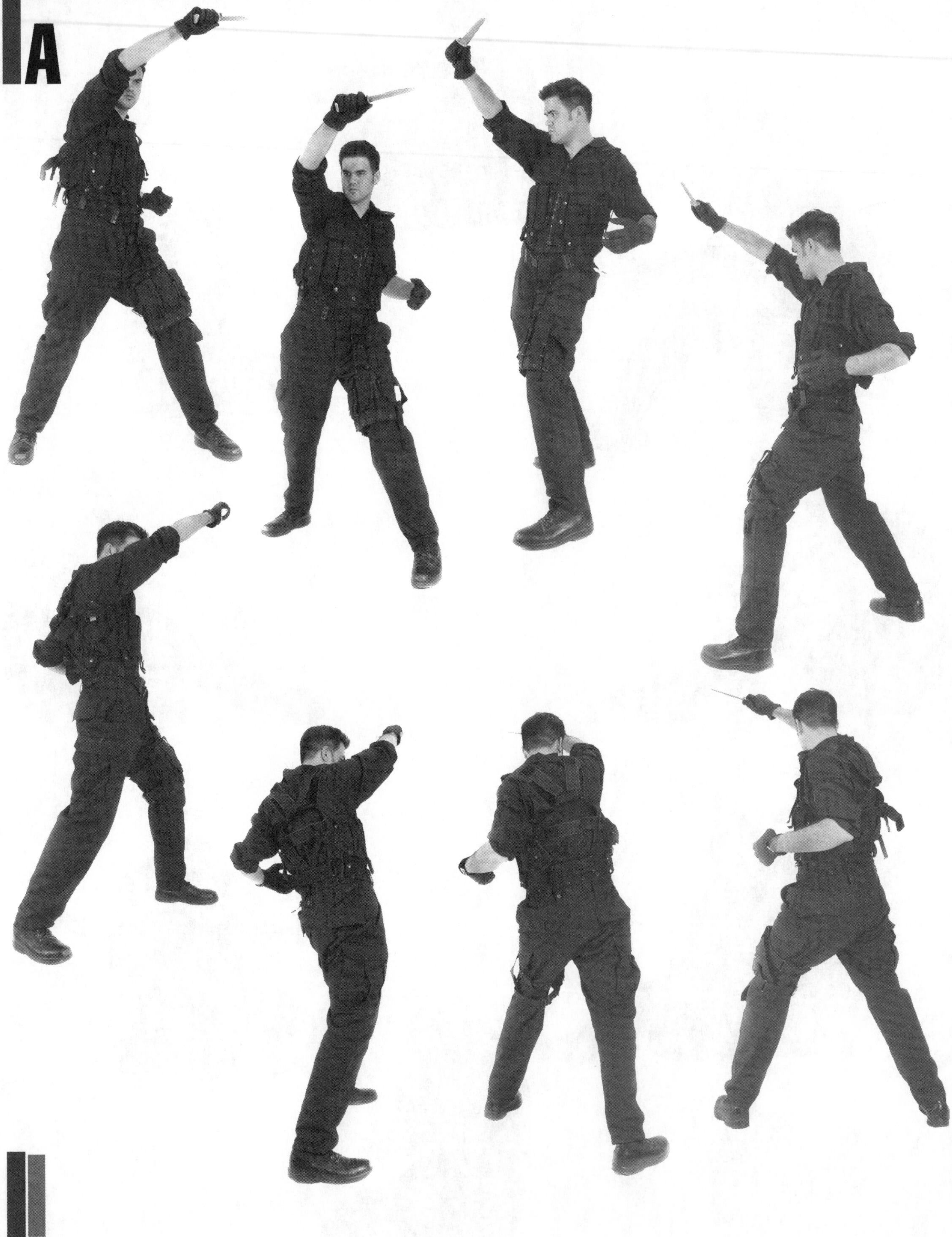

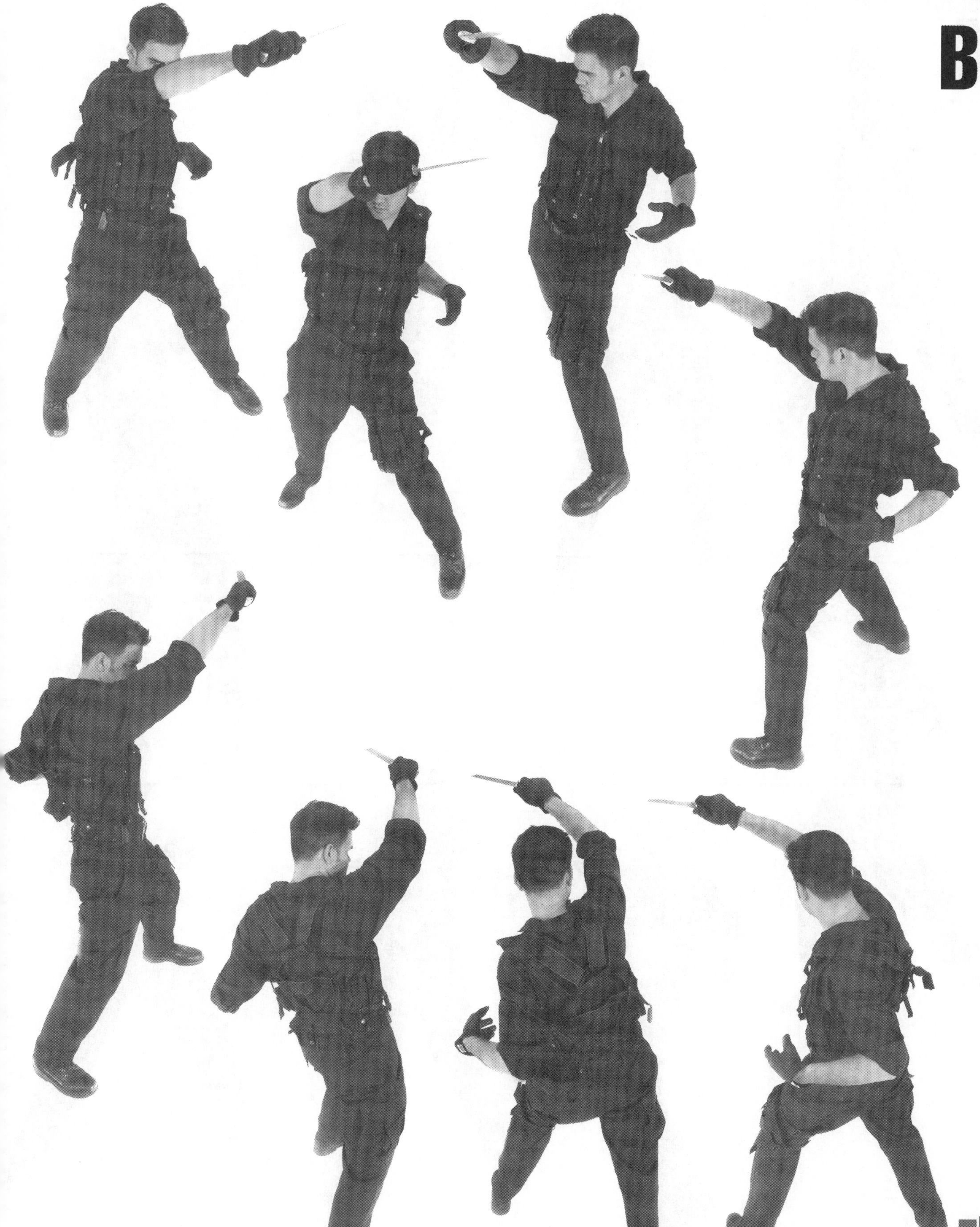

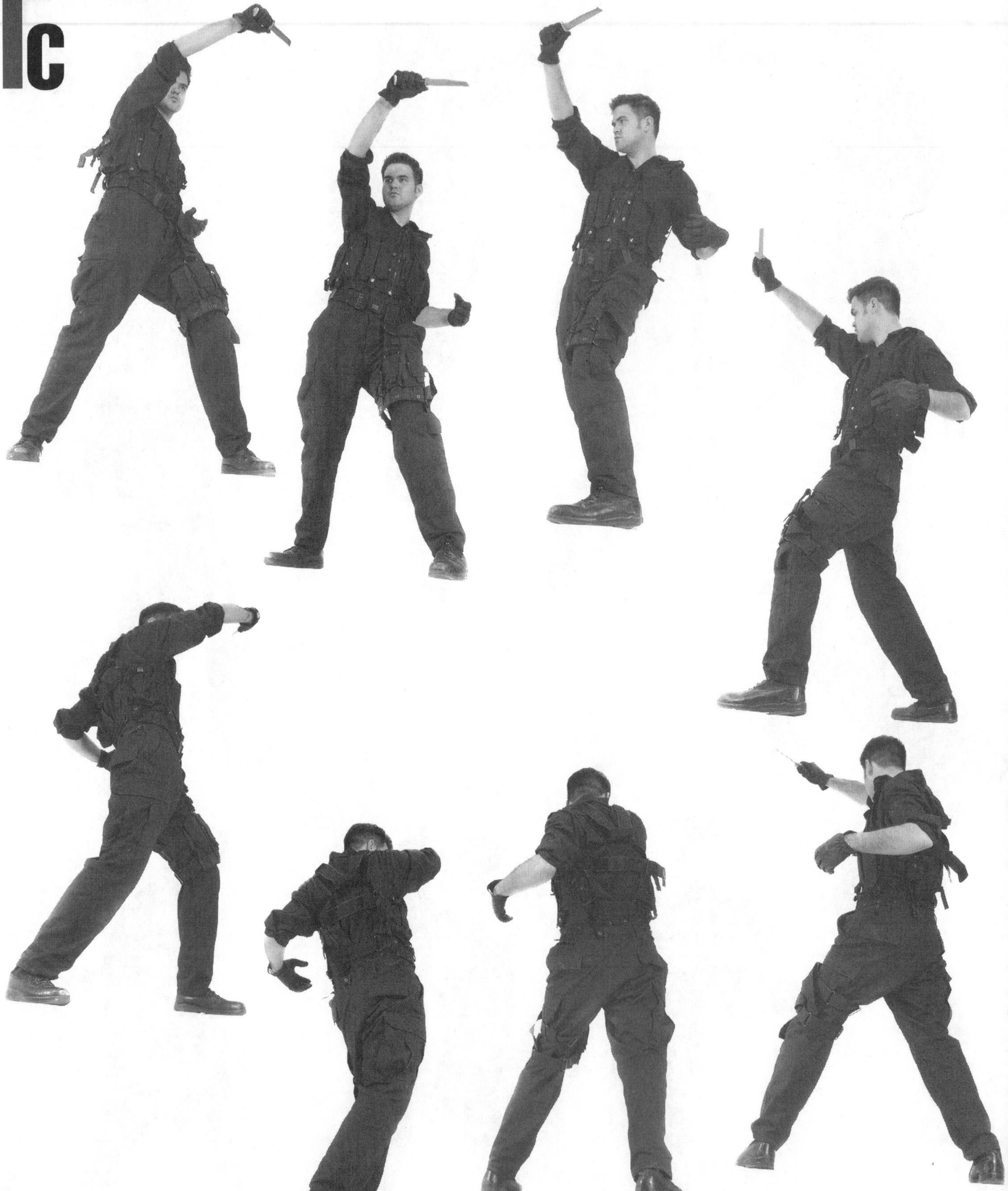

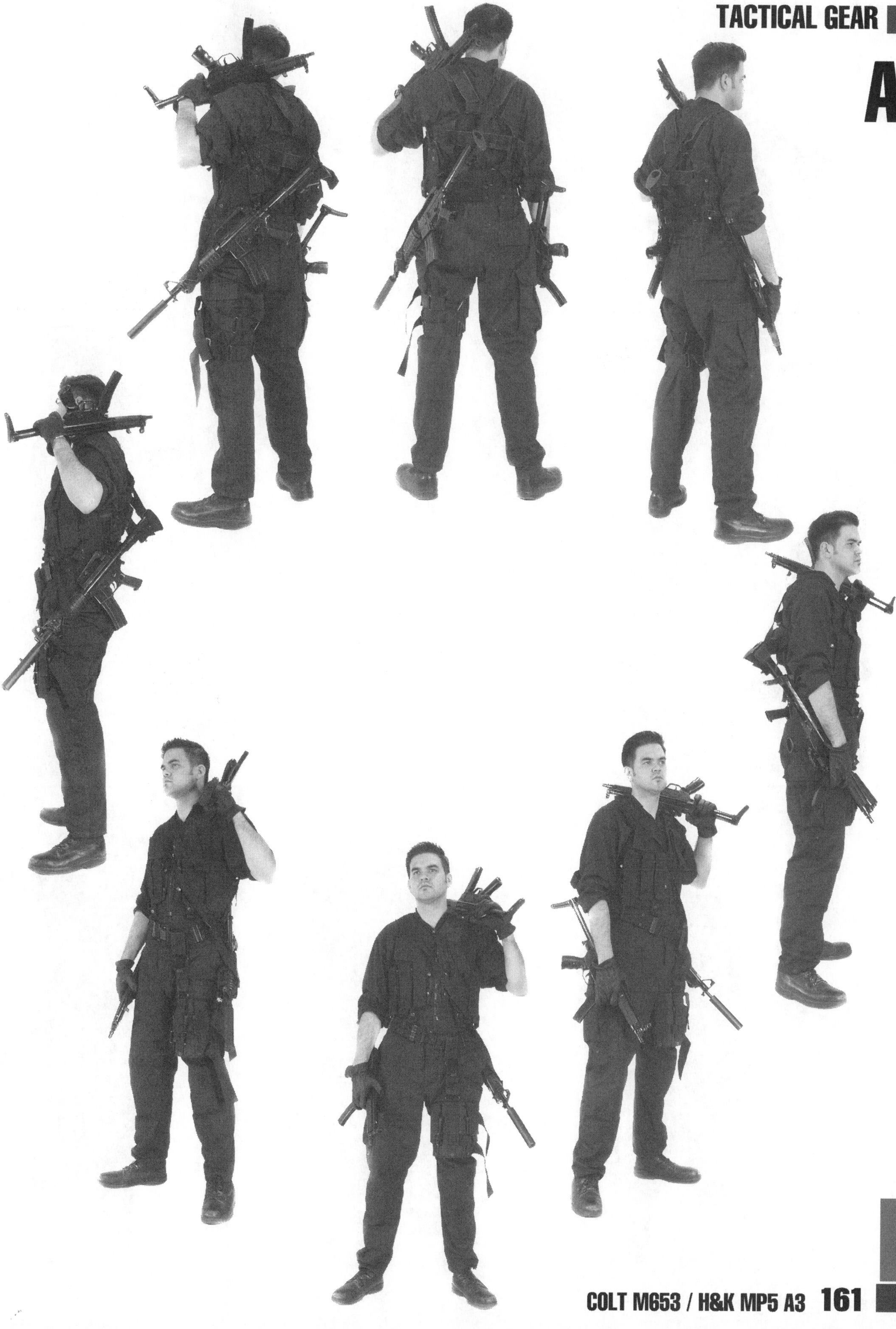

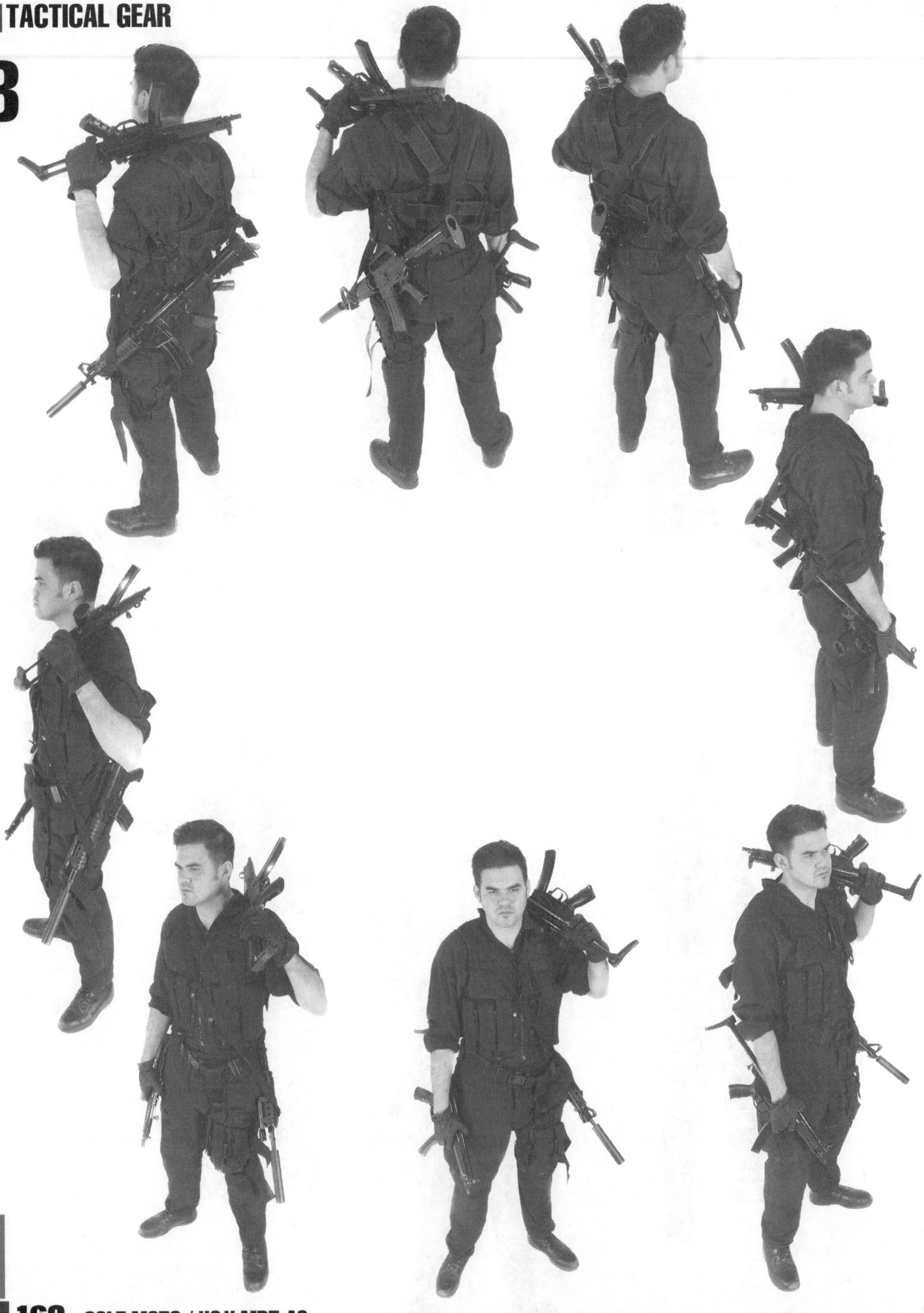

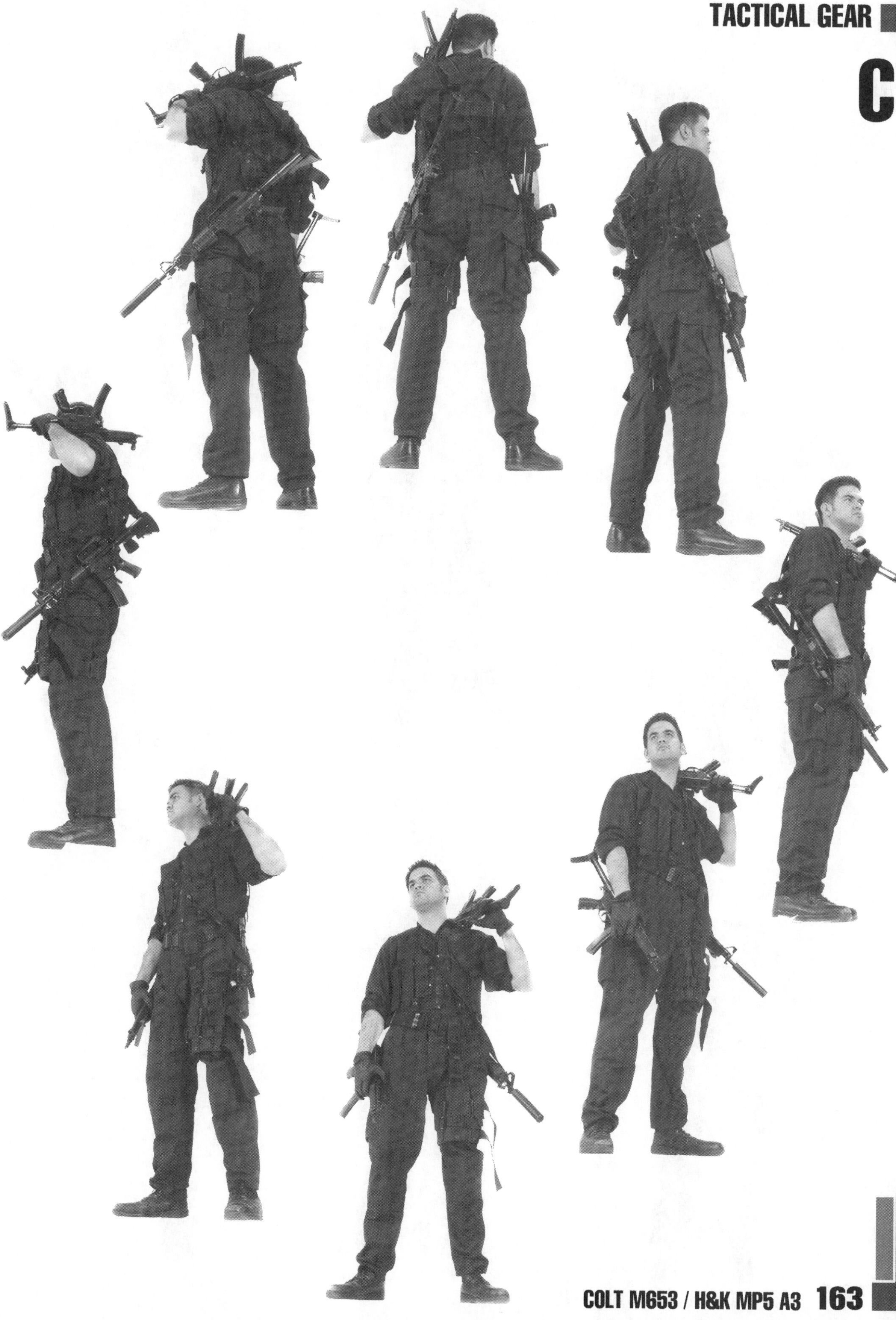

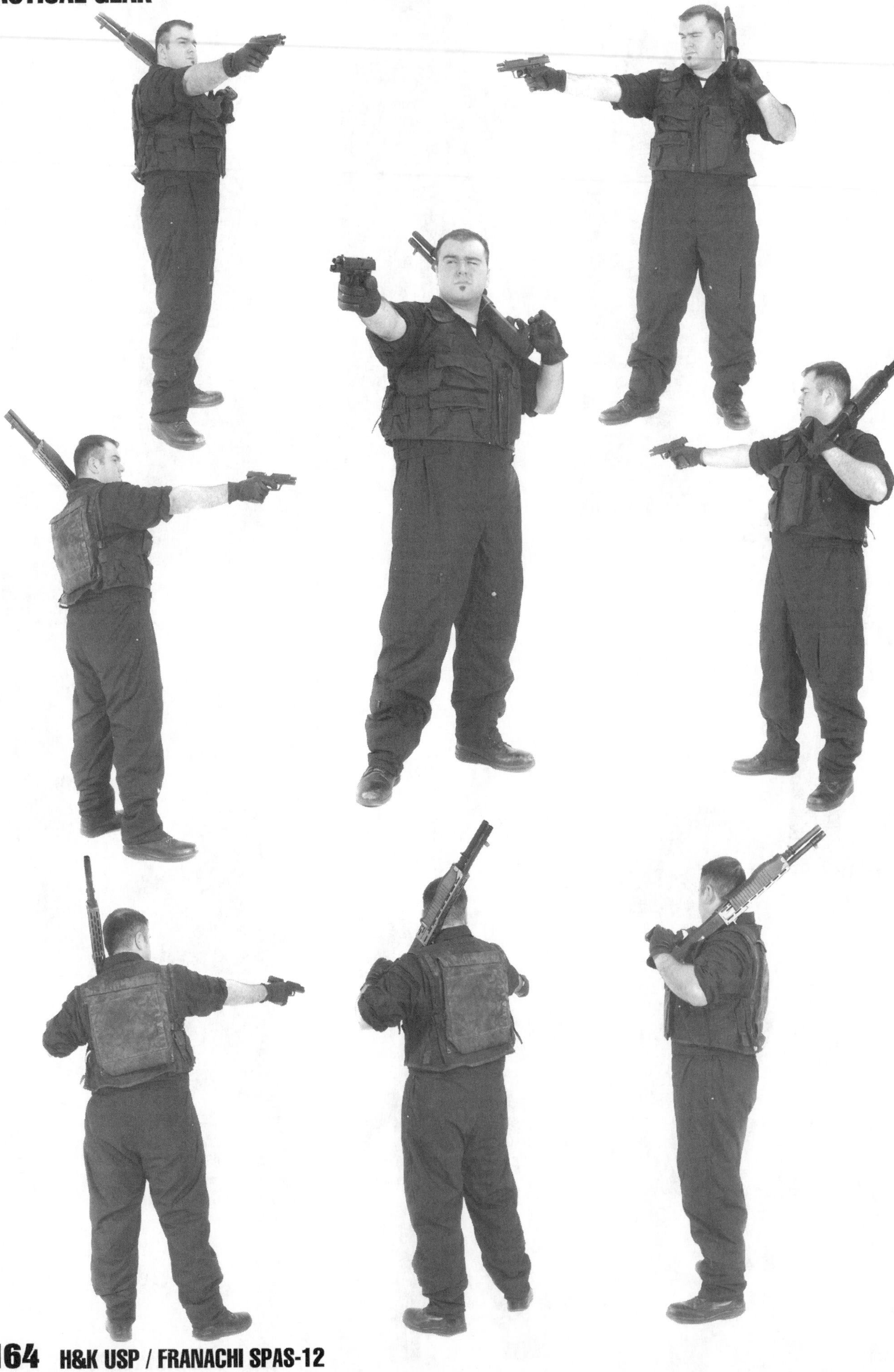

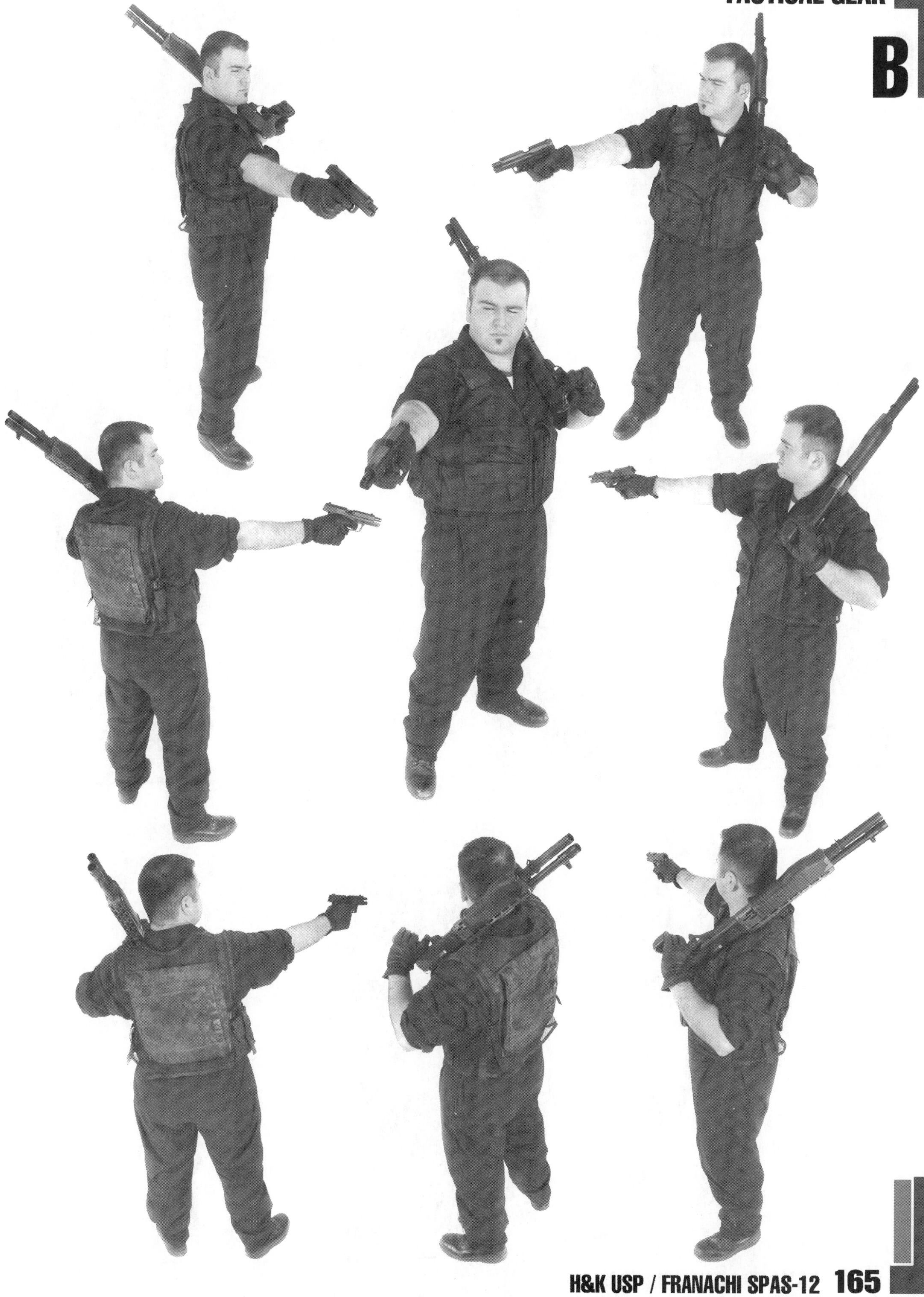

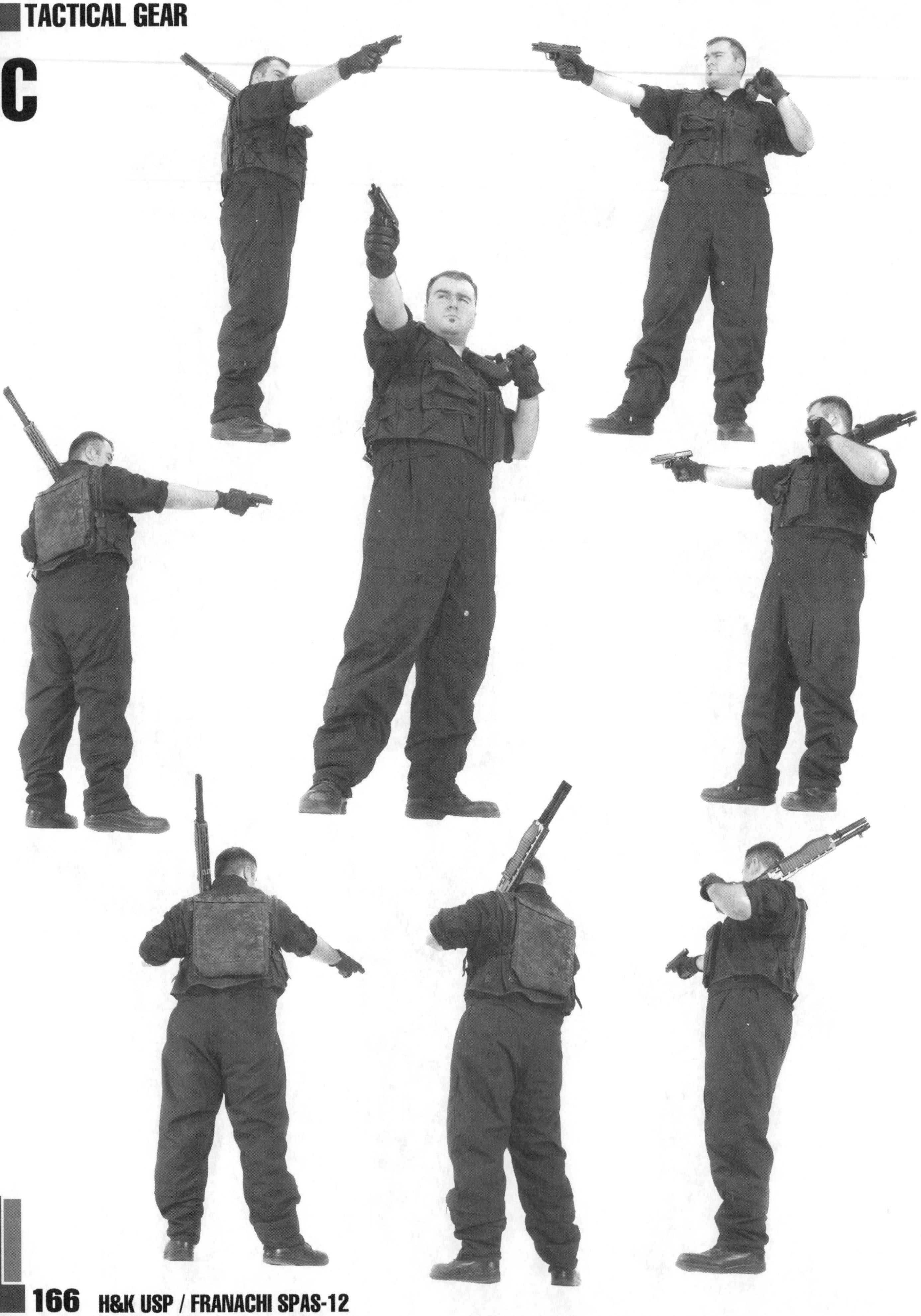

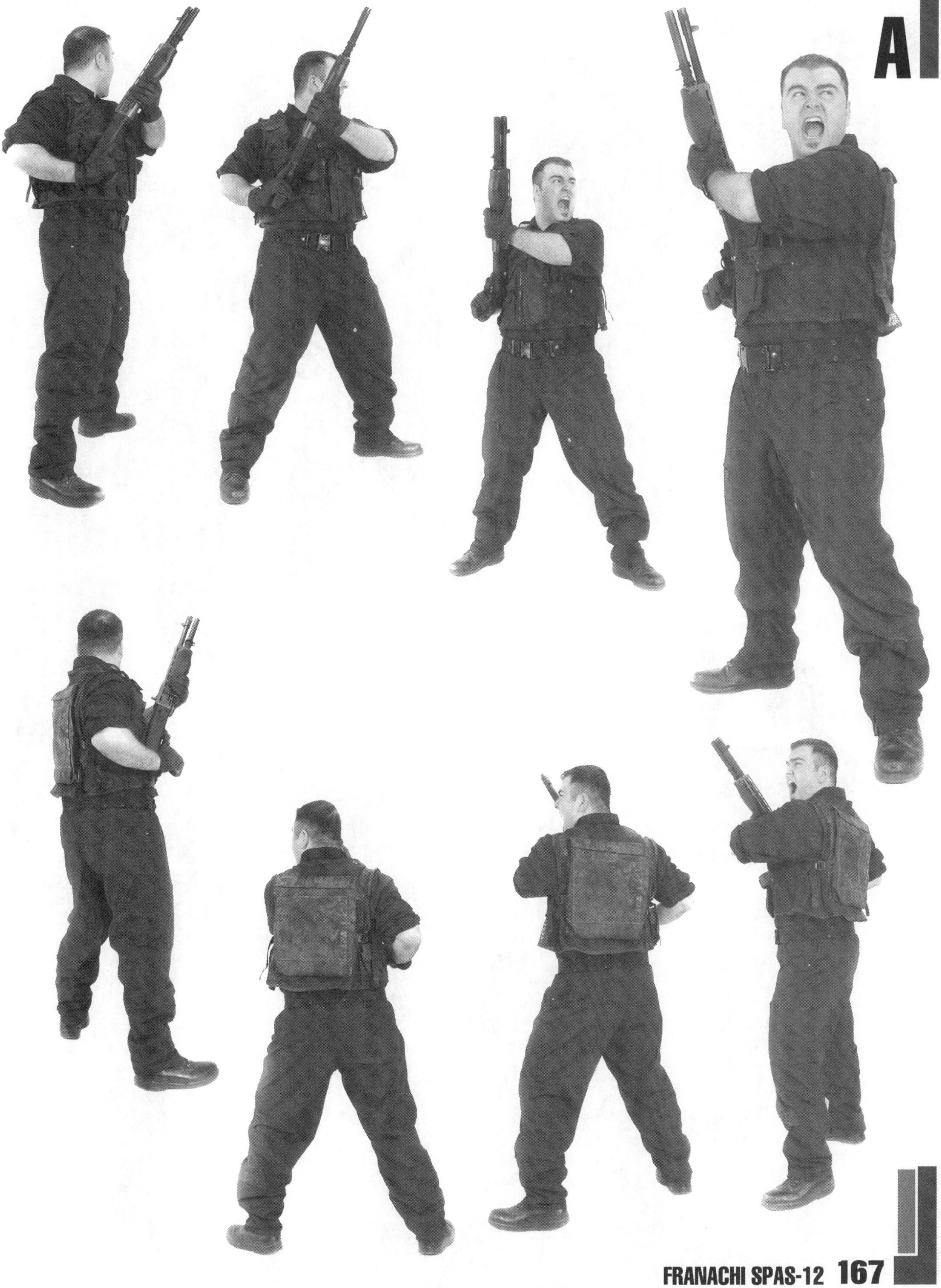

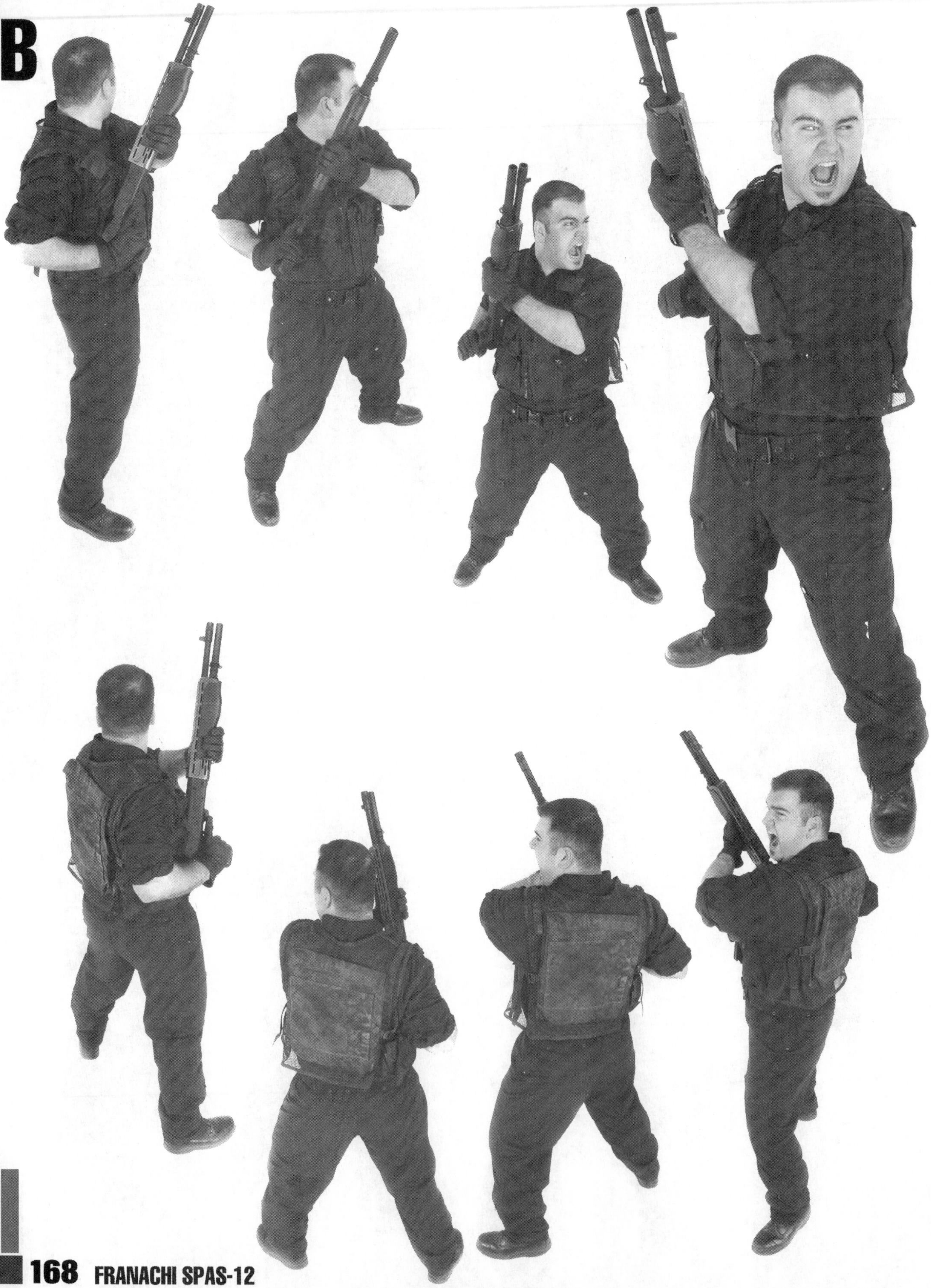

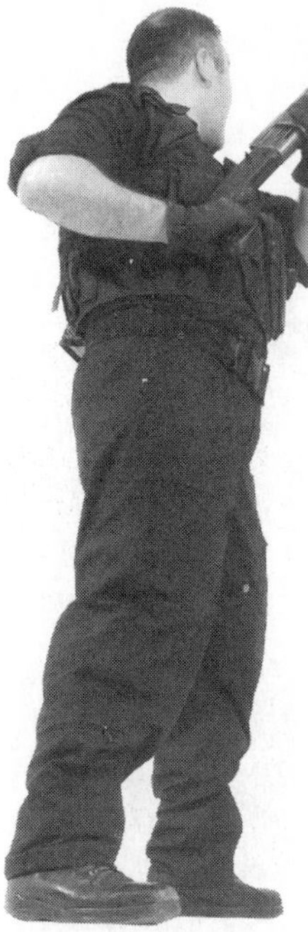
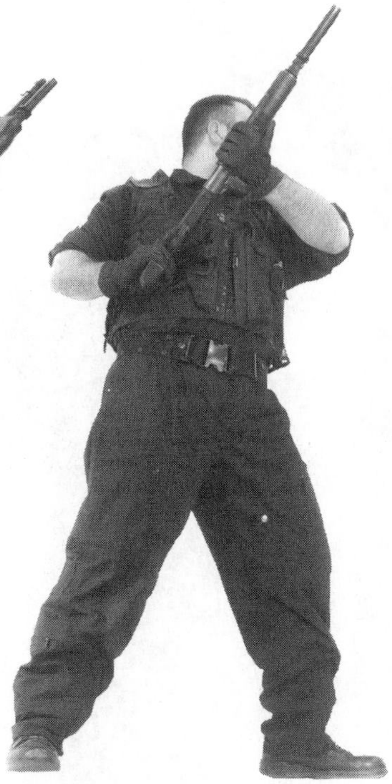
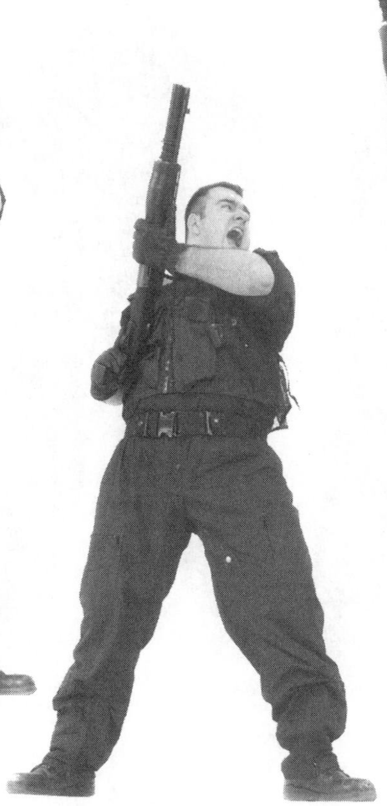
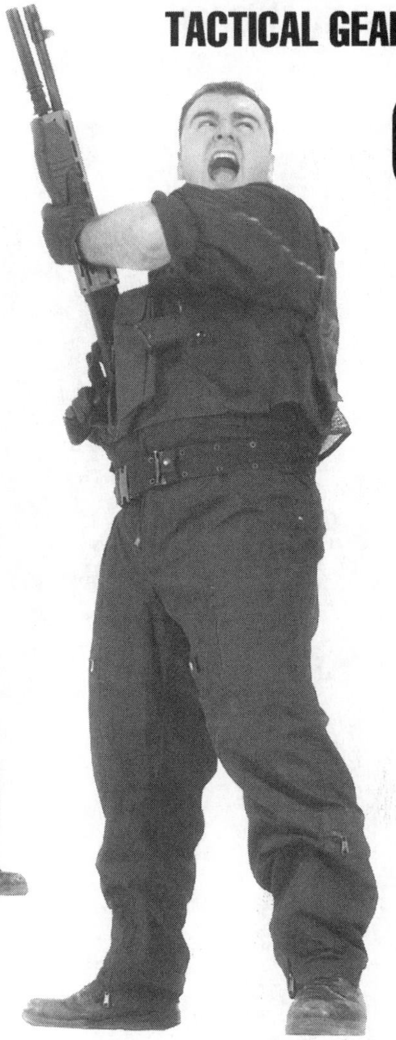
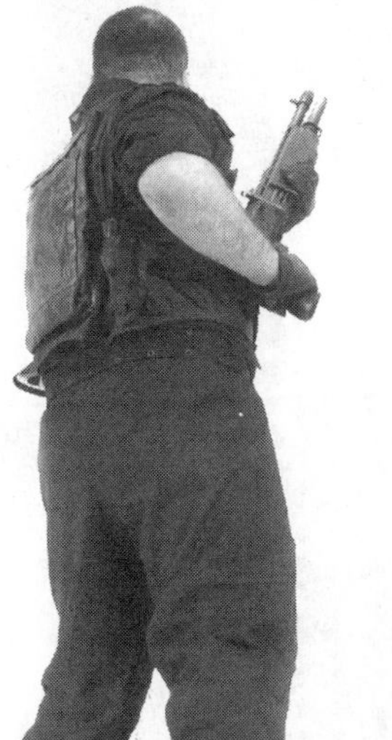
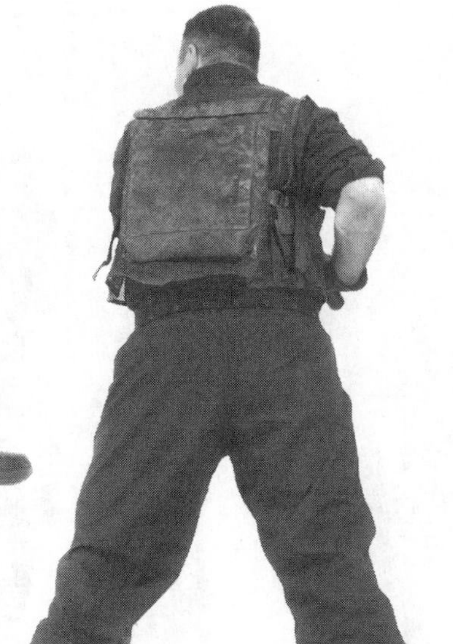
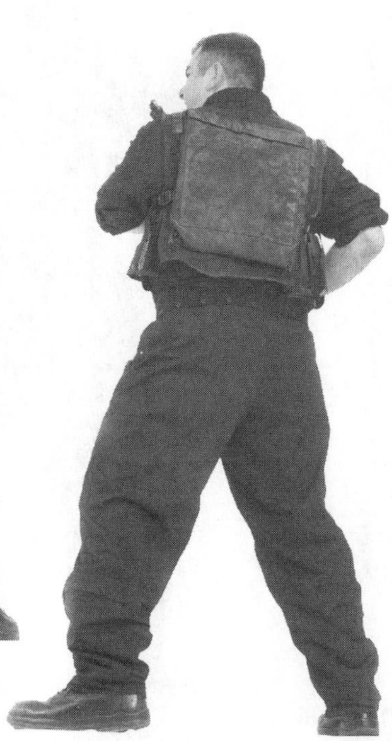
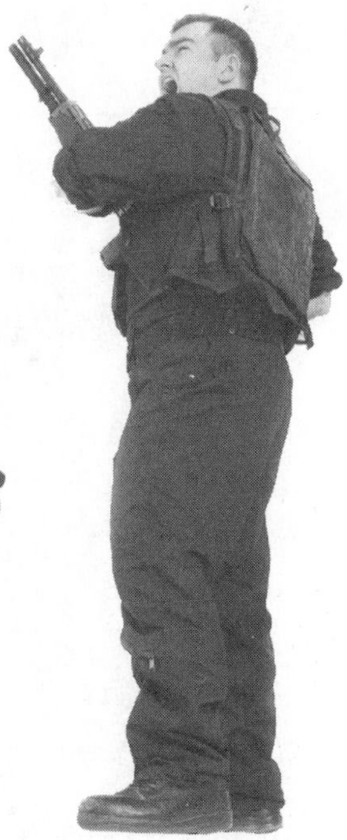

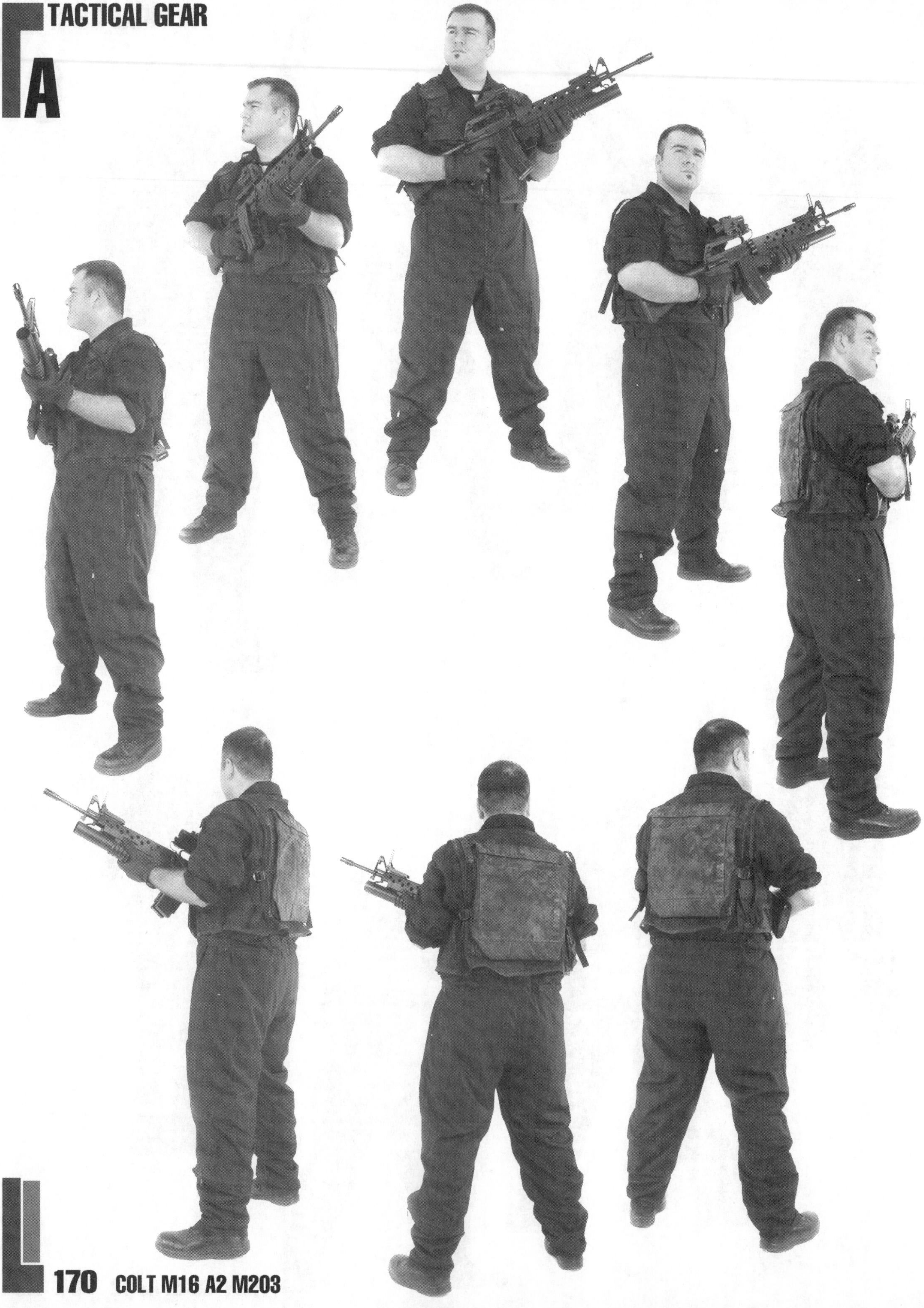

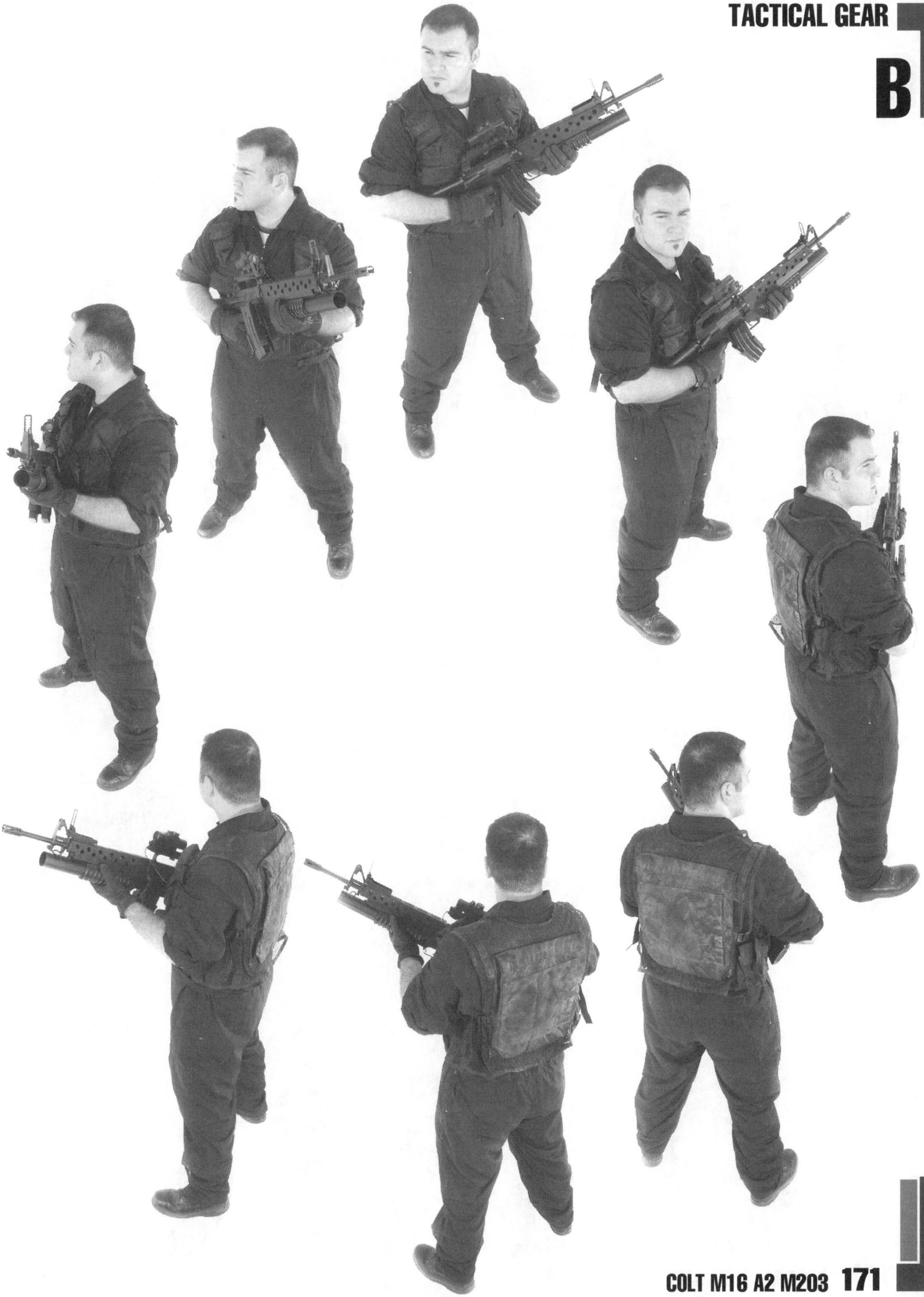

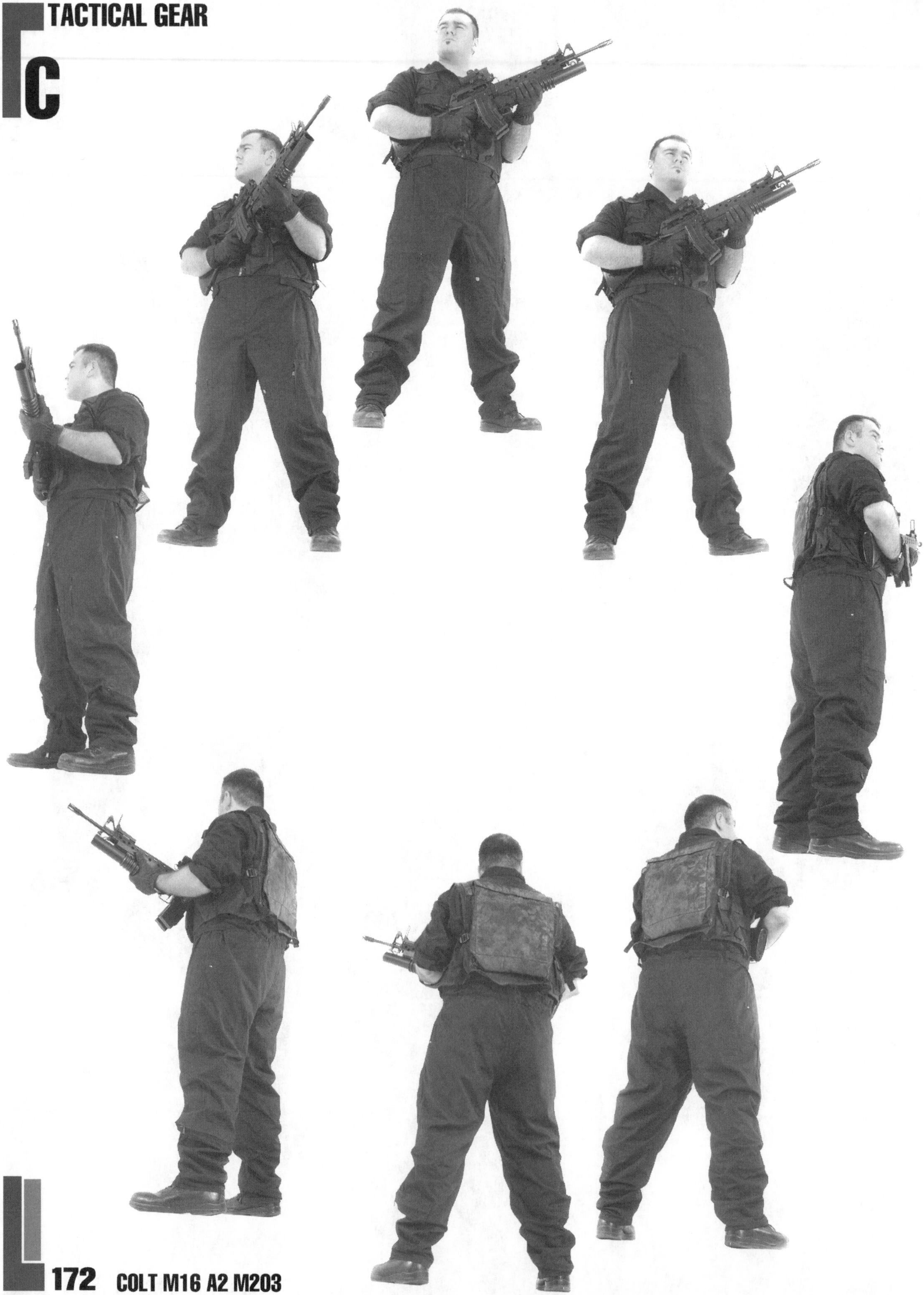

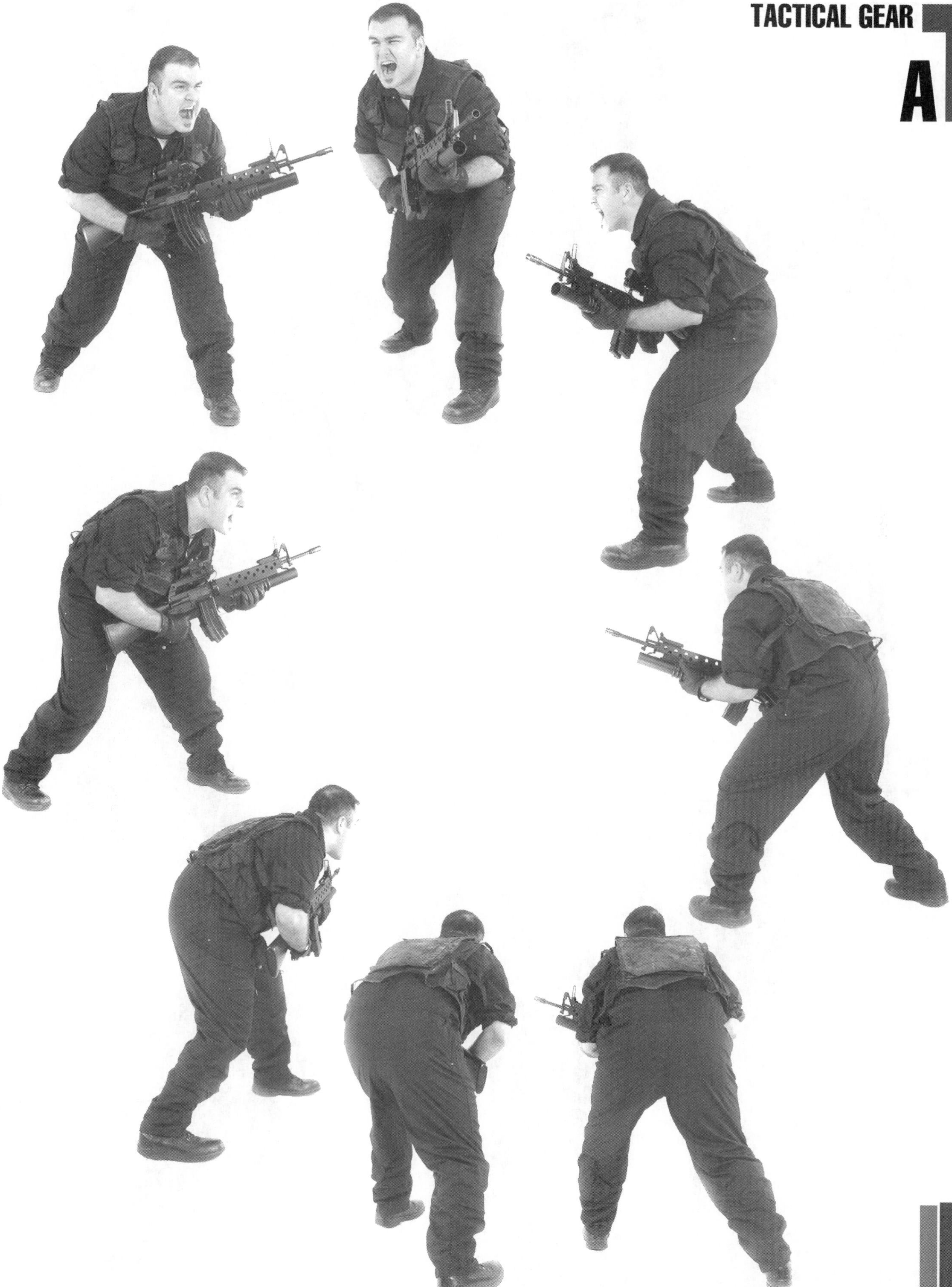

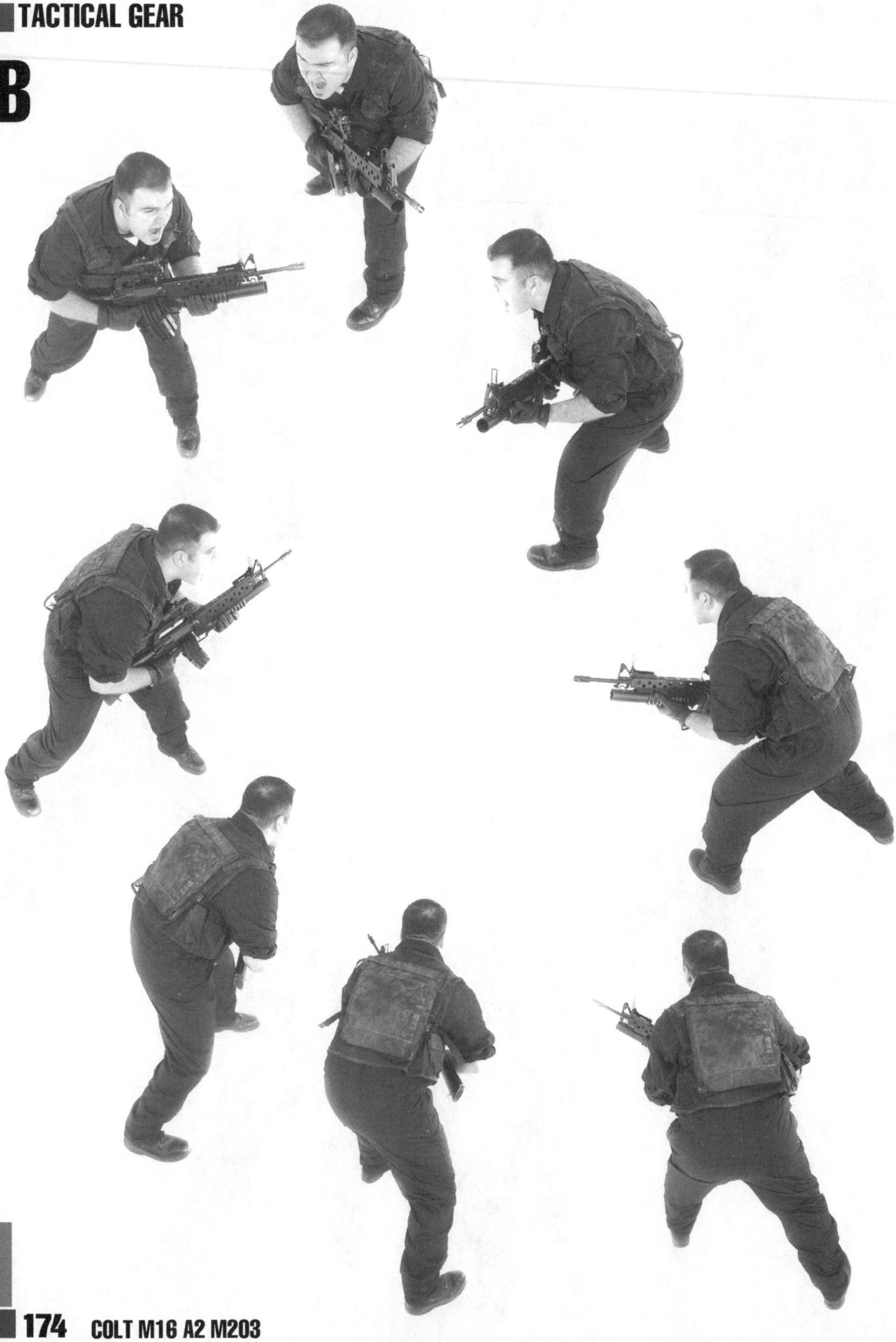

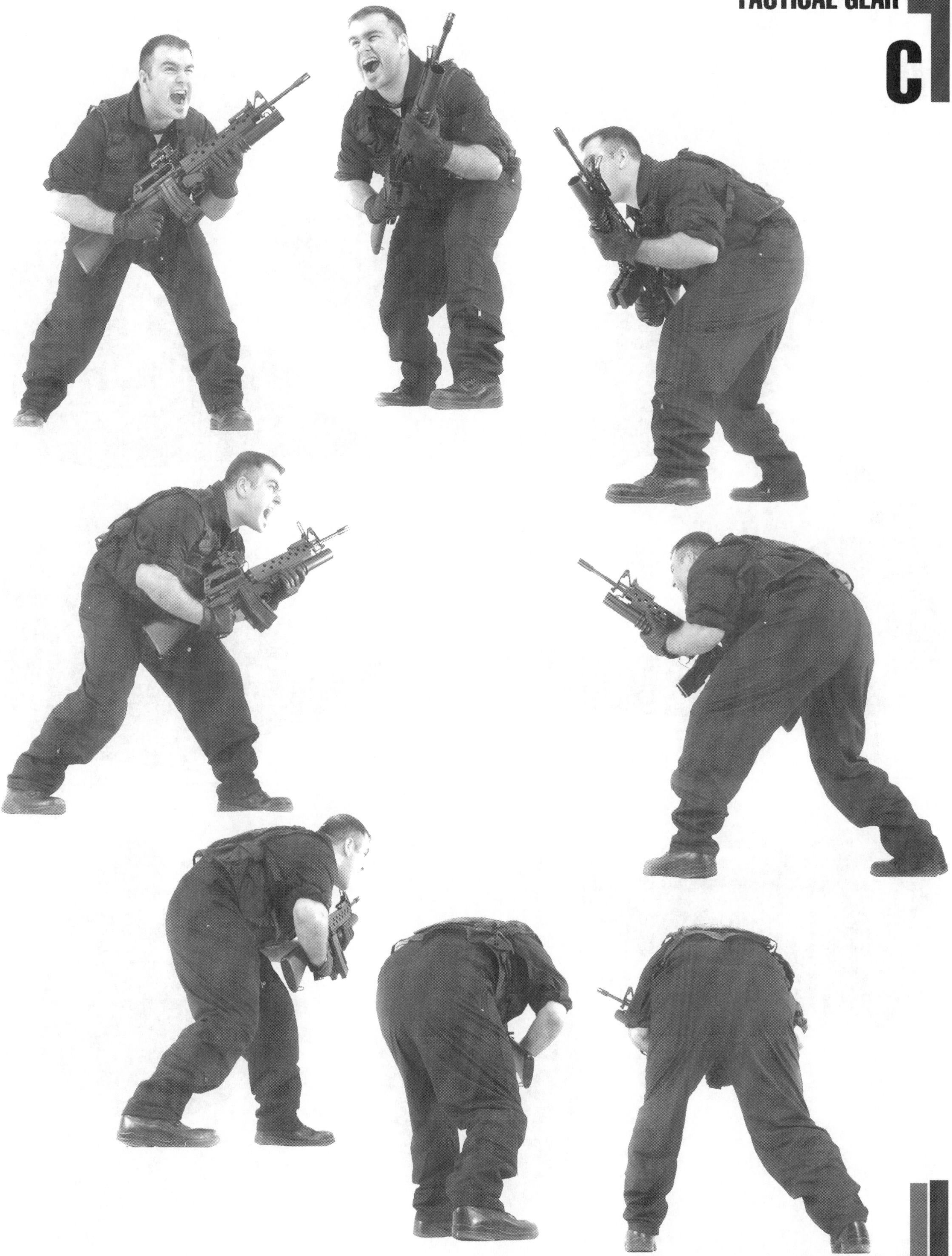

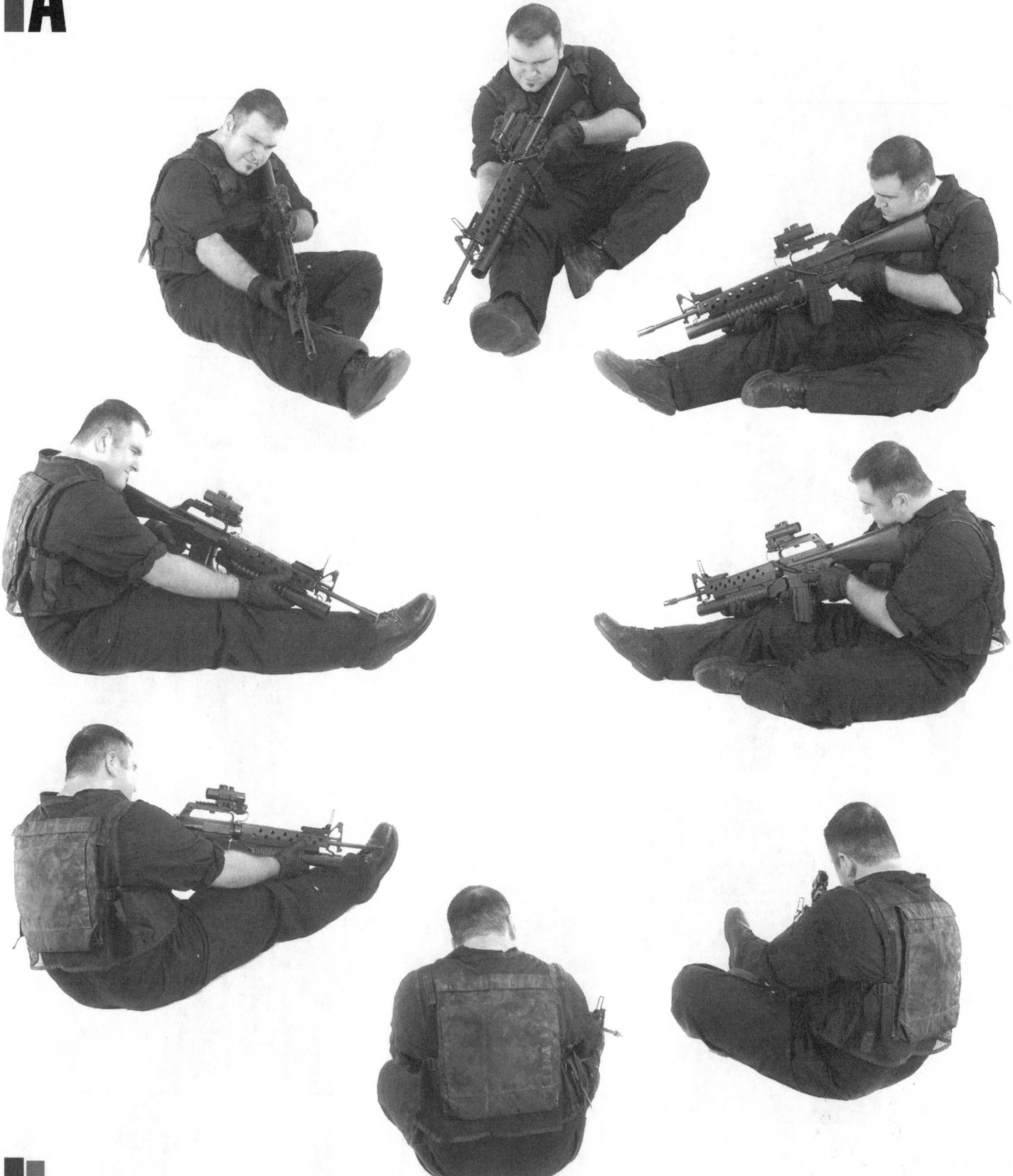

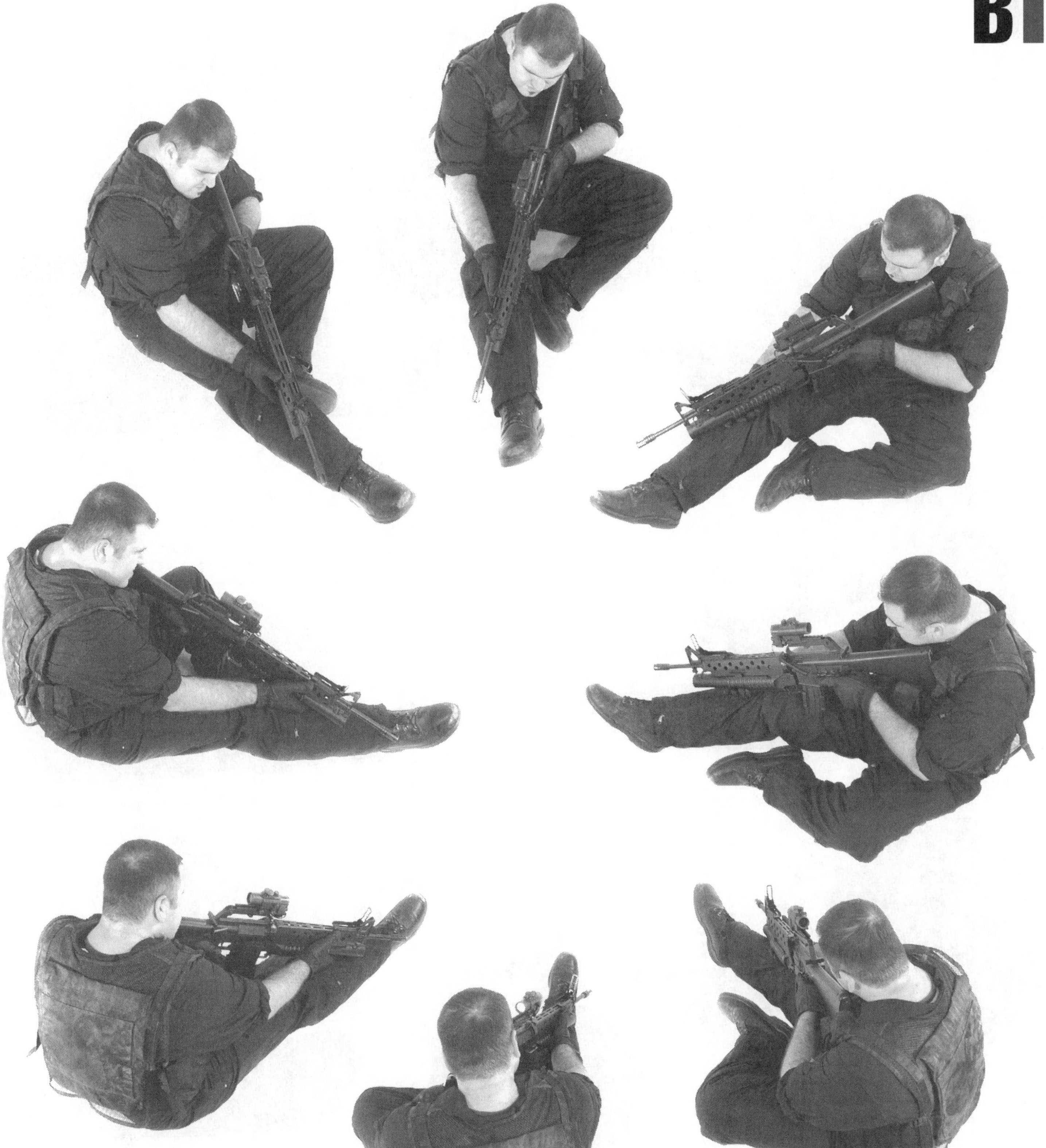

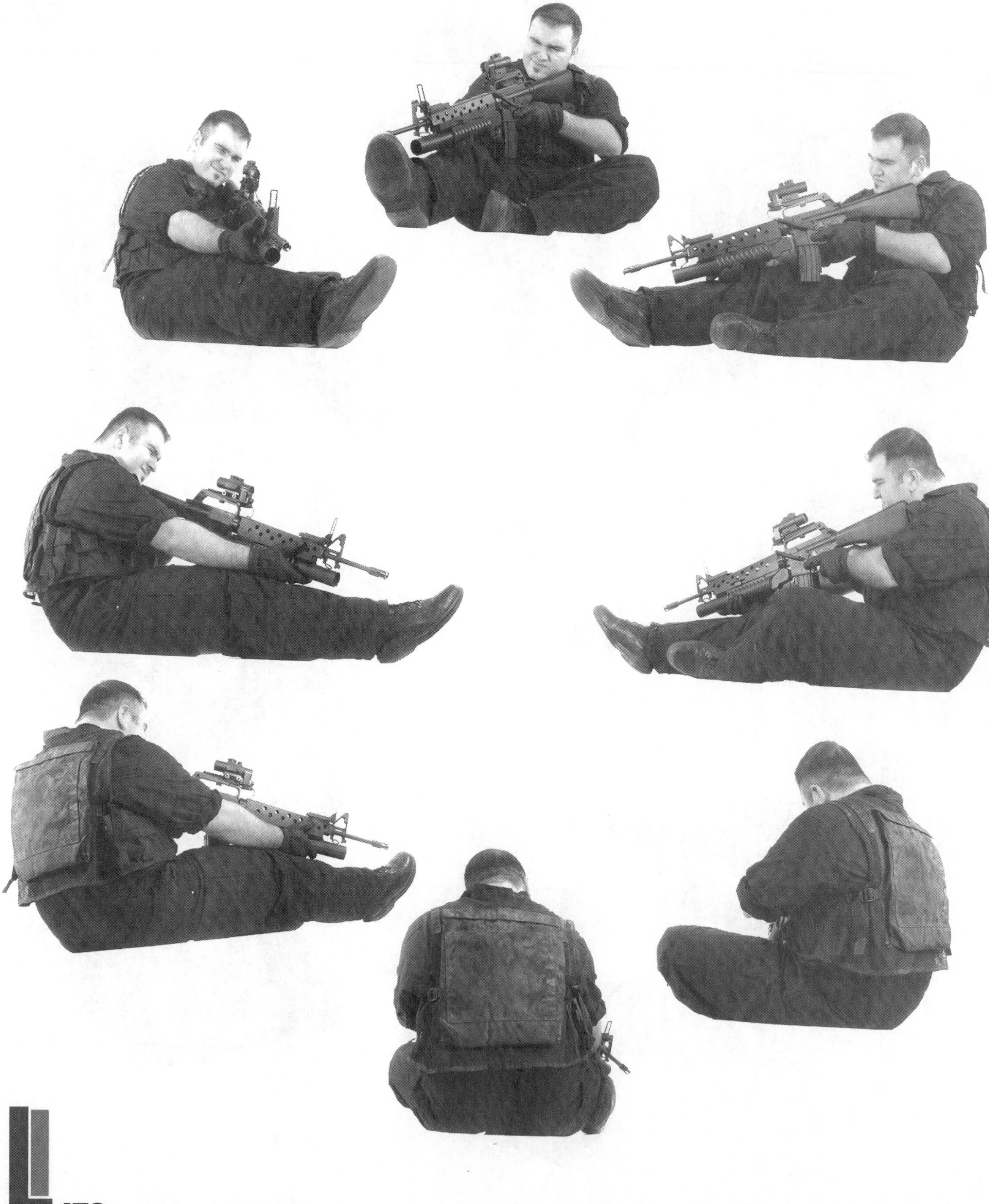

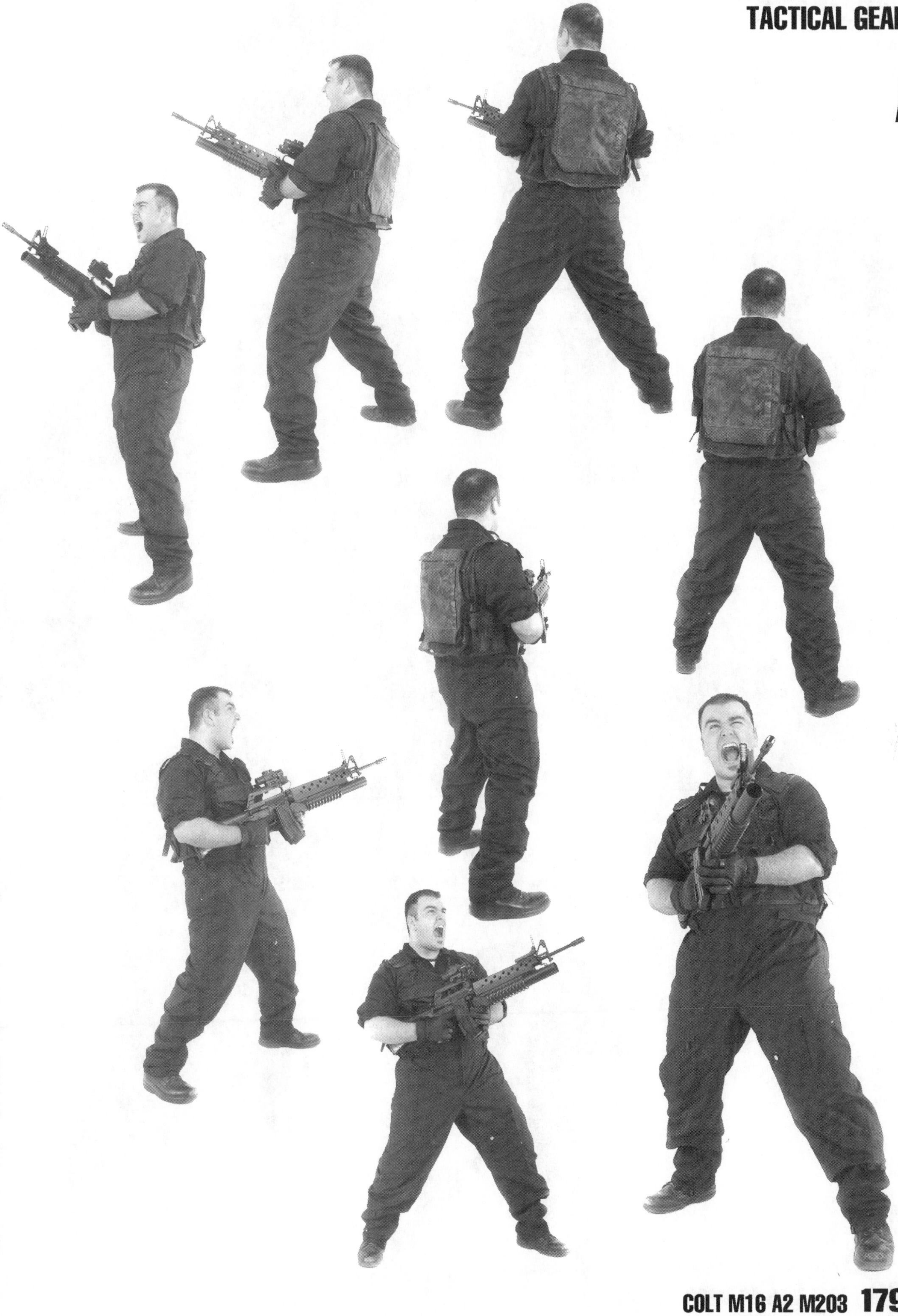

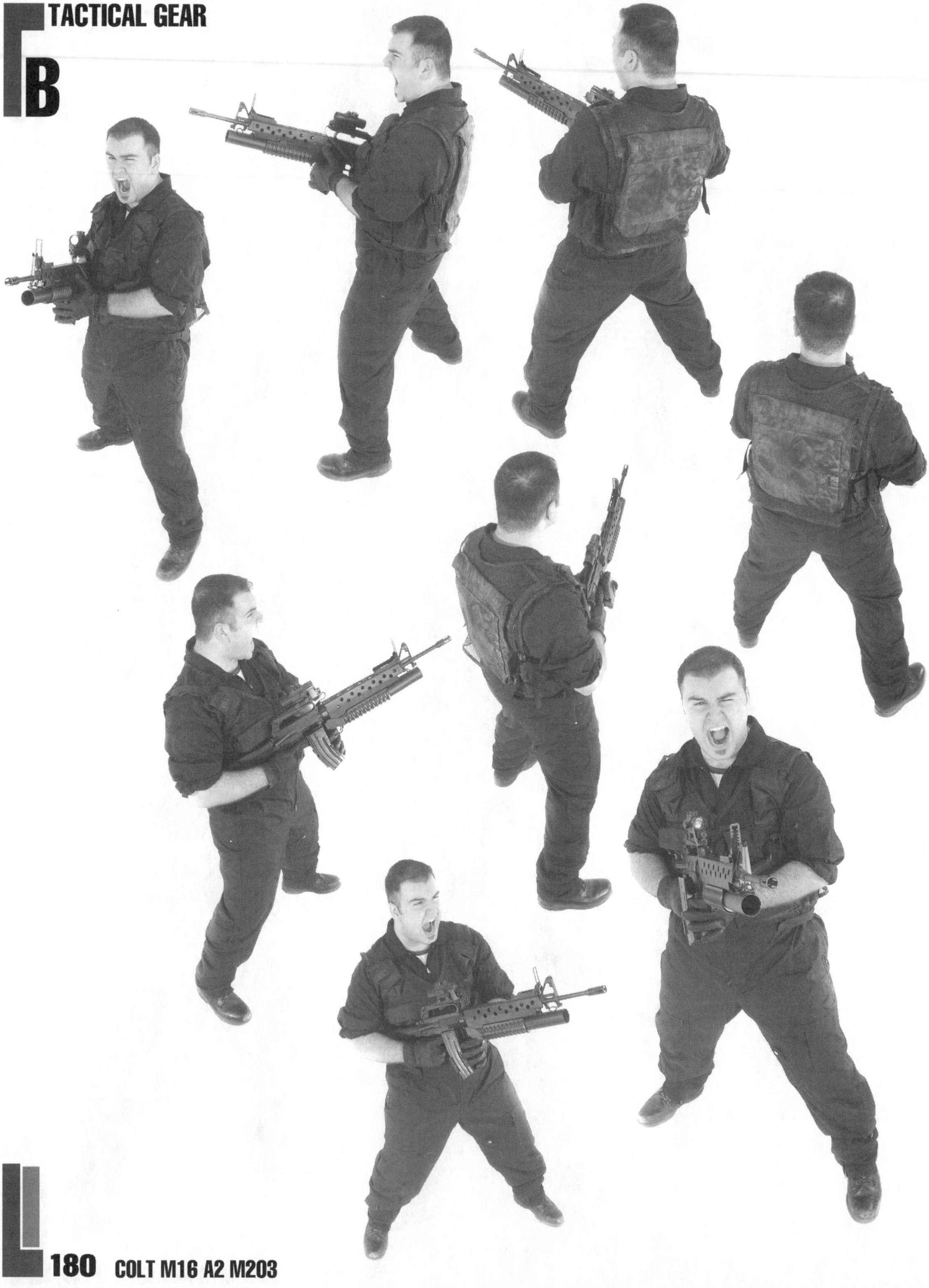

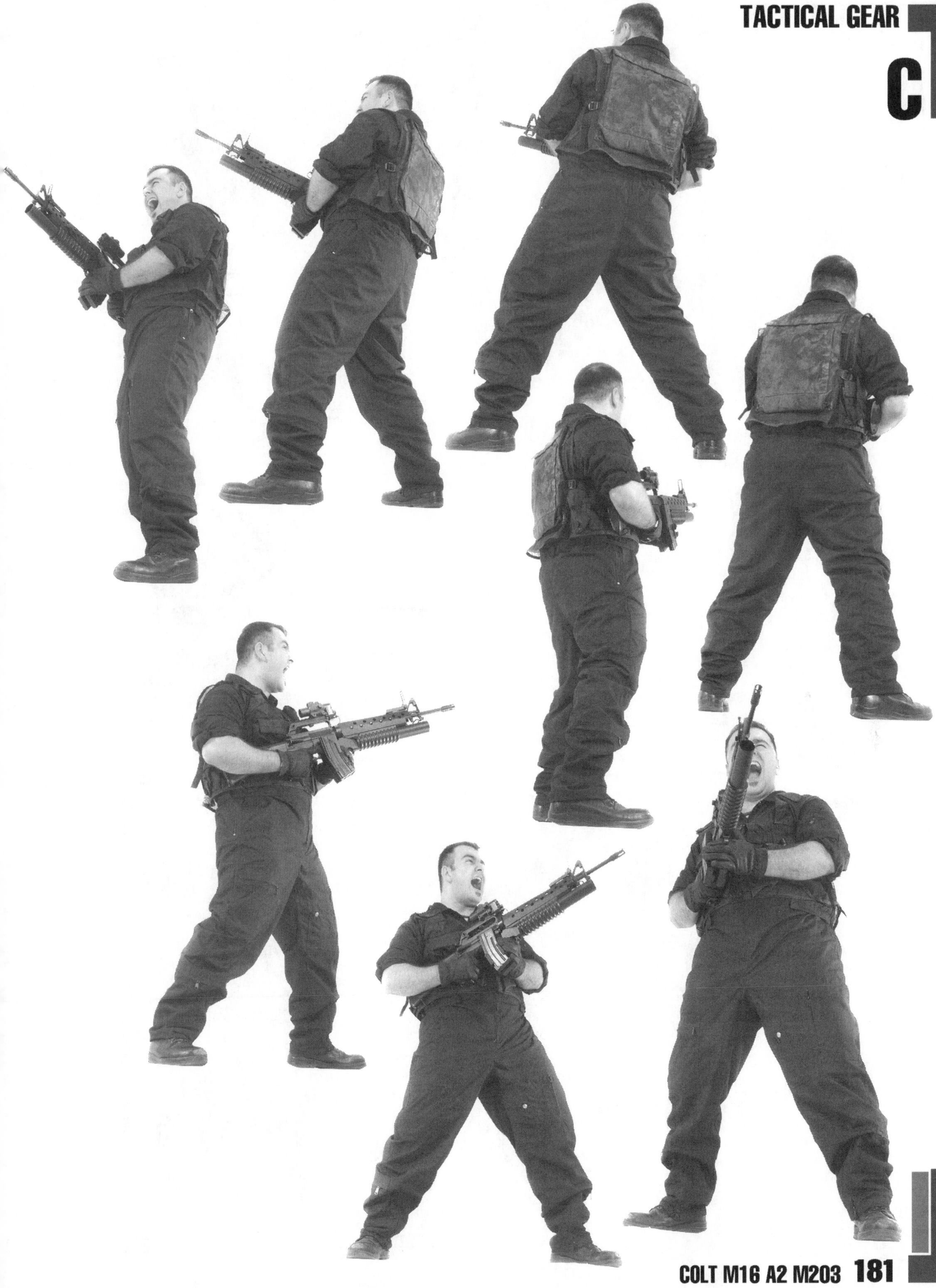

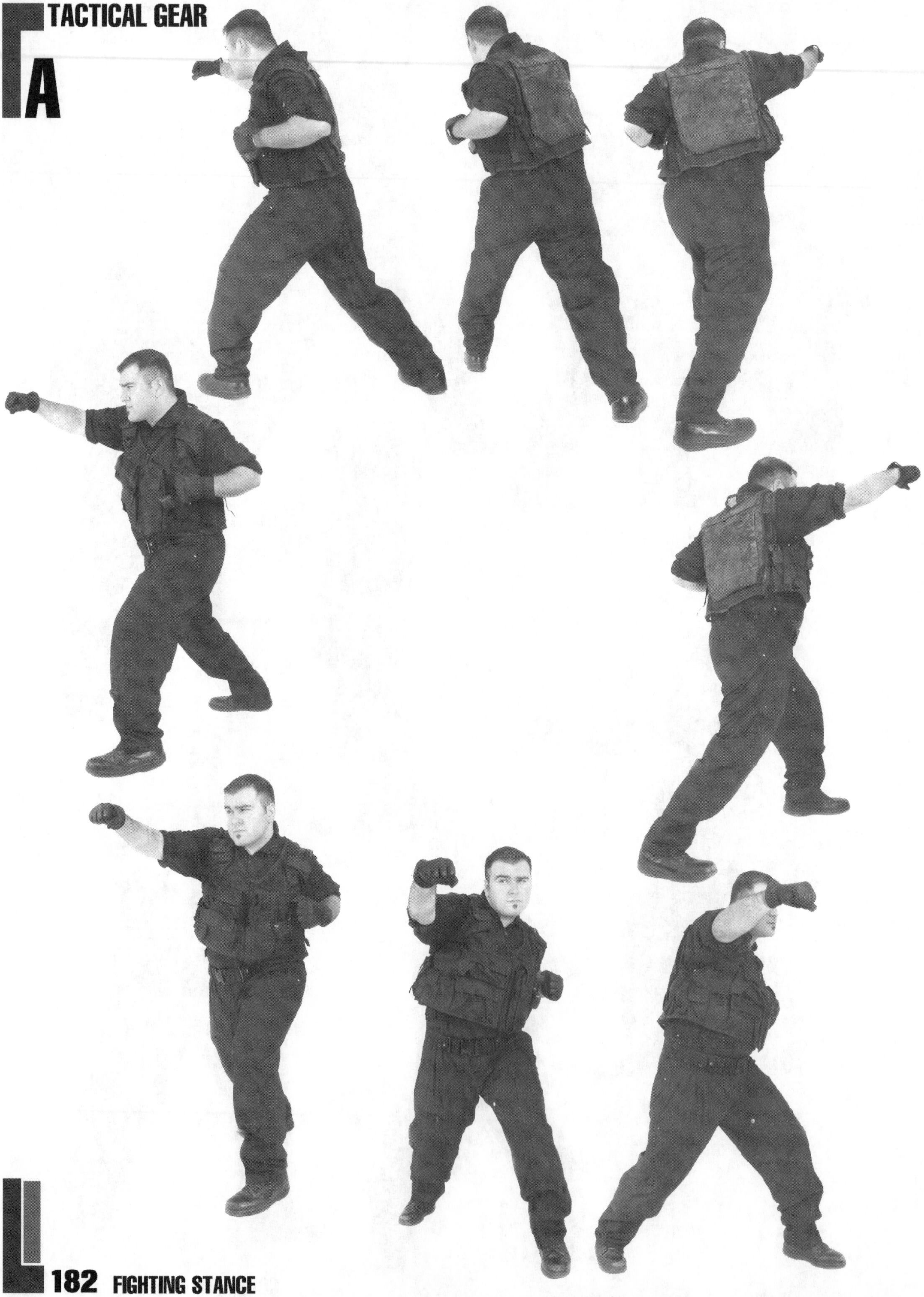

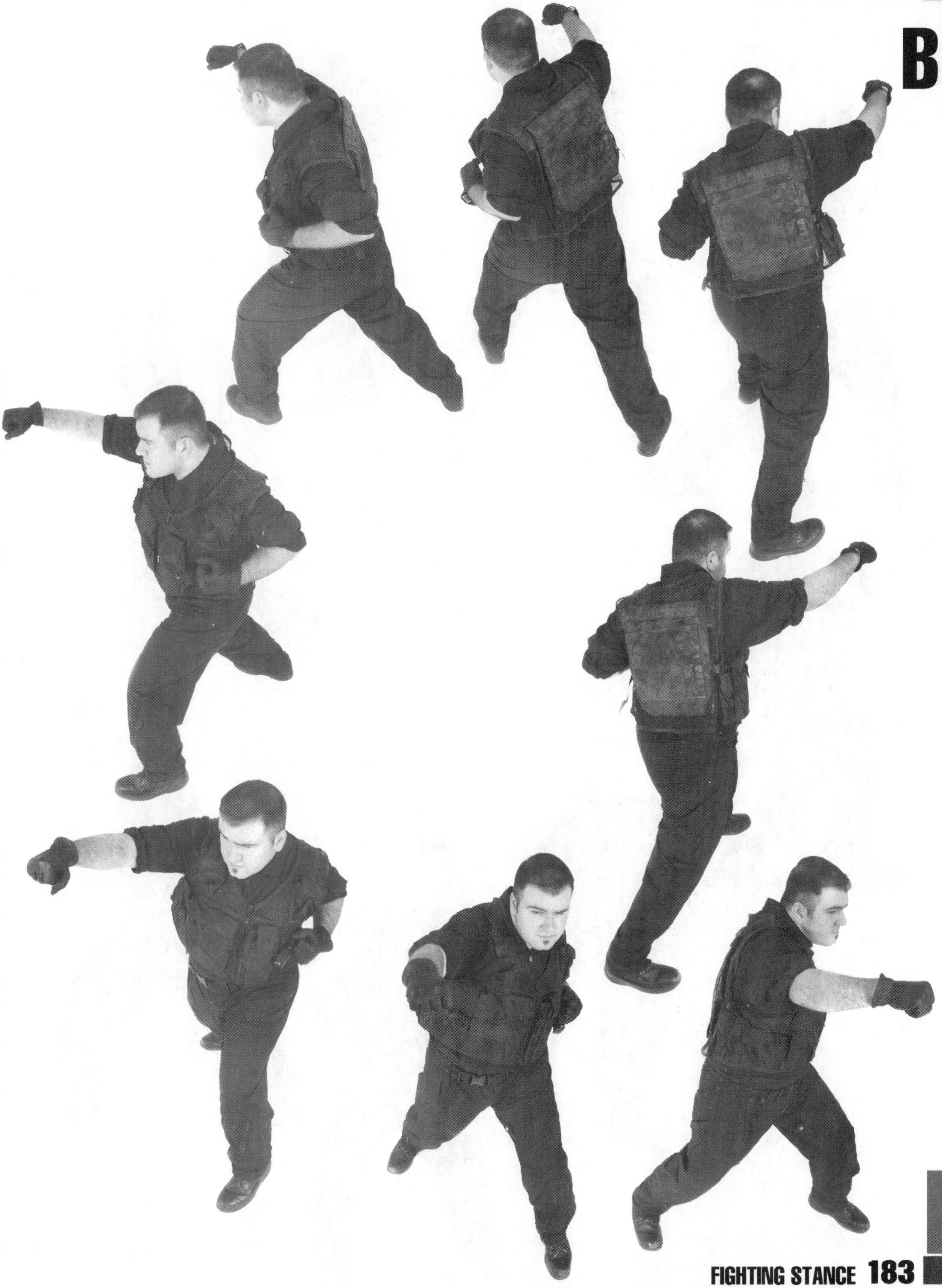

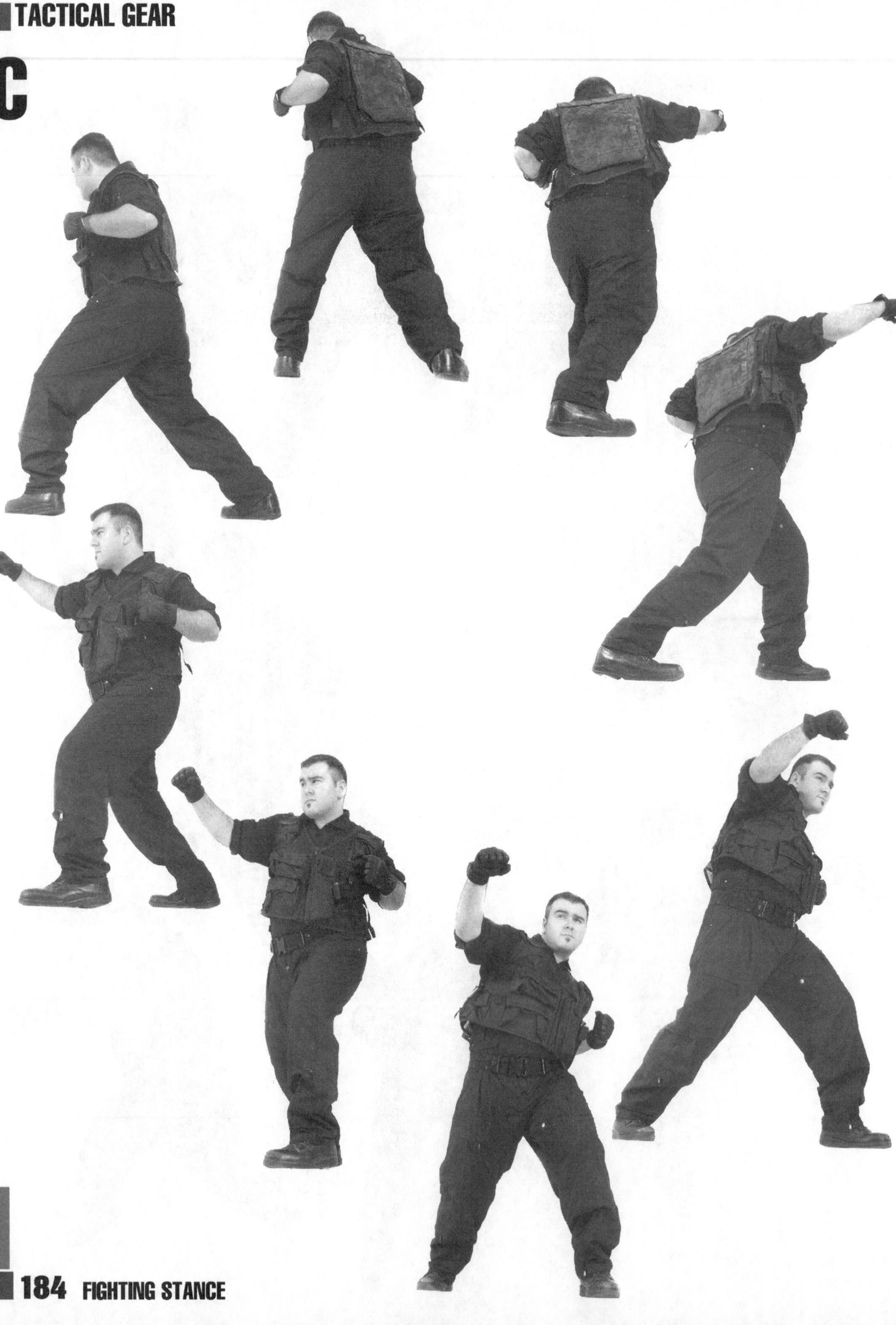

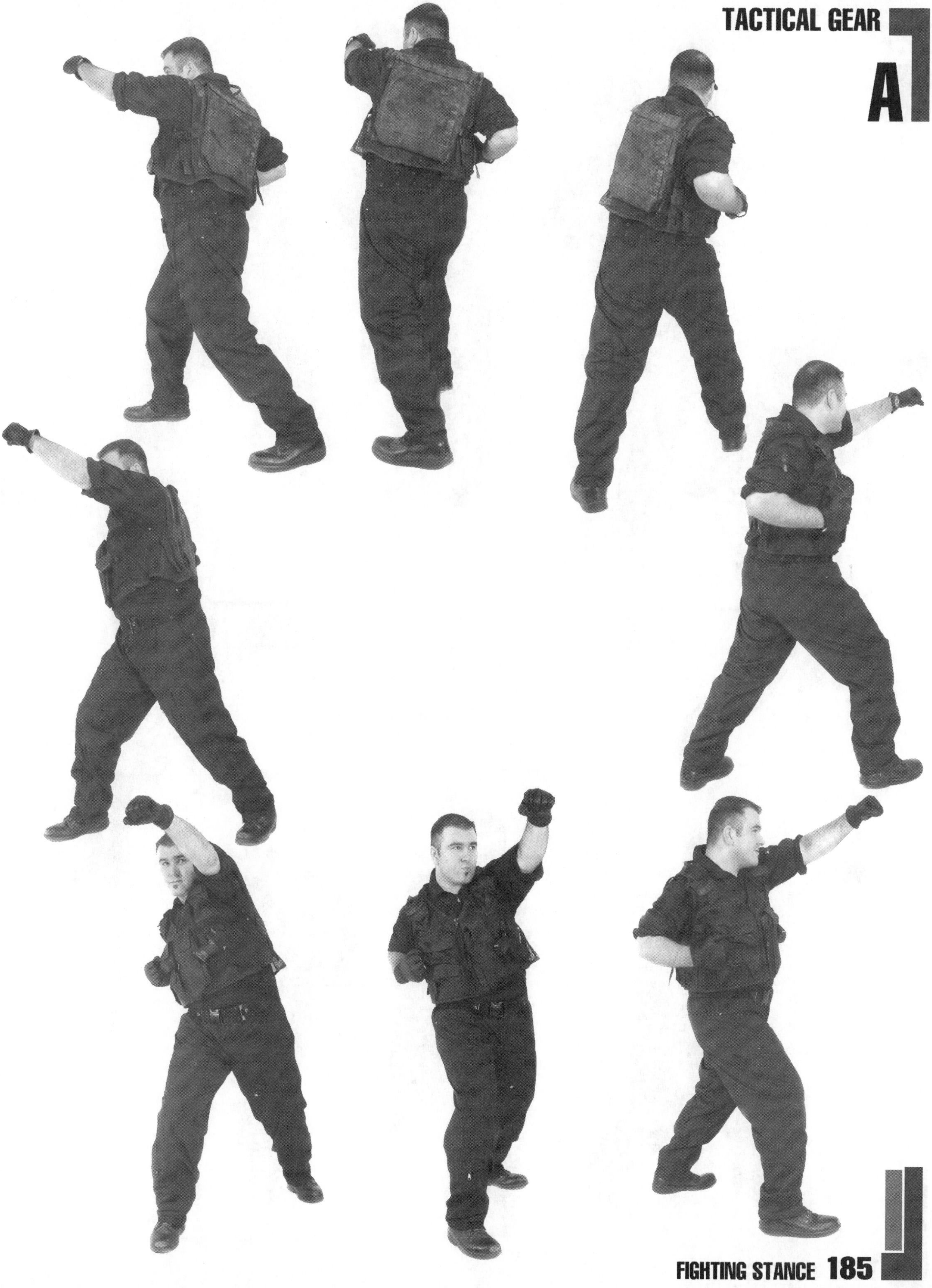

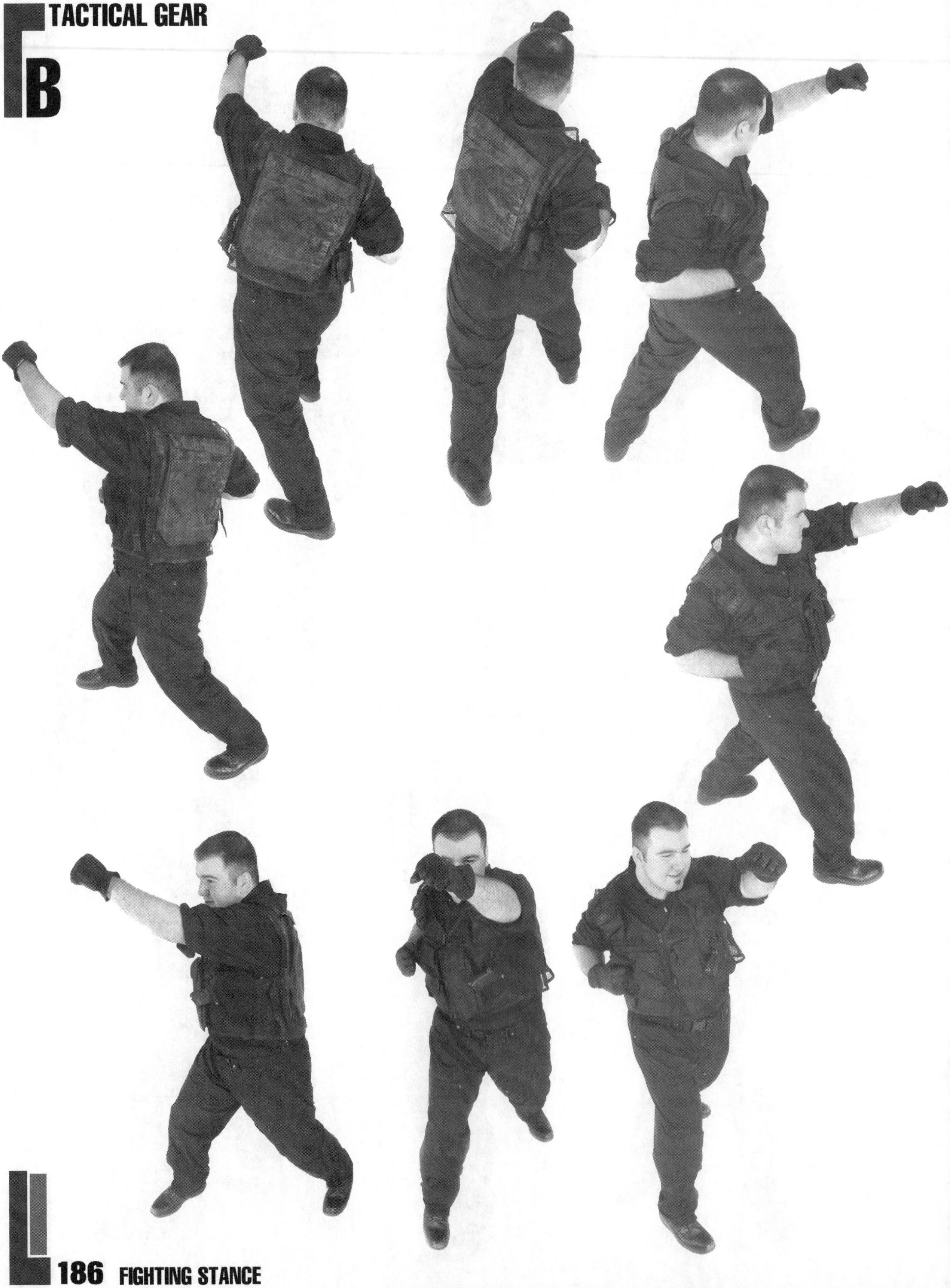

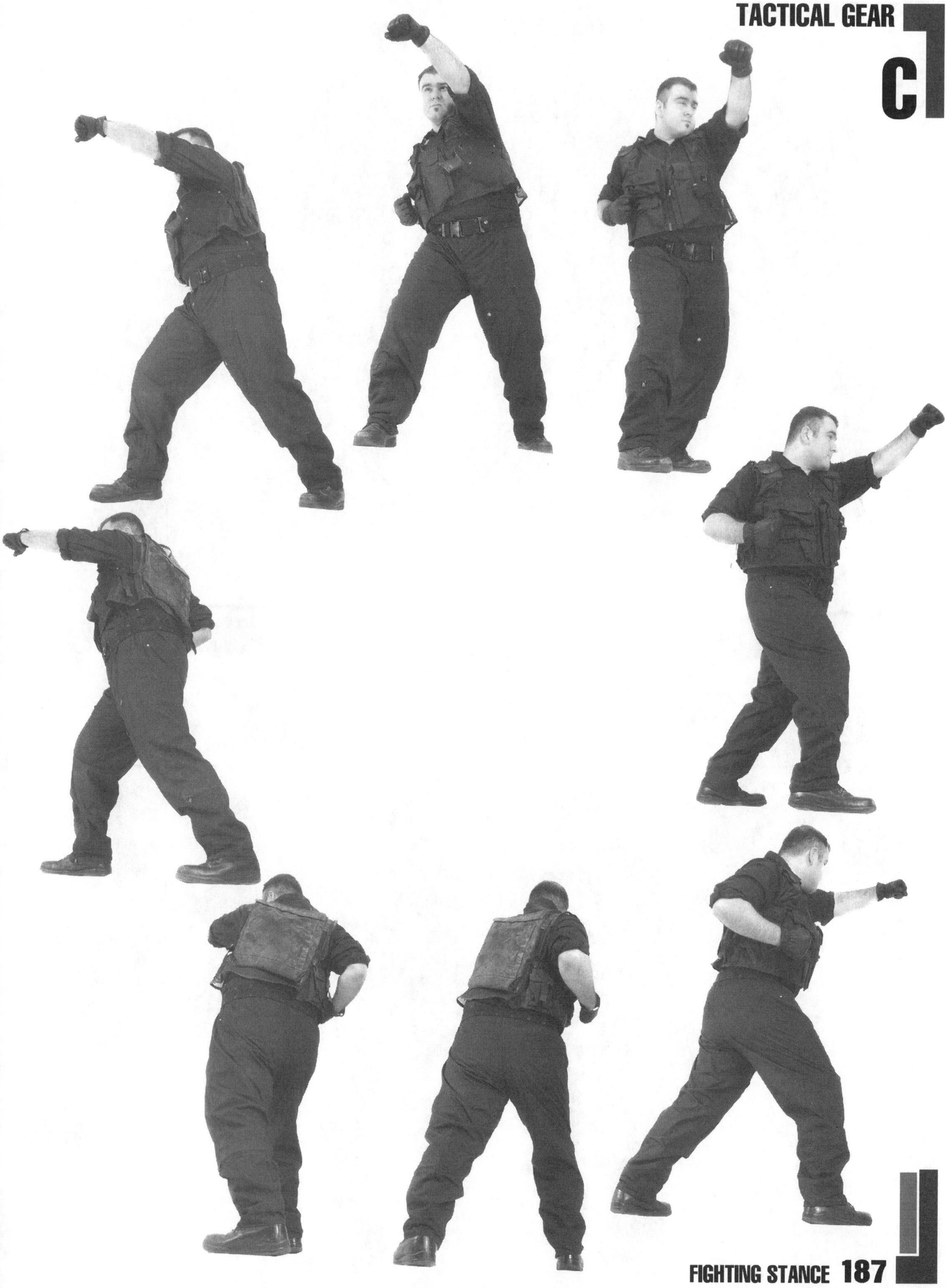

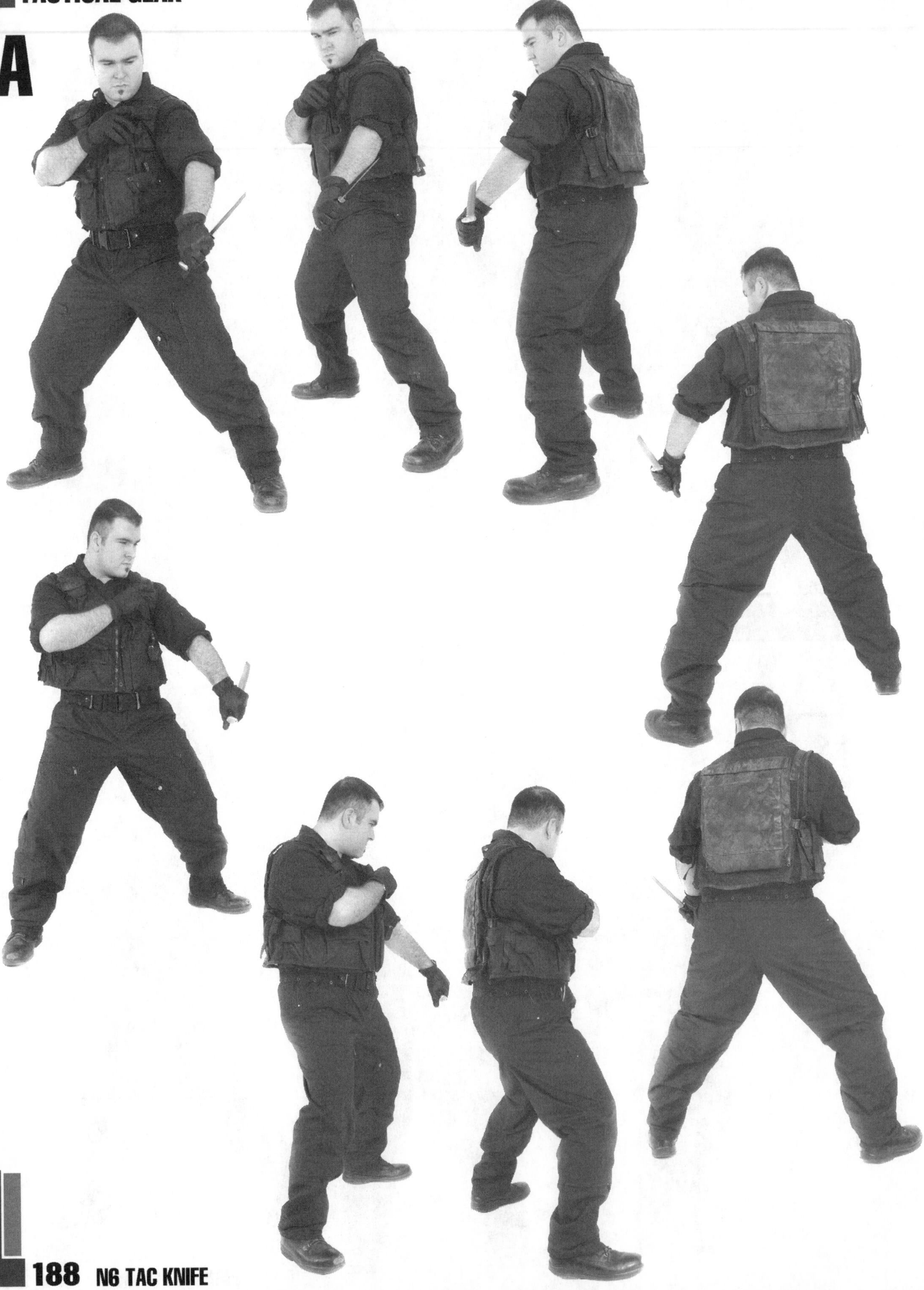

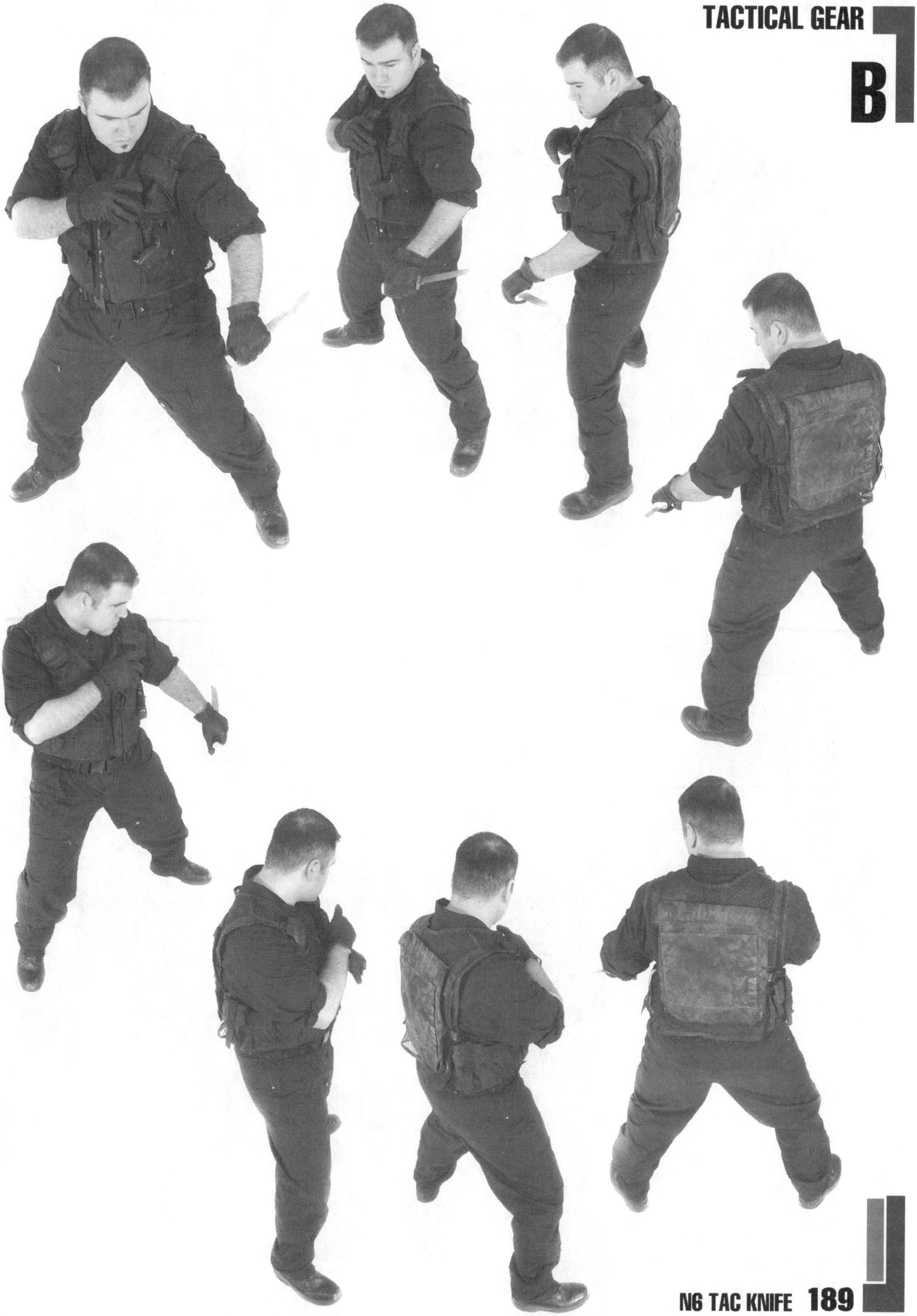

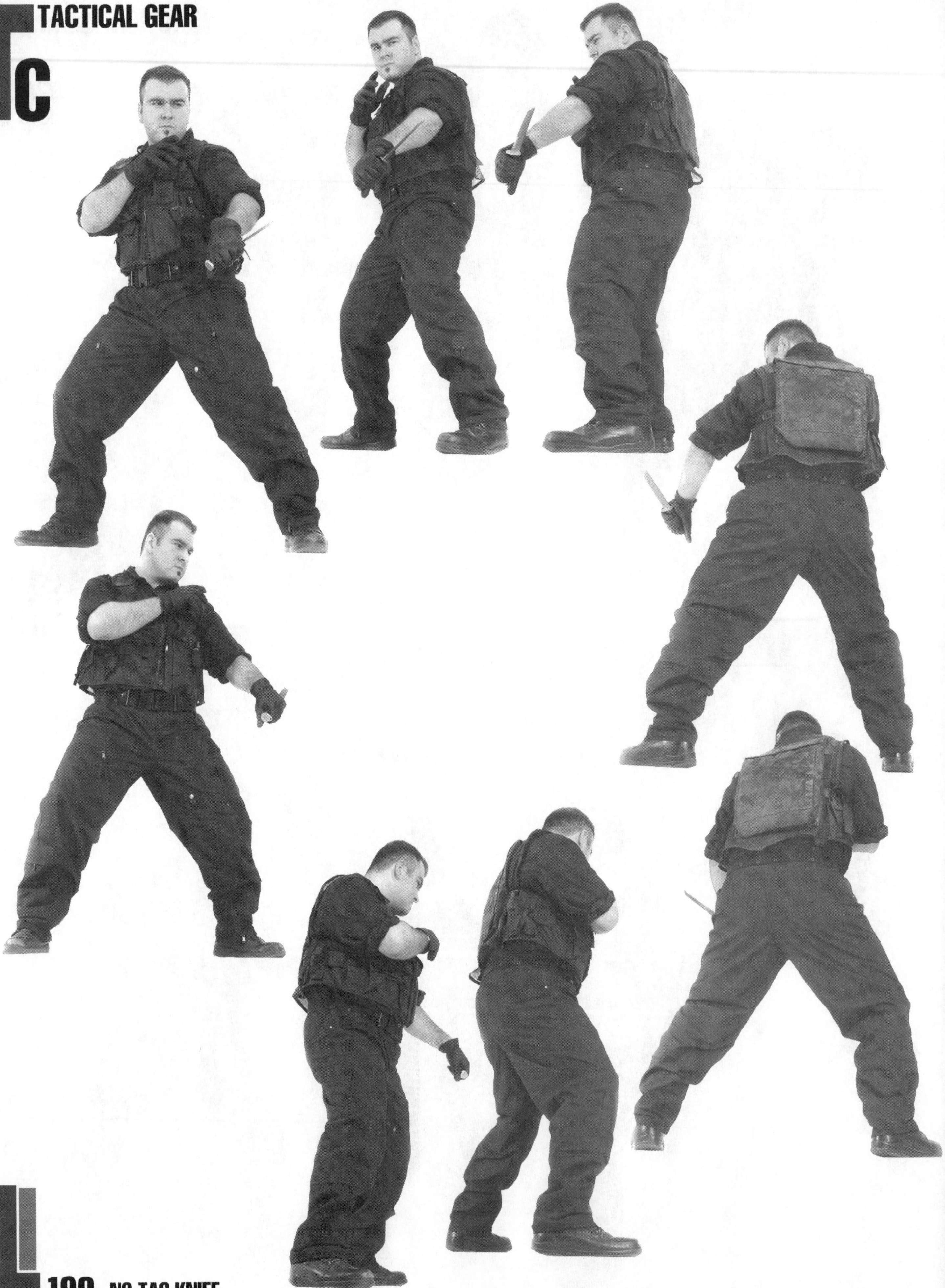

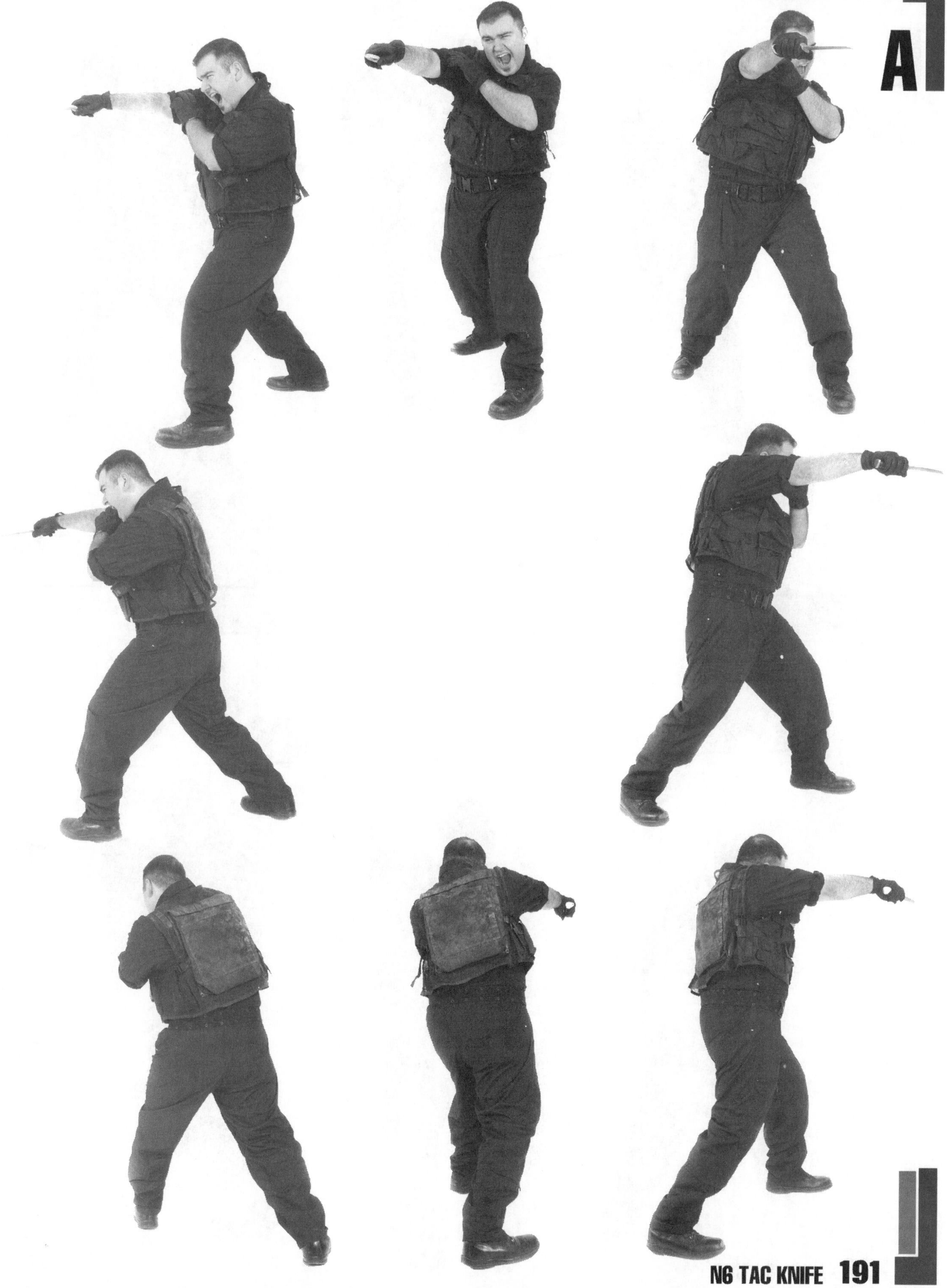

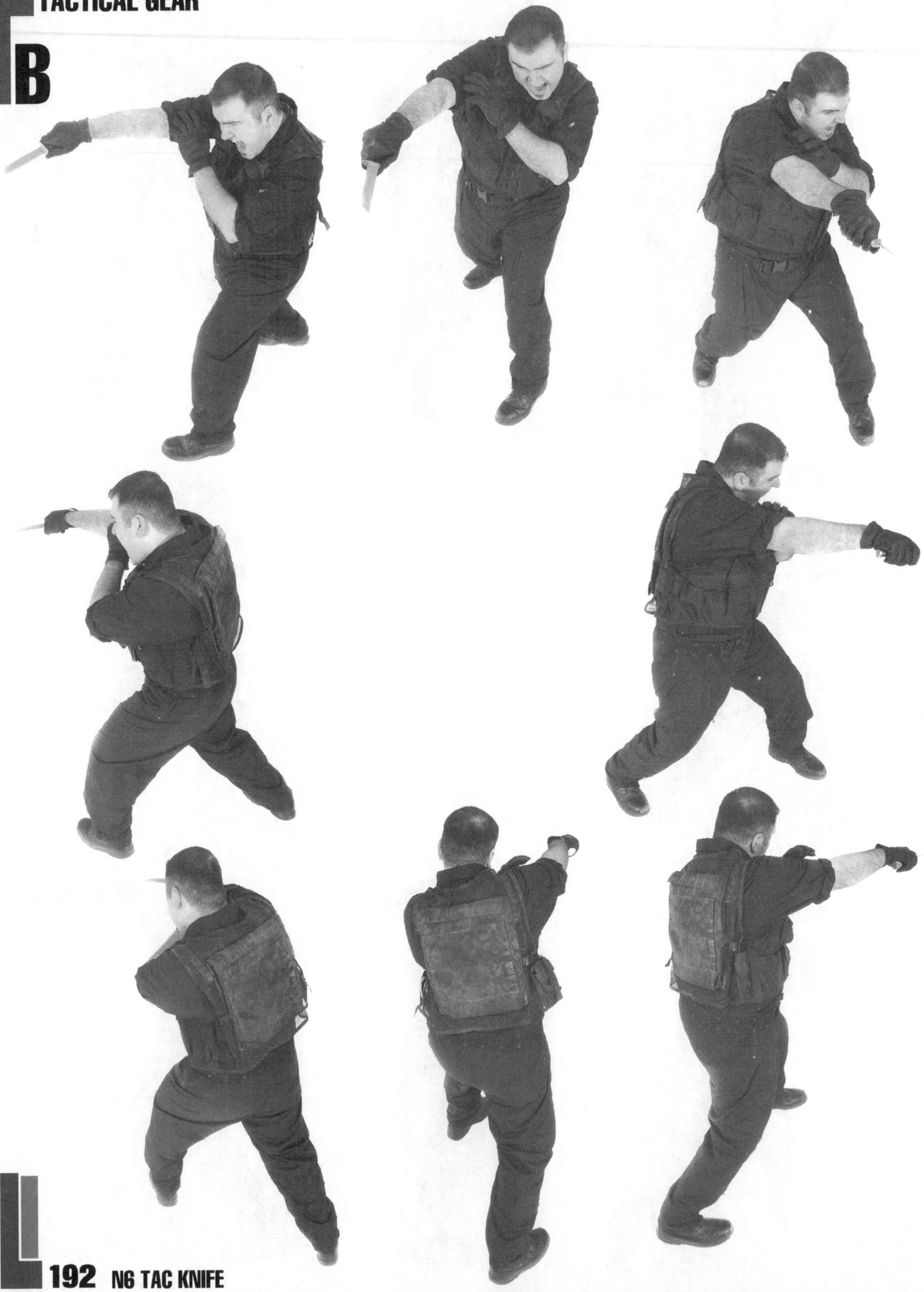

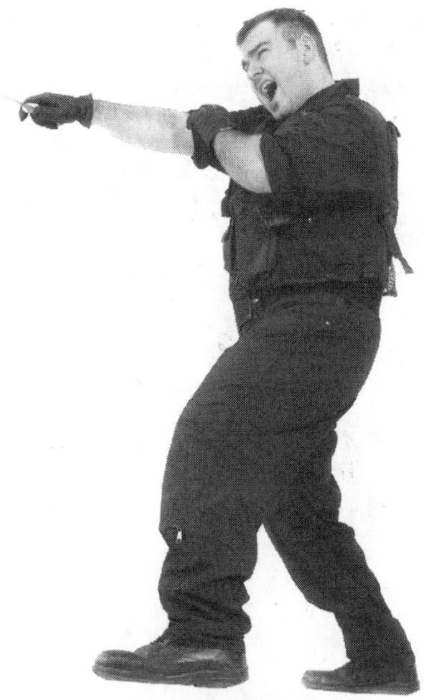
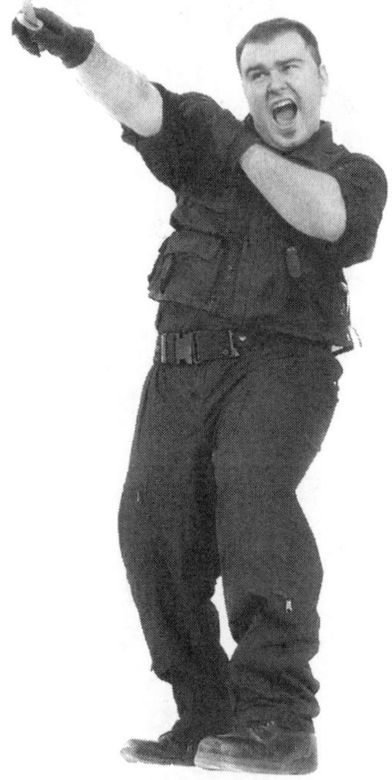
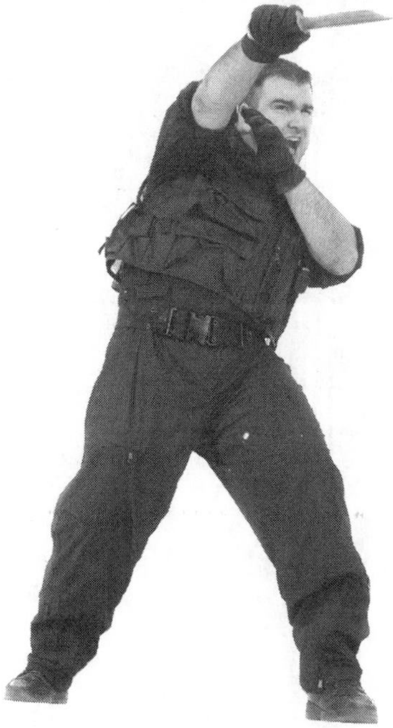
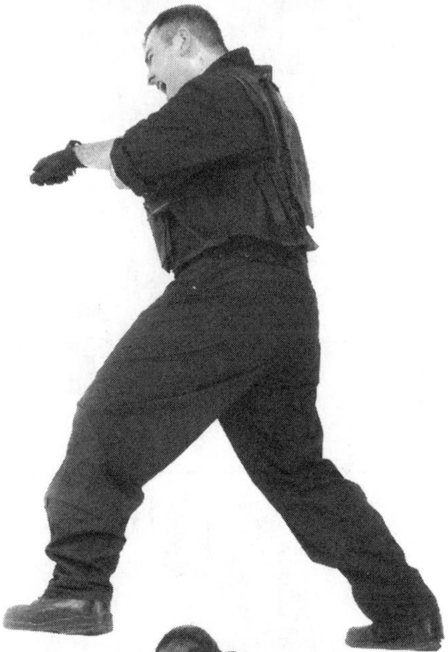
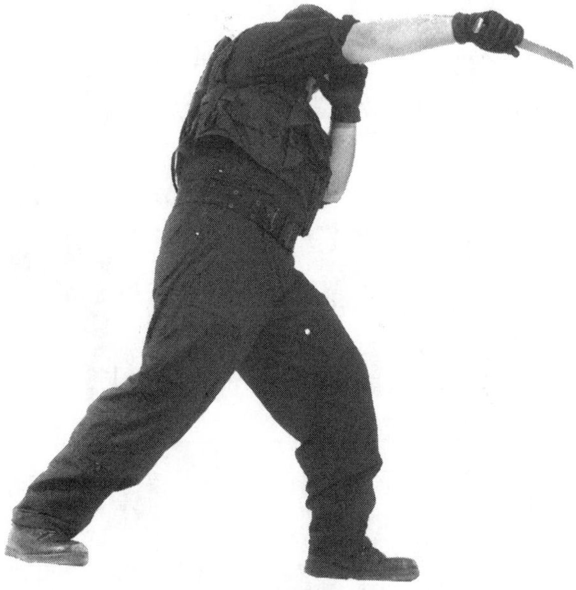
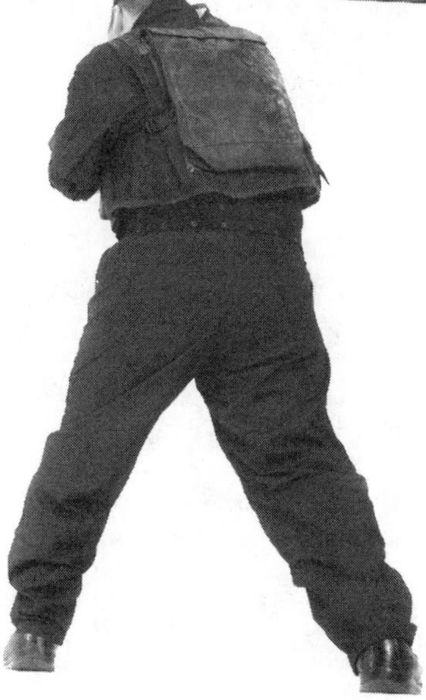
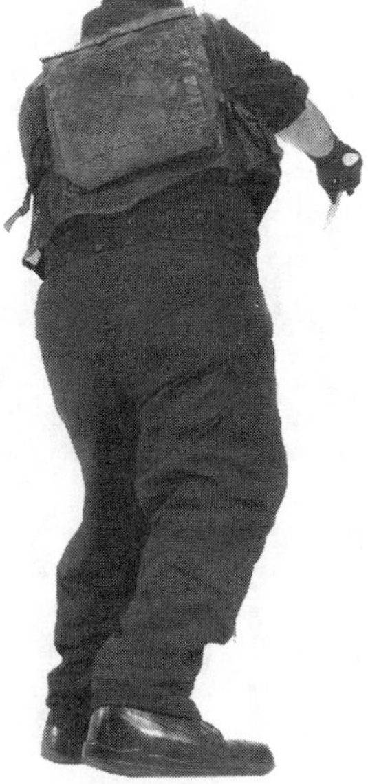
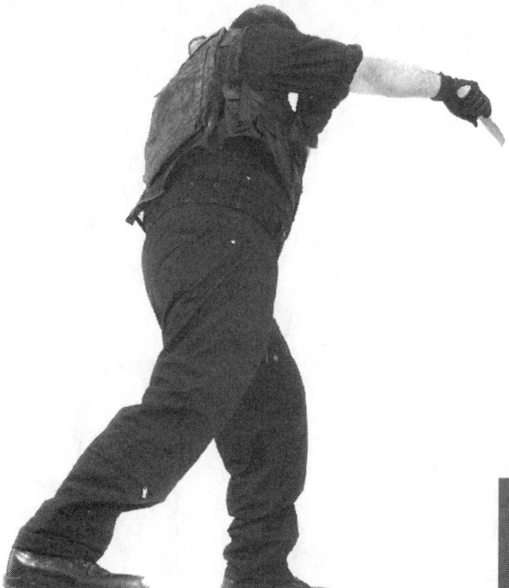

ACTION POSES

POSE

REFE

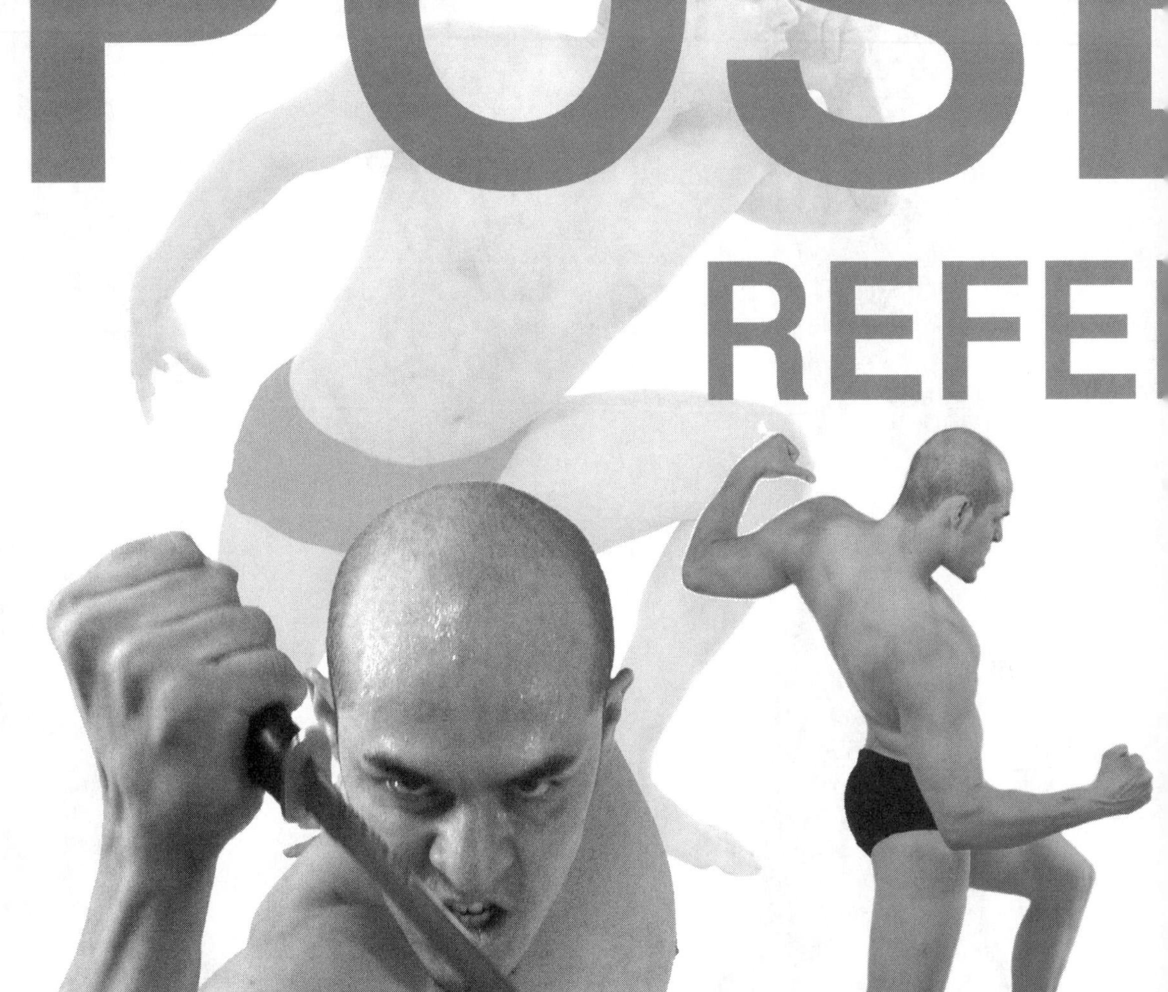

ACTION POSE COLLECTION

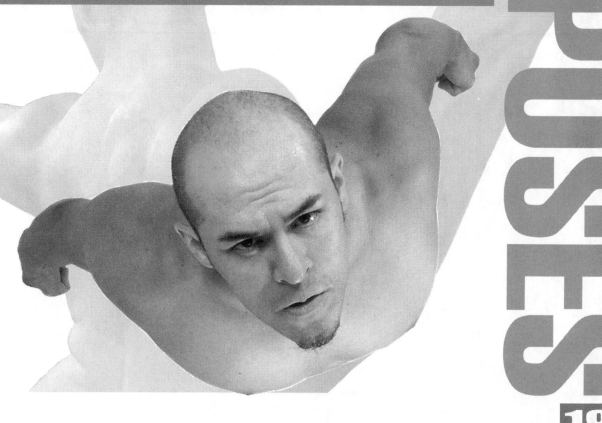

EFILE

ENCE

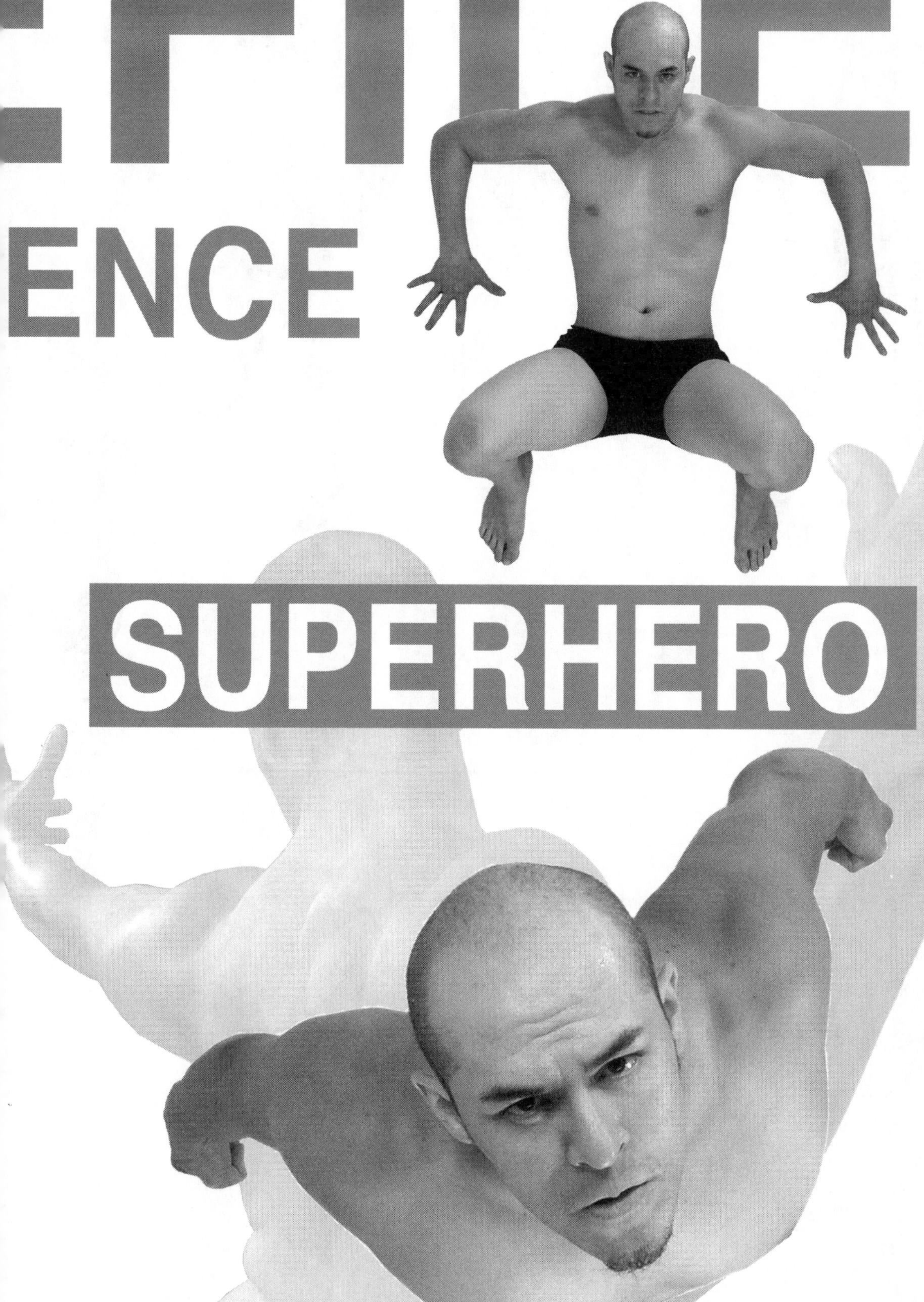

SUPERHERO

ACTION POSES

A

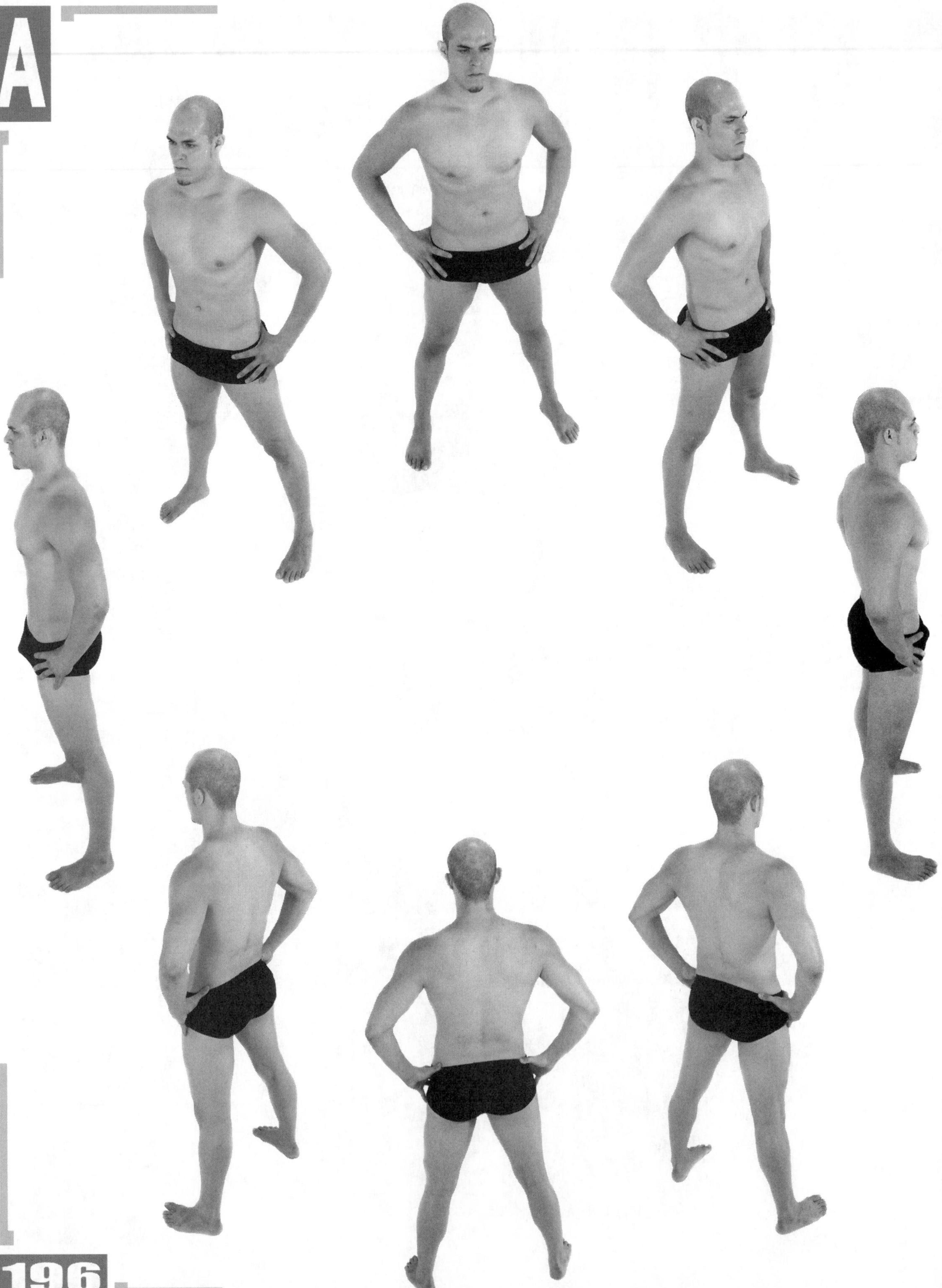

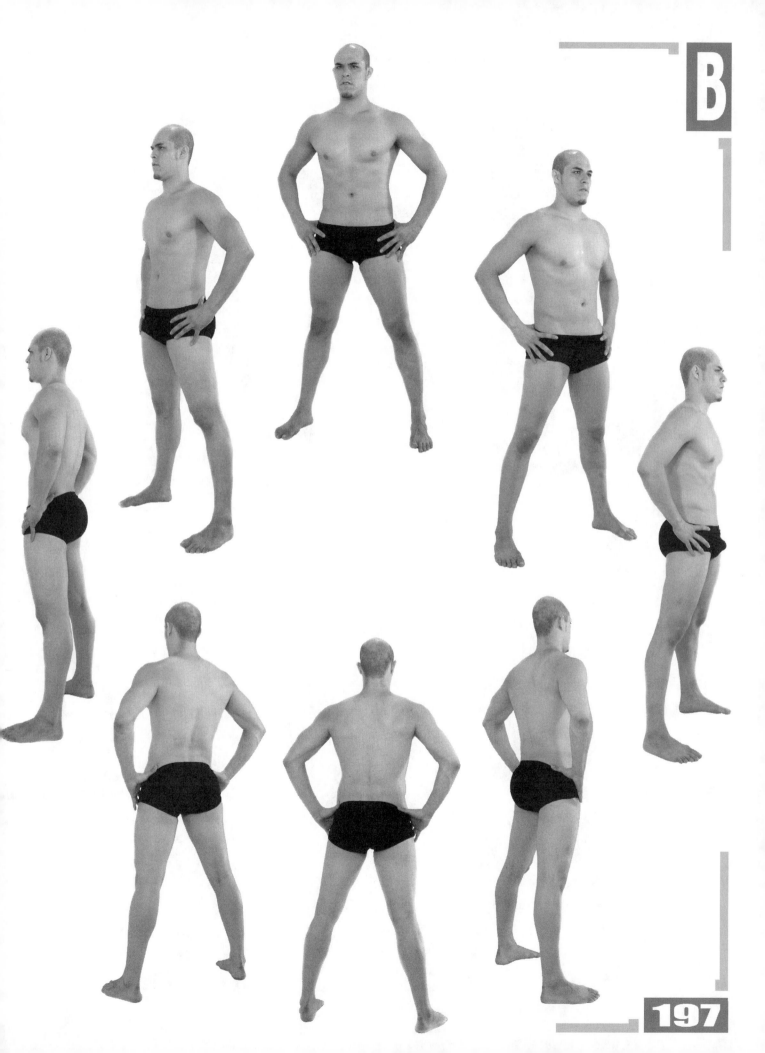

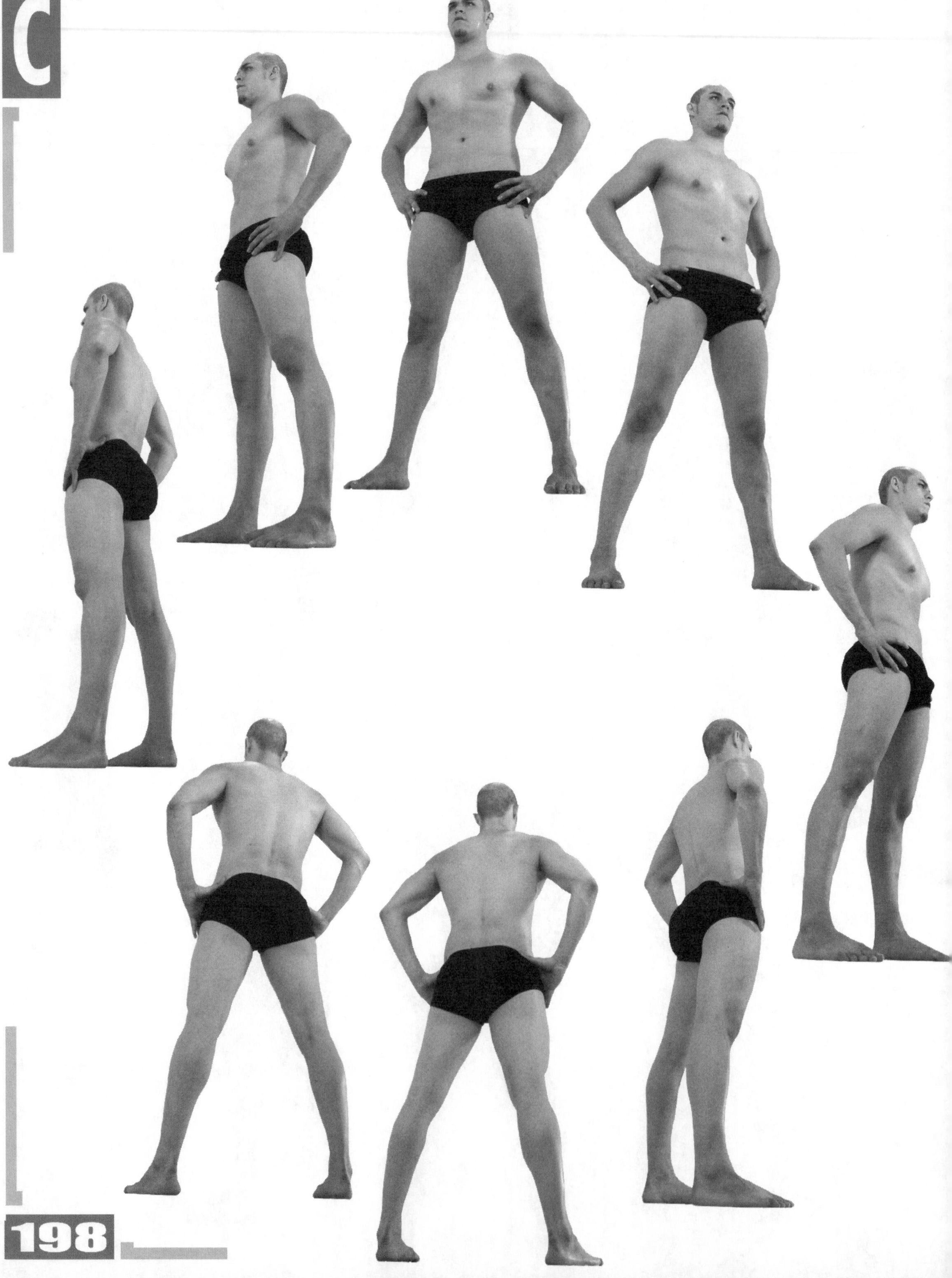

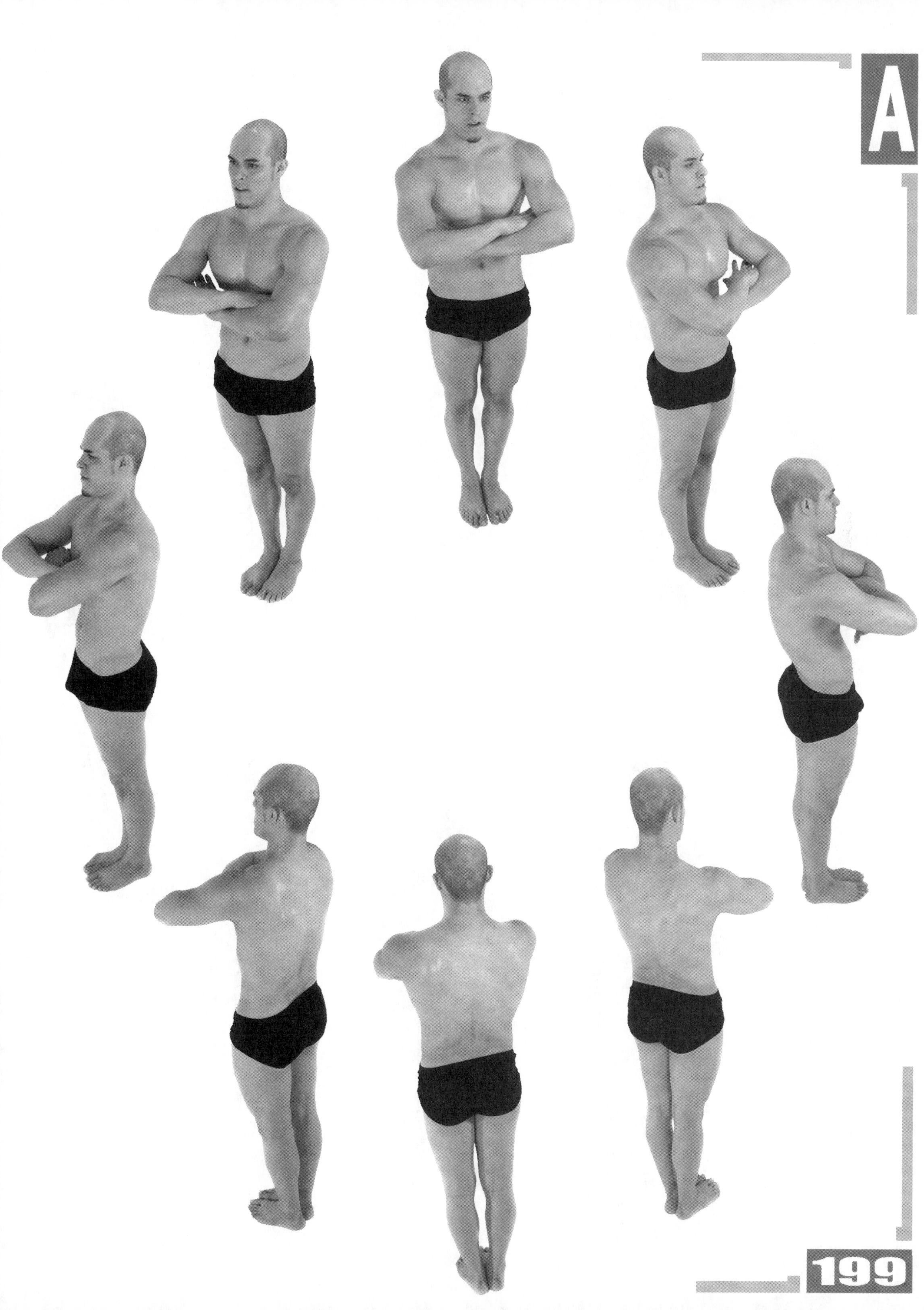

B

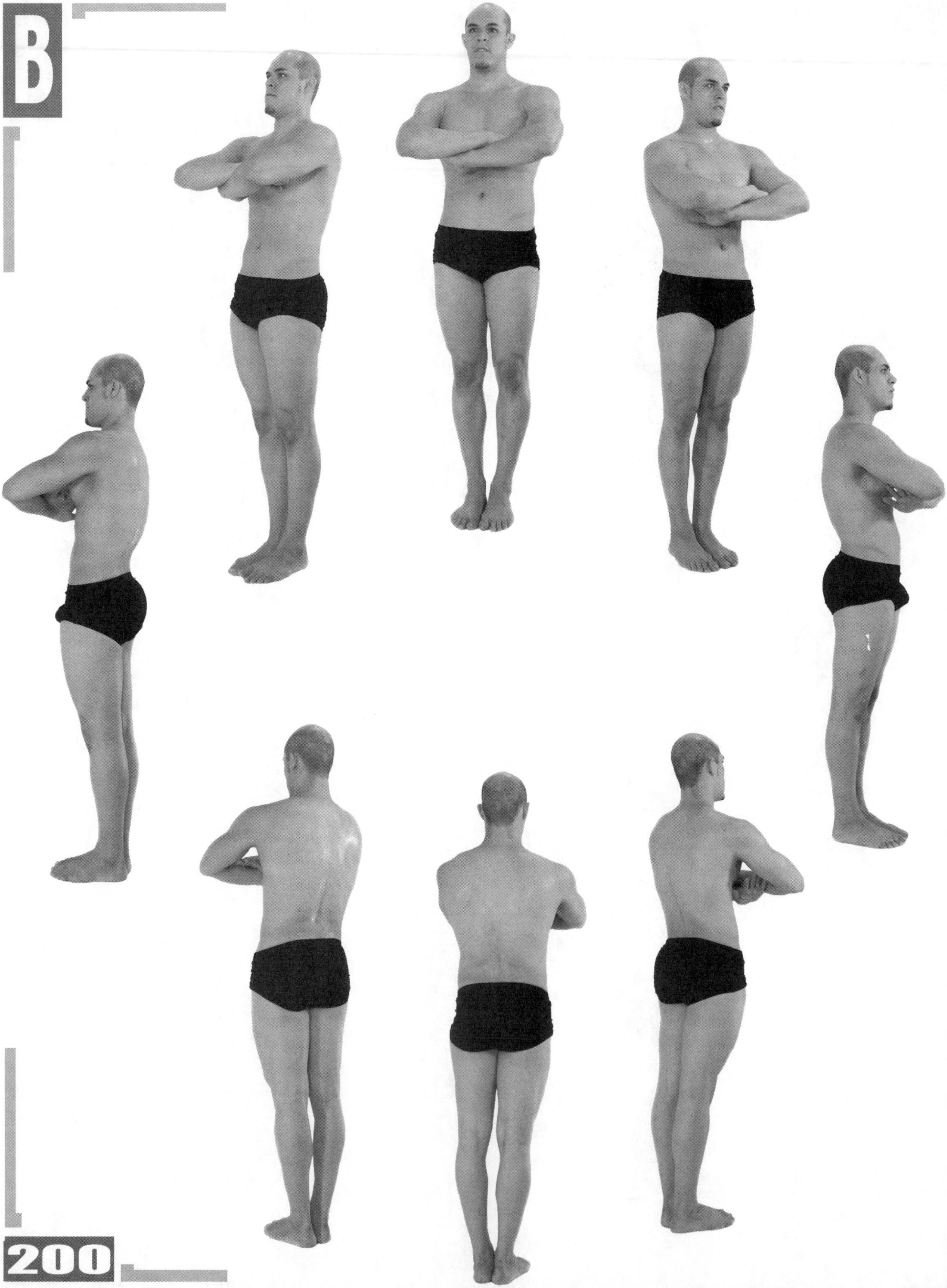

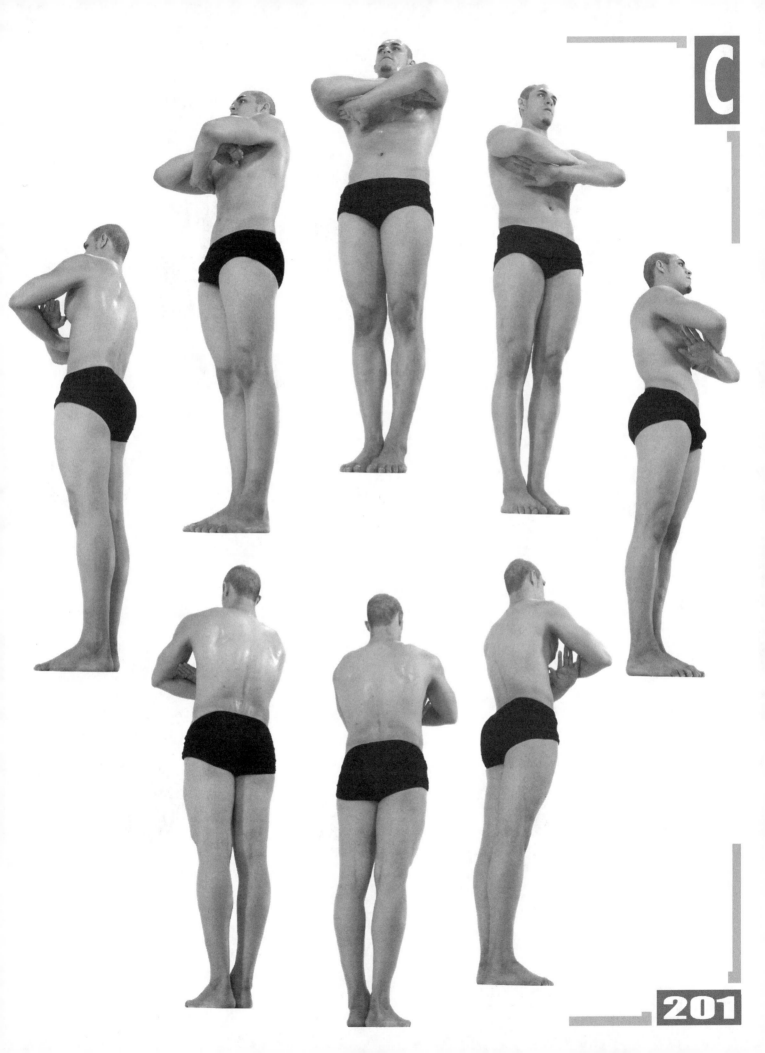

A

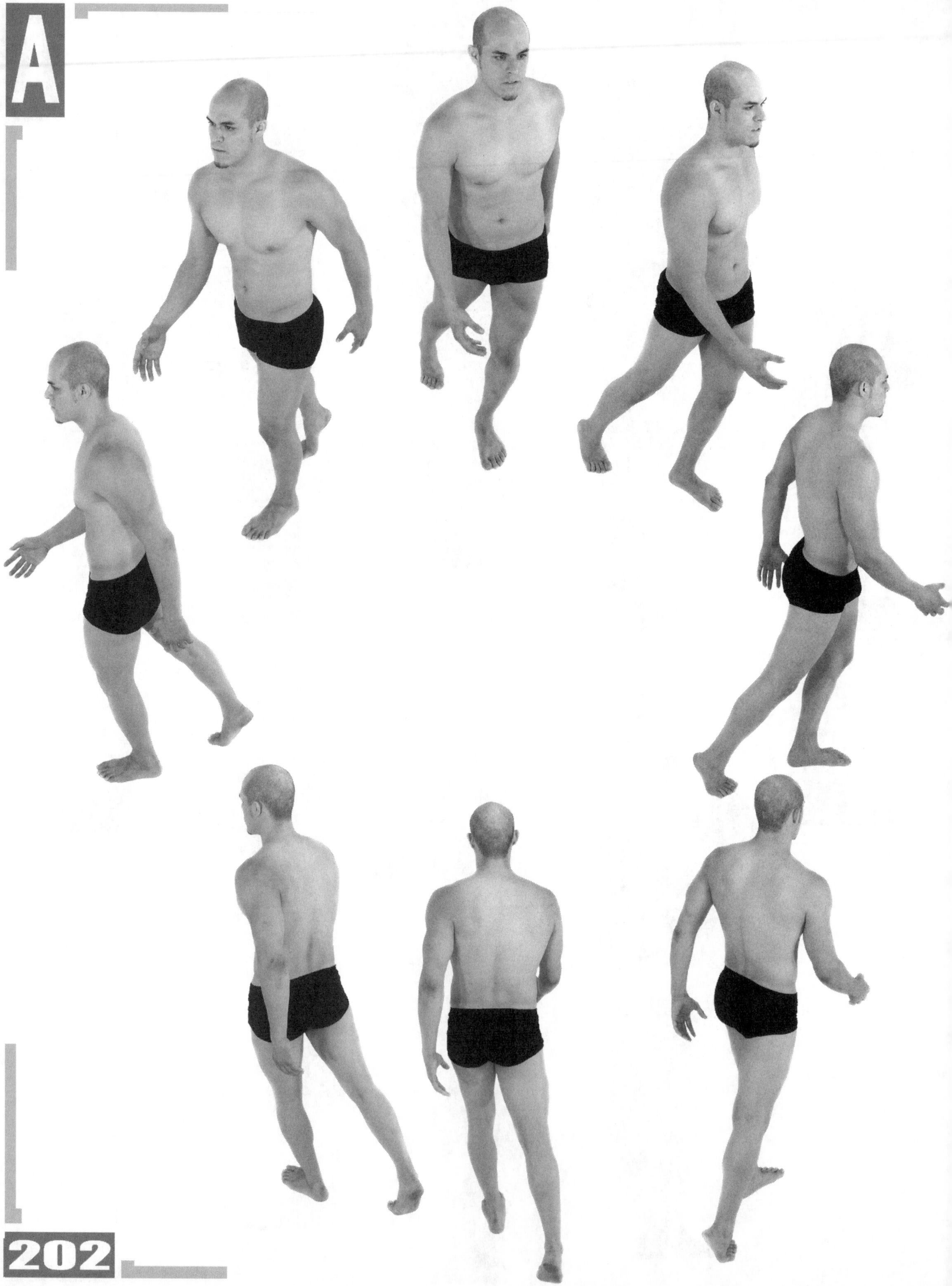

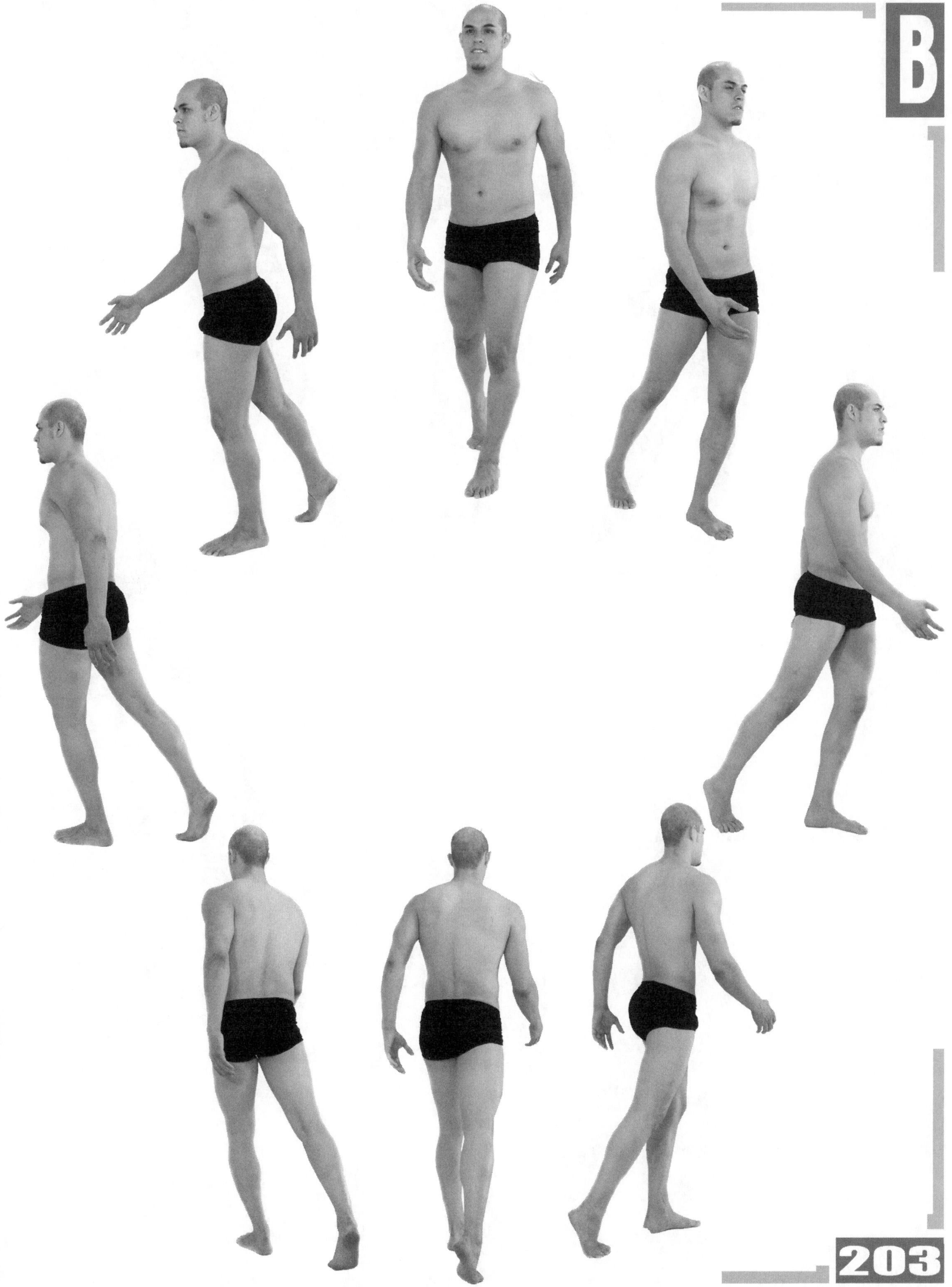

C

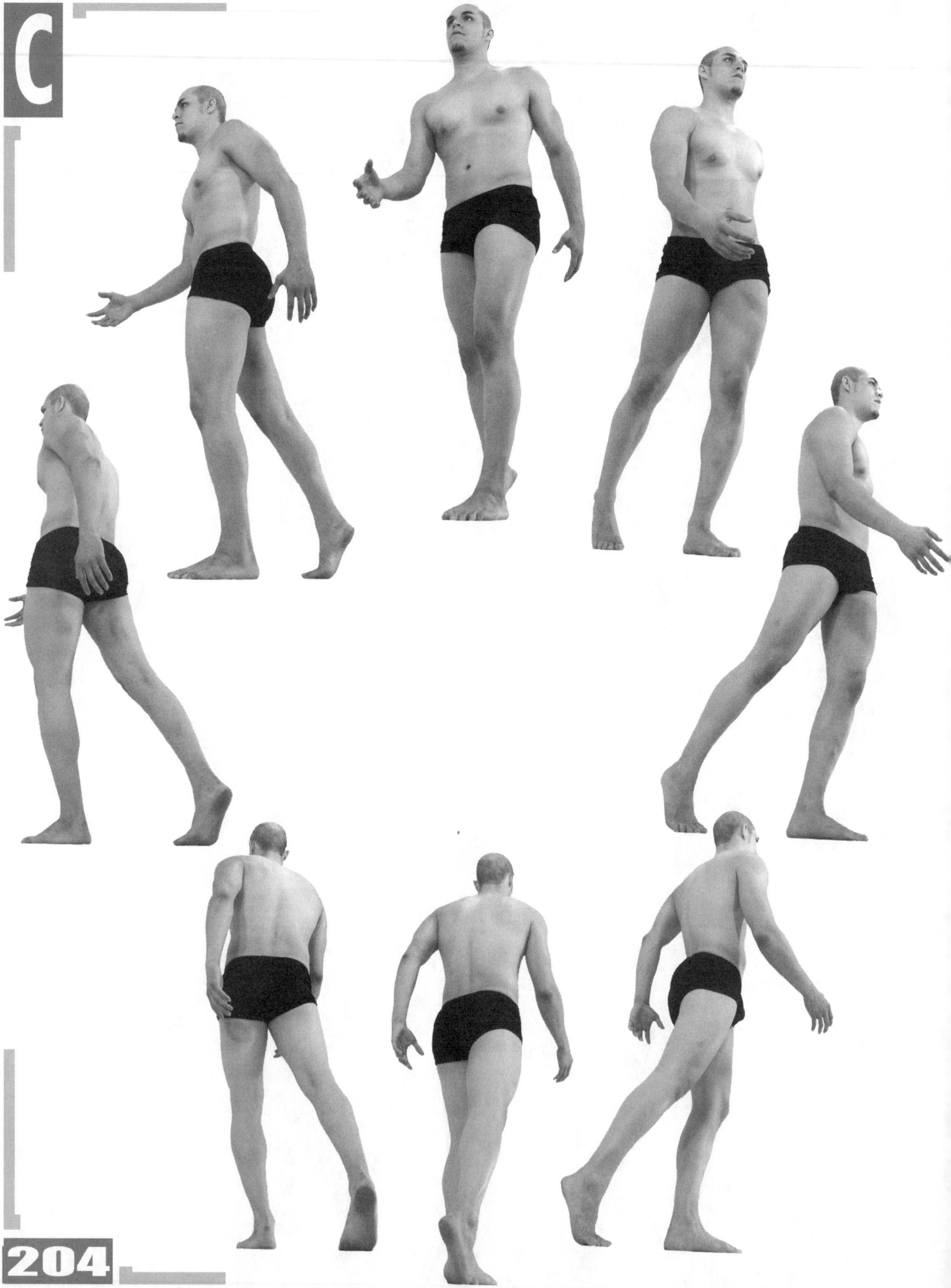

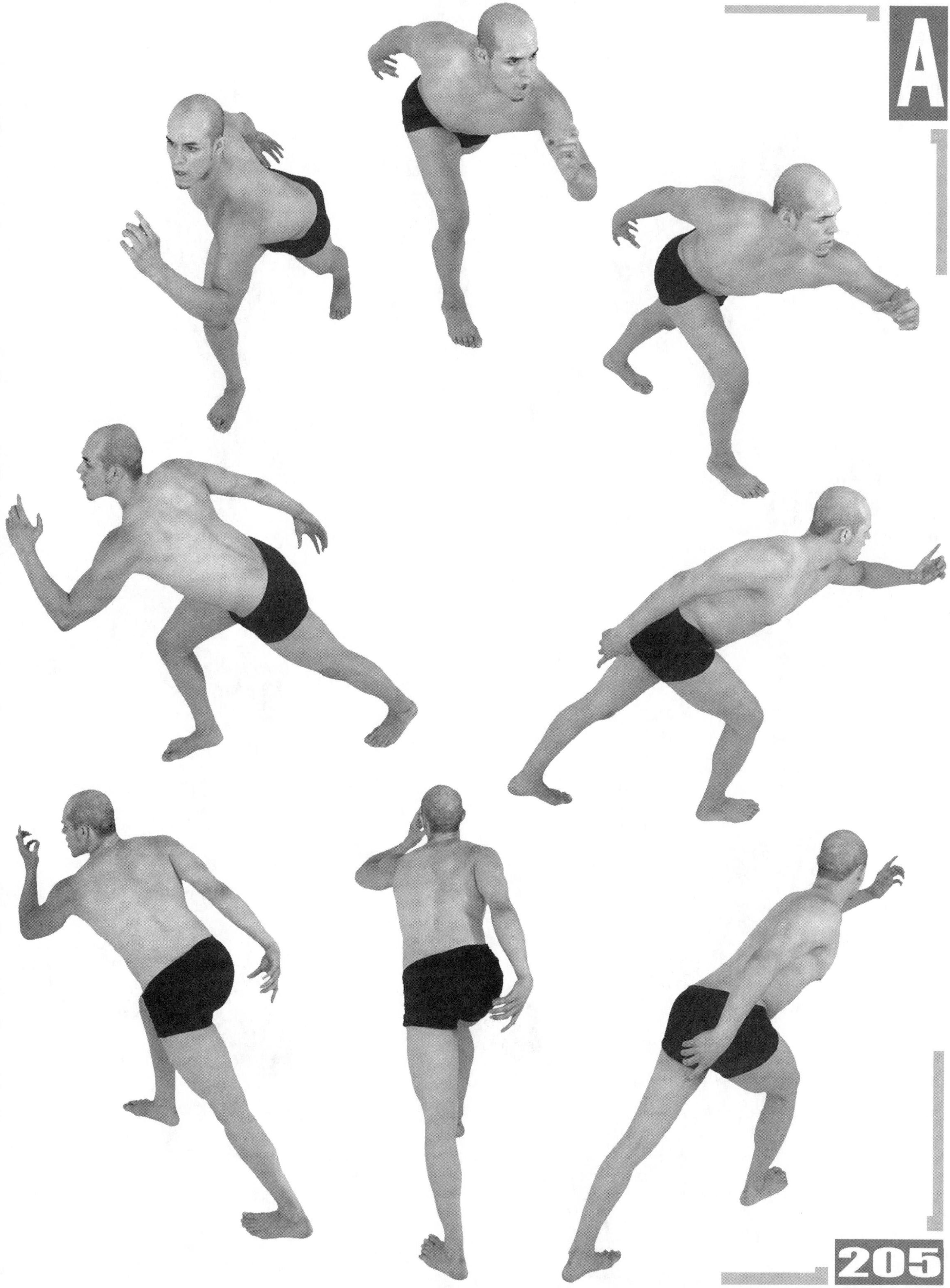

B

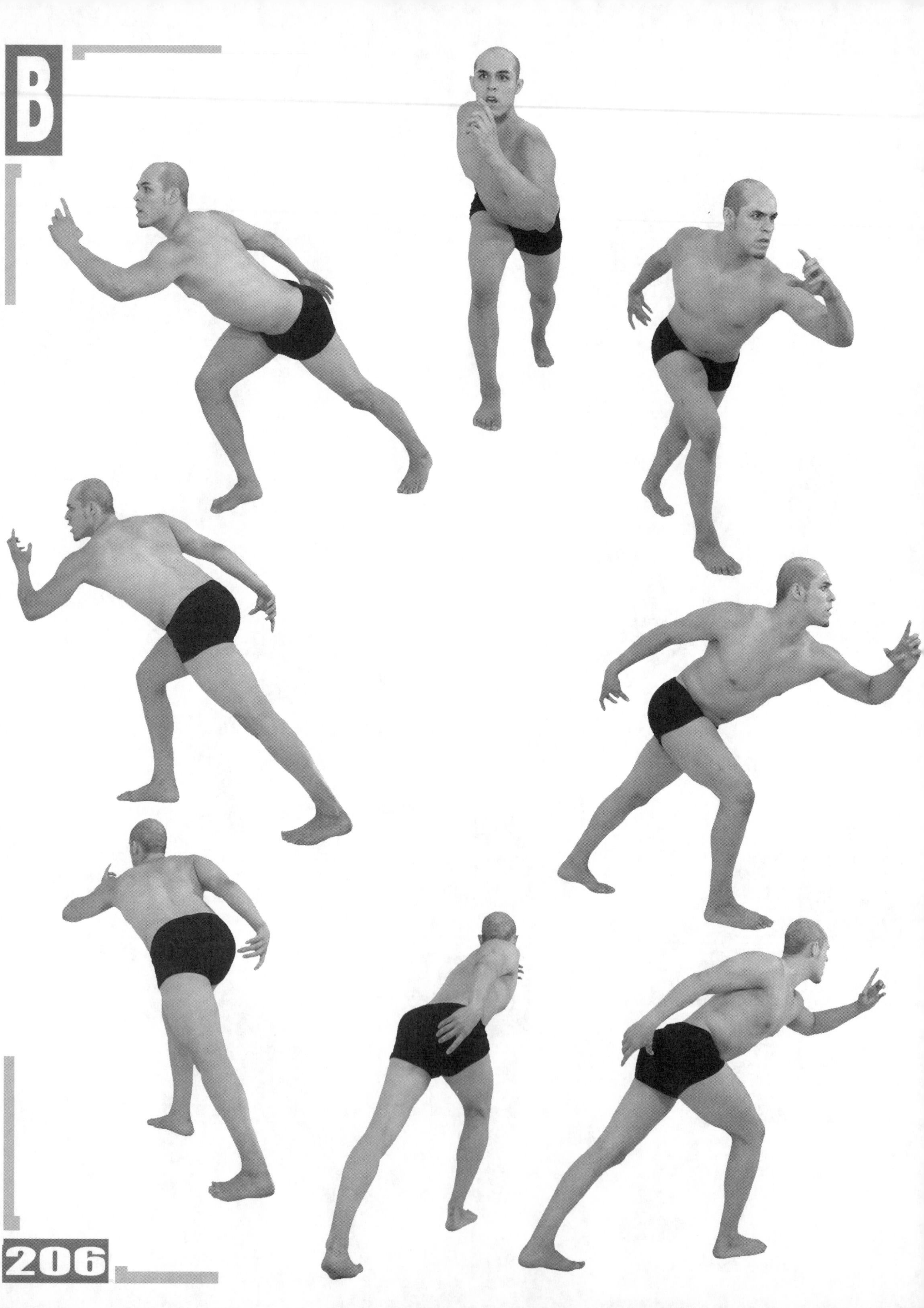

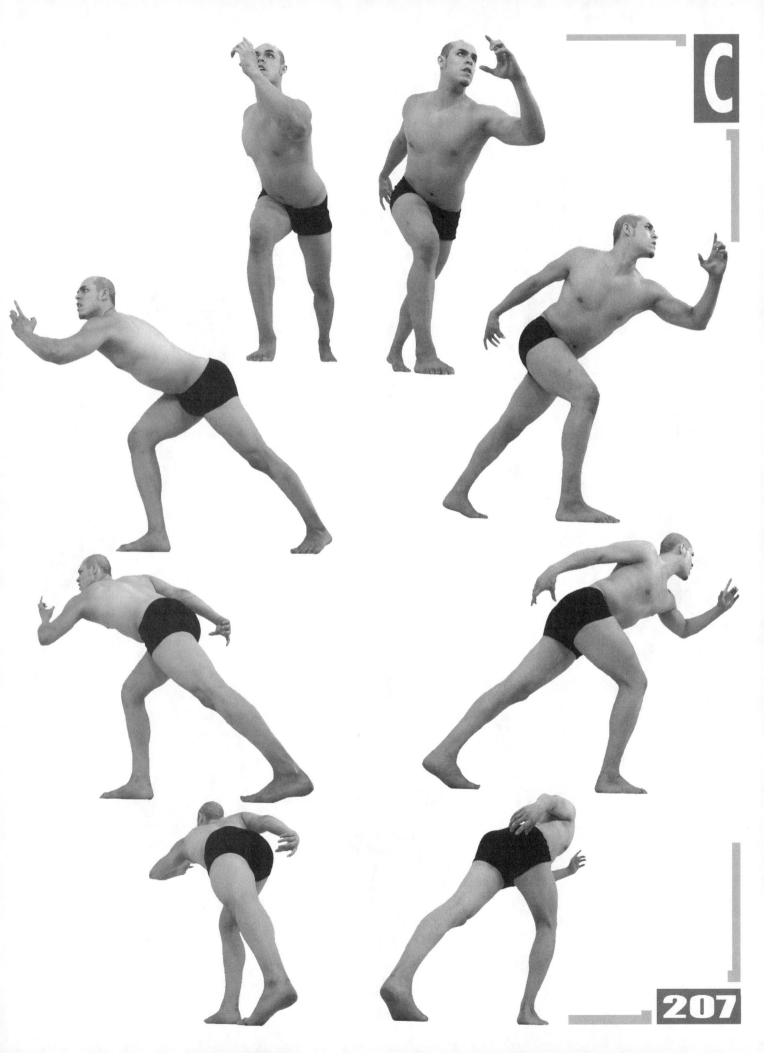

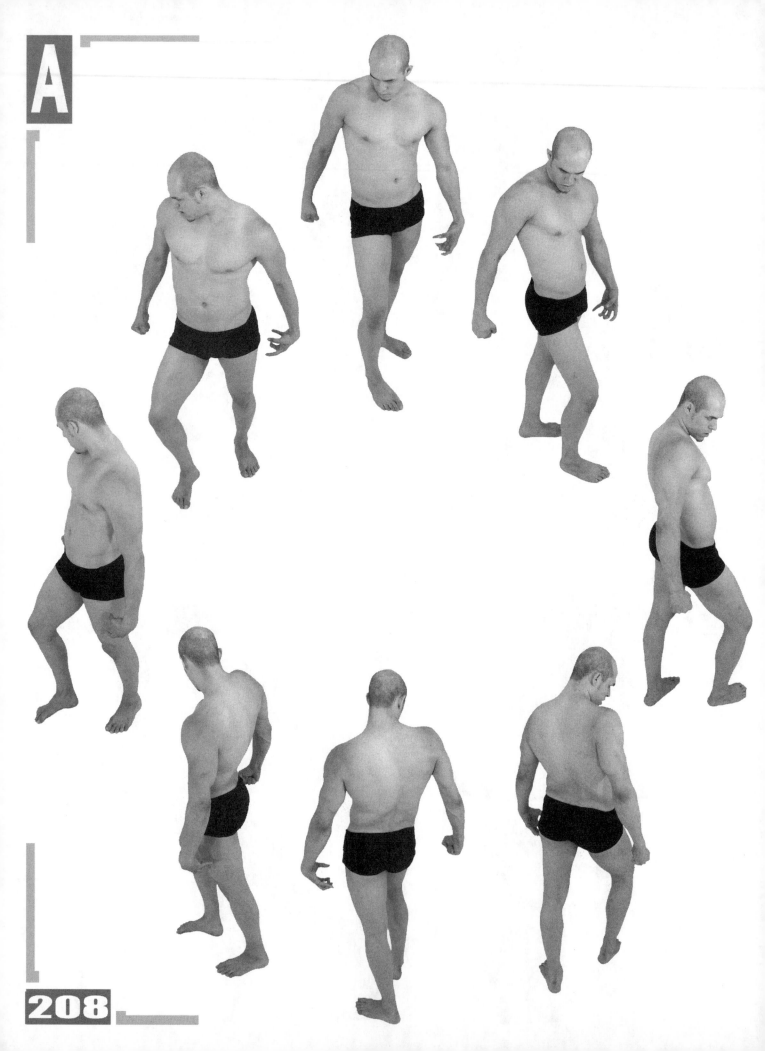

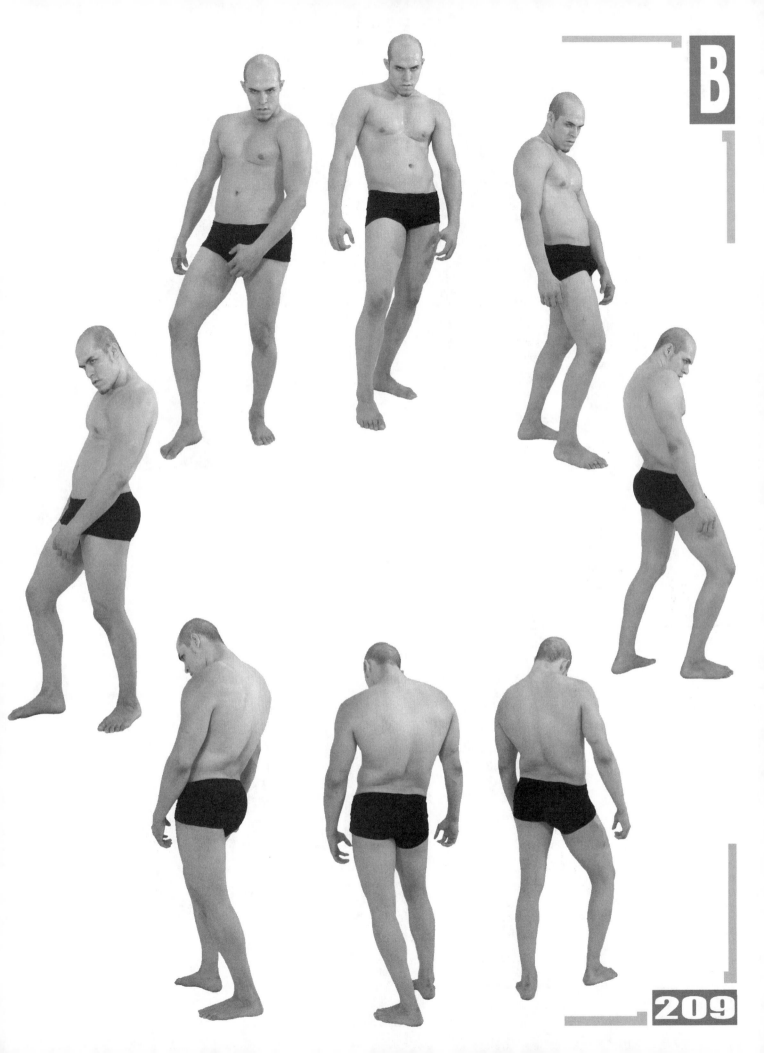

C

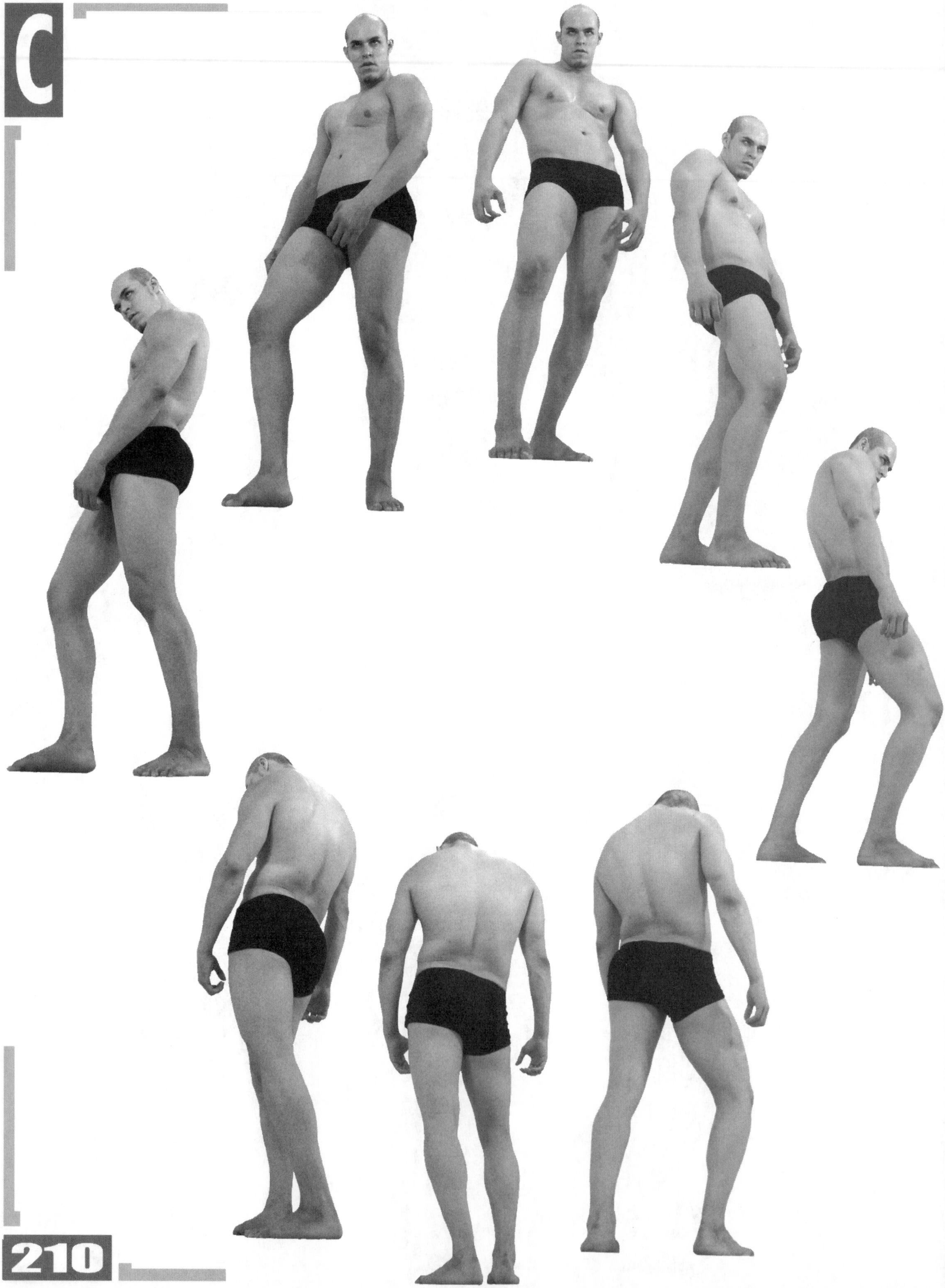

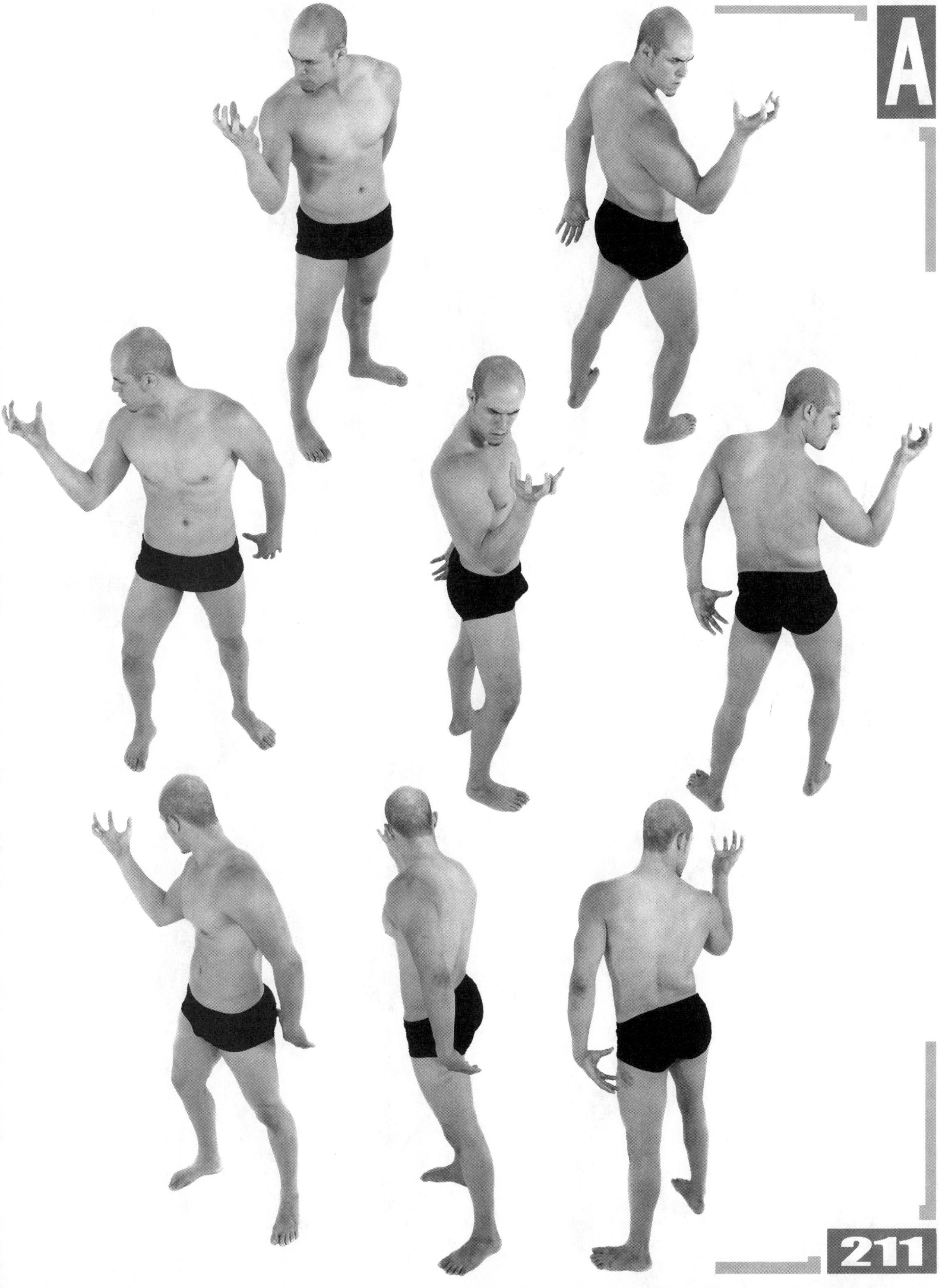

B

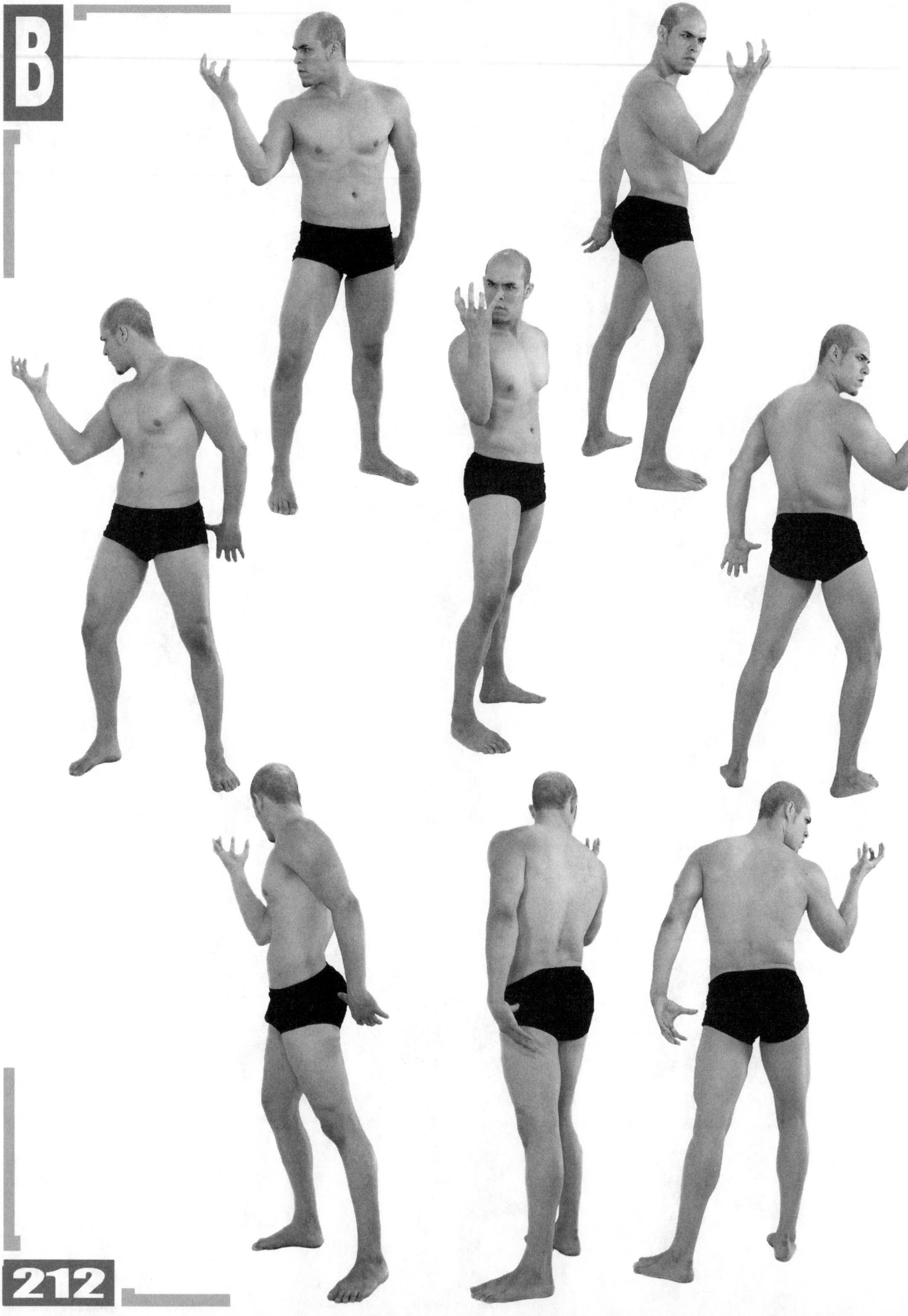

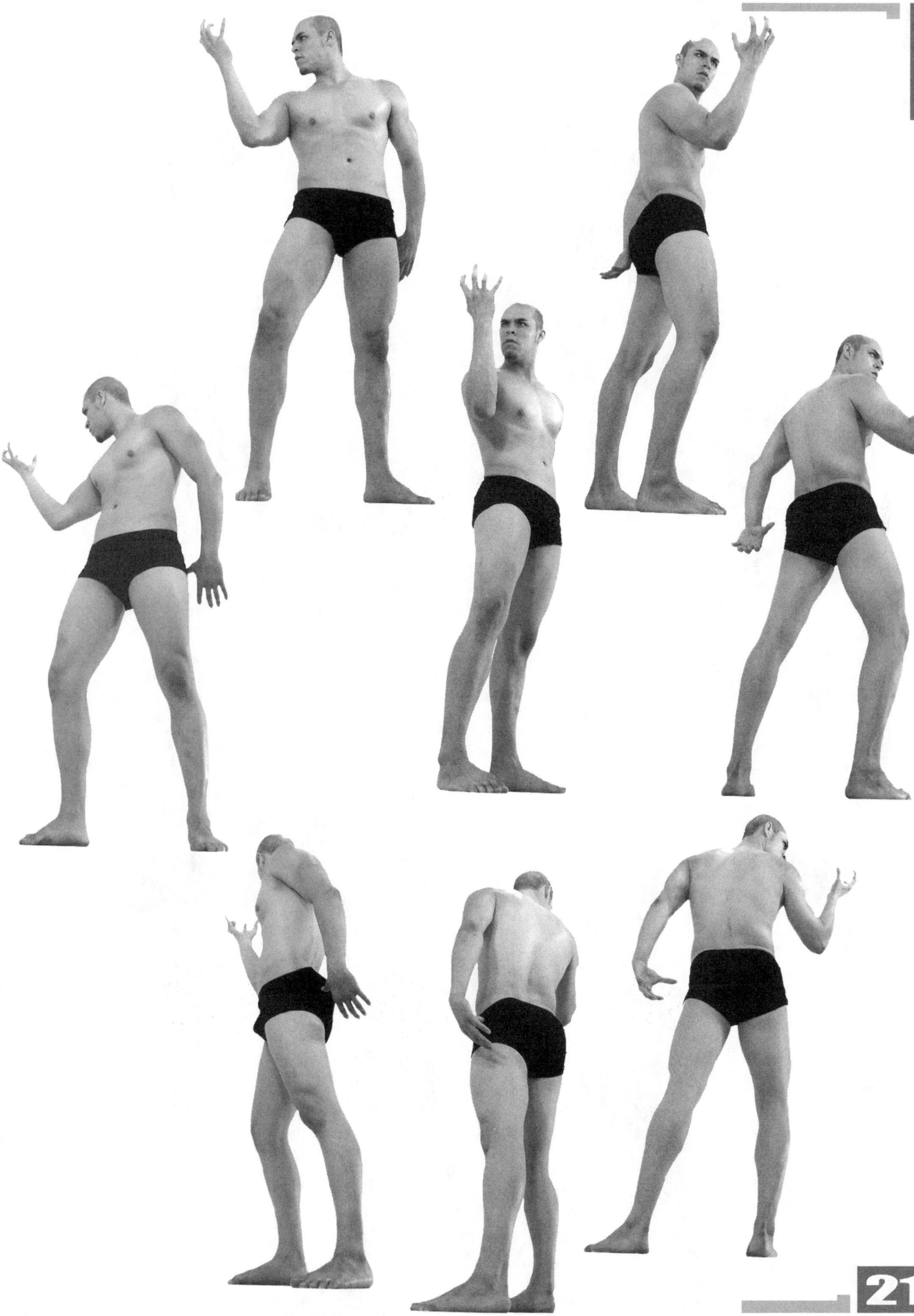

A

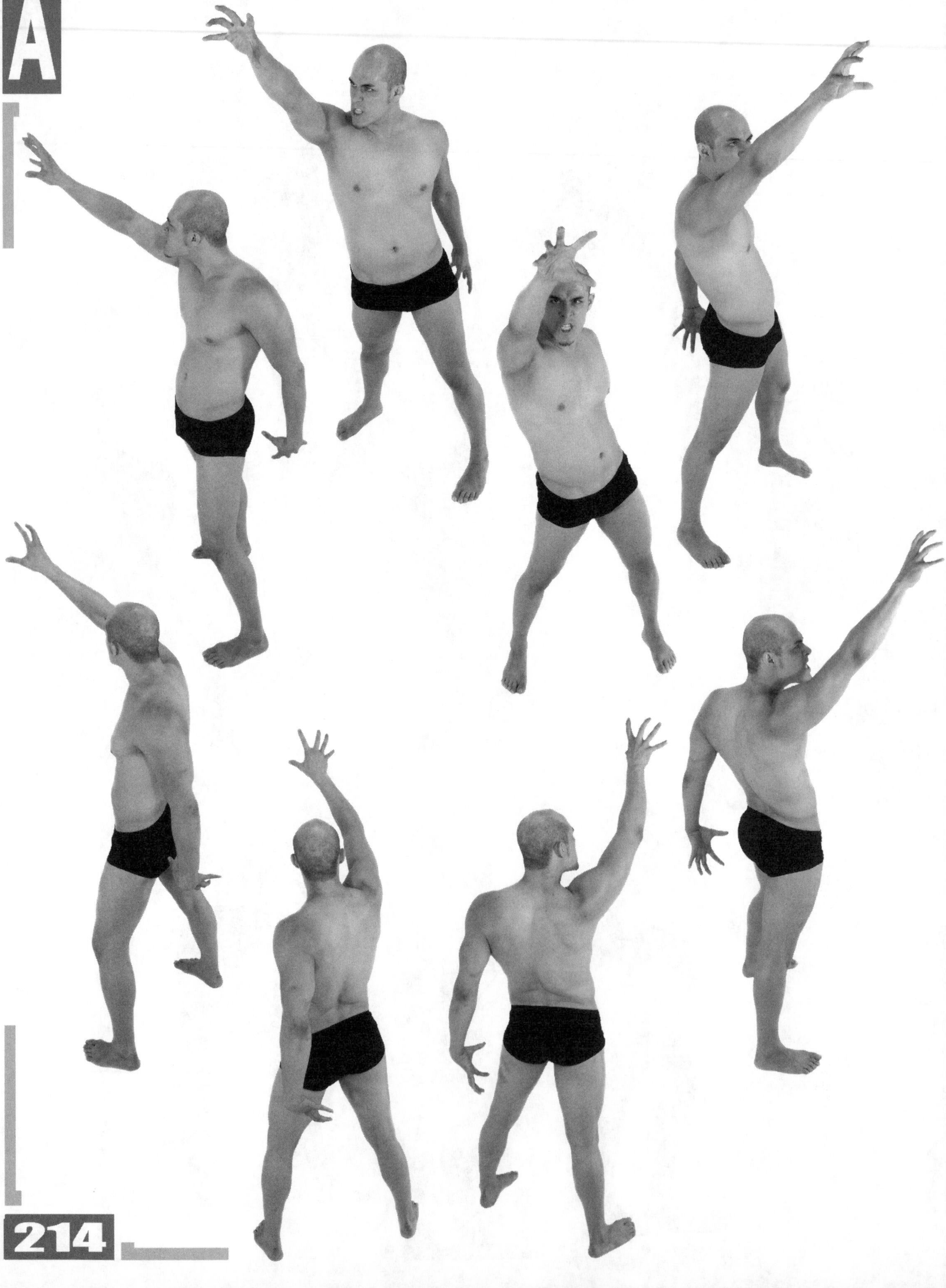

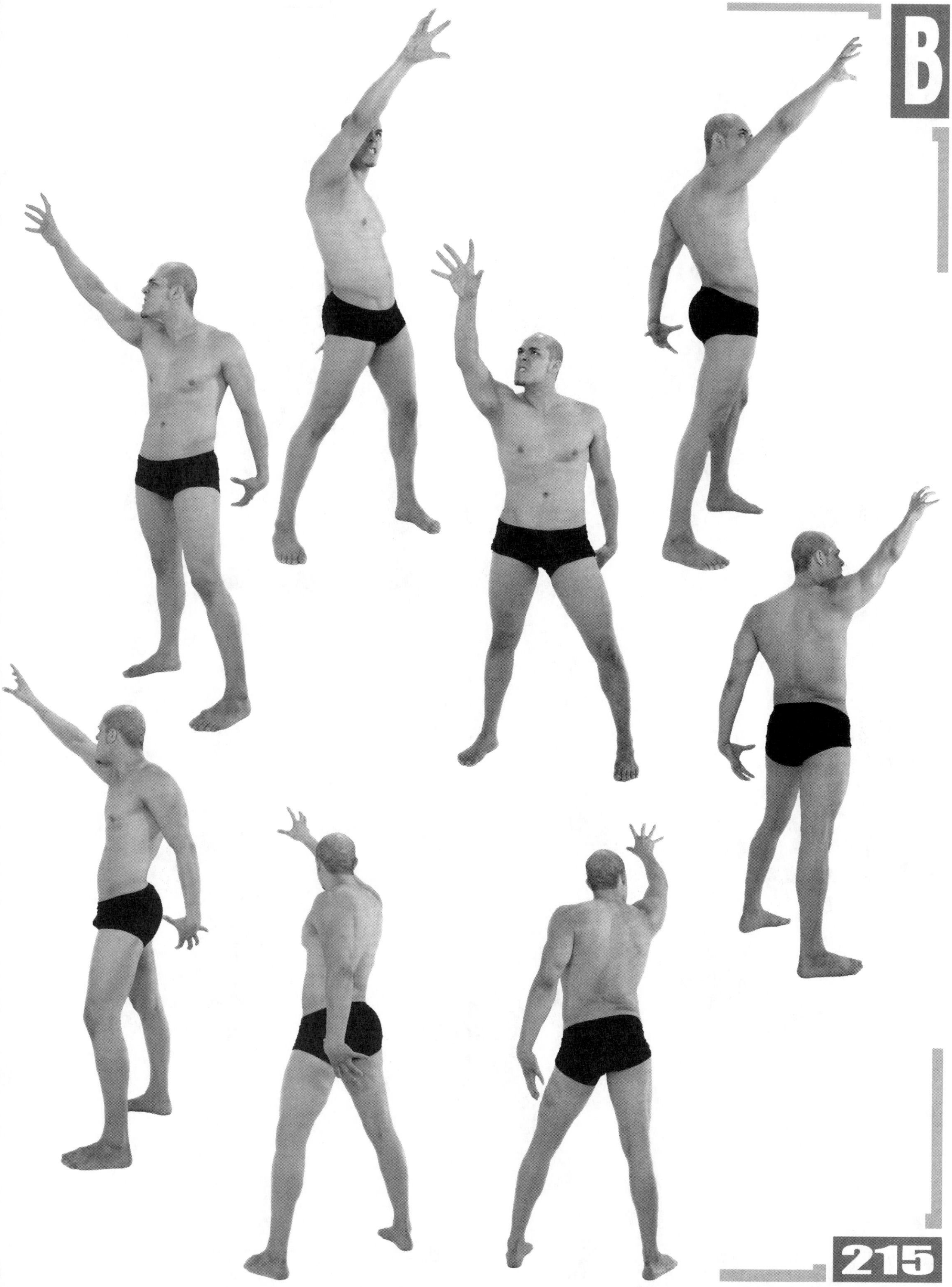

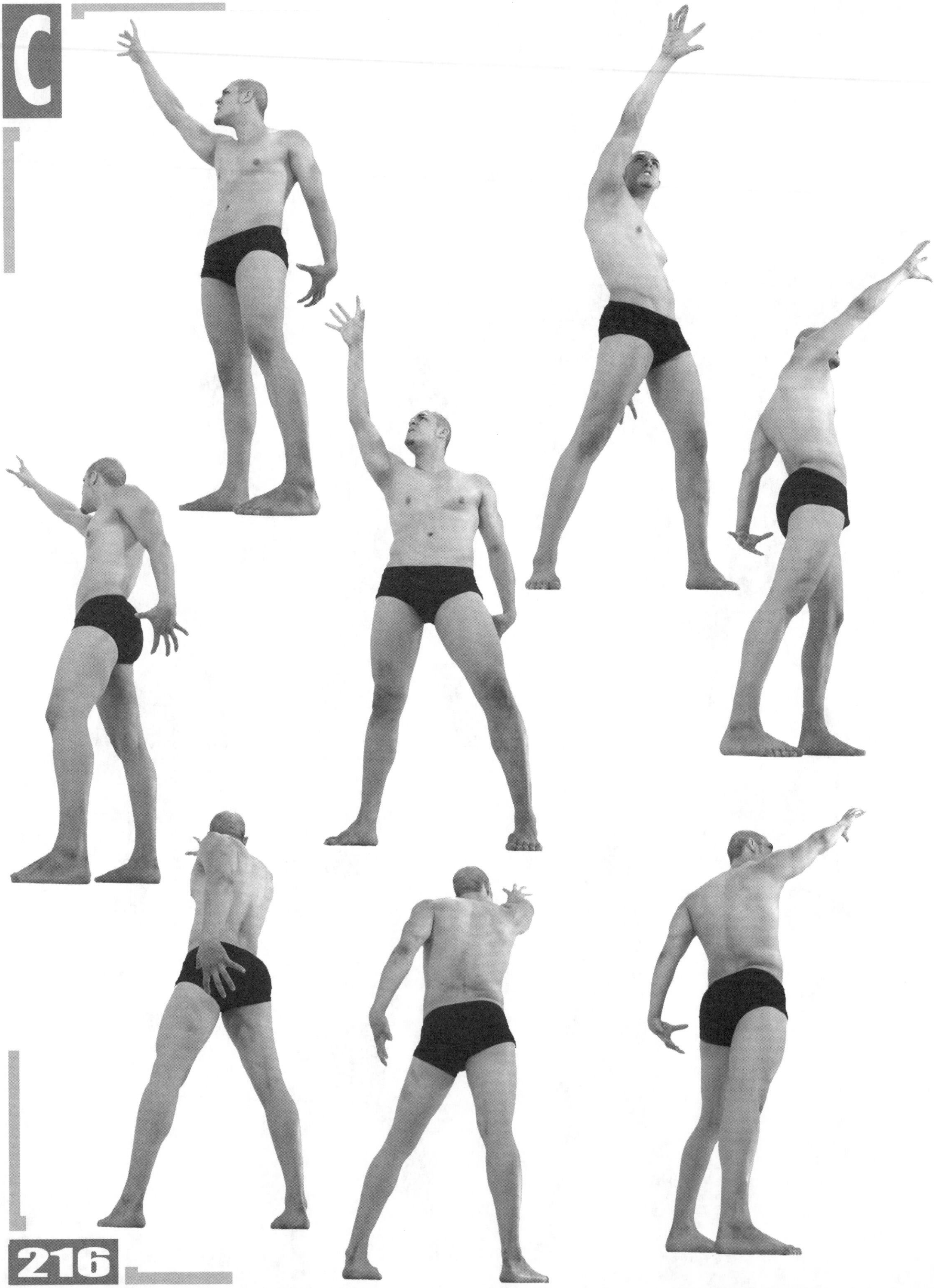

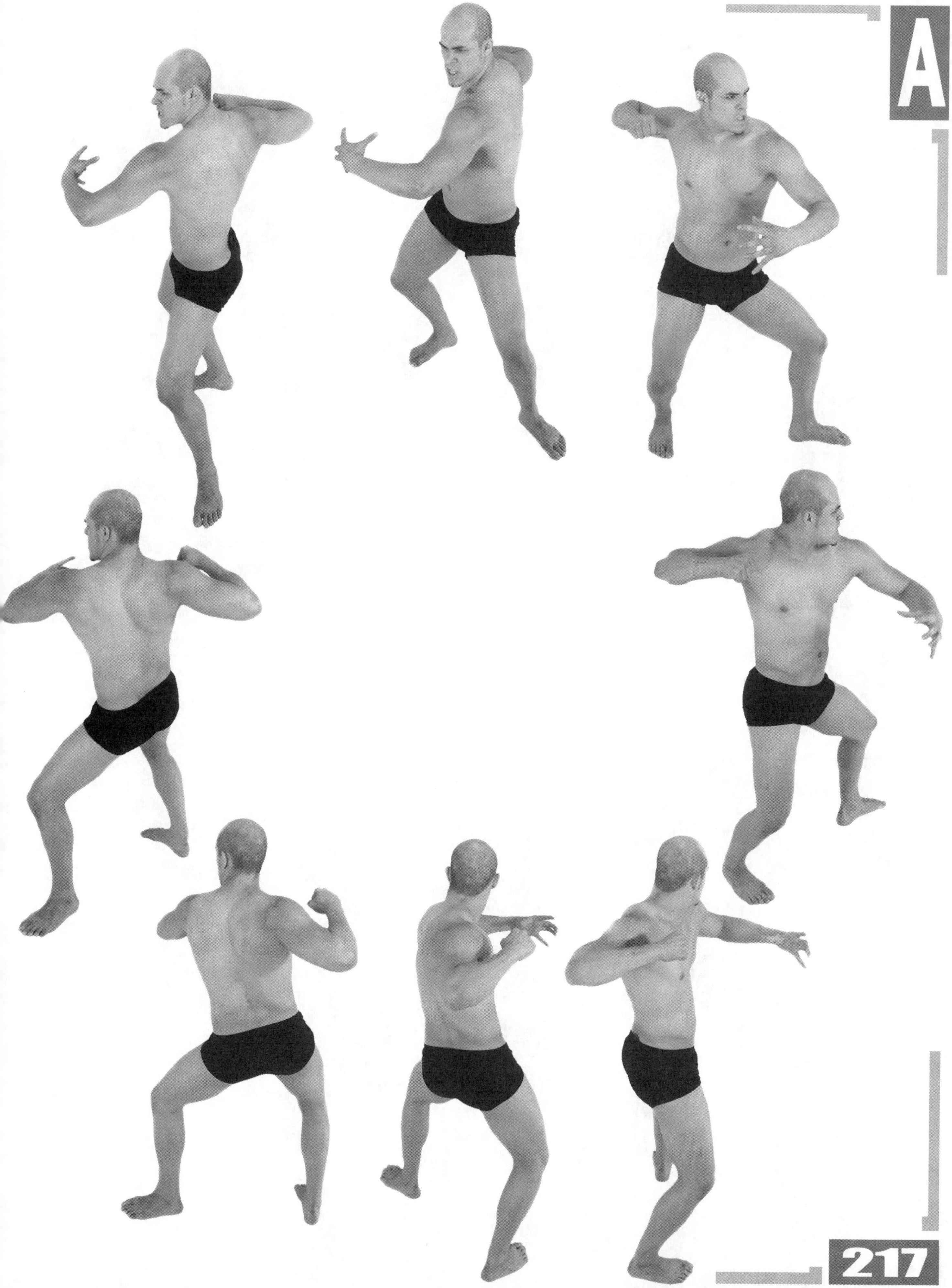

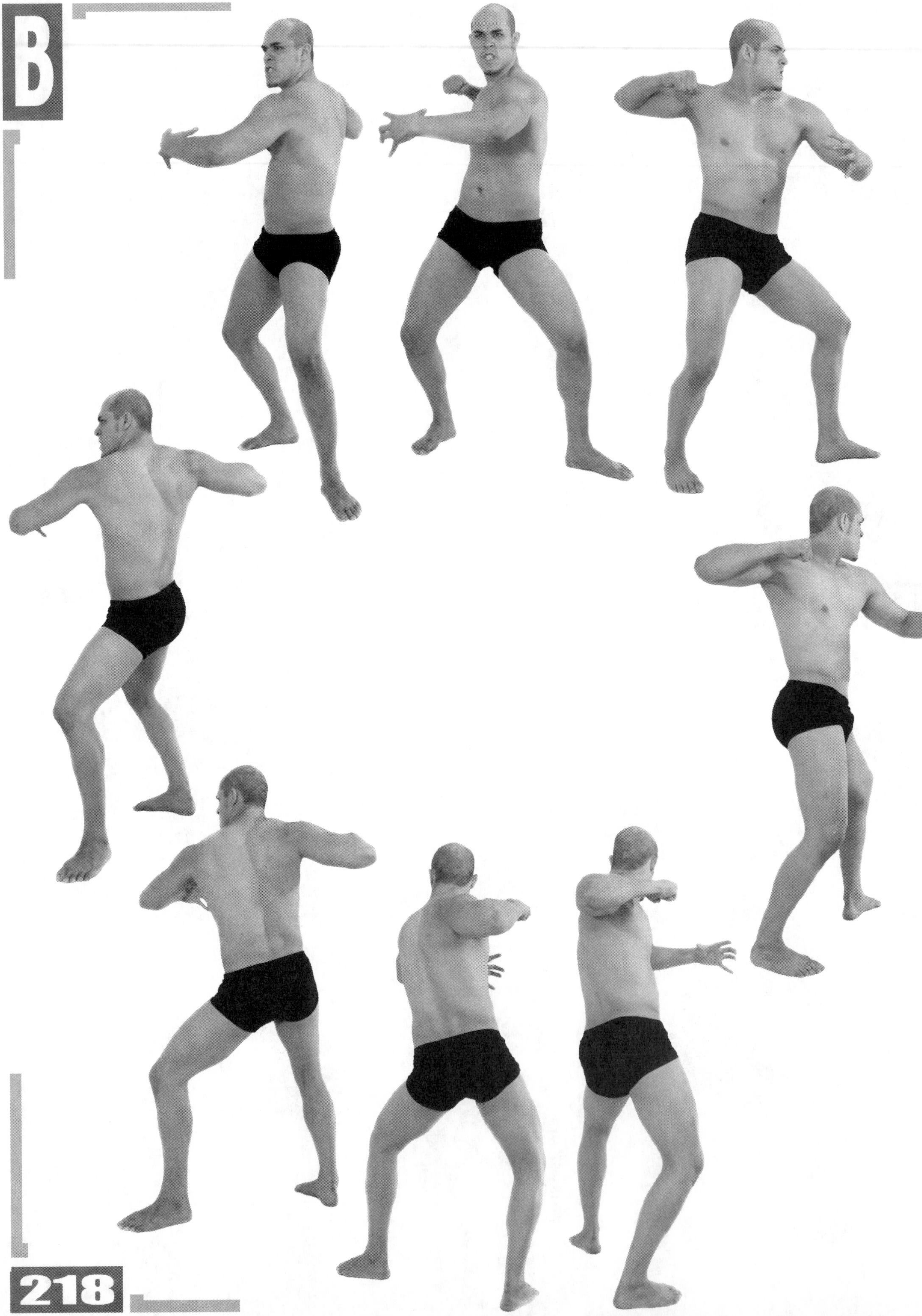

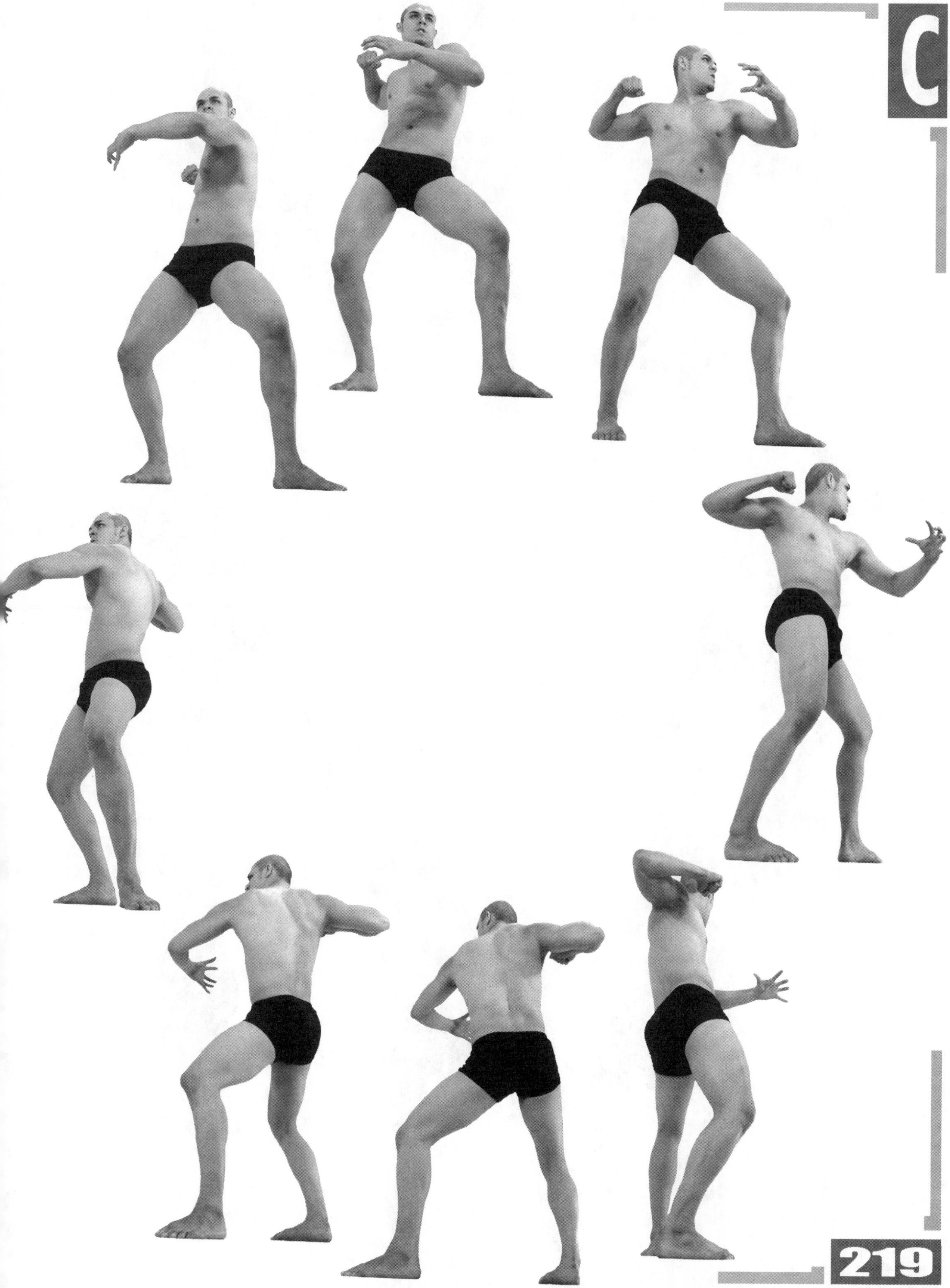

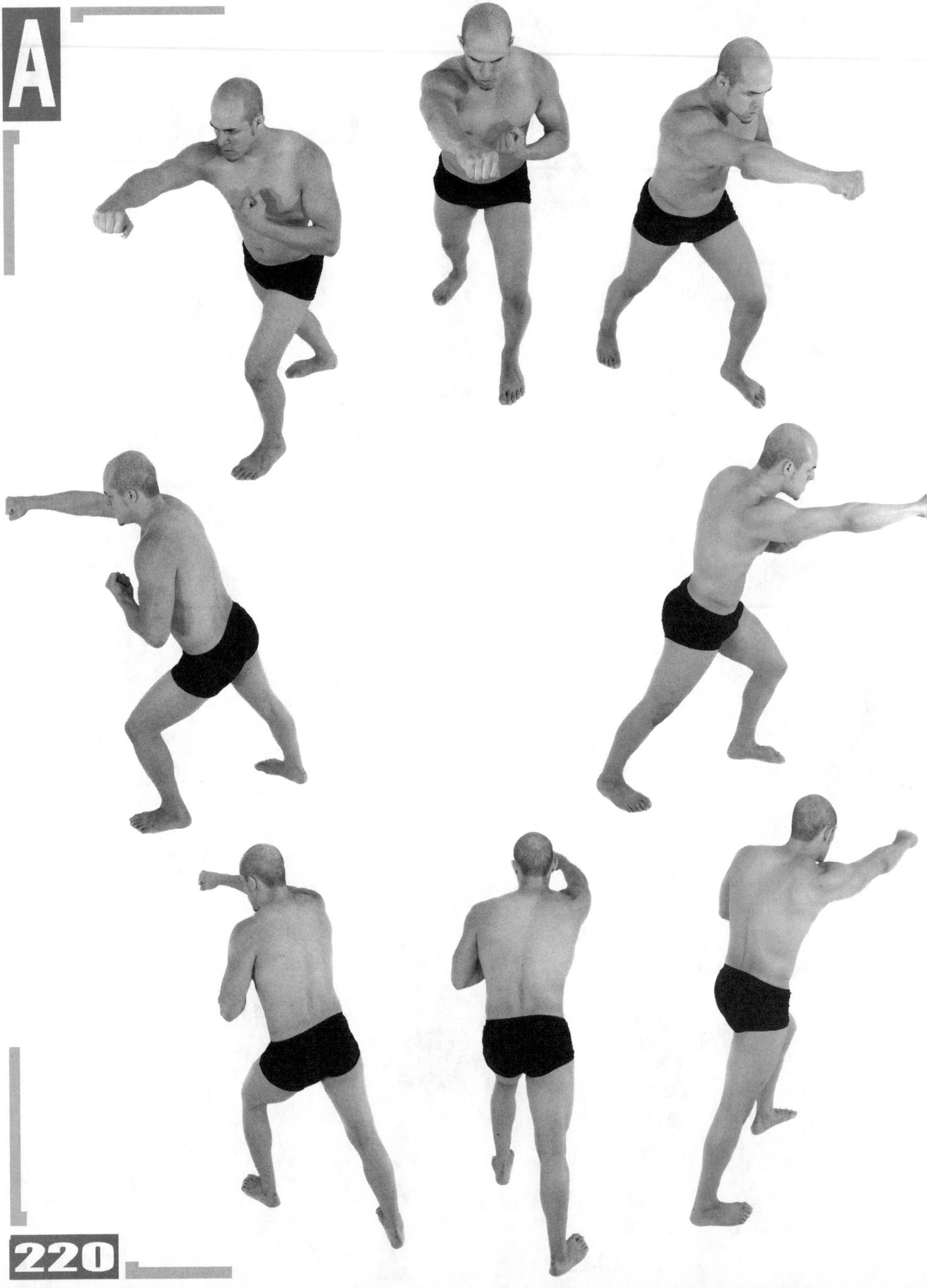

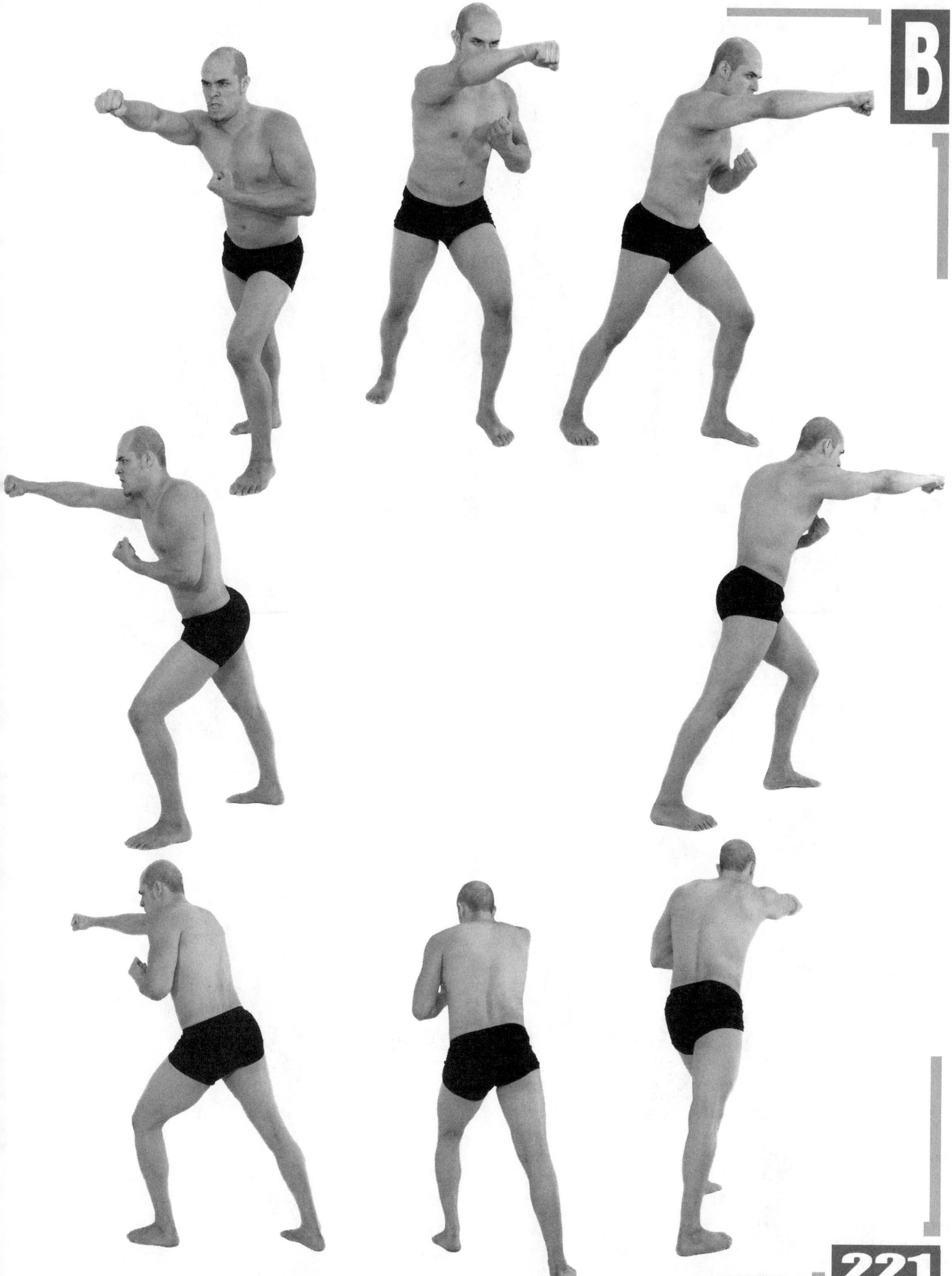

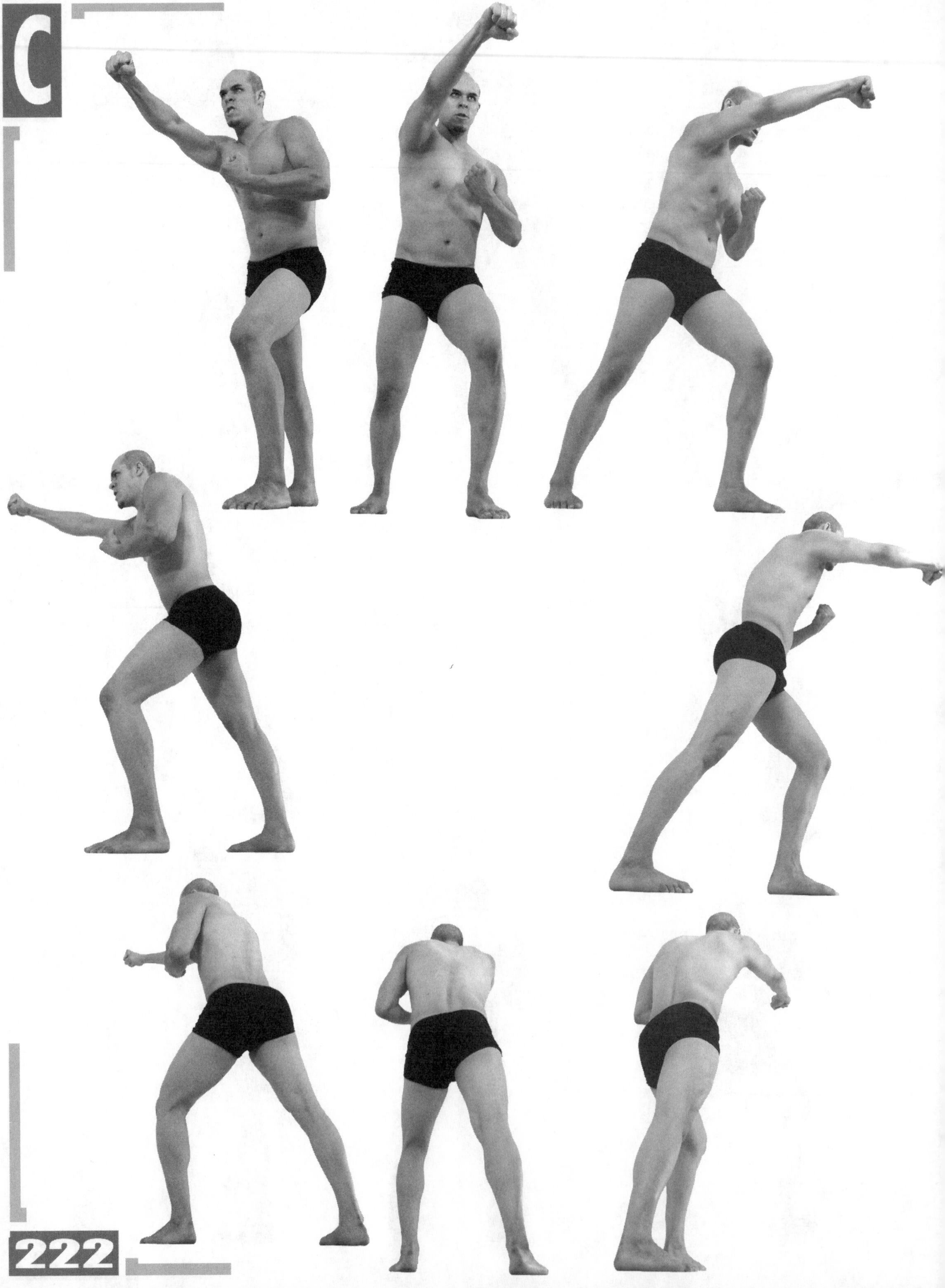

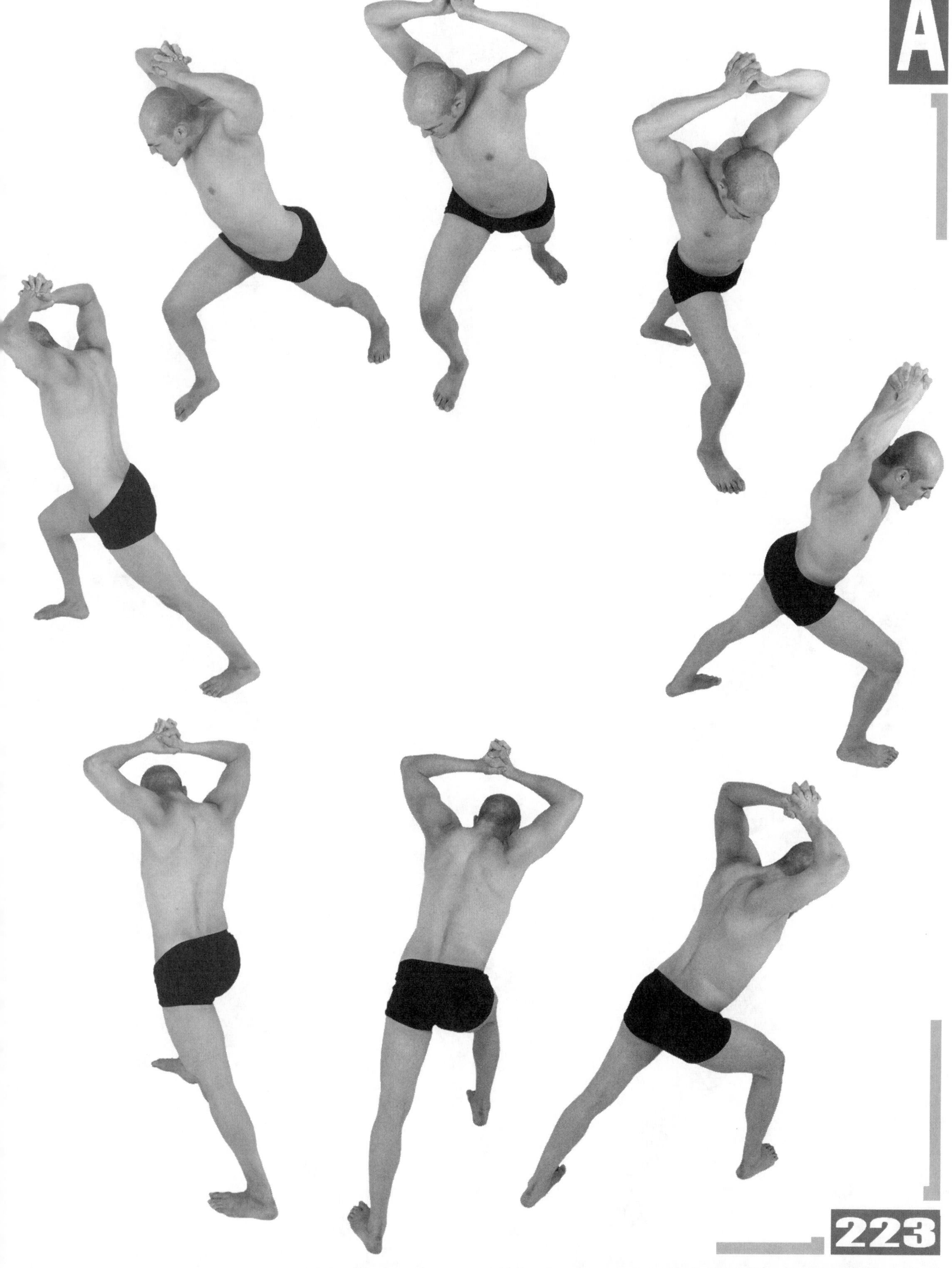

A

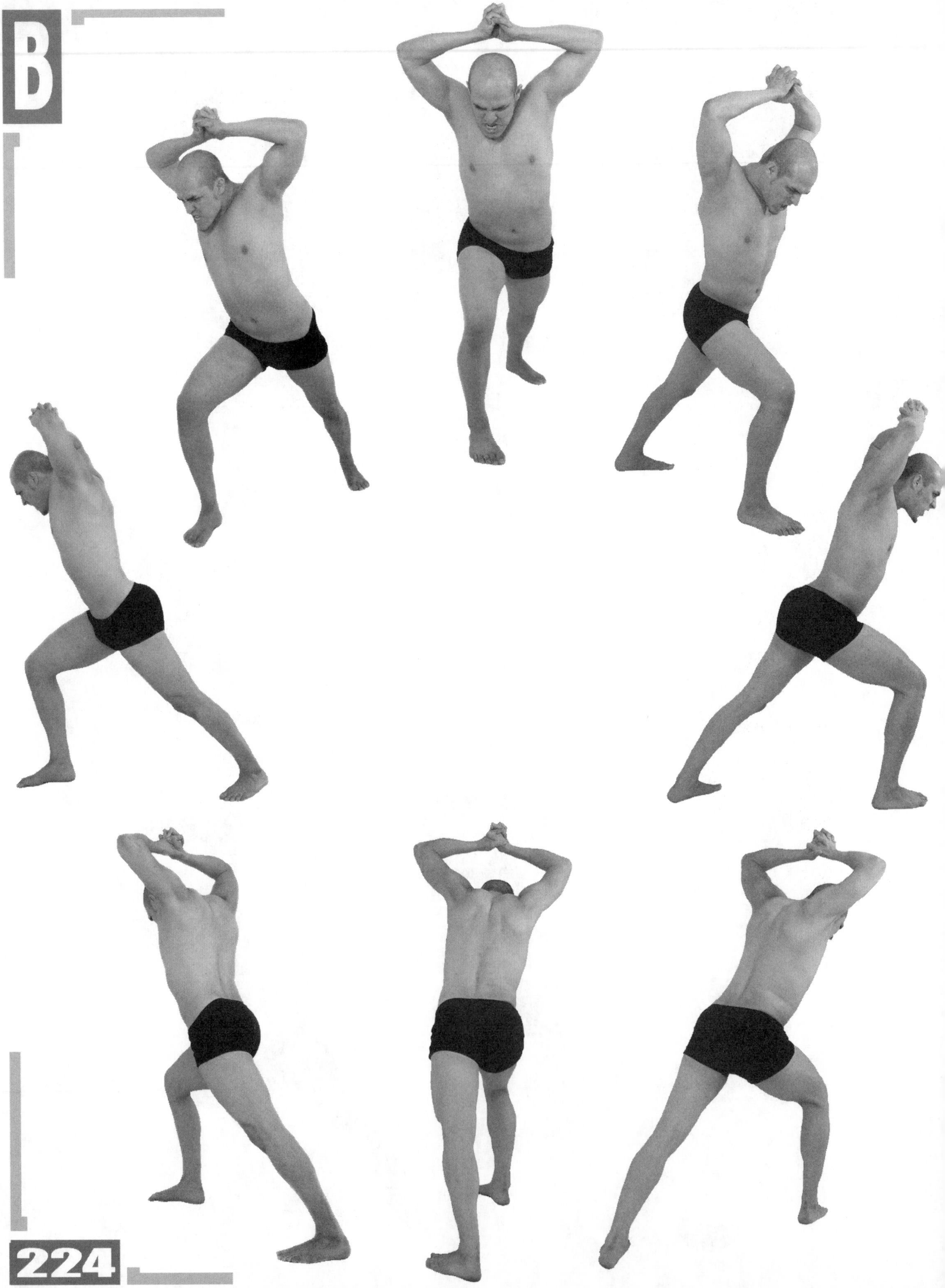

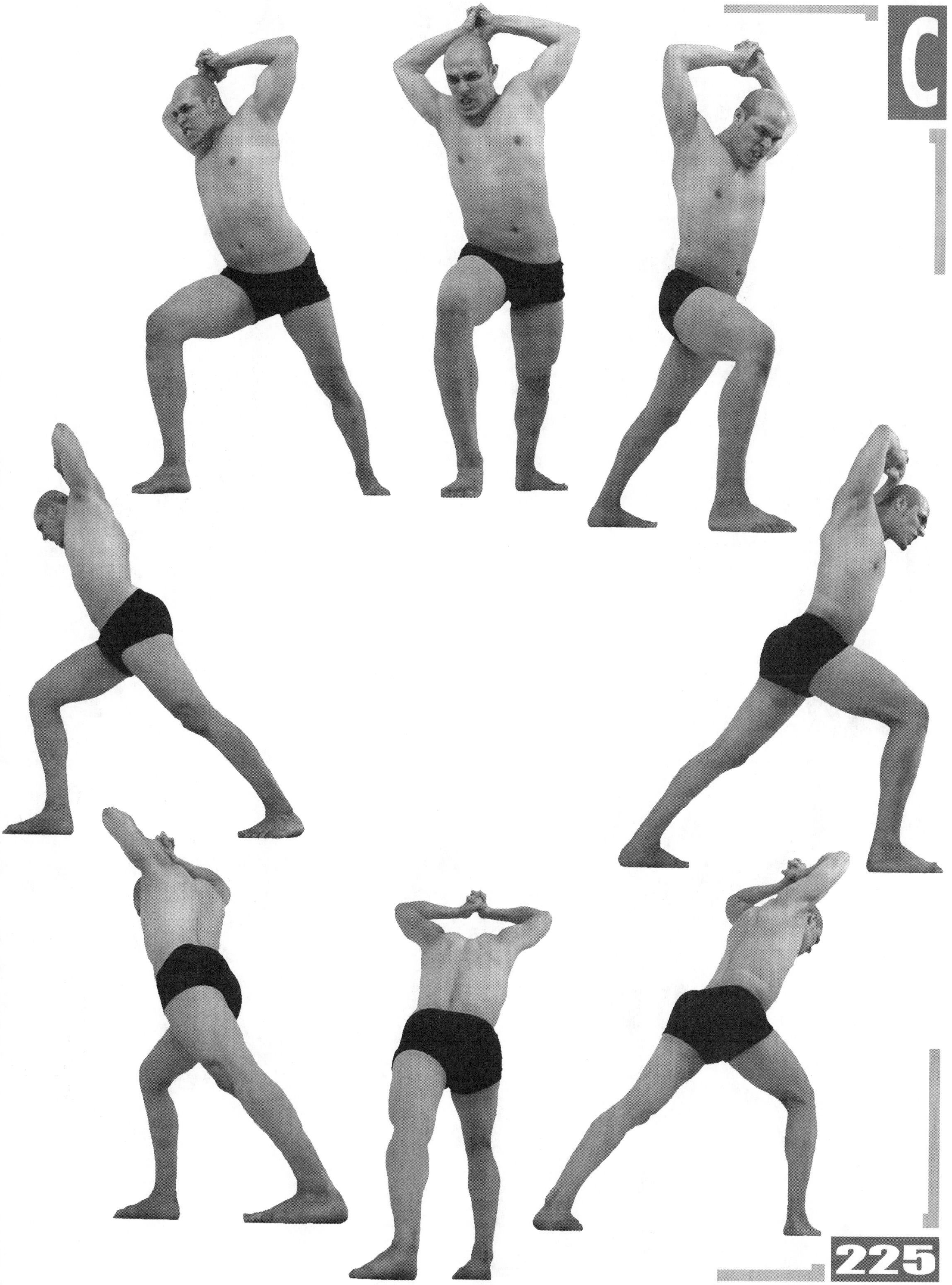

A

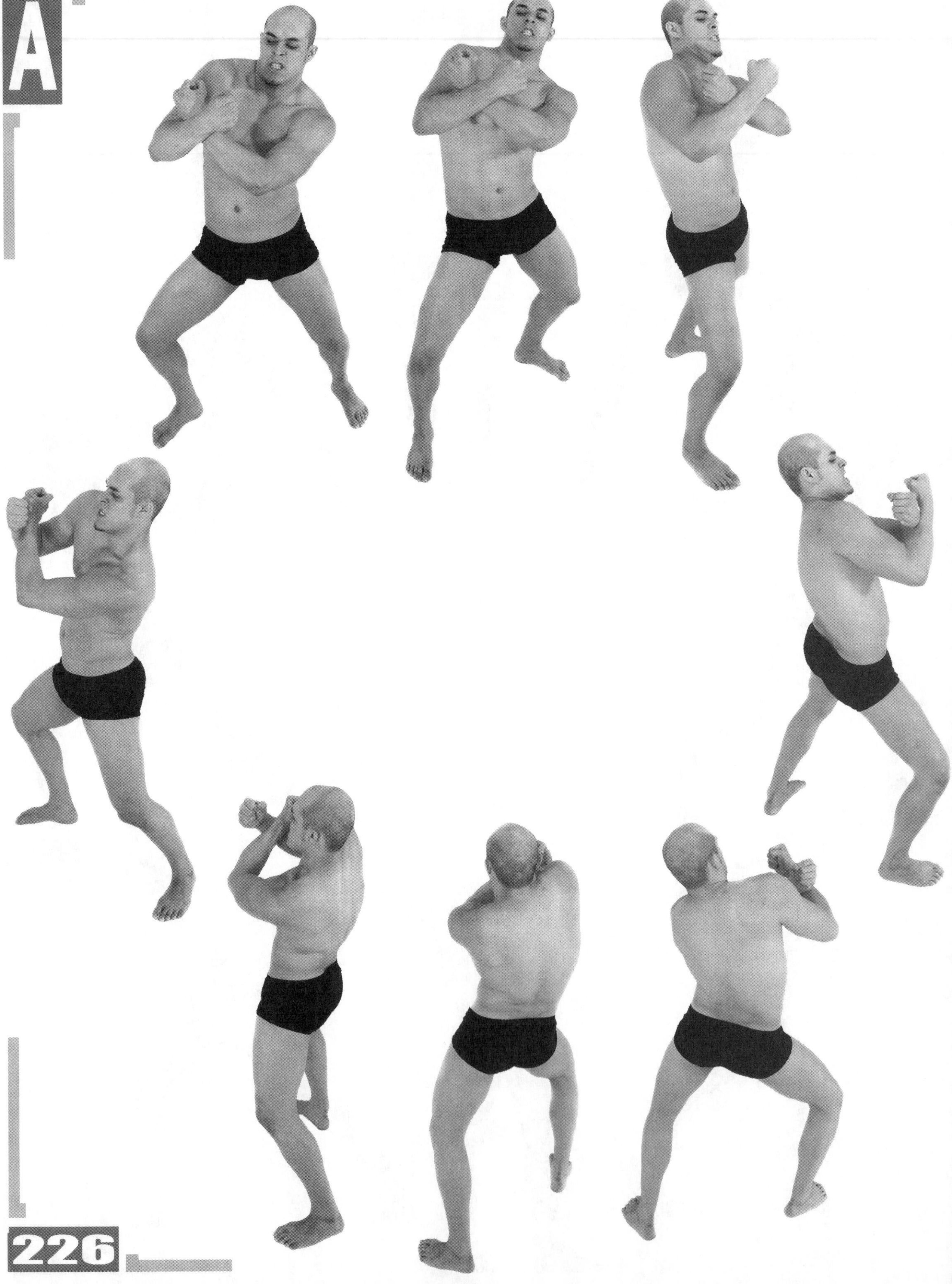

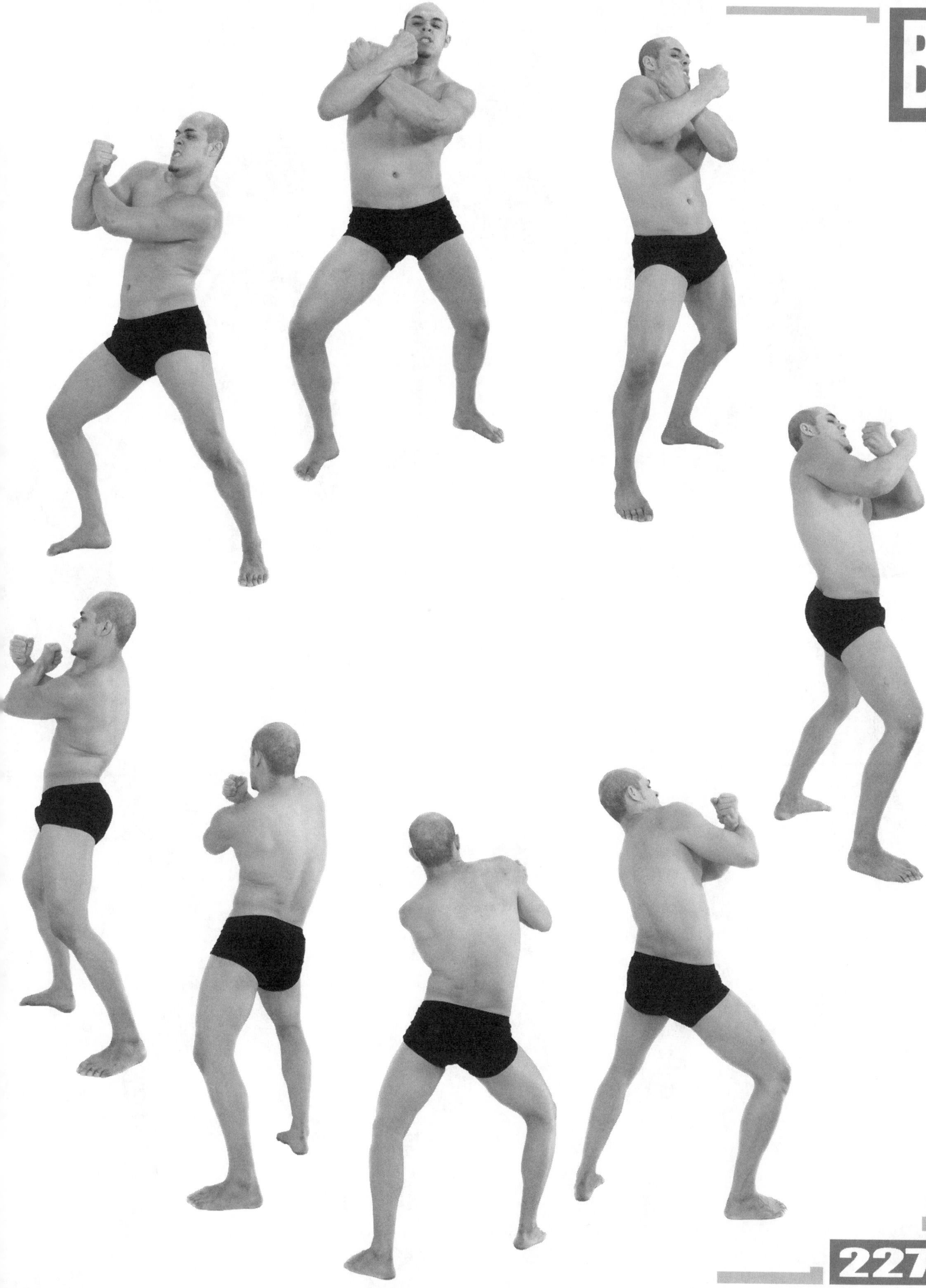

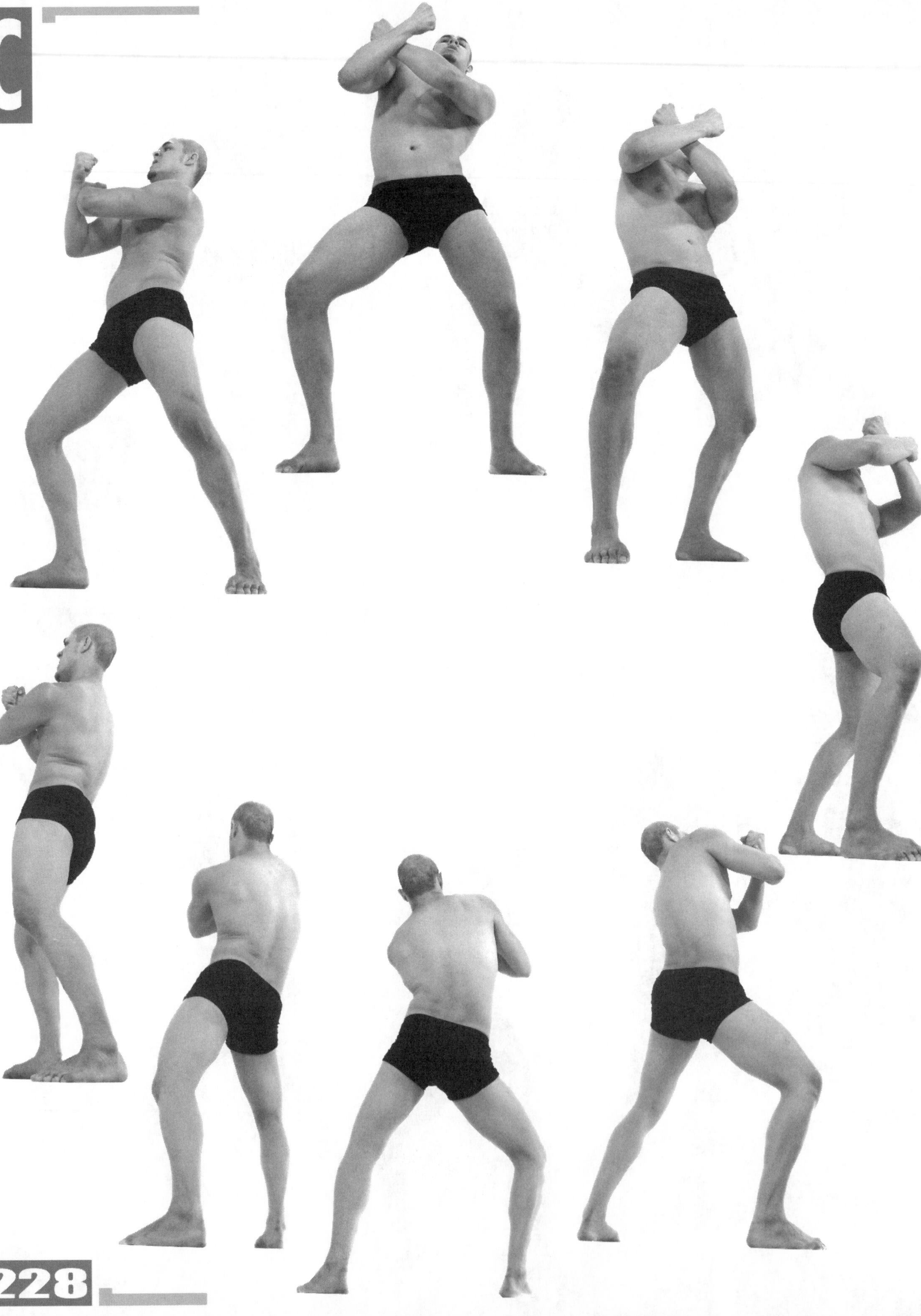

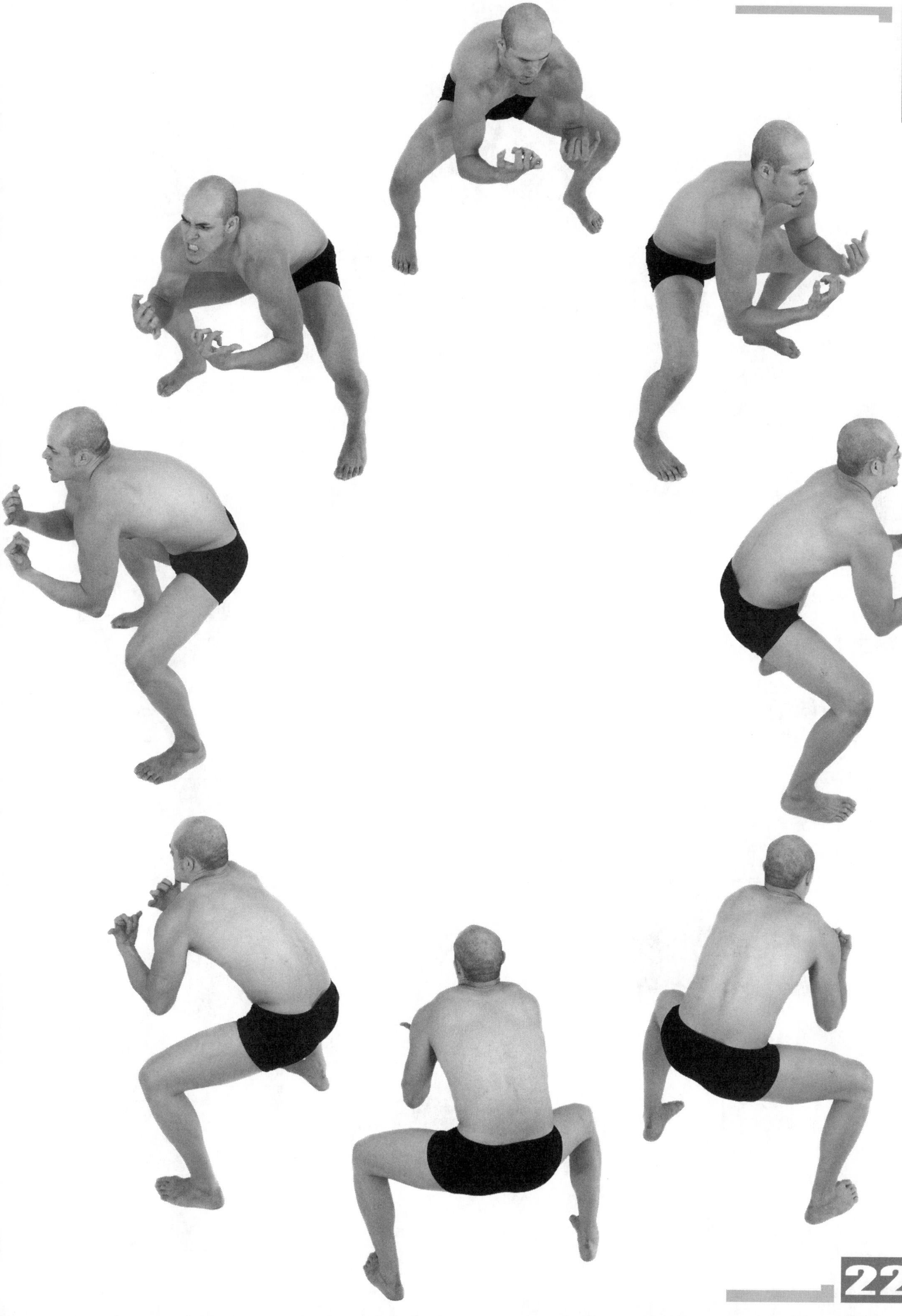

B

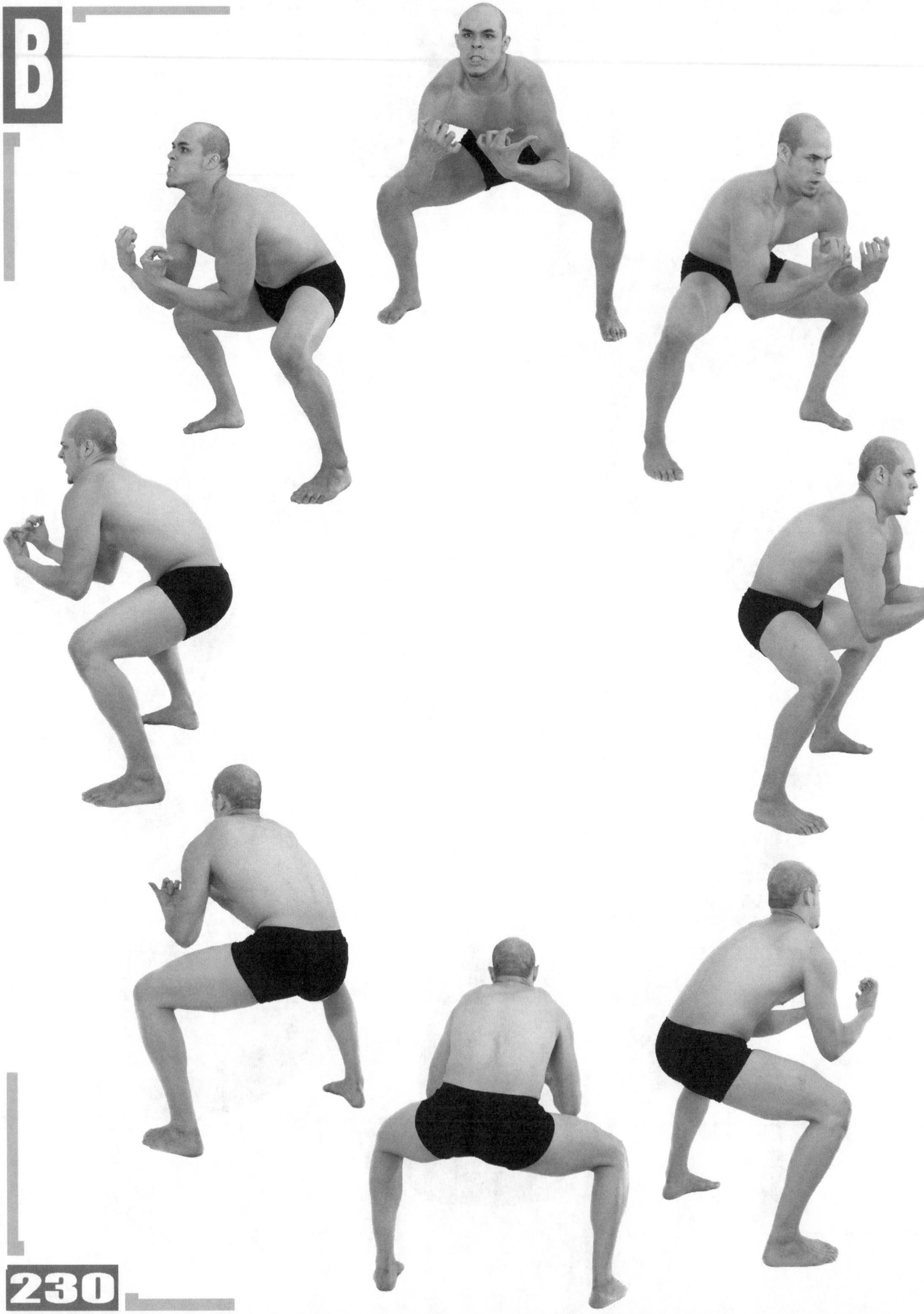

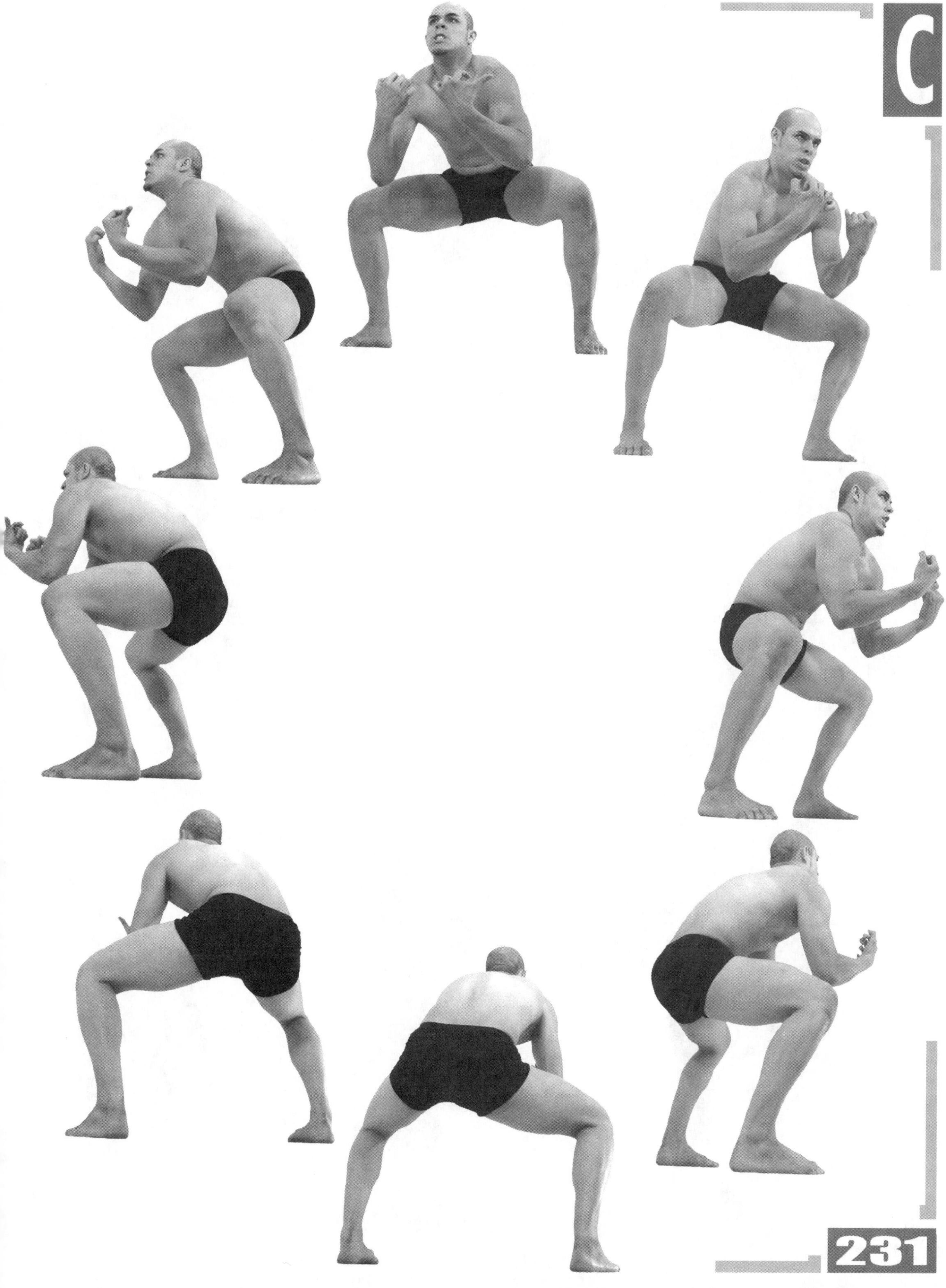

A

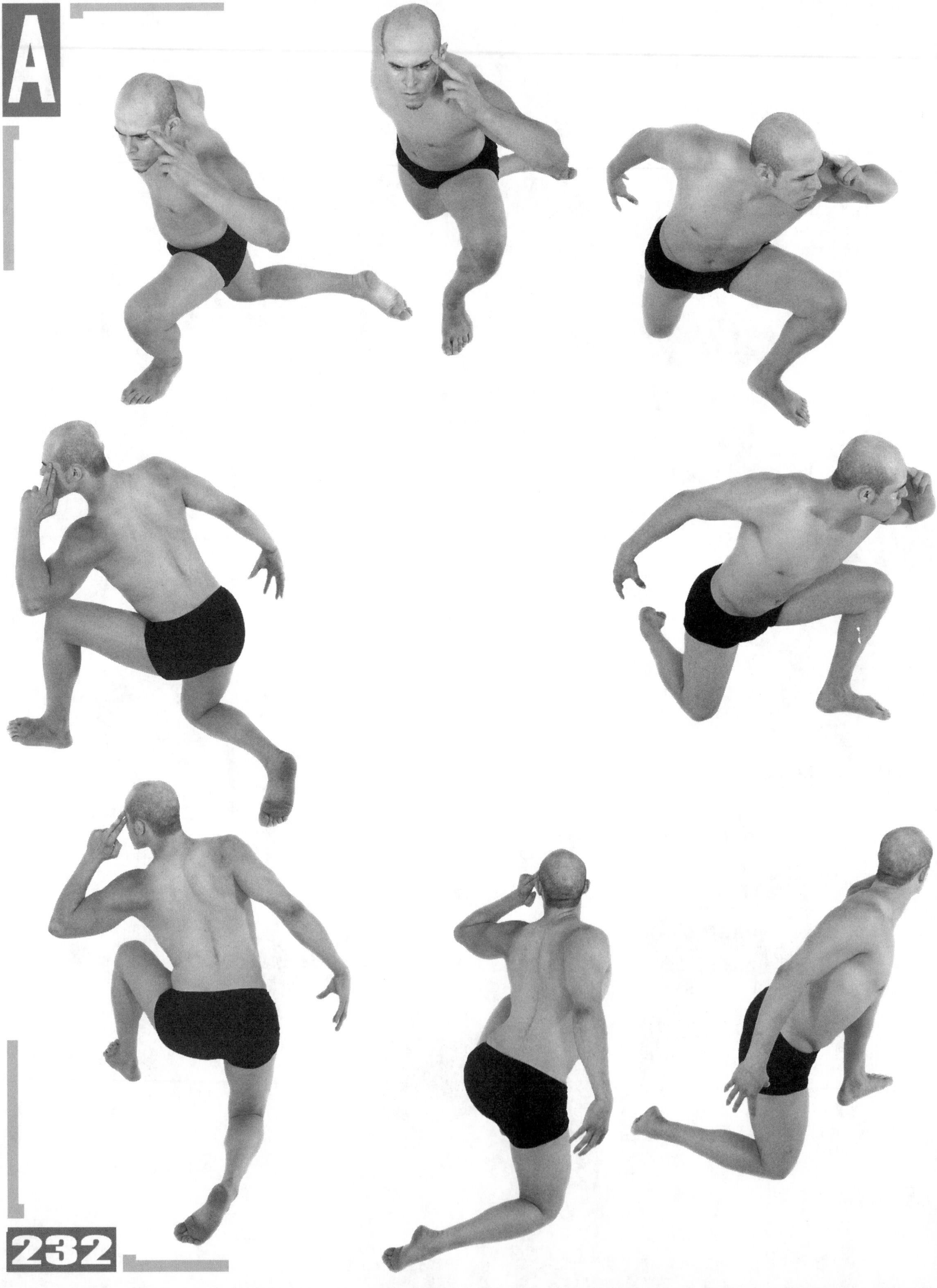

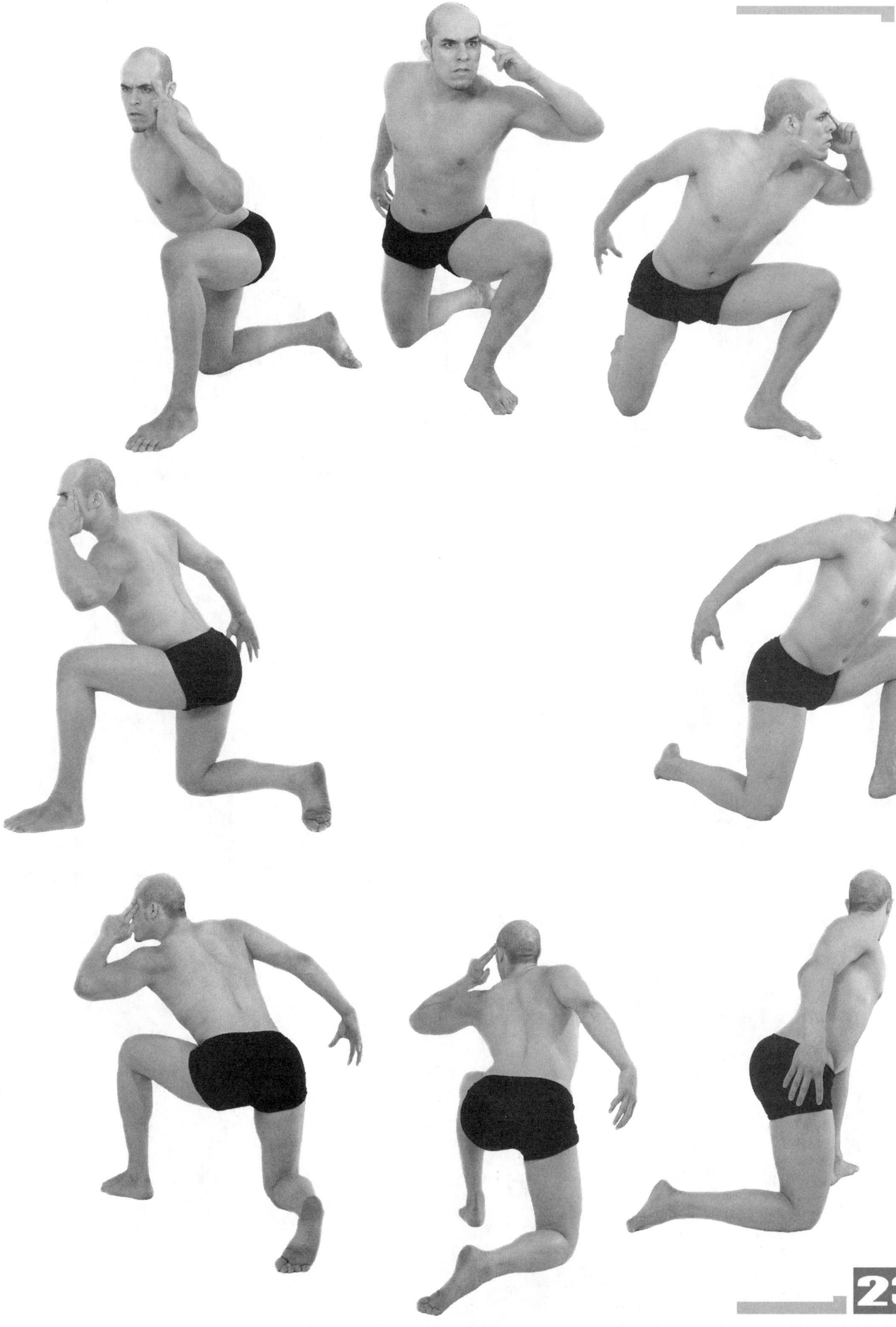

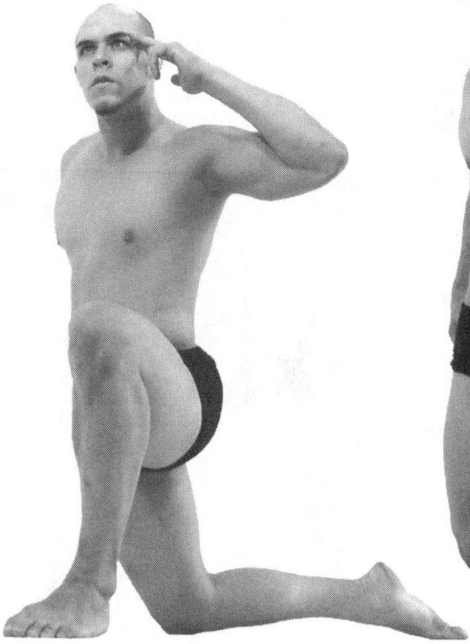
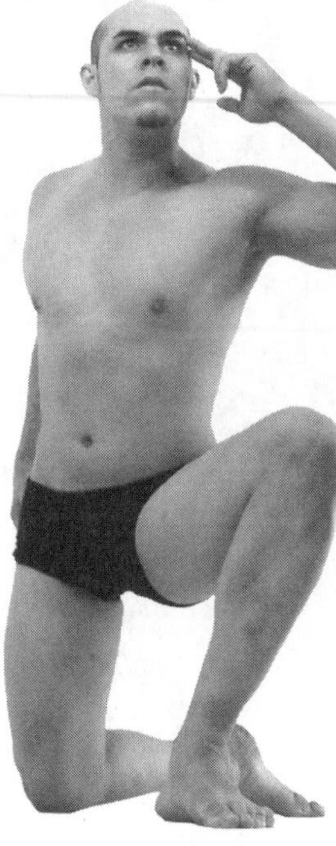
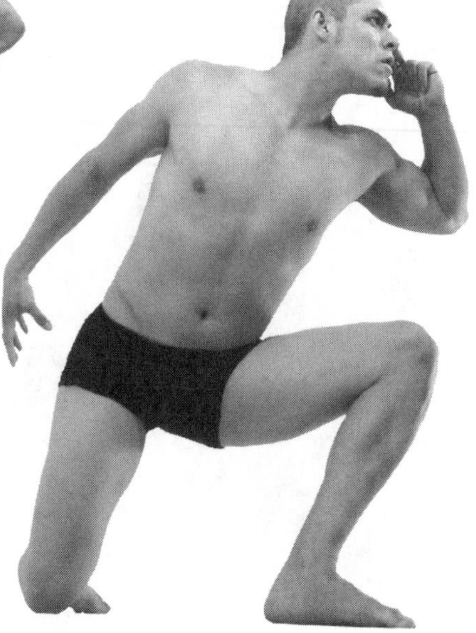
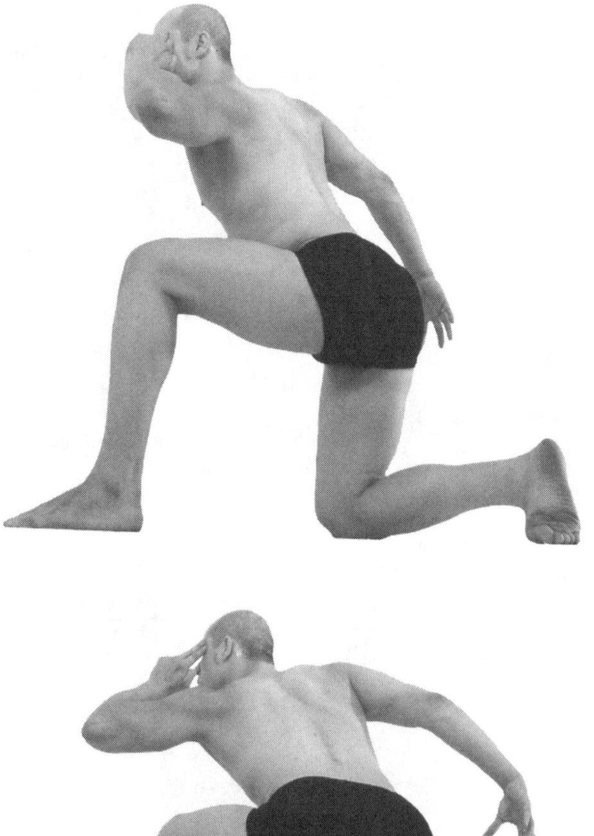
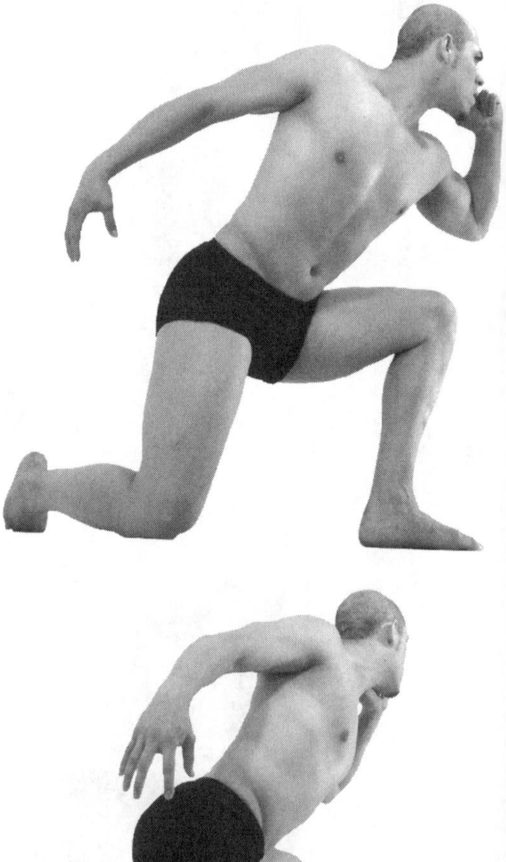
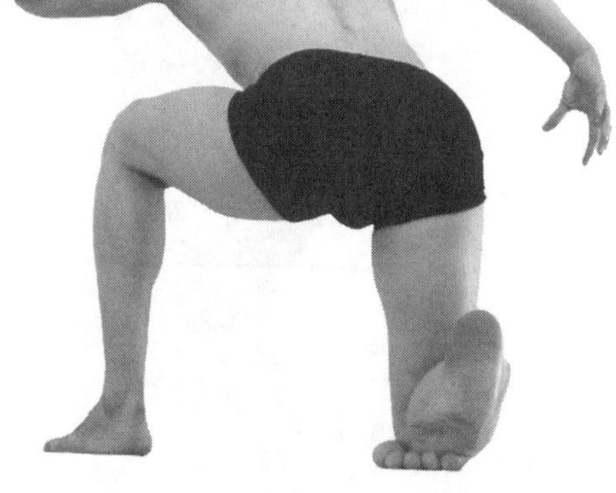
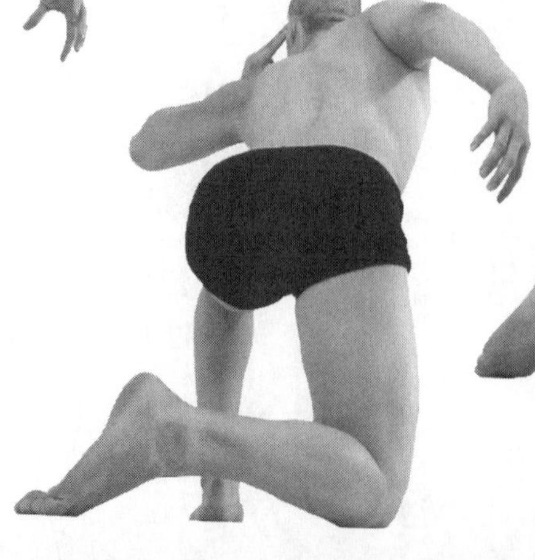
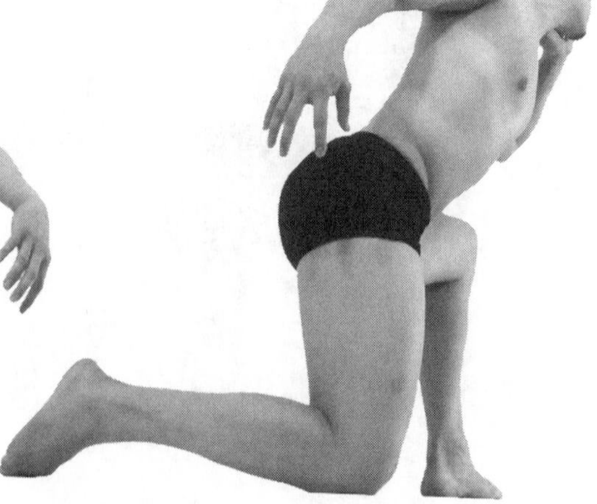

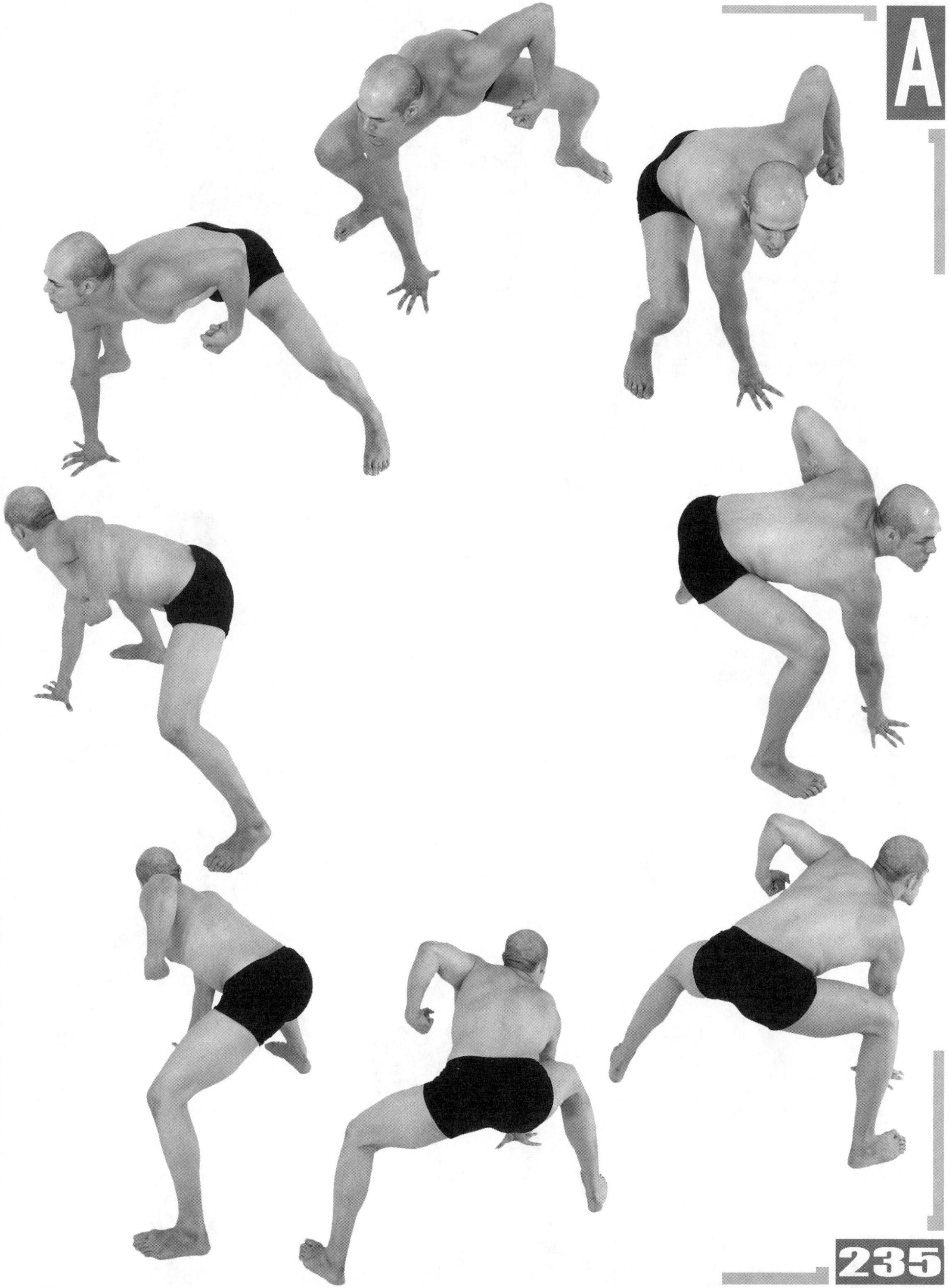

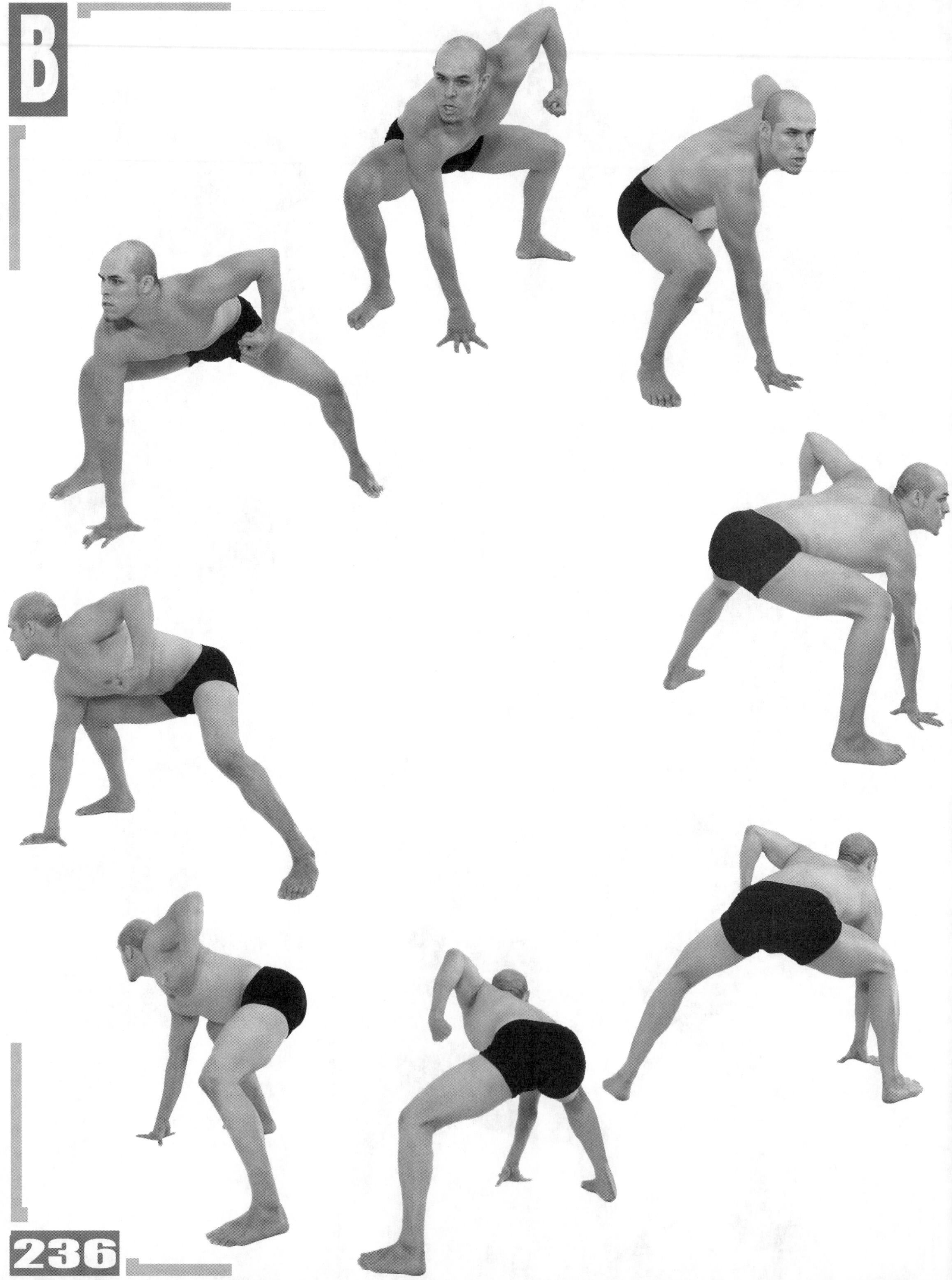

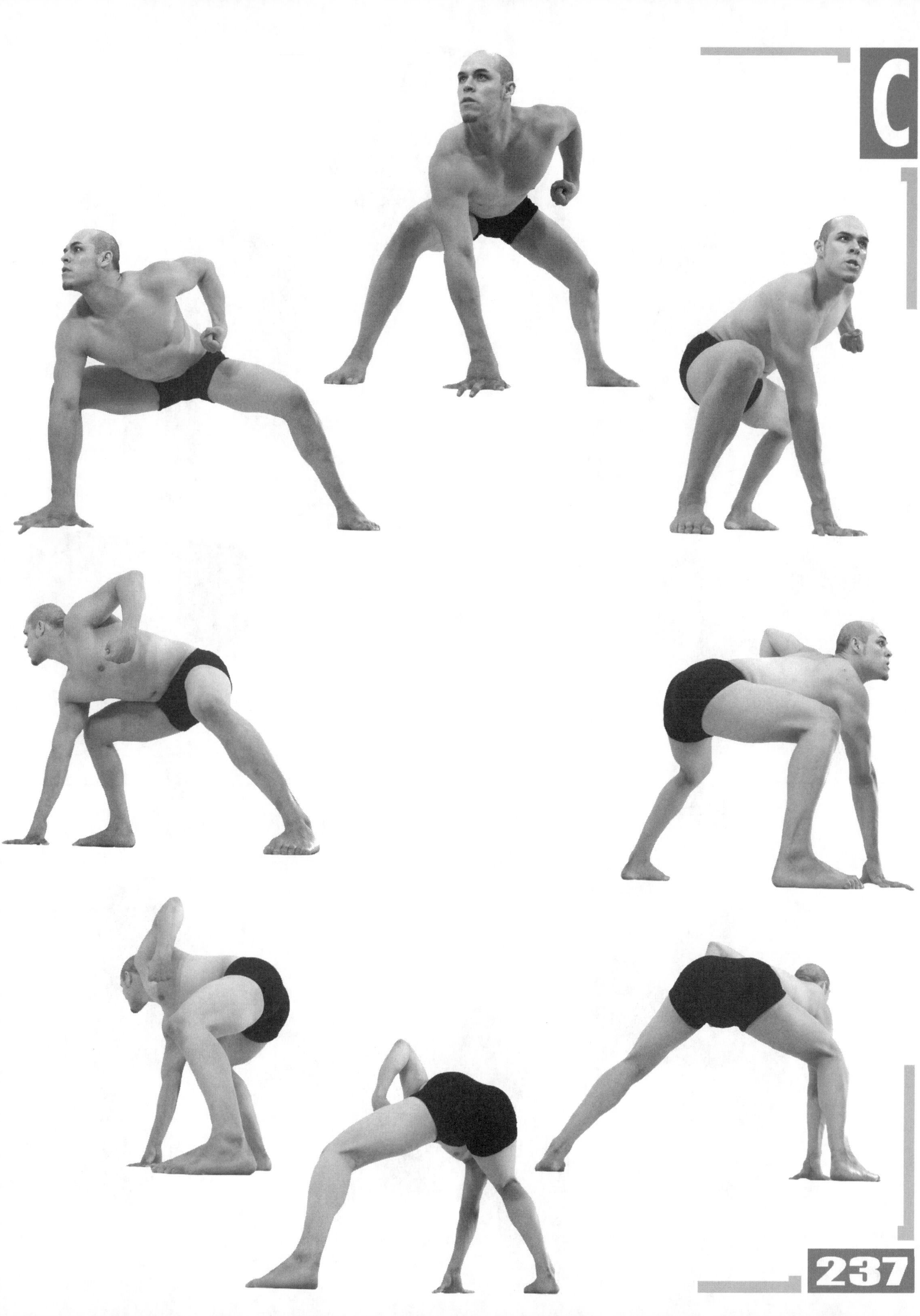

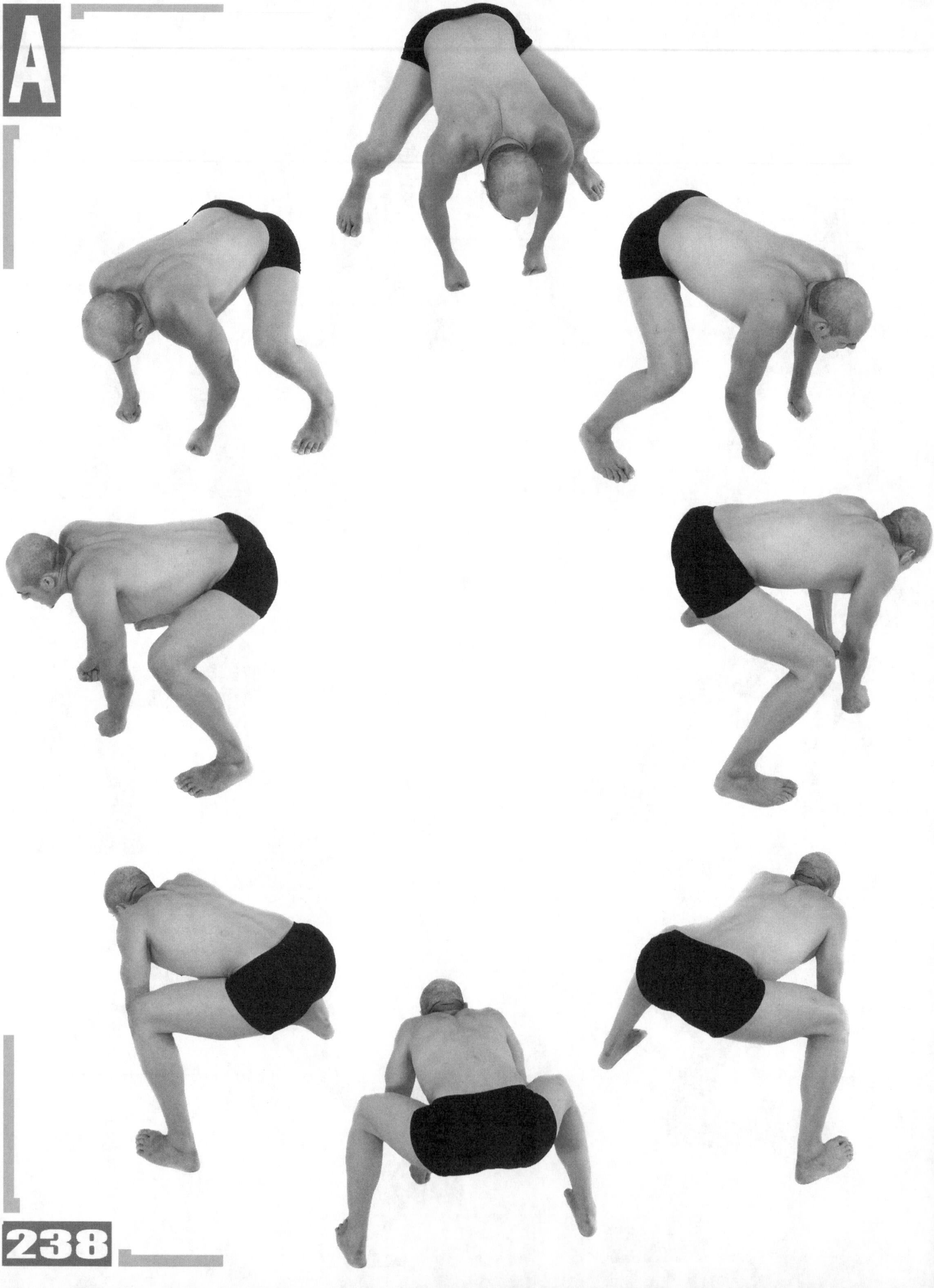

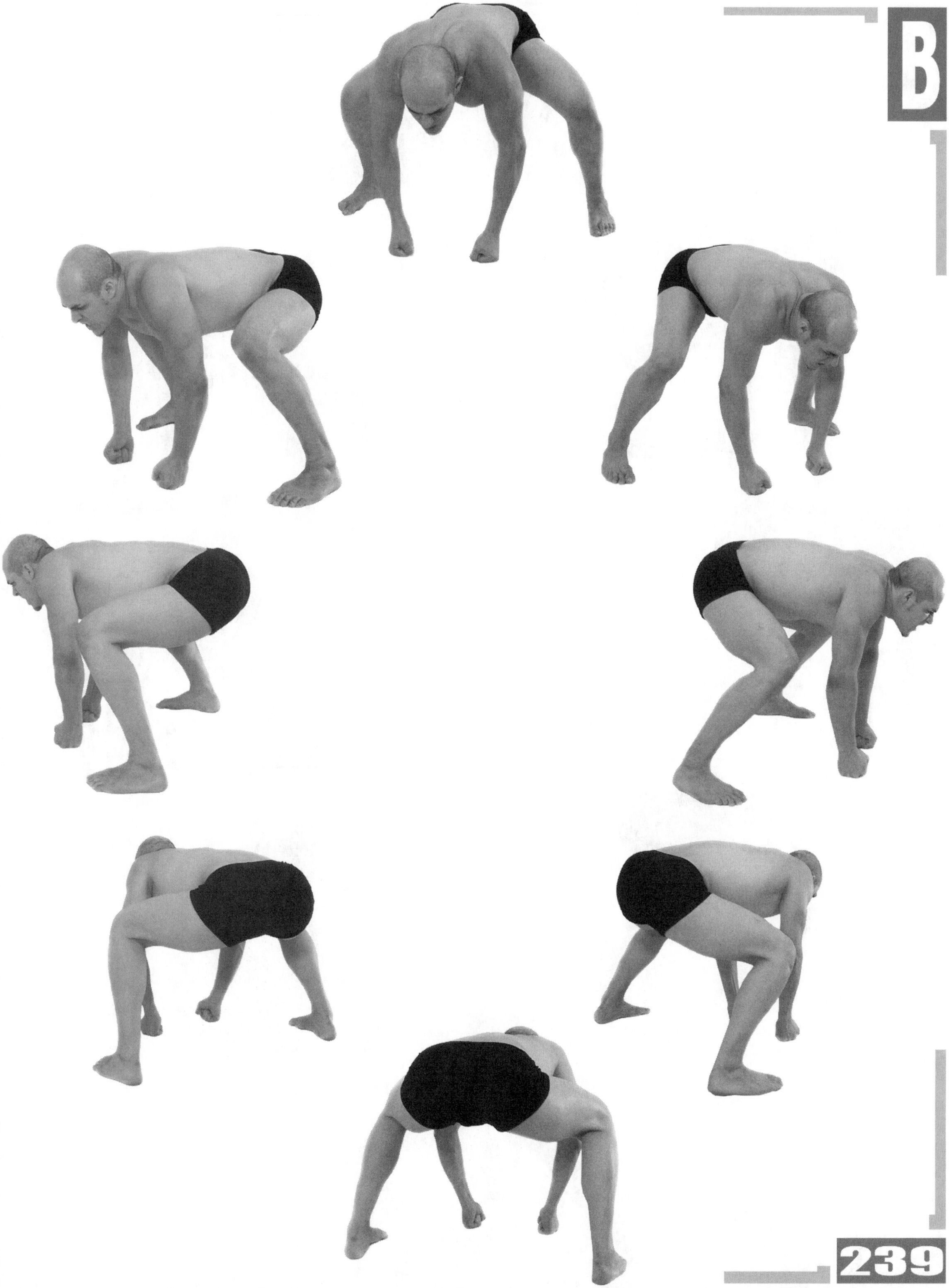

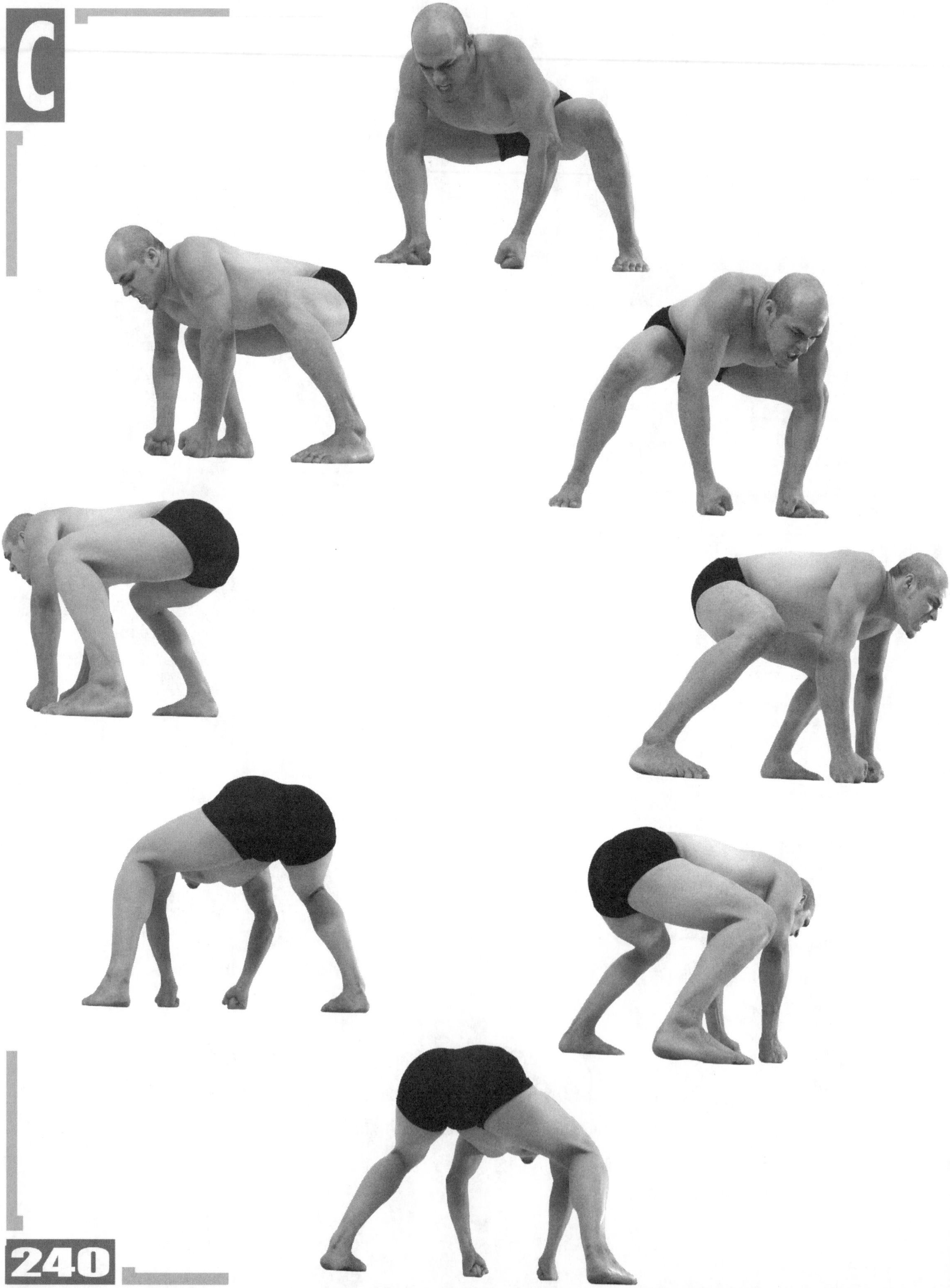

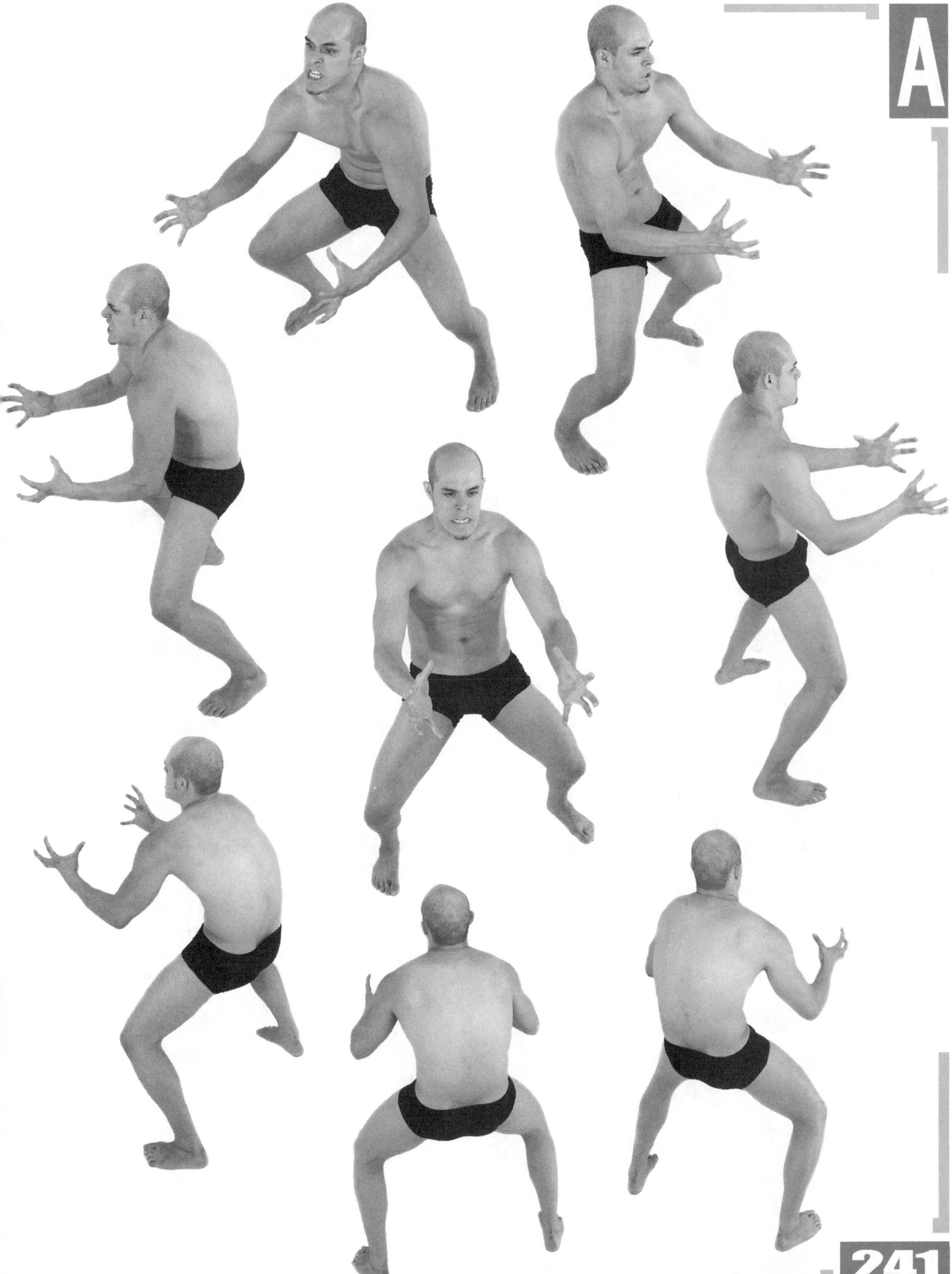

B

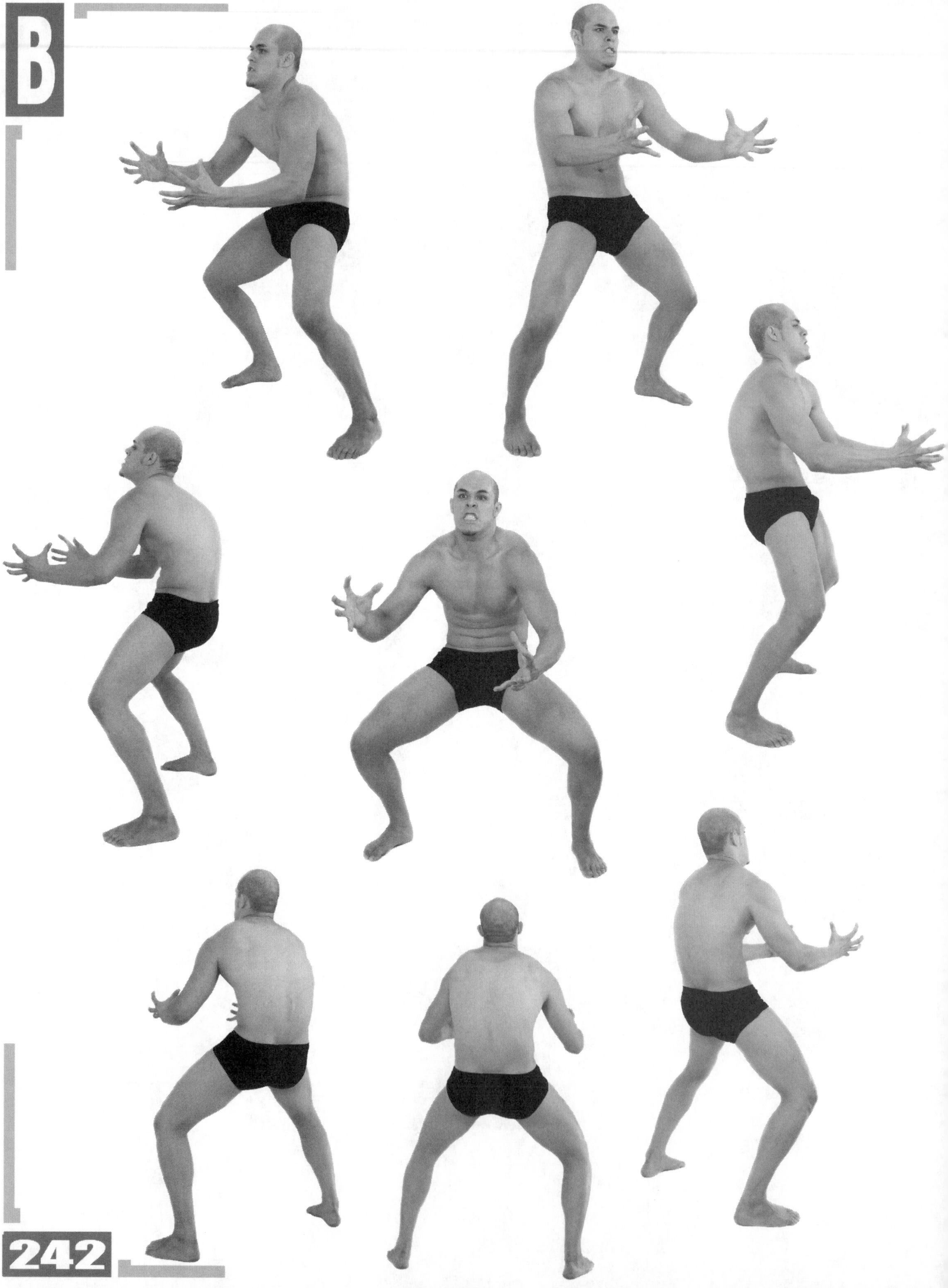

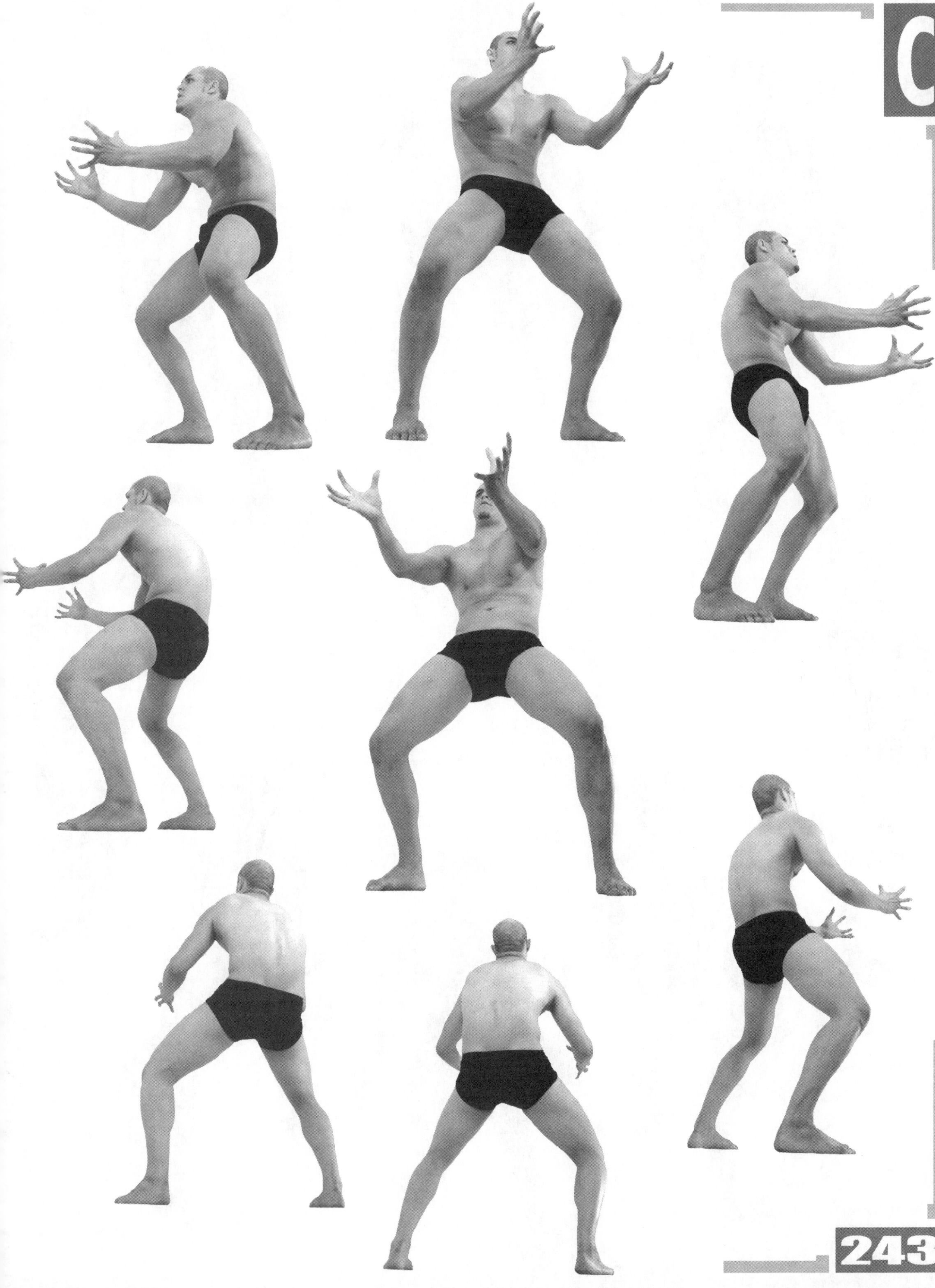

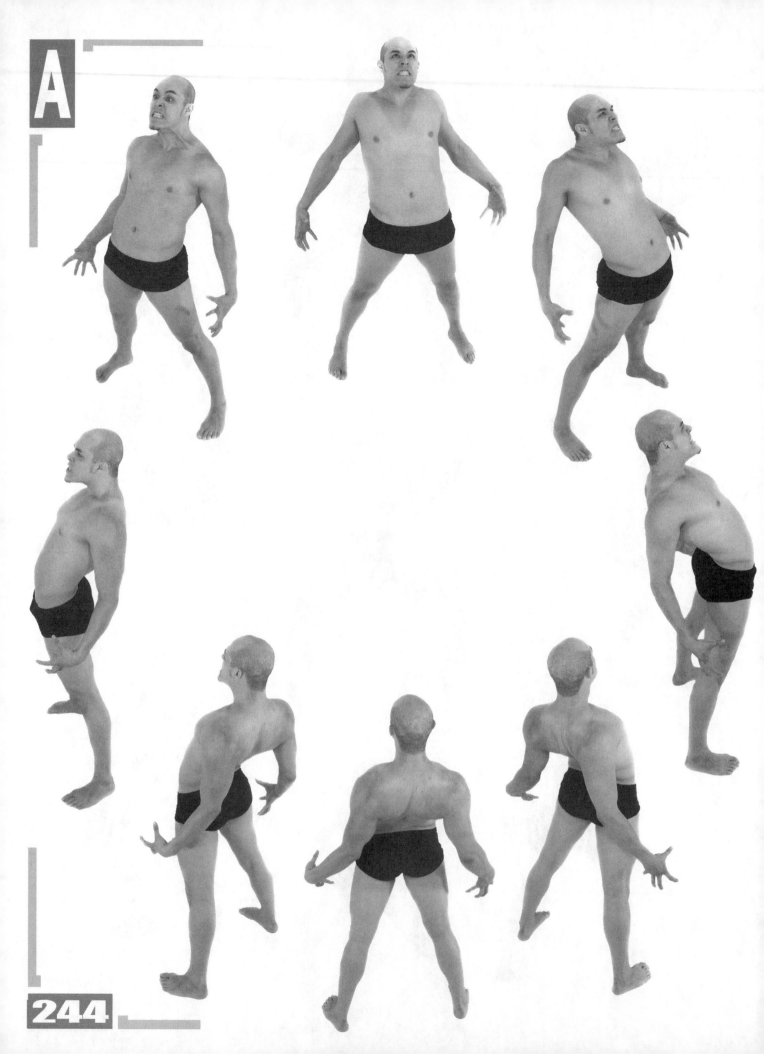

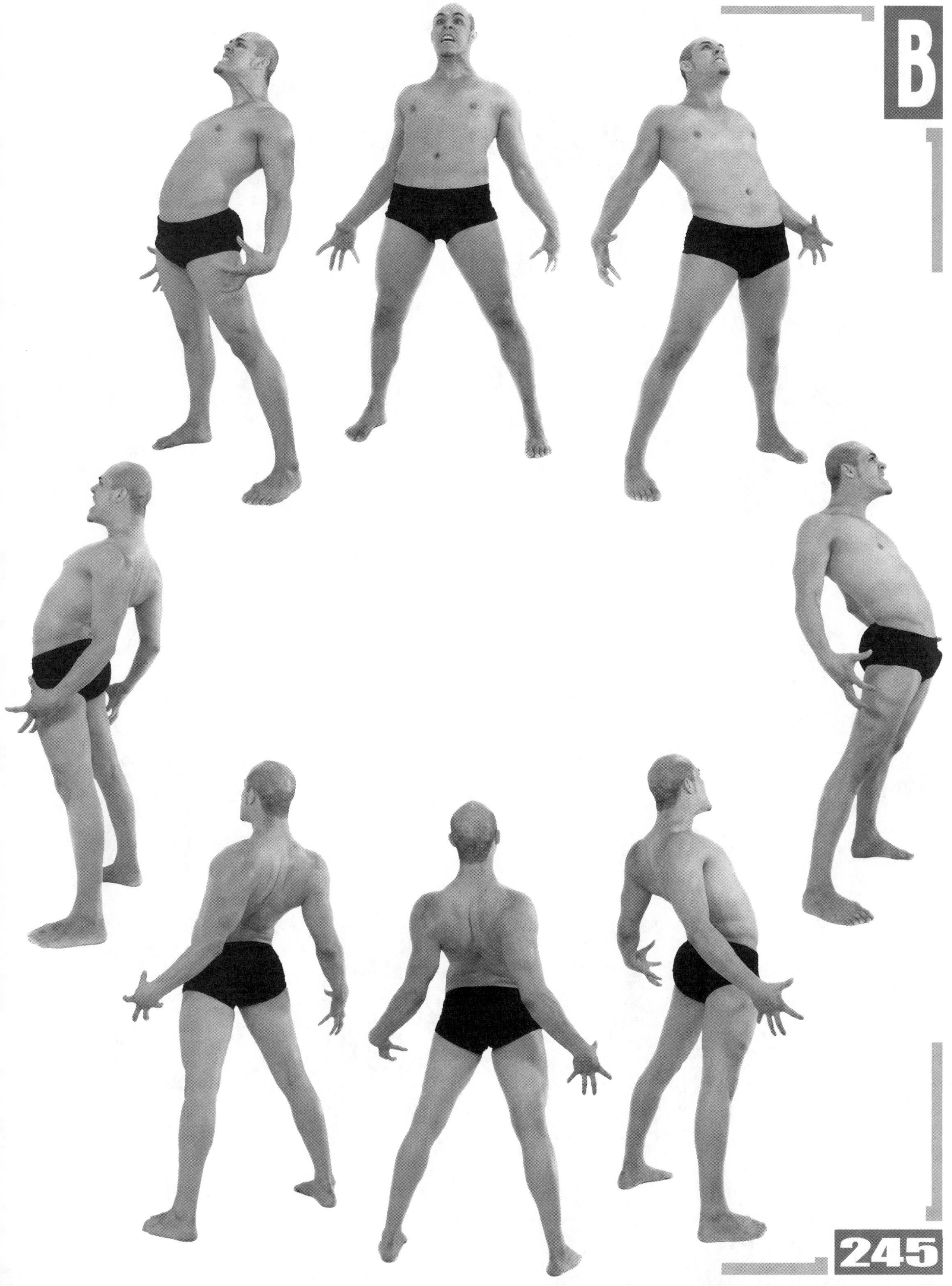

B

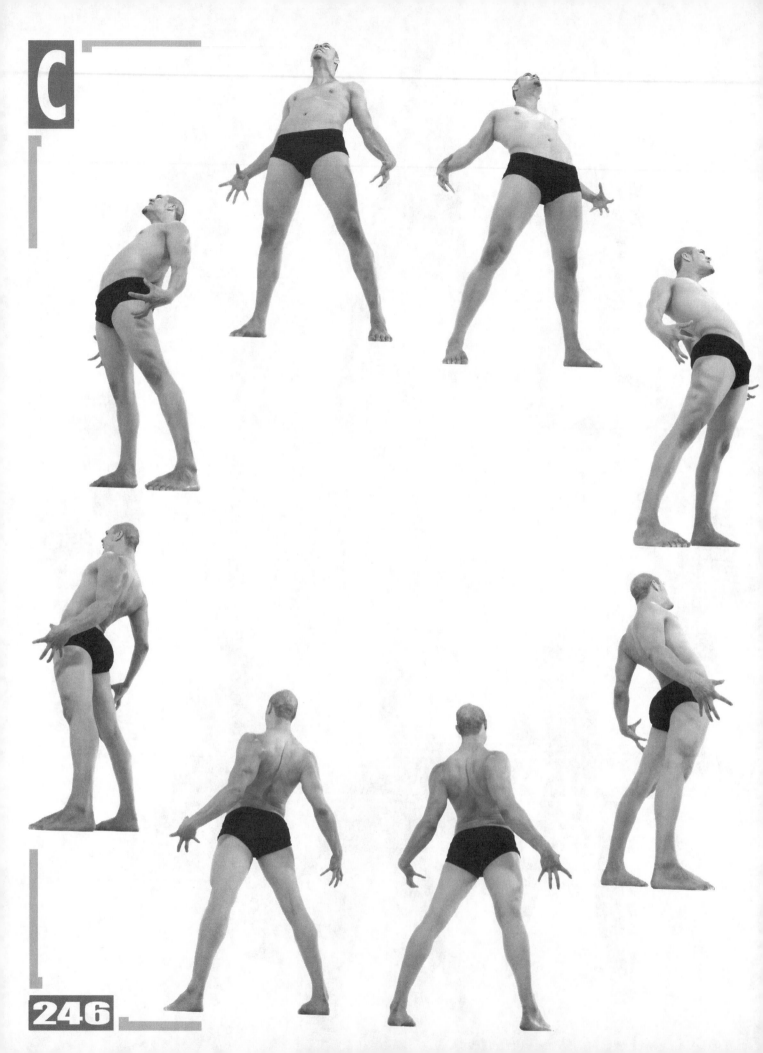

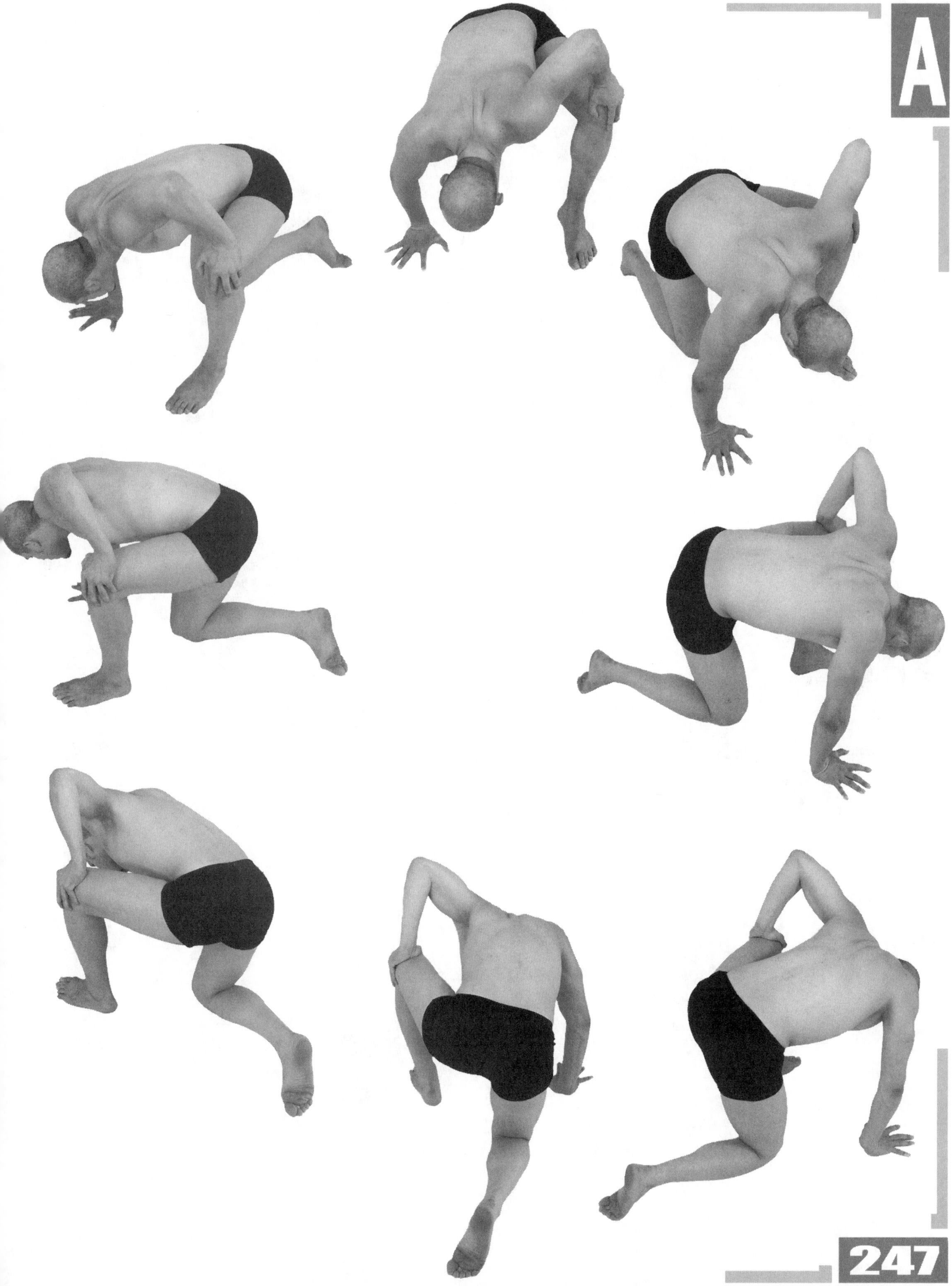

B

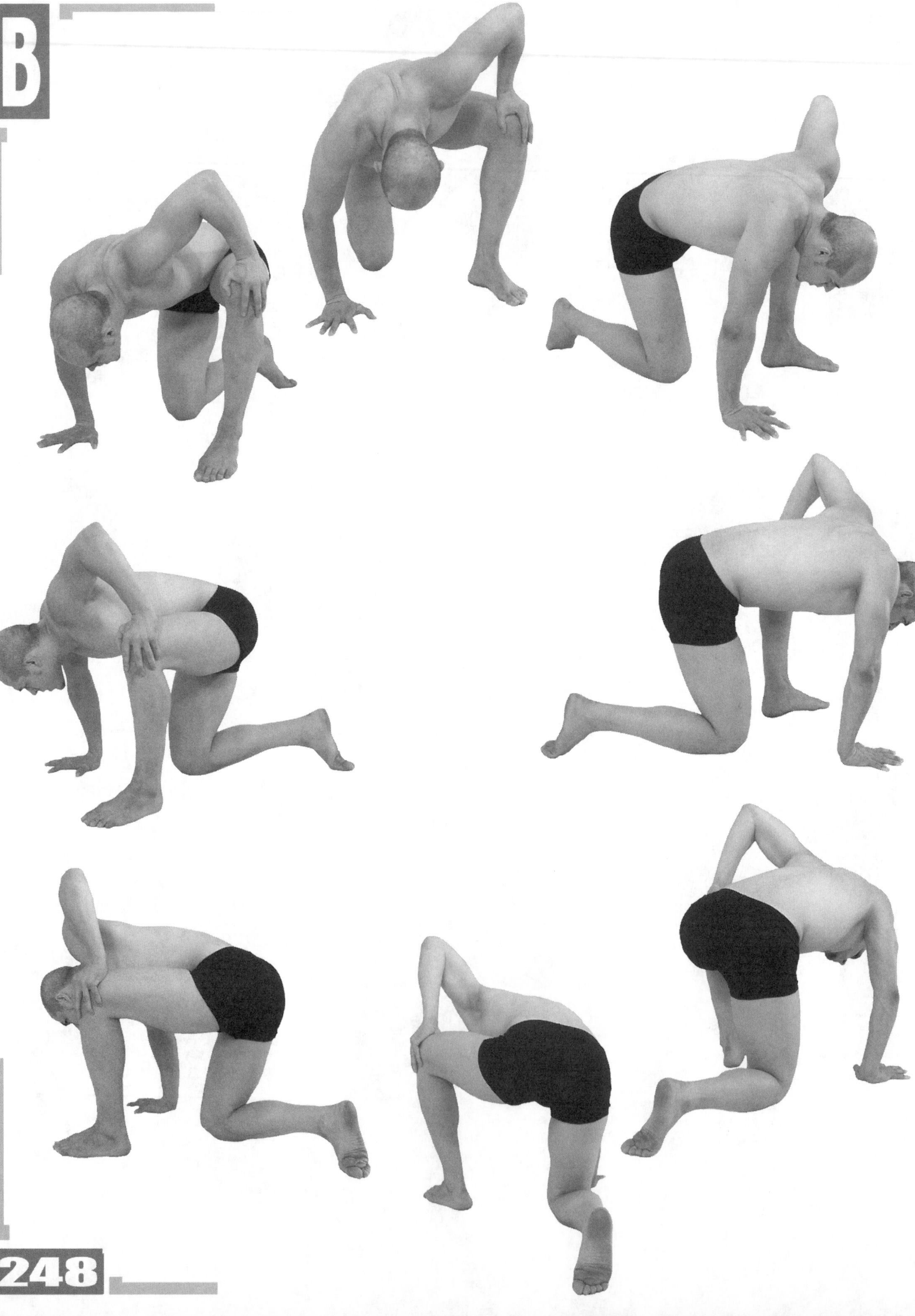

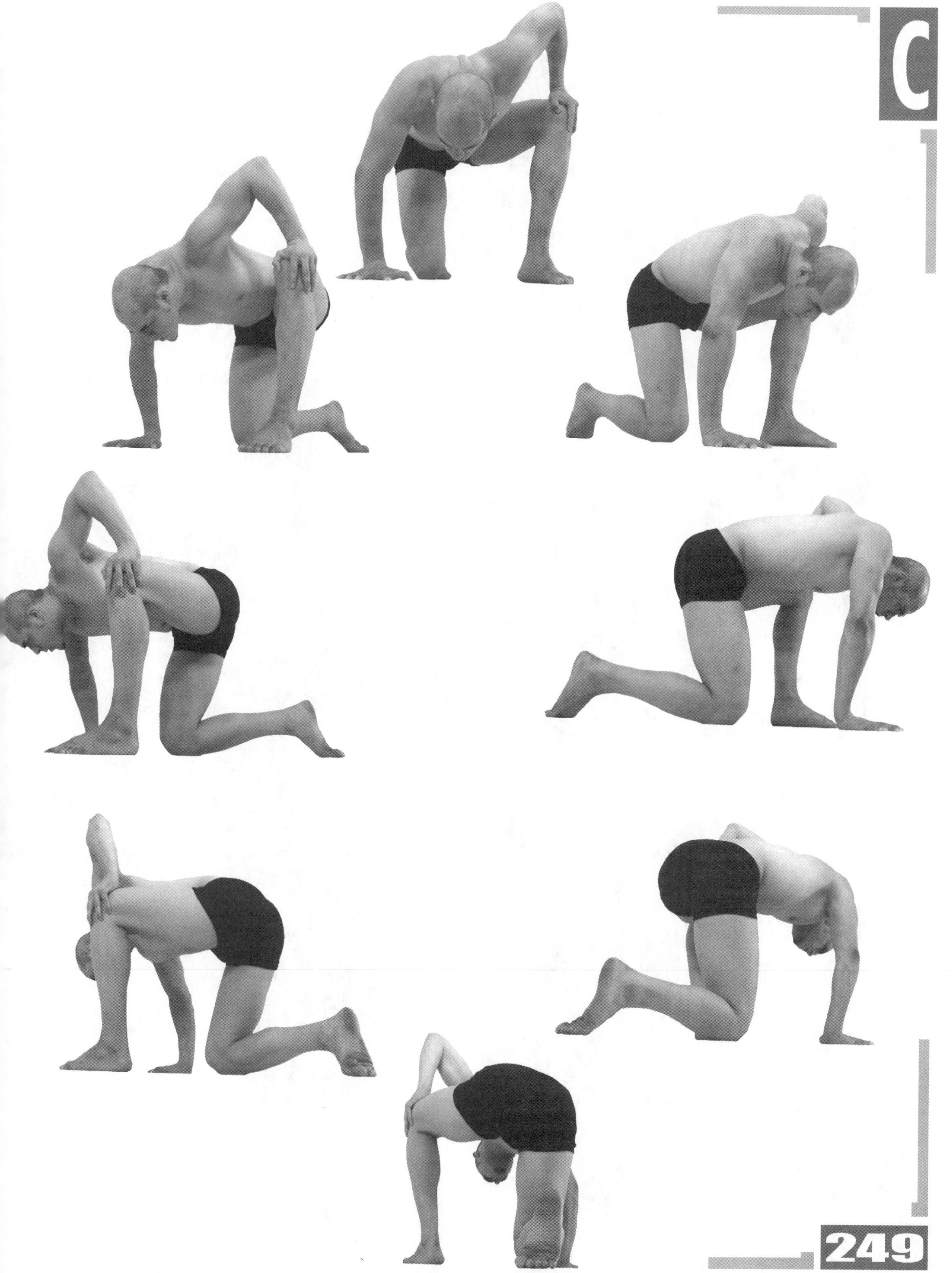

CAPES POSES

POSE

250

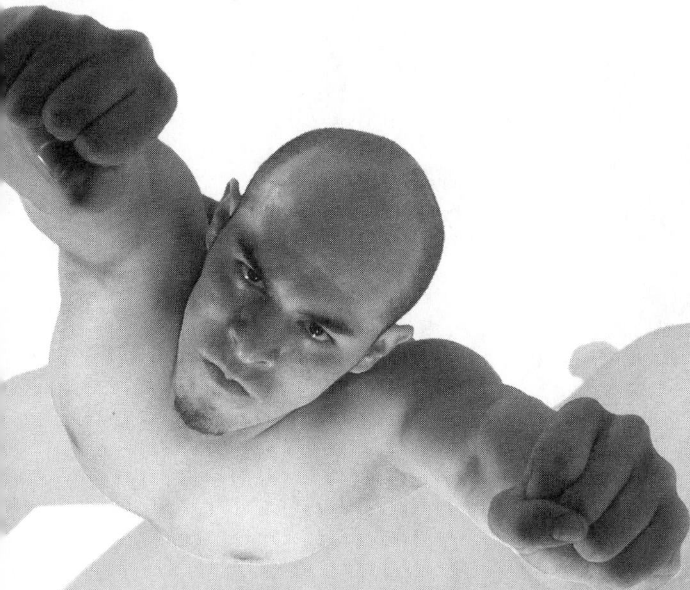

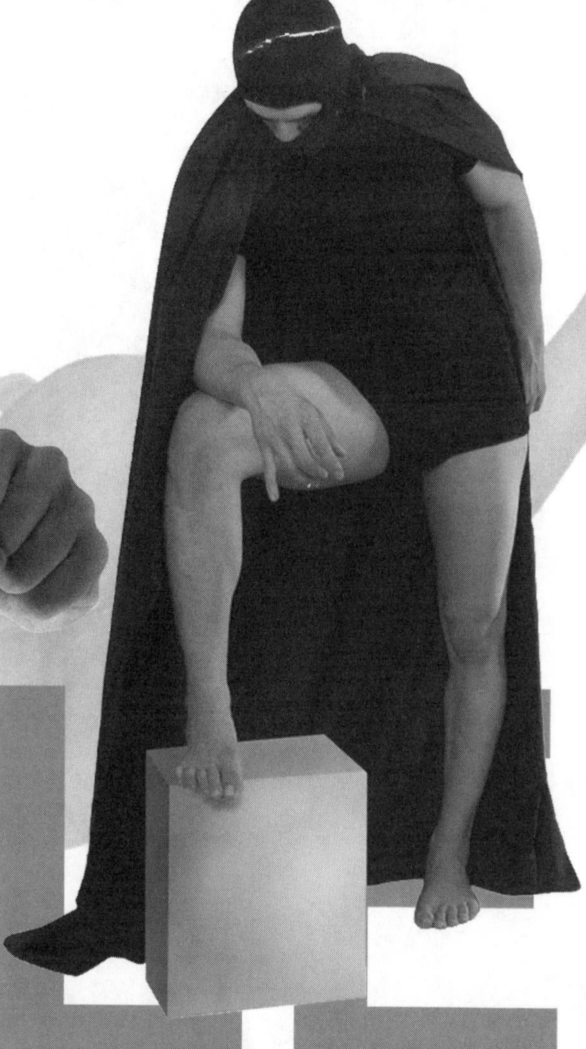

CAPE POSES

FILE

REFERENCE

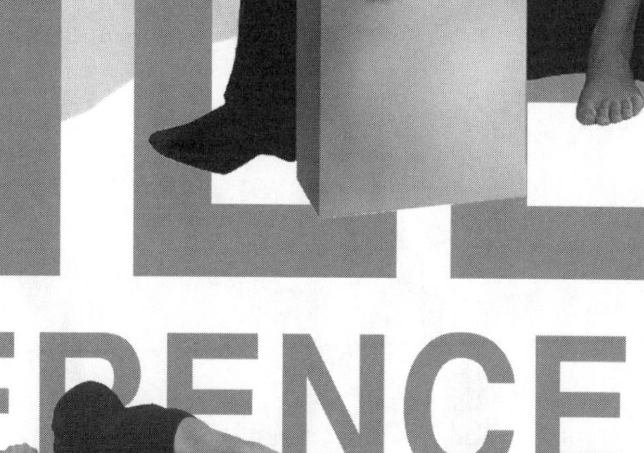

ACTION POSE COLLECTION

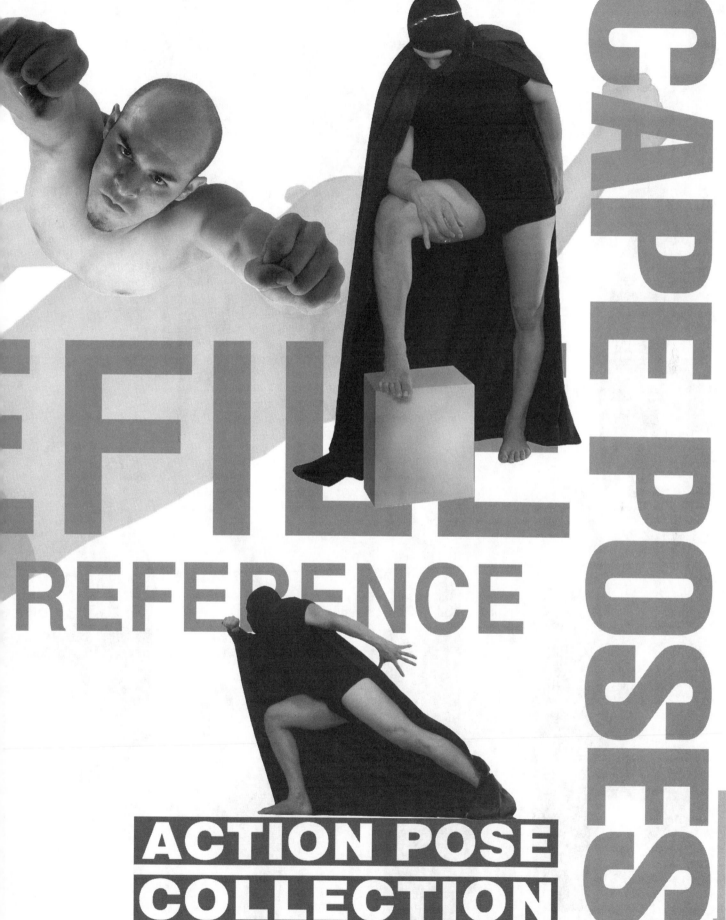

A

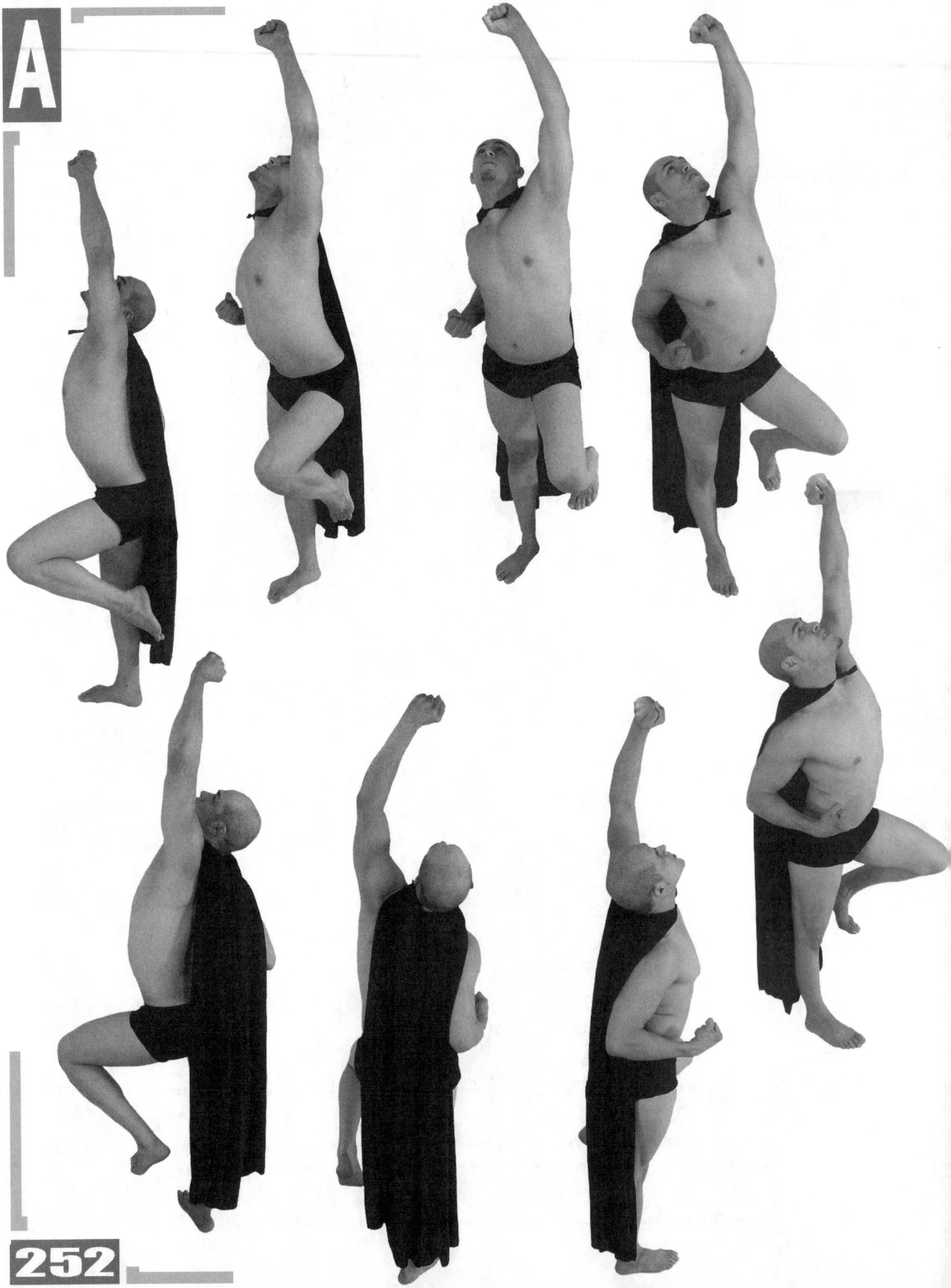

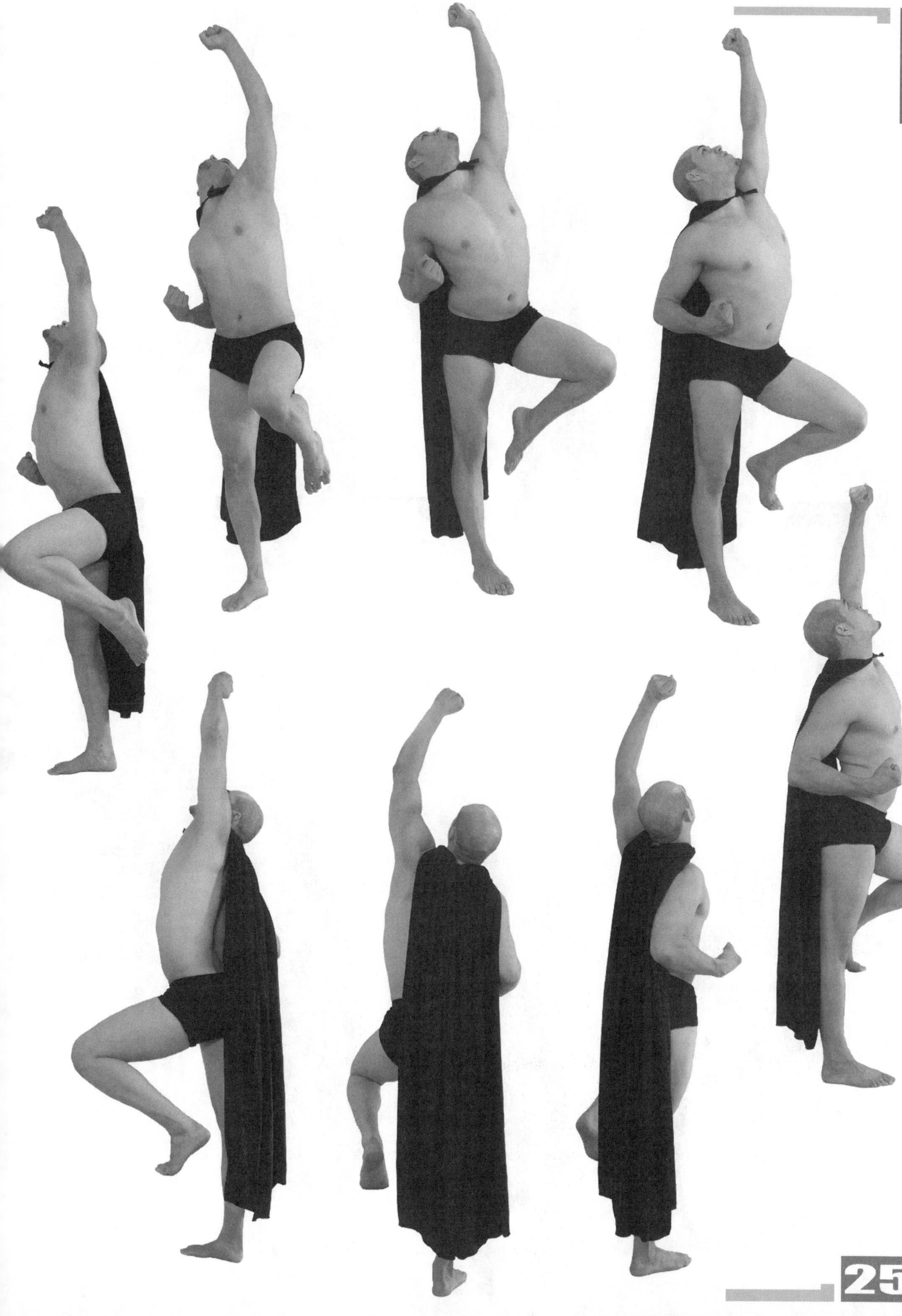

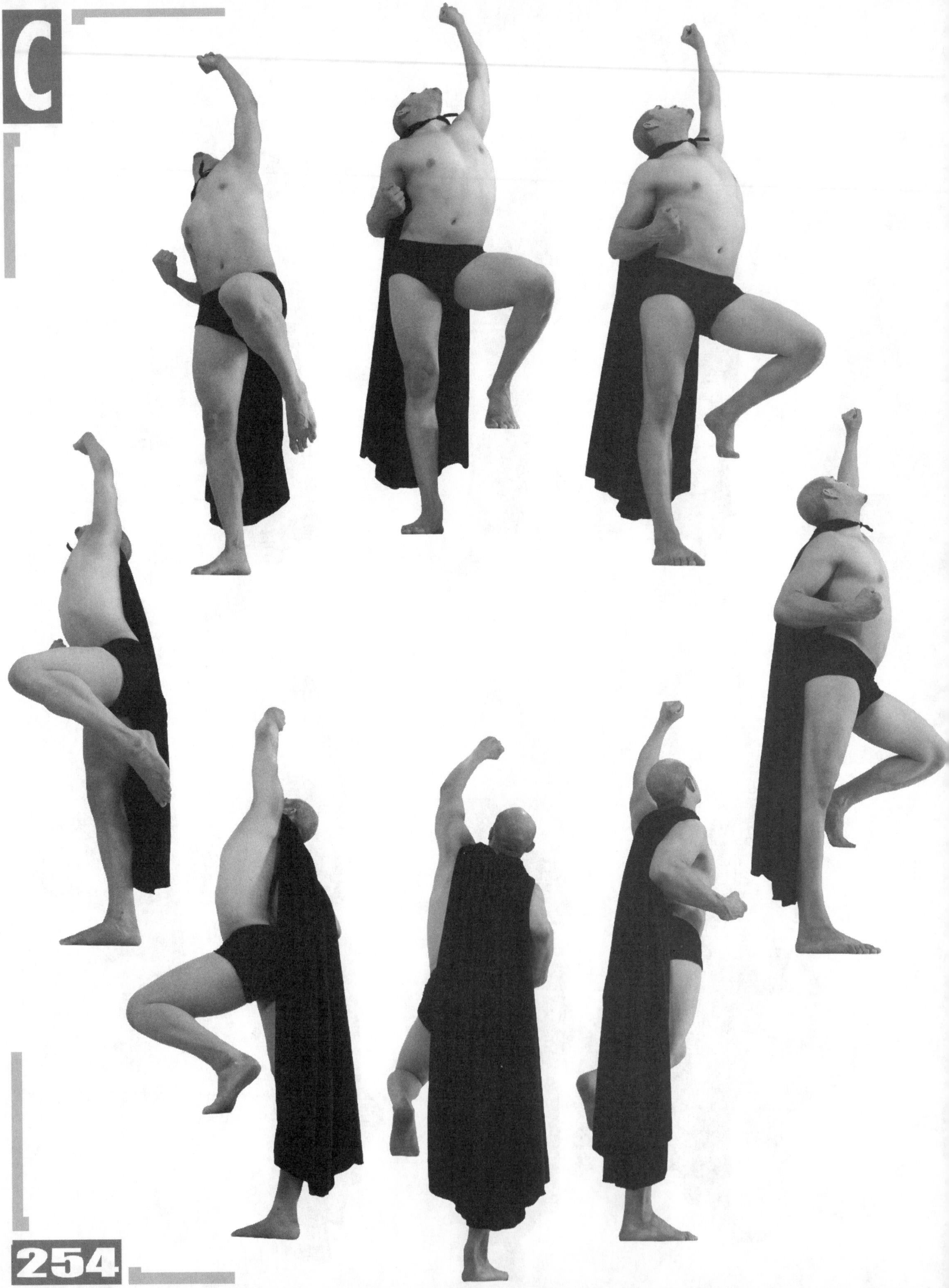

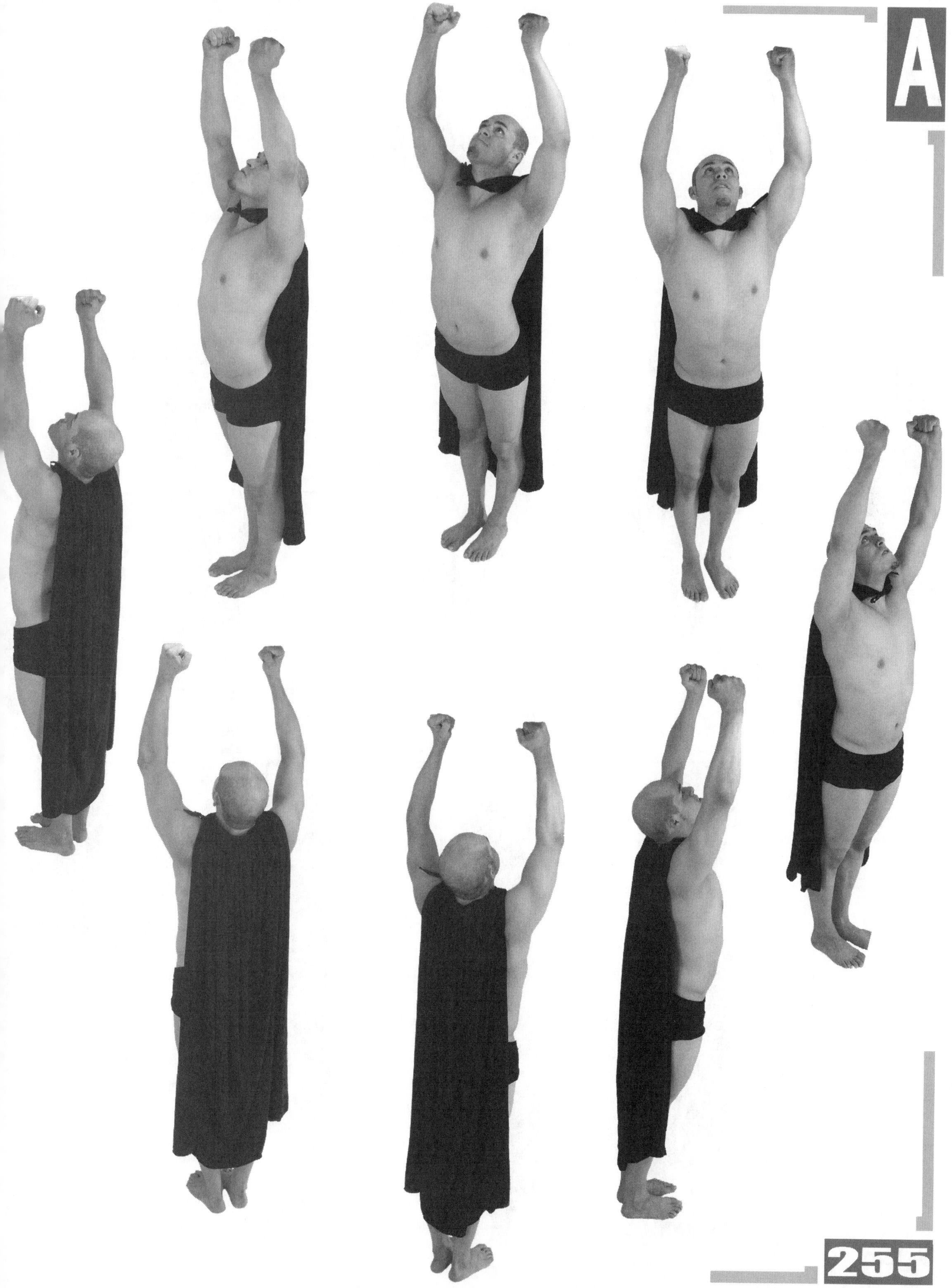

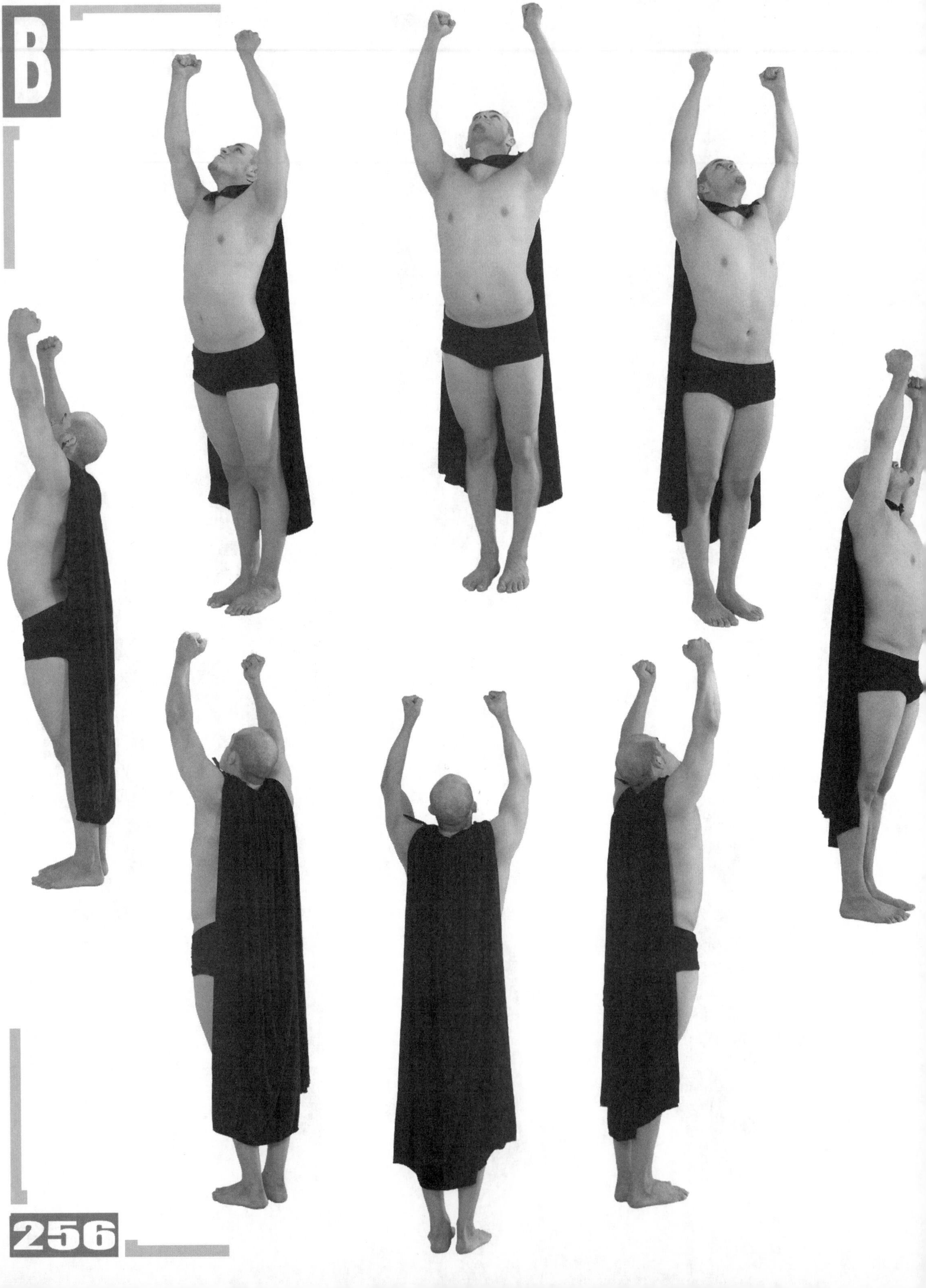

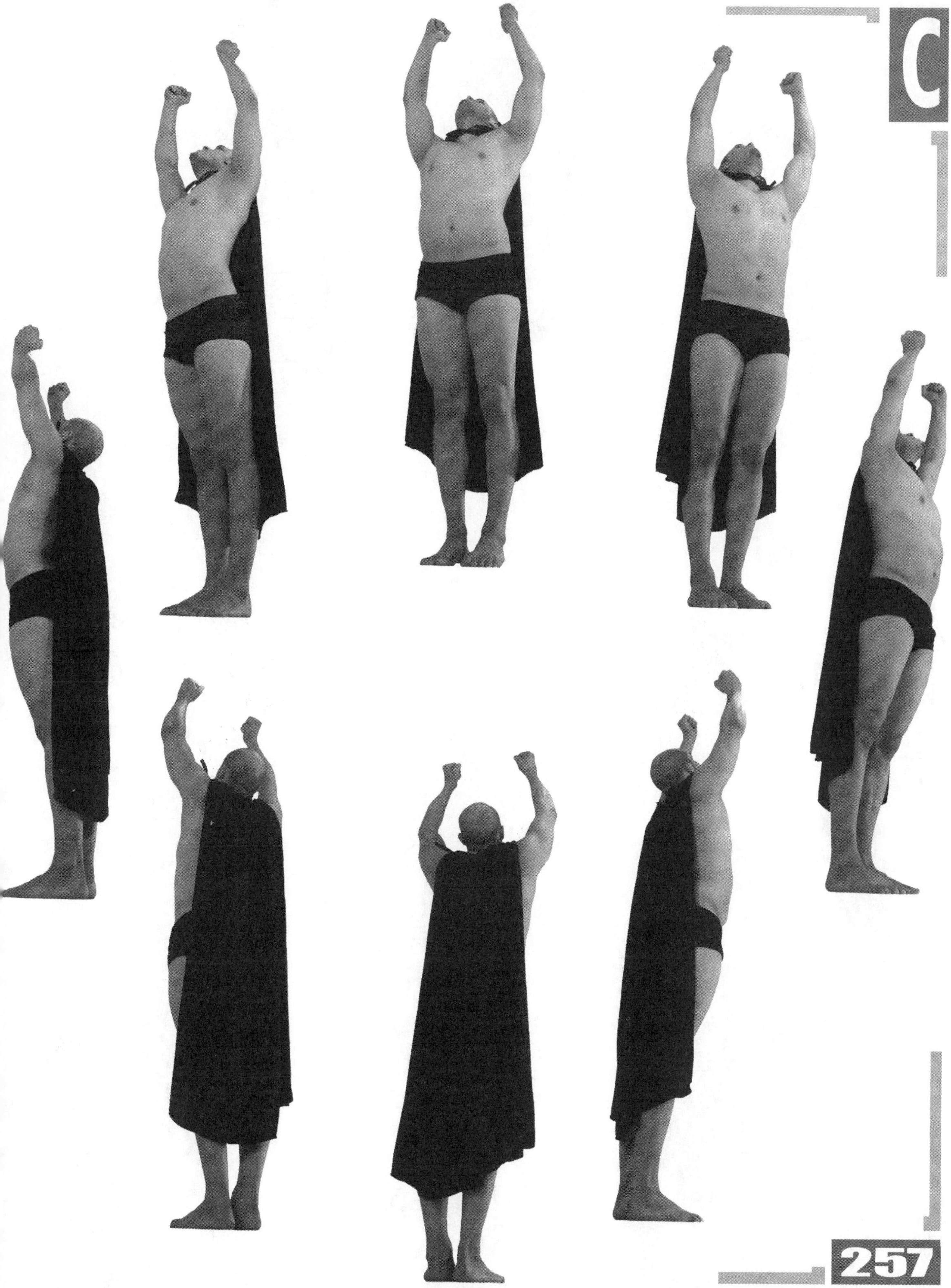

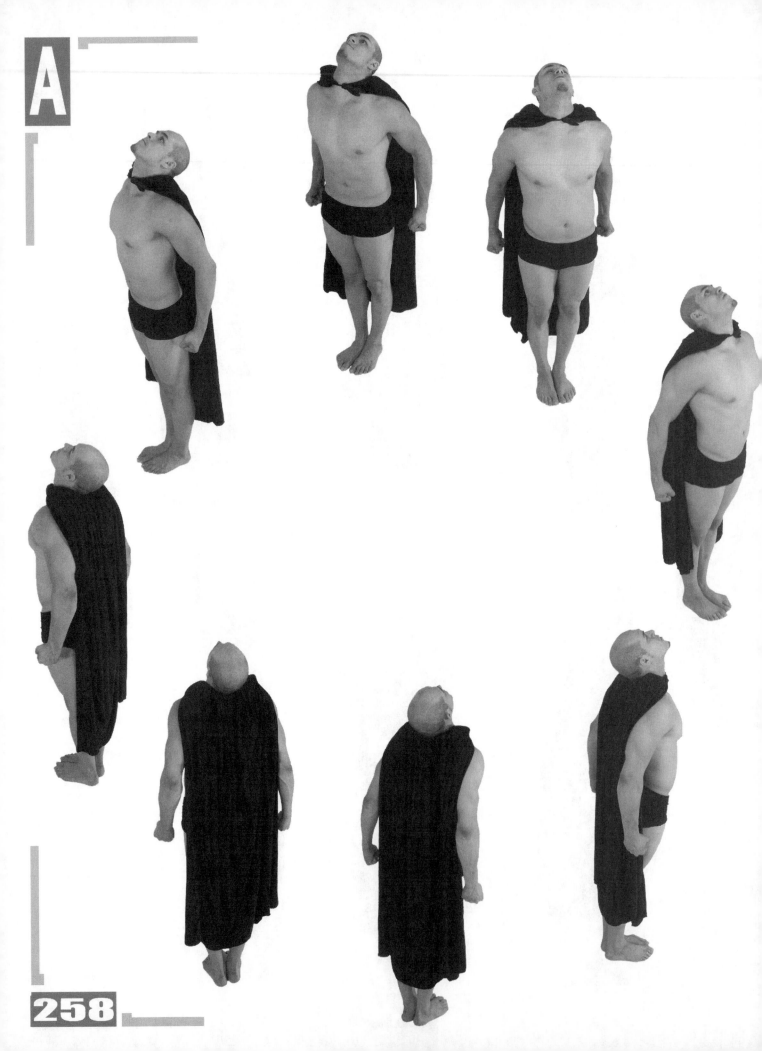

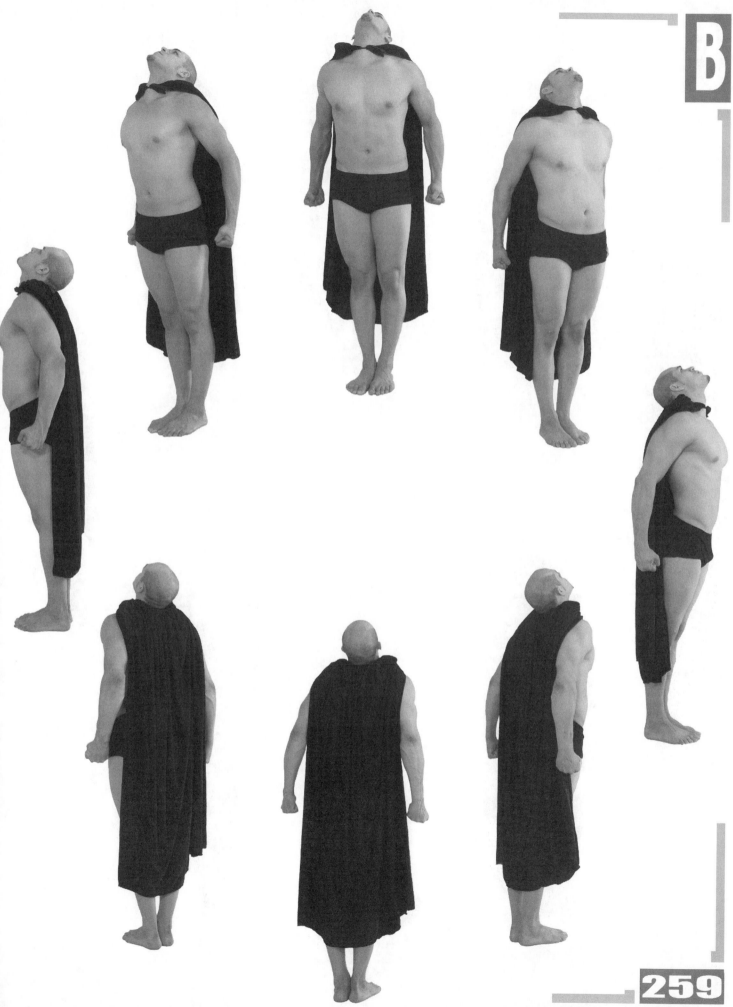

C

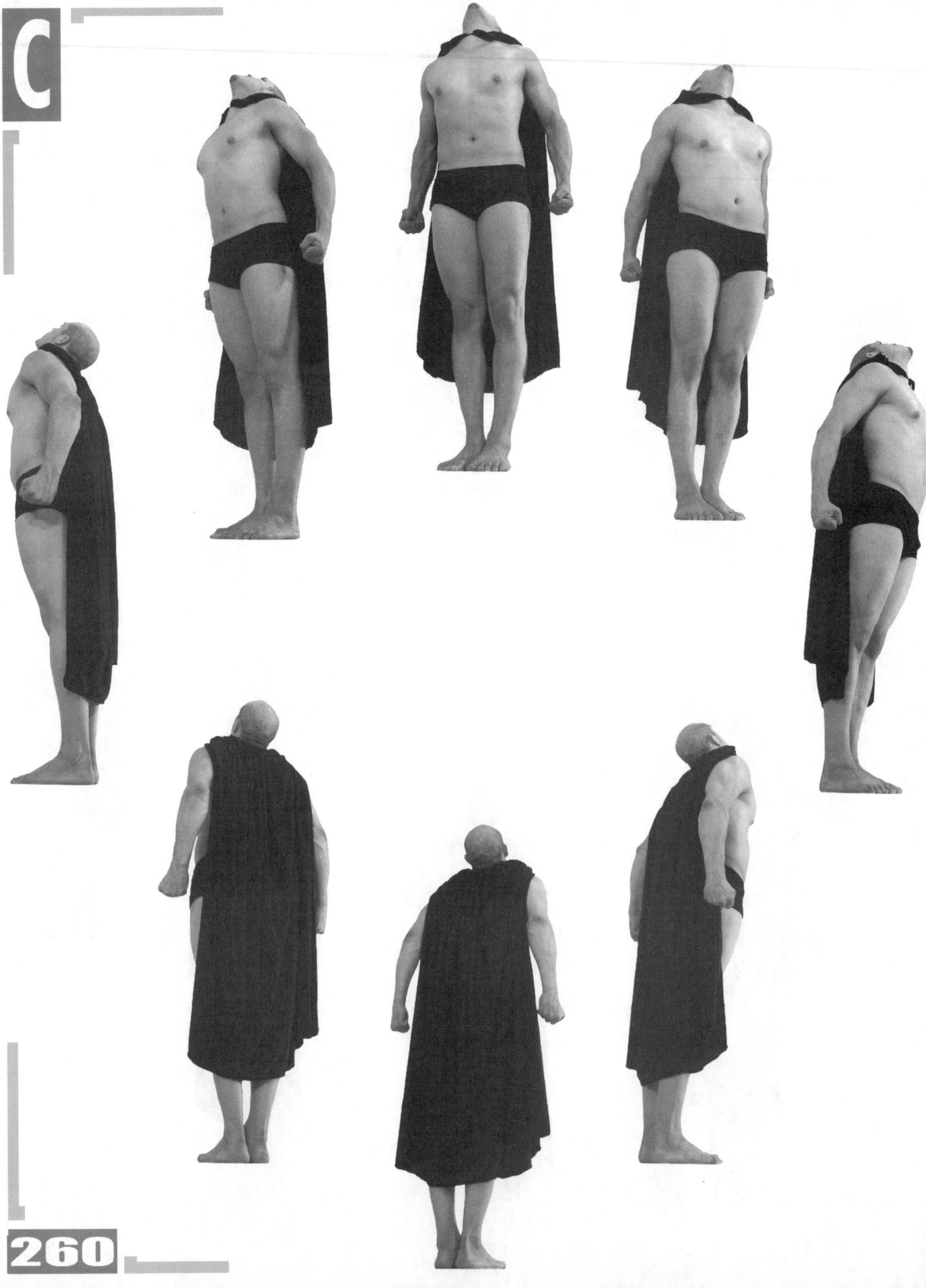

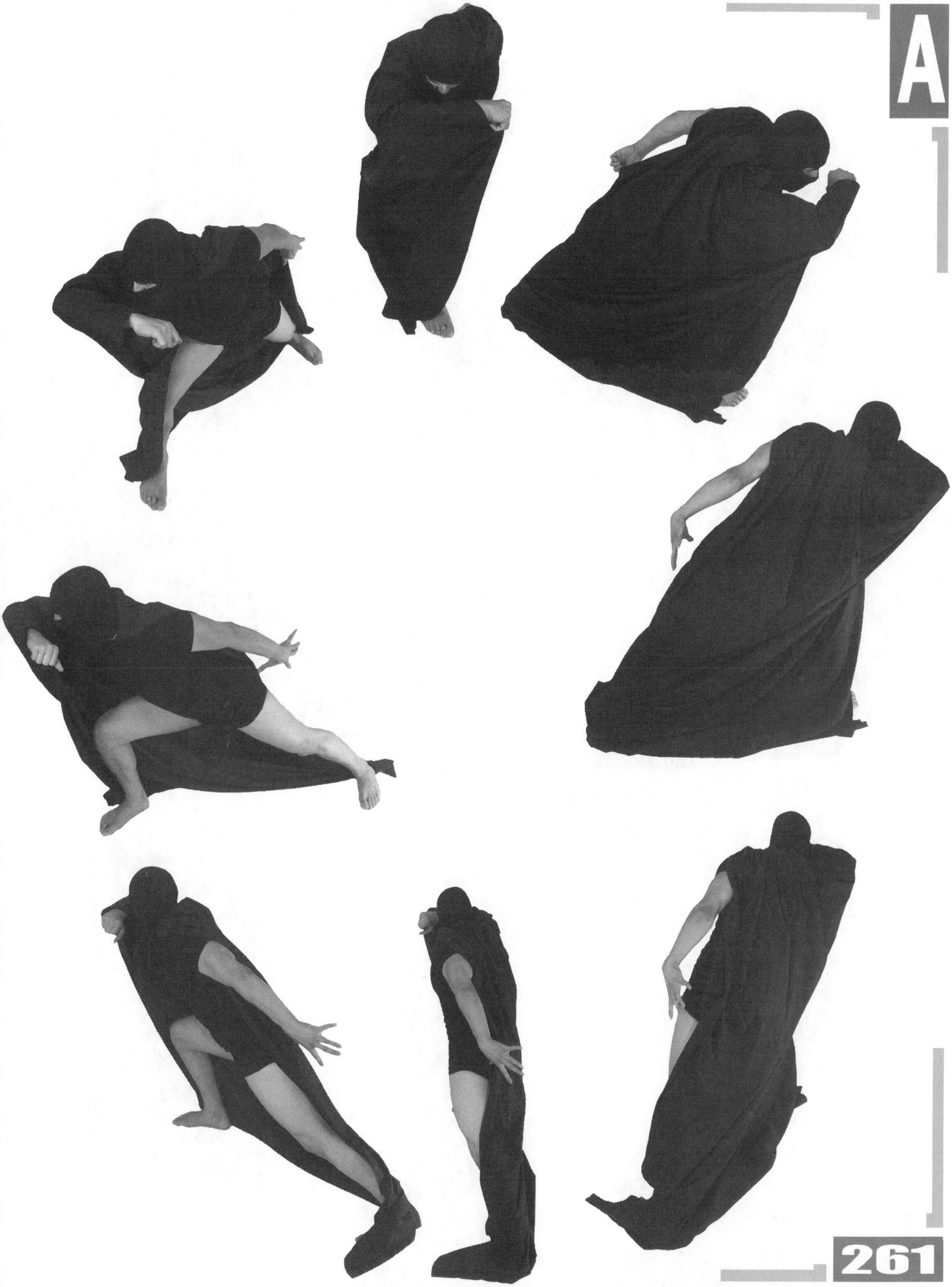

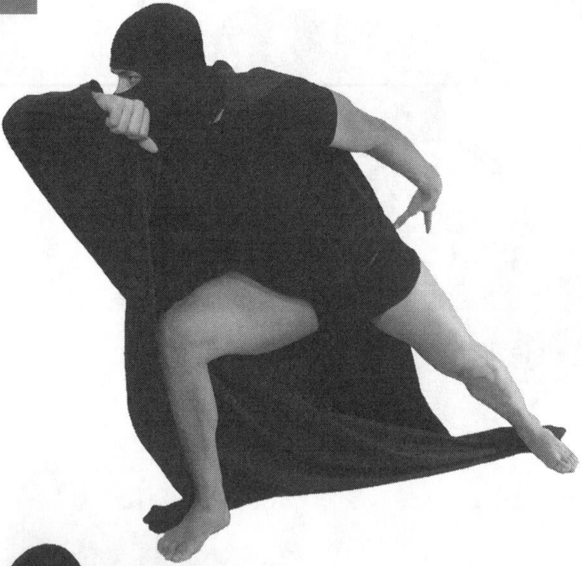
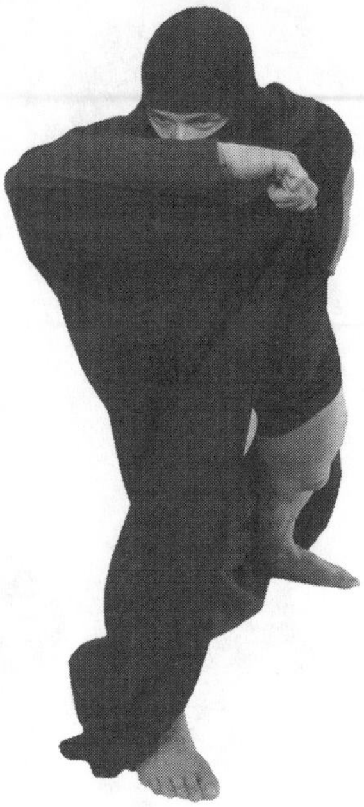
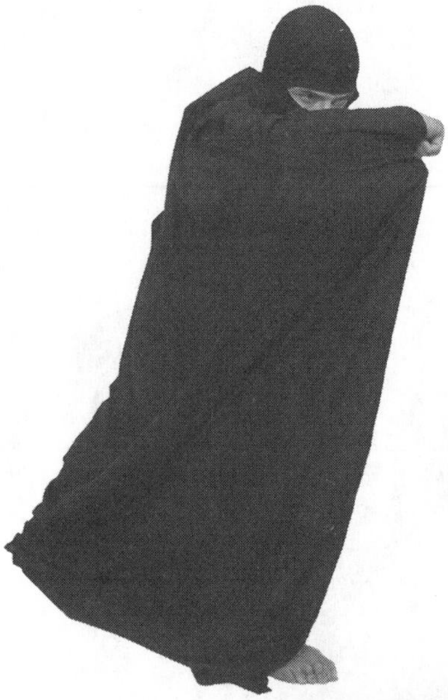
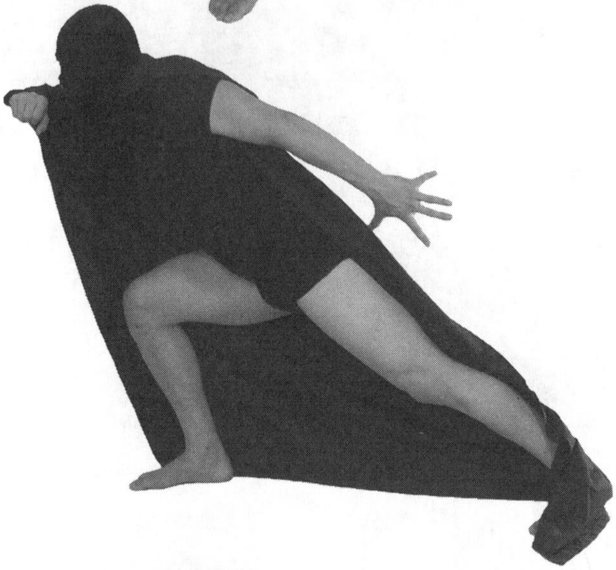
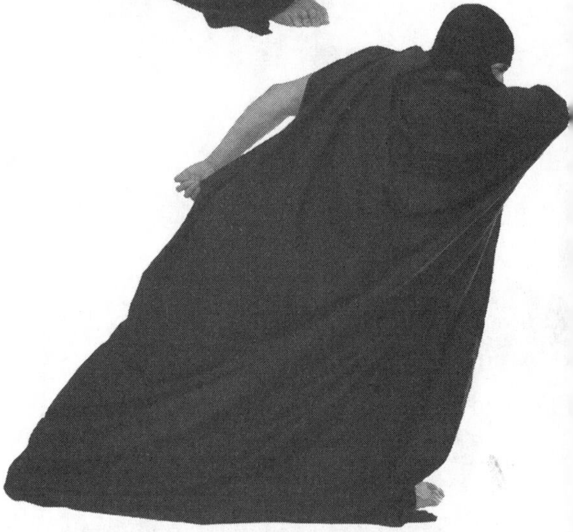
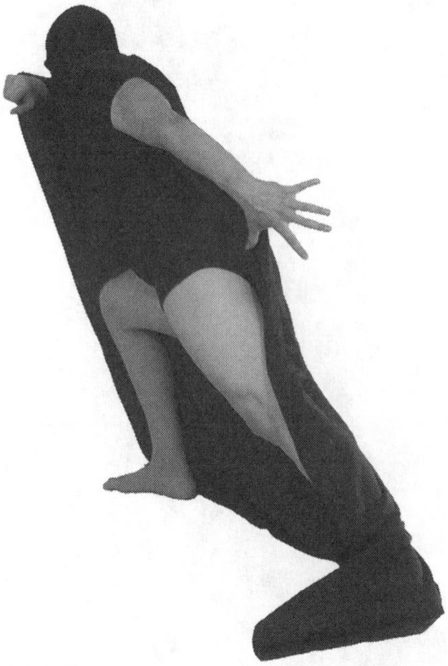
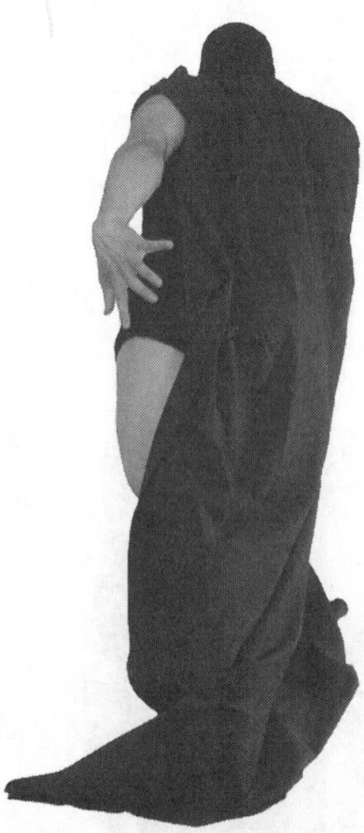
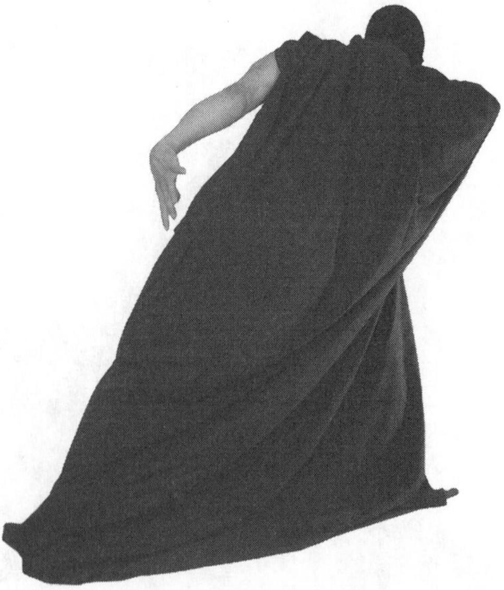

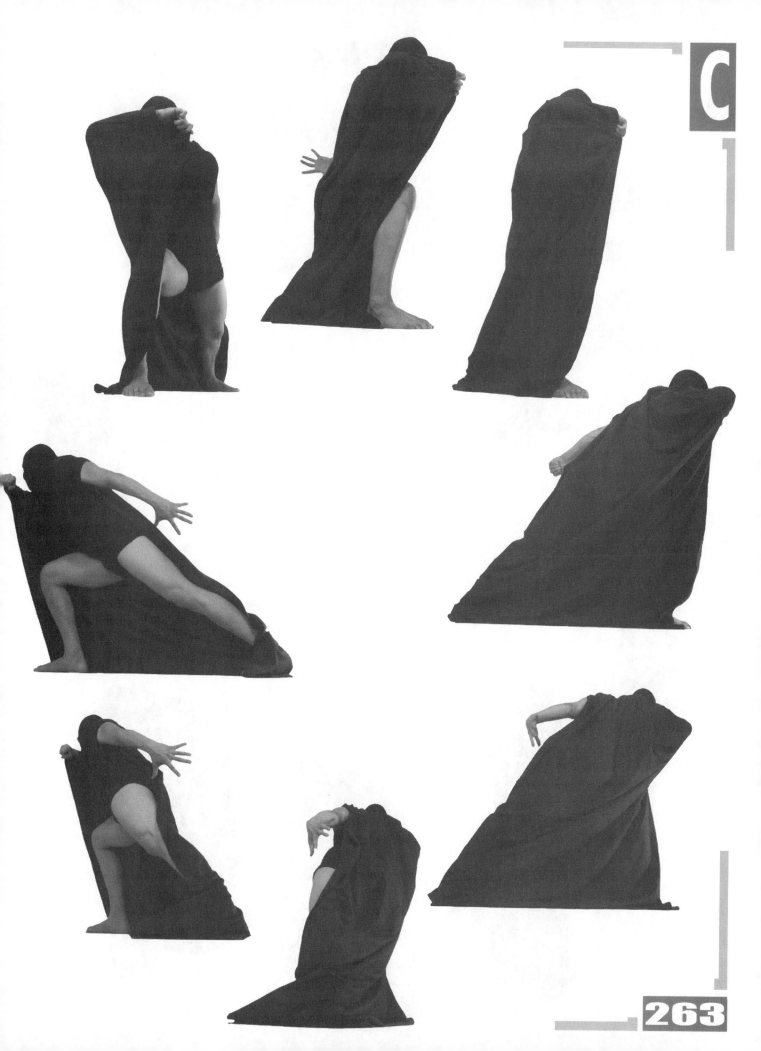

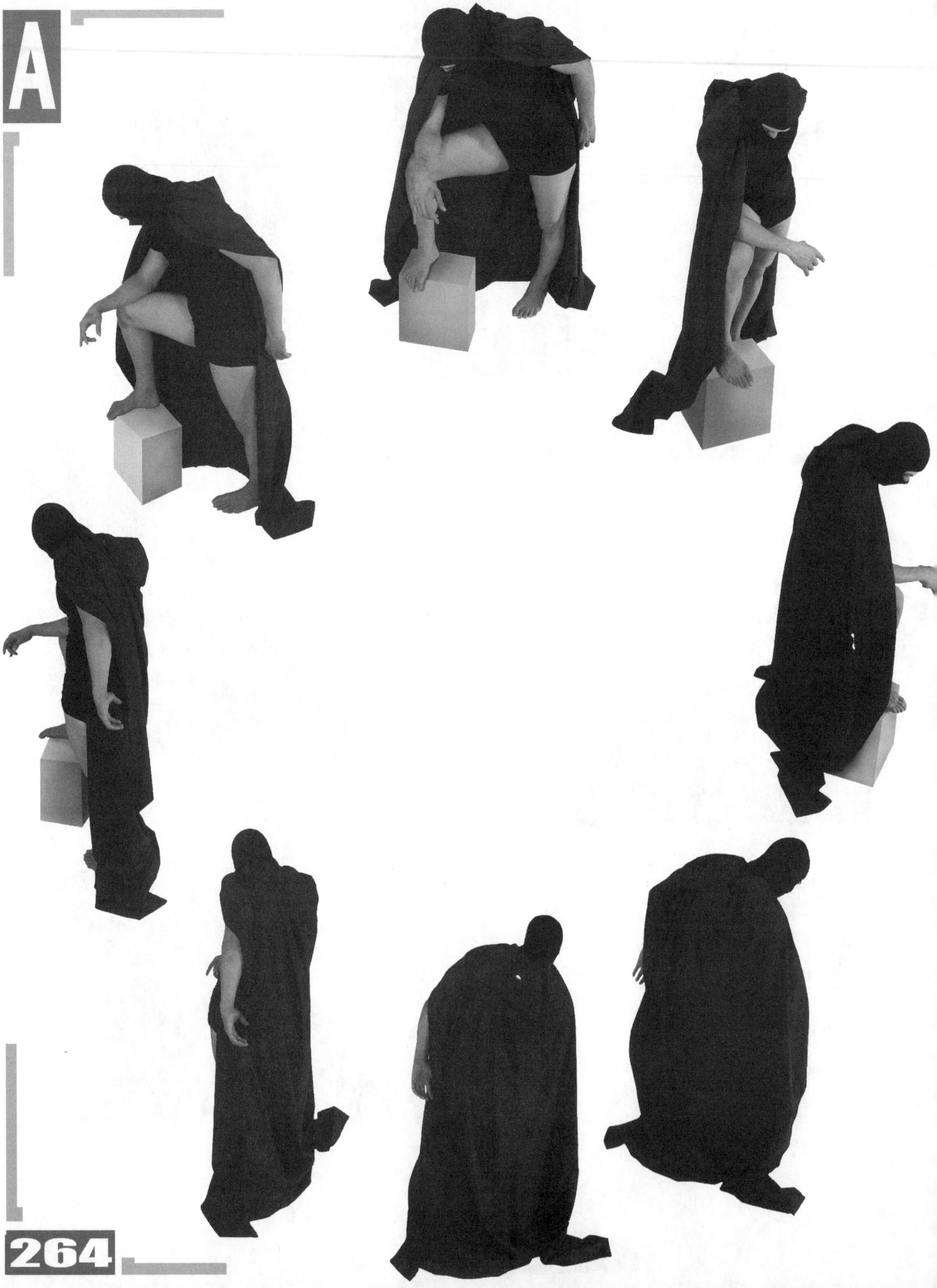

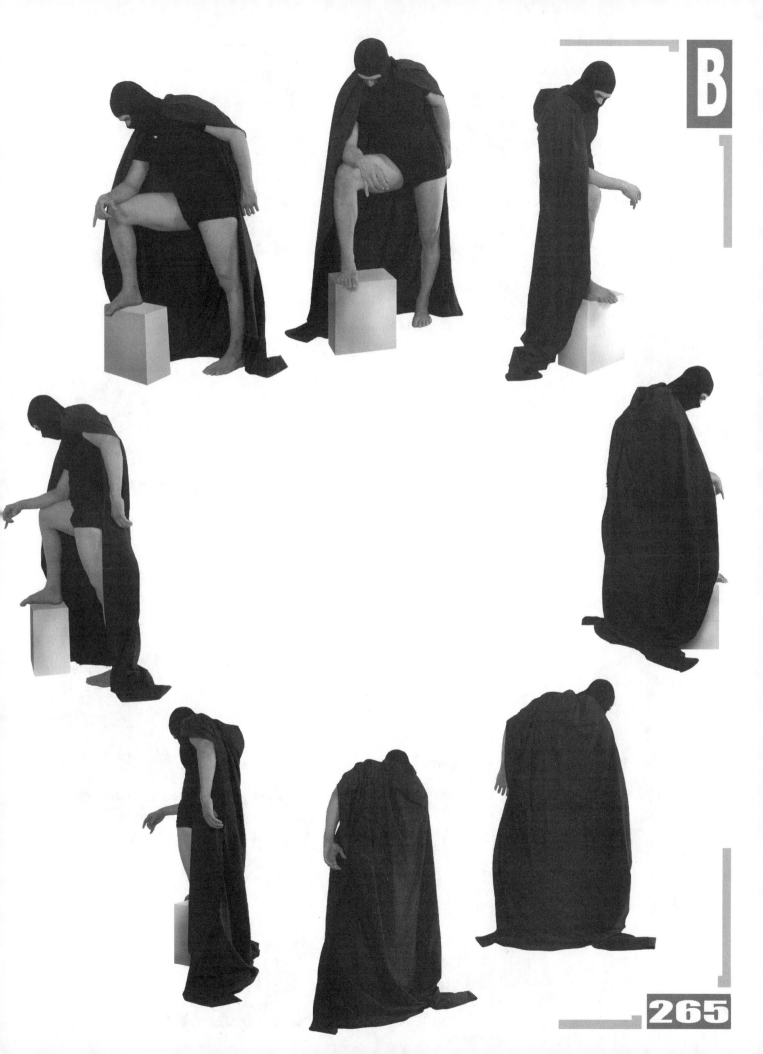

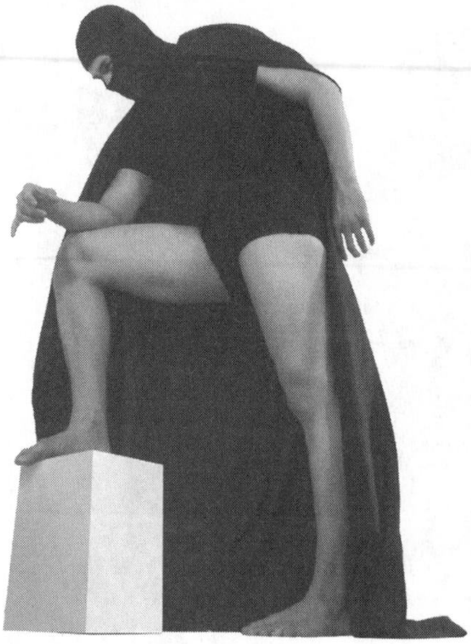

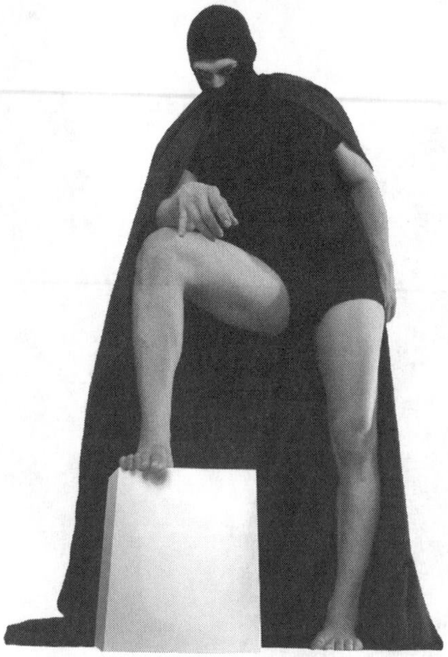

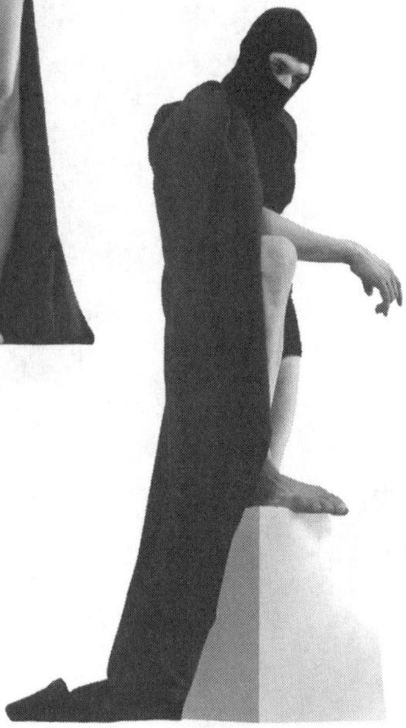

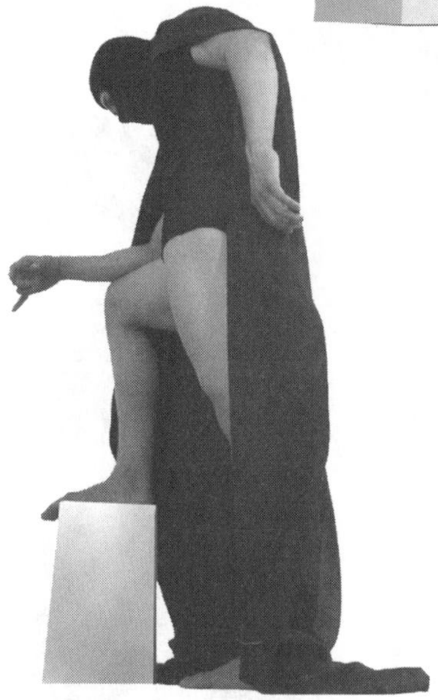

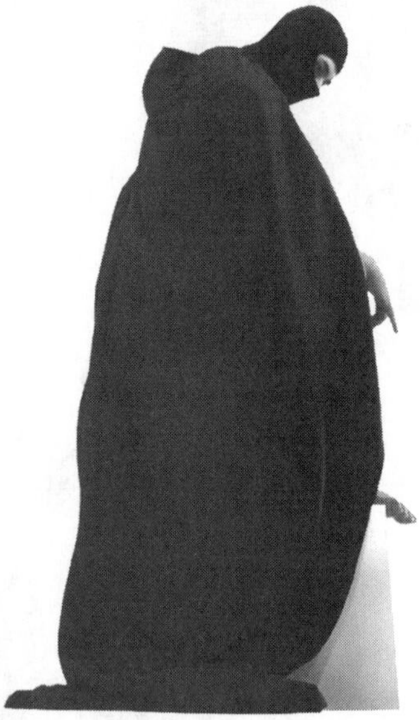

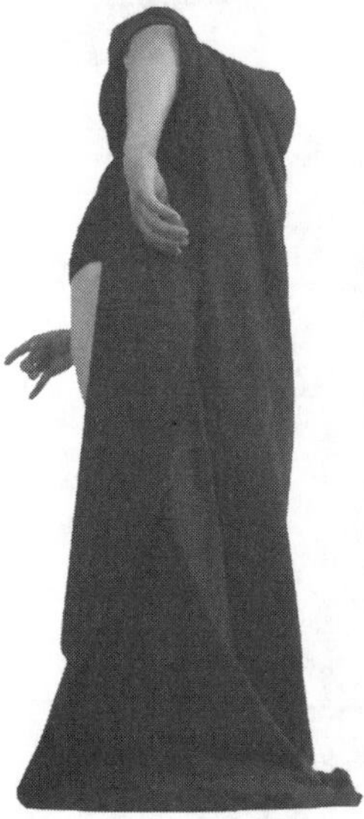

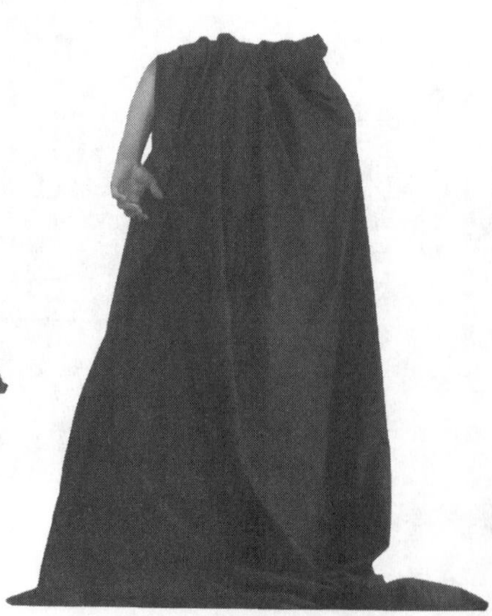

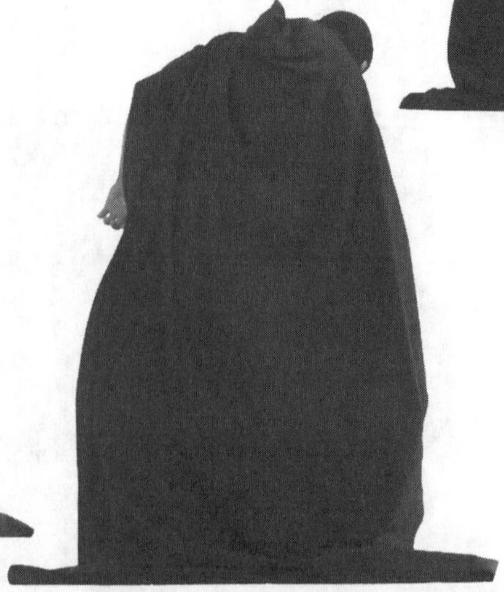

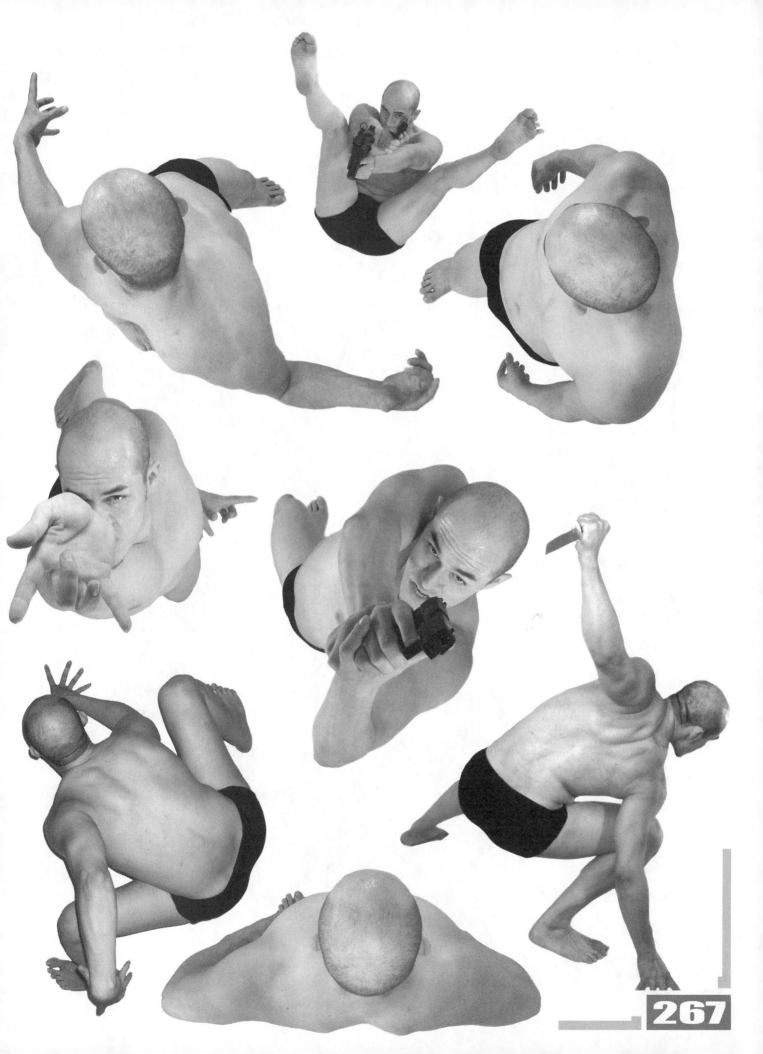

SPANDEX POSES

SUPERHE

POSE

RO

PROFILE
REFERENCE

SPANDEX POSES

ACTION POSE
COLLECTION

269

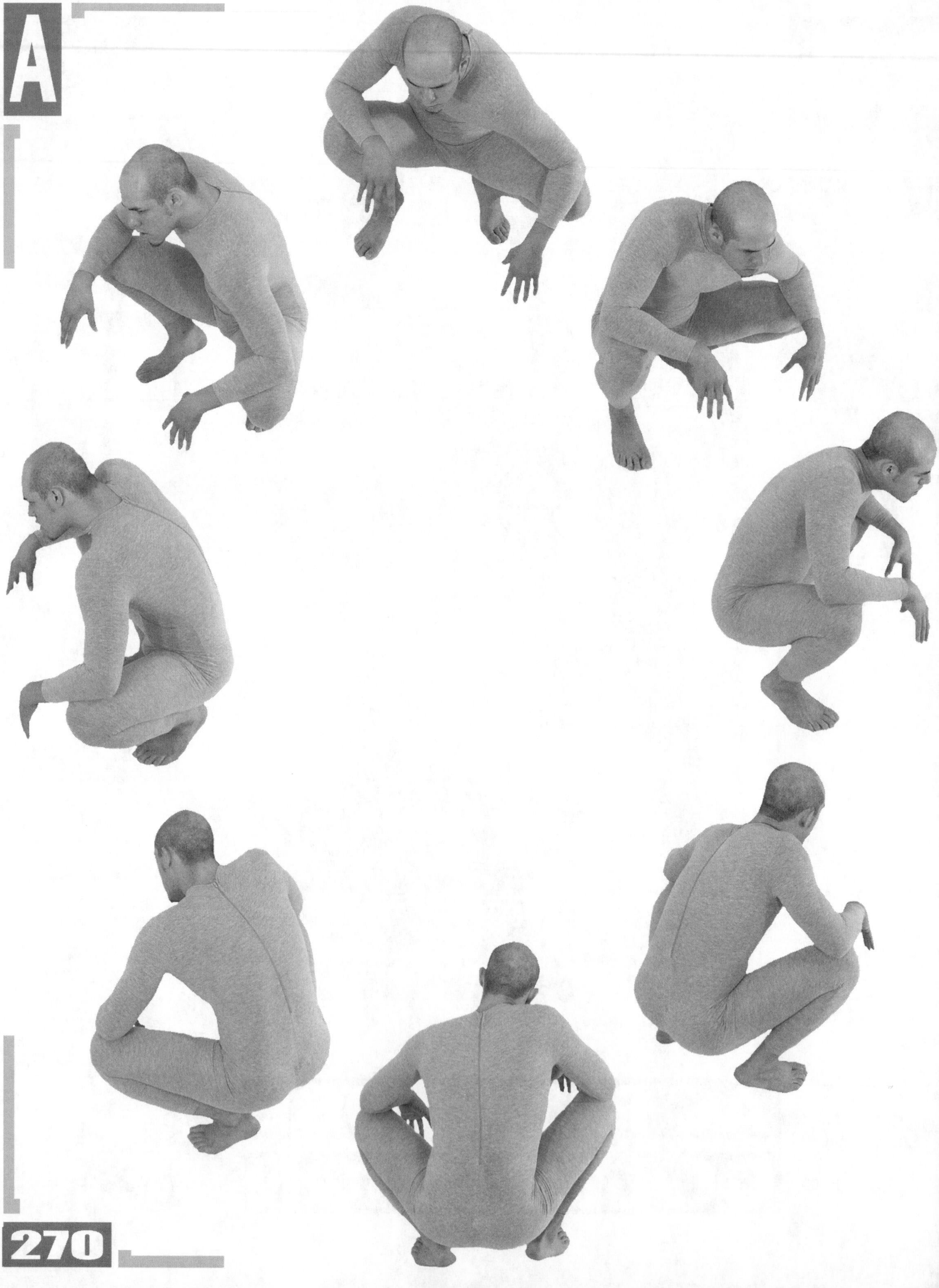

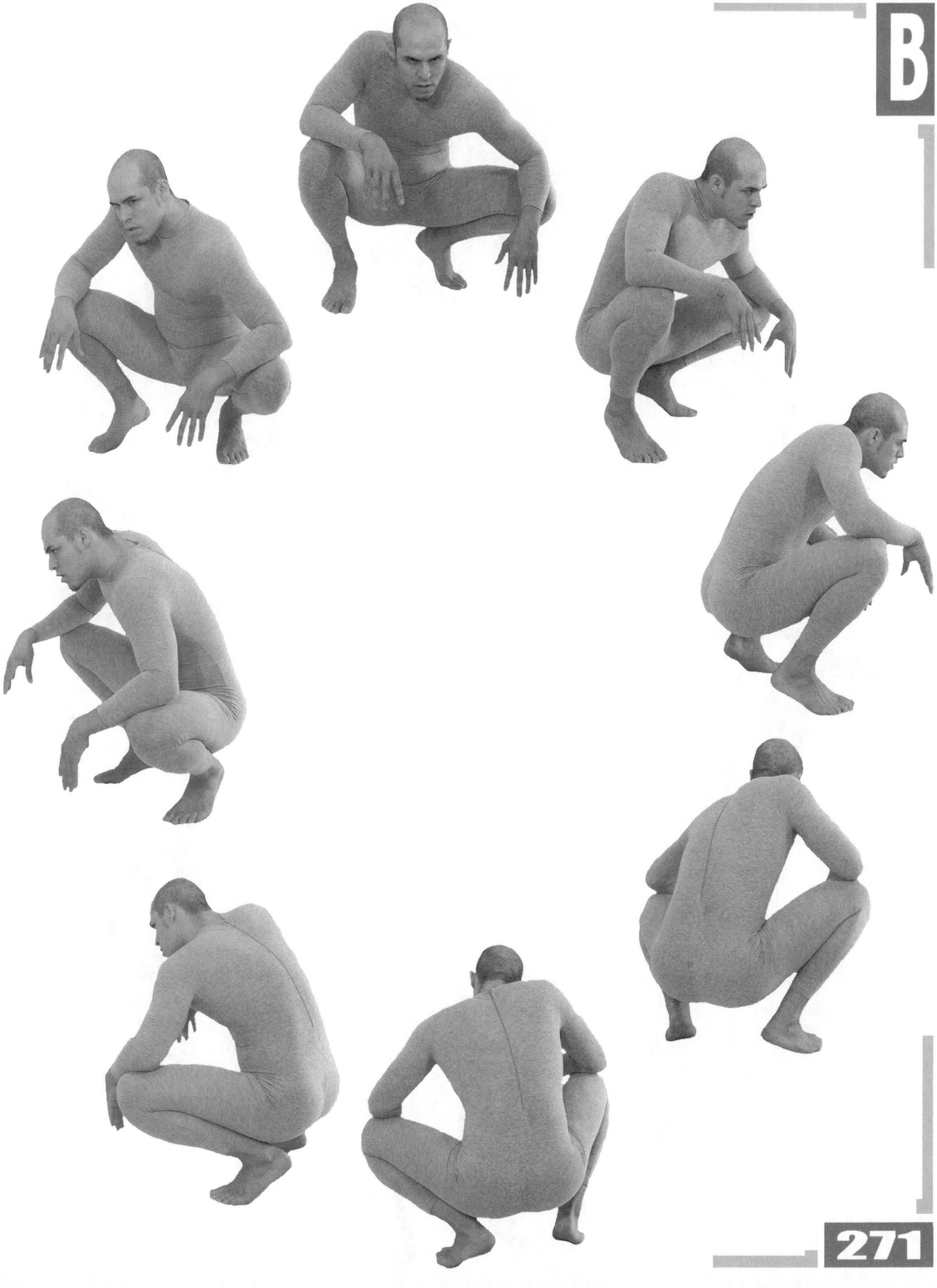

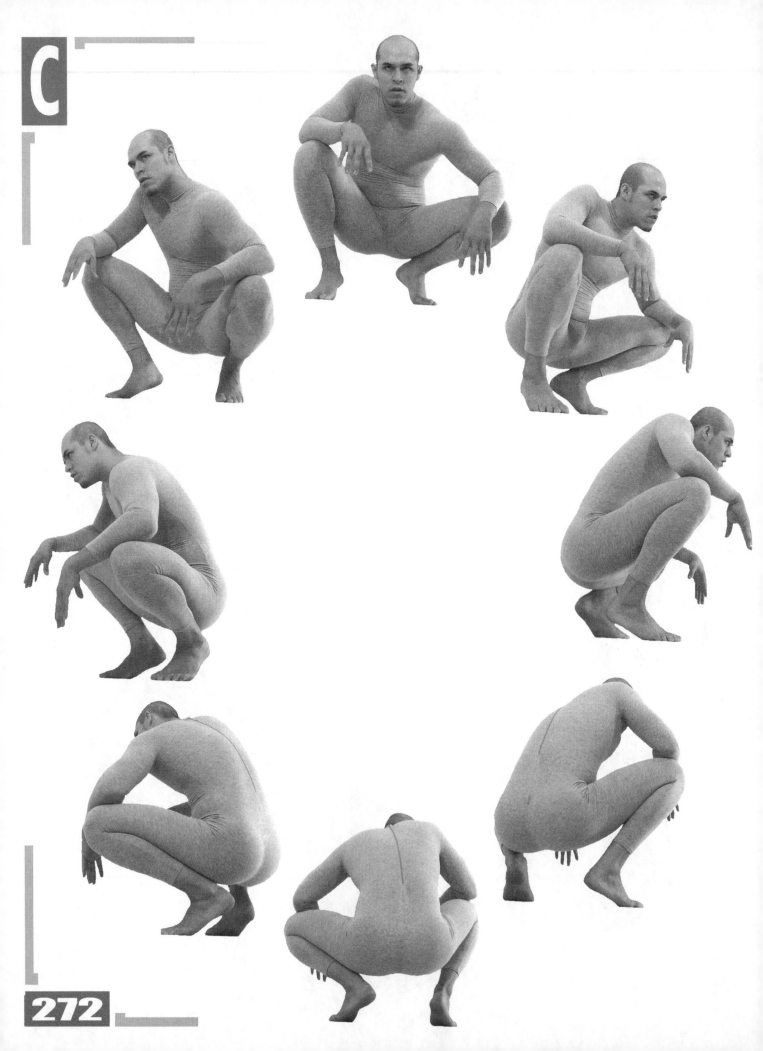

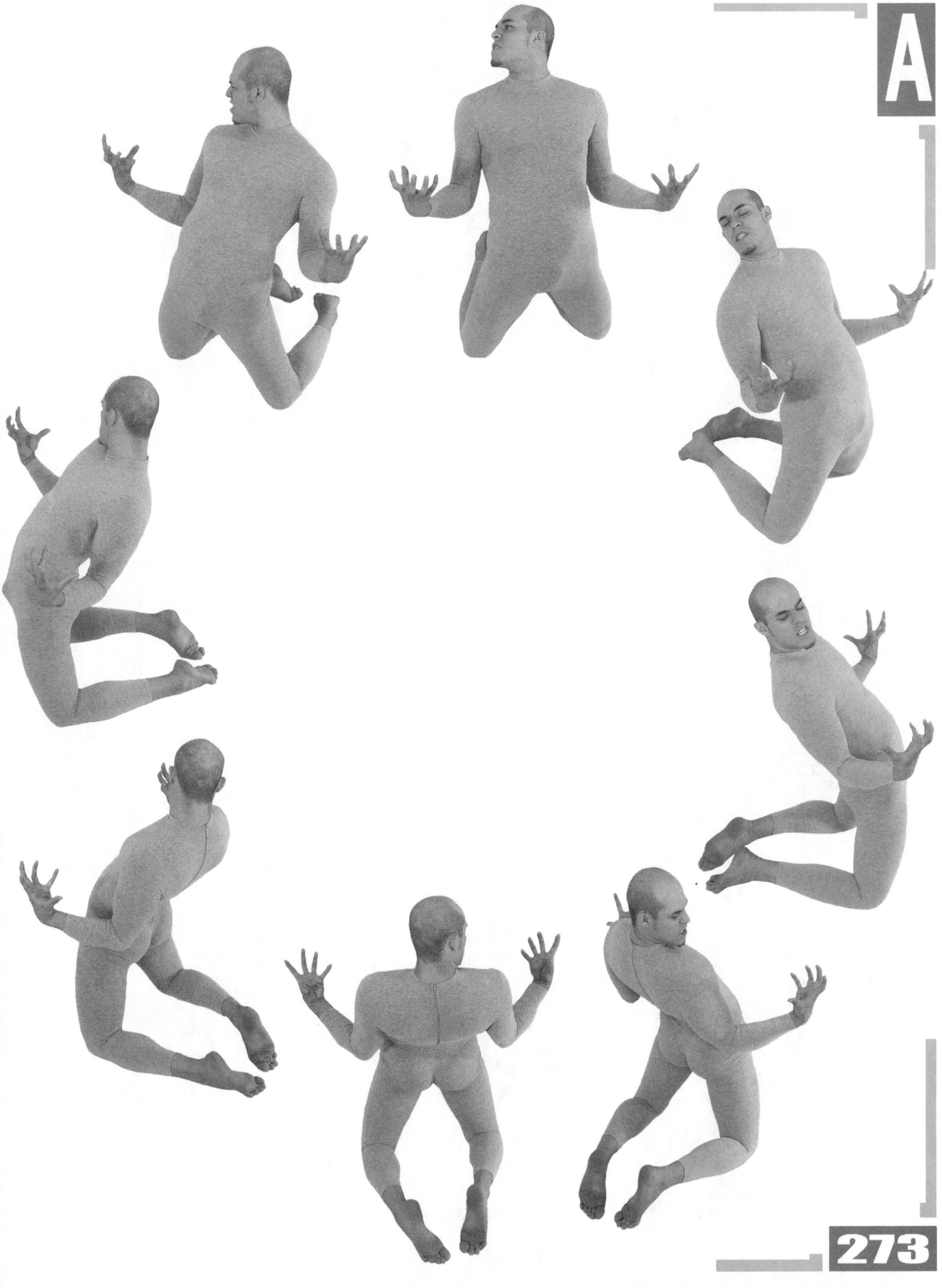

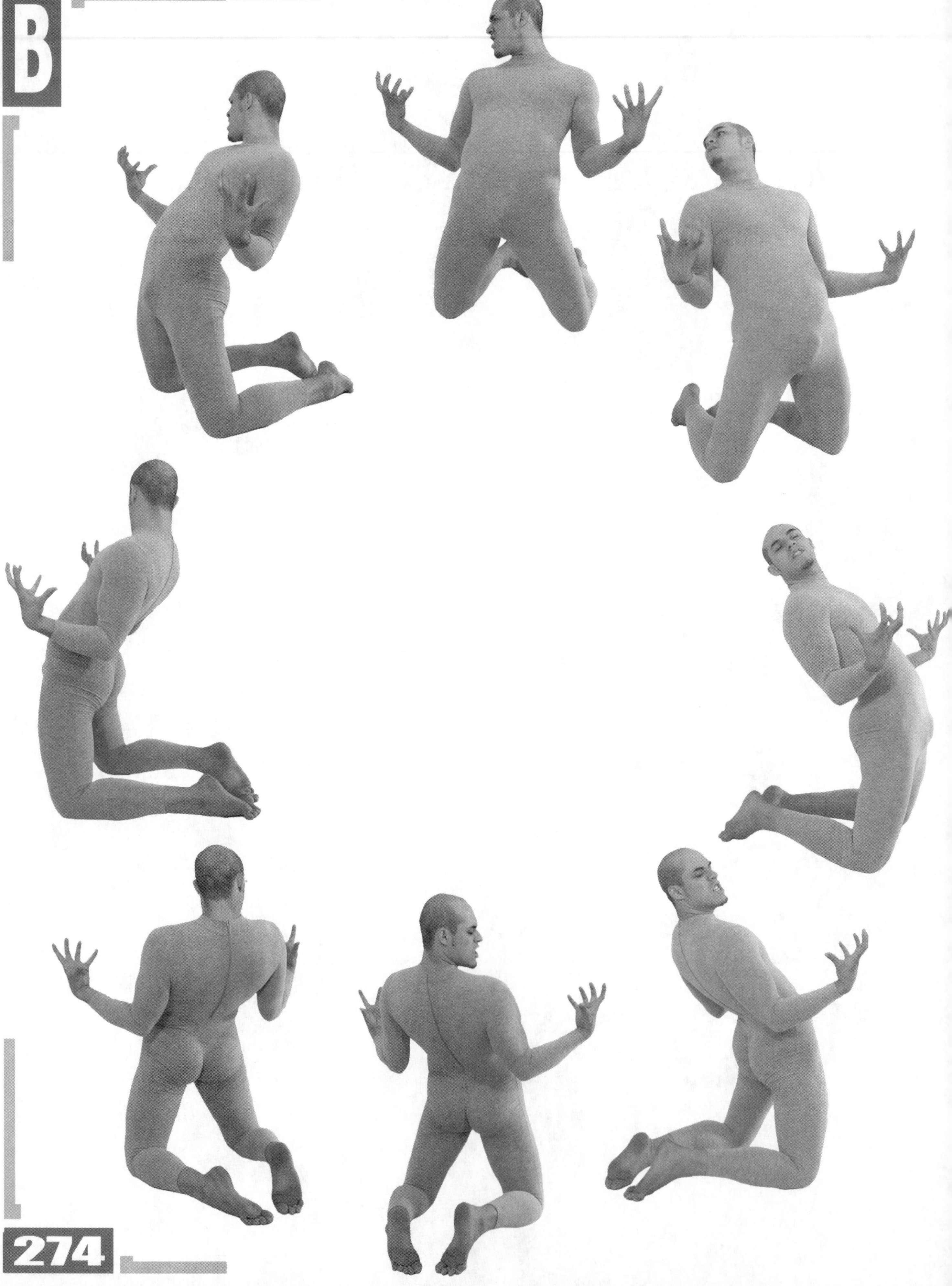

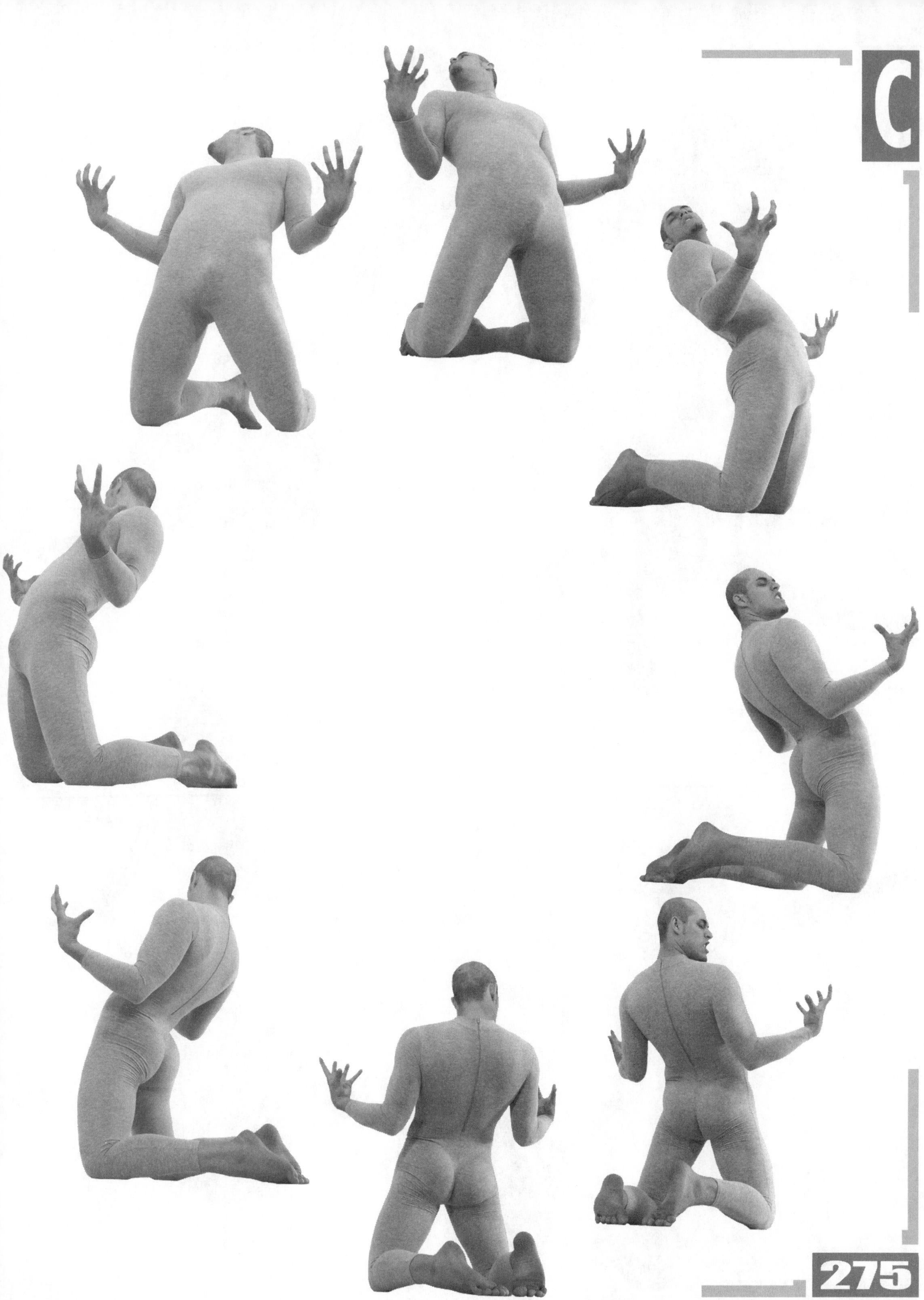

A

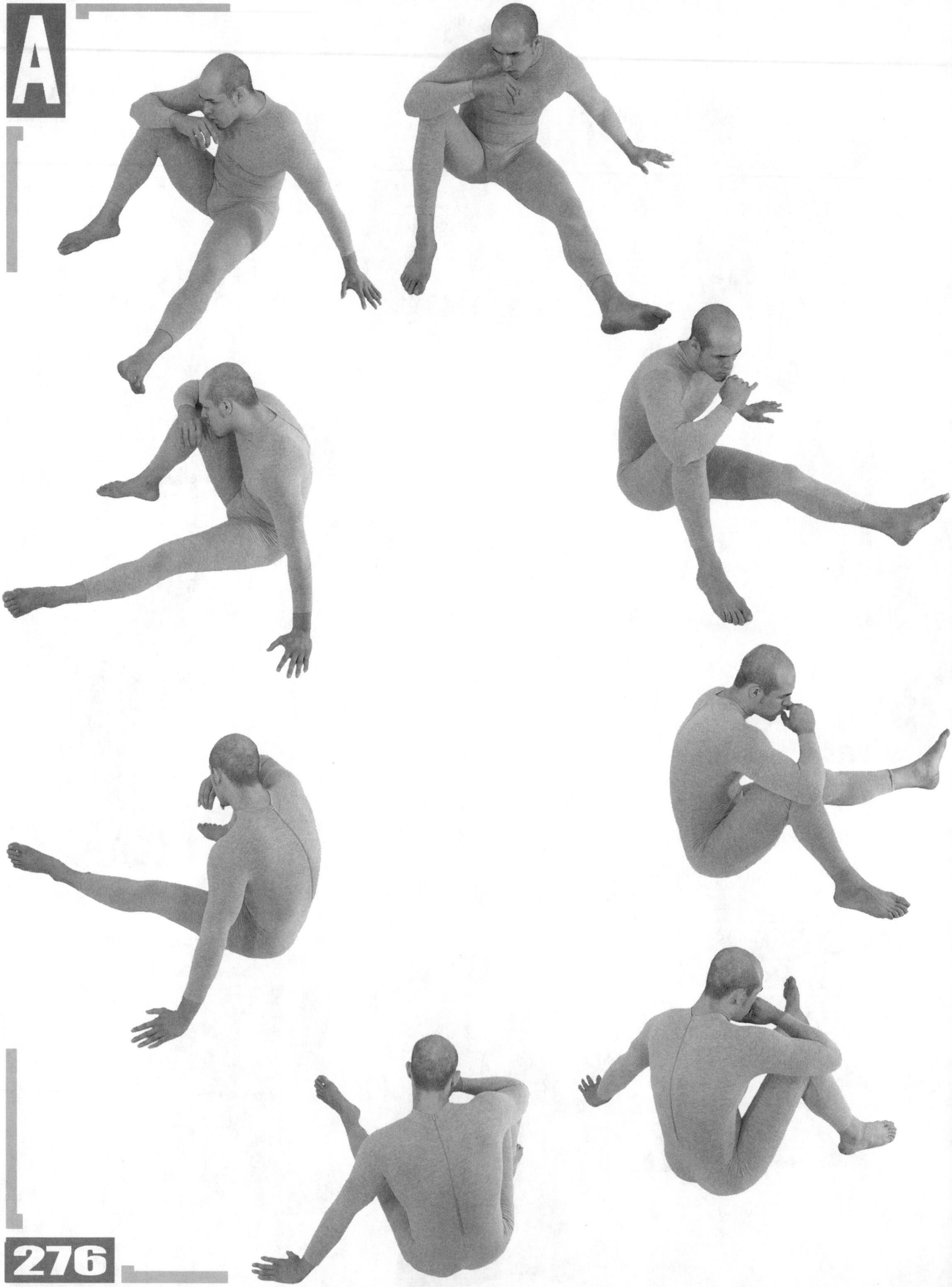

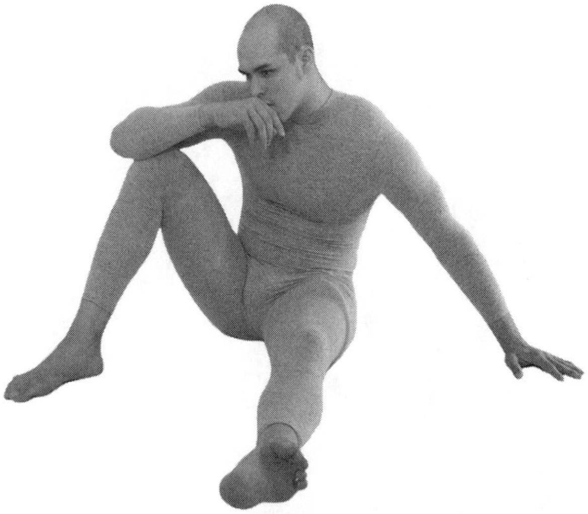

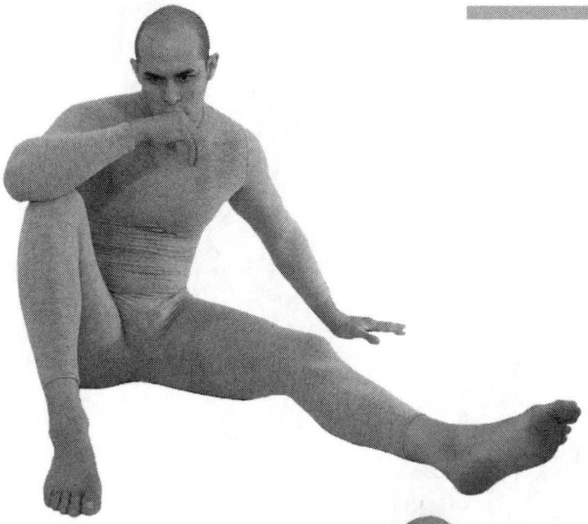

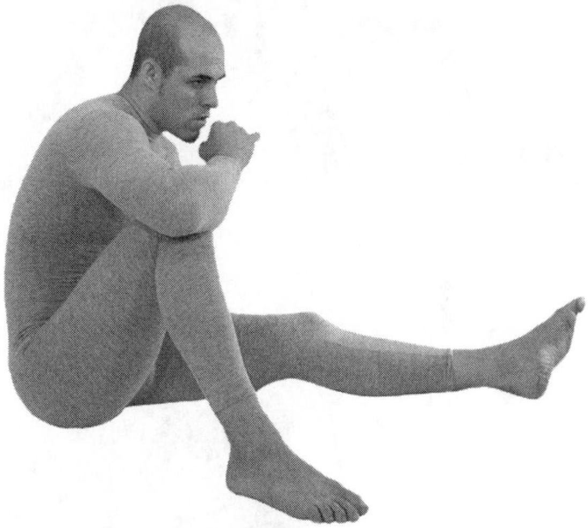

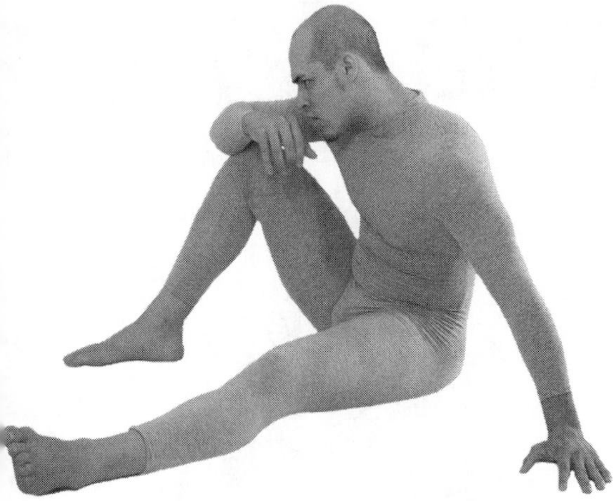

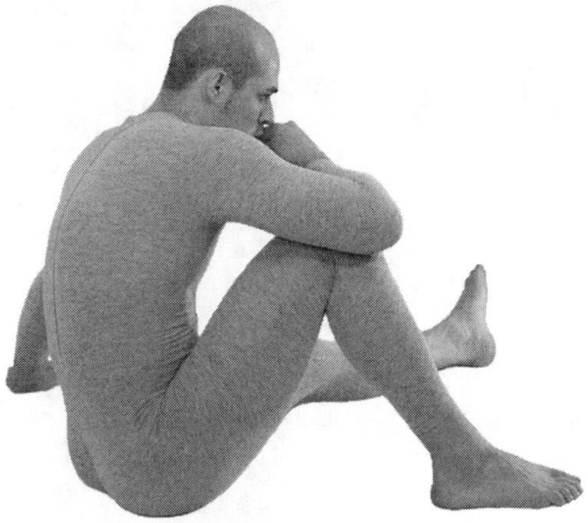

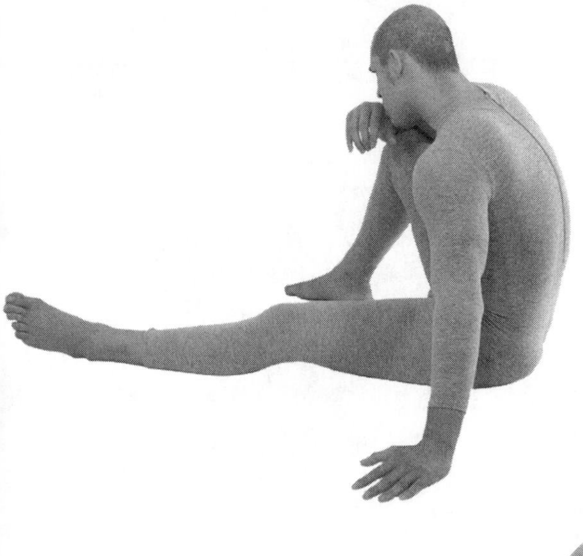

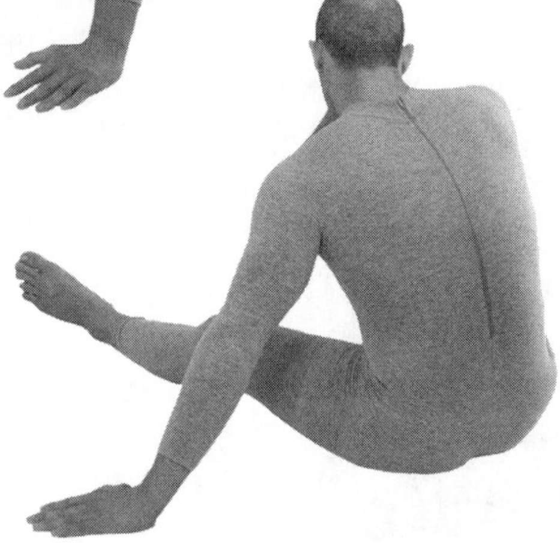

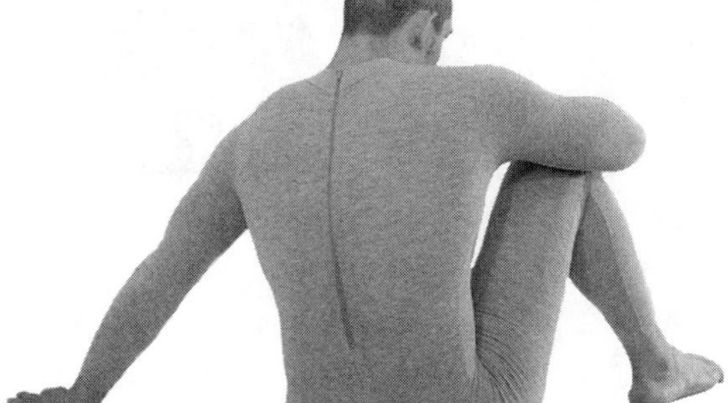

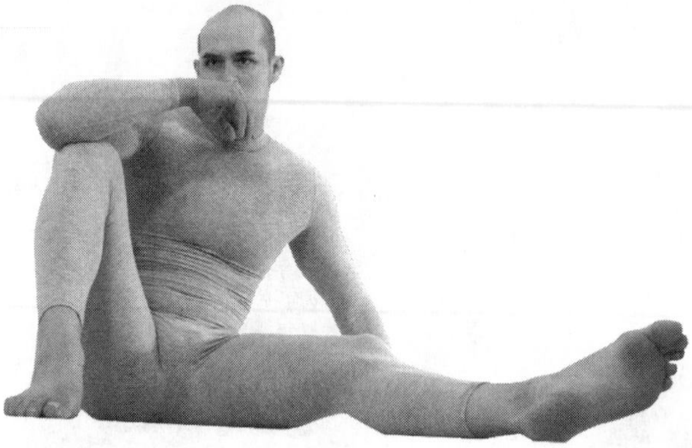

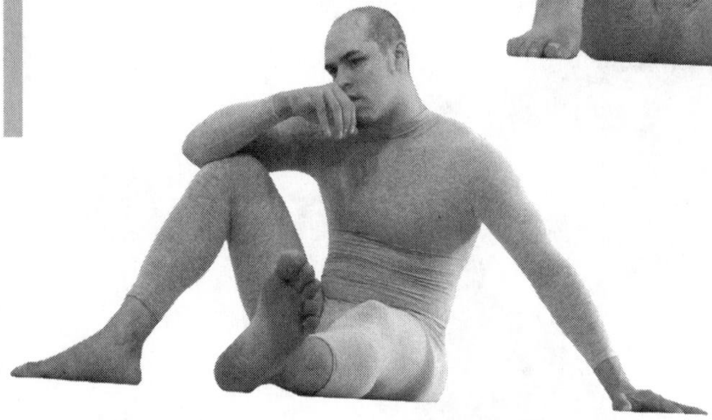

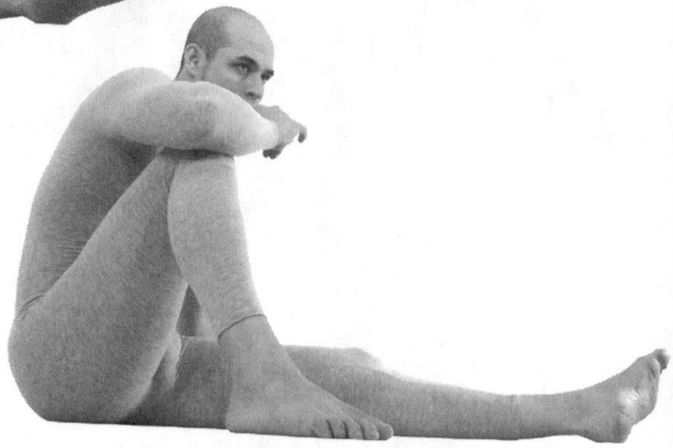

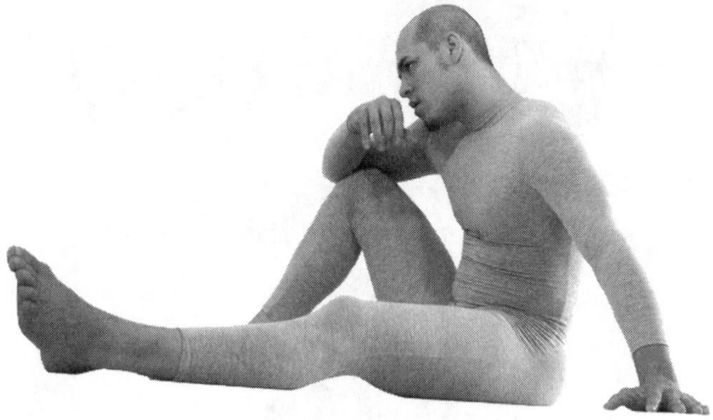

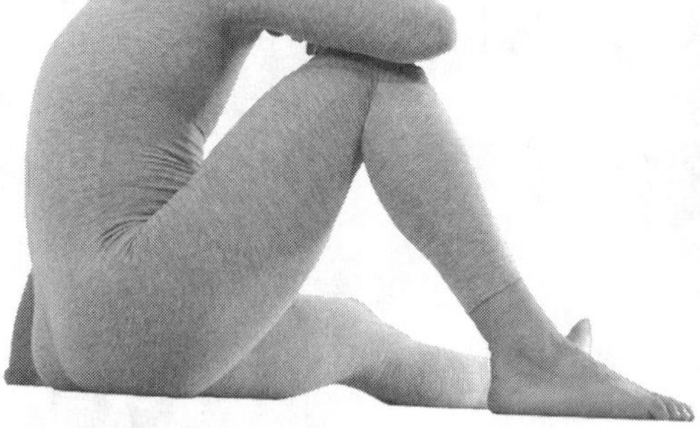

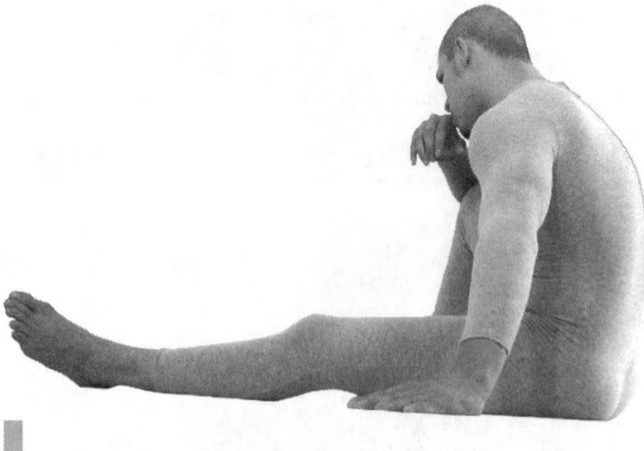

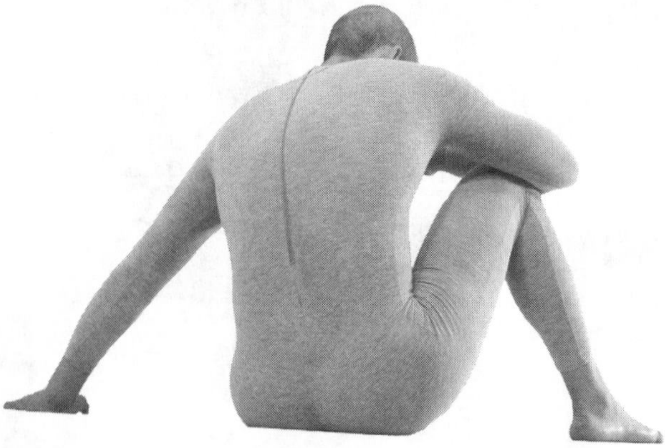

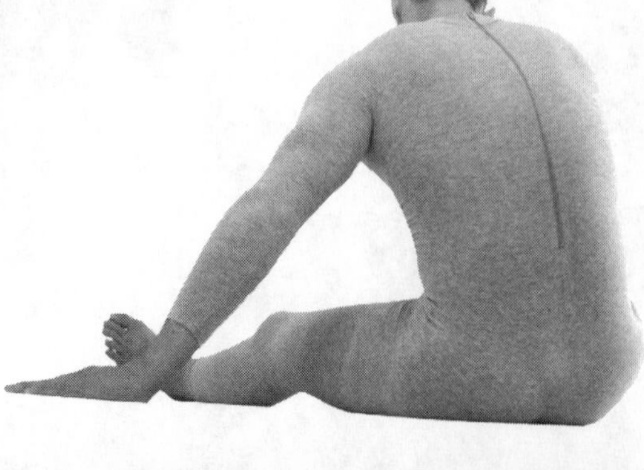

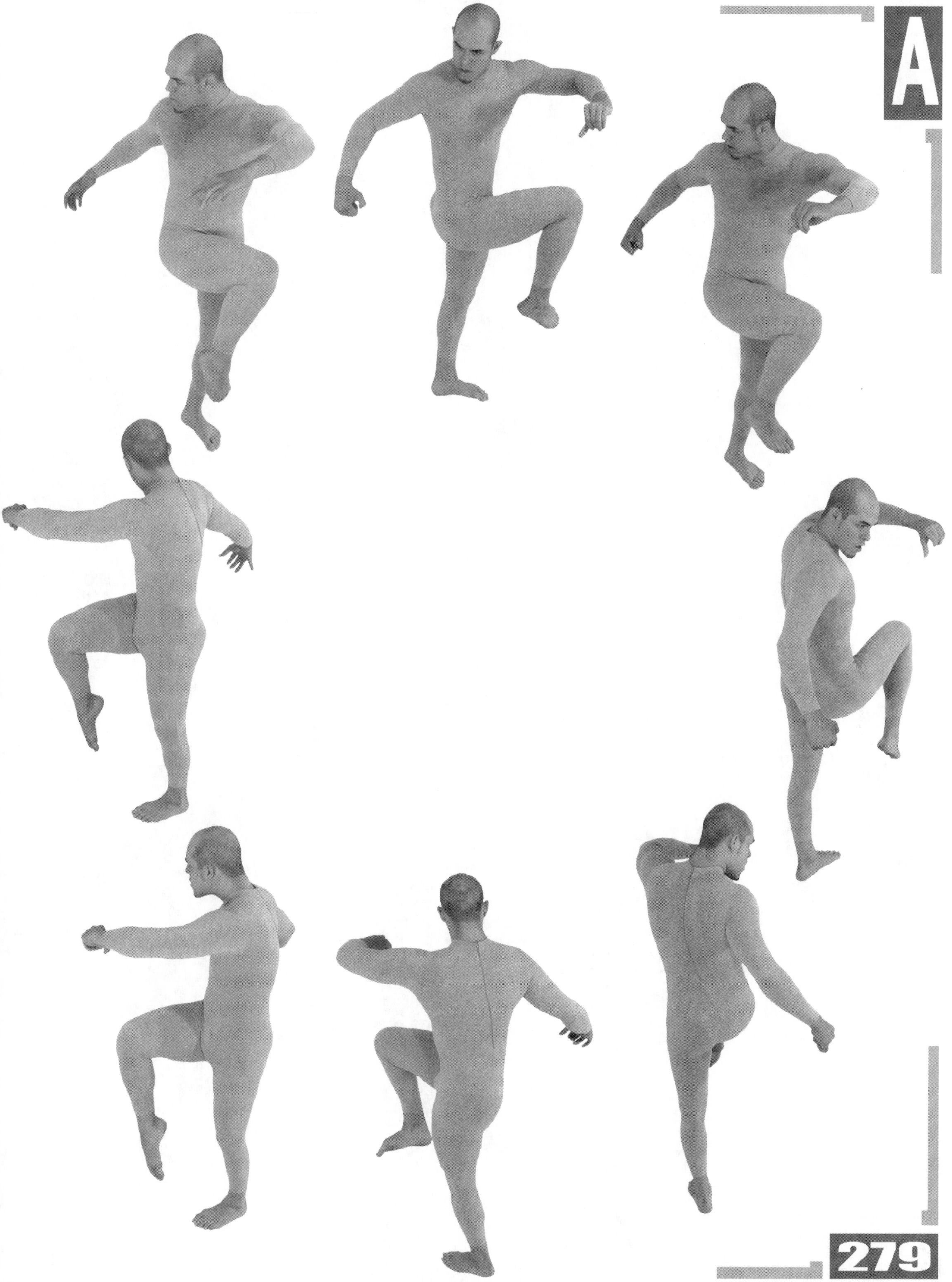

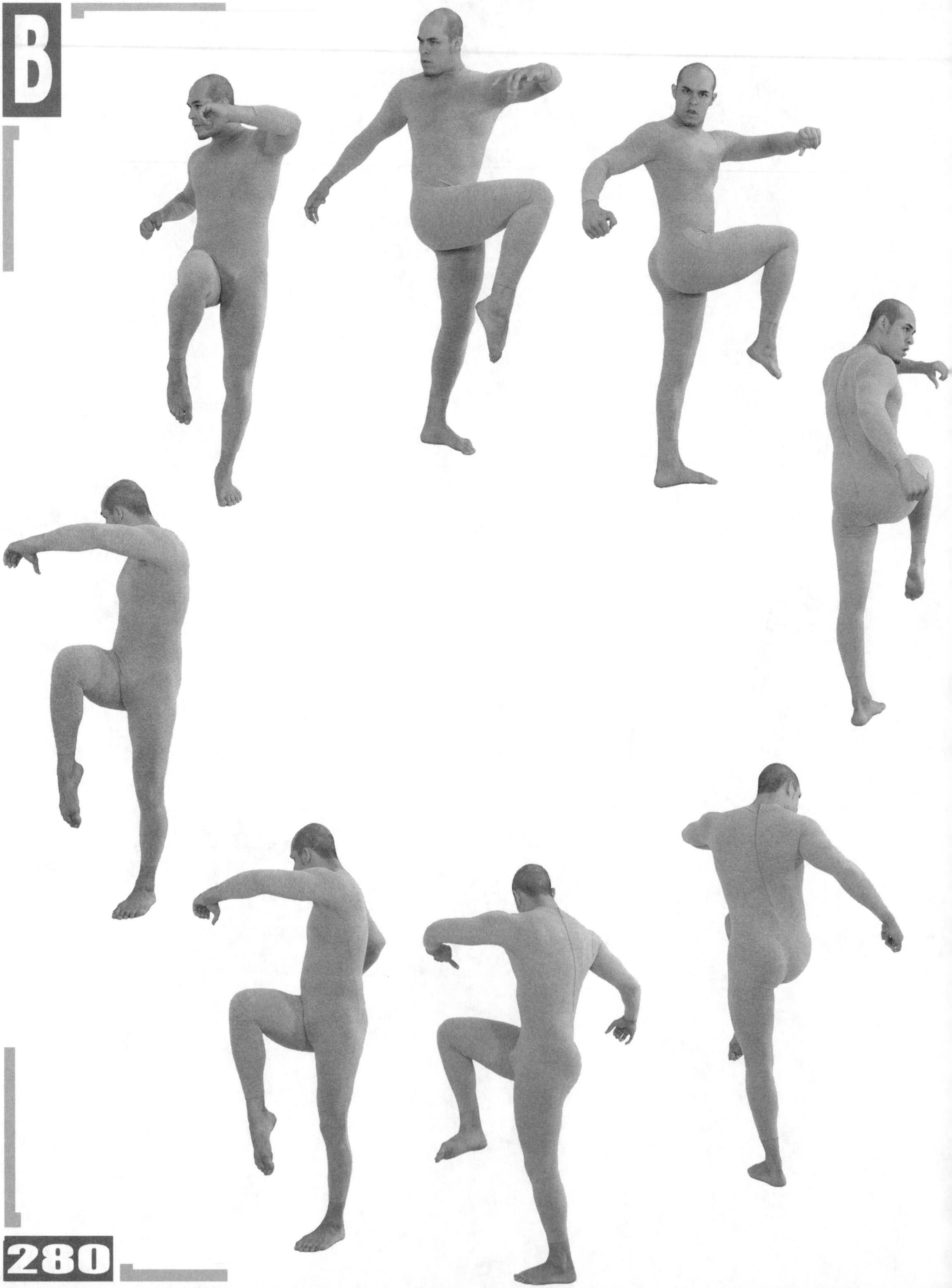

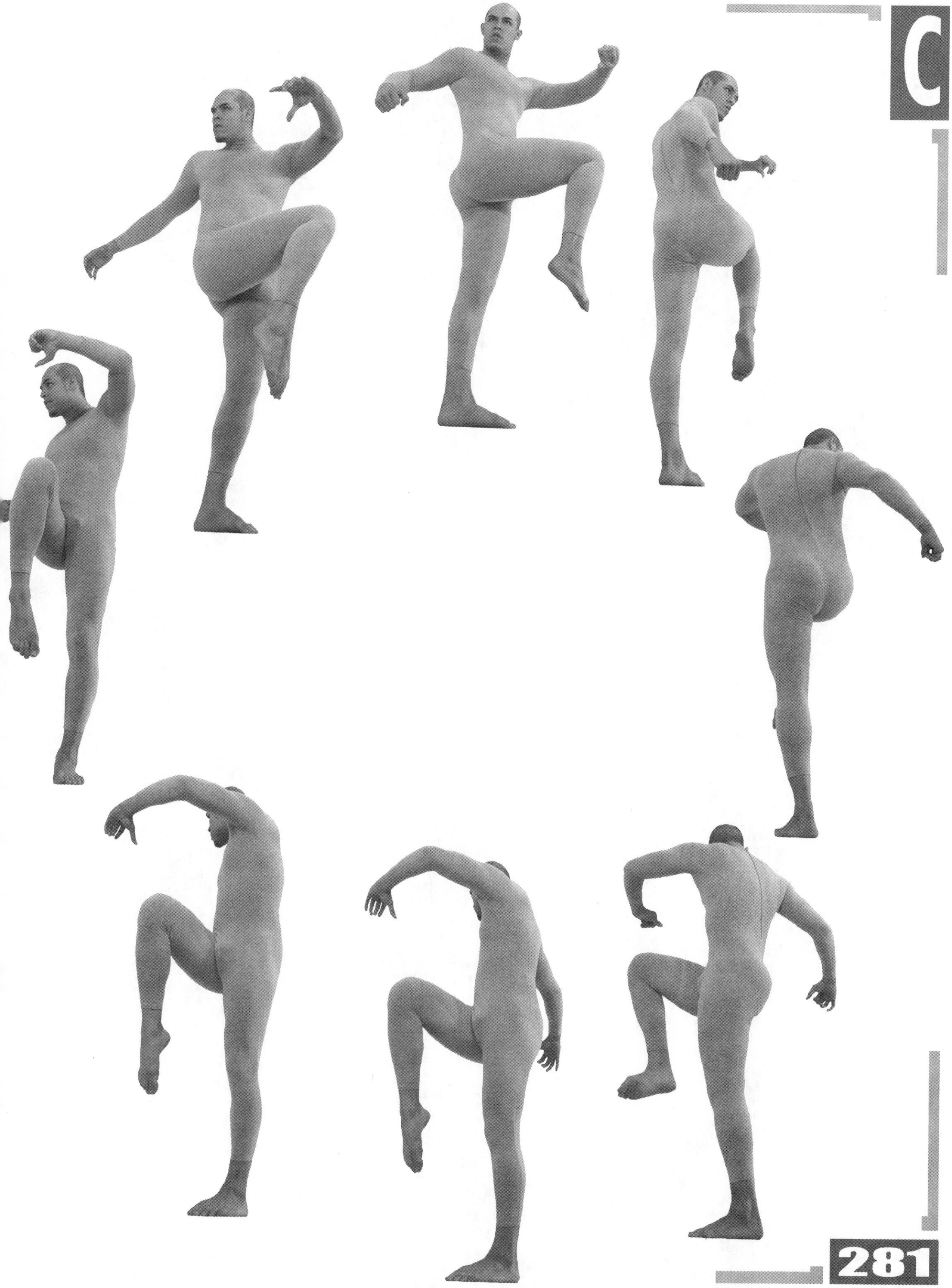

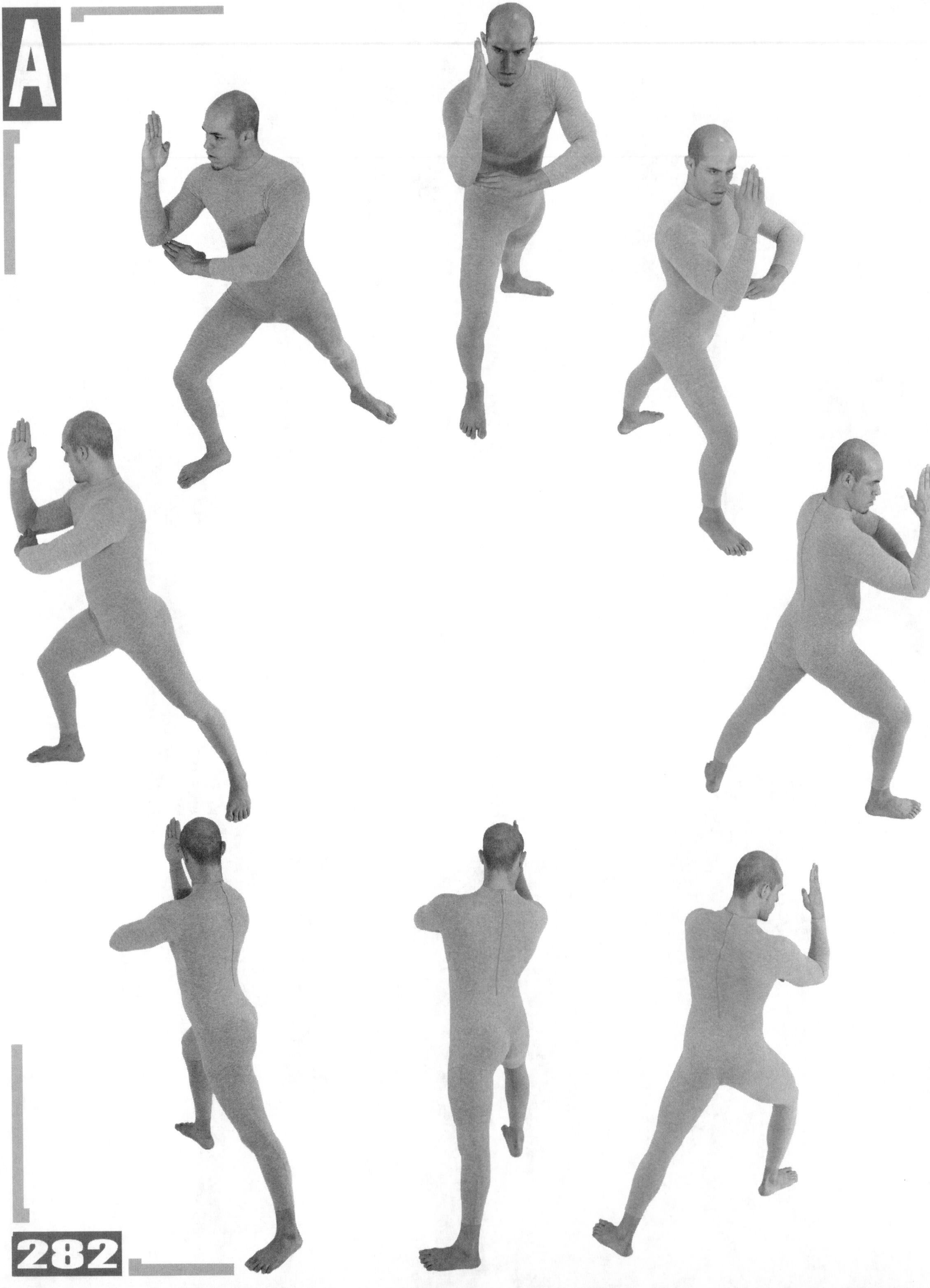

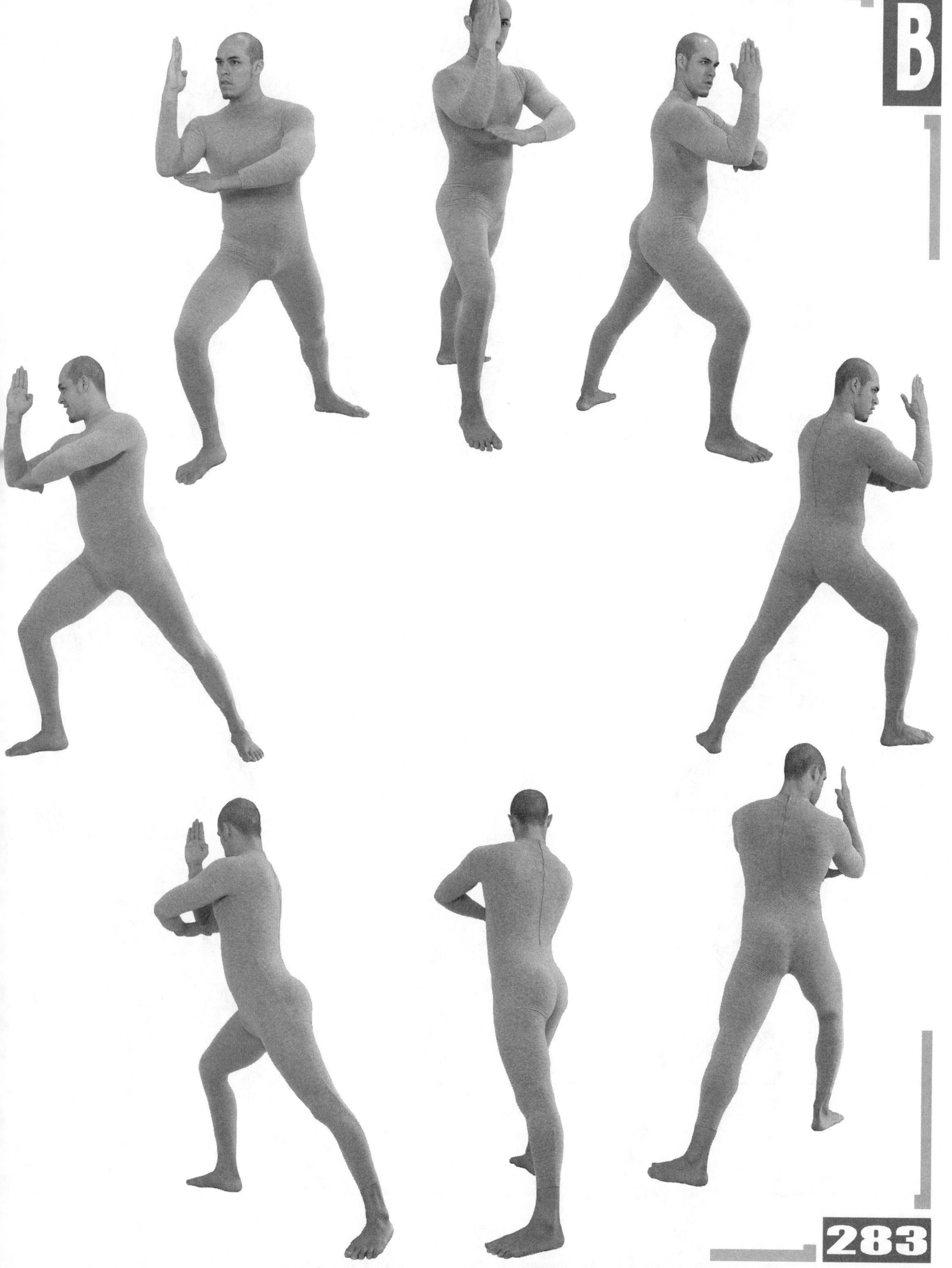

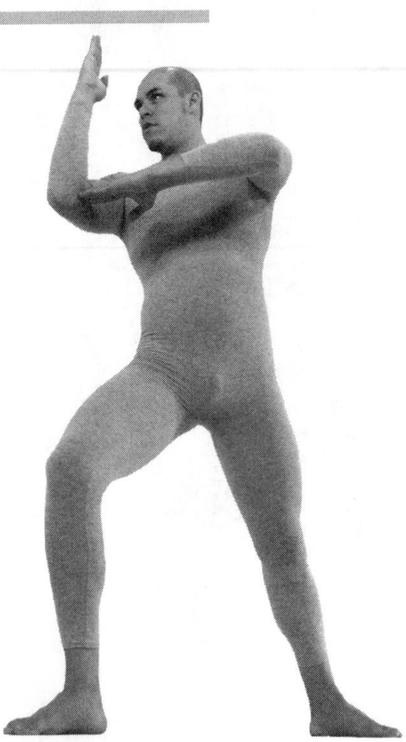

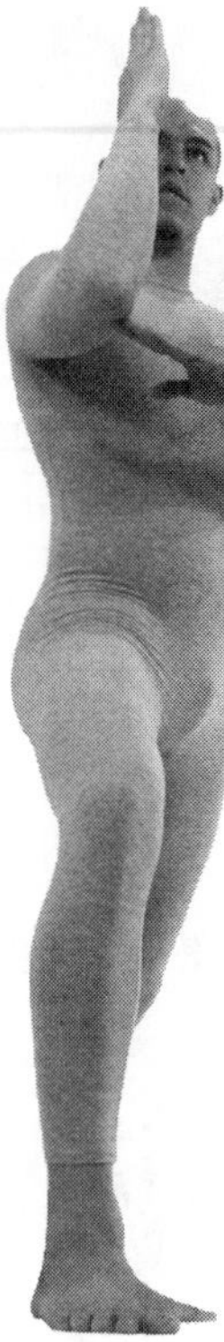

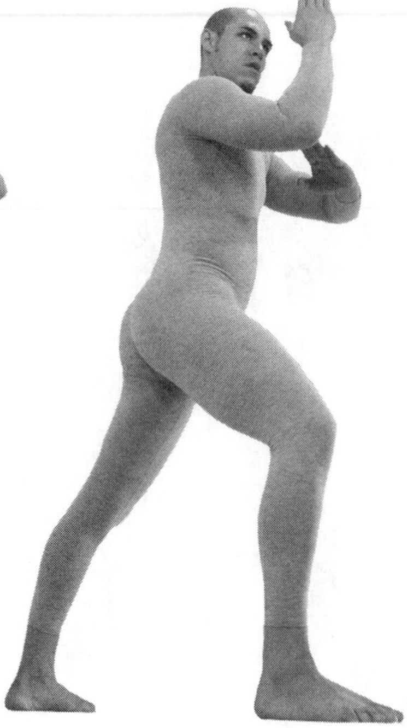

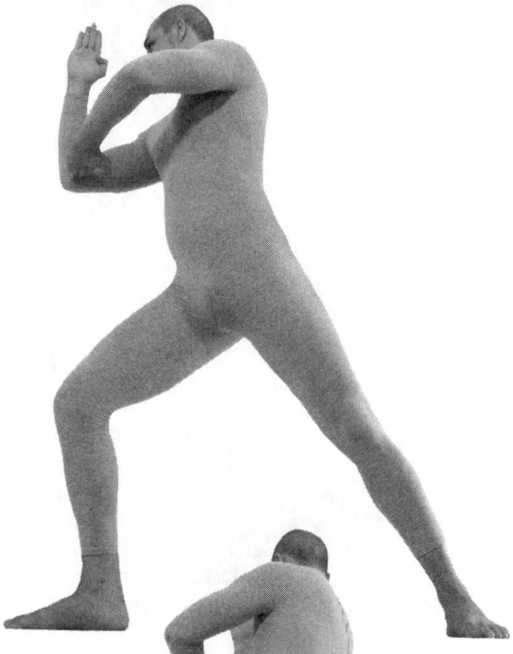

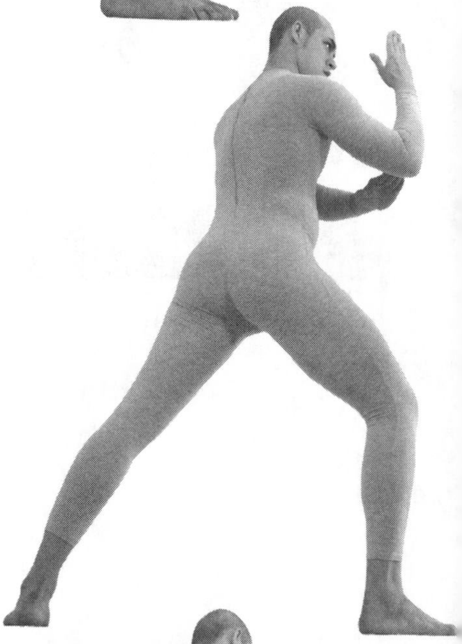

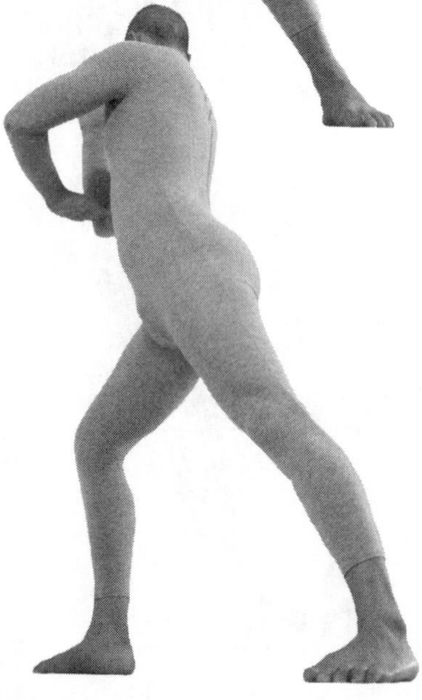

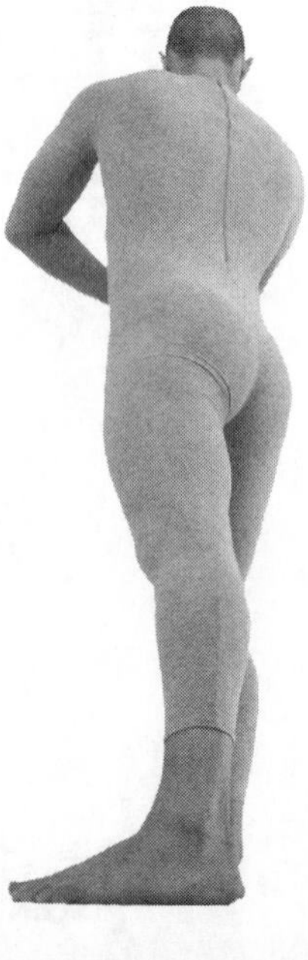

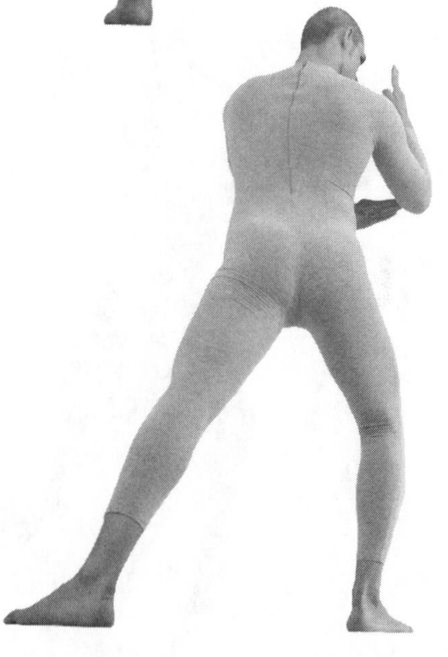

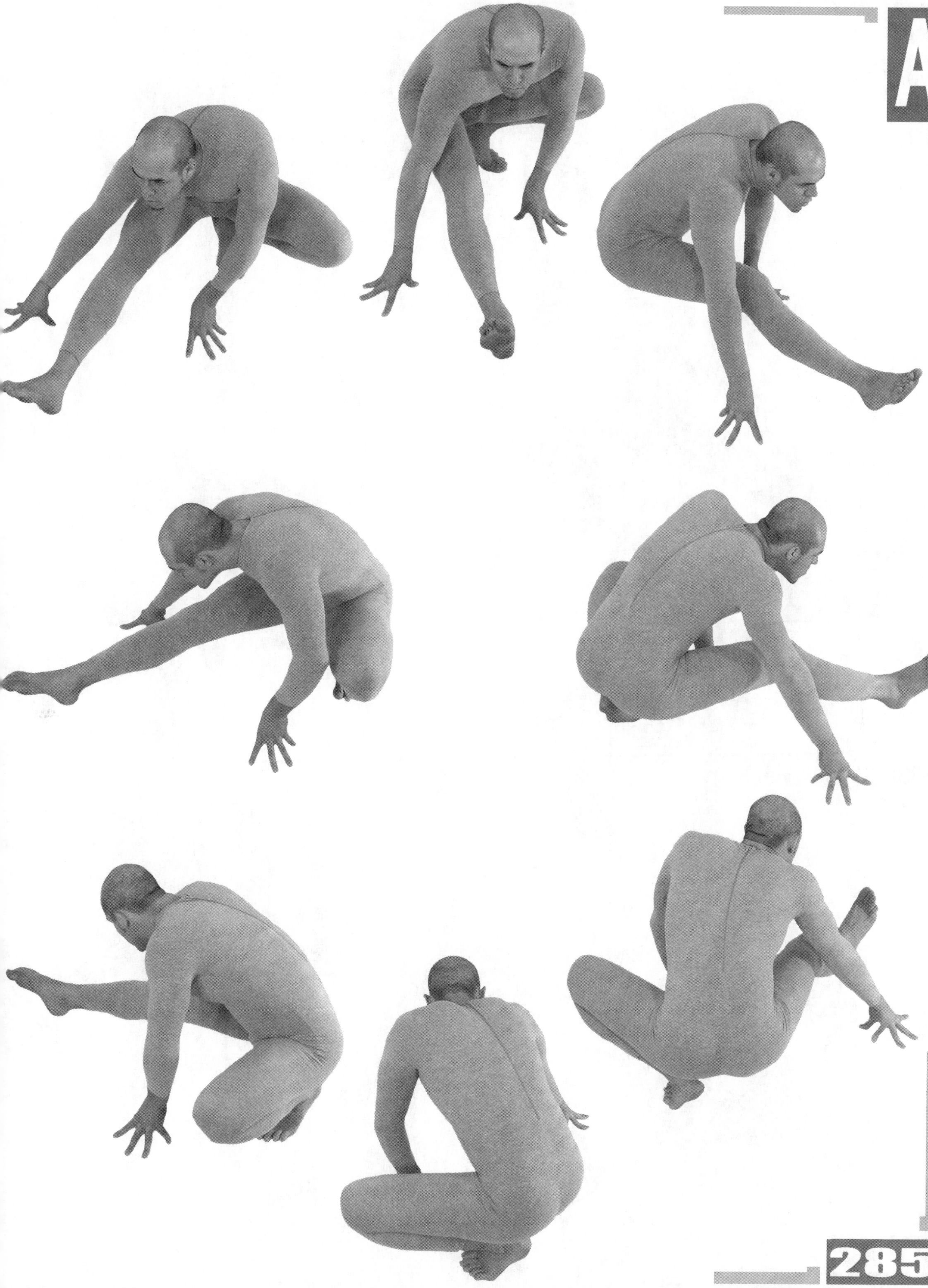

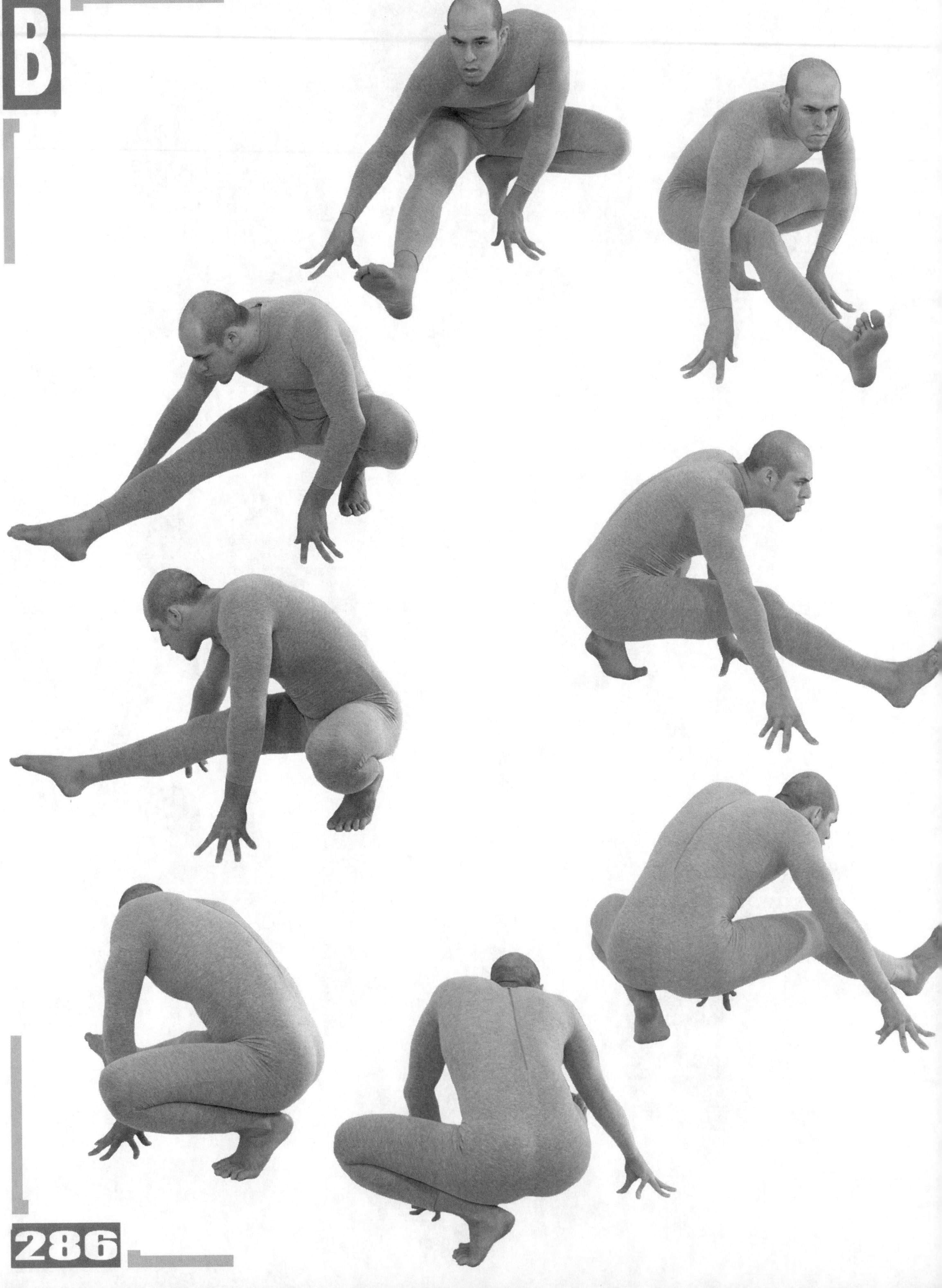

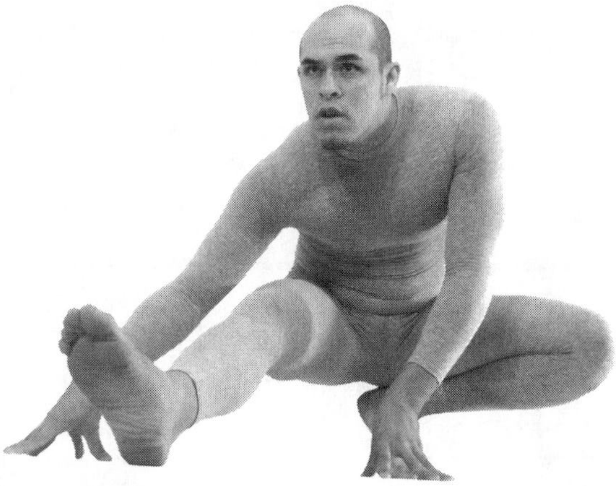

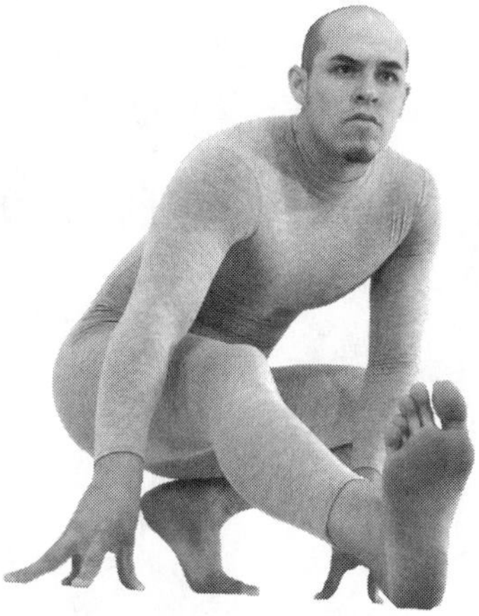

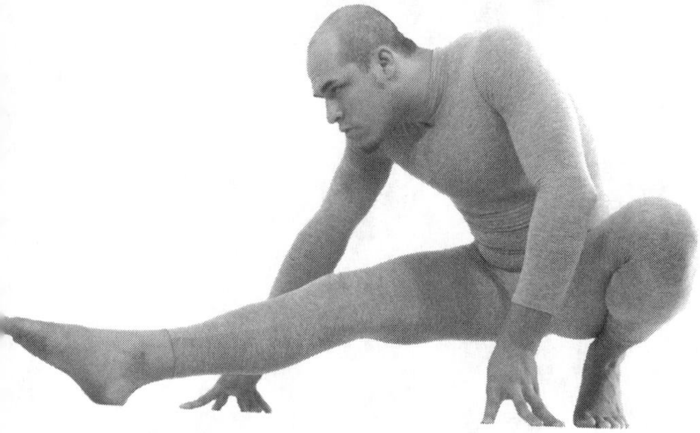

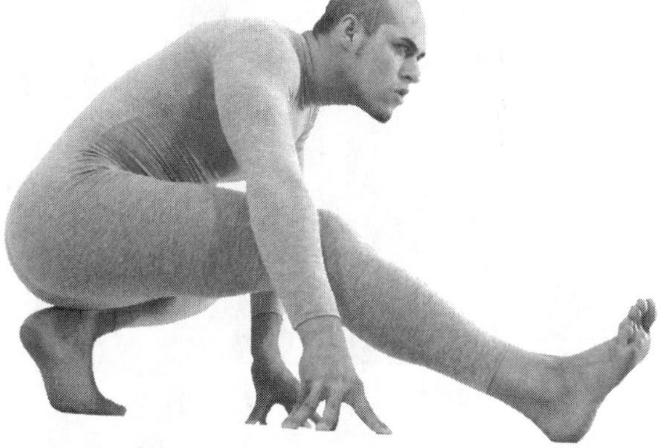

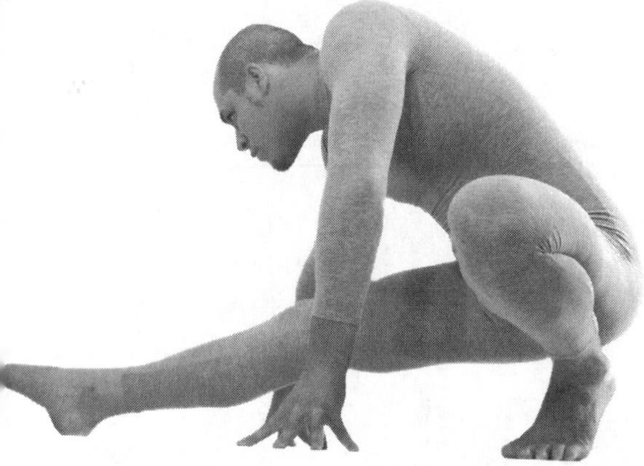

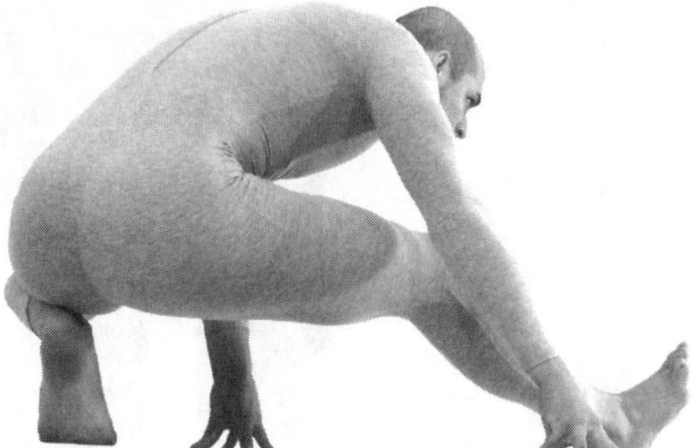

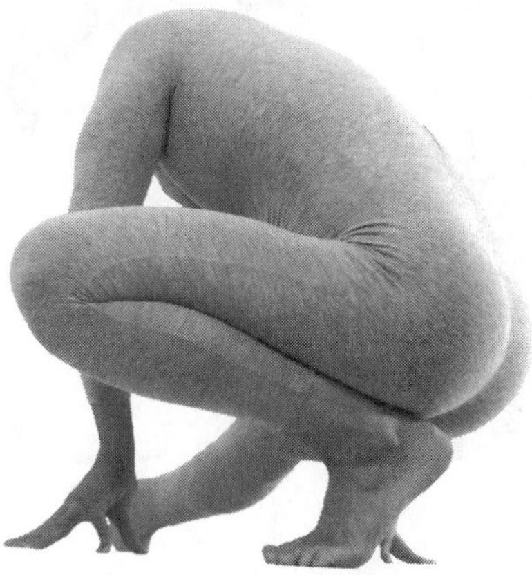

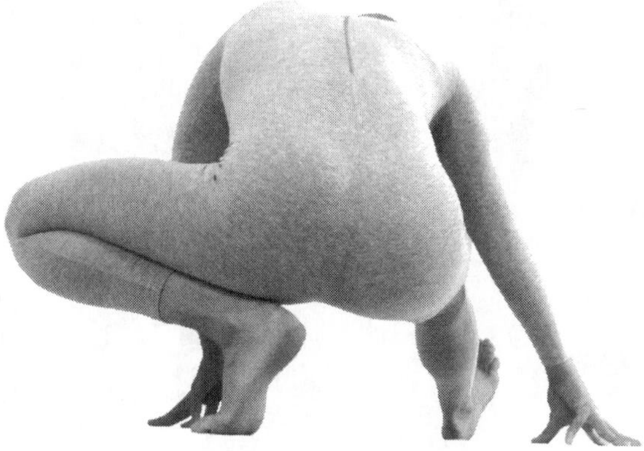

ACTION POSE COLLECTION

WEAPONS POSES

POSE REFERENCE

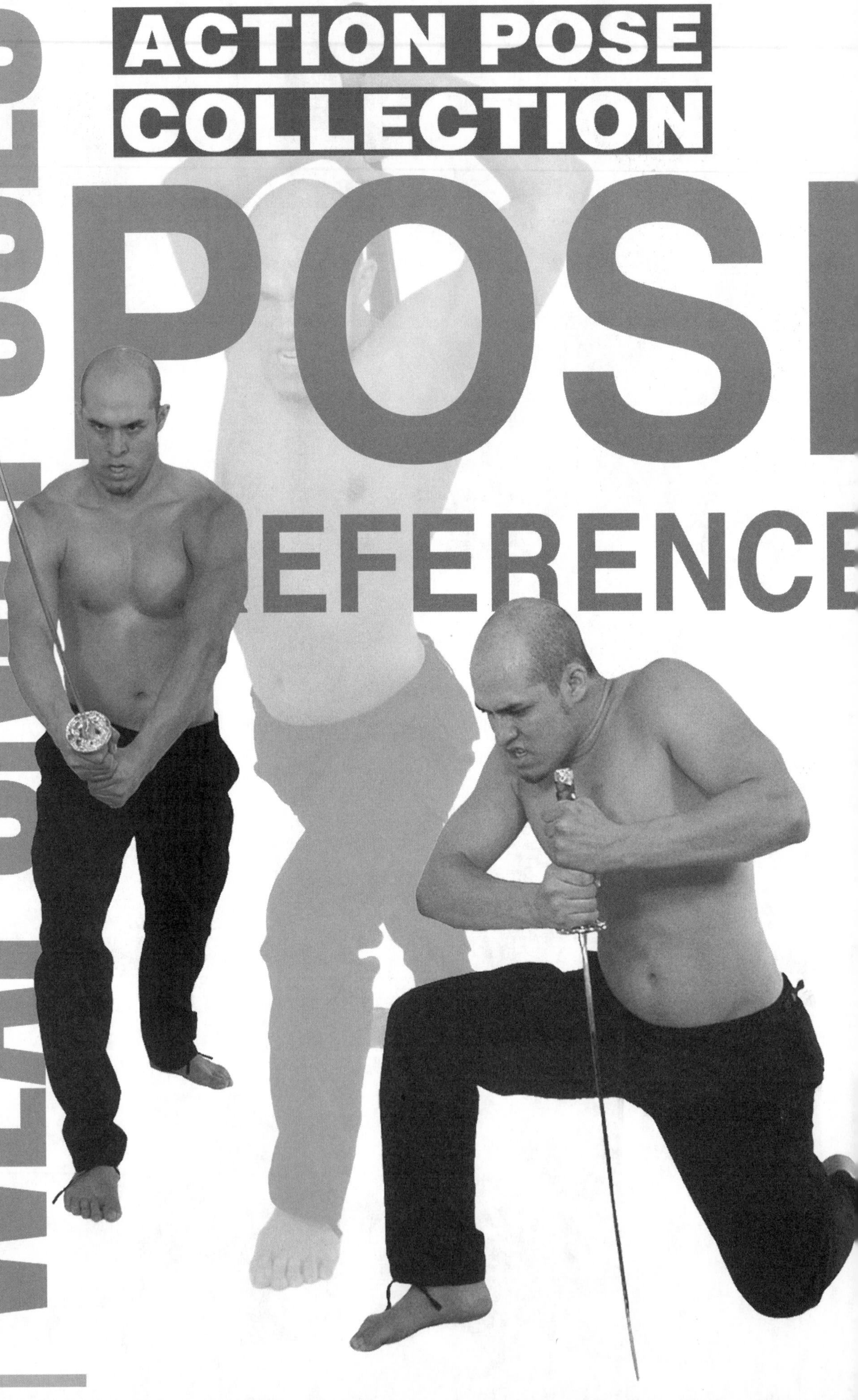

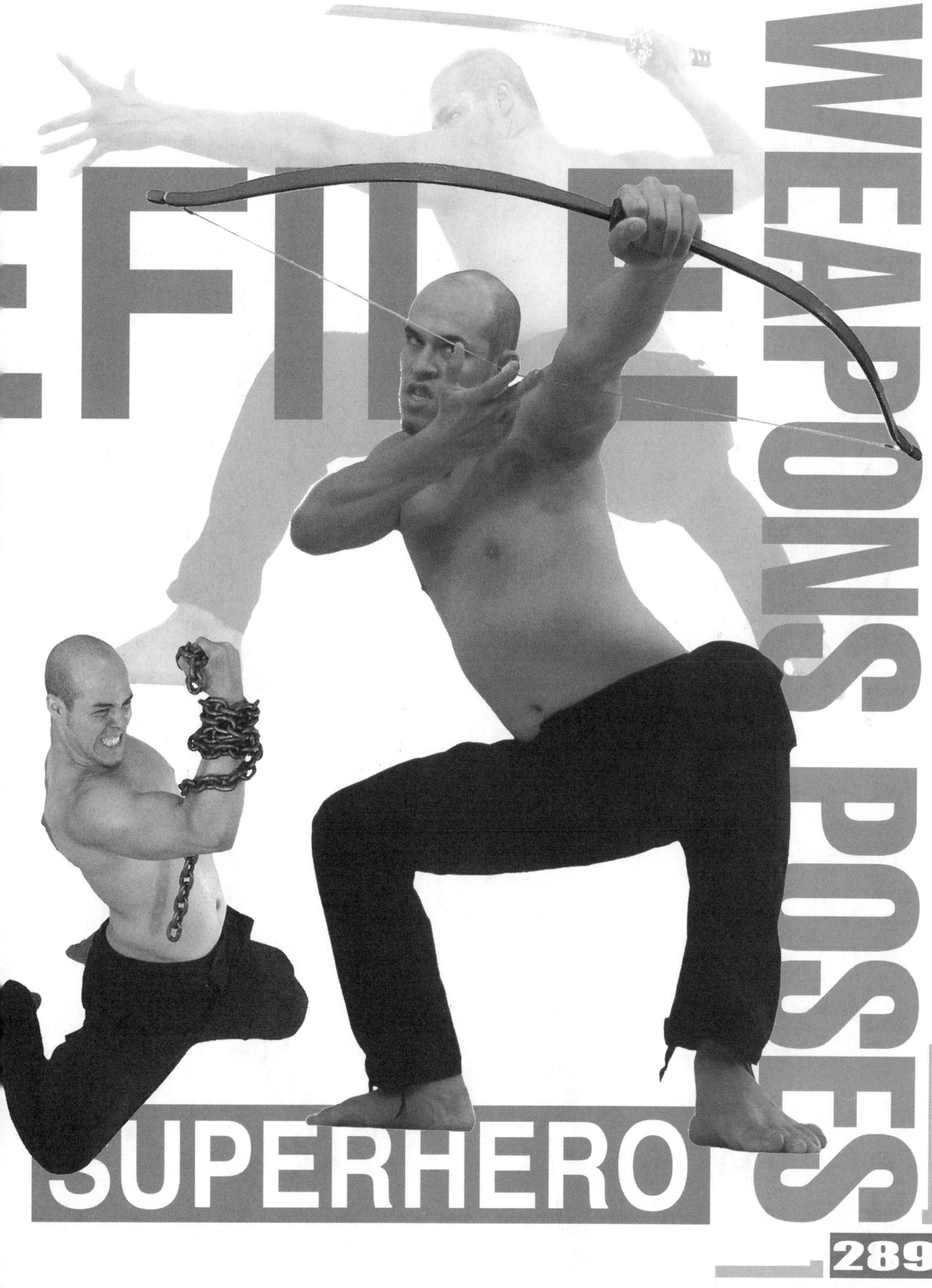
WEAPONS POSES
SUPERHERO

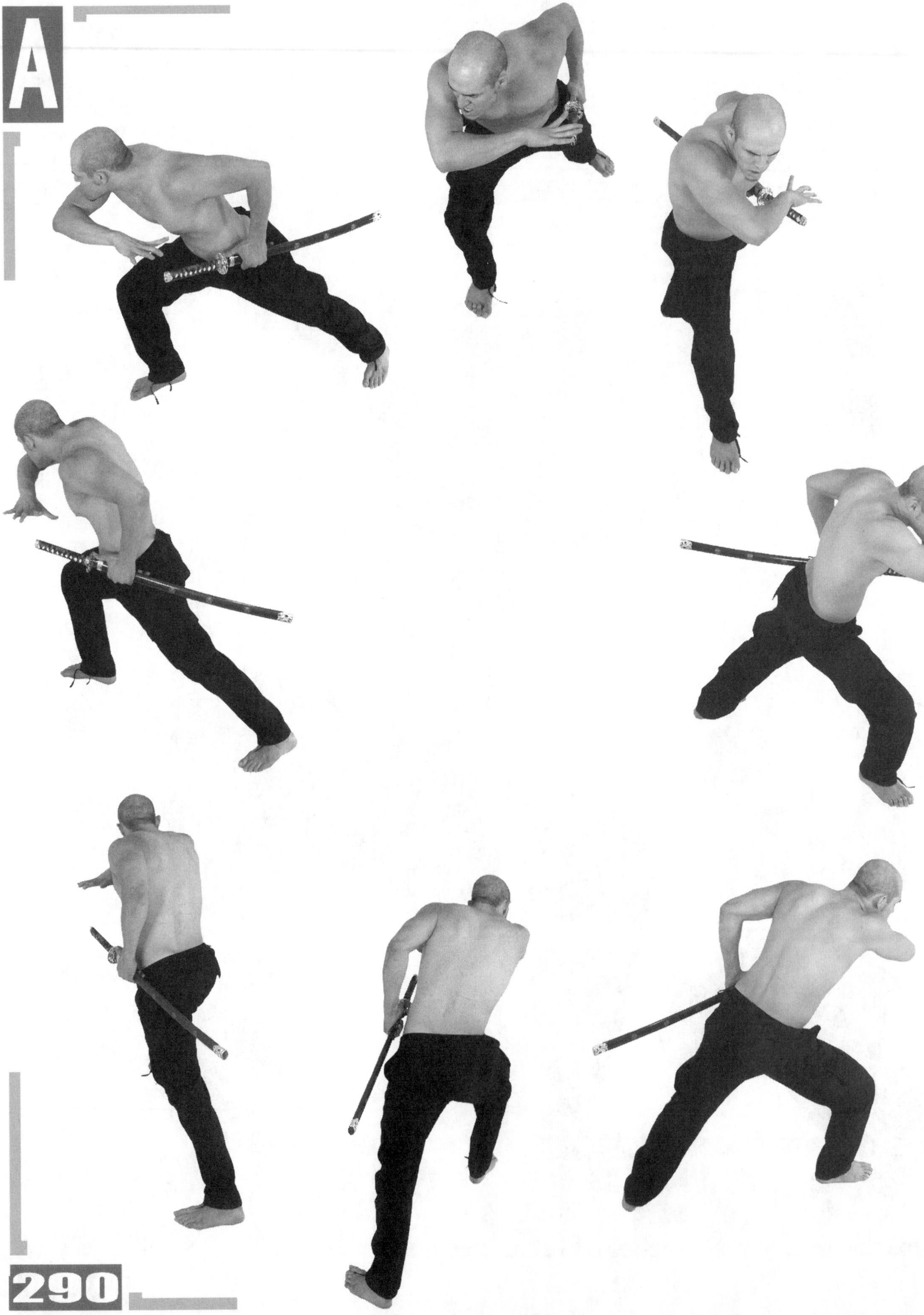

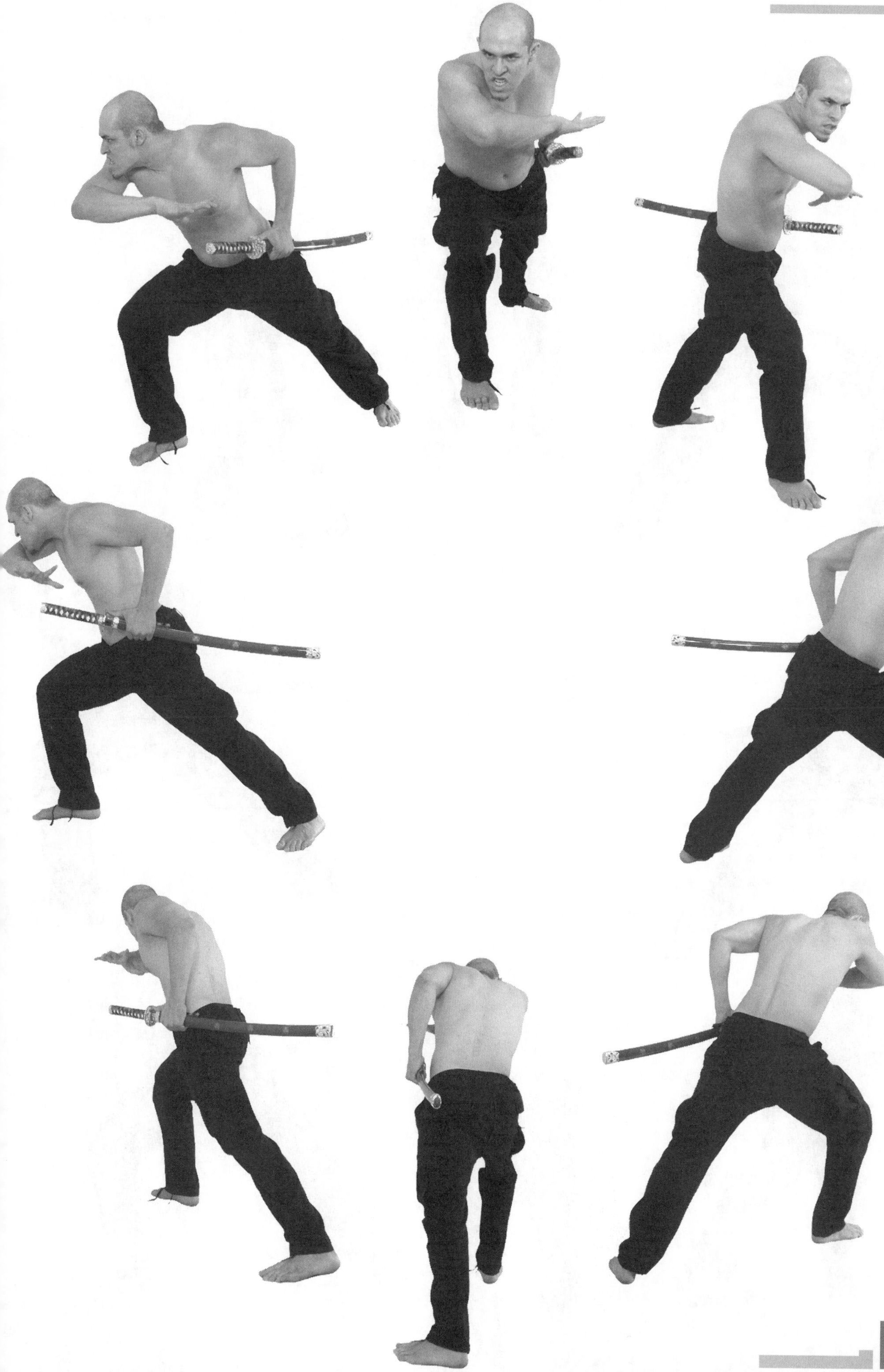

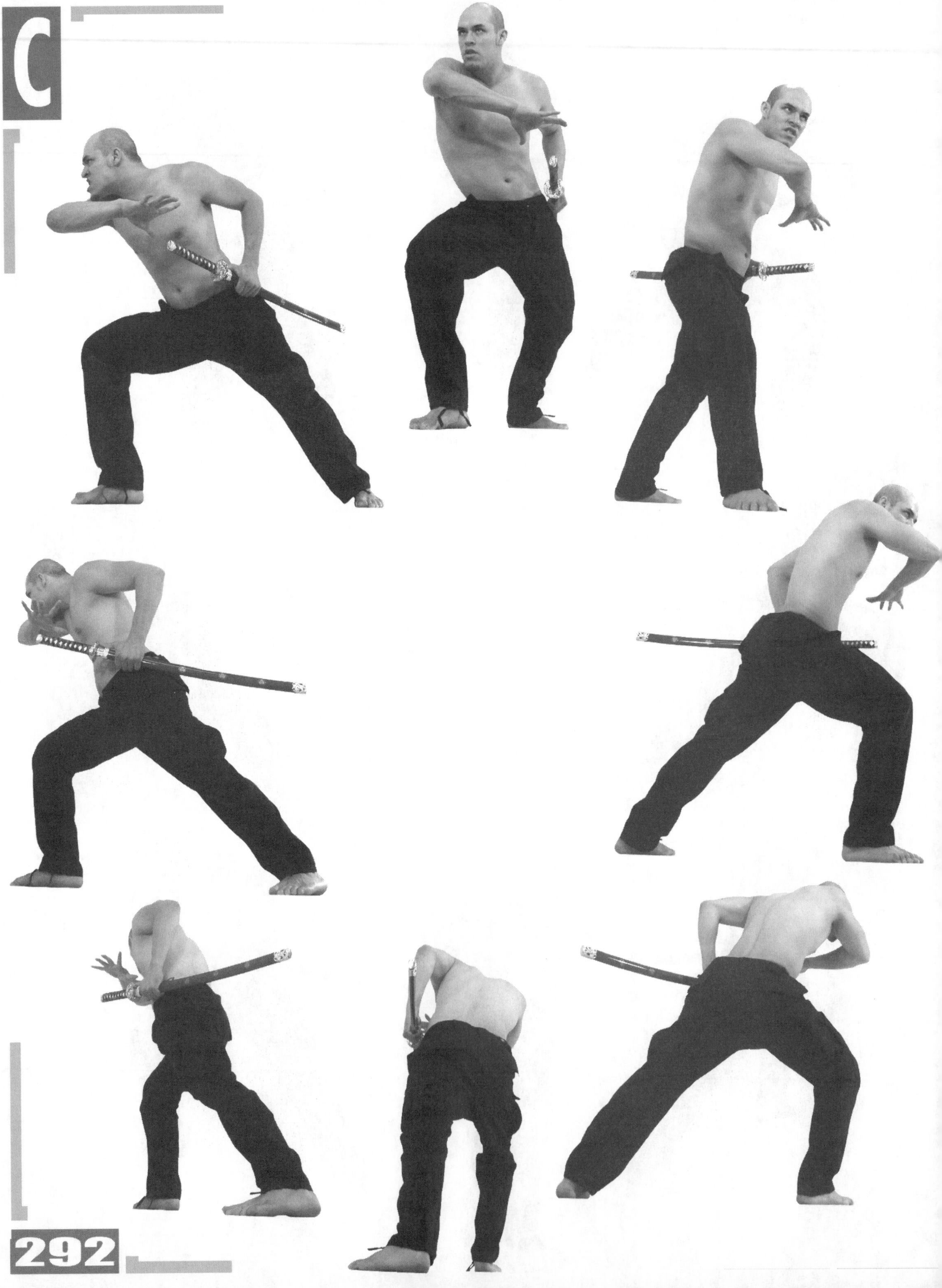

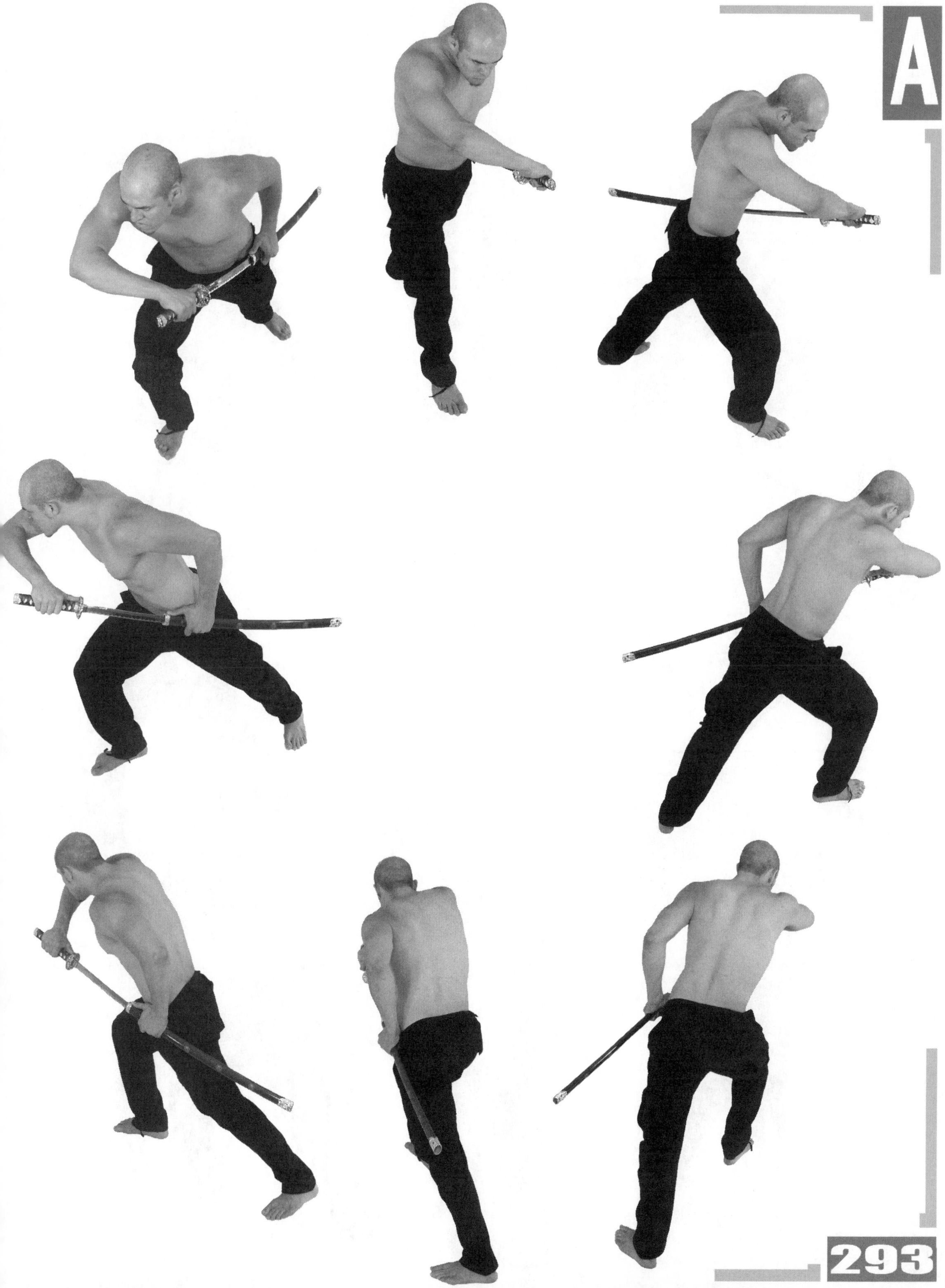

A

B

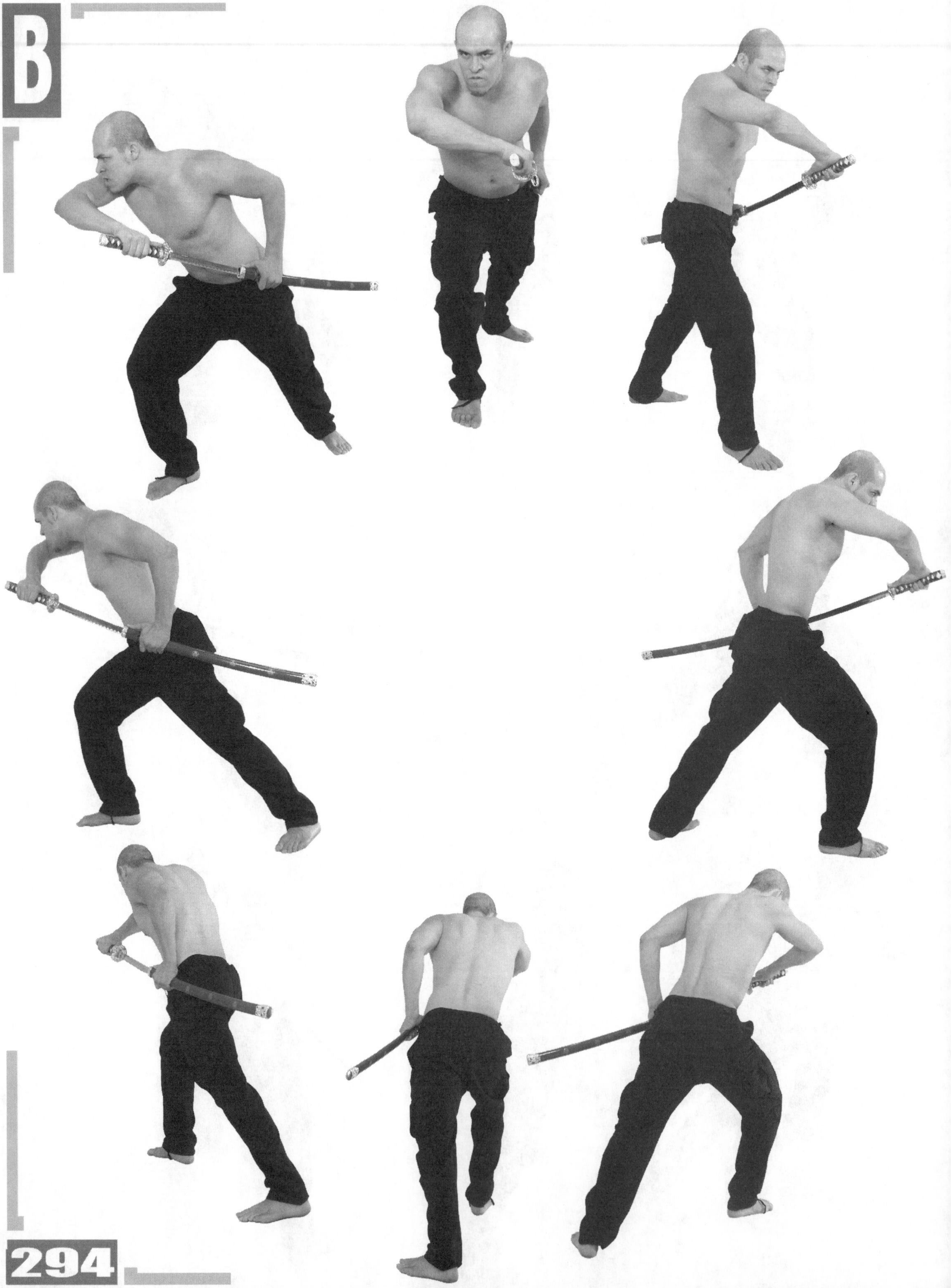

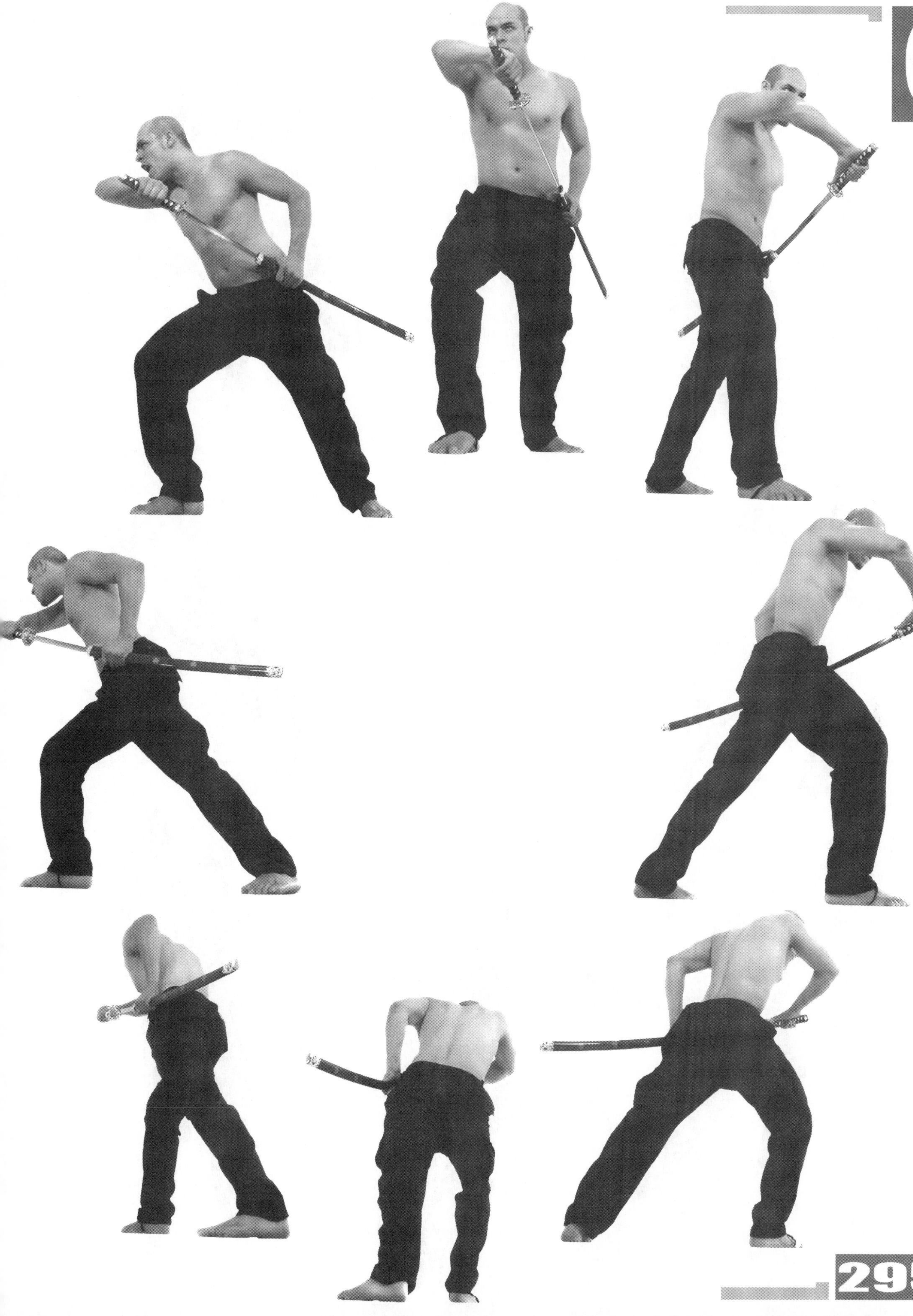

A

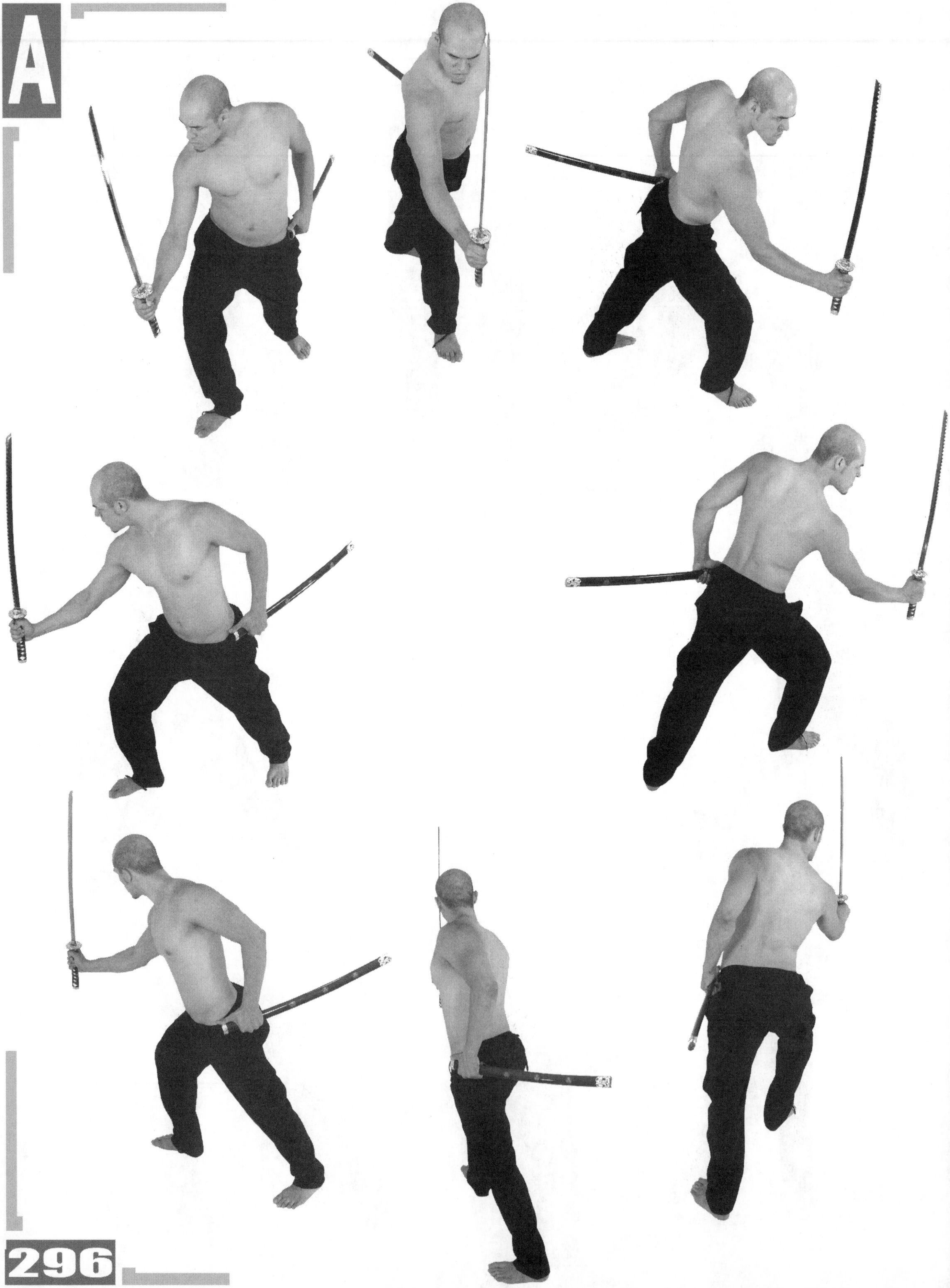

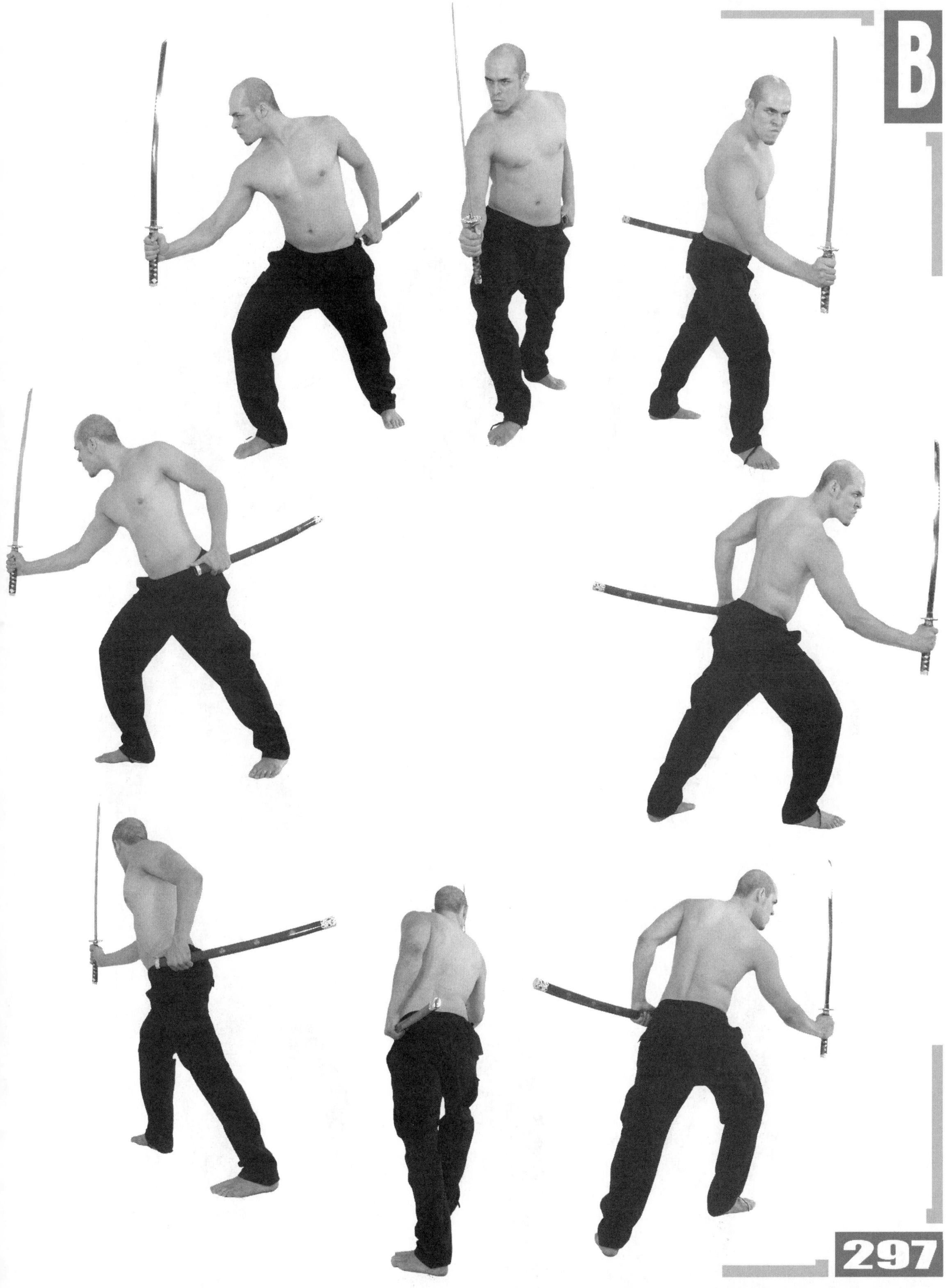

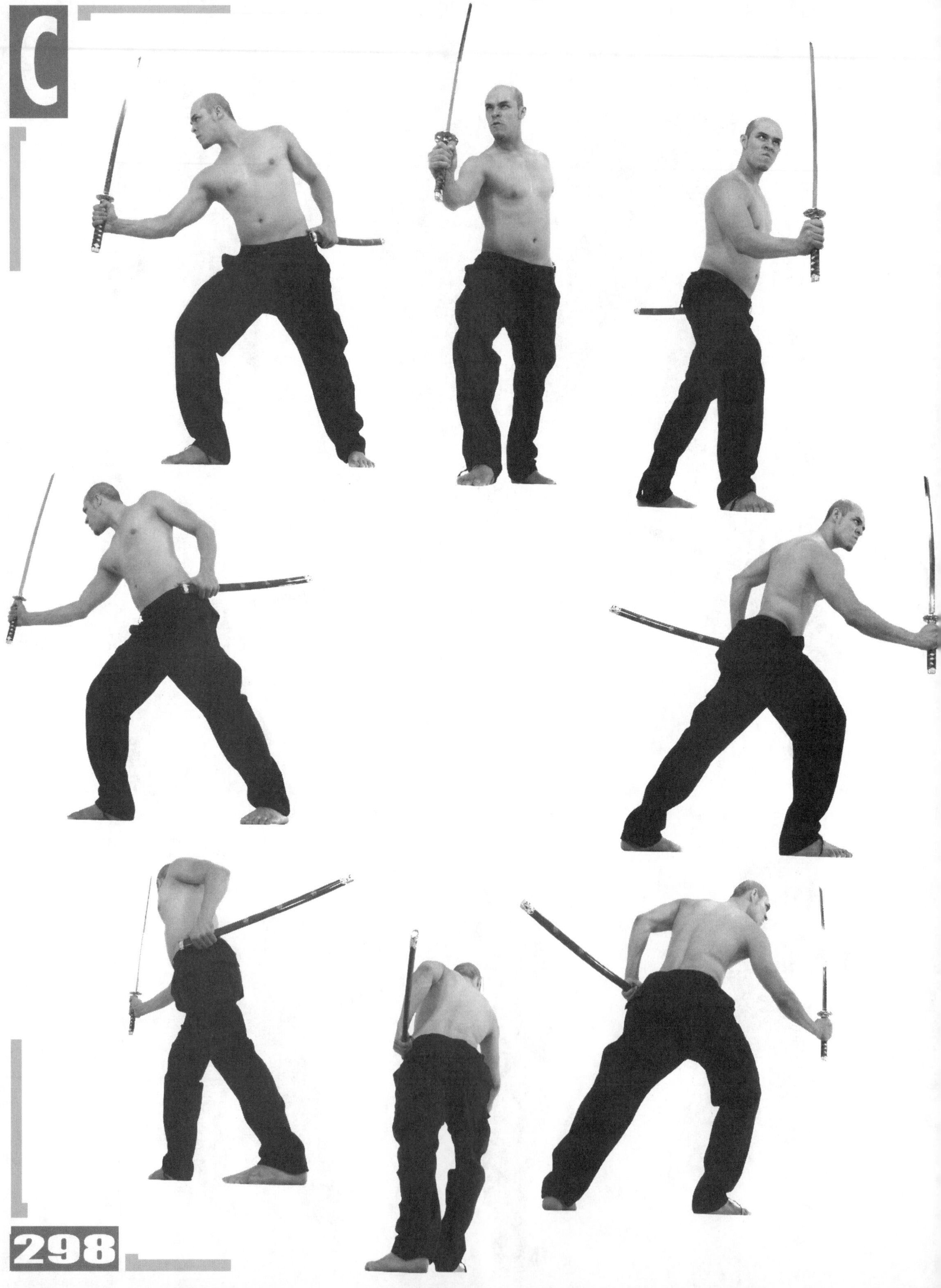

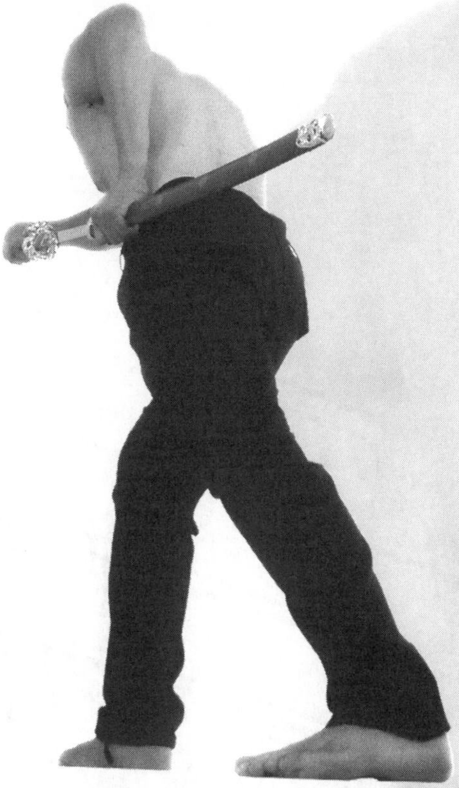

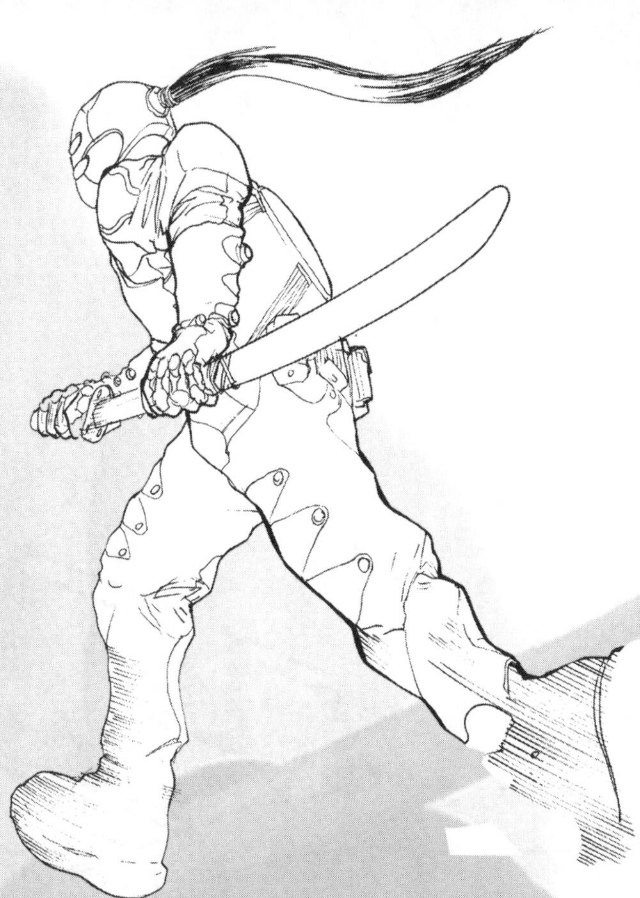

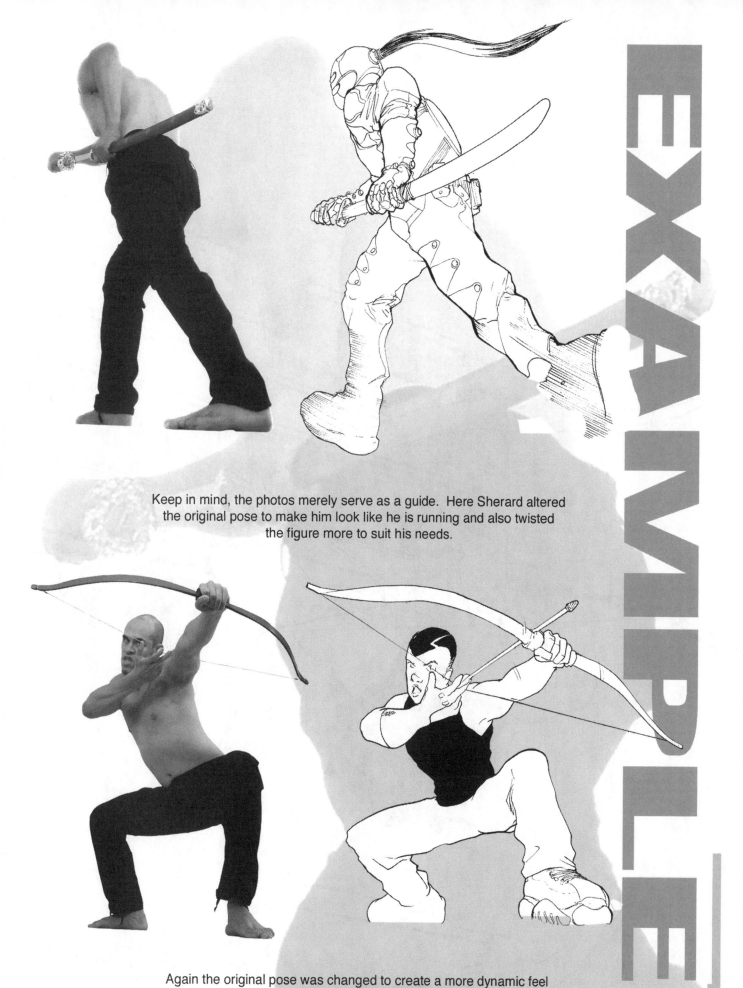

Keep in mind, the photos merely serve as a guide. Here Sherard altered the original pose to make him look like he is running and also twisted the figure more to suit his needs.

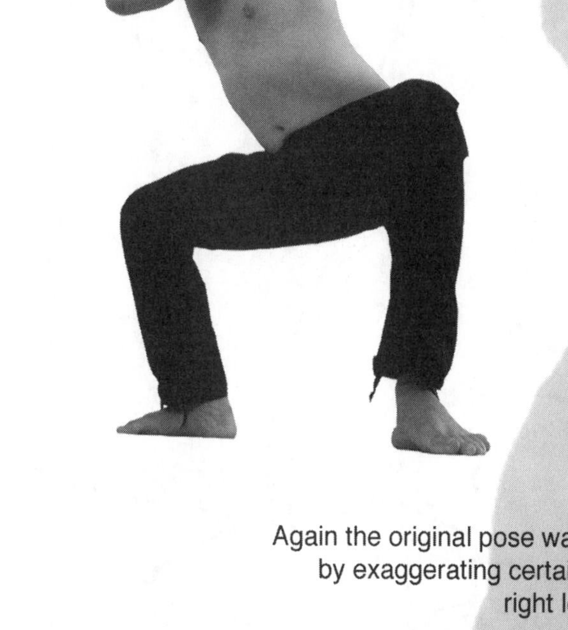

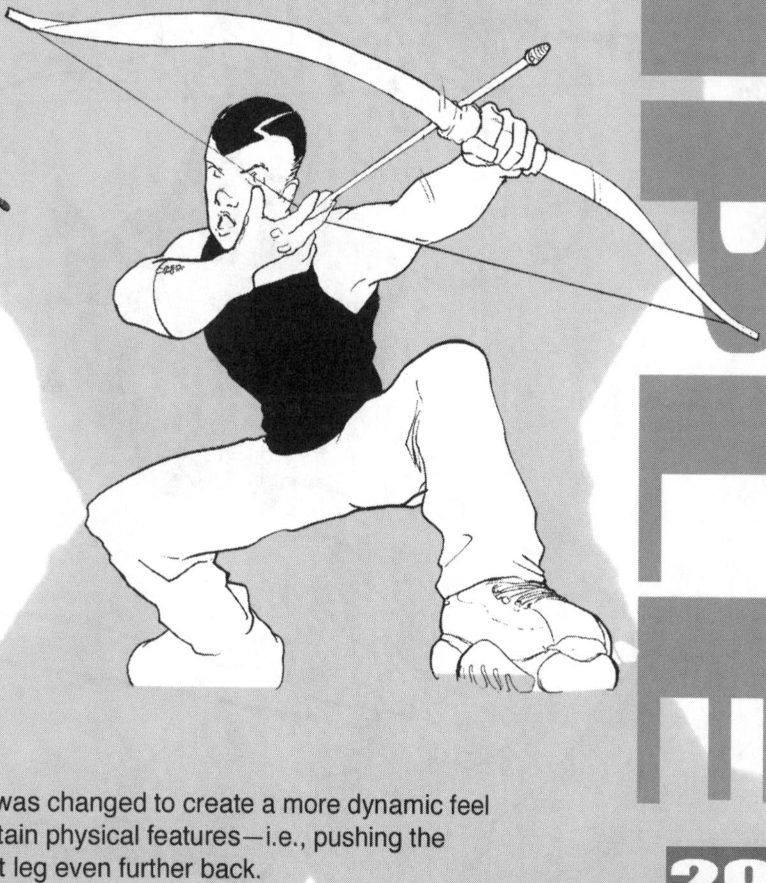

Again the original pose was changed to create a more dynamic feel by exaggerating certain physical features—i.e., pushing the right leg even further back.

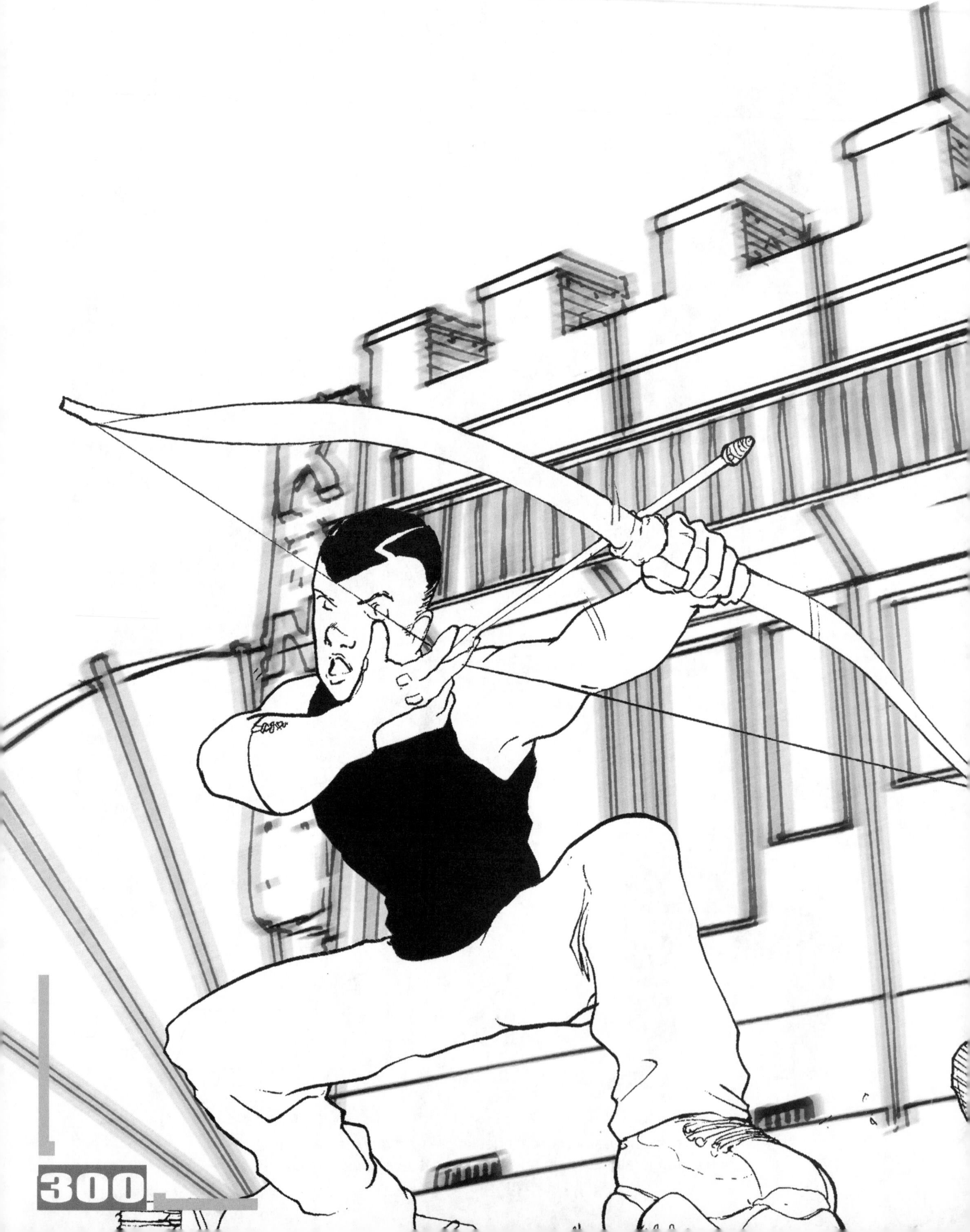

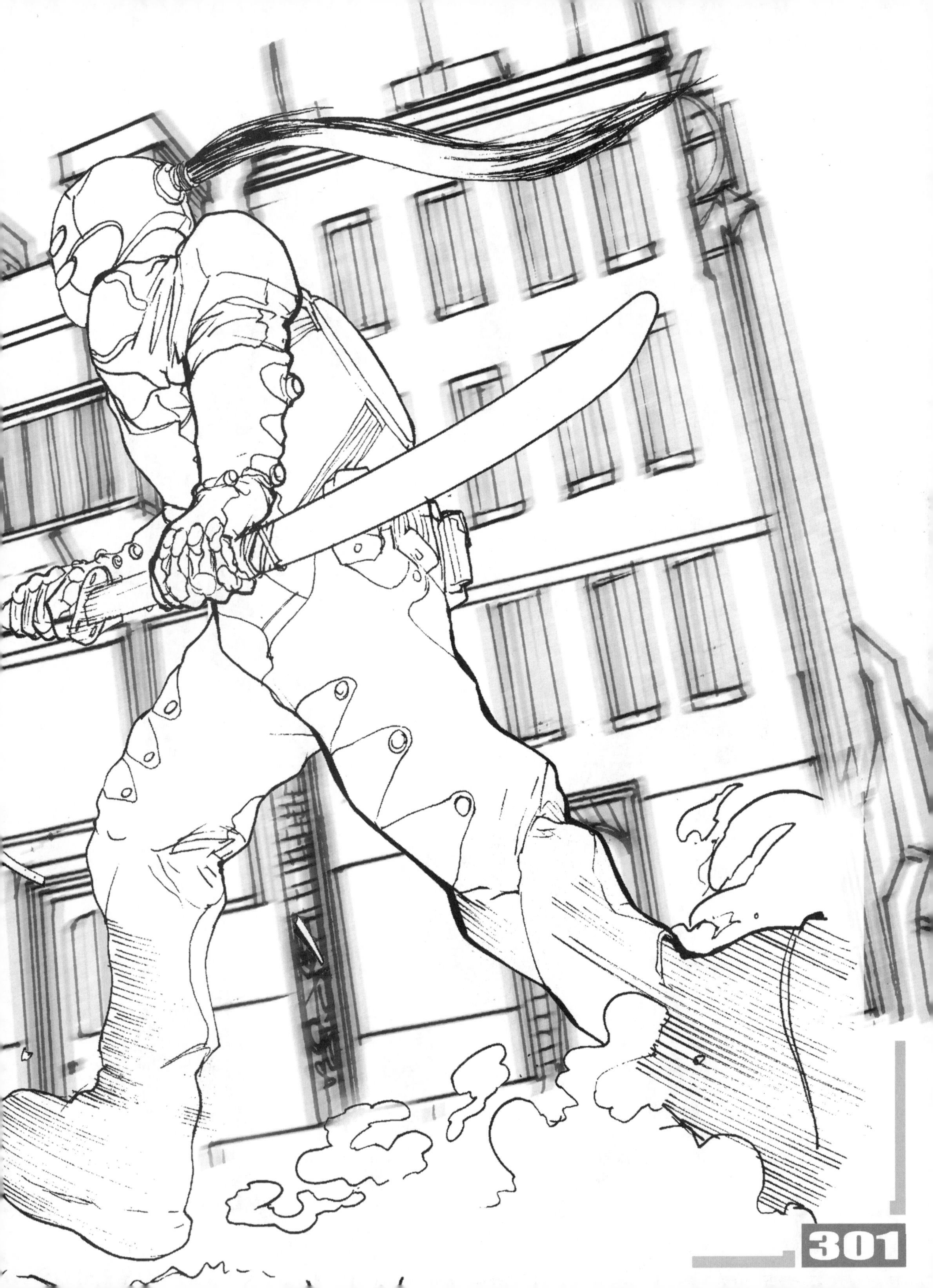

A

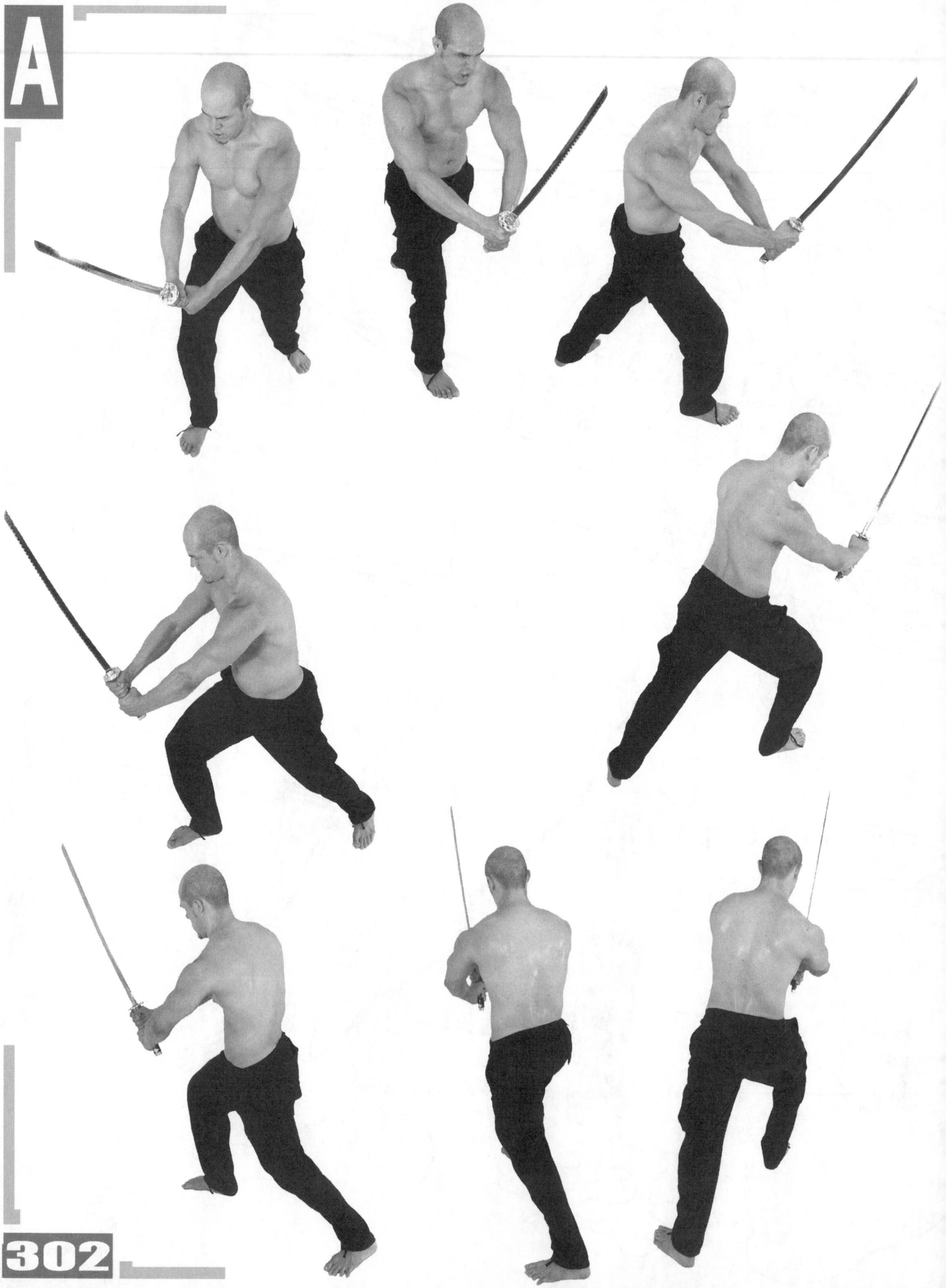

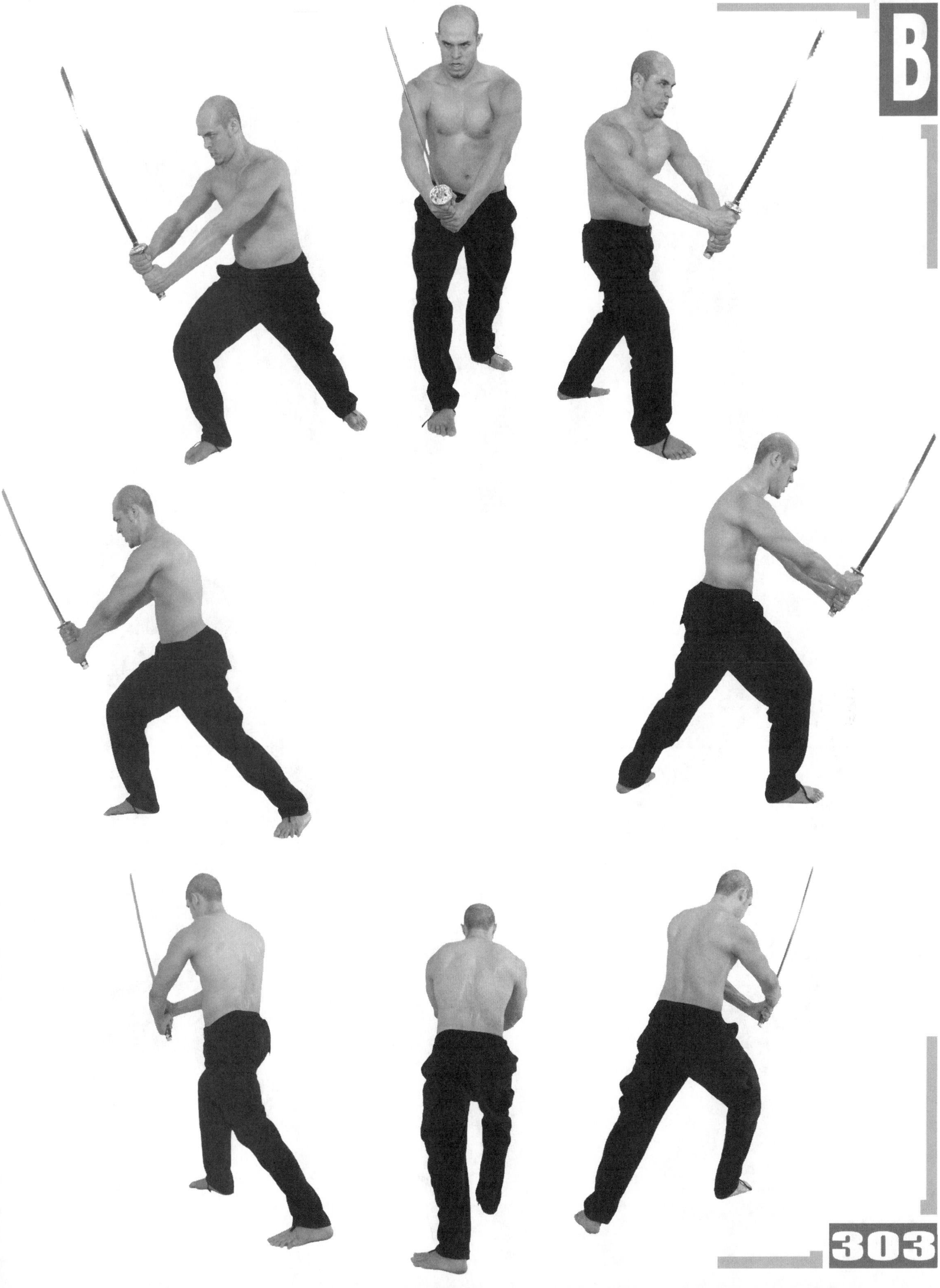

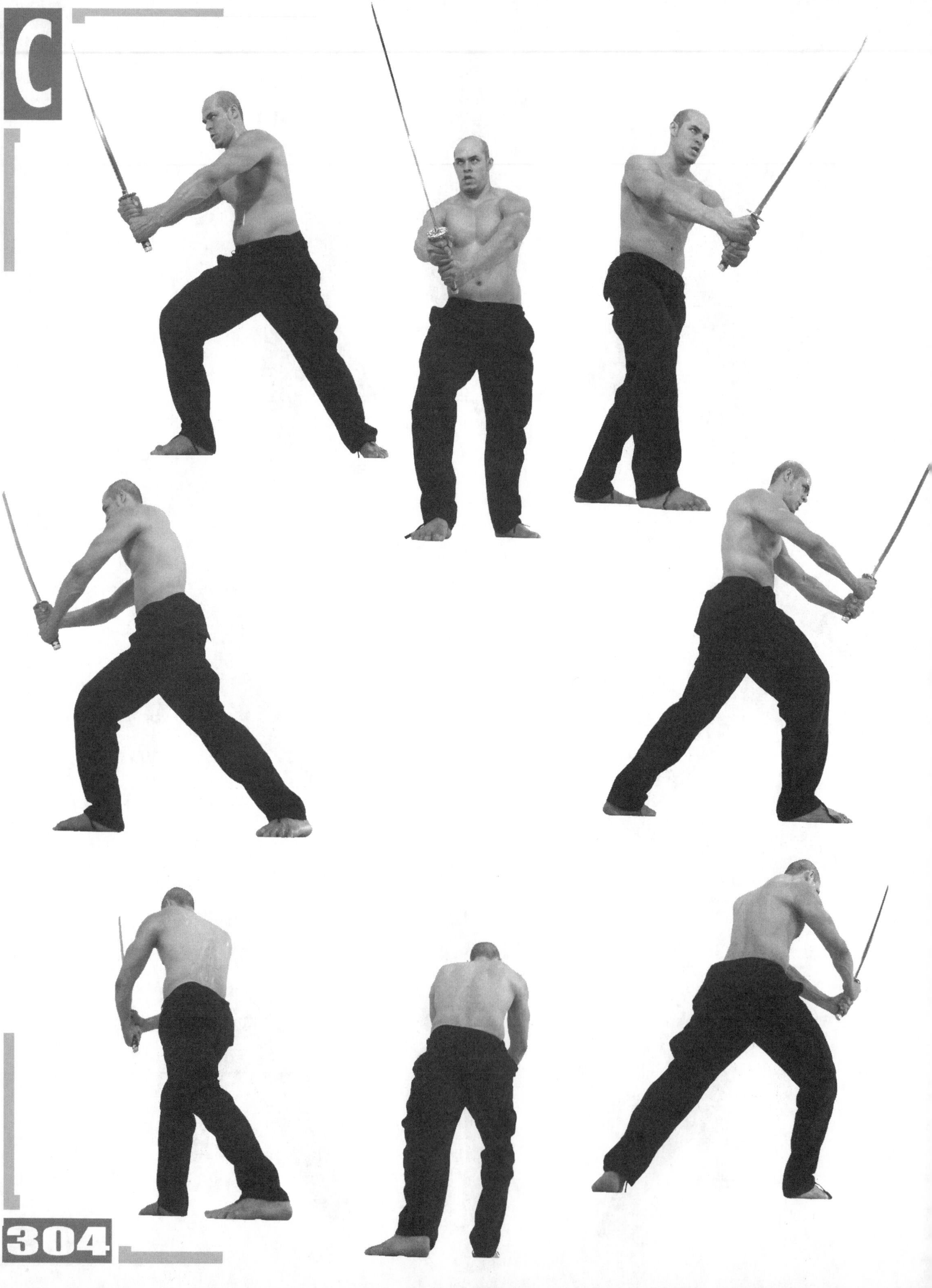

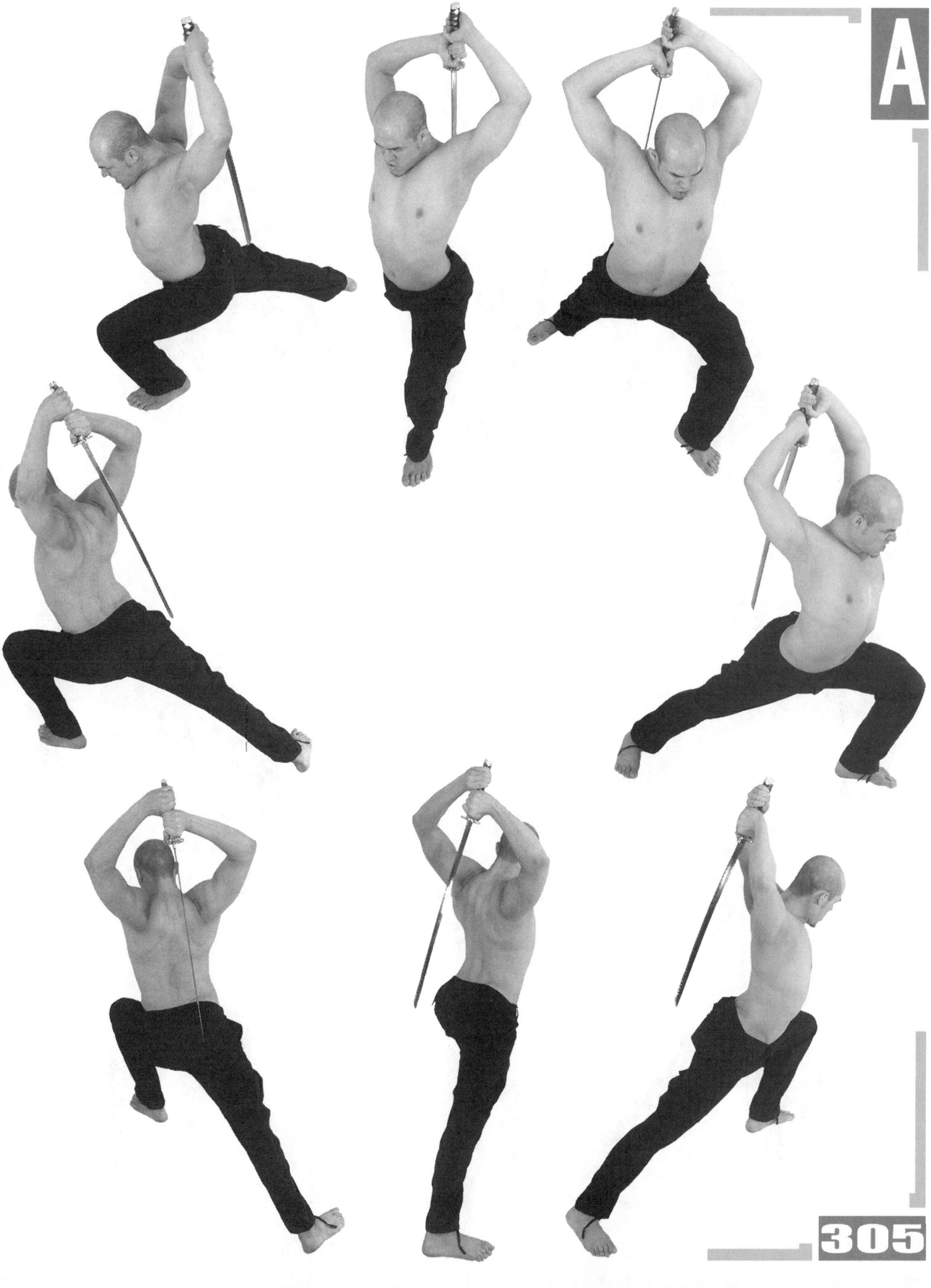

B

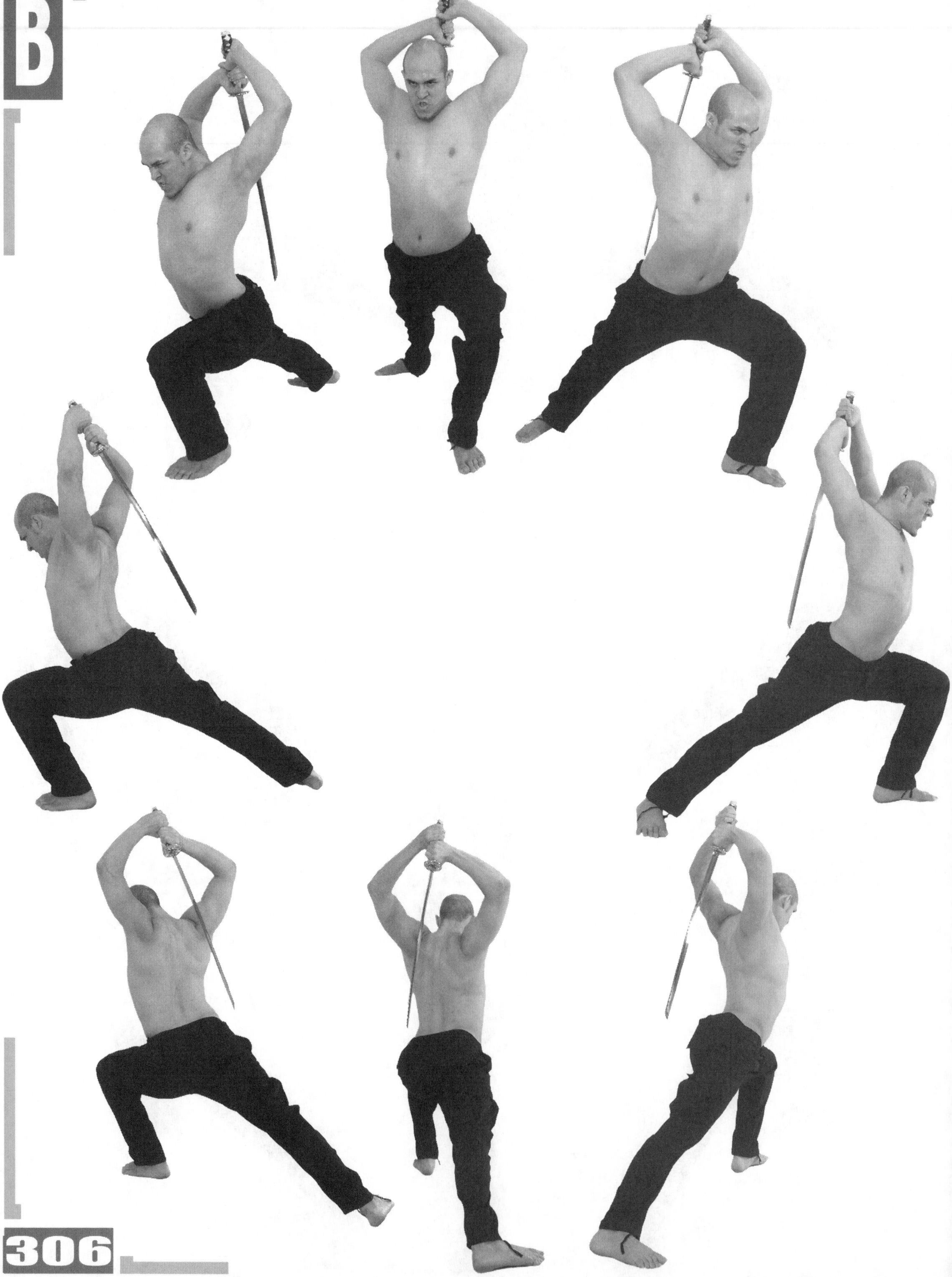

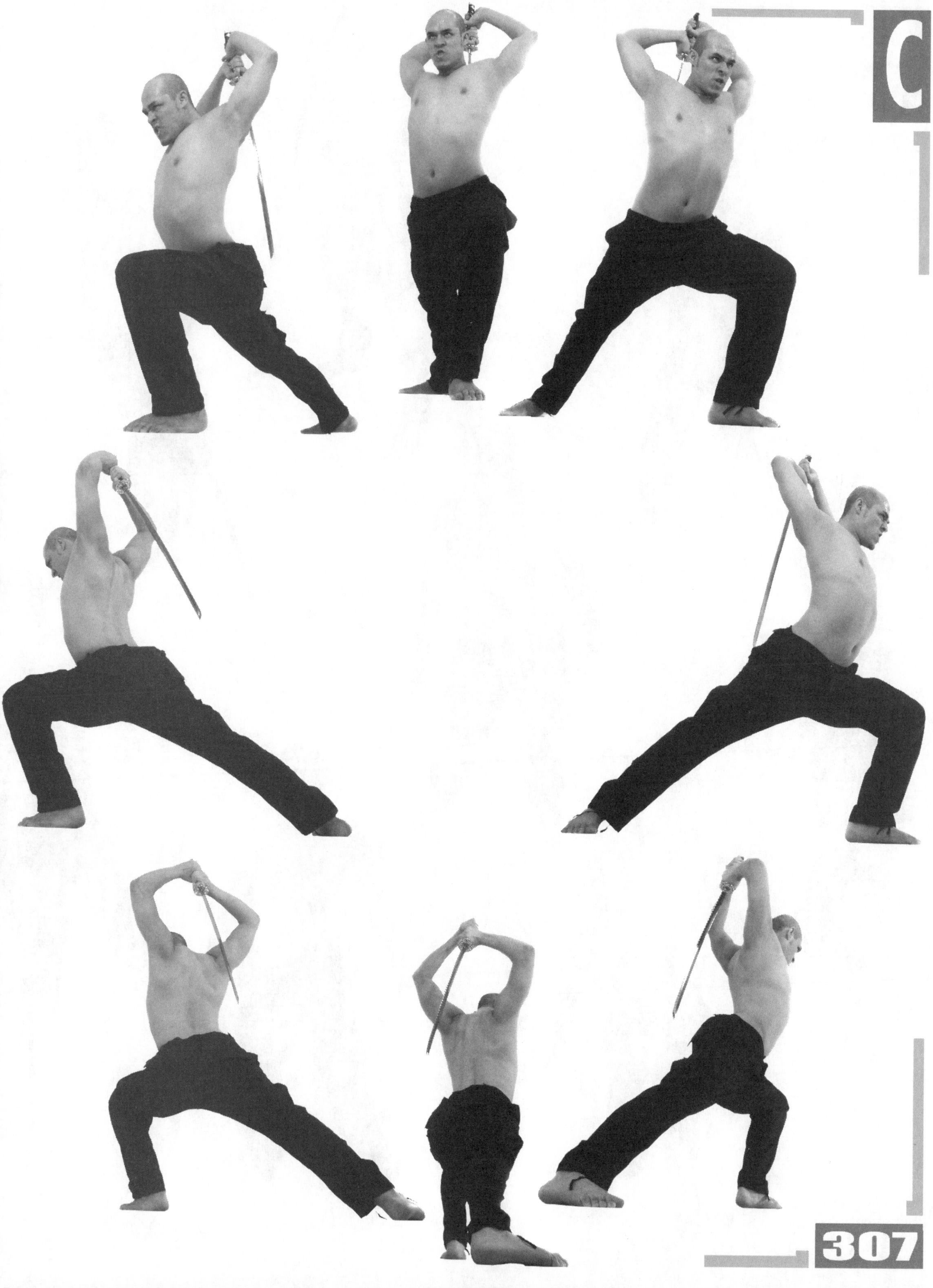

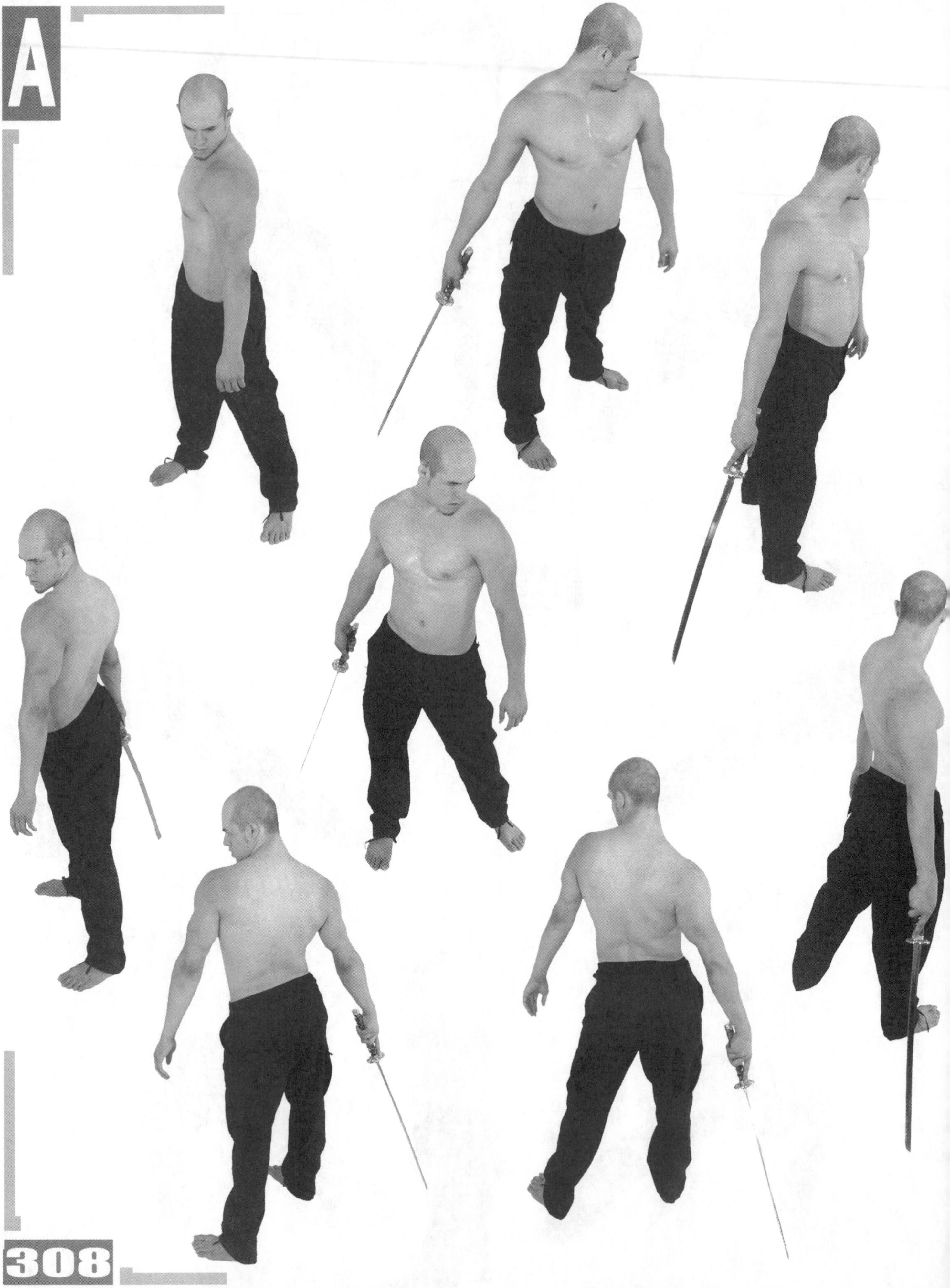

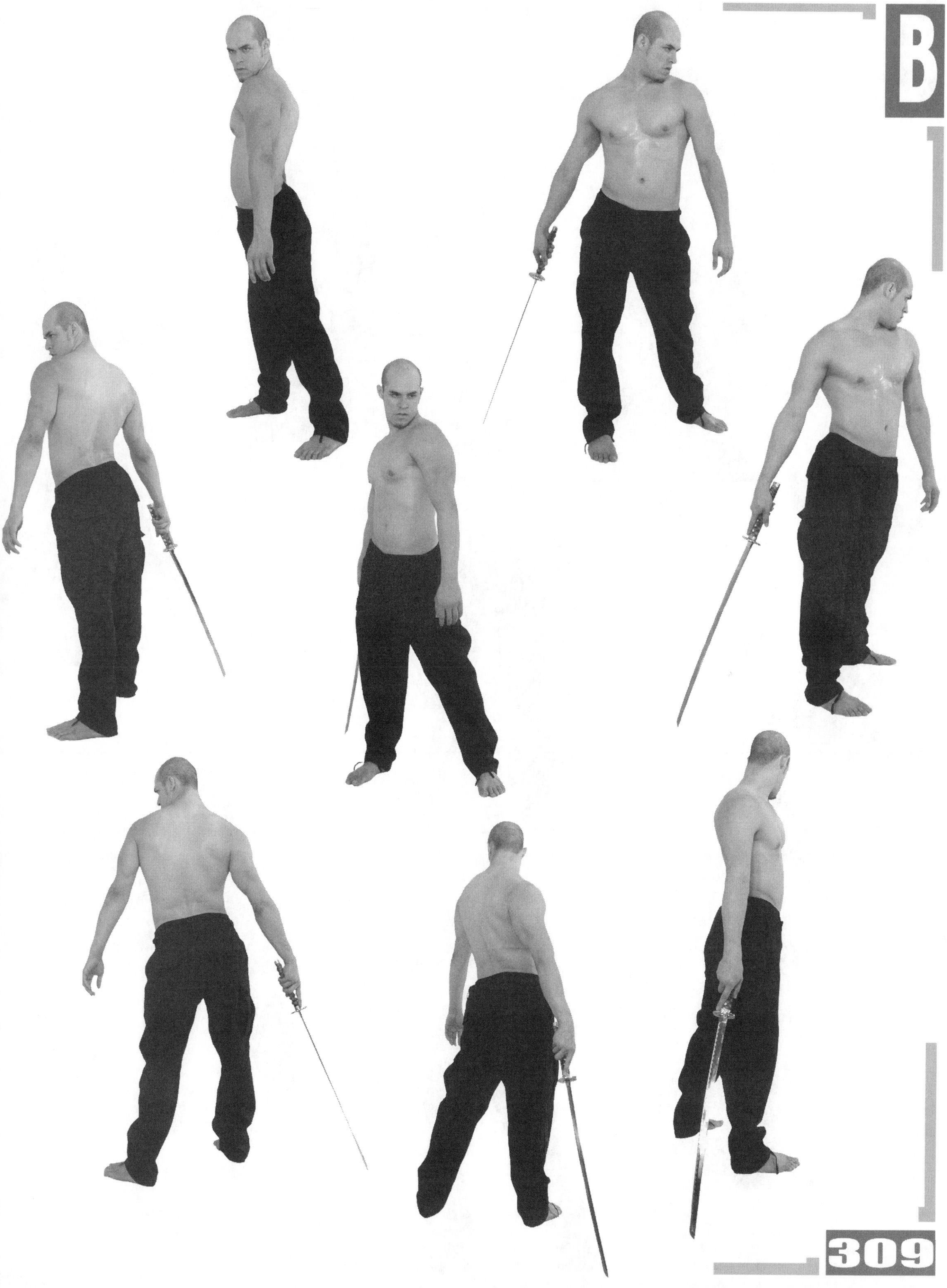

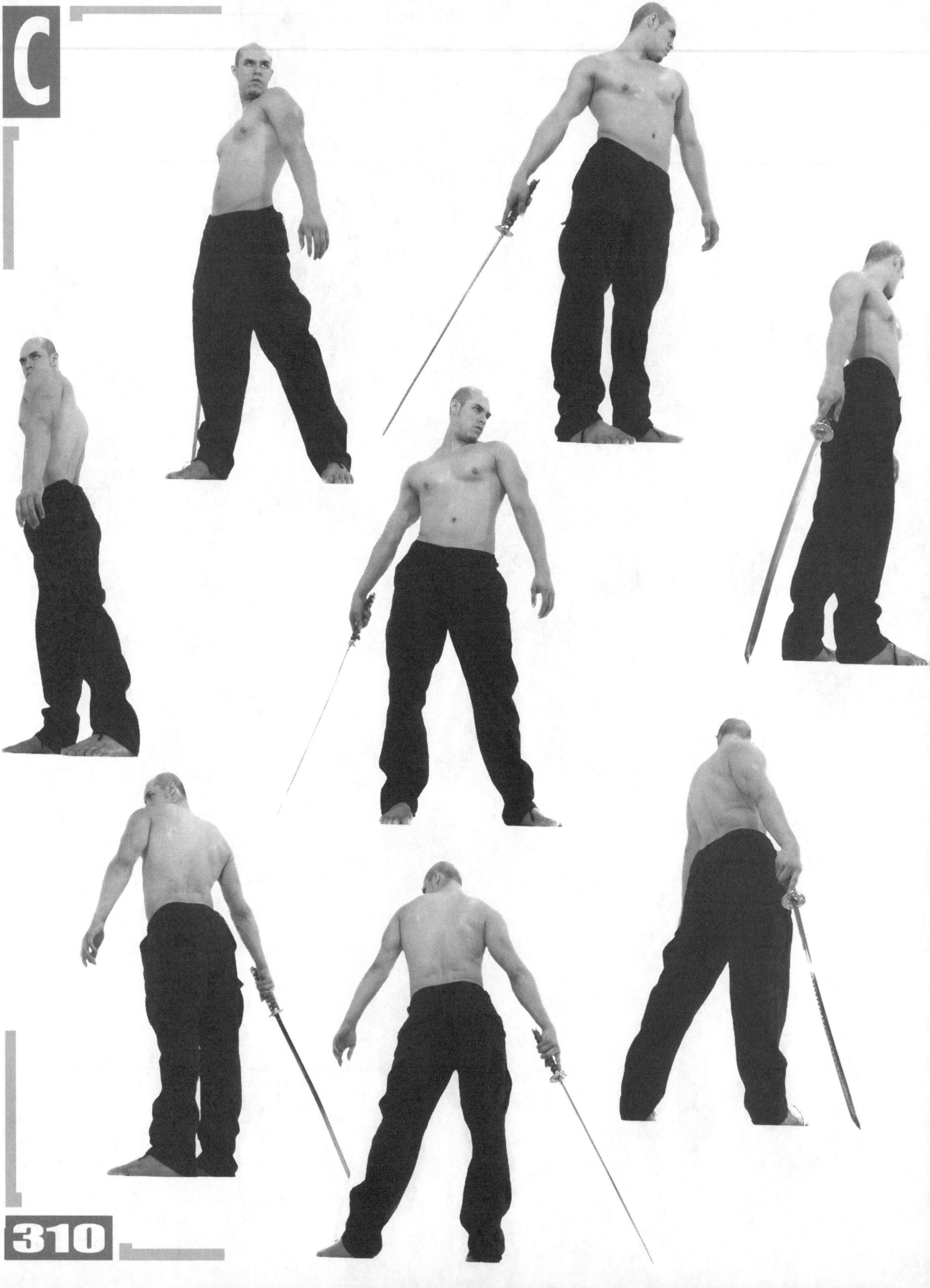

EXAMPLE

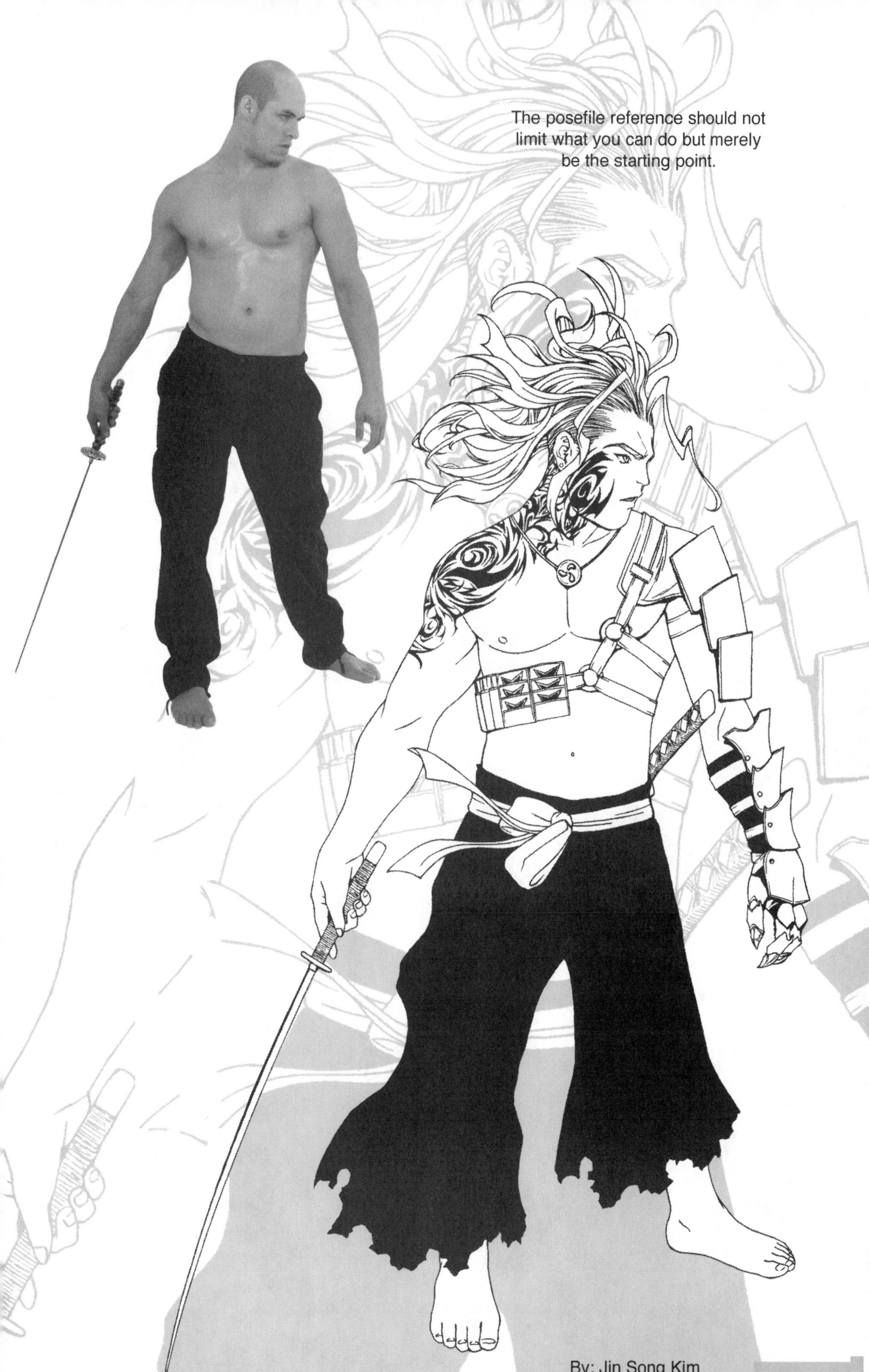

The posefile reference should not limit what you can do but merely be the starting point.

By: Jin Song Kim

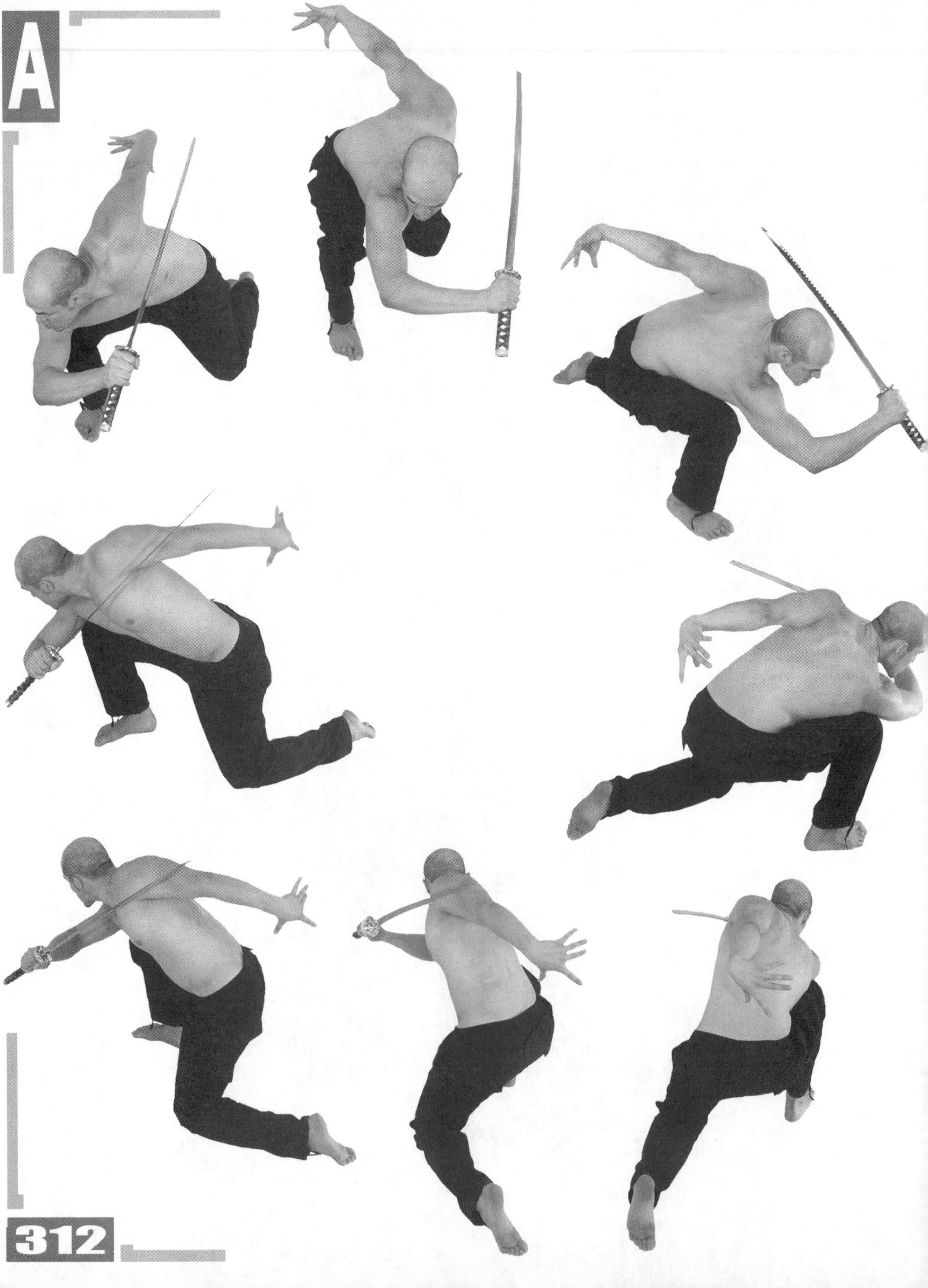

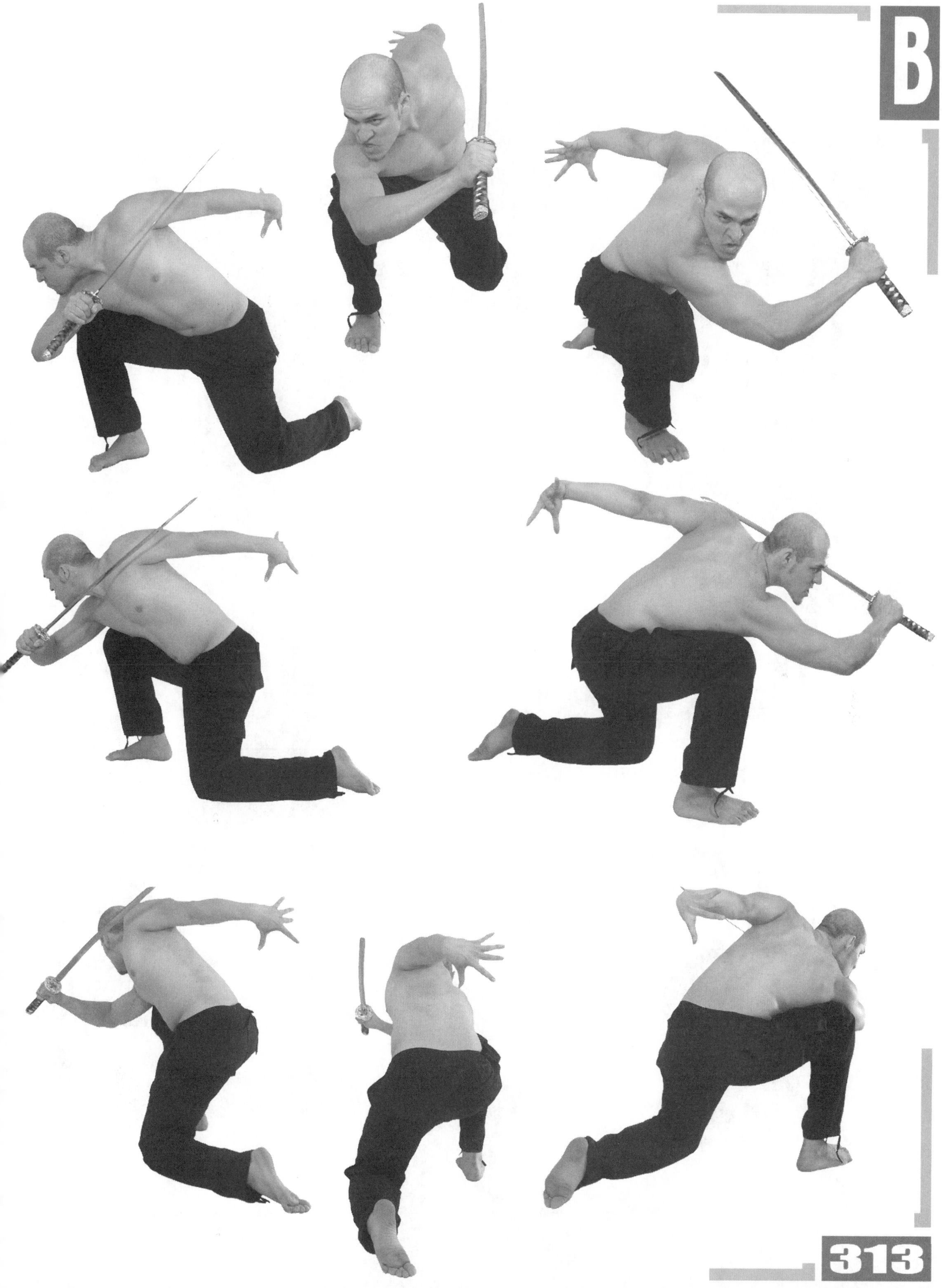

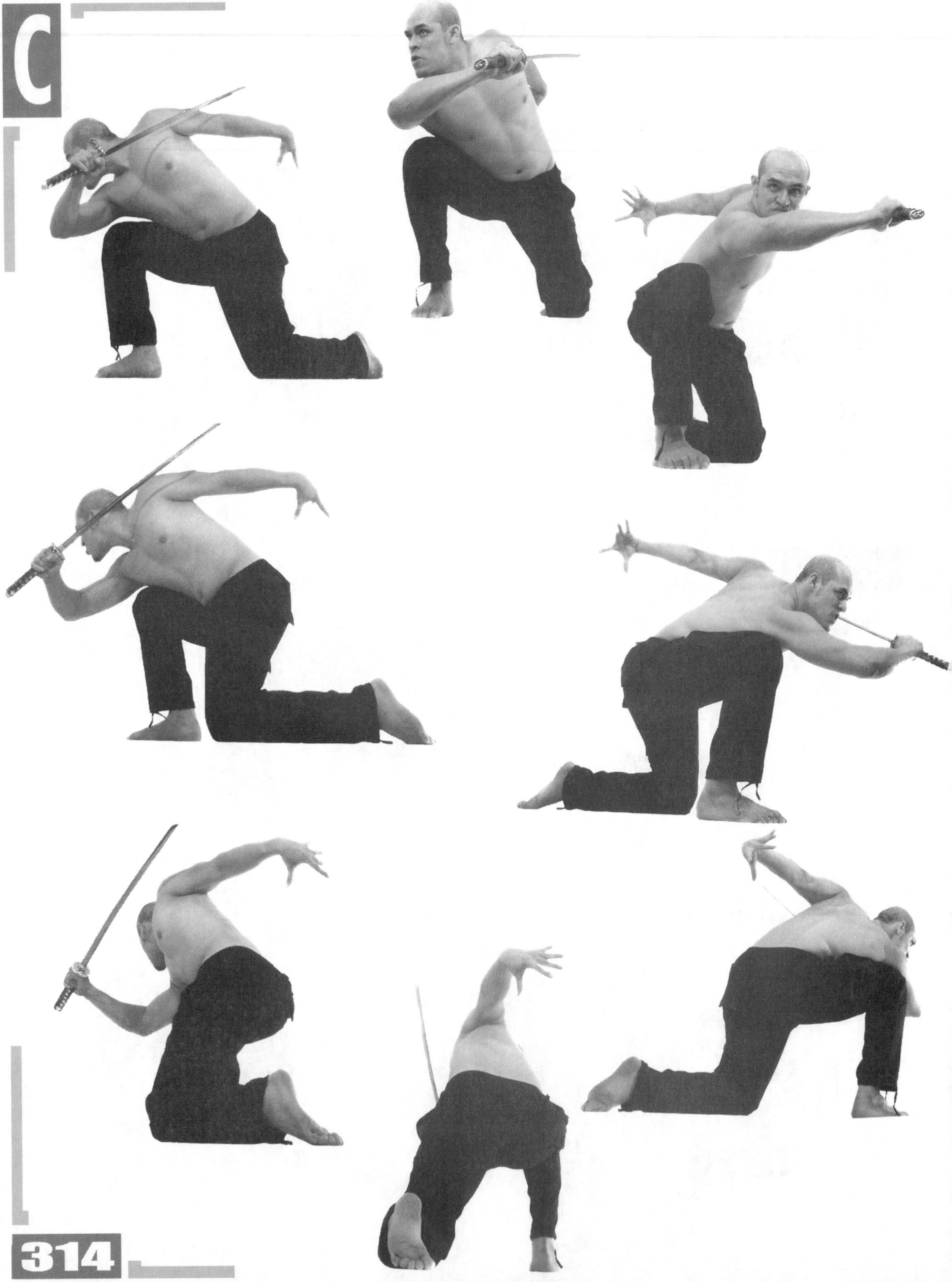

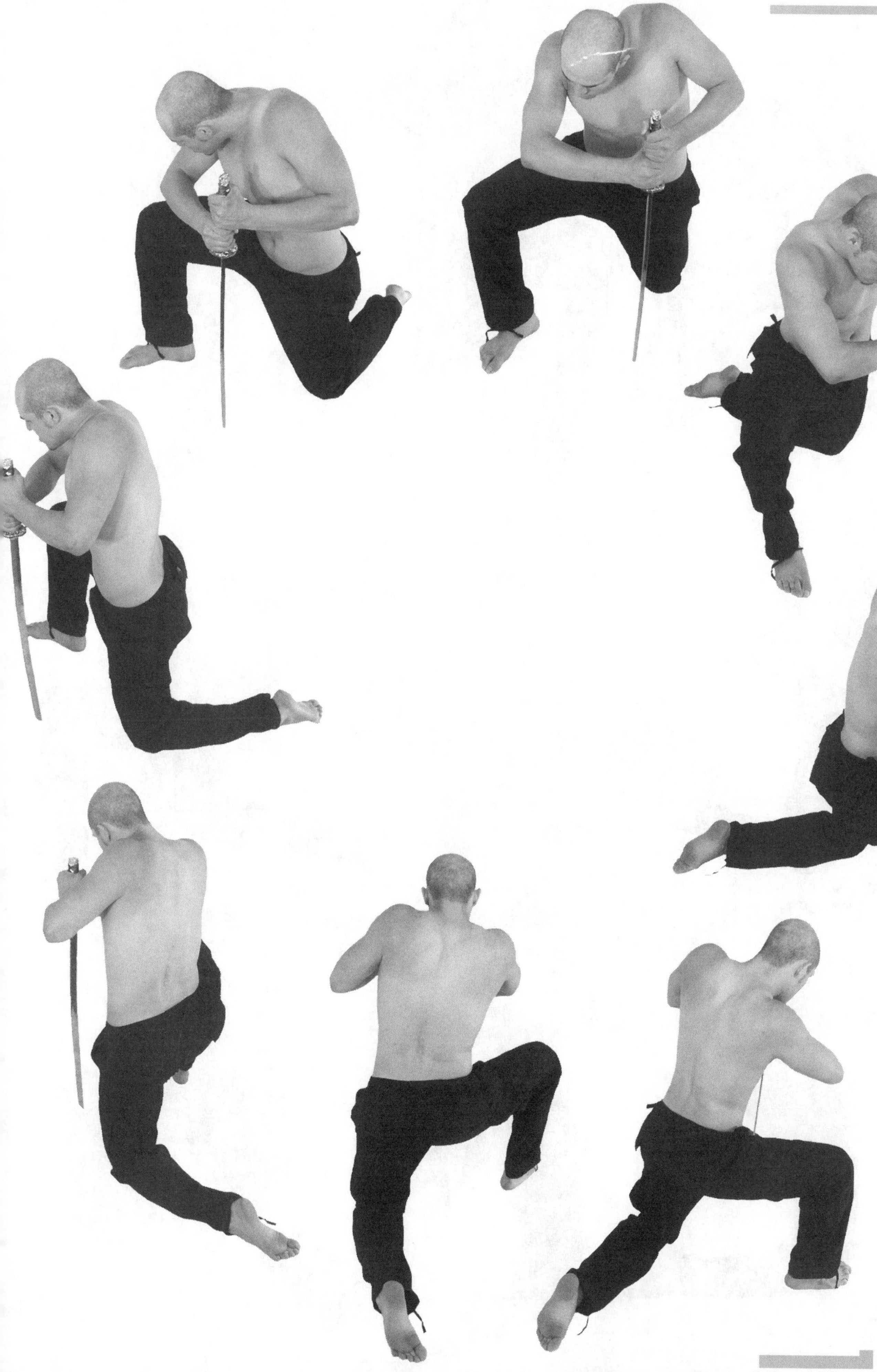

B

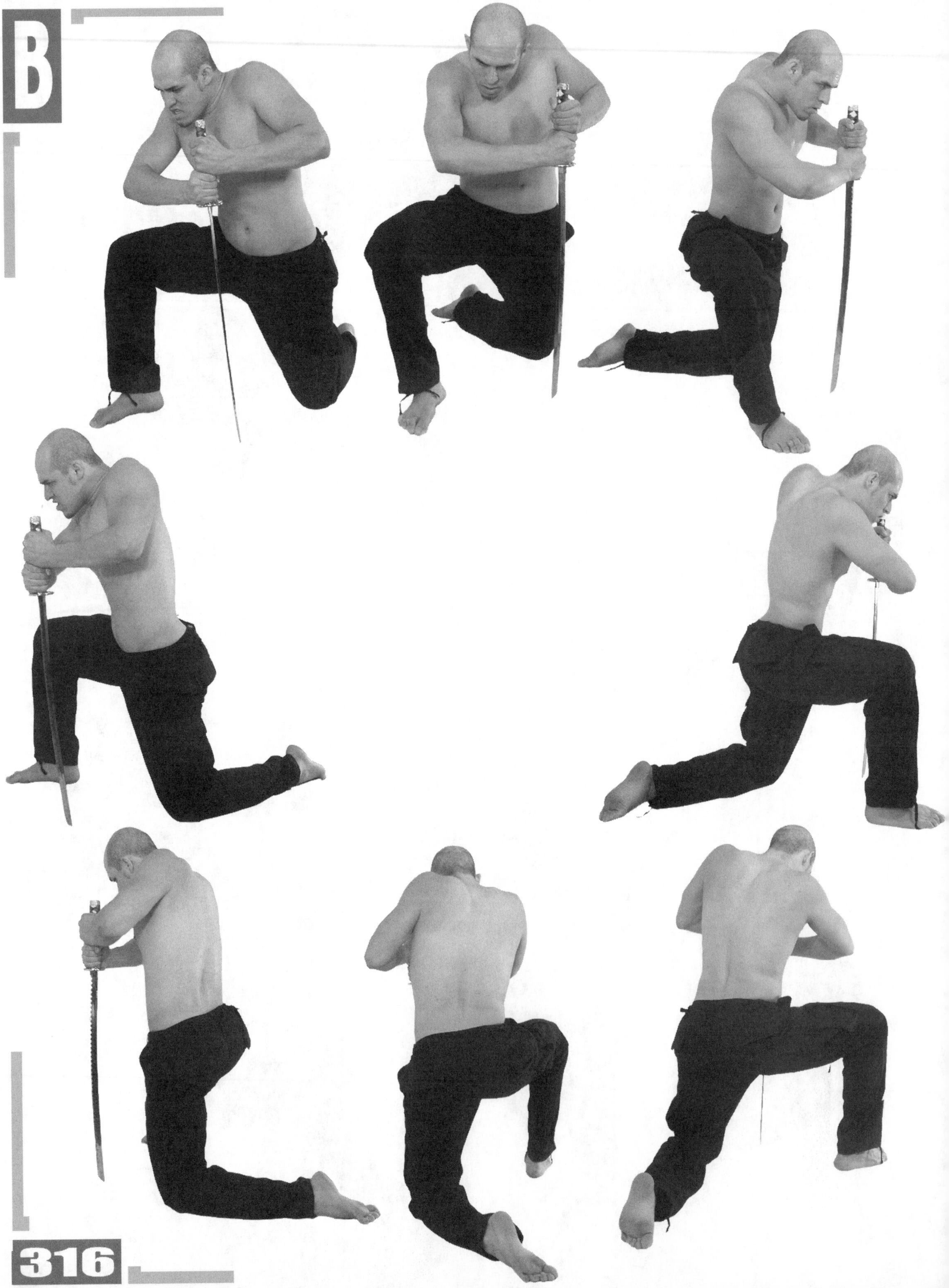

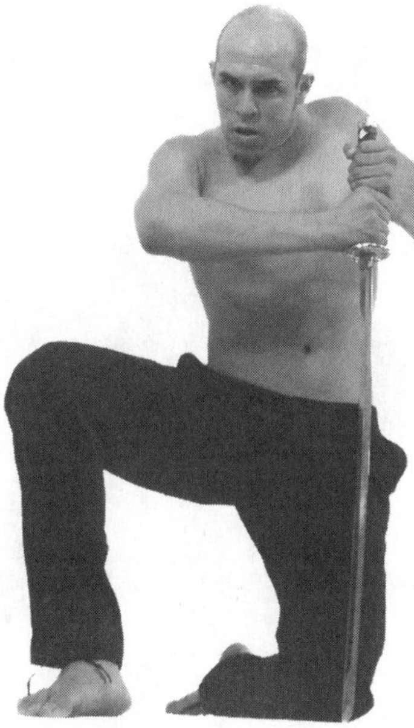

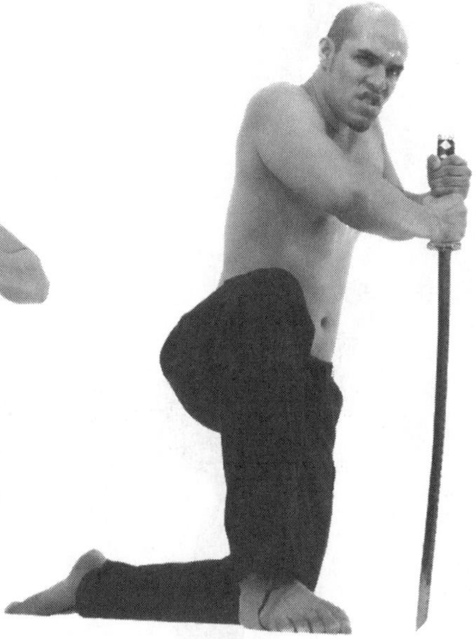

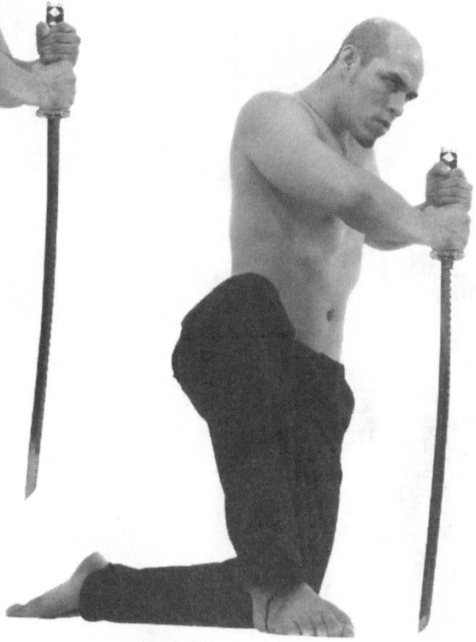

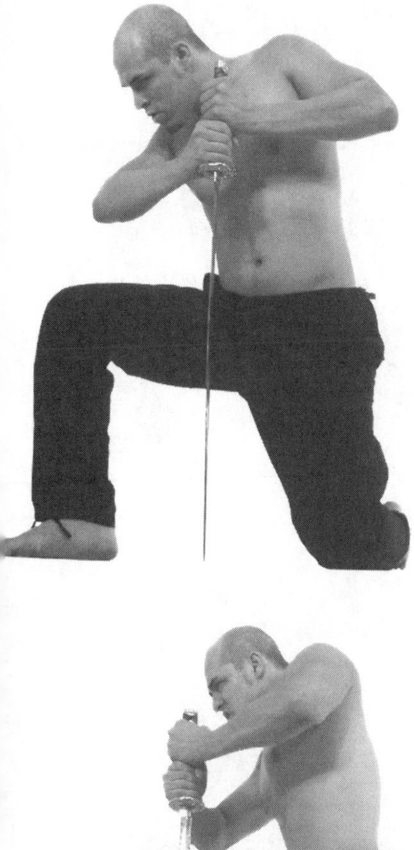

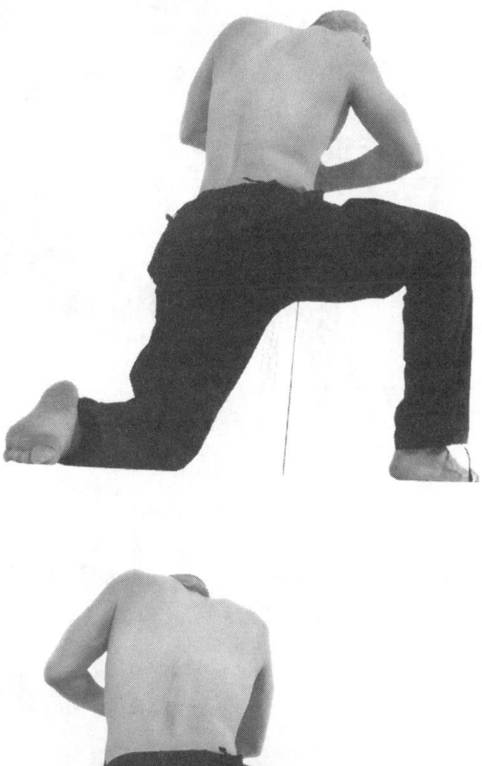

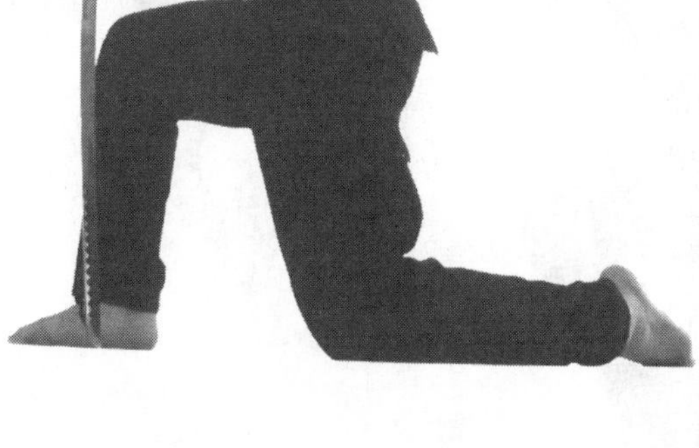

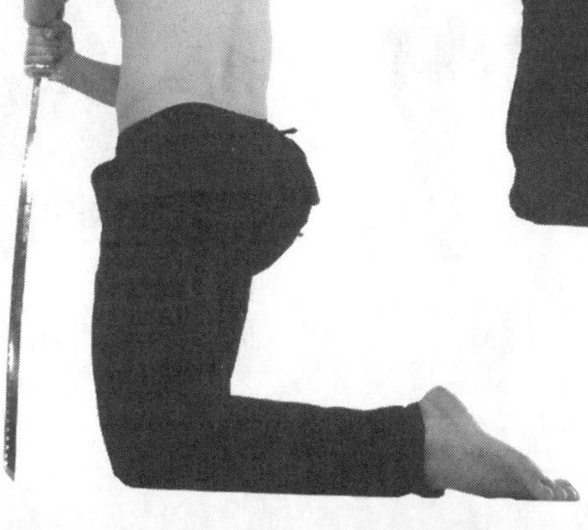

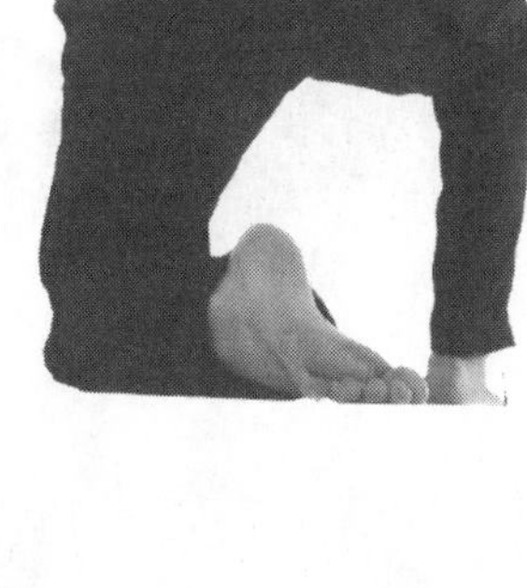

A

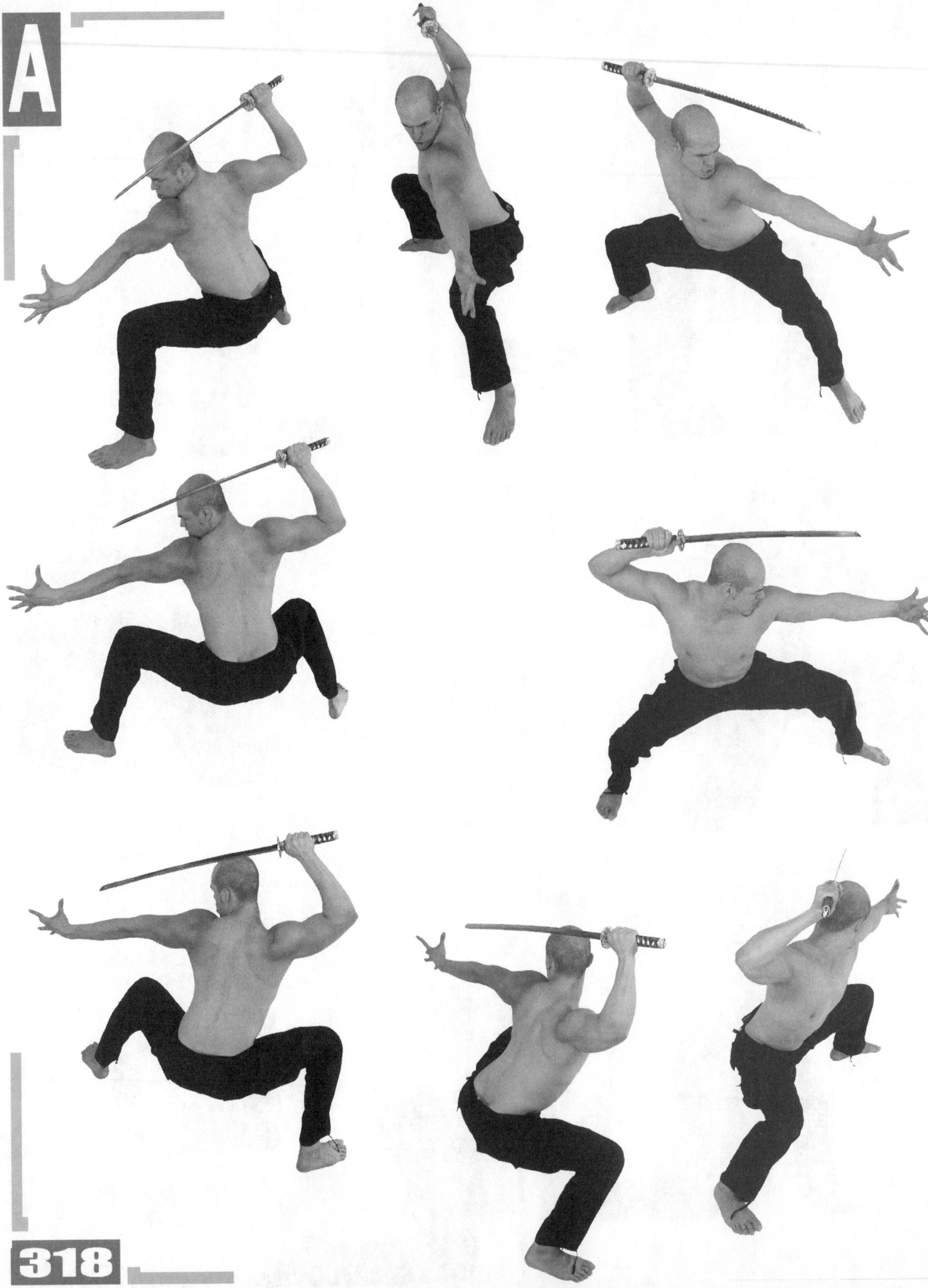

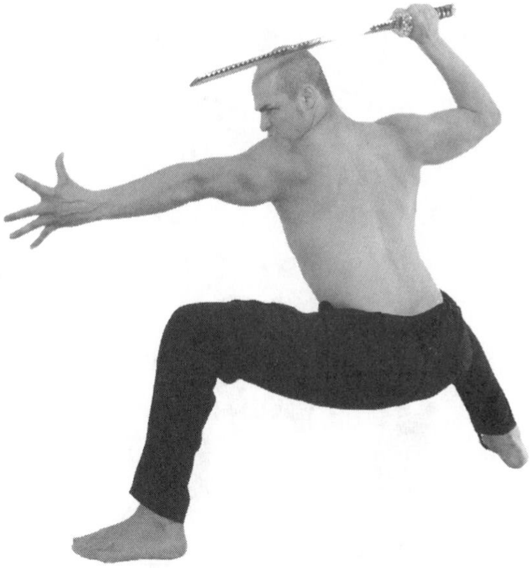

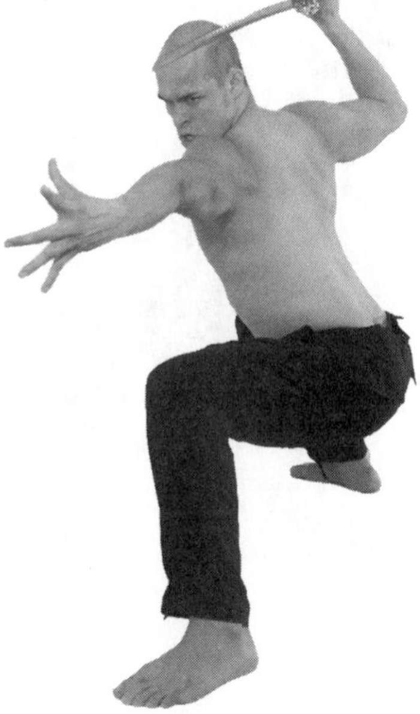

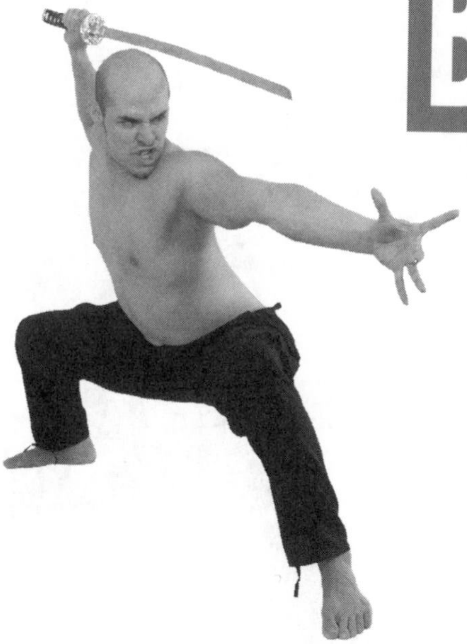

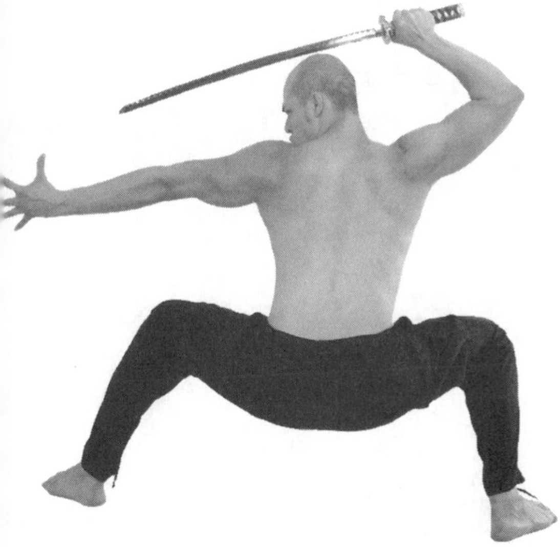

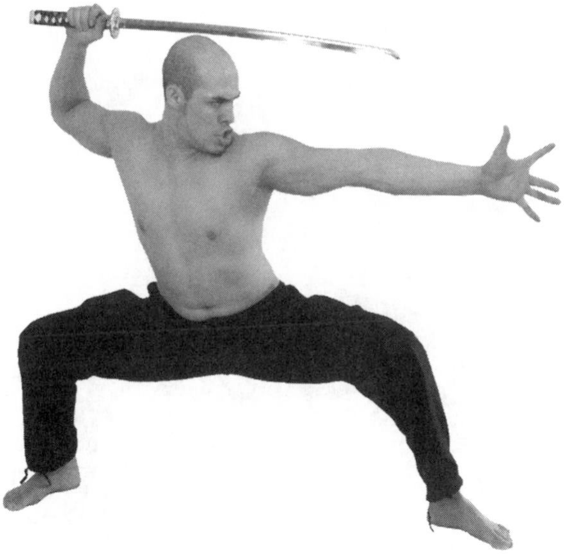

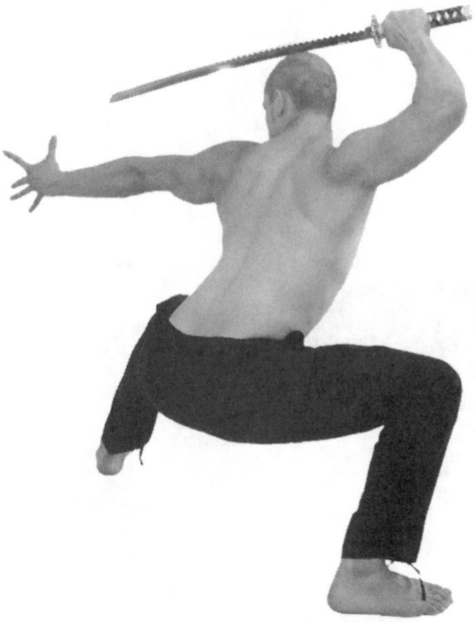

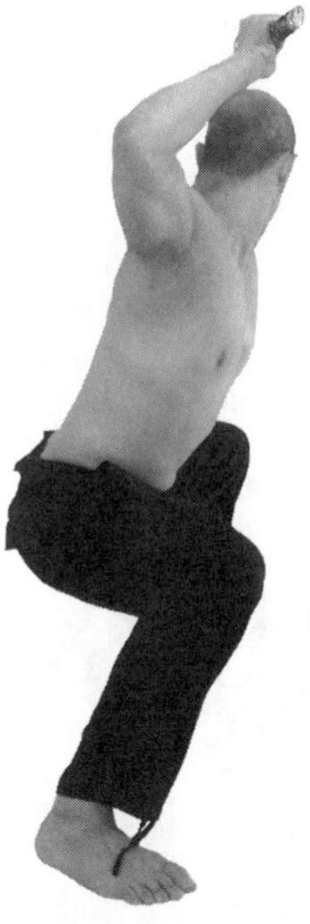

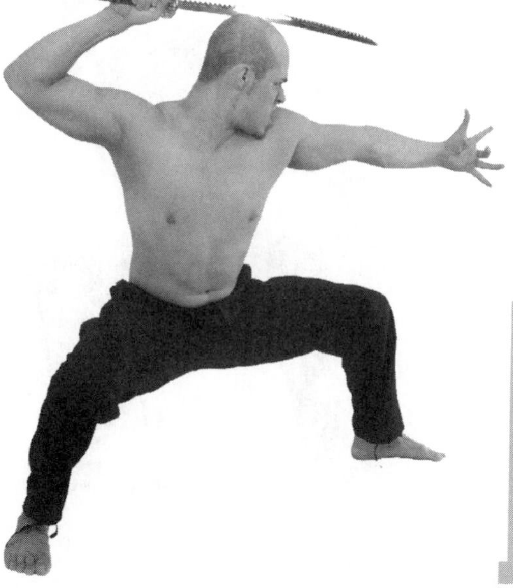

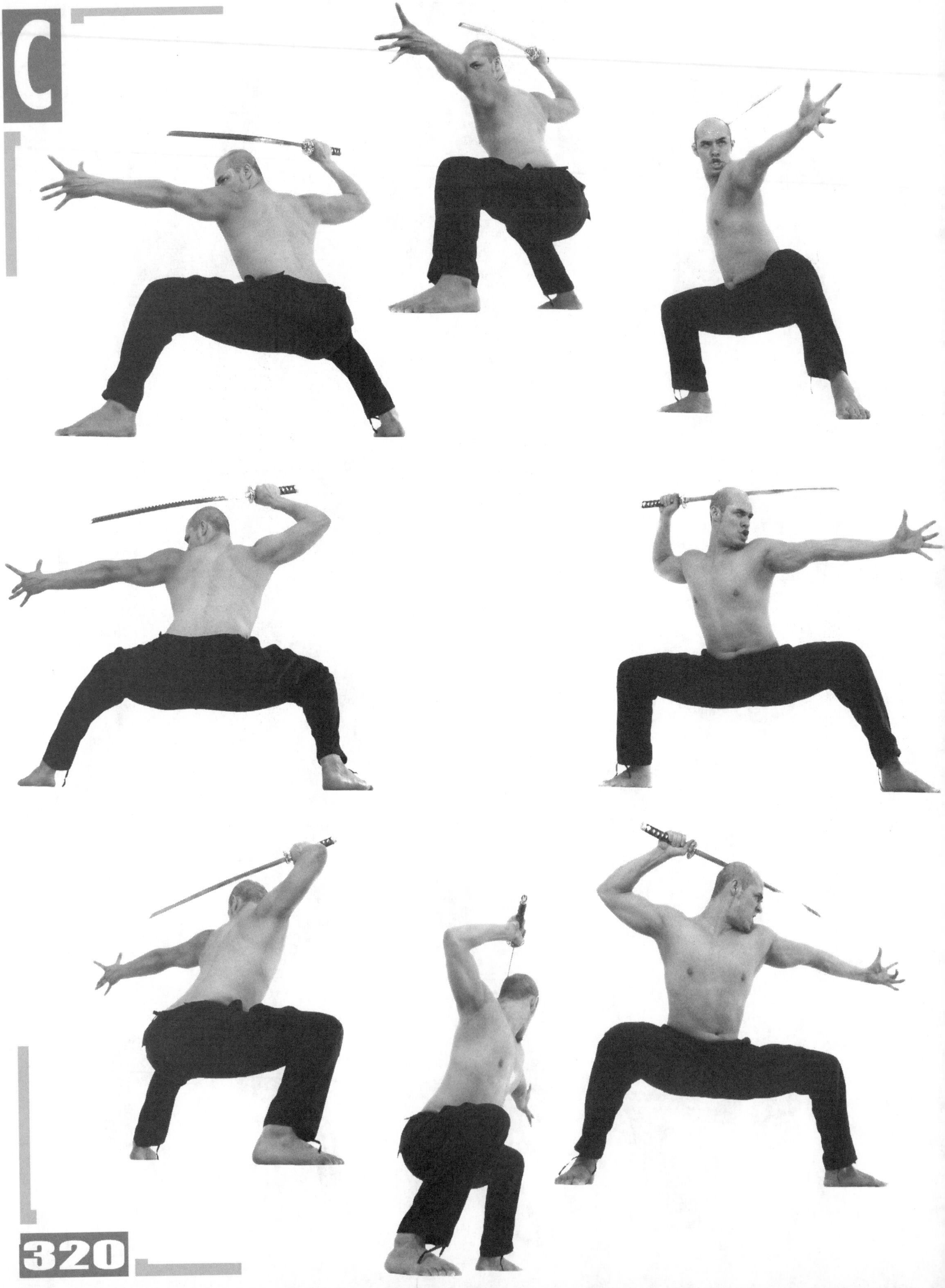

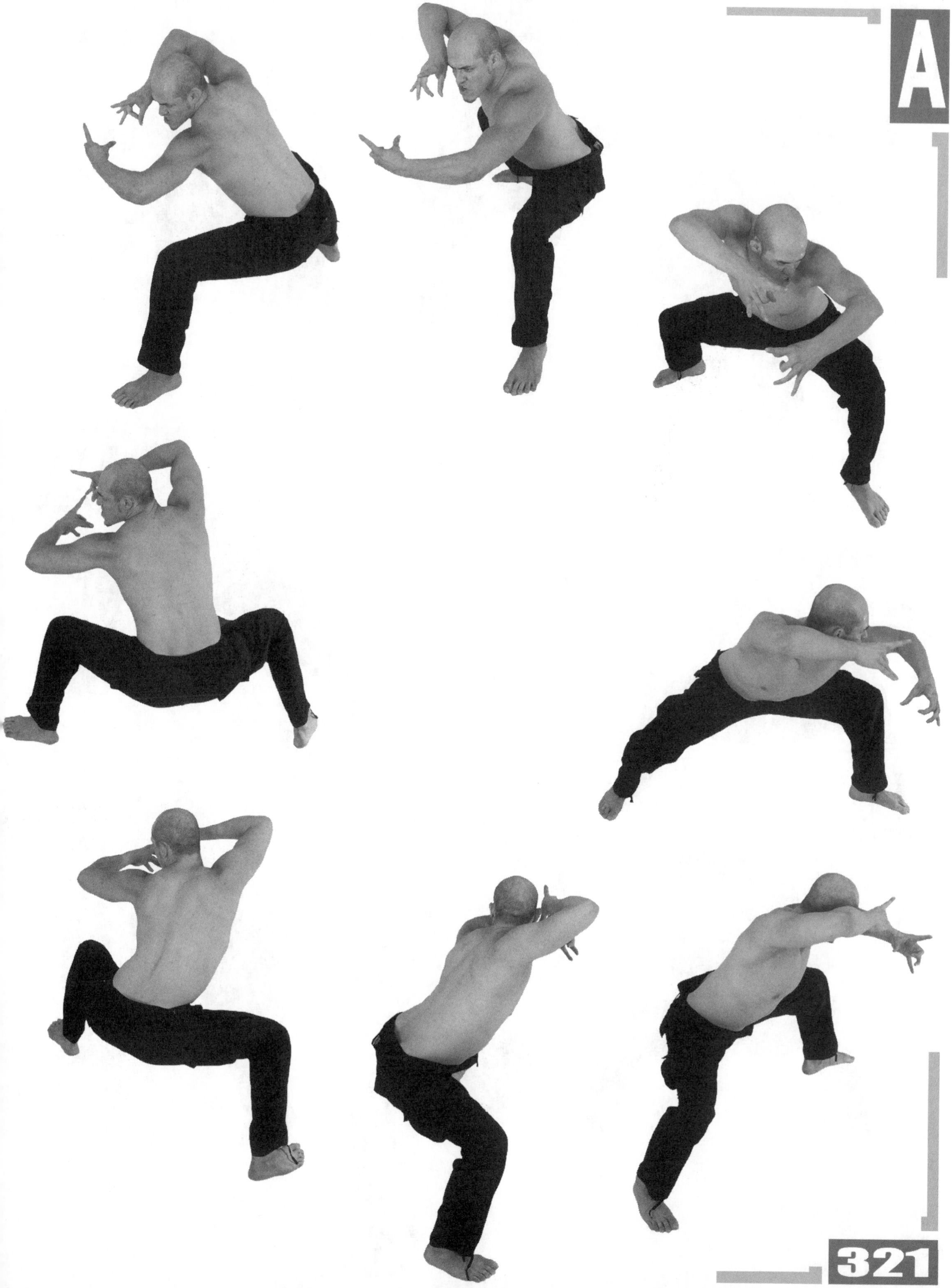

B

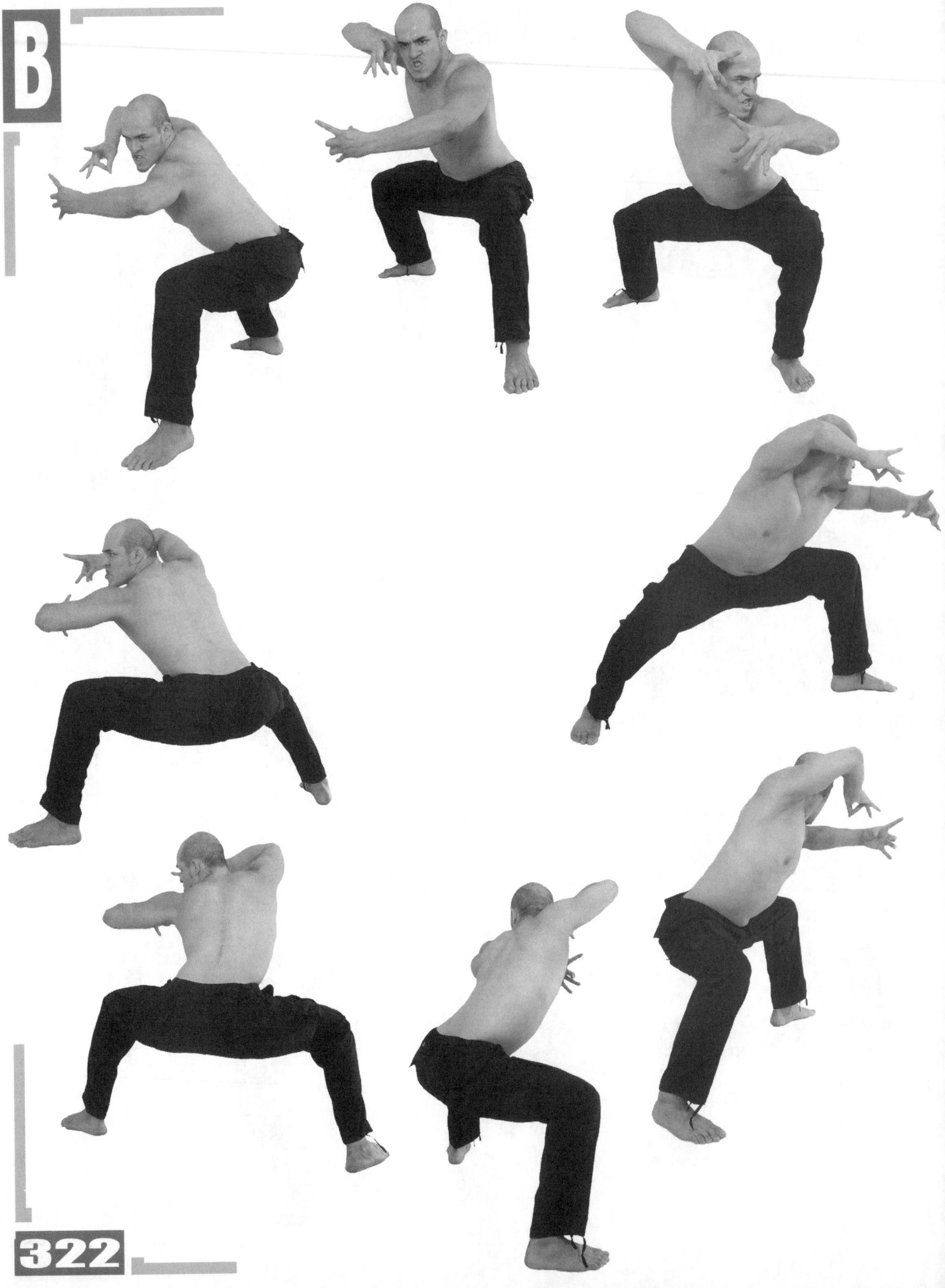

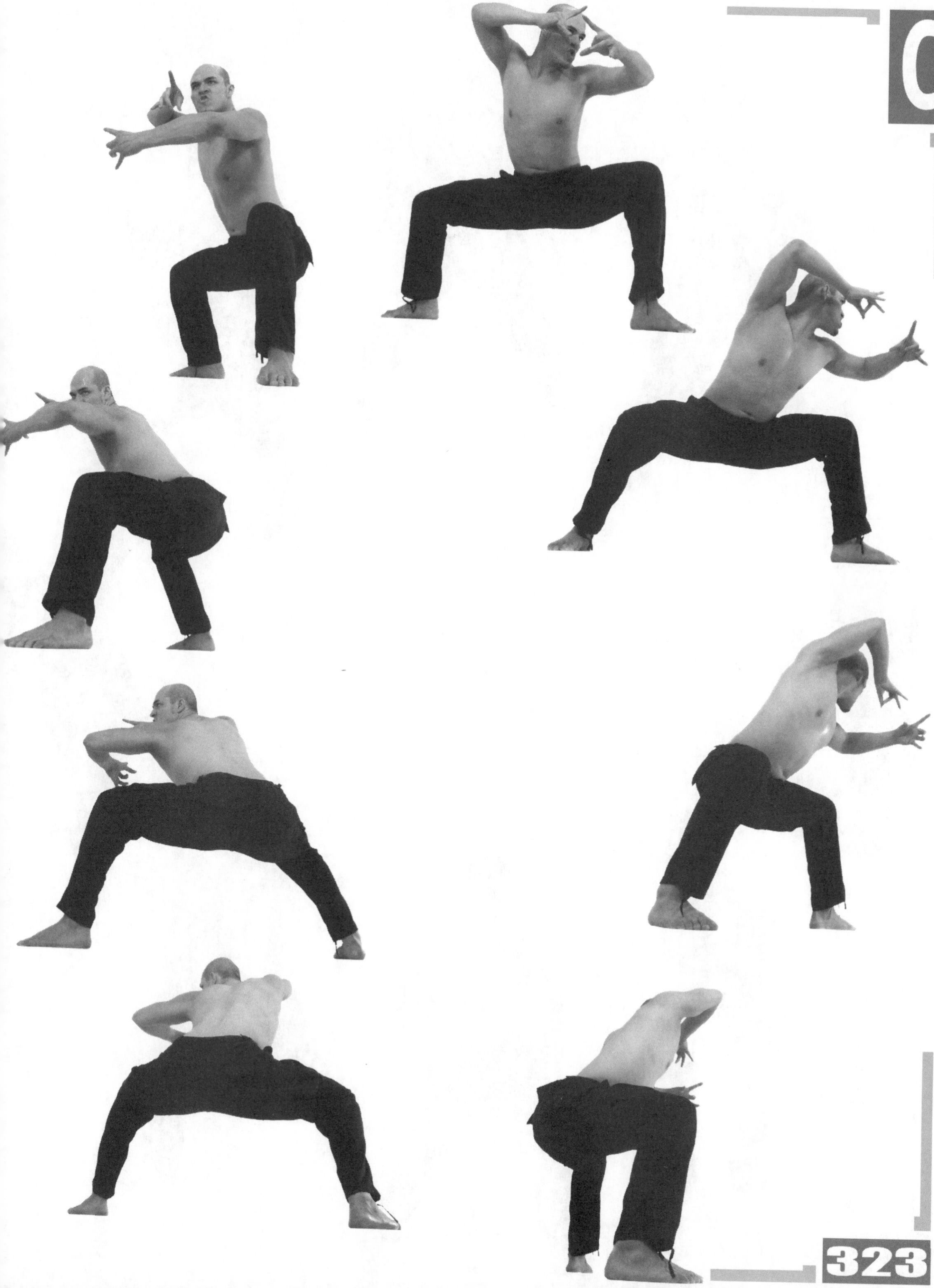

A

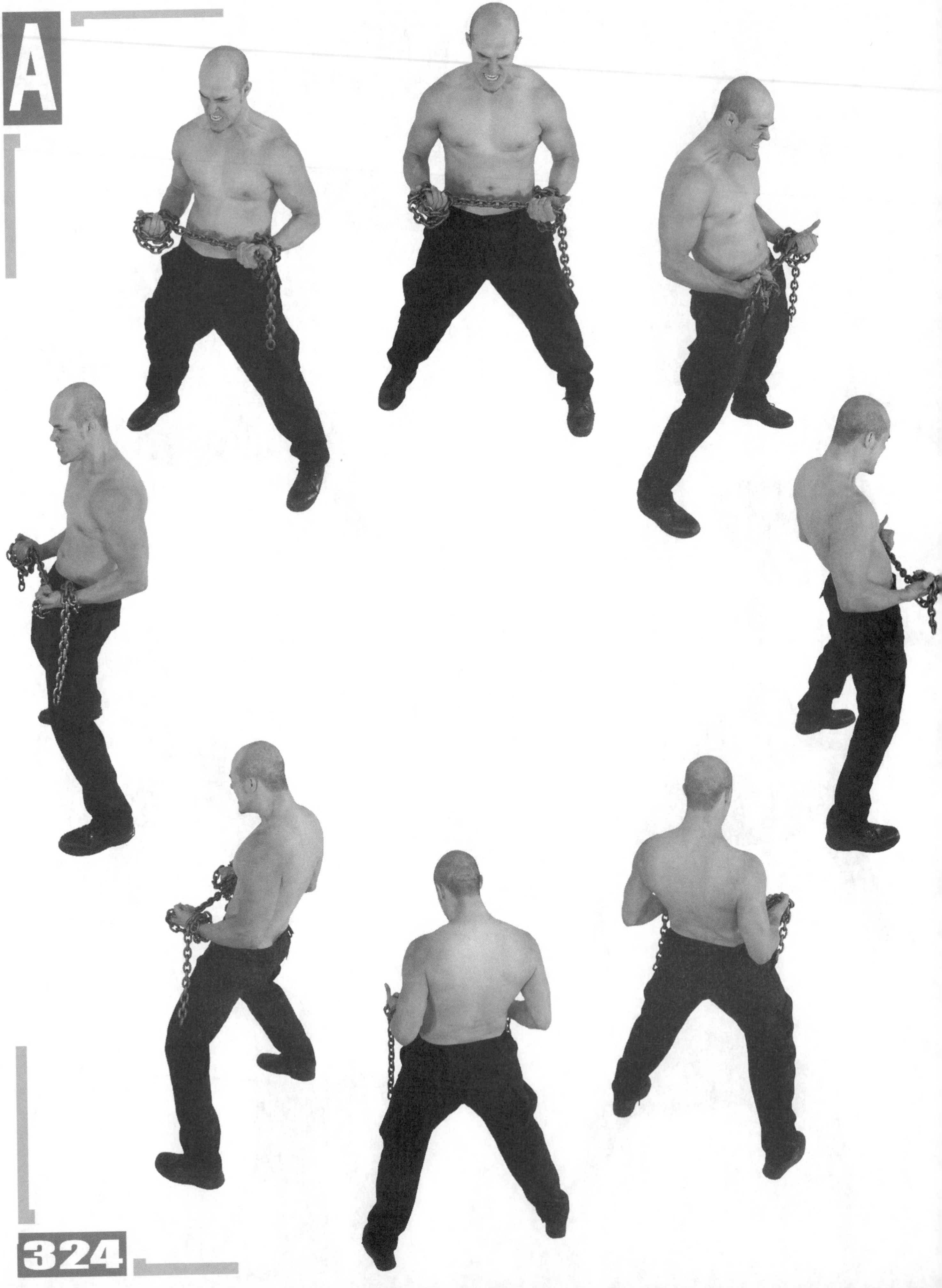

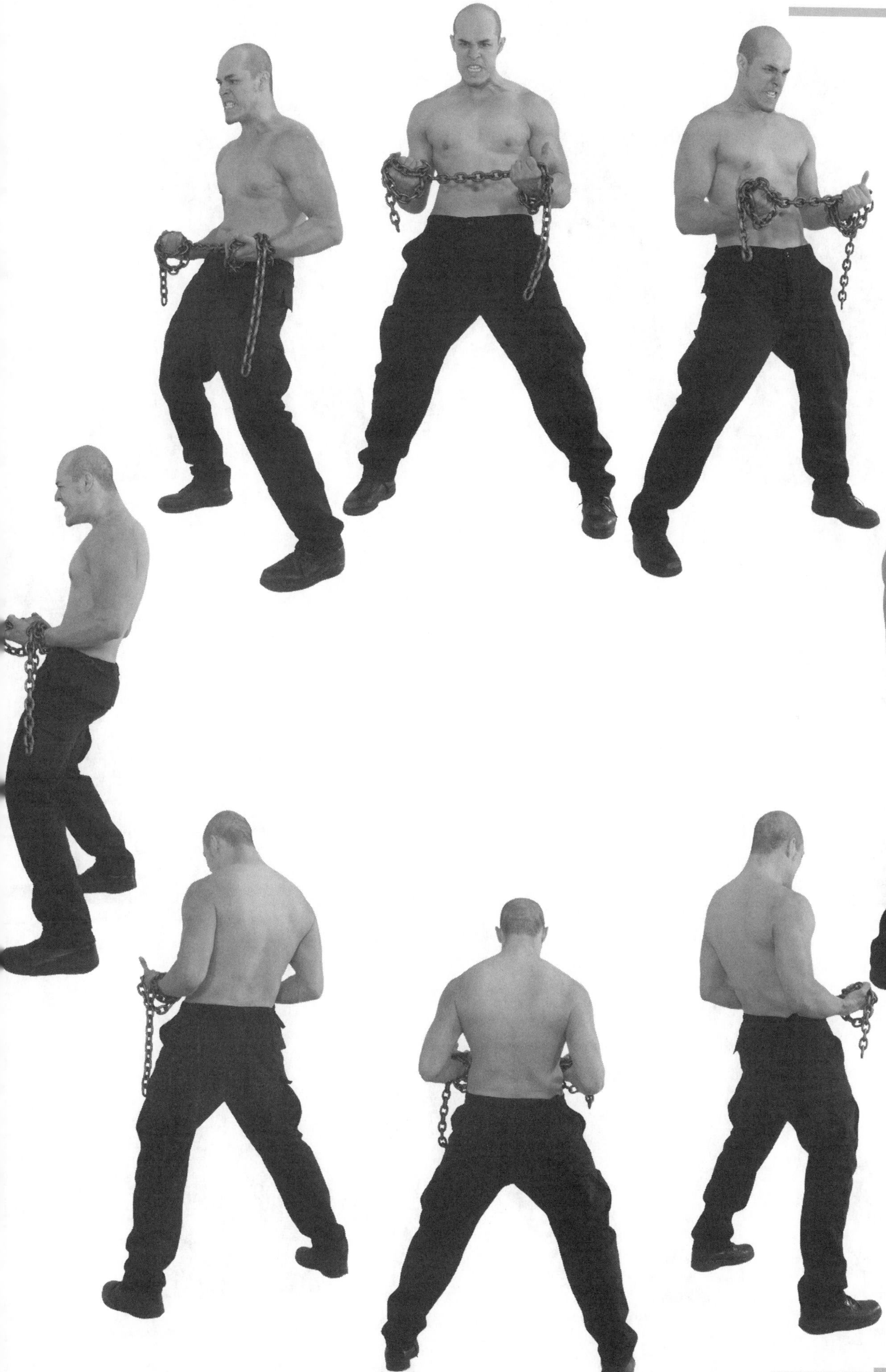

C

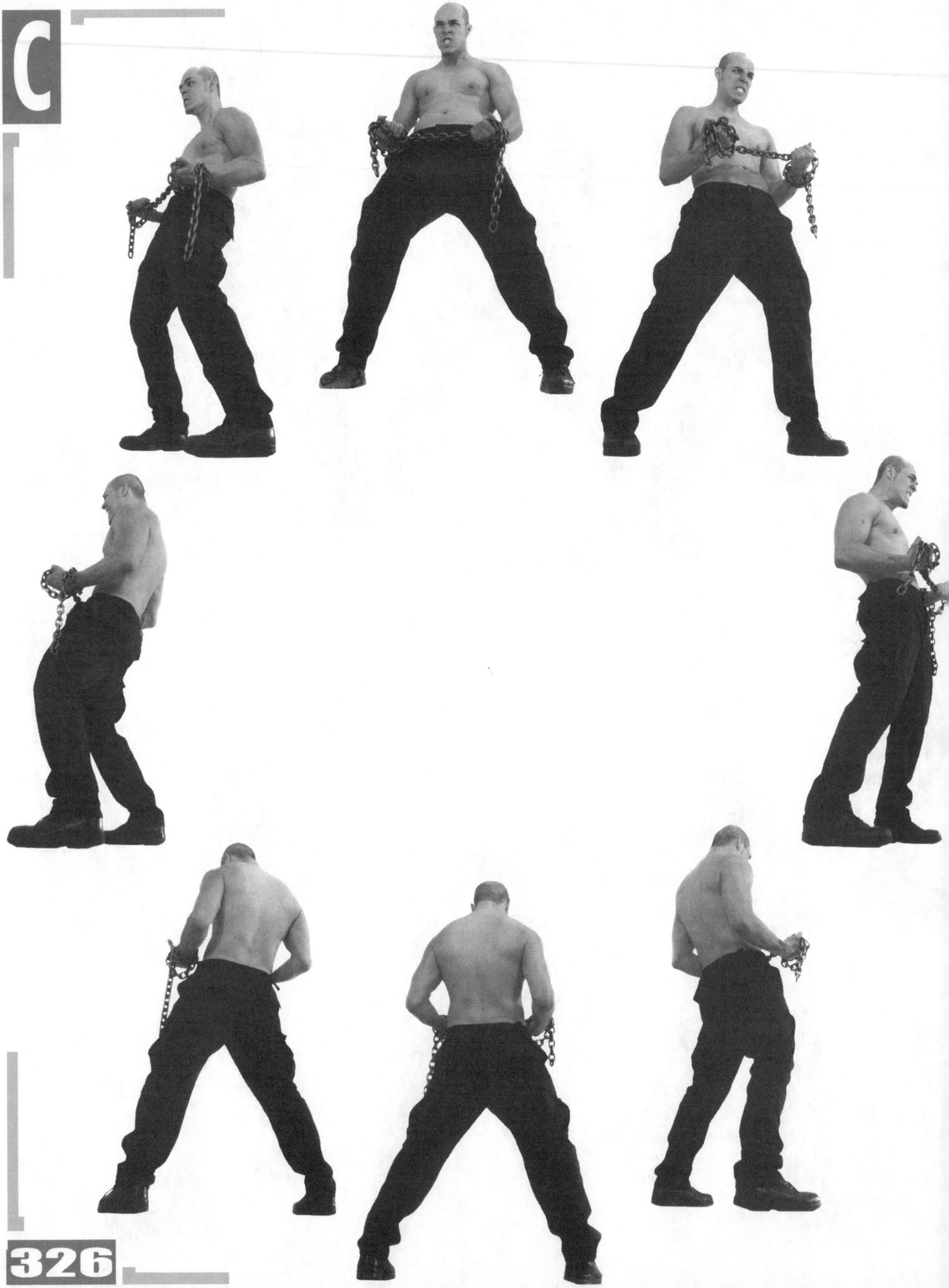

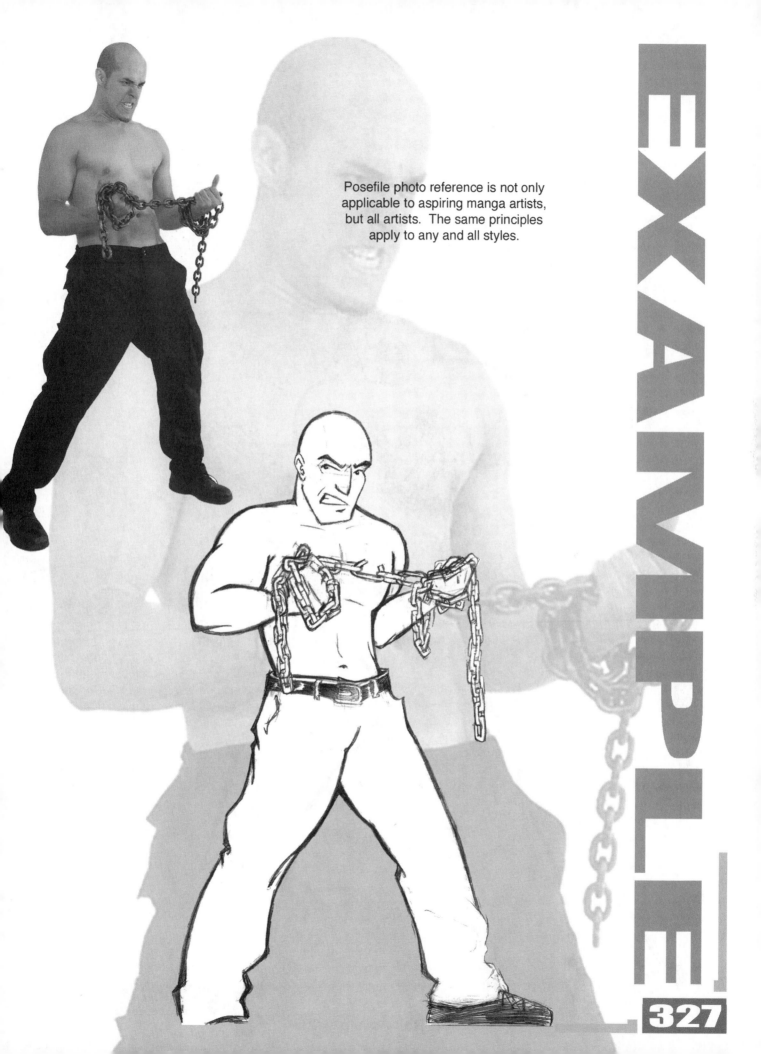

Posefile photo reference is not only applicable to aspiring manga artists, but all artists. The same principles apply to any and all styles.

EXAMPLE

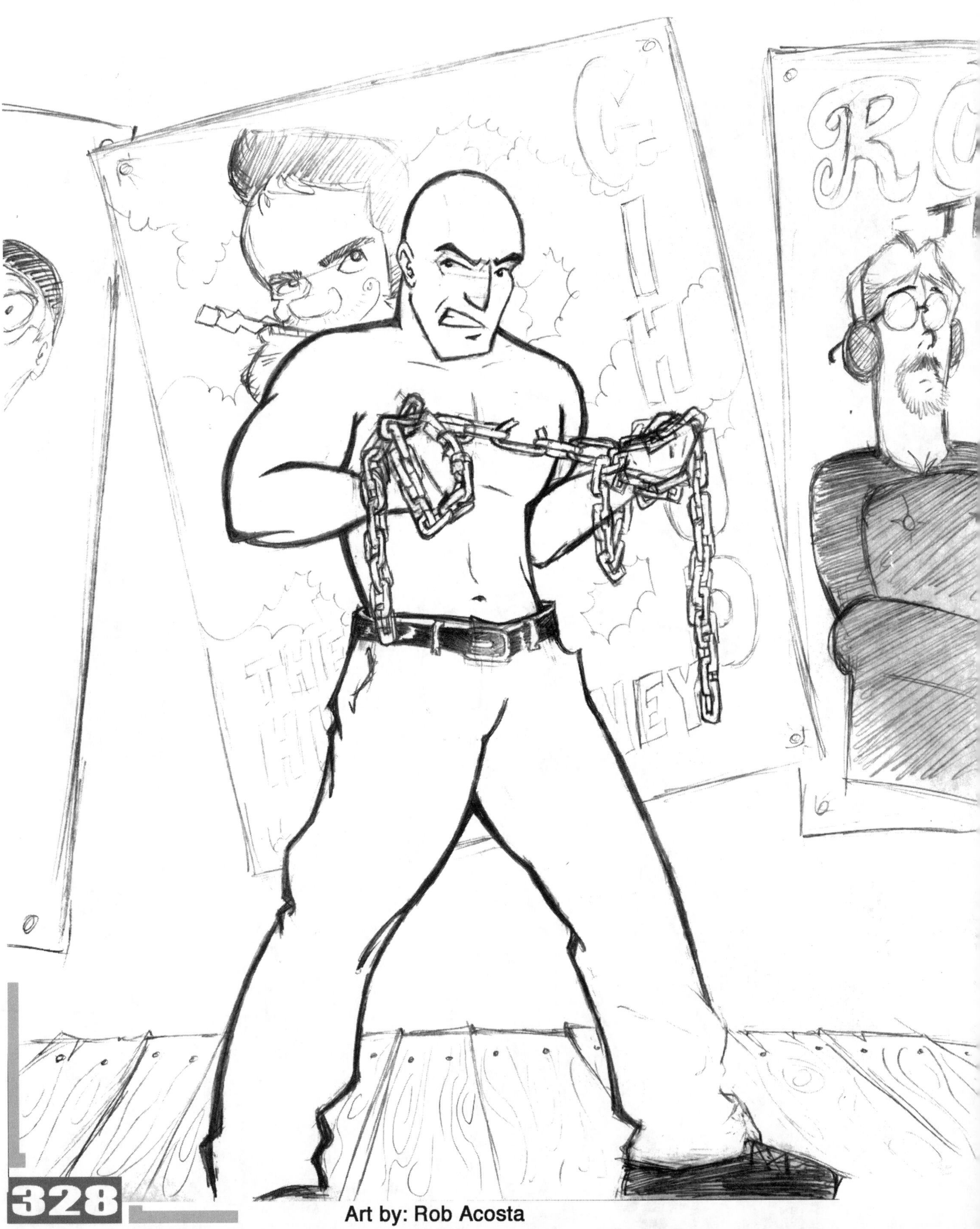

Art by: Rob Acosta

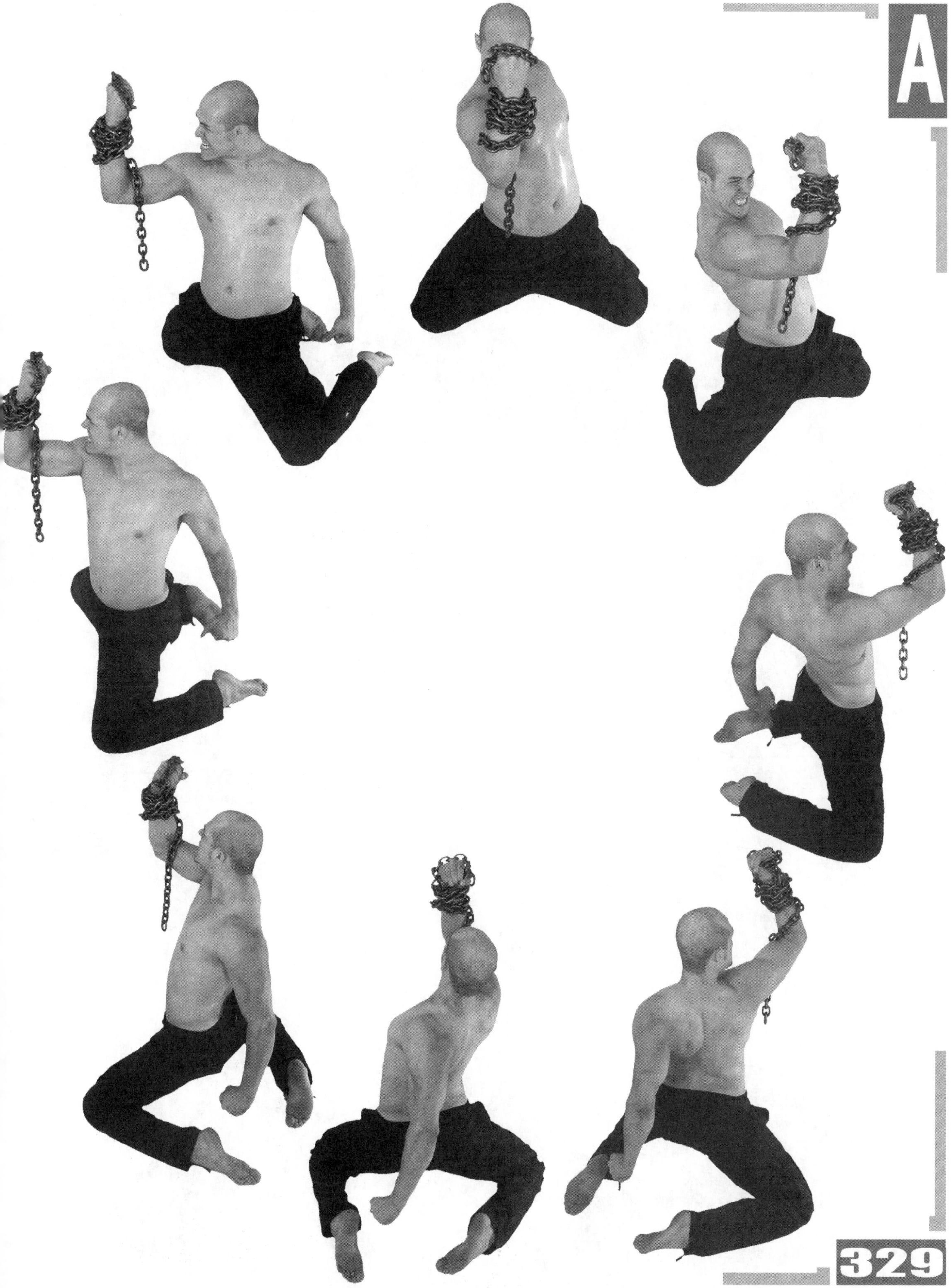

B

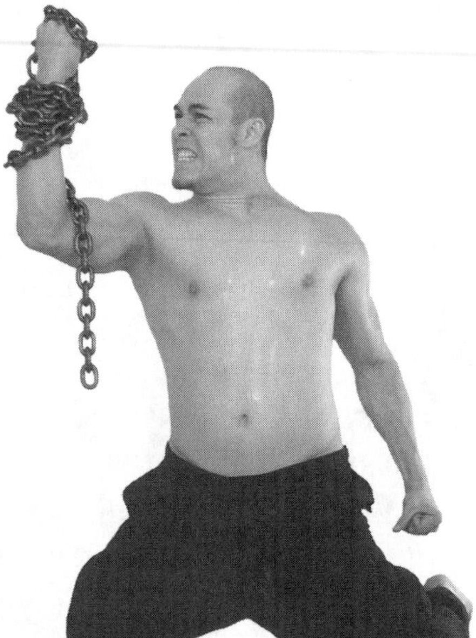
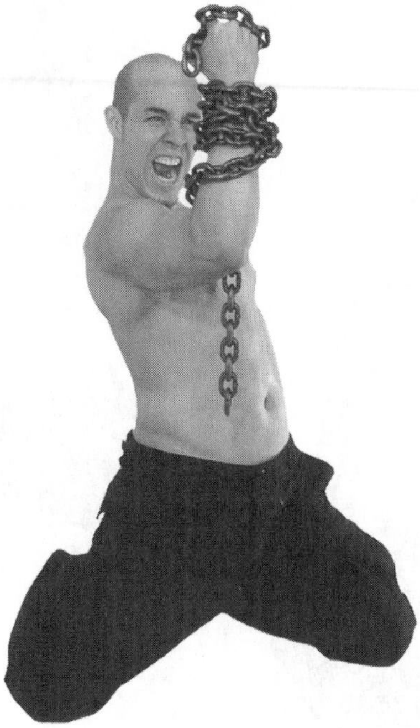
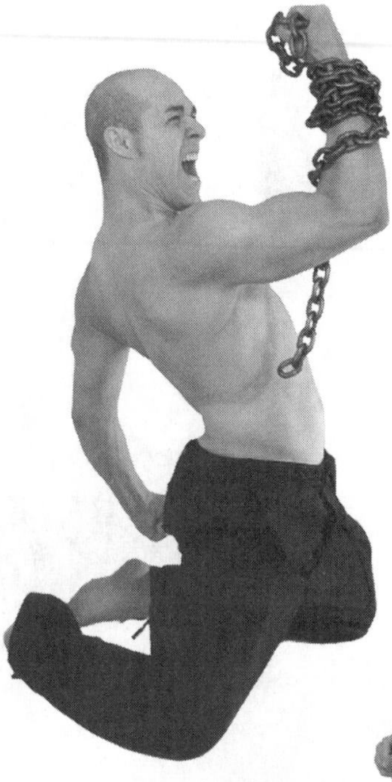
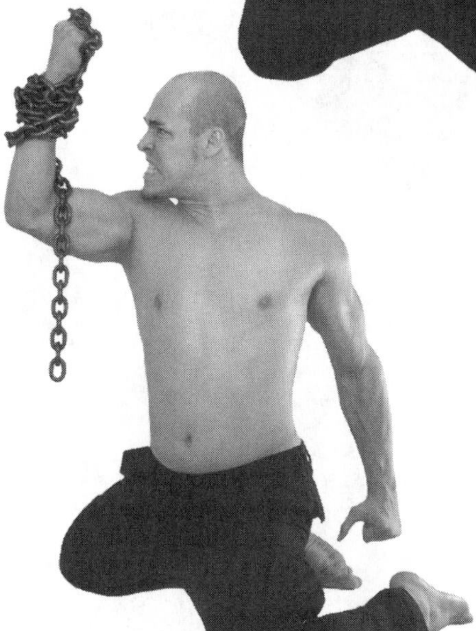
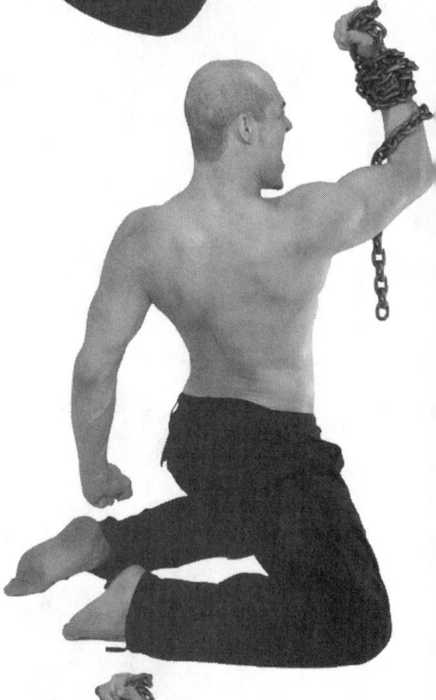
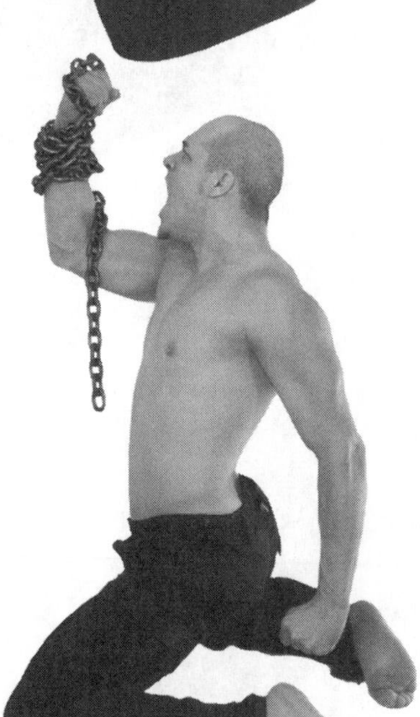
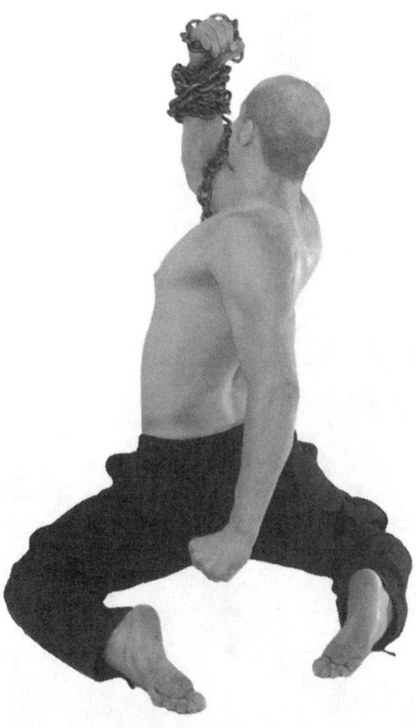
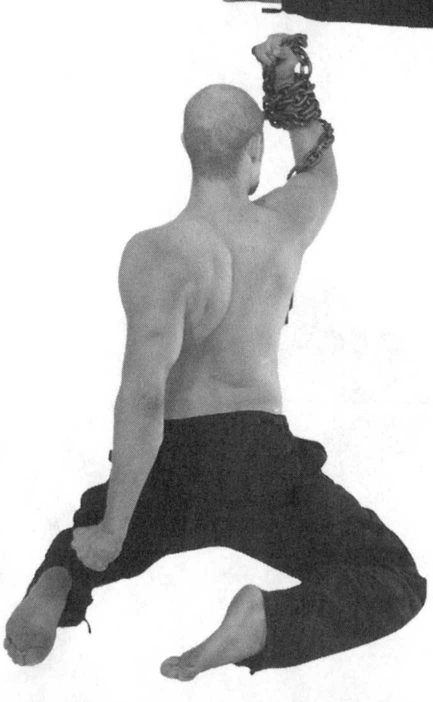

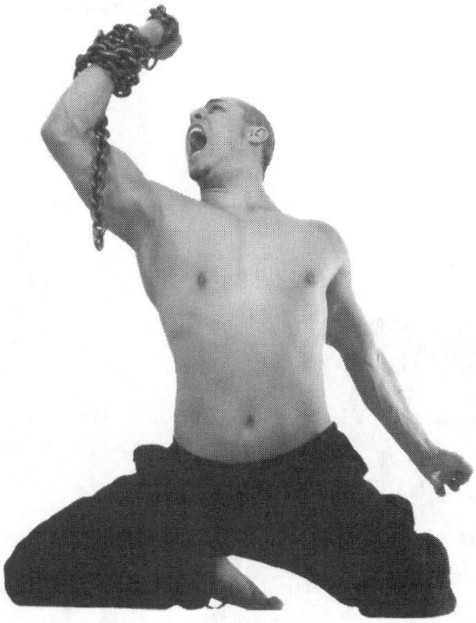

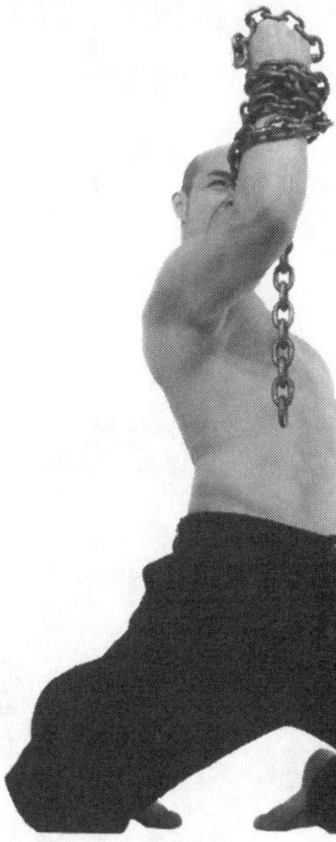

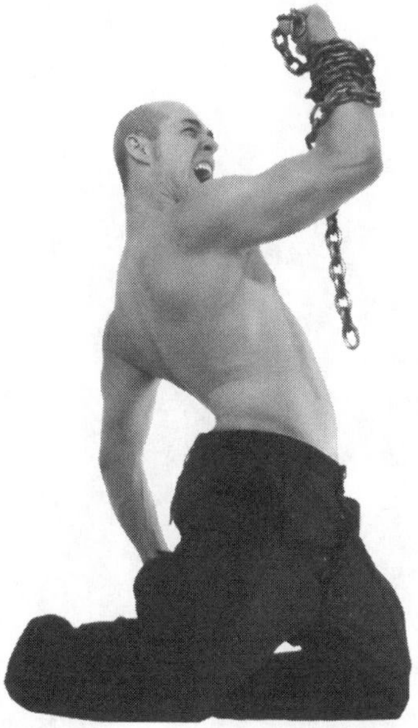

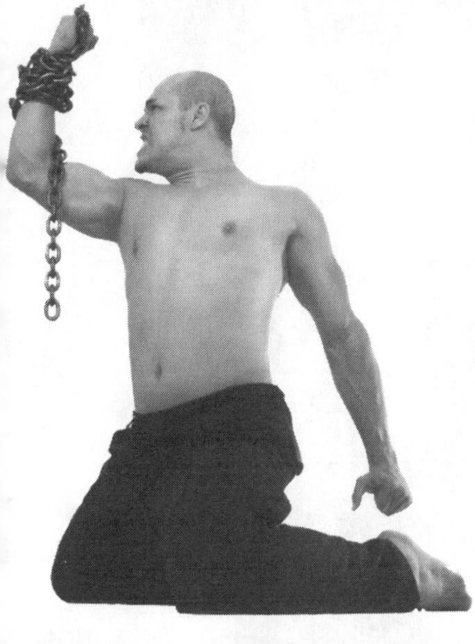

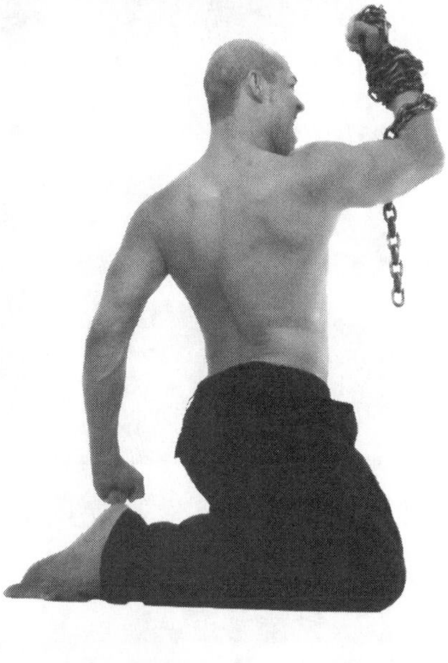

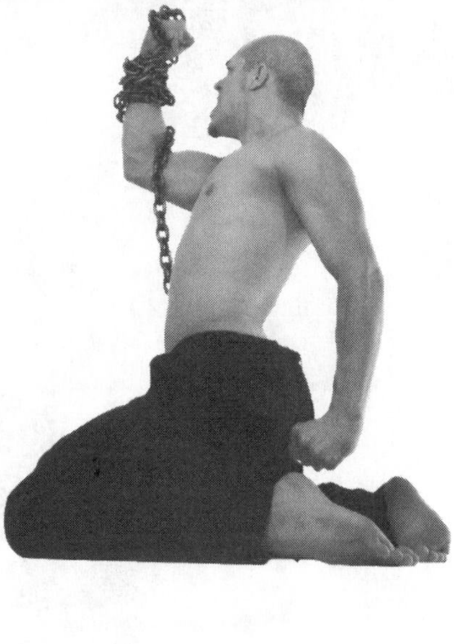

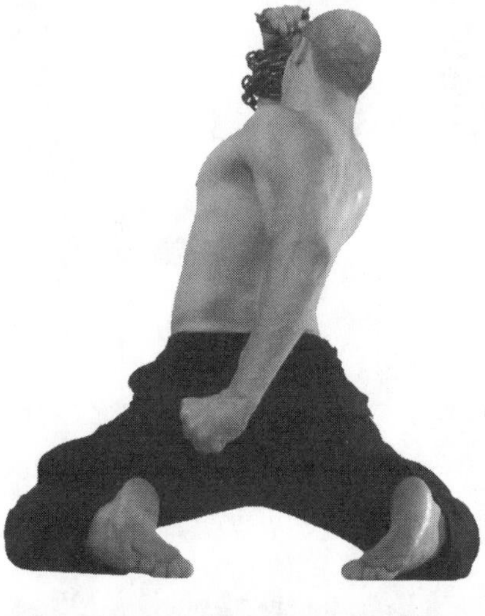

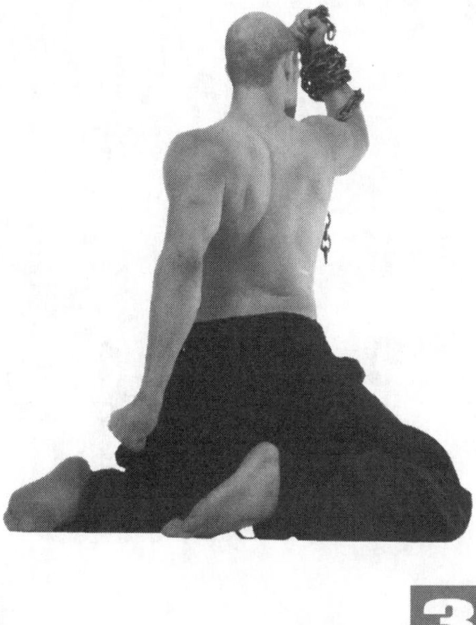

SUPERHERO POSE

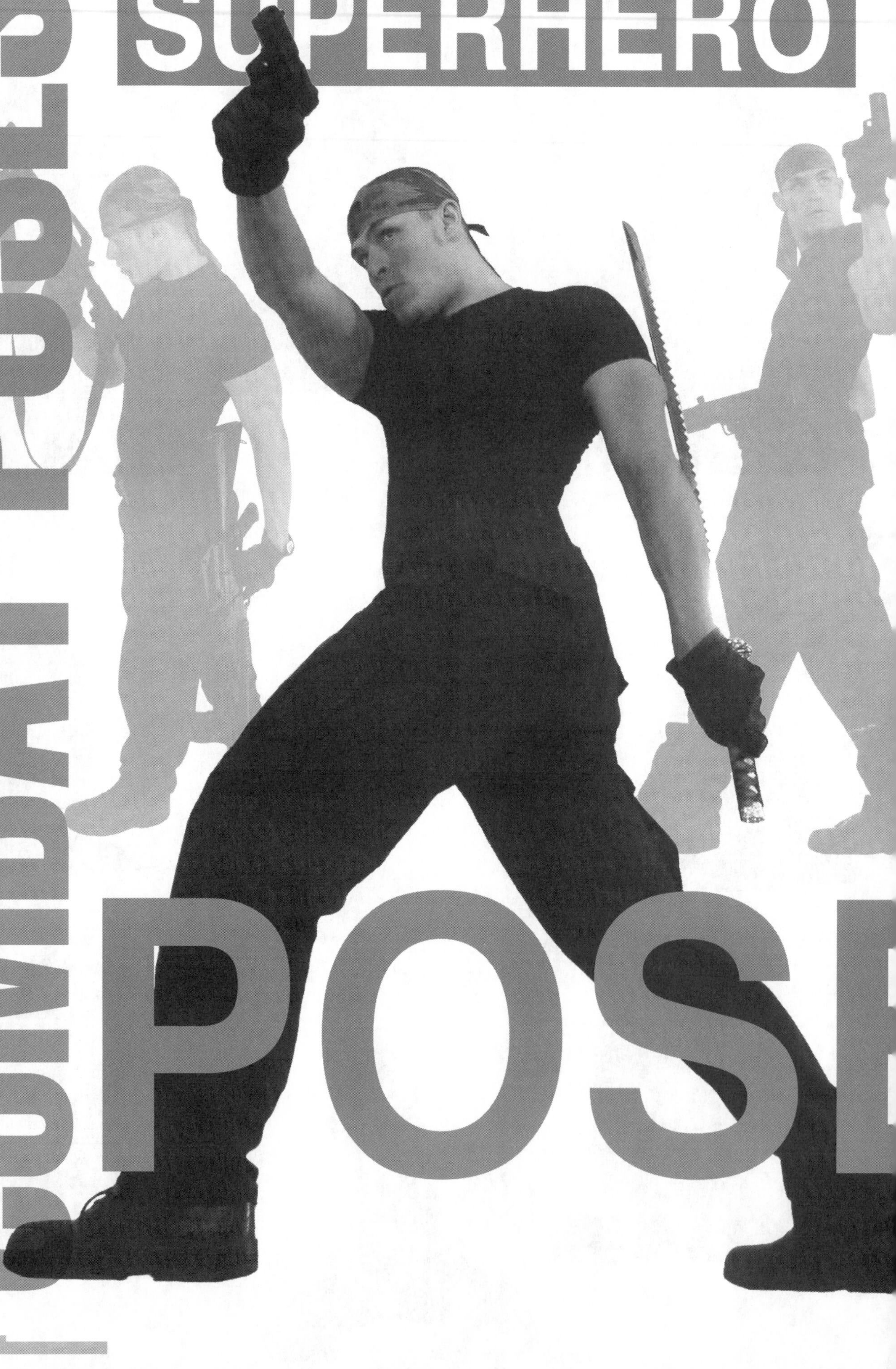

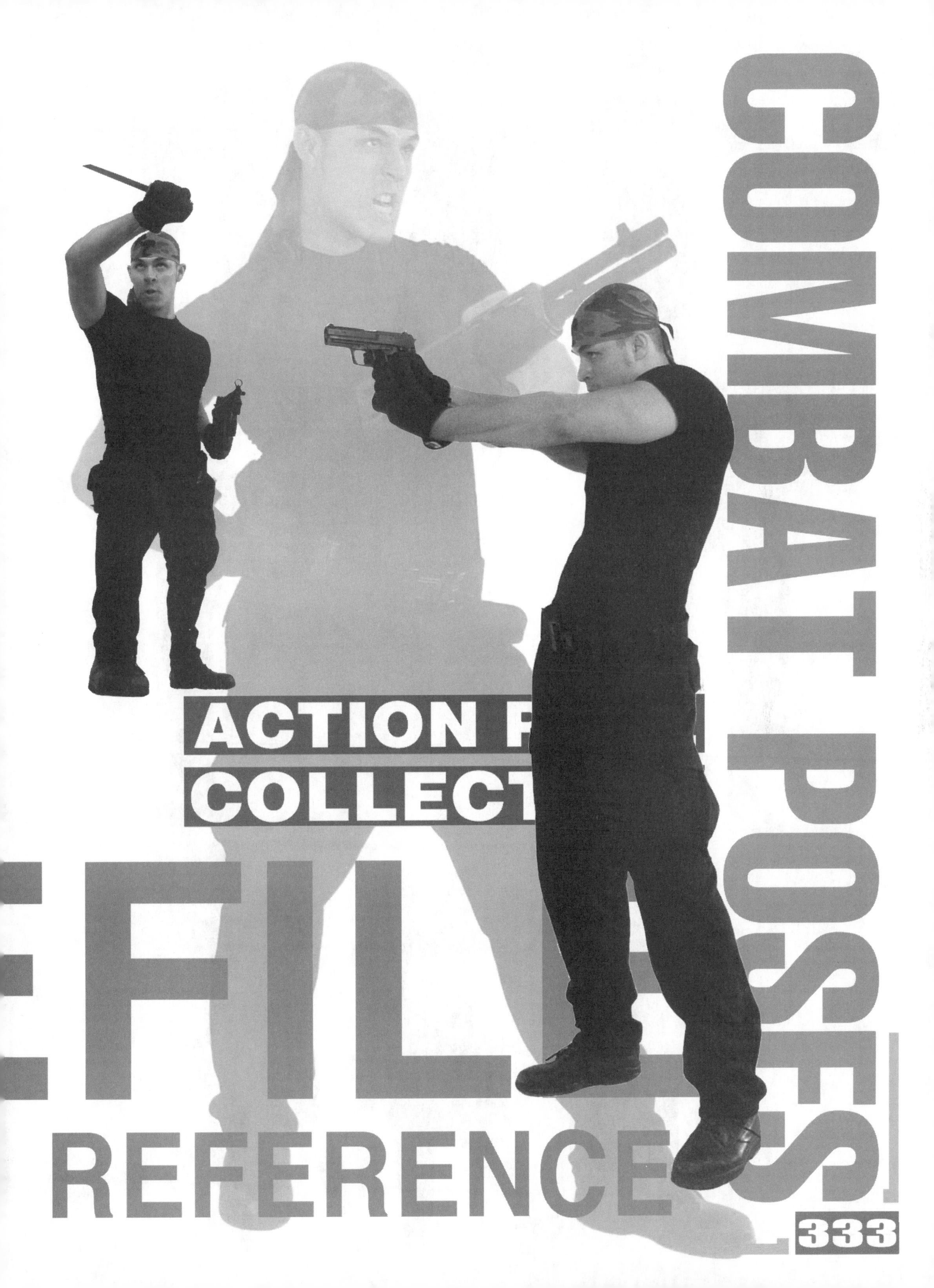
COMBAT POSES
ACTION P
COLLECT
FIL
REFERENCE

A

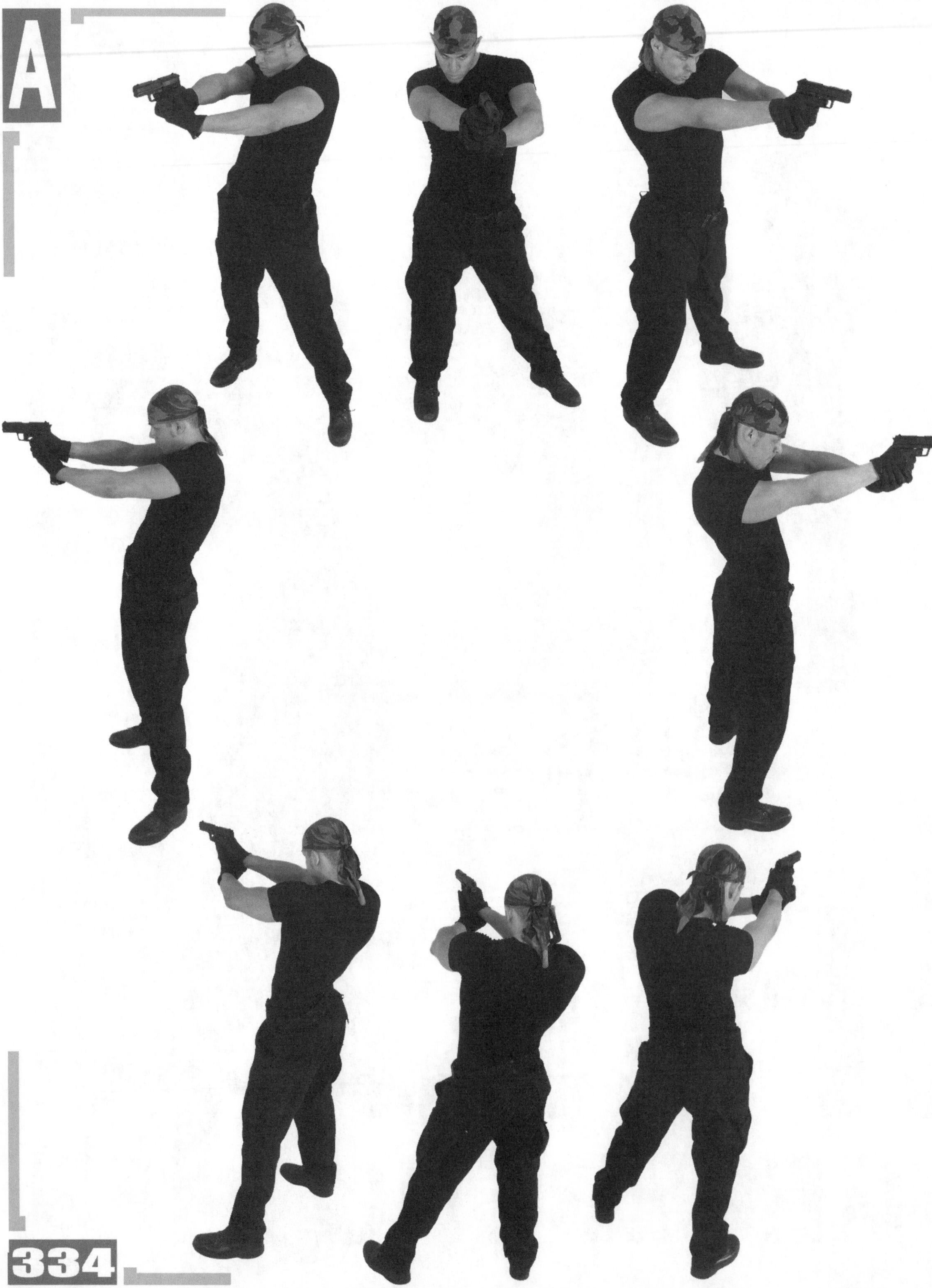

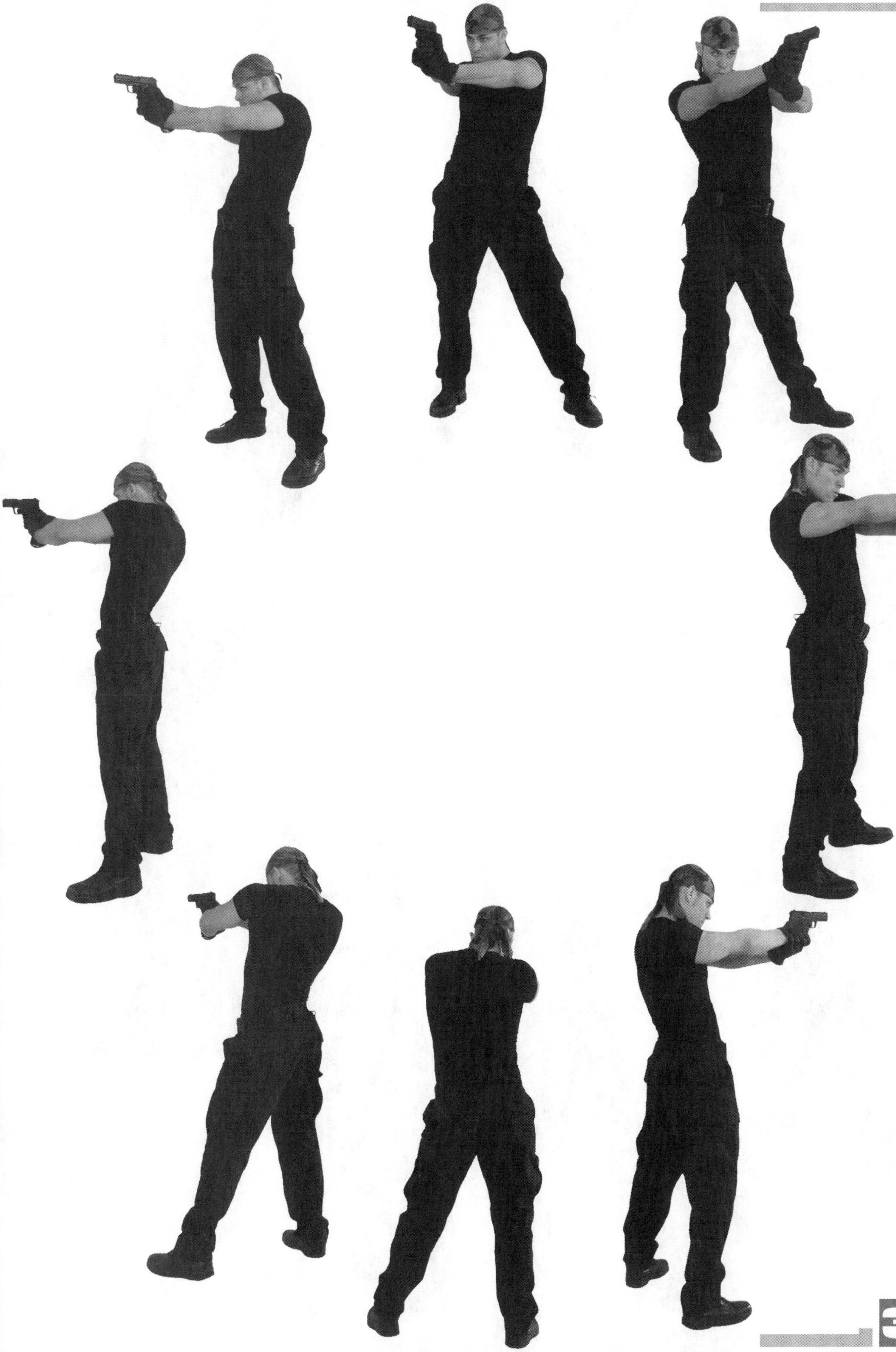

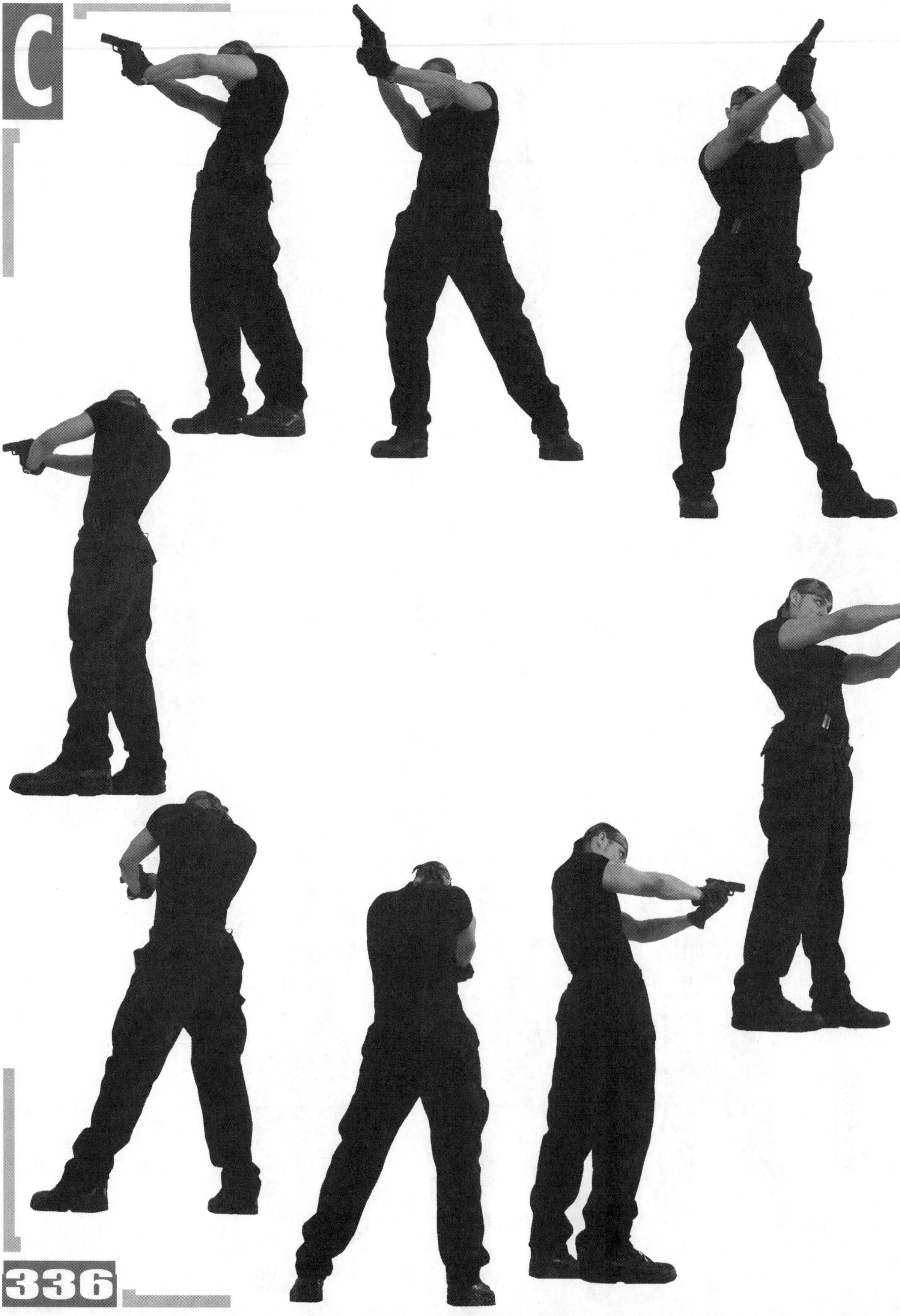

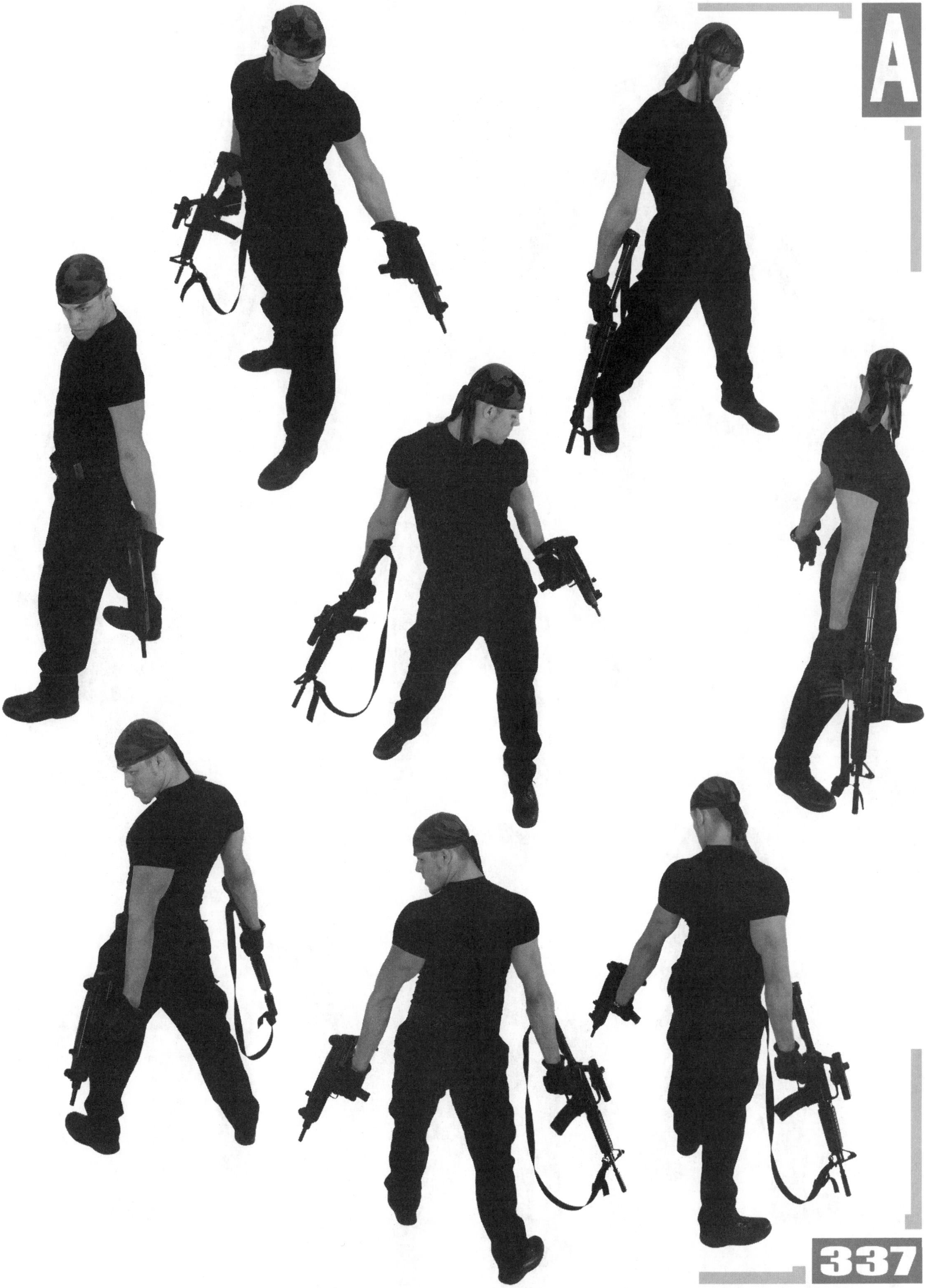

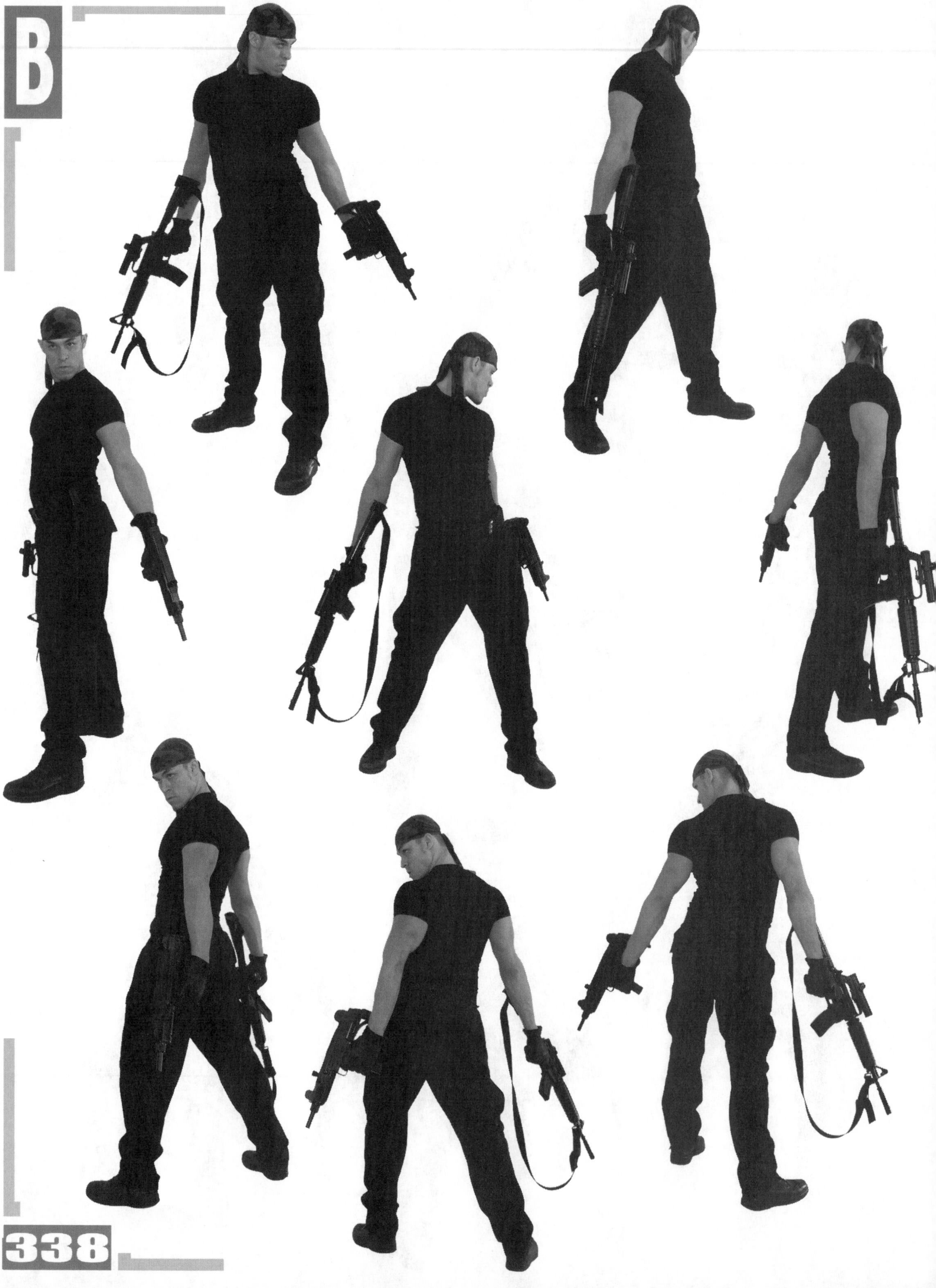

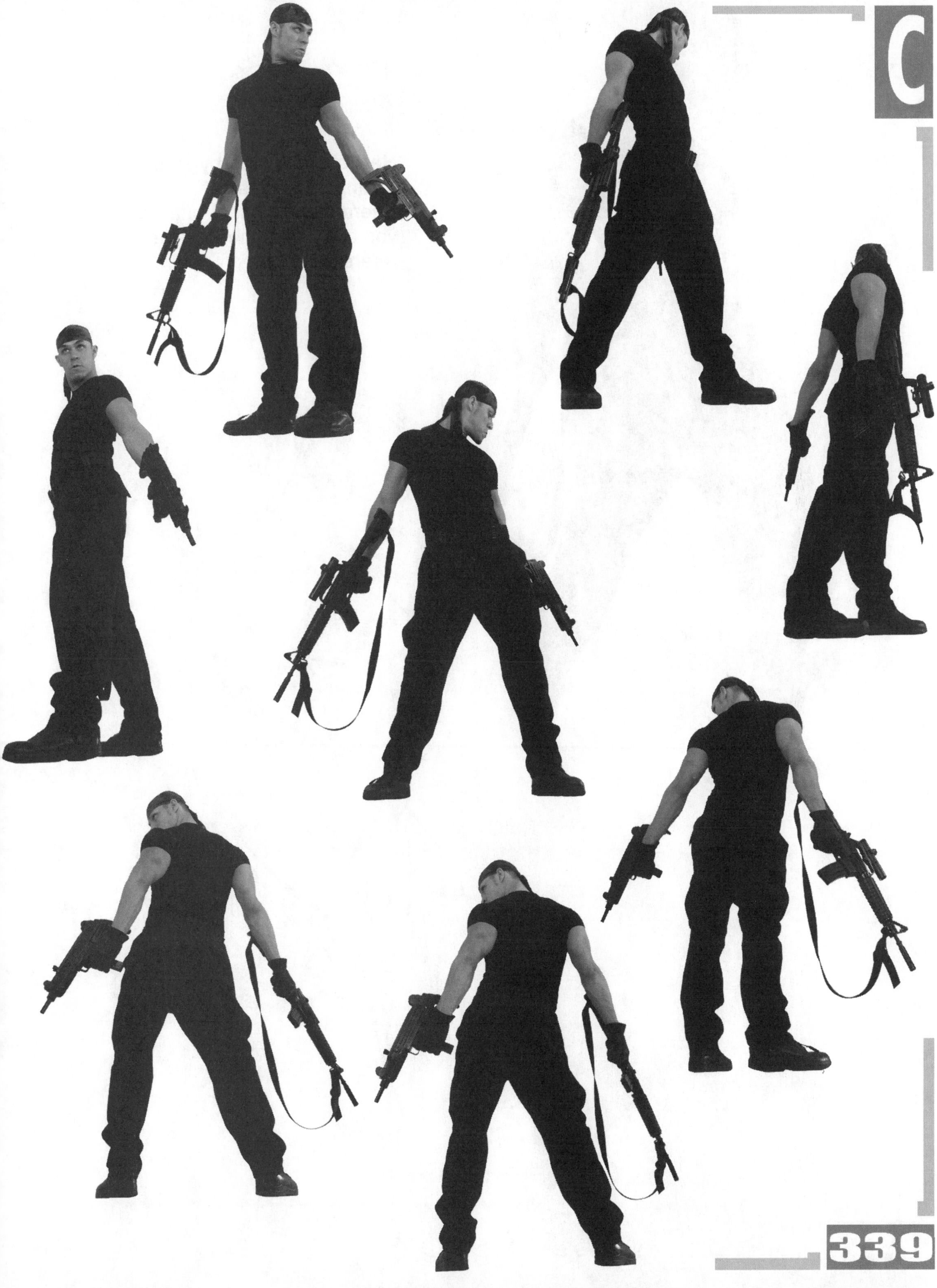

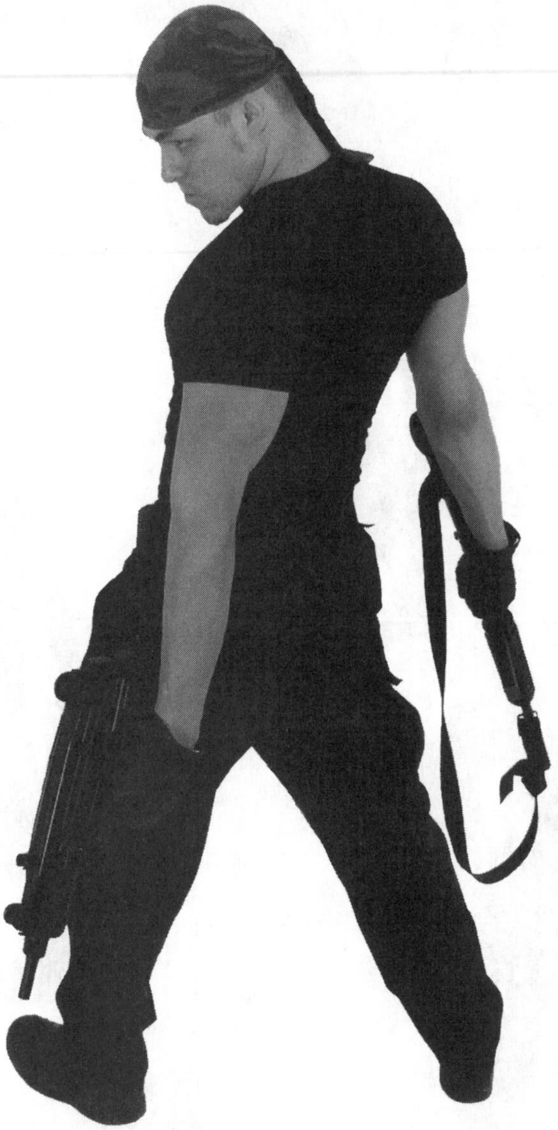

Here's a little step-by-step example, courtesy of Sherard Jackson, of one way you can utilize the Posefile reference.

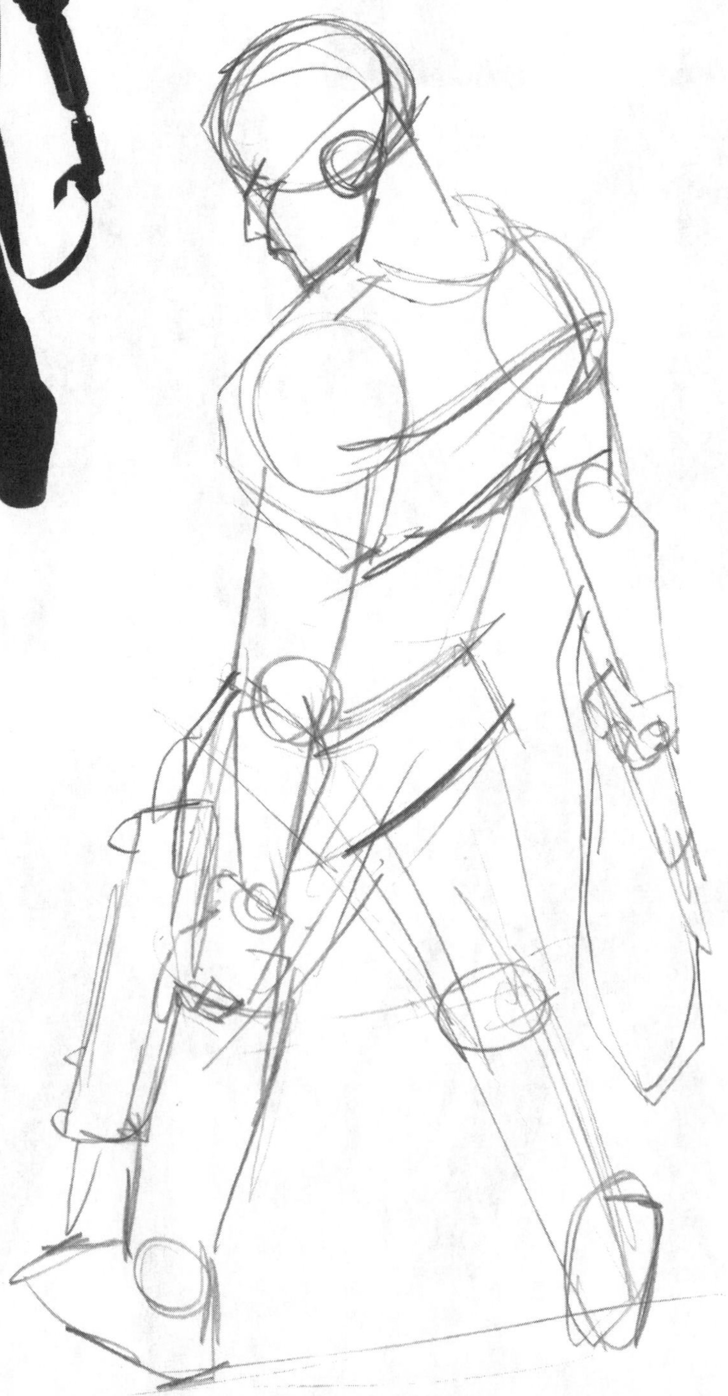

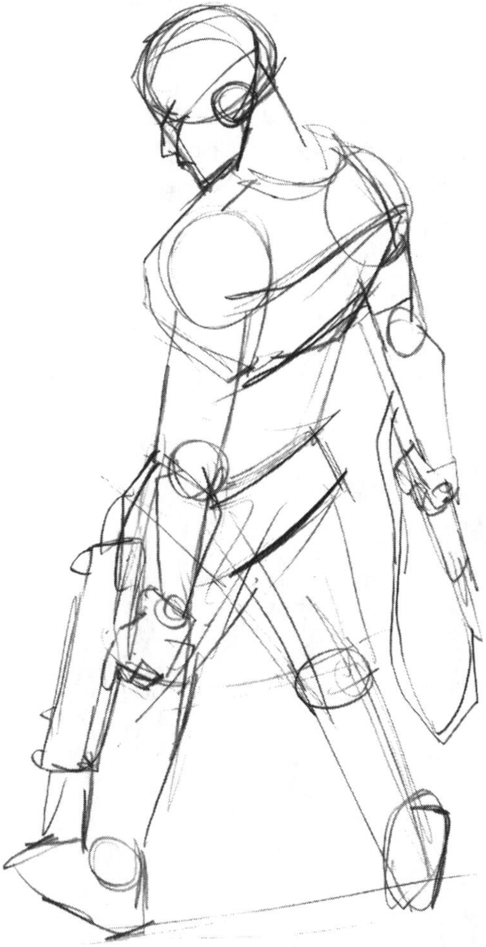

You can see how accessories are added to the figure to create the basic structure of his robot.

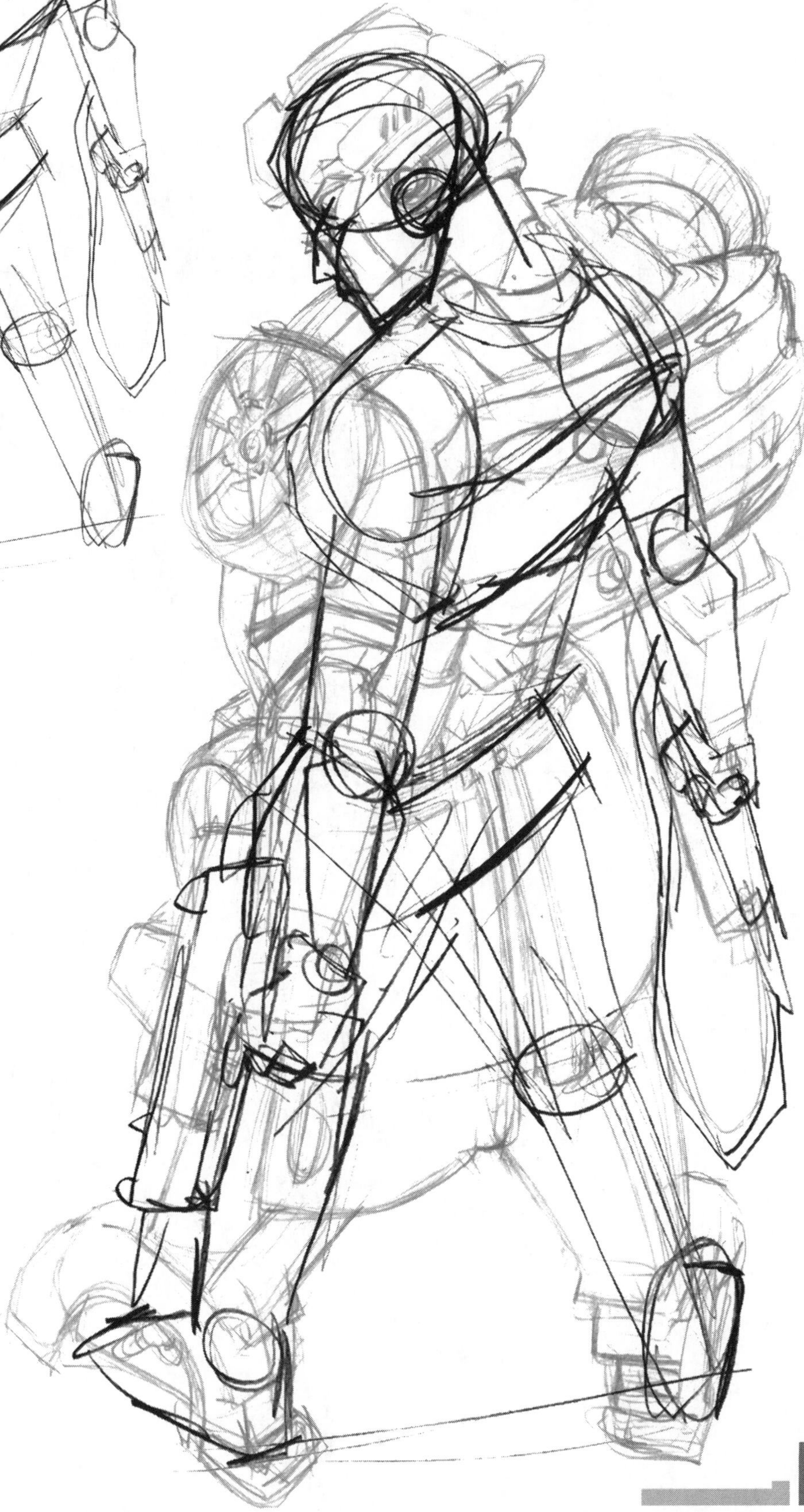

Further steps are taken to define the structure and details are starting to be added.

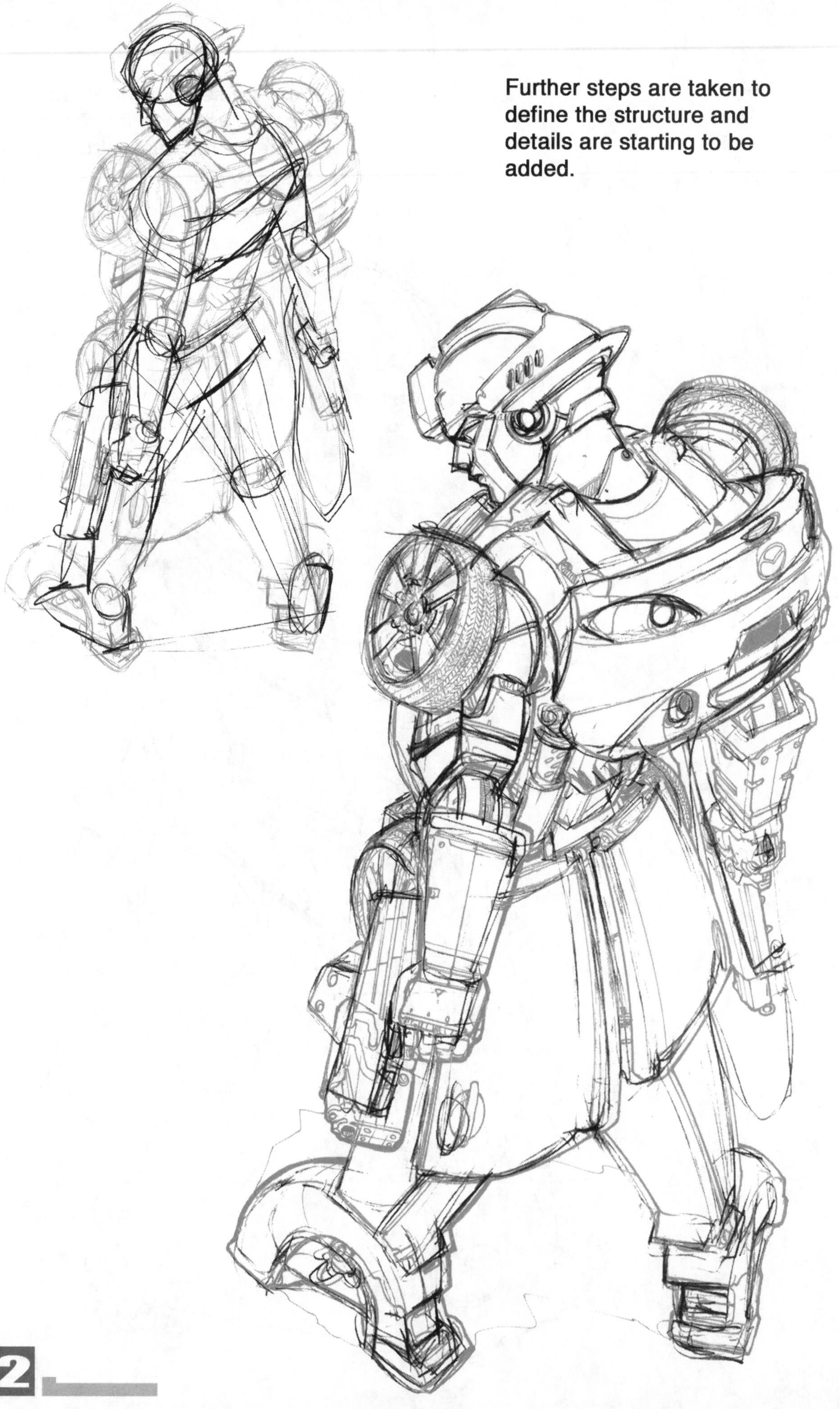

That's cool, right?

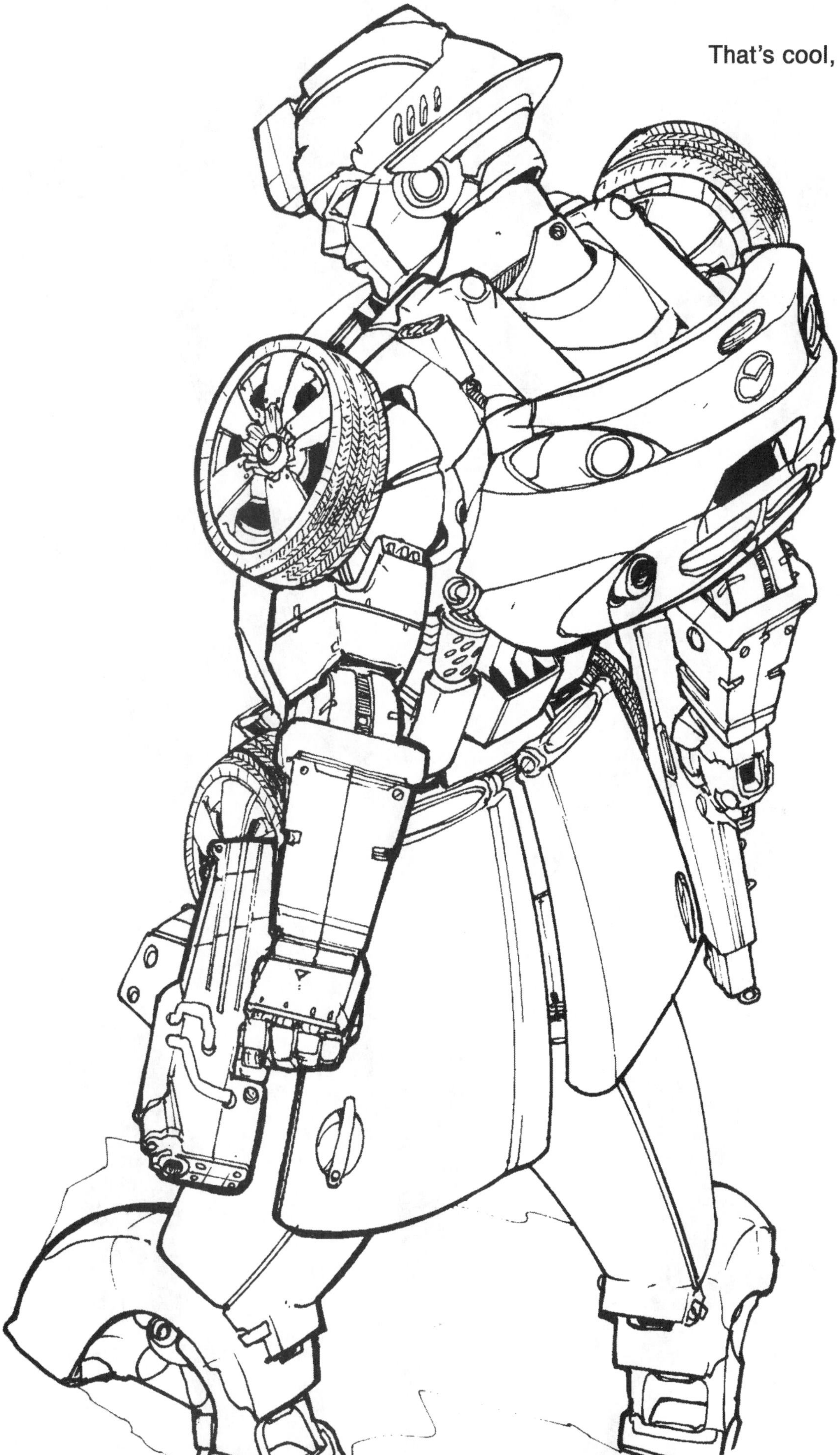

Art by Sherard Jackson

A

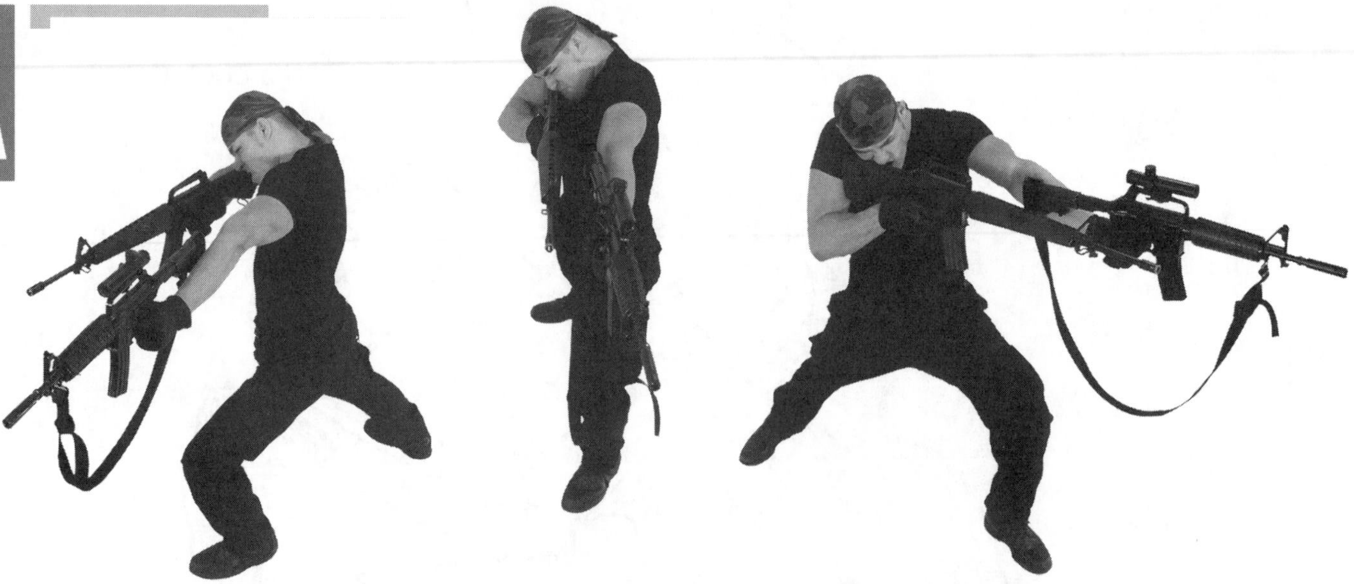

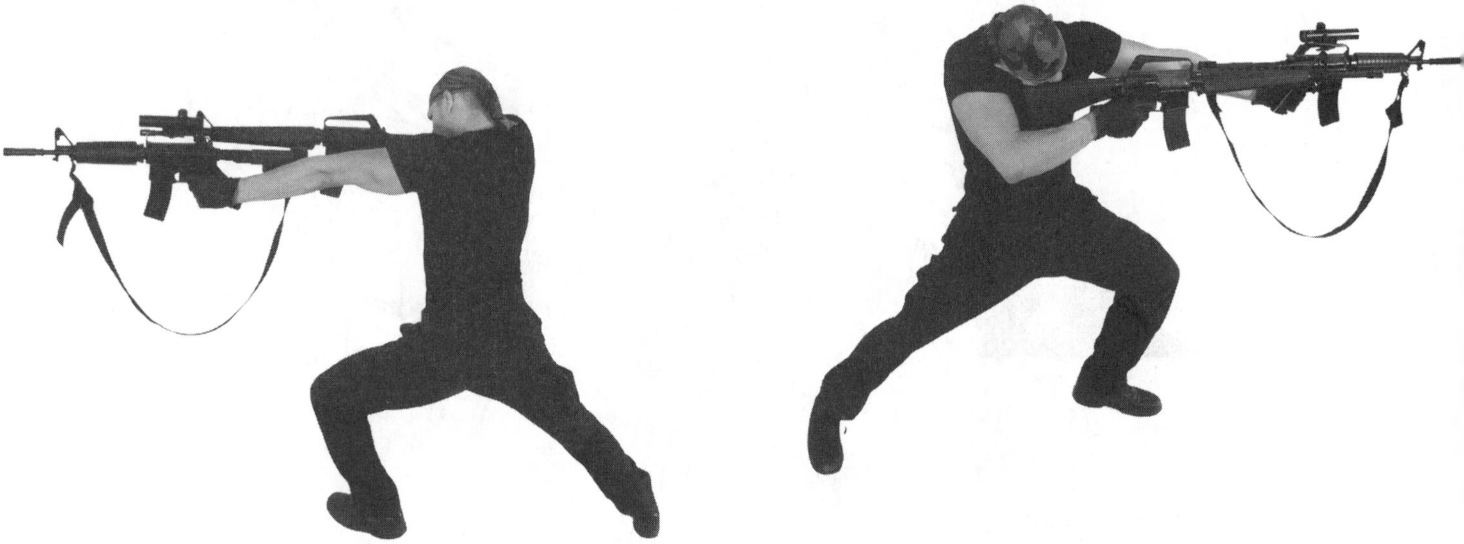

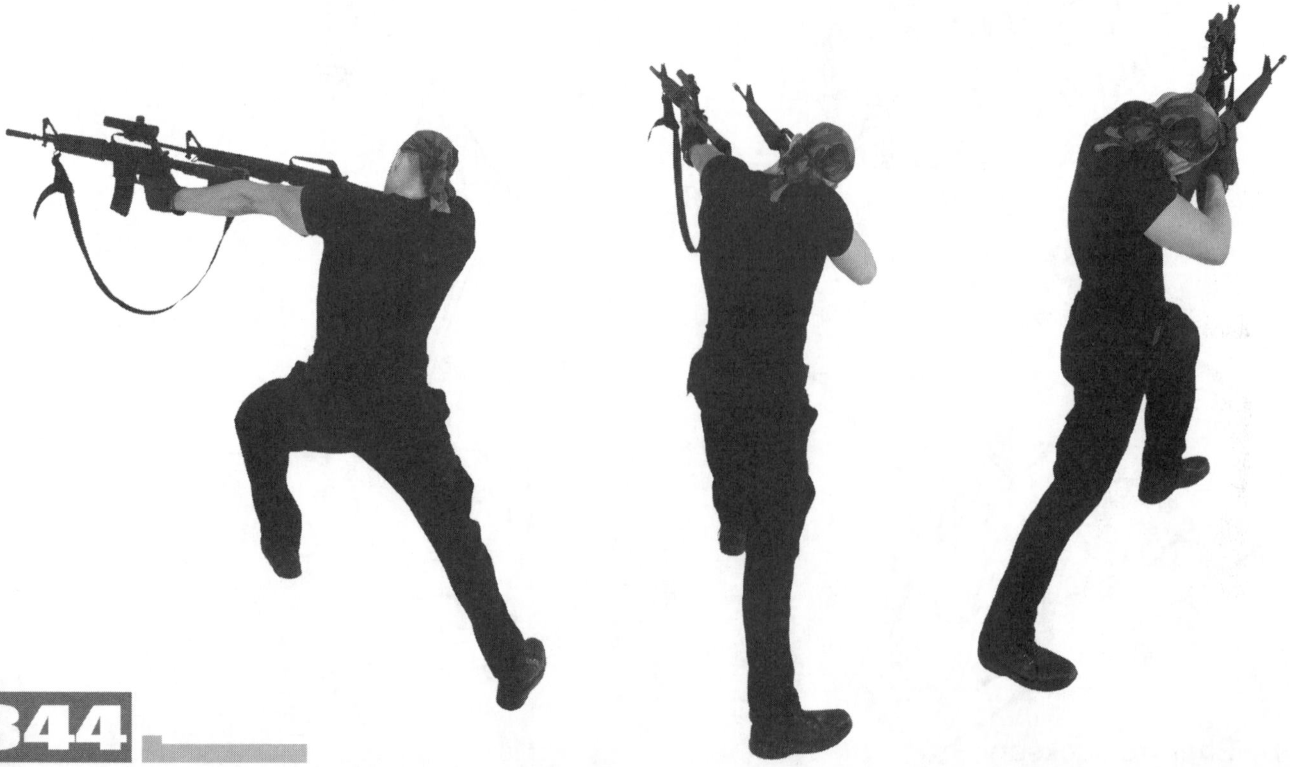

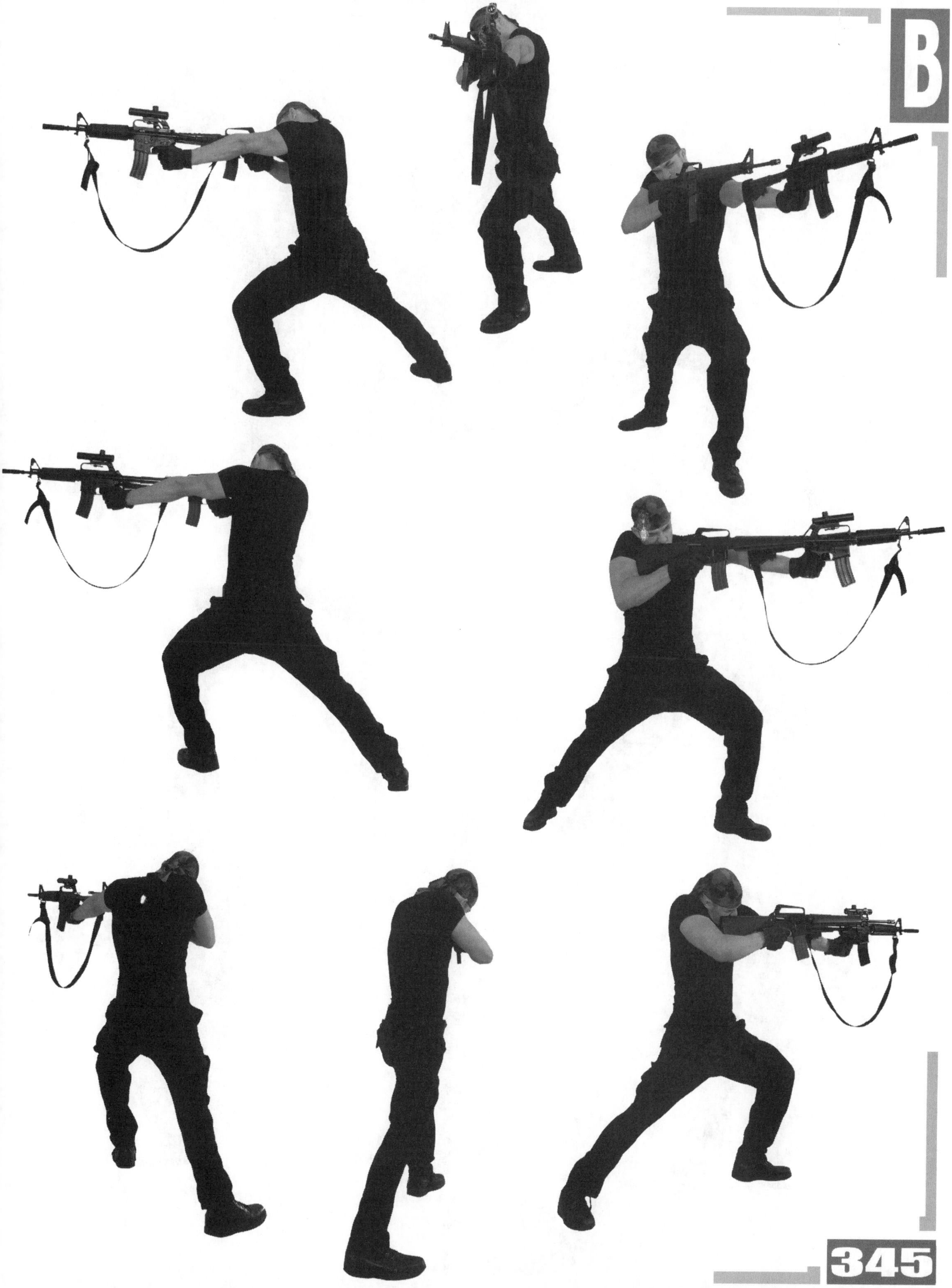

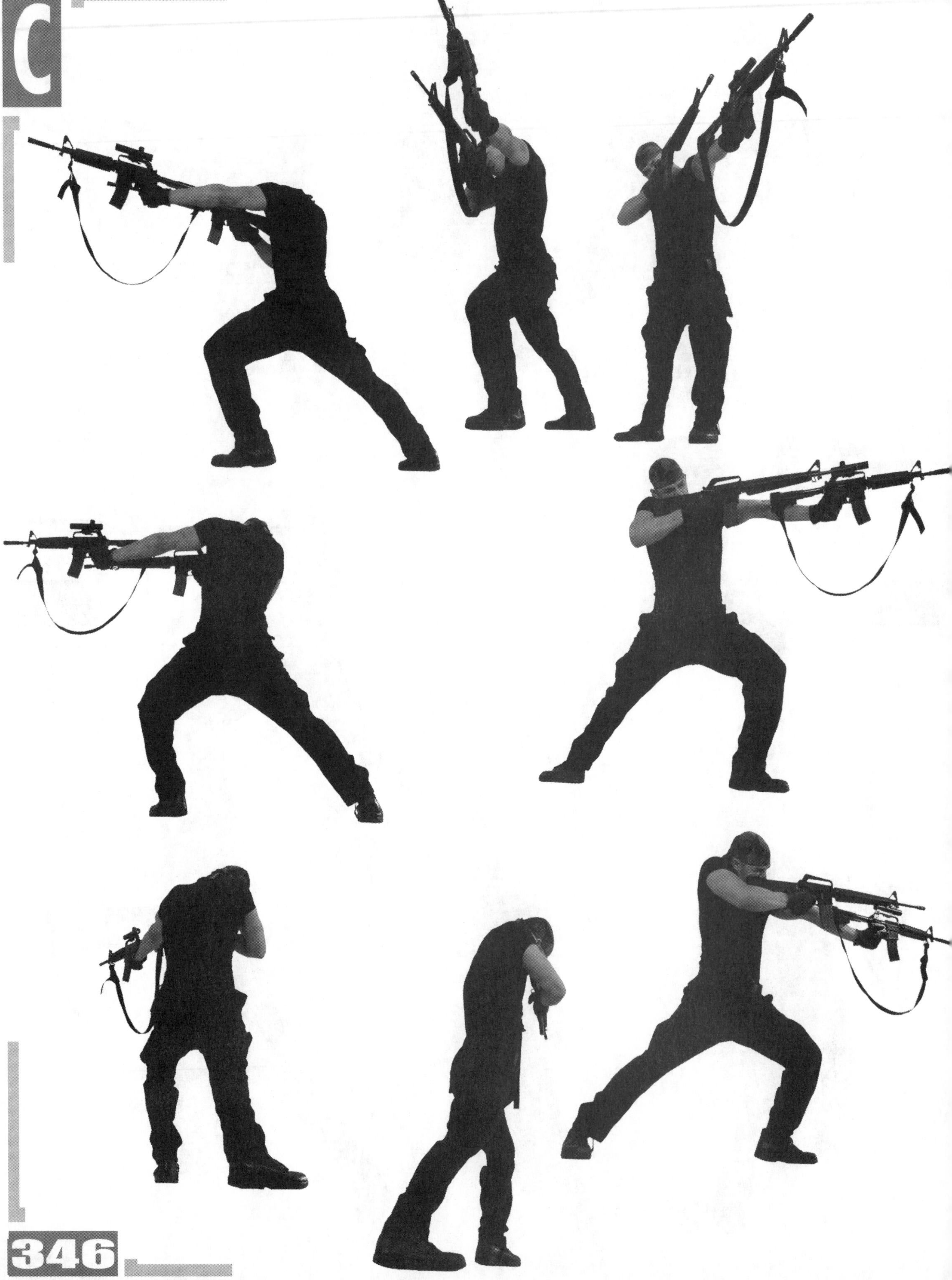

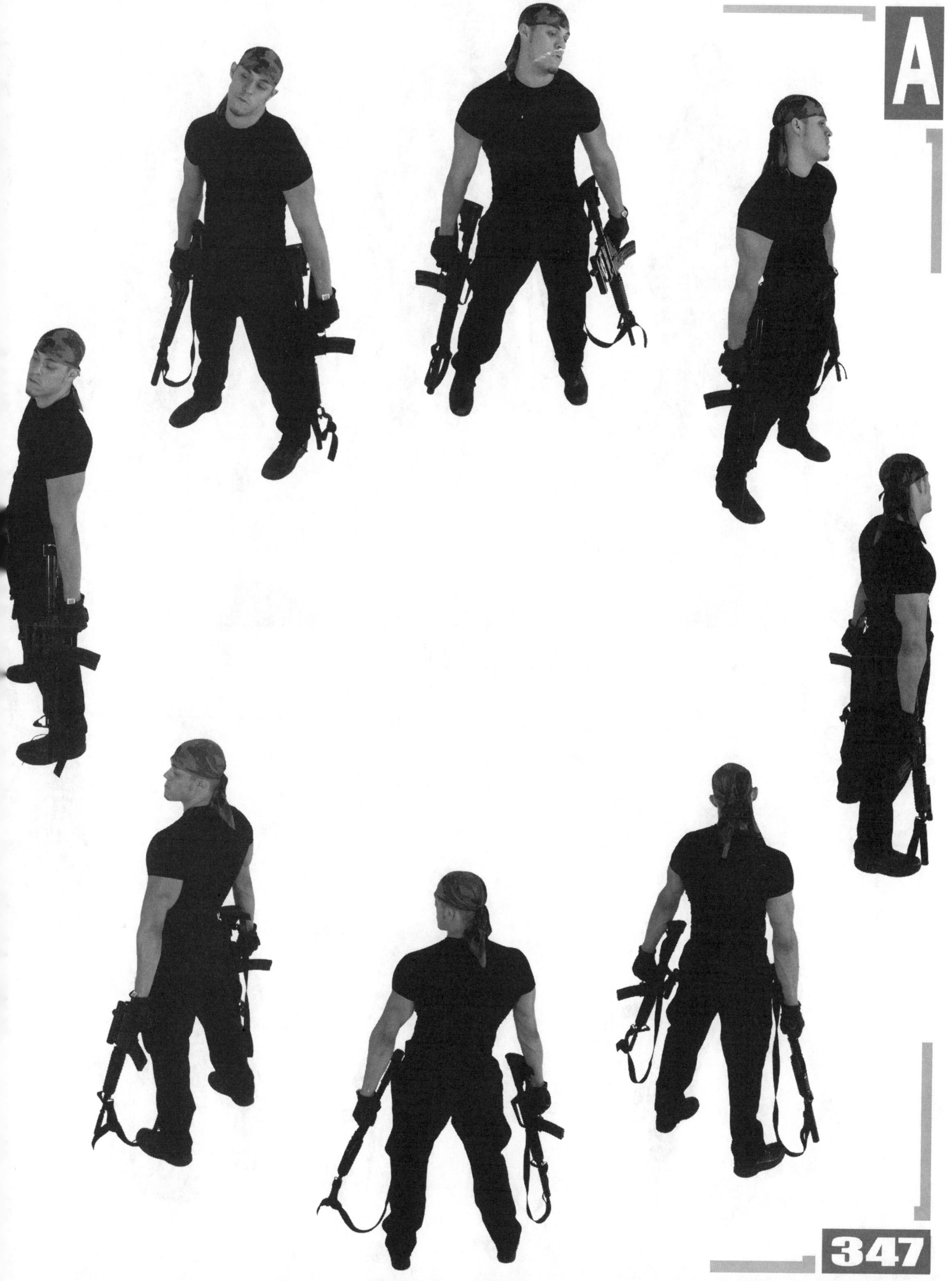

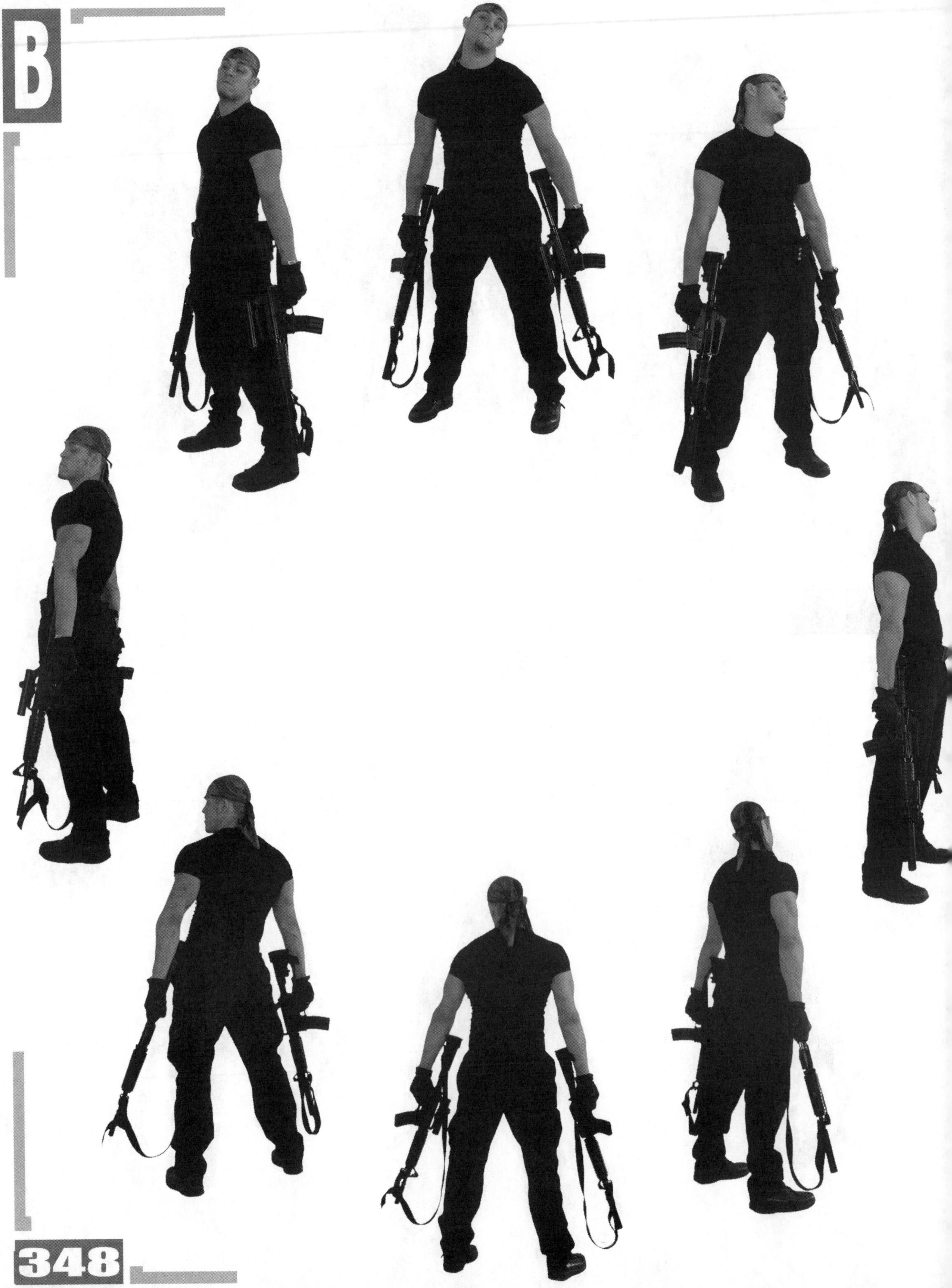

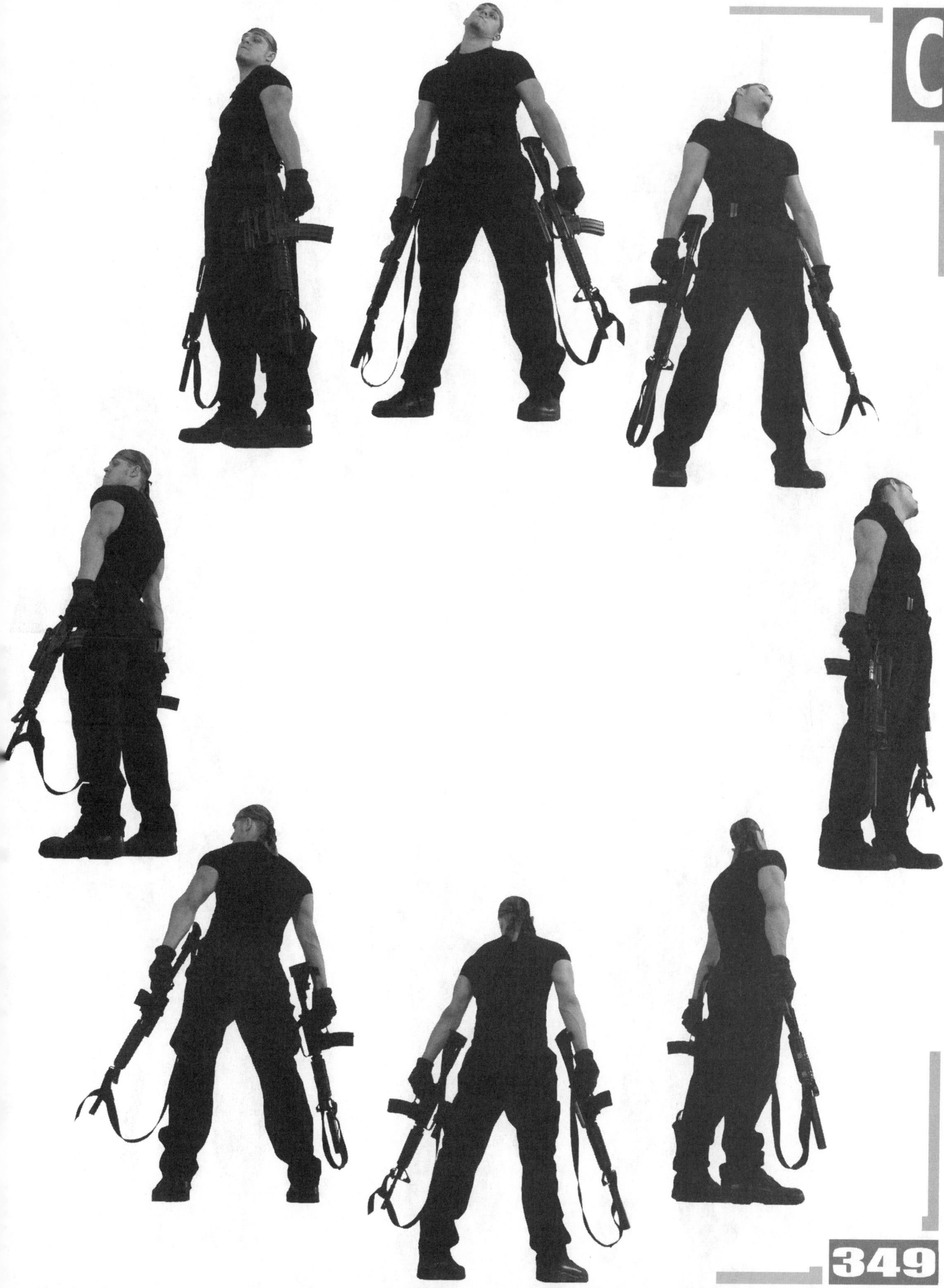

A

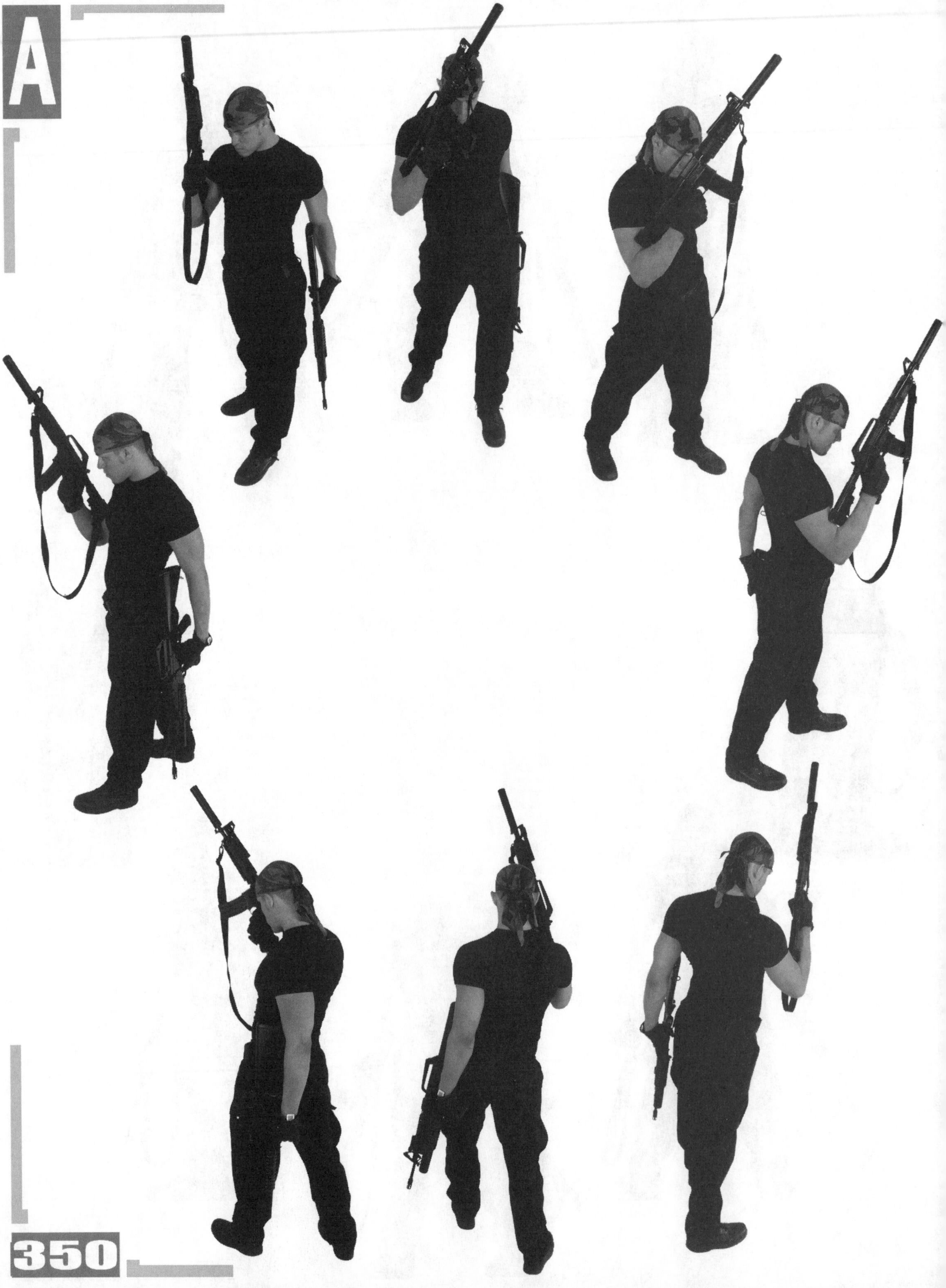

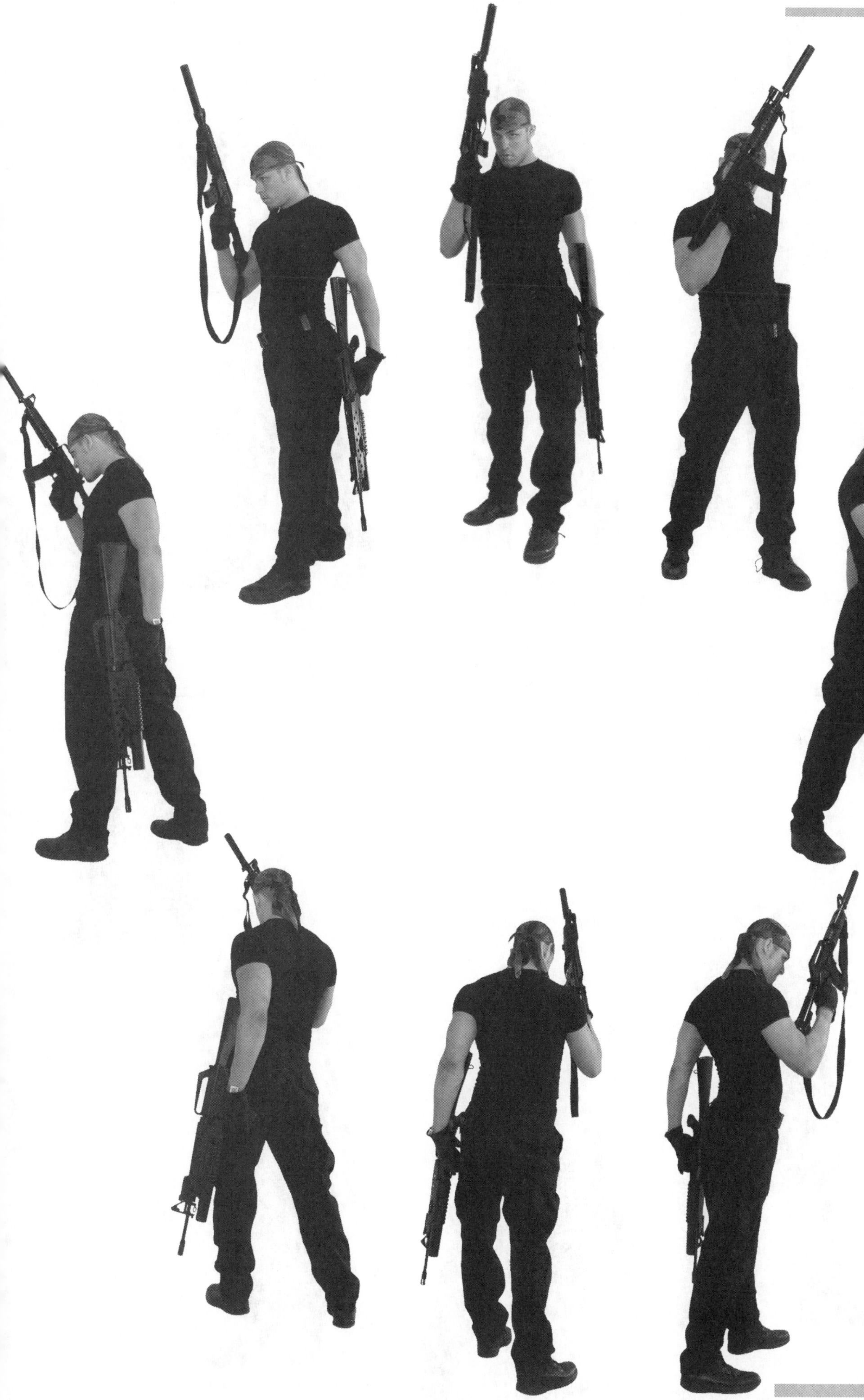

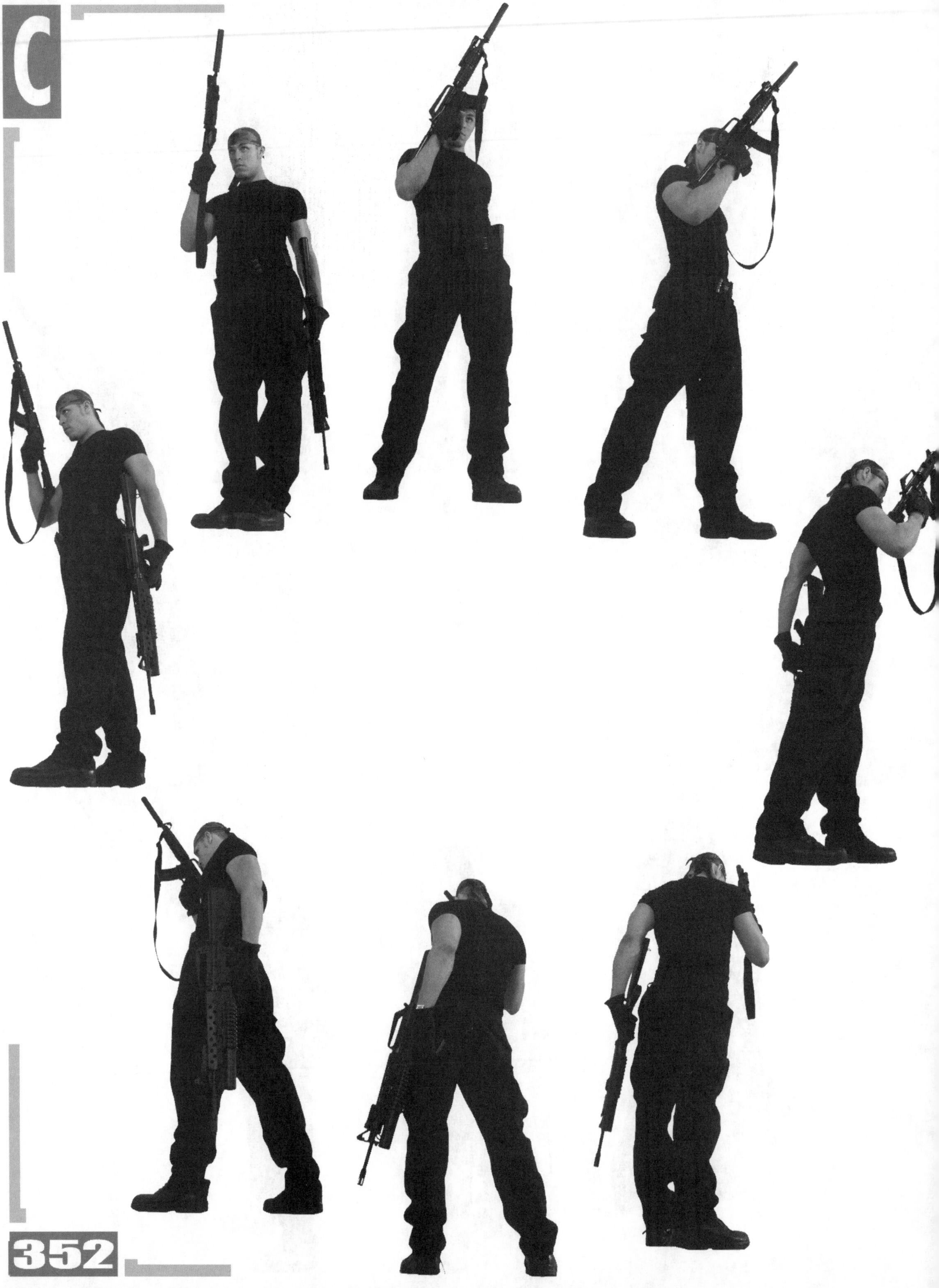

With a printout or a xerox
copy, a light box can be used
to lay down your rough
pencils.

From your initial sketch, your pencils can be refined and inked to get the desired look and feel of your character. Of course, once your image is inked, you can always go in and give it a little sumthin'-sumthin'.

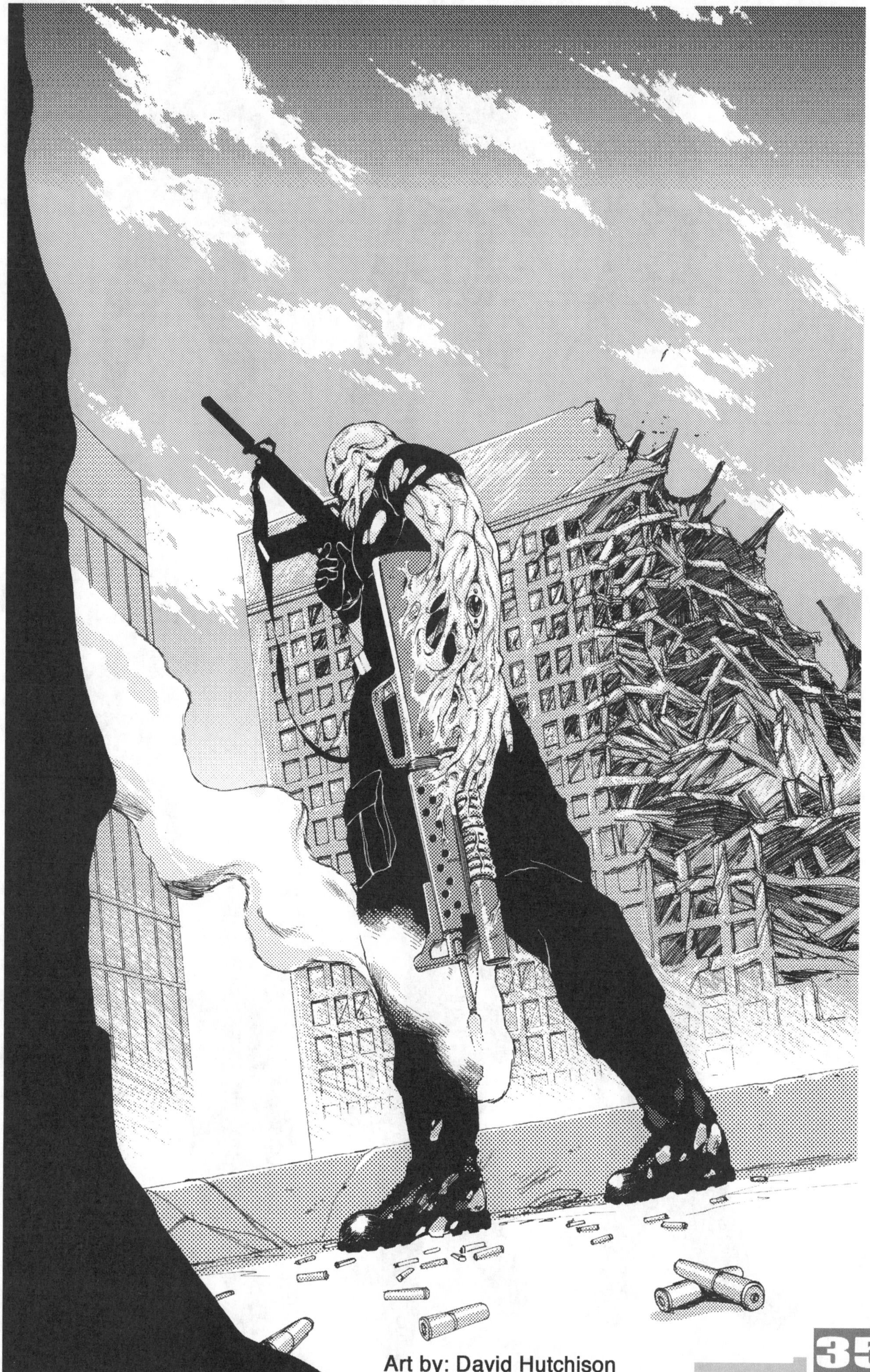

Art by: David Hutchison

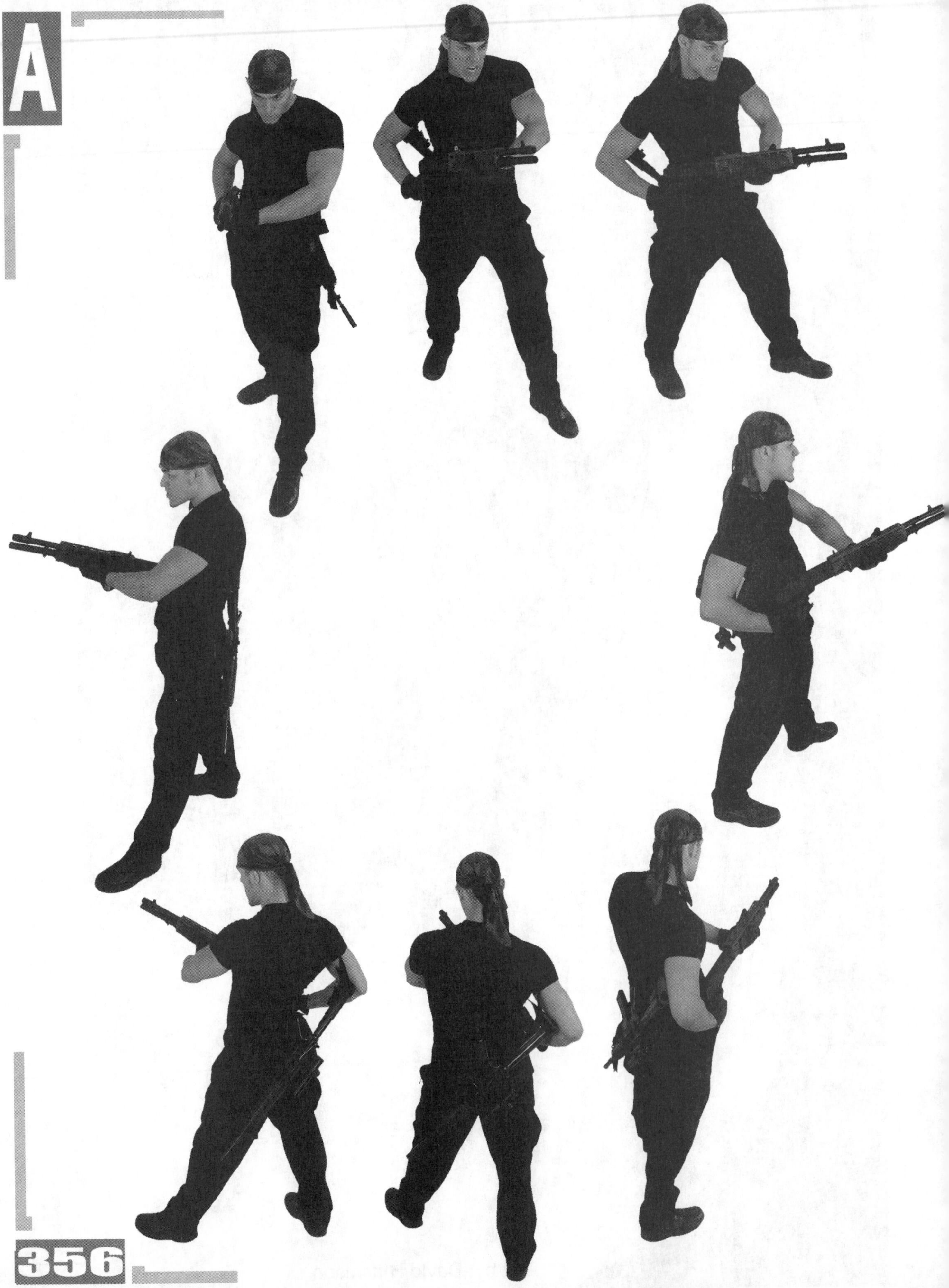

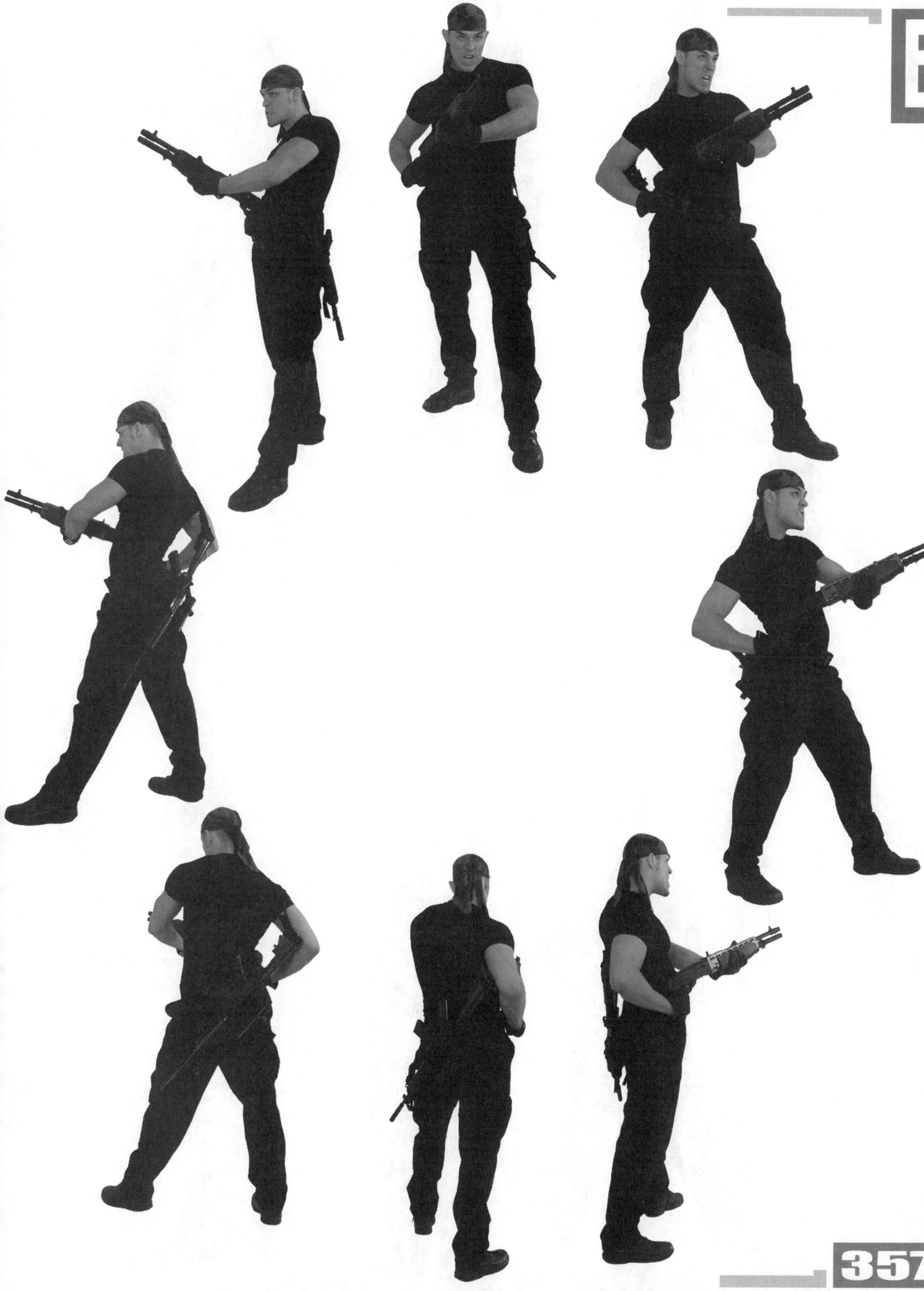

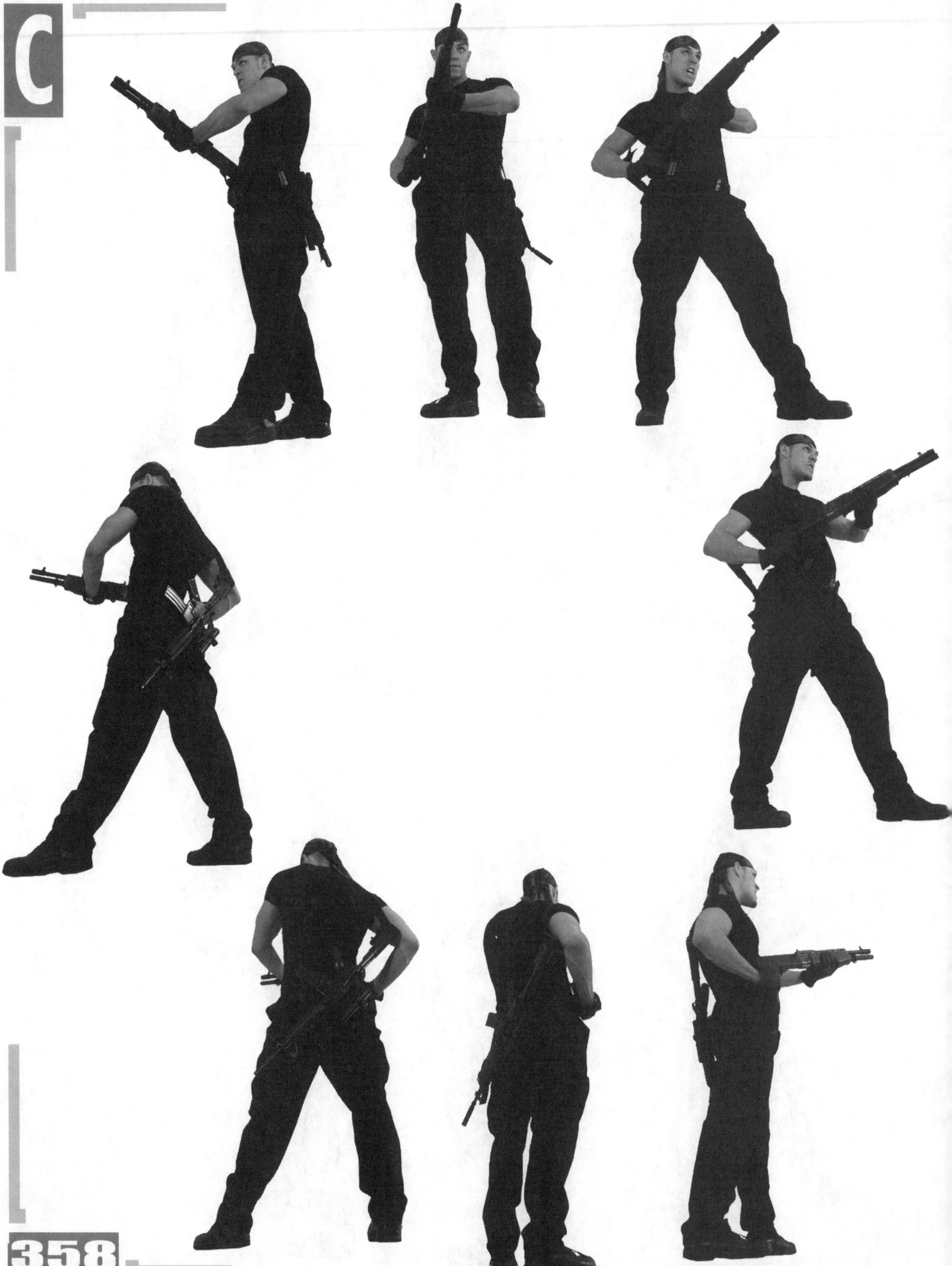

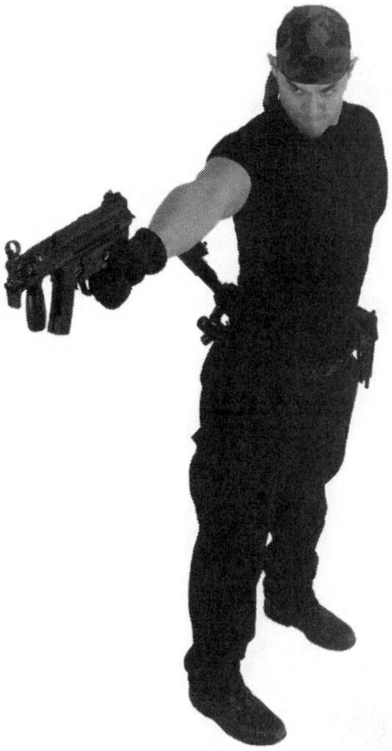

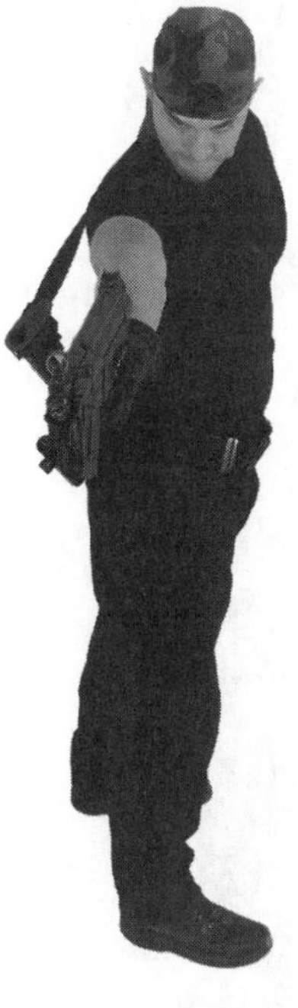

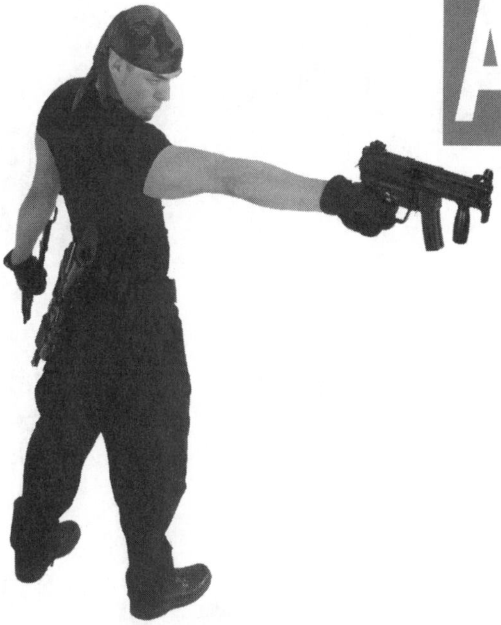

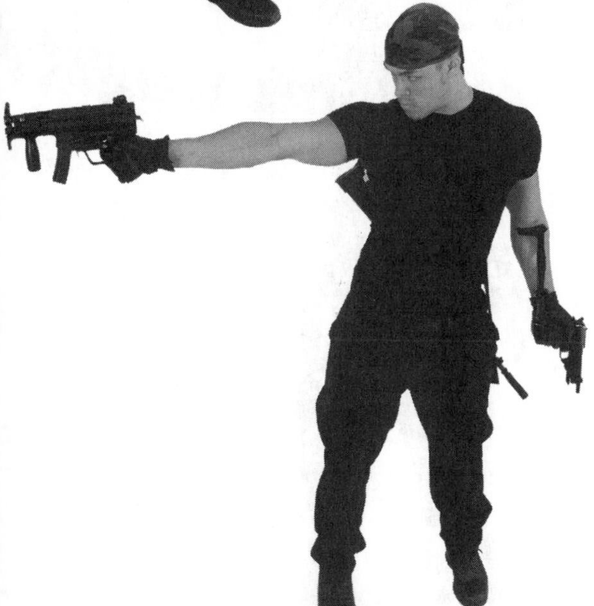

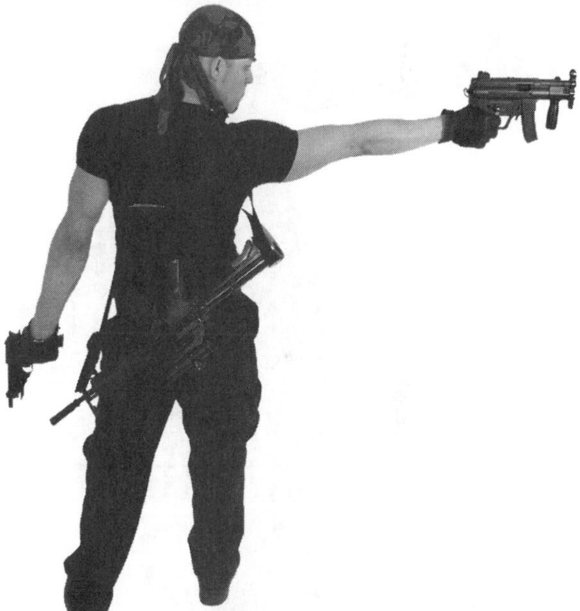

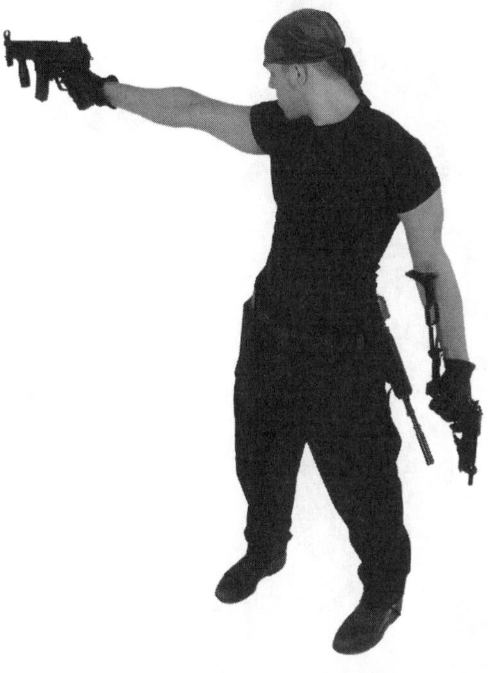

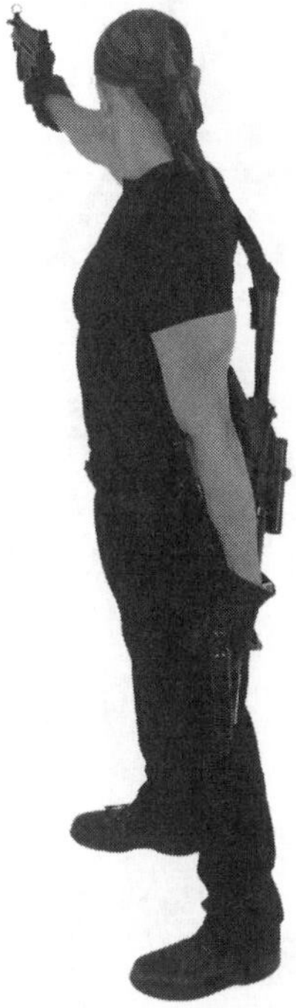

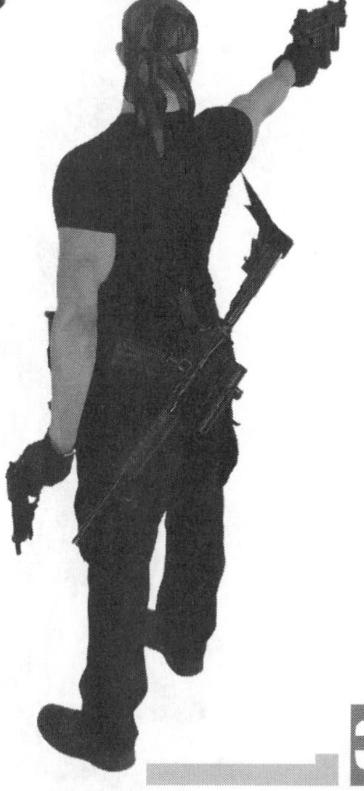

B

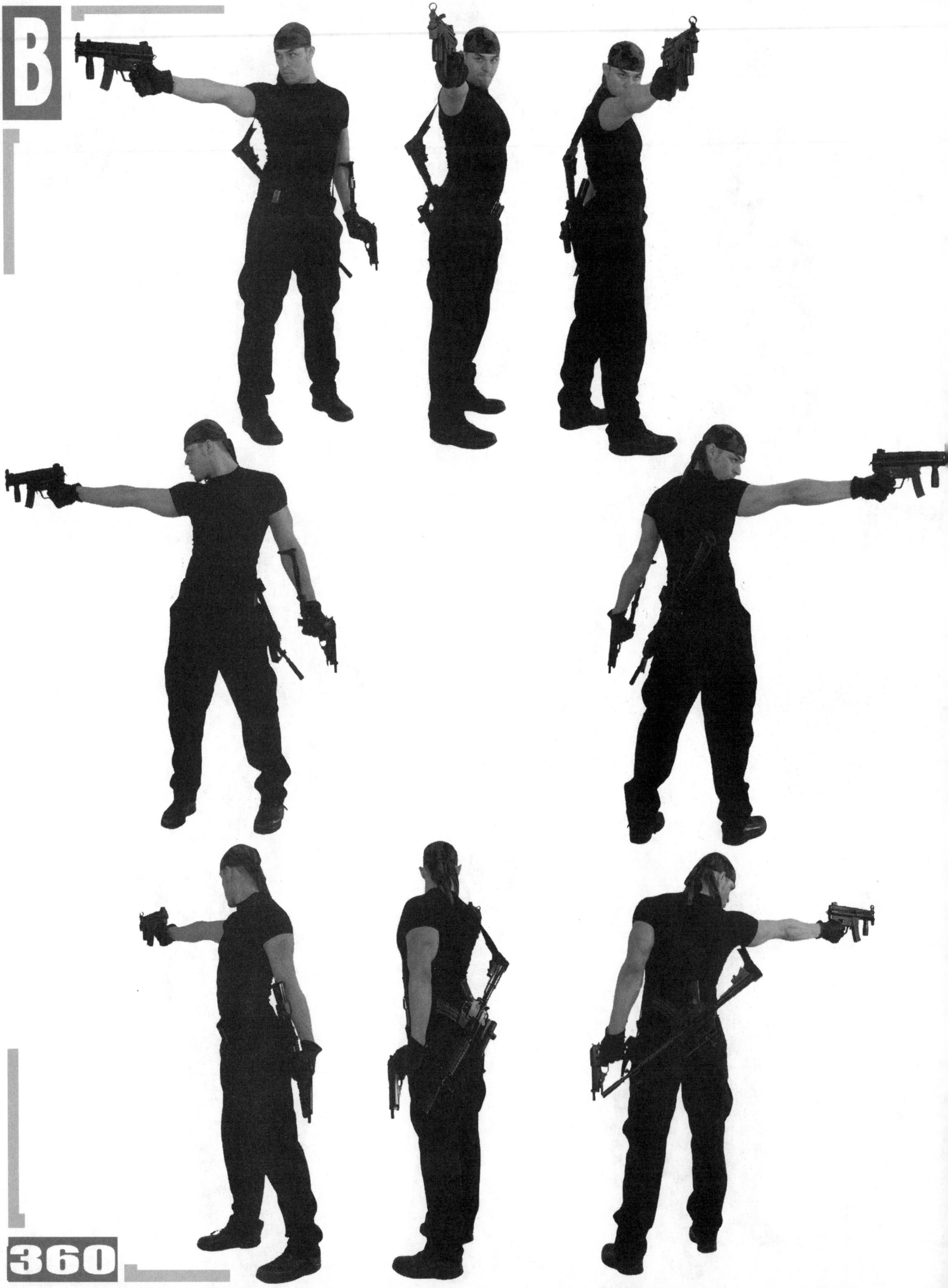

360

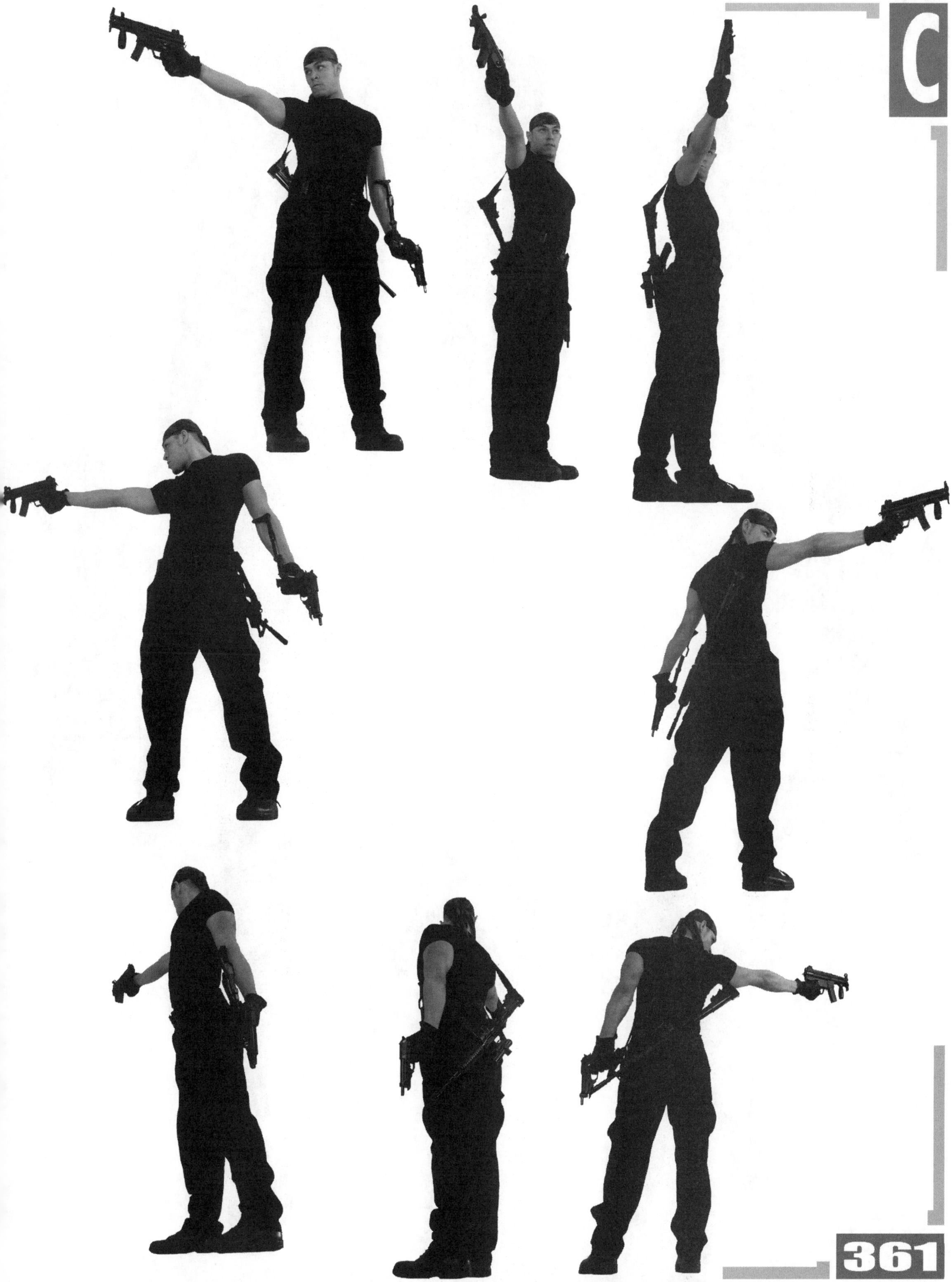

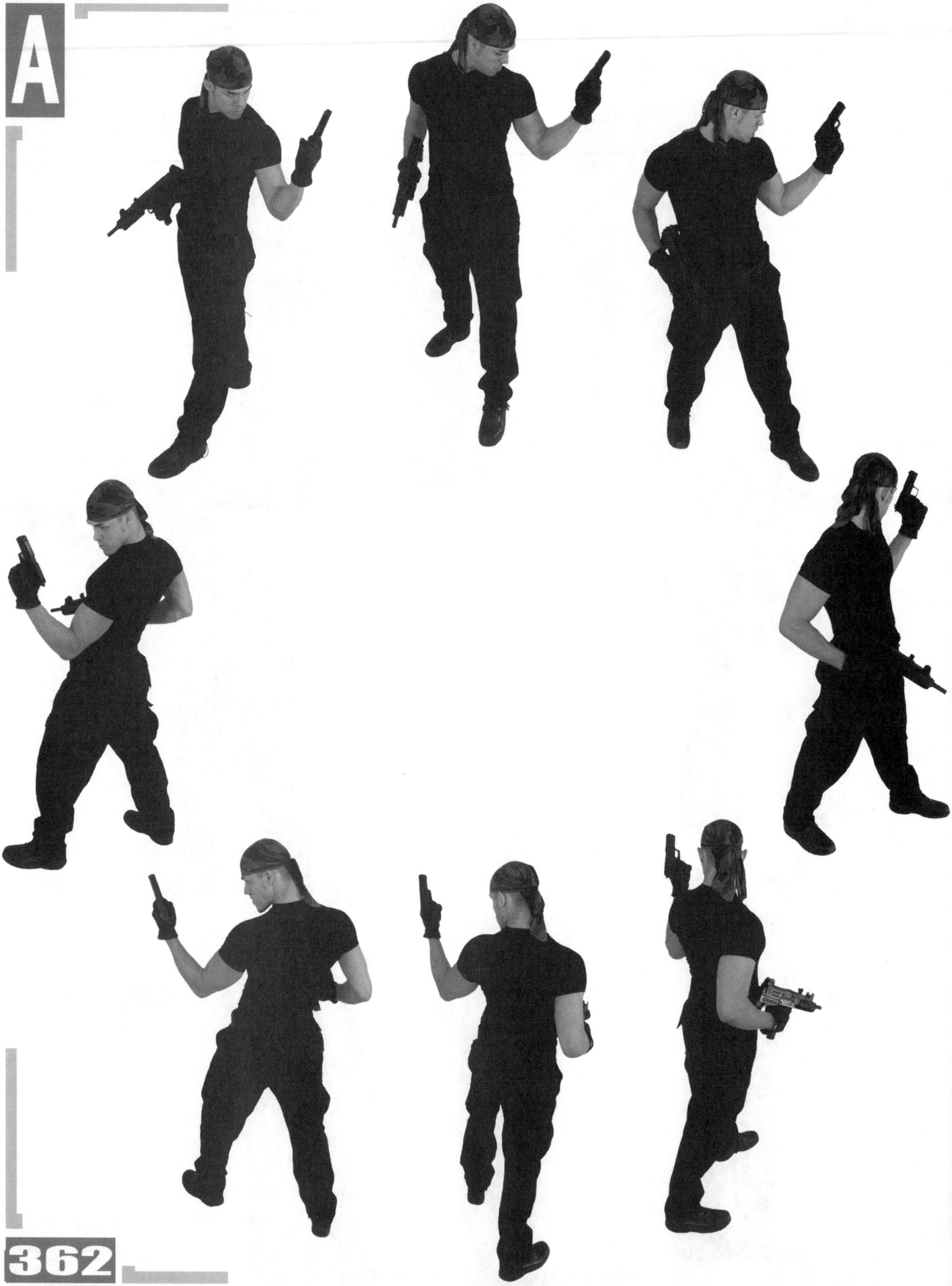

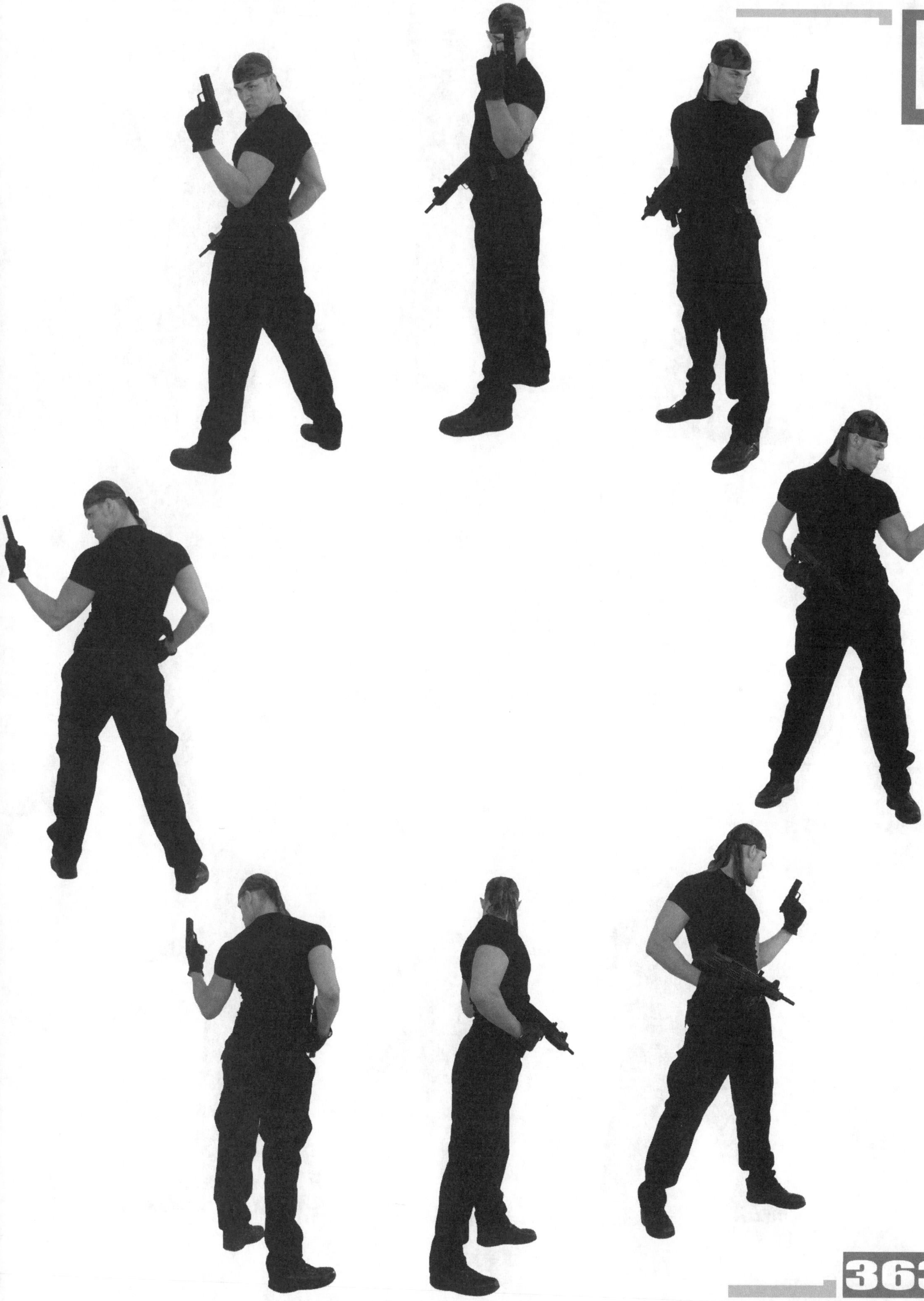

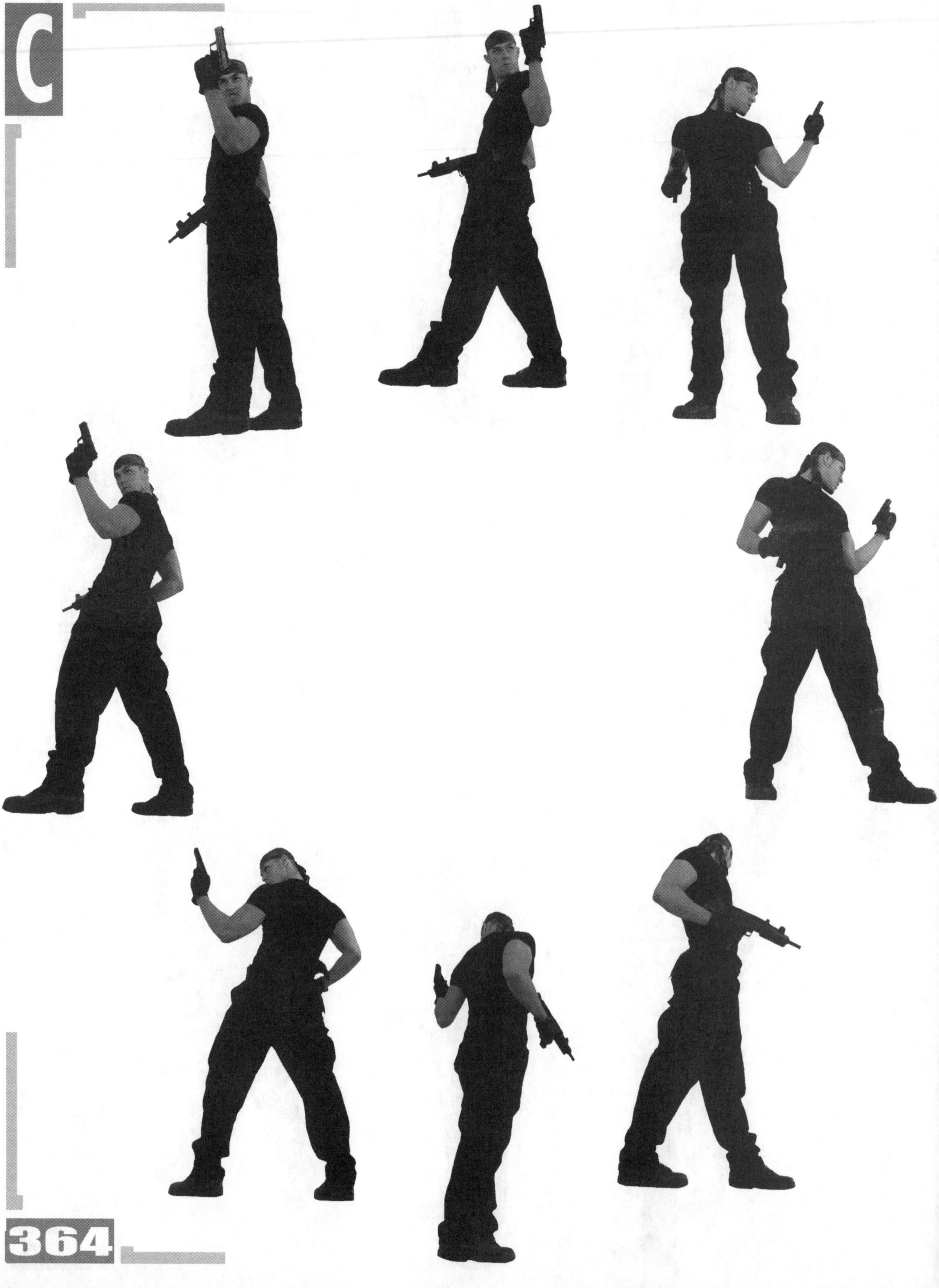

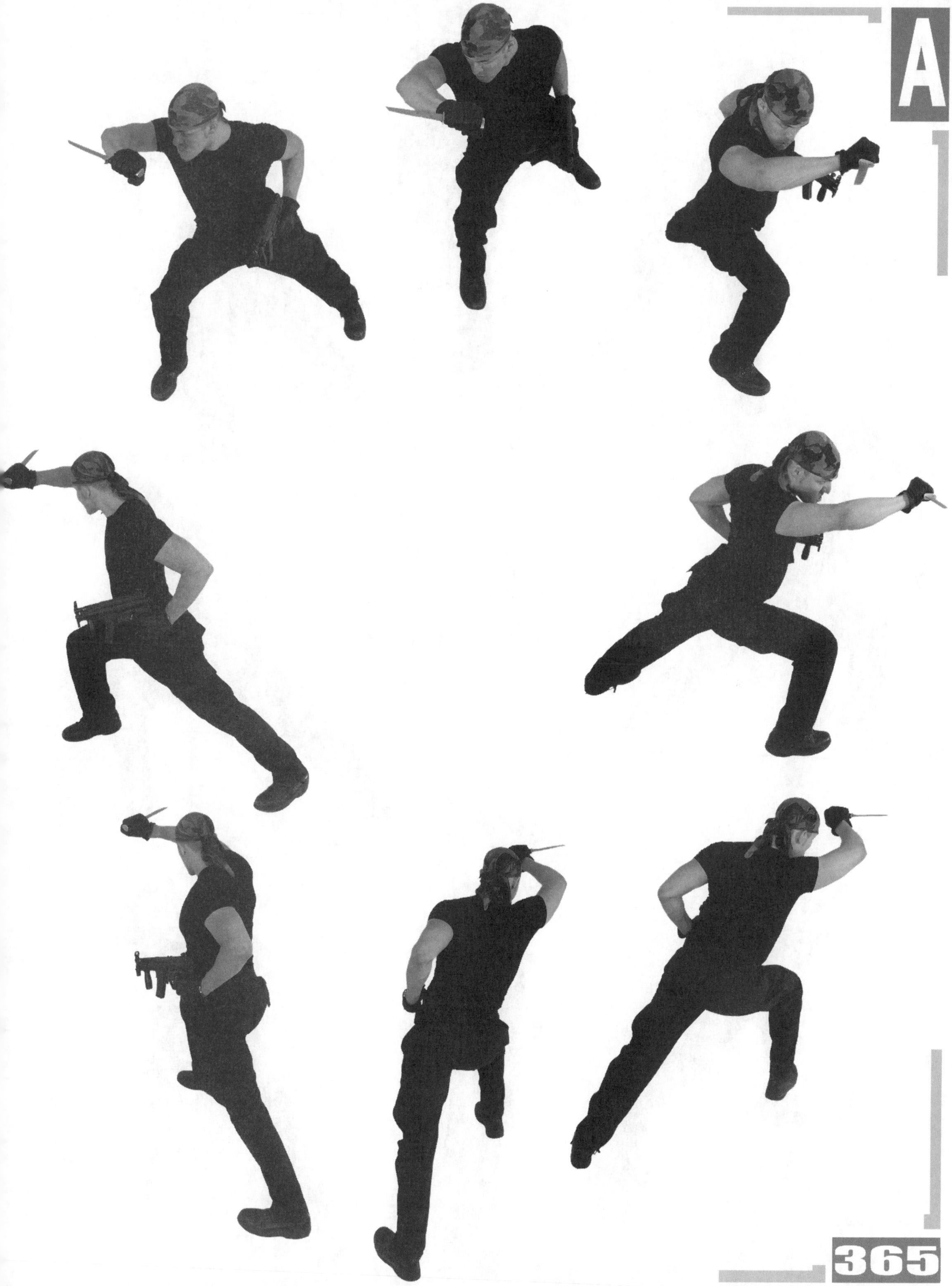

B

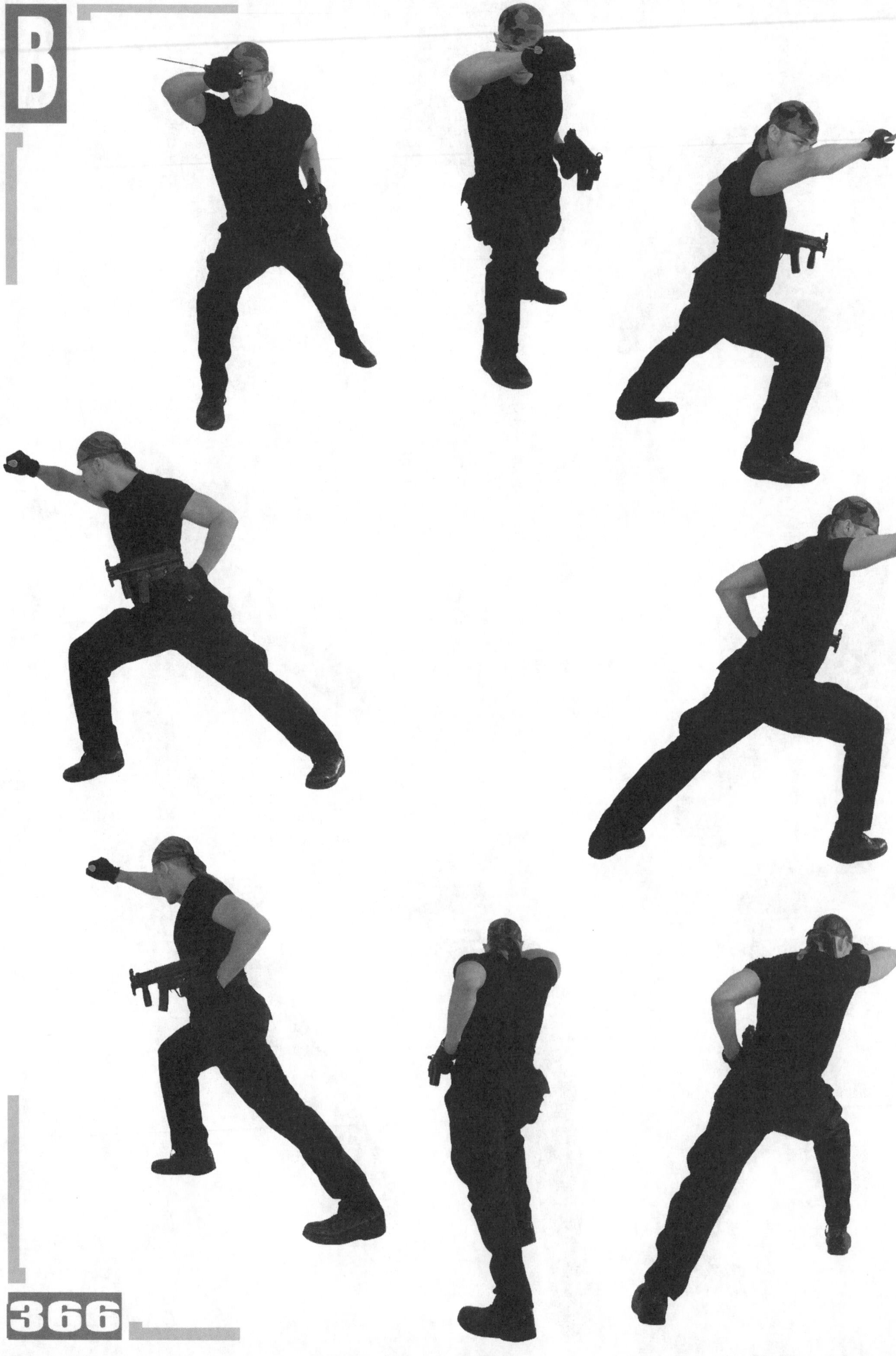

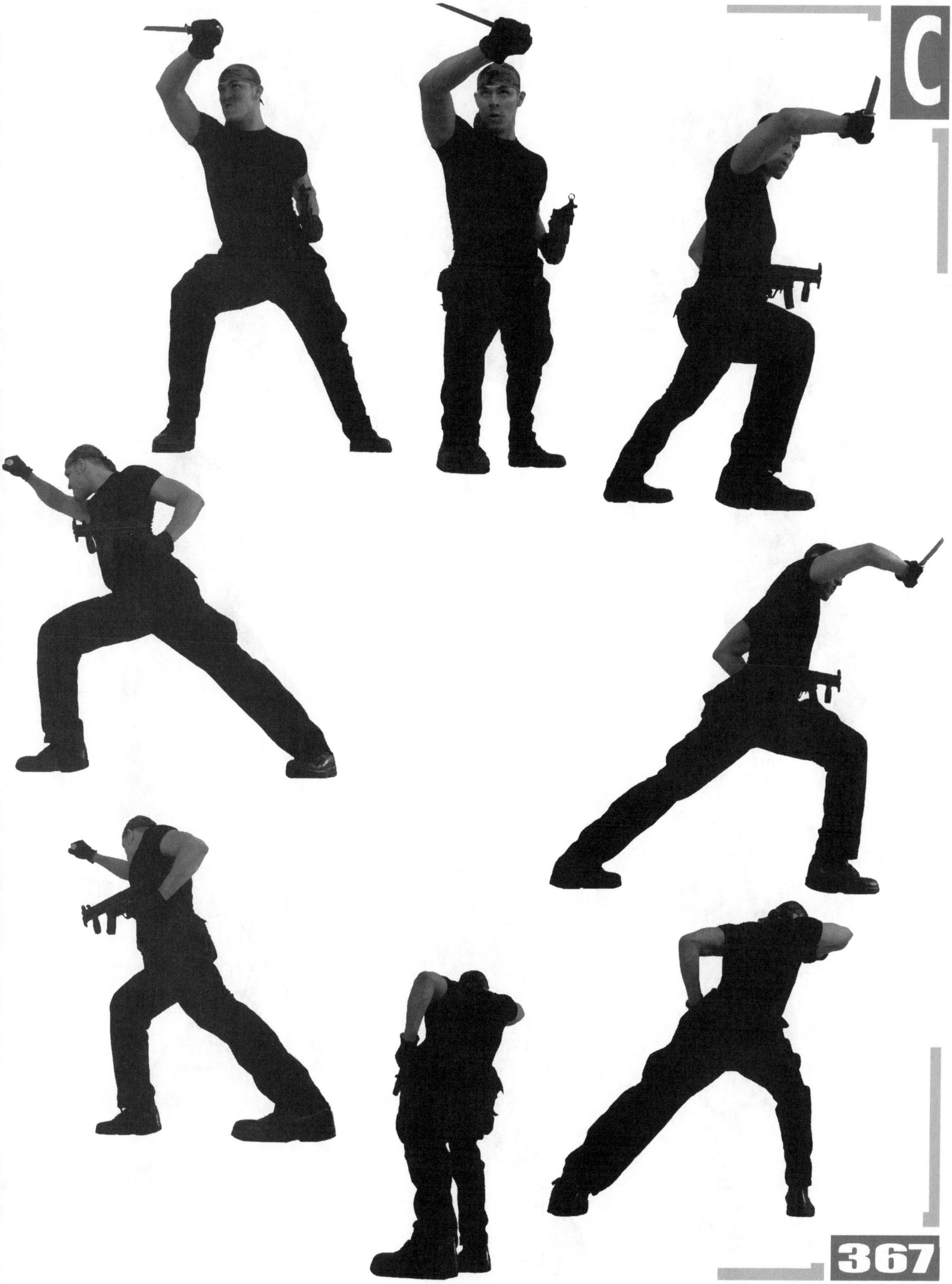

A

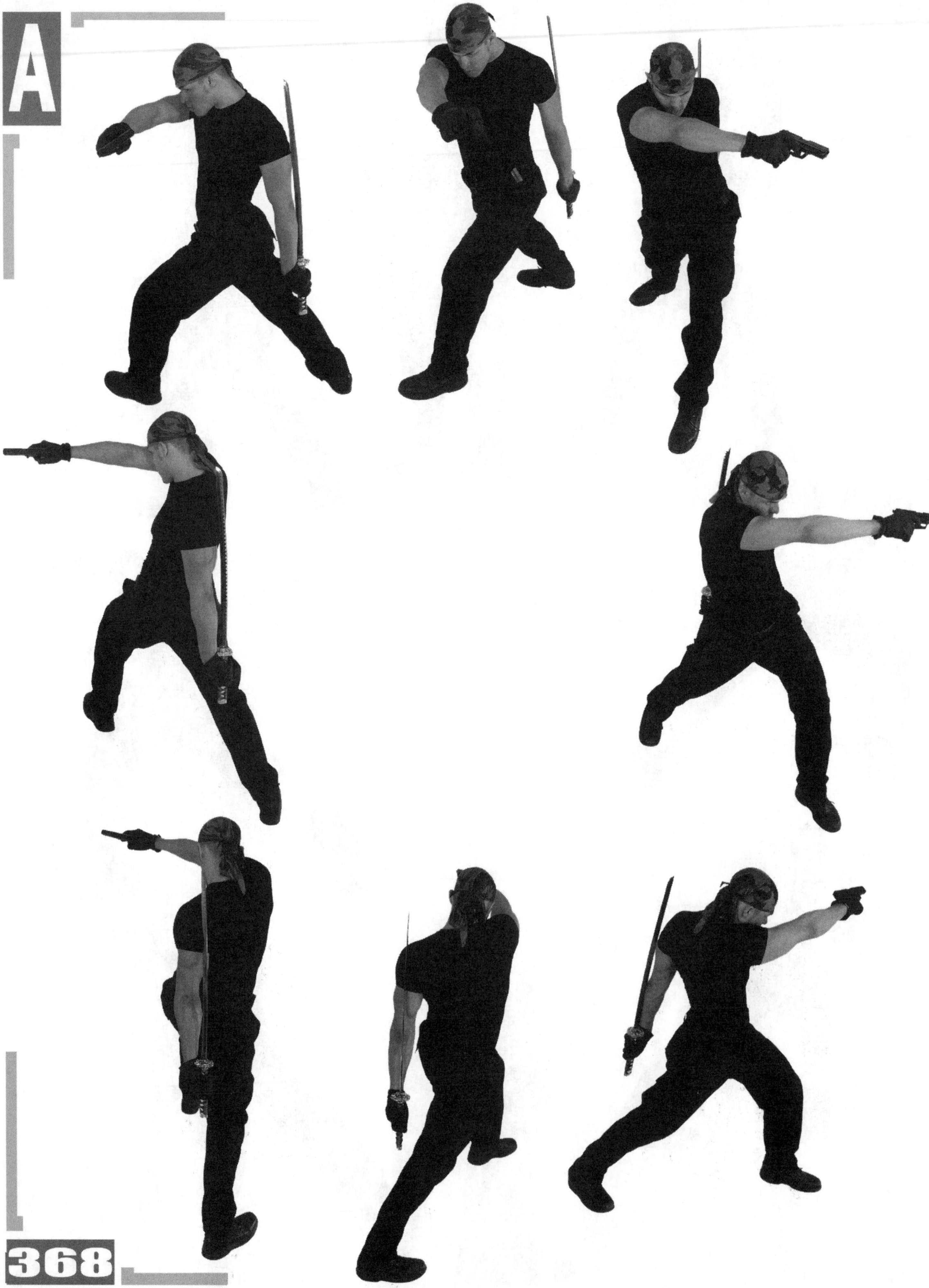

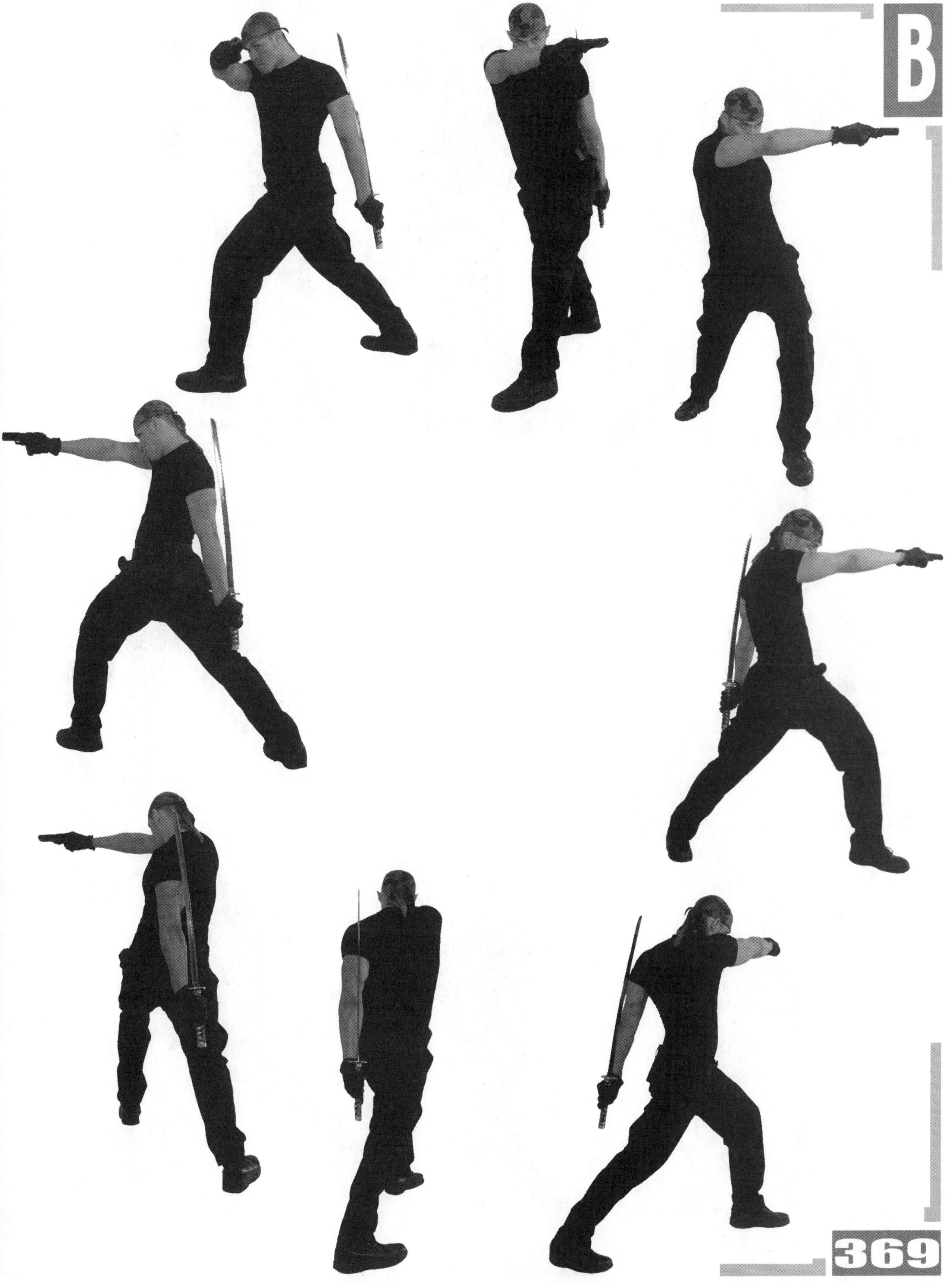

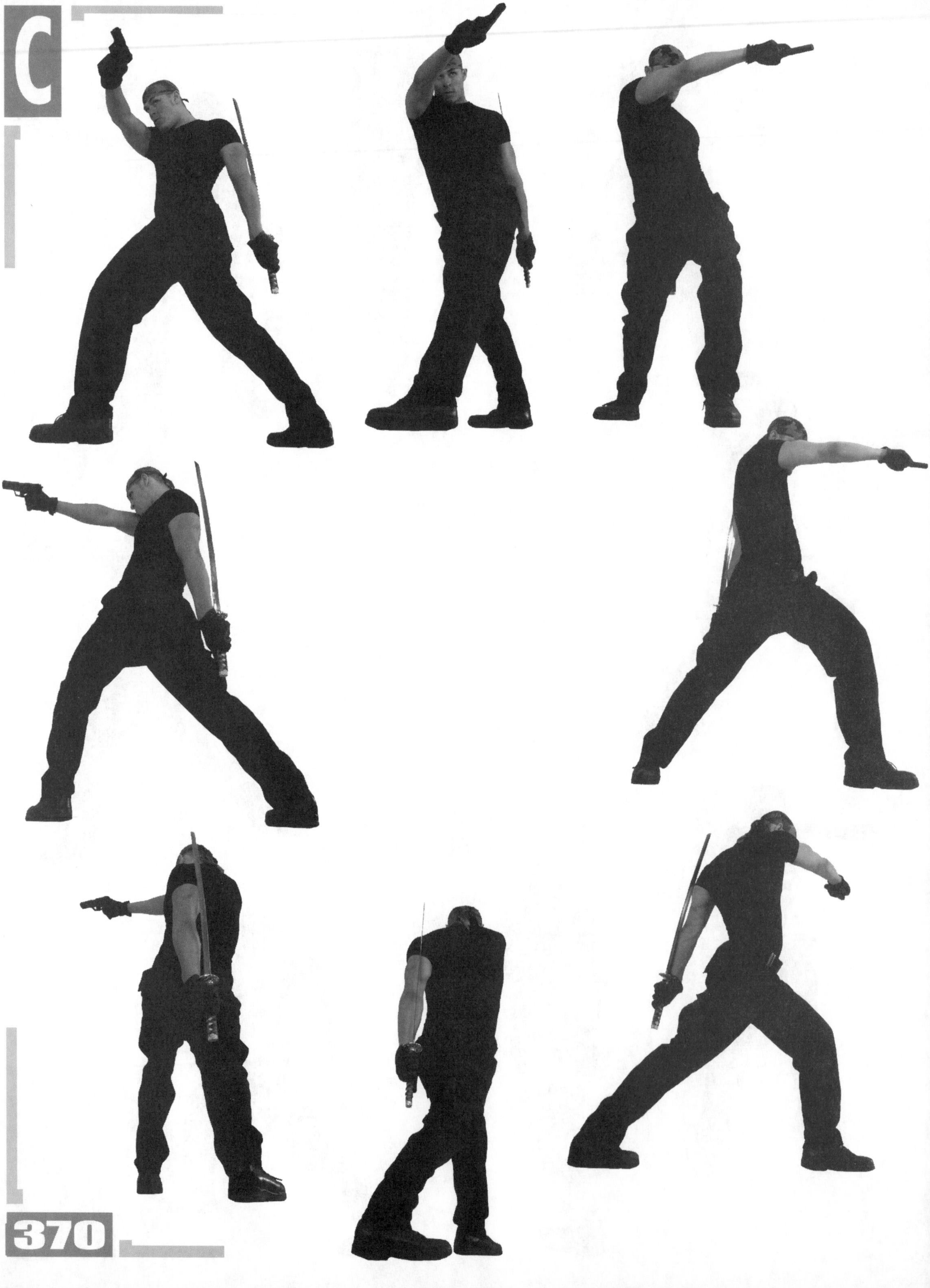

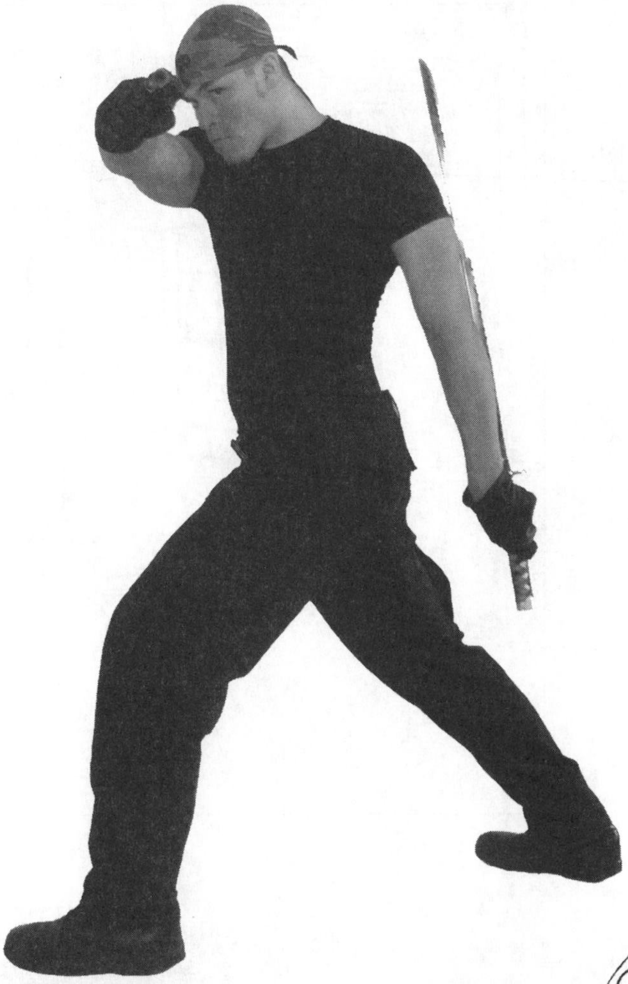

As this example shows, the clothes don't always make the man. Because the reference may not look exactly like what you're trying to do, use that artistic side and change it to your heart's content. It is just a starting point, after all.

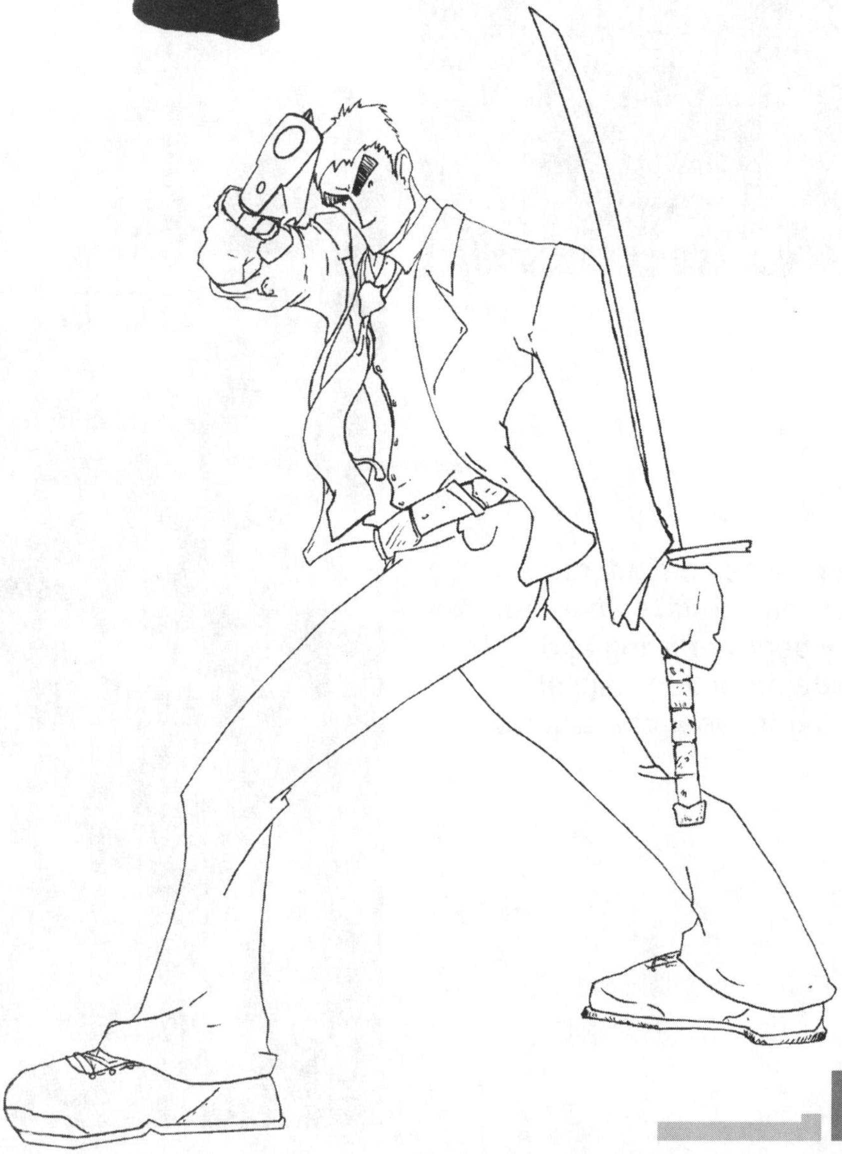

The internet is also a valuable artist's tool. A quick image search located a picture of of an office space filled with cubicles, the perfect setting for our blade-wielding businessman.

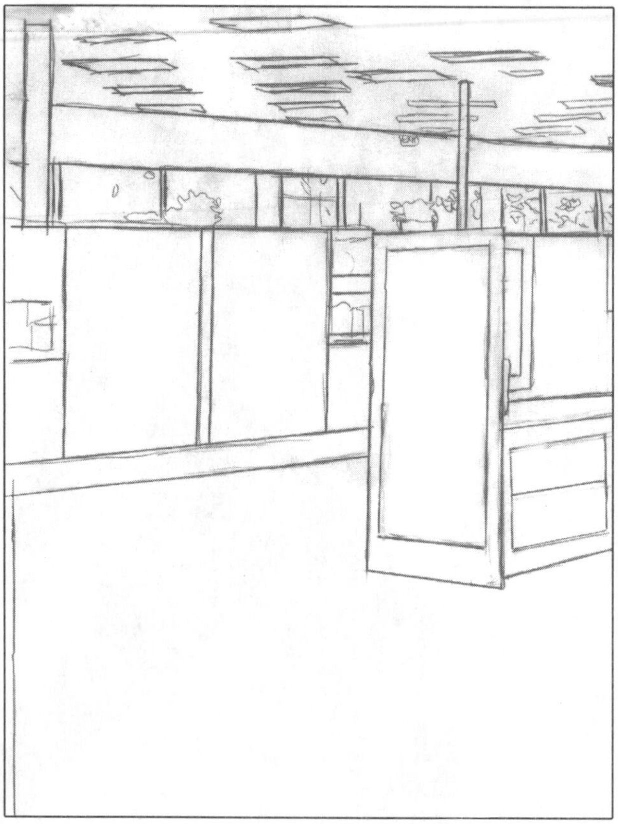

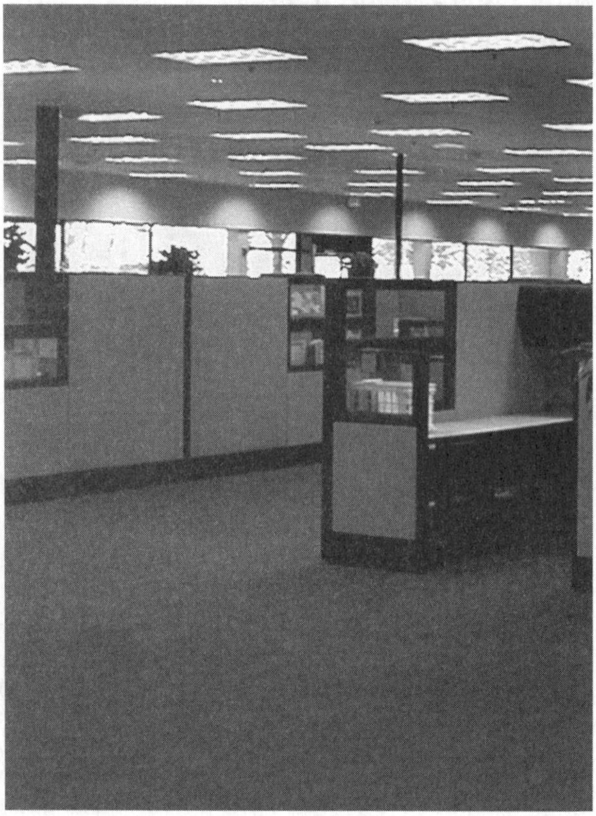

With a little computer know-how you can take your ordinary pencil drawing and create an entirely digital setting for your character(s).

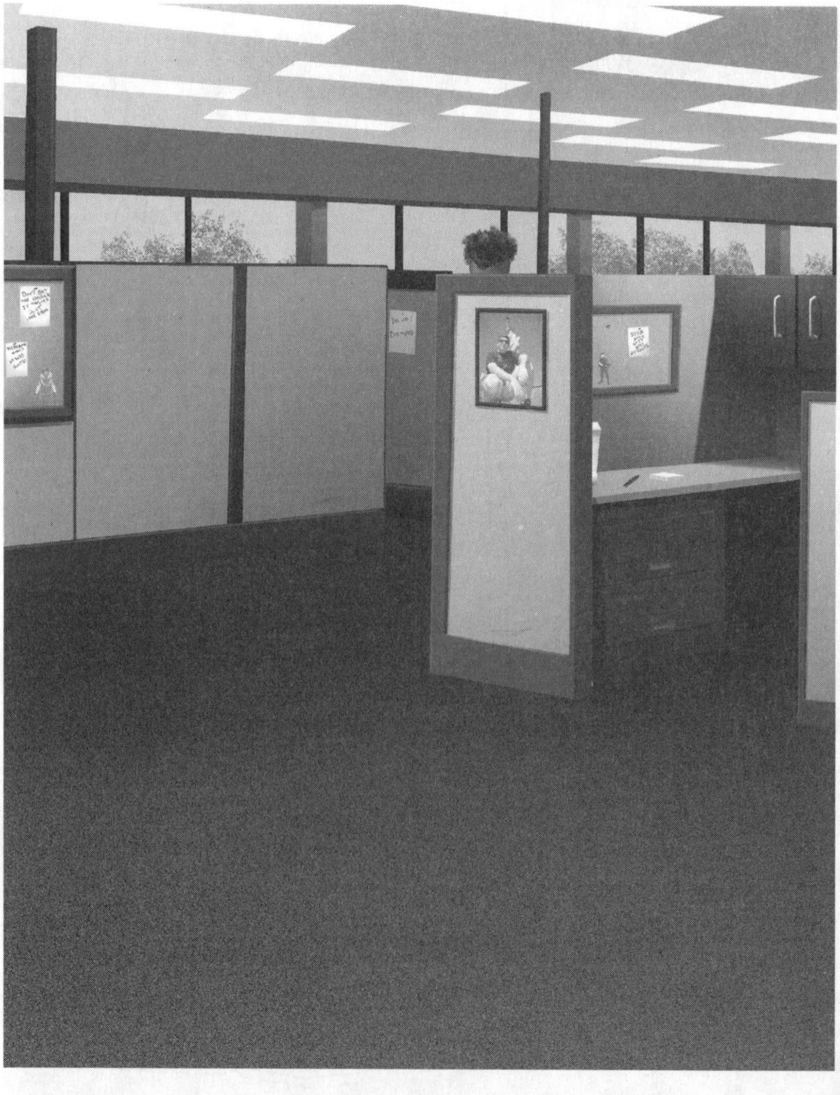

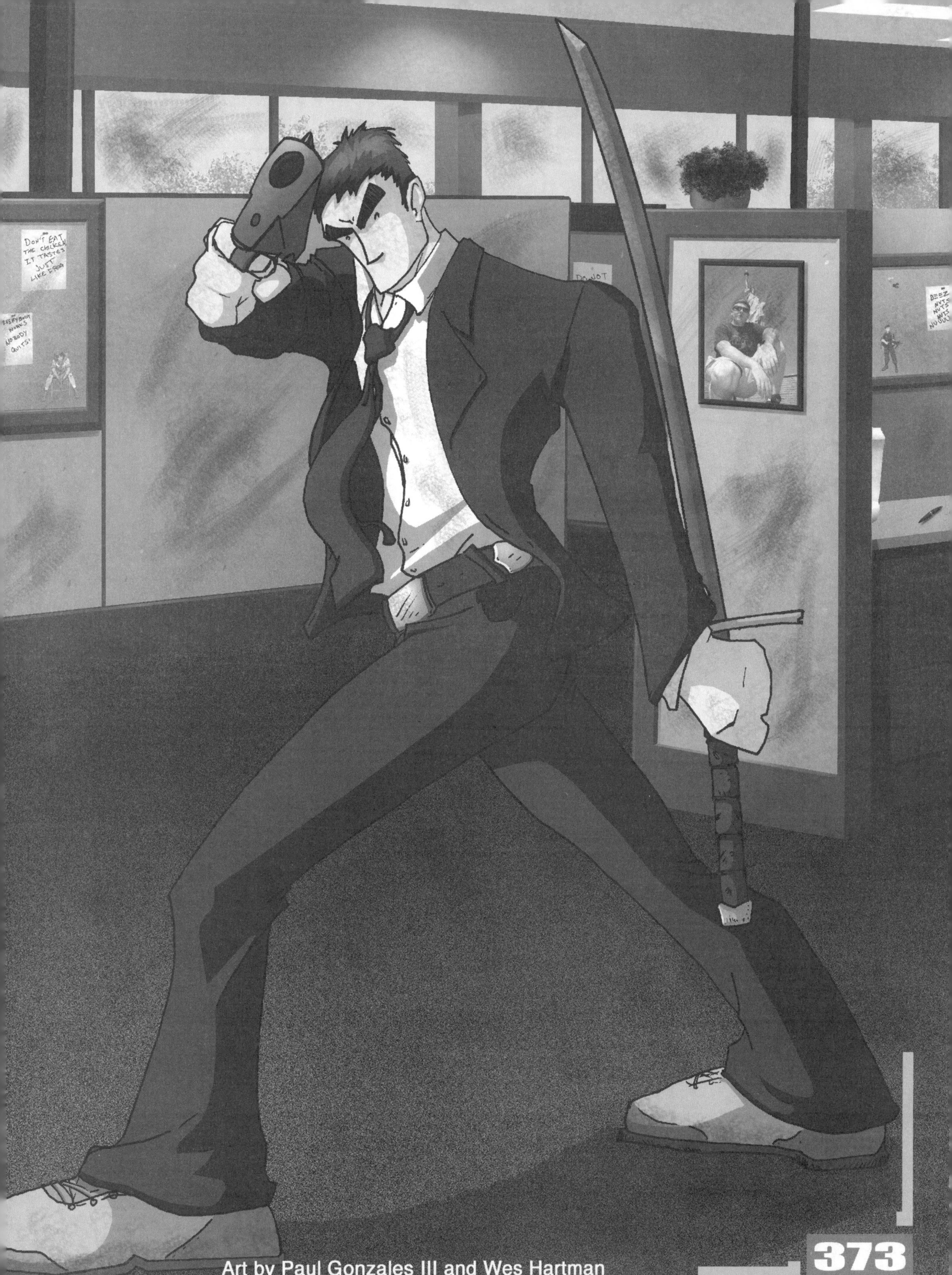
DON'T EAT THE CHICKEN IT TASTES JUST LIKE FROG
EVERYBODY WORKS NOBODY QUITS!
DO NOT
DEEZ NUTS

Art by Paul Gonzales III and Wes Hartman

URBAN COMMANDO

POSE

REFE

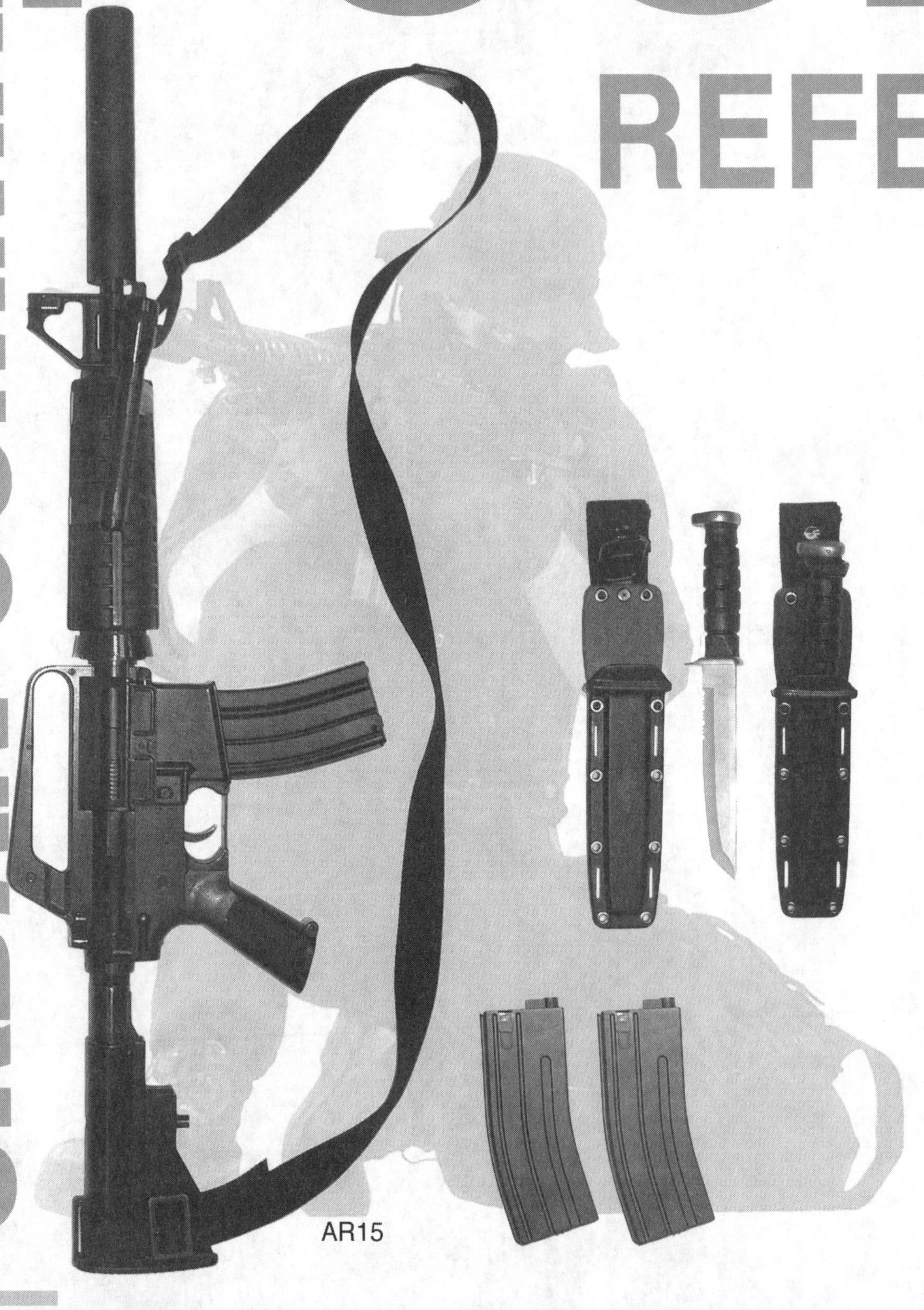

AR15

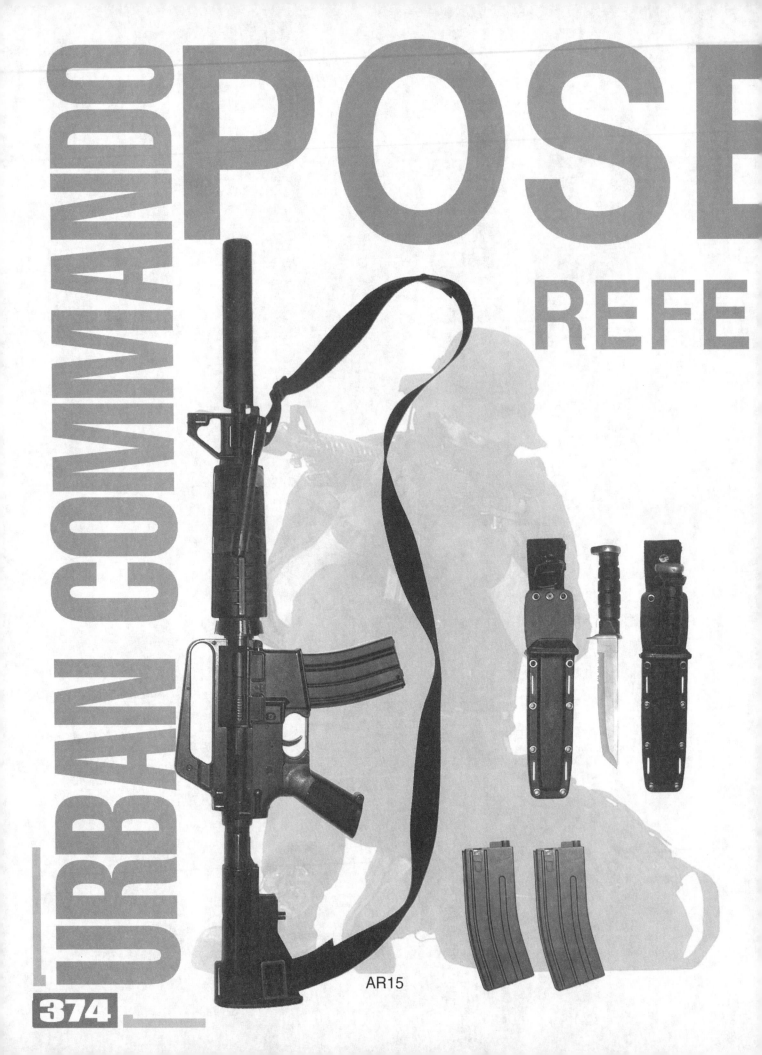

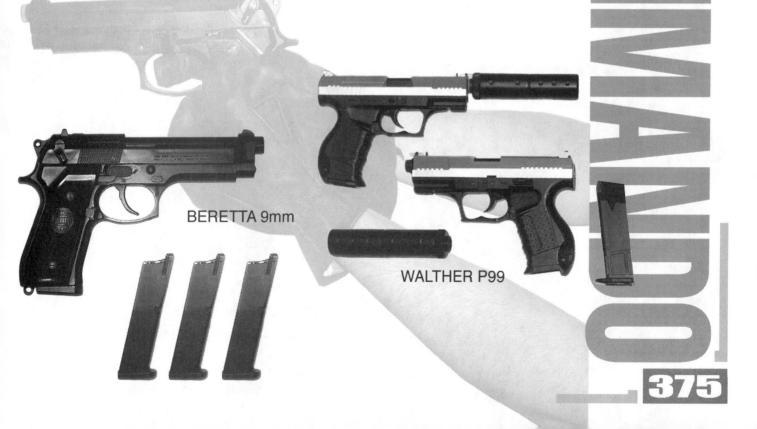

FILE

ENCE

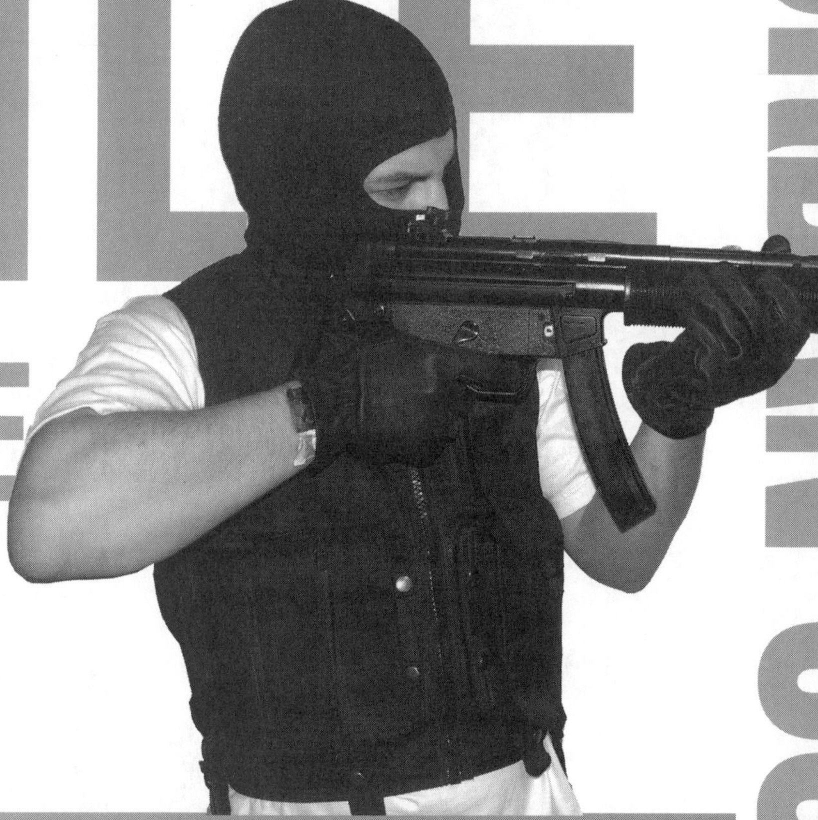

TACTICAL GEAR

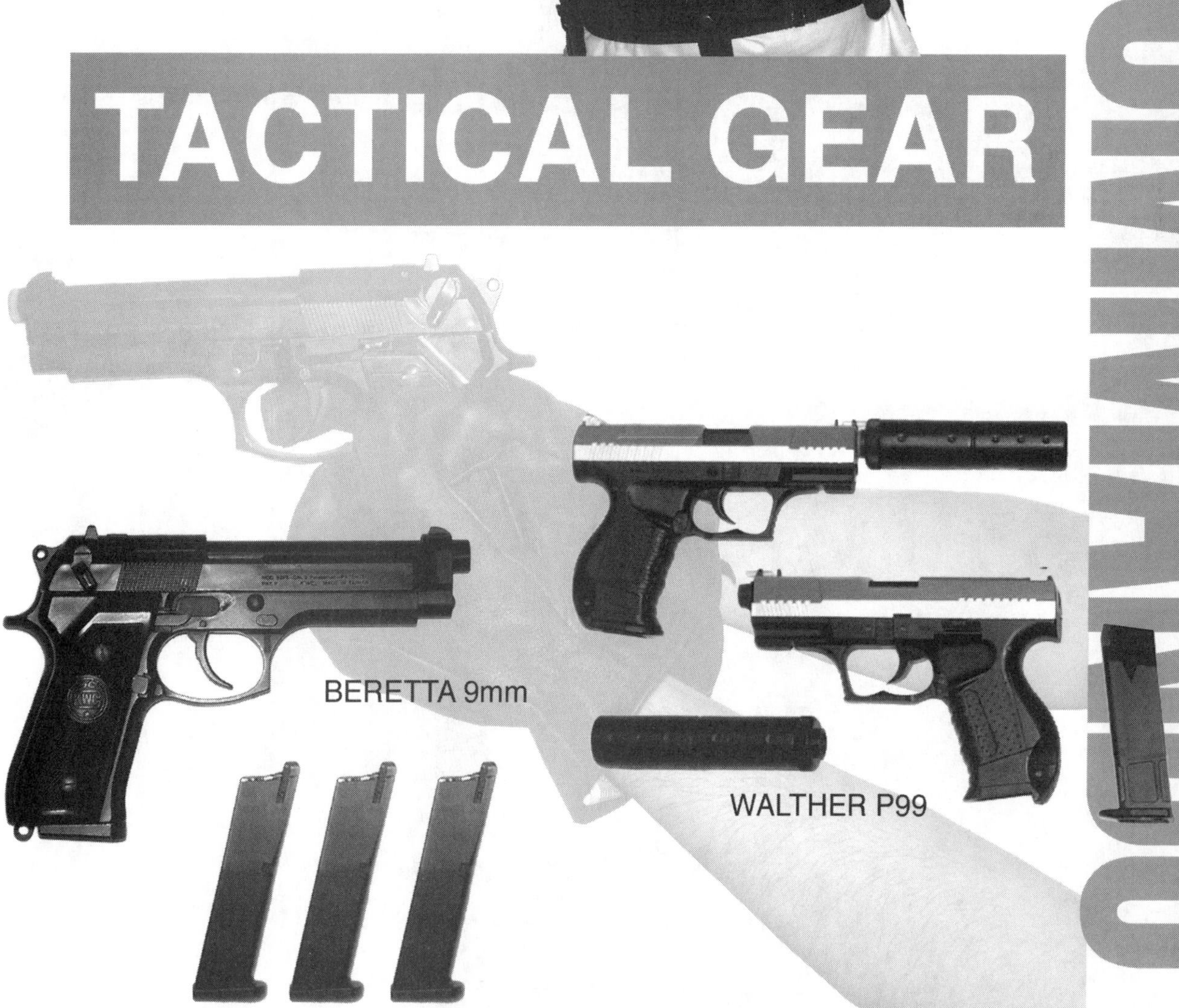

BERETTA 9mm

WALTHER P99

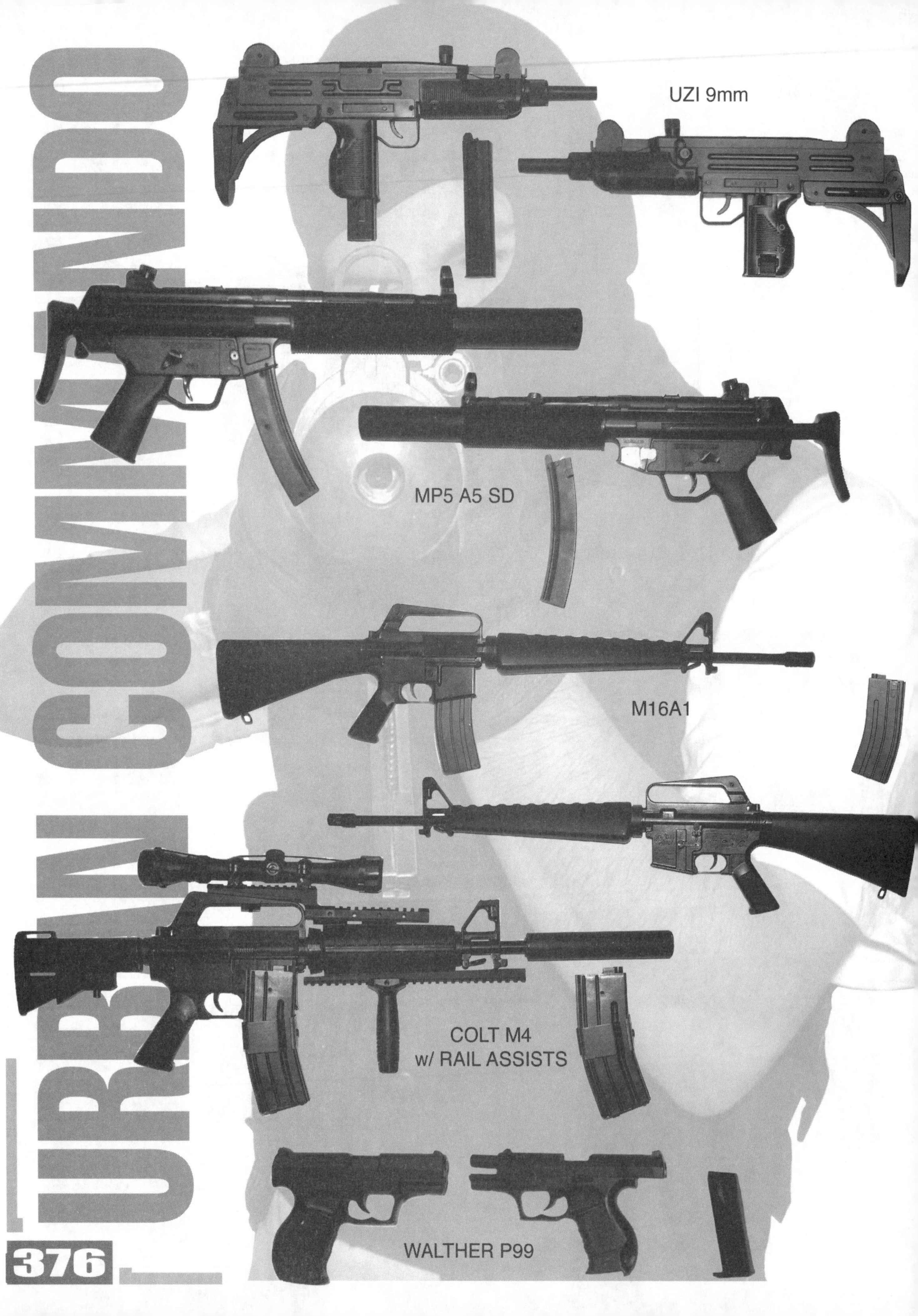
UZI 9mm
MP5 A5 SD
M16A1
COLT M4
w/ RAIL ASSISTS
WALTHER P99

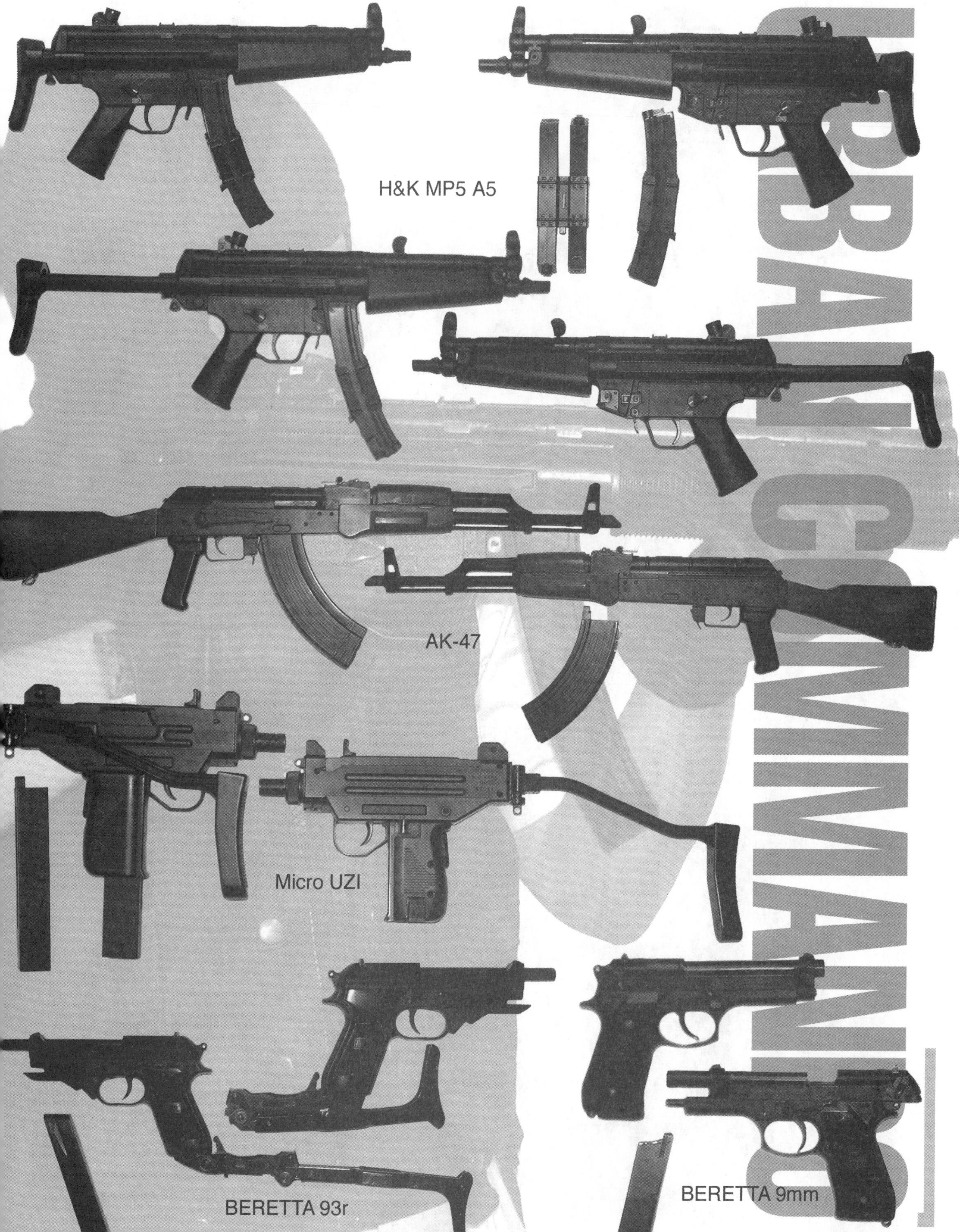
H&K MP5 A5
AK-47
Micro UZI
BERETTA 93r
BERETTA 9mm

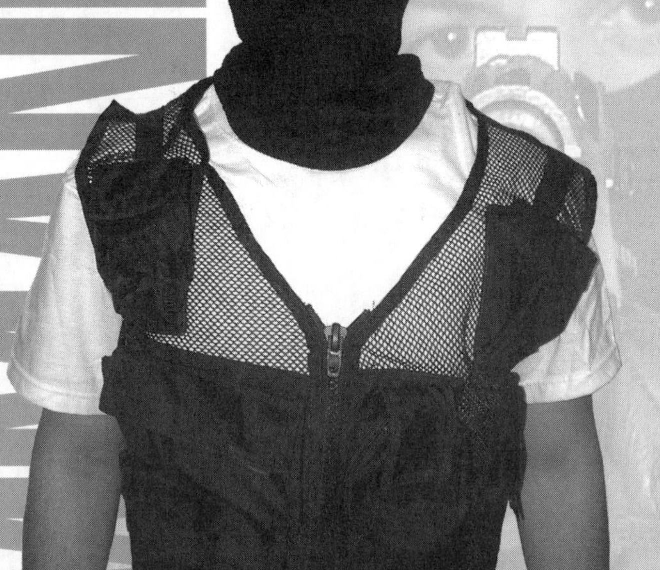

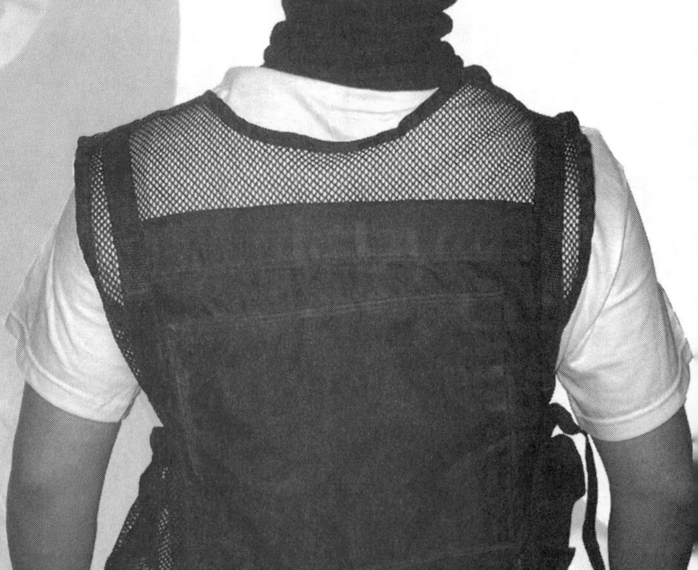

TACTICAL VESTS

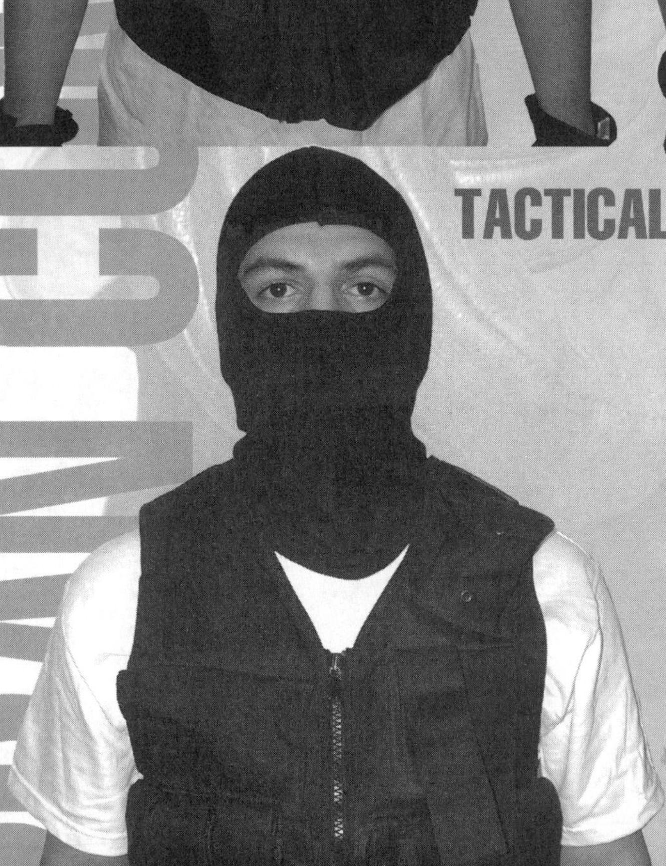

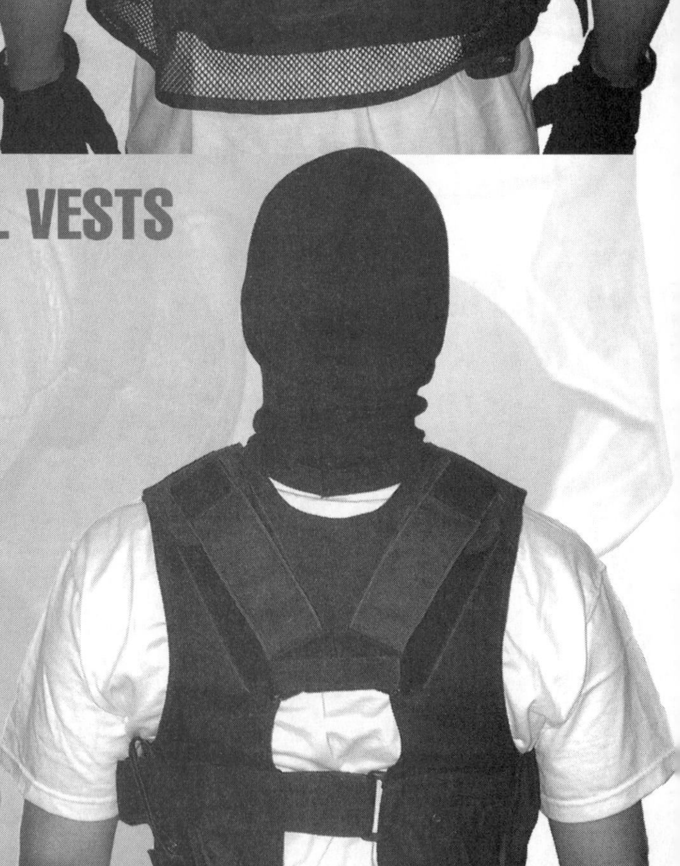

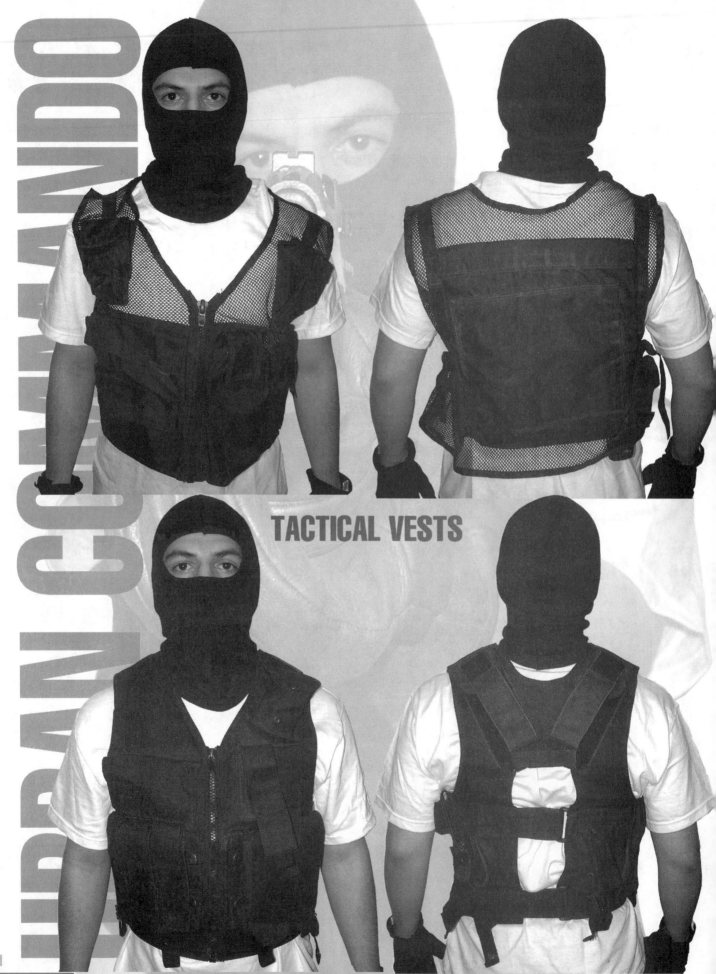

MASKS

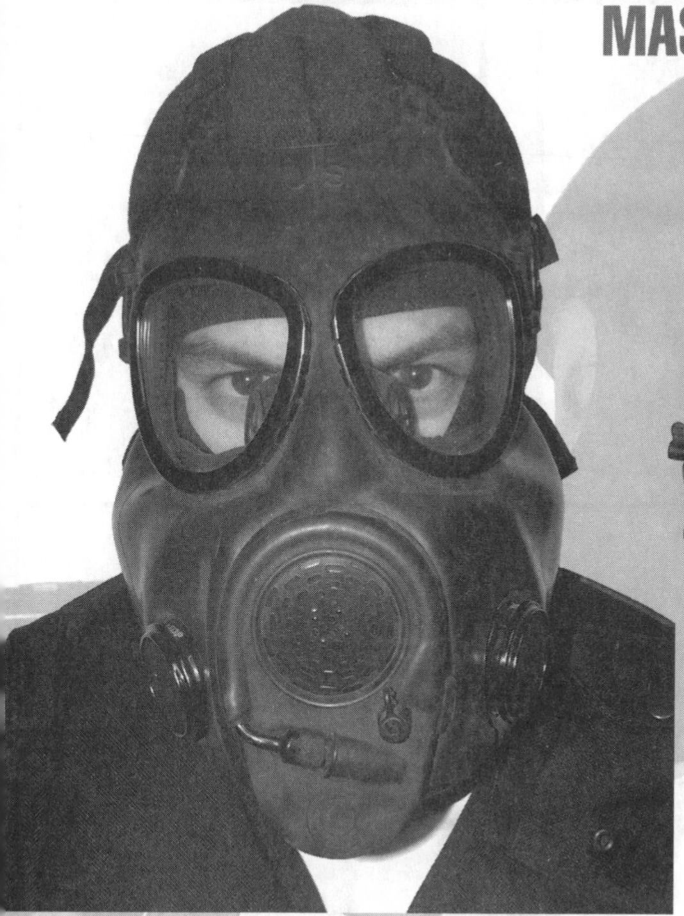

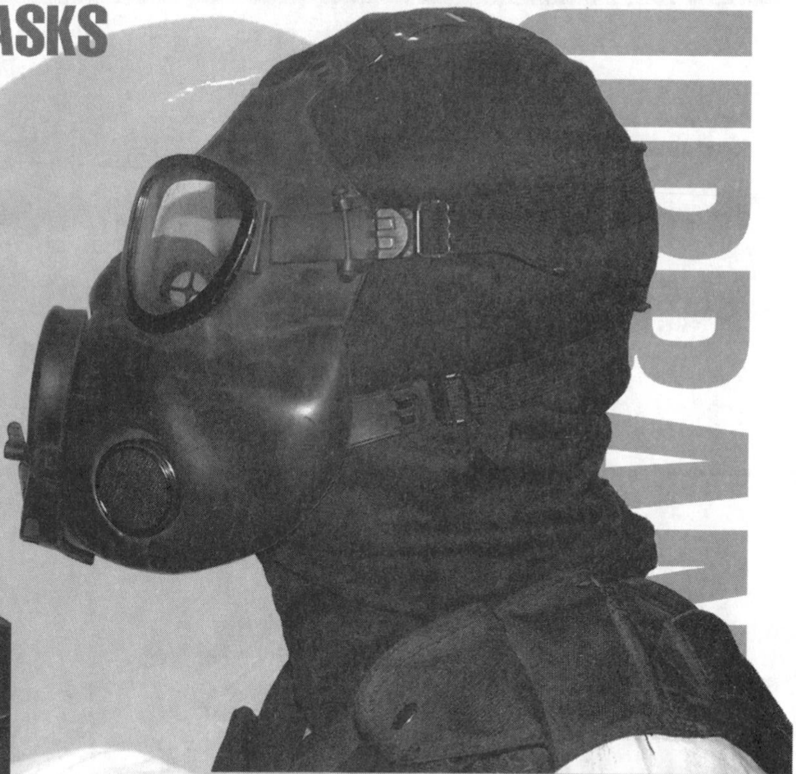

M2 GAS MASK

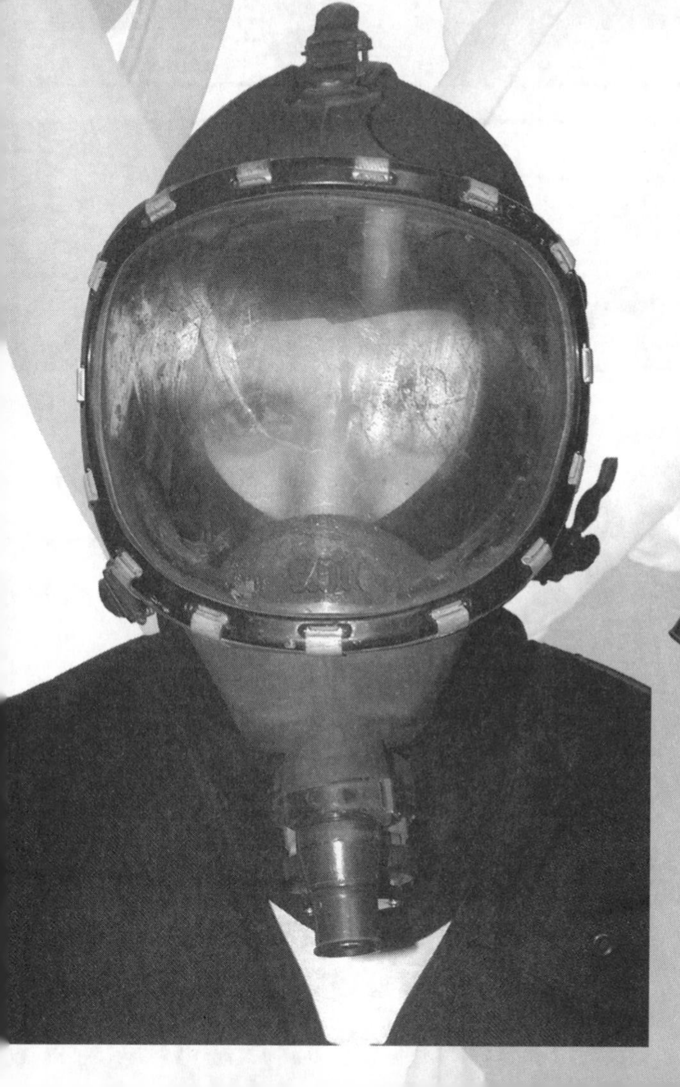

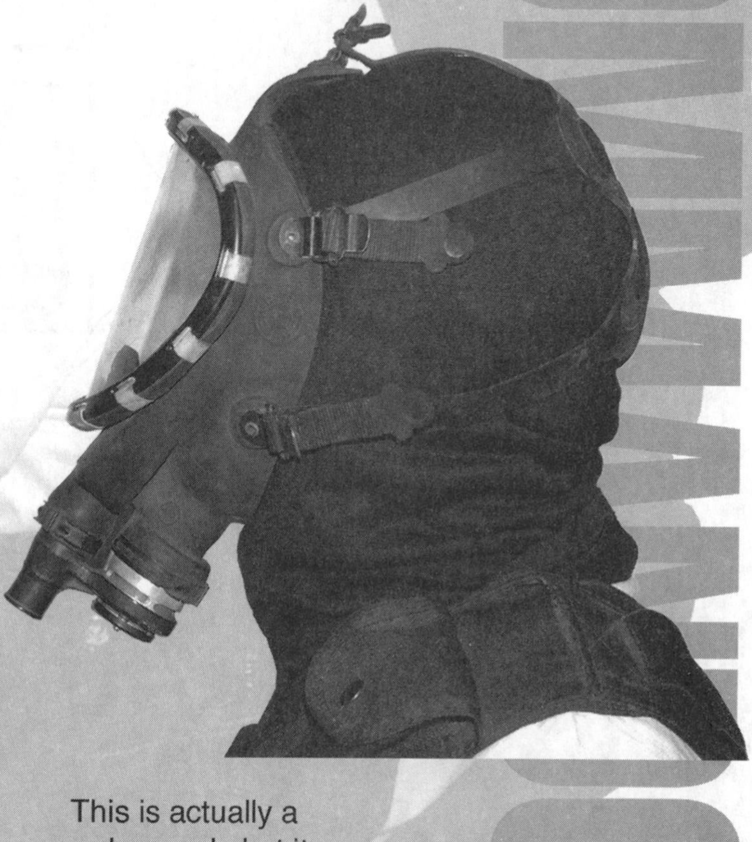

This is actually a scuba mask, but it looked cool so I used it.

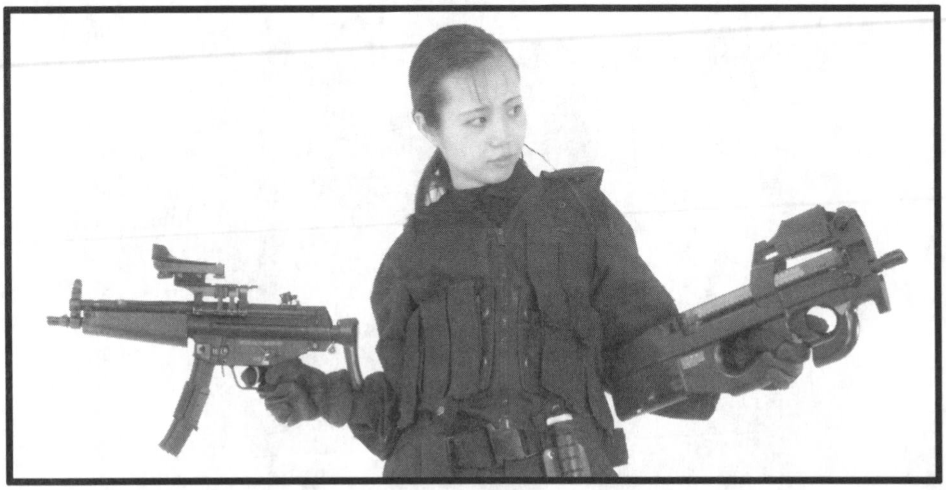

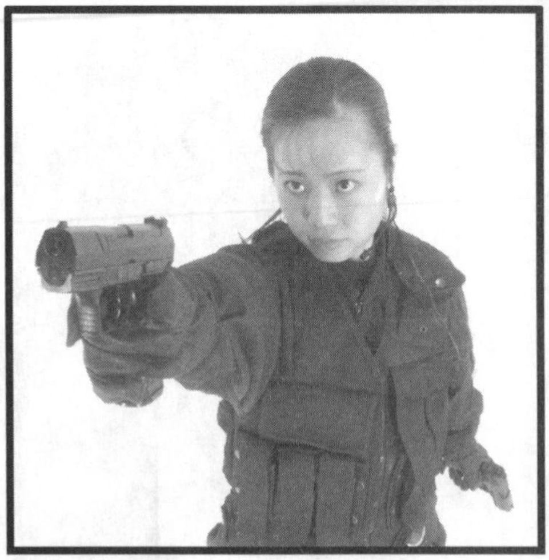

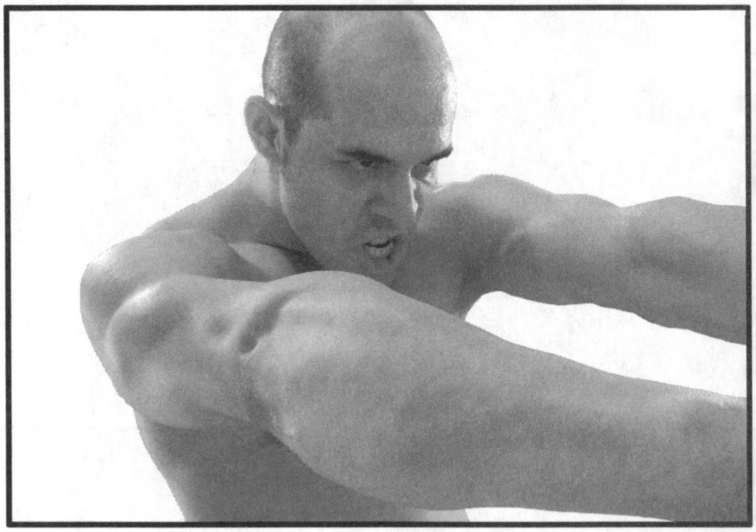

MODELS:

**HIROKO YARNELL,
JESUS SANTOS,
PAUL GONZALES III,
LEE DUHIG, AND
SAM LOTFI**

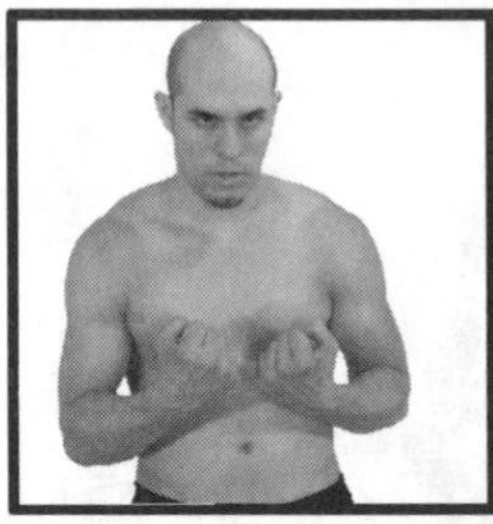

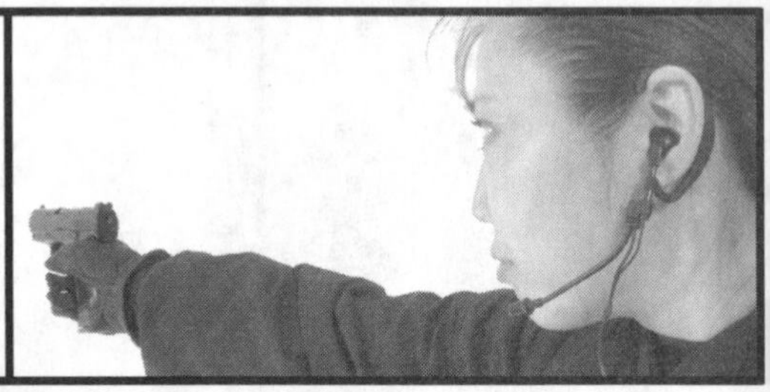

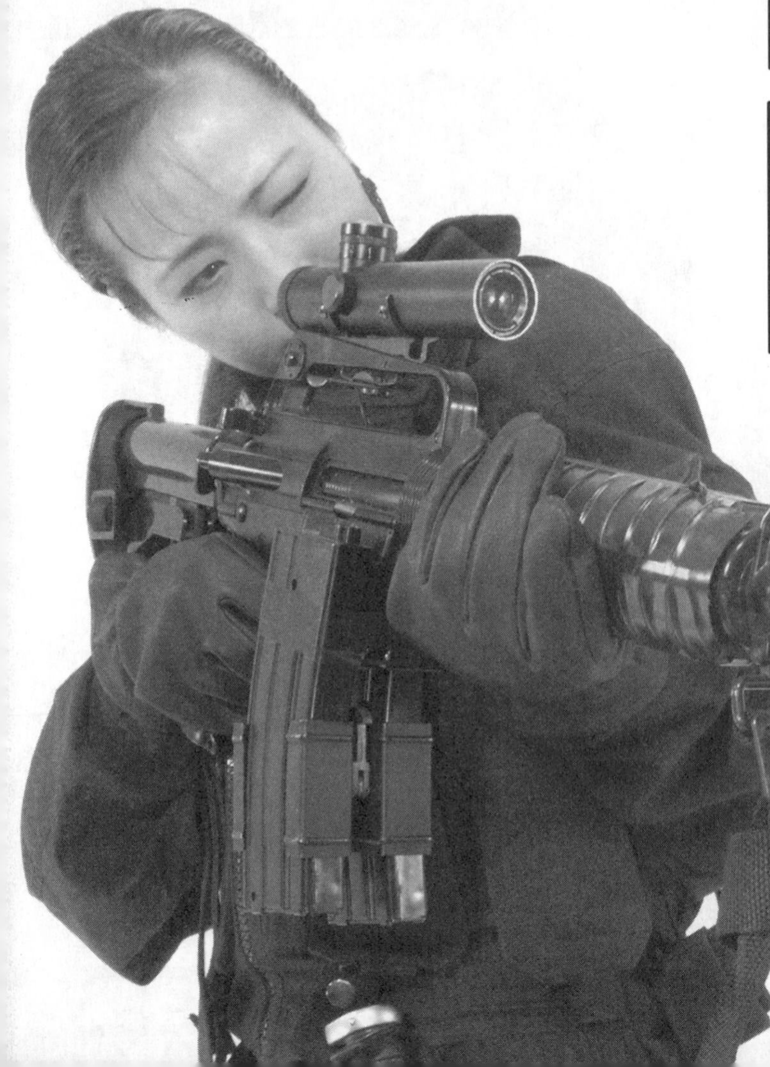

WWW.ANTARCTIC-PRESS.COM

BOOK DESIGN/LAYOUT:

**GURU-eFX and
WES HARTMAN**

PHOTOGRAPHY:

**GURU-eFX,
PAUL GONZALES III,
WES HARTMAN, AND
PAUL KILPATRICK**

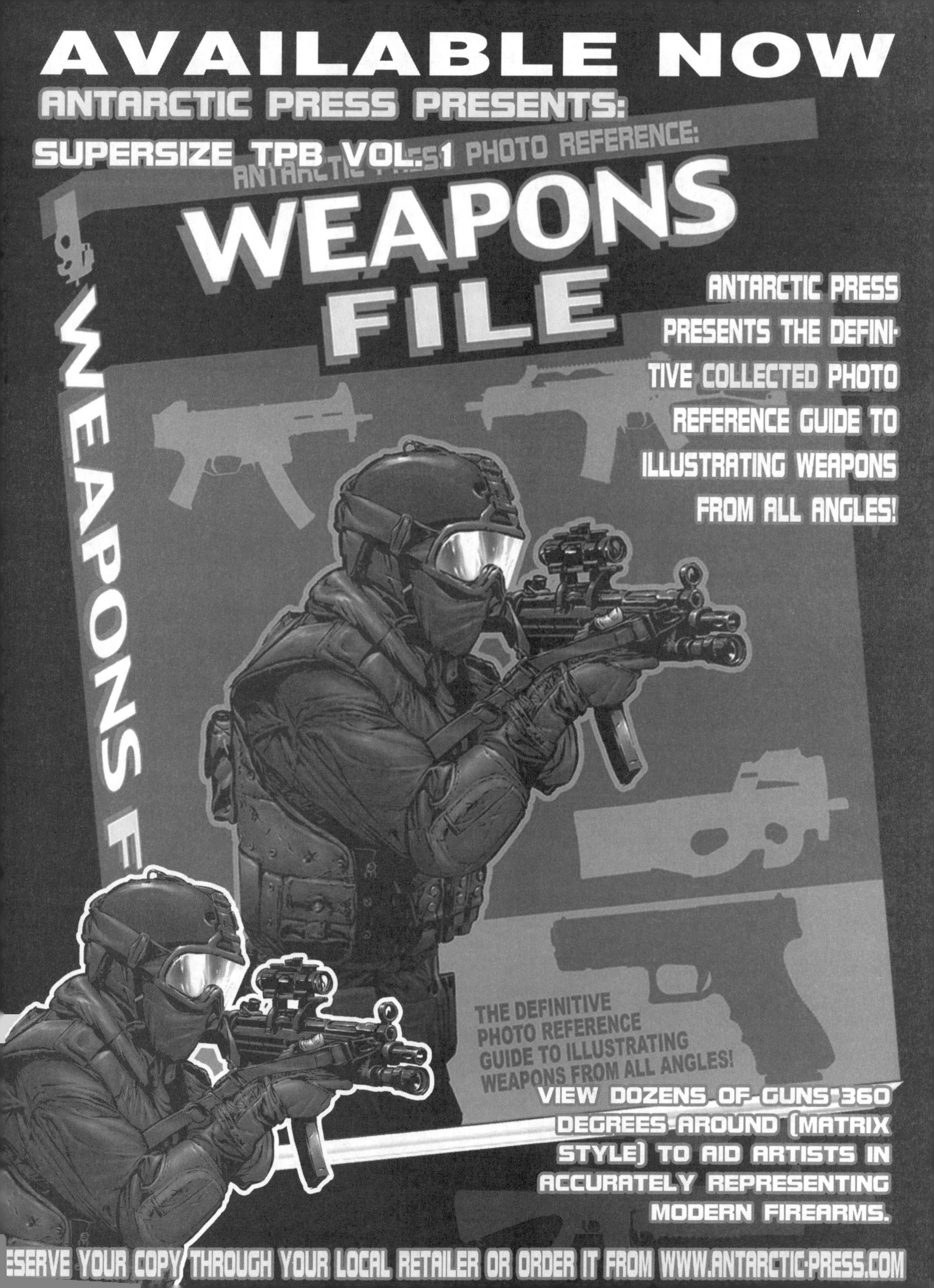
AVAILABLE NOW
ANTARCTIC PRESS PRESENTS:
SUPERSIZE TPB VOL. 1
ANTARCTIC PRESS PHOTO REFERENCE:
WEAPONS FILE
ANTARCTIC PRESS PRESENTS THE DEFINITIVE COLLECTED PHOTO REFERENCE GUIDE TO ILLUSTRATING WEAPONS FROM ALL ANGLES!
WEAPONS F
THE DEFINITIVE PHOTO REFERENCE GUIDE TO ILLUSTRATING WEAPONS FROM ALL ANGLES!
VIEW DOZENS OF GUNS 360 DEGREES AROUND (MATRIX STYLE) TO AID ARTISTS IN ACCURATELY REPRESENTING MODERN FIREARMS.
ESERVE YOUR COPY THROUGH YOUR LOCAL RETAILER OR ORDER IT FROM WWW.ANTARCTIC-PRESS.COM

ATTENTION, CLASS!

CHECK OUT THIS REQUIRED READING LIST OF GREAT HOW-TO MATERIAL!

HOW TO DRAW MANGA™

HOW to COLOR for COMICS™

YOU CAN! DRAW MANGA™

WEAPONS FILE™

(photocopy if you do not wish to cut up your book)

MAIL ORDER FORM

You can order online at: www.antarctic-press.com

CHECK BOX	Title	Price (US)
☐	How To Draw Manga SSZ #1	$19.95
☐	How To Draw Manga SSZ #2	$22.95
☐	How To Draw Manga SSZ #3	$22.95
☐	How To Draw Manga SSZ #4	$22.95
☐	How To Draw Shoujo	SOLD OUT
☐	How NOT To Draw Manga	$20.95
☐	How To Draw Chibi	$20.95
☐	How To Draw Ninja & Samurai	$22.95
☐	How To Tone	$20.95
☐	How To Tone (CD edition)	$25.95
☐	How to Color for Comics SSZ #1 (CD included)	$30.95
☐	How To Draw Manga Next Generation SSZ #1	$20.95
☐	You Can Draw Manga SSZ #1	$20.95
☐	You Can Draw Mecha	$20.95
☐	You Can Draw Monsters	$20.95
☐	You Can Draw Transforming Robots	$20.95
☐	Posefile Reference SSZ #1	SOLD OUT
☐	Posefile Reference SSZ #2	$20.95
☐	Posefile Reference SSZ #1 (cd edition)	SOLD OUT
☐	Posefile Reference SSZ #2 (cd edition)	$30.95
☐	Weapons File Reference #1	$5.95
☐	Weapons File Reference #2	$5.95
☐	Weapons File Reference #3	$5.95
☐	Weapons File SSZ #1	$20.95

All prices include domestic postage. Canadian/Mexican customers please add $0.25/book. All others outside North America please add $1.00/book.

Non-U.S. Postage: ________

TOTAL: ________

CHECK IT OUT!

If you don't see what you want in this ad, our website is always there to provide you, our friend, an exciting and easy browsing and buying experience. Give it a look-see, and be sure to visit the forums so you can give a shout out to all of us here in the Antarctic and let us know what you think of the site.

☐ I enclose cheque/money order/cash

☐ I wish to pay by

☐ Visa ☐ Mastercard

Card No: |_|_|_|_|_|_|_|_|_|_|_|_|_|_|_|_|

Expiry Date__________

Signature____________ Date_________

Name______________________________

Address____________________________

____

____

www.antarctic-press.com

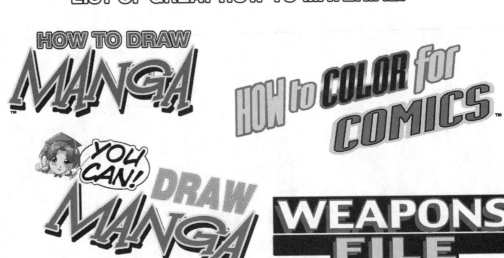